10,001 of the WORLD'S WORST JOKES

geddes & grosset

BEANObooks

© D. C. Thomson & Co., Ltd, 2001

Published 2001 by Geddes & Grosset,
David Dale House, New Lanark ML11 9DJ, Scotland.
Reprinted 2002

ISBN 1 84205 140 7

Printed and bound in the UK.

Why did the sailor grab a piece of soap when he was sinking?
So he could wash himself ashore.

What are the best kind of letters to read in hot weather?
Fan mail!

What is out of bounds?
An exhausted kangaroo!

Wife – Doctor, doctor, my husband's broken his leg.
Doctor – But madam, I'm a doctor of music.
Wife – That's all right, it was the piano that fell on him!

What do you call a toffee train?
A chew chew!

What do you give a deaf fisherman?
A herring aid?

What birds are cowboys afraid of?
Toma-hawks.

Why is Cinderella such a rotten footballer?
Because her coach is a pumpkin!

What did the Mona Lisa say to the gallery attendant?
I've been framed!

What is short, green and goes camping?
A boy sprout!

Eck – Why wouldn't they let the butterfly into the dance?
Bob – Because it was a moth ball!

How should you dress on a cold day?
Quickly!

Doctor, my husband thinks he's a clothes line.
Bring him round to the surgery.
What, and have all my washing fall on the ground?

Ticket collector – Are you first class?
Second-class passenger – Oh, yes, I'm fine, thank you. How's yourself?

Knock! Knock!
Who's there?
Senor.
Senor who?
Senor father out and let me in!

Why is a fish shop always crowded?
Because the fish fillet!

Boastful angler – I once had a three-hour fight with a salmon.
Bored friend – Yes, tin openers can be a nuisance at times.

Landlady – I don't allow cats, dogs, radios or record players in my house!
New lodger – Er … do you mind if my shoes squeak a little?

Teacher – What happens to gold when it is exposed to the air?
Smiffy – It's stolen!

Mrs McDougall – I want a pair of fur gloves!
Assistant – Yes, madam. What fur?
Mrs McDougall – What fur? To keep my hands warm, of course!

Father – Sidney, are you tall enough to reach that package on the mantelpiece?
Sidney – Not if it's my cough mixture!

Diner – I find that I have just enough money to pay the dinner, but I have nothing left to give you a tip.
Waiter – Let me add up that bill again, sir.

Farmer to man – If you can guess how many chickens I have, I'll give you both of them!

What do you get when you cross a sparrow with a haddock?
Cheep fish.

Doctor, doctor. Every time I drink a cup of hot tea, I get a pain in my eye.
Try taking the spoon out.

Why is it useless telling shopkeepers to be quiet?
Because they don't shut up till the end of the day.

**Why did Smiffy stand in
front of the mirror with his eyes closed?**
*To see what he looked like when
he was sleeping.*

**What do you get if you cross a
football team with an ice cream?**
Aston Vanilla!

**Smiffy couldn't tell the difference
between toothpaste and putty.**
All his windows fell out.

Why is a football pitch always wet?
Because of all the dribbling during matches.

Danny – Why do you call your new dog Ginger?
Sidney – Because he snaps!

Brring! Brring!
Who's there?
Hurd.
Hurd who?
Hurd my hand, so couldn't Knock!
Knock!

Smiffy – I went to the dentist yesterday.
Toots – Does your tooth still hurt?
Smiffy – I don't know – the dentist kept it.

First tramp – I have heard of a millionaire who wears a suit of clothes only once.
Second tramp – So do we, but it's a longer once.

Teacher – What is the name of the pine with the longest and sharpest needles?
Danny – The porcupine.

Fisherman – Do the fish in this river bite?
Gamekeeper – Bite? They're so fierce that you have to hide behind a tree while you are baiting your hook.

Minnie – There's something without any legs running across the yard.
Dad – What is it?
Minnie – Water. You left the tap on.

Smith – Did I leave an umbrella here yesterday?
Restaurant manager – What kind of umbrella?
Smith – Oh, any kind. I'm not particular.

Wilfrid – Why does it rain, Dad?
Dad – To make the grass grow.
Wilfrid – Then why does it rain on the streets?

Who became a space hero by mistake?
Fluke Skywalker.

Teacher – If you use this text book, you will get your homework done in half the time.
Danny – Great! Can I have two?

Teacher – Brian, how old were you on your last birthday?
Brian – Seven, Miss.
Teacher – Very good! That means you'll be eight on your next birthday.
Brian – No, Miss. I'll be nine!
Teacher – But that's impossible!
Brian – No it isn't. I'm eight today, Miss!

Danny – What has ten legs, a yellow back, a green eye and a long, horned tail?
Cuthbert – I don't know.

Danny – Neither do I, but I've just seen one swimming in your soup!

Plug – What is black and white and red all over?
Teacher – I know that one, Plug, a newspaper!
Plug – No sir, a zebra with a sun tan!

Boss – So you can do anything? Can you wheel a barrow full of smoke?
Workman – Yes, if you fill it for me.

Lazy Larry – Well, here I am to see about the job you advertised.
Contractor – Oh, do you think you are fit to work?
Lazy Larry – Work? I thought you wanted a foreman!

Why are you running?
There's a lion loose.
Which way did it go?
Do you think I'm following it?

Speaker – How long have I been speaking? I haven't got a watch with me.
Danny – There's a calendar behind you.

Teacher – What is meant by extravagance?
Sidney – Wearing a tie below a beard.

Waiter – Are you the filleted kipper, sir?
Diner – No. I'm the lonely sole with an empty plaice waiting for someone to fil-let

Old lady – I suppose sailors are very careful when you are at sea?
Old sailor – No, not at all, ma'am. In fact, we try to be as wreckless as possible.

Doctor – Do your teeth chatter when you are in bed?
Patient – I dunno. I put them on the dressing-table at night.

Teacher – If I stand on my head, the blood rushes into it. Now tell me, when I stand on my feet why doesn't the blood rush into them?
Danny – Because your feet aren't empty, sir!

Headmaster (to boy who has been fighting) – You should be ashamed of yourself. You shouldn't hurt a hair of your friend's head.
Boy – I didn't. I punched him on the nose.

Airman (after crashing into a tree) – I was trying to make a record.
Farmer – You did. You're the first man to climb down that tree before climbing up it.

Jones – What do you think of my dia-mond tie-pin?
Smith – It's quite nice, but, of course, it's not a real diamond.
Jones – Isn't it? Then, by jove, I've been swindled out of £2.

'Erbert – I can hear a pin drop twenty yards away.
Wilfrid – Really?
'Erbert – Yes, a rolling pin.

Where does a monkey cook its toast?
Under a gorilla!

Smith – I hear your car goes like a top.
Brown – Yes, I've just been out for a spin.

Mr McTavish – Don't run up any more bills. I can't face them.
Mrs McTavish – I don't want you to face them, dear. I want you to "foot" them.

Office boy – The cashier kicked me, sir.
Boss – Well, what about it? I can't do everything myself.

Lawyer – So you want me to defend you? Have you any money?
The accused – No, but I have a sports car.
Lawyer – Well, you can raise some money on that. Now, what are you accused of stealing?
The accused – A sports car.

Spotty – Why did the disco dancer put a stone to her left ear, and a bun to her right ear?
Fatty – I don't know.
Spotty – Because she wanted to hear rock and roll!

What do you buy only to throw out?
Streamers!

First salesman – How's the trampoline selling business going?
Second salesman – Oh, up and down!

Patient – So the x-rays show I'm perfectly normal?
Doctor – Yes, both your heads are all right.

What is the fastest part of a car?
The dashboard!

Old man – Here's £1. It makes me happy to think I'm helping you to get a bit of food.
Tramp – Make it a fiver guv'nor, and thoroughly enjoy yourself!

Why did the burglar take a bath before breaking out of jail?
He wanted to make a clean getaway!

What does a frog with no money say?
Broke! Broke!

Toots – Is the Headmaster really mean?
Sidney – Mean? Why, if he were a ghost he wouldn't even give you a fright!

Smiffy – What is the date?
Toots – I dunno. Why don't you look at that newspaper that's on the table.
Smiffy – Oh, that's no use – it's yesterday's.

Teacher (after a lesson about a rhinoceros) – Now, tell me something that has a big horn and is very dangerous?
Smiffy – A motor car.

Mac – Can I see that new device of yours for preventing the theft of a watch?
Jock – I can't show you it, it was stolen from me yesterday by a pickpocket.

Teacher – What is hail?
Smiffy – Please, sir, it's hard-boiled rain.

Where does Dracula live when he's in New York?
The Vampire State Building!

Why do witches fly about on broomsticks?
Because vacuum cleaners don't have a long enough cord?

Teacher – What's the shape of the world?
Toots – Round.
Teacher – How do you know it's round?
Toots – All right, it's square, then. I don't want to start an argument about it.

Captain – Wash the prisoner and put him in irons.
Stowaway – First I was collared and now I'm being washed and ironed. Is this a ship or a laundry?

What's worse than a snake with sore ribs?
A centipede with athlete's foot!

If you get referees in football, and umpires in cricket, what do you get in bowls?
Goldfish!

Teacher – Now, Smiffy, what does the word "asset" mean?
Smiffy – A young donkey, sir

Knock! Knock!
Who's there?
Doris.
Doris who?
Door isn't locked, just come in.

What rides at the amusement park do ghosts like best?
The scary-go-round and the roller ghoster!

Headmaster (to visitor) – By the way, what was the first thing that struck you about the school chemistry lab?
Visitor – A pea from a pea-shooter.

Mother – What? You've been fighting with Billy Biggs? I thought he was a peaceable child. He had such a nice face, too.
Freddie – Well, he hasn't now.

Tourist – Hey! One of your bees stung me. What are you going to do about it?
Beekeeper – Sorry. Just tell me which one did it, and I'll punish him.

King – You shall die, but you may choose to die any way you wish.
Slave – Then, Your Majesty, I choose to die of old age.

Librarian – Please be quiet, Tim. Those people beside you can't read!
Tim – They should be ashamed of themselves! I've been able to read since I was six!

Smiffy went to the dentist to get wisdom teeth put in.

When Smiffy went hitch-hiking, he left early to avoid the traffic.

Smiffy was listening to the match last night and burnt his ear.

WHAT'S ROUND, WHITE AND GIGGLES?
A tickled onion.

WHAT DO YOU GET WHEN YOU CROSS A HYENA WITH A BEEF CUBE?
A laughing stock.

Little Willie – Gran, was Dad a very bad boy when he was small?
Gran – Why?
Little Willie – Because he knows exactly what questions to ask when he wants to know what I've been doing.

Mother – Dennis, what are you reading?
Dennis – I don't know, Mum.
Mother – But you were reading aloud.
Dennis – I know, but I wasn't listening.

What did the rocket's door say?
Gone to launch!

Teacher – Sidney, what is that swelling on your nose?
Sidney – I bent down to smell a brose, sir.
Teacher – There's no "B" in rose, Sidney.
Sidney – There was in this one.

What is the fastest liquid in the world? Milk, because it is pasteurised before you see it.

Paperboy – Special! Read all about it. Forty-nine people swindled!
McSporran – I don't see anything here about a swindle.
Paperboy- Special! Read all about it! Fifty people swindled.

'Erbert – How do you spell blind pig?
Wilfrid – Easy – B.L.I.N.D. P.I.G.
'Erbert – Wrong! B.L.N.D. P.G.
Wilfrid – Why is that?
'Erbert – Because if it had two "I"s it wouldn't be a blind pig.

McGraw – How old is old Archie?
McGill – I dunno, but everybody was overcome by the heat from his candles at his last birthday party.

Doctor – Now take a deep breath and say nine three times.
Smart Alec (after inhaling) – Twenty-seven!

Frankie – Please, Mrs Smart, is Bobby coming out to play?
Mrs Smart – No, Frankie, it's too wet.
Frankie – Well, is his football coming out, then?

Bob – With patience, you can do anything.
Bill – Can I fill this sieve with water?
Bob – Yes, if you wait till it freezes.

Teacher – Now, Billy, what letter in the alphabet comes before "J"?
Billy – I dunno.
Teacher – What have I on both sides of my nose?
Billy – Freckles.

Judge – You are sentenced to ten years' imprisonment. Have you anything to add?
Prisoner – No, but I'd like to subtract.

Doctor – Have you taken the box of pills I gave you?
Oswald – Yes, but I feel worse. Perhaps the cardboard disagreed with me.

Mrs Perkins – Have you eaten these sandwiches?
Mr Perkins – Yes.
Mrs Perkins – Well, you'll have to clean your shoes with meat paste, for I put the boot polish on the sandwiches by mistake.

Policeman – I arrested a man for stealing a calendar yesterday!
Joe – What did he get?
Policeman – Twelve months!

If "L" on a car means learner, what does "GB" mean?
Getting better.

Why is a baby like a diamond?
Because it's such a dear little thing.

What sort of fish sings songs?
Tuna fish.

What vegetable is green and strong?
A muscle sprout.

Plug – I saw something last night that I'll never get over.
Danny – What was that?
Plug – The moon!

Diner – I say, waiter, bring my hat.
Waiter – It's on your head, sir.
Diner -Then don't bother. I'll look for it myself.

Smiffy – I wish I'd lived at the very beginning of the world.
Toots – Why?
Smiffy – Because I wouldn't have had to learn history.

It was my wife's birthday yesterday, so I bought her a rocket.
Was she delighted?
Yes, over the moon.

What was awarded to the inventor of door knockers?
The No-bell prize!

Mum – What are you doing, Tommy?
Tommy – I'm writing a letter to my sister.
Mum – Don't be silly, you can't write.
Tommy – That doesn't matter, she can't read.

Patient – Doctor, my family think I'm a little odd.
Doctor – Why?
Patient – Because I like sausages.
Doctor – Nonsense. I like sausages too.
Patient – You do? You must come round to see my collection. I have hundreds.

Danny – I have a great memory. I can recite all the names on five pages of the telephone directory.
Wifrid – I don't believe you!
Danny – Right then – Smith, Smith, Smith, Smith, Smith …

Why did you give up singing in the choir?
I was ill last week and didn't go, and after the service someone asked if the organ had been mended.

Angler (telling tall story) – Yes, the fish I caught was so big that I simple couldn't pull it out of the water.
Sarcastic listener – It was a whale, I suppose?
Angler – A whale? Goodness, no! I was baiting with whales.

Diner – Waiter, this bread has got sand on it.
Waiter – Yes, sir, it helps to keep the butter from sliding off.

What is white and goes up?
A stupid snowflake!

Grandpa – How long have you been going to school, Angus?
Angus – Too . . .
Grandpa – Two years?
Angus – No, too long.

Auntie – Do you ever help your little brother, Andrew?

Andrew – Yes, Auntie, I helped him to spend the five pounds you gave him yesterday!

What do you get if you cross a chip shop with a famous train?
The Frying Scotsman!

The new bank clerk's hobby is climbing trees.
He must want to be a branch manager!

Knock, knock!
Who's there?
The Invisible Man.
Tell him I can't see him at the moment!

What are the two fastest fish in the sea?
A motor pike and a side carp!

Fat Fred – What? Four pounds for a shave? Your sign says two pounds!
Barber – That's right, but you've got a double chin!

Boy to teacher wearing dark glasses – Why do you wear these glasses?
Teacher – Because my pupils are very bright!

Tourist at the edge of high cliff – Don't you think there should be a warning sign here? It's a very dangerous cliff!
Tour guide – They did have one, but nobody fell over so they took it down!

Fatty – I'm going to grow a moustache and beard when I grow up.
Wilfrid – Why?
Fatty – So that I won't have so much face to wash.

Baker – Good morning, madam. Bread's gone up another penny today.
Mrs Hardup – Oh, has it? Well, give me a yesterday's loaf.

Captain – Let's find out just how much you know about a boat. What would you do if a sudden storm sprang up on the starboard?
Danny – Throw out the anchor.
Captain – What would you do if another storm sprang up aft?
Danny – Throw out another anchor.
Captain – And if another storm sprang up forward, what would you do?
Danny – Throw out another anchor.
Captain – Hold on. Where are you getting all your anchors from?
Danny – From the same place you're getting your storms.

Gamekeeper – Don't you know you're not allowed to fish here?
Sandy – I'm not fishing. I'm teaching a worm to swim!

Waiter – How did you find your steak?
Diner – Easy. I'm a detective!

Tim – My Dad's got a leading position in a circus!
Tom – Gosh! What does he do?
Tim – He leads in the elephants!

Danny – Why are you looking at the mirror with your eyes shut?
'Erbert – I want to see what I look like when I'm asleep.

How did the witch know she wasn't well?
She had a dizzy spell.

Diner – Waiter, waiter, there's a spider in my soup.
Waiter – Oh, yes, sir. All the flies are on holiday.

Teacher – Toots, can you name the four seasons?
Toots – Yes, sir! Salt, mustard, vinegar and pepper!

Mother – What's wrong, Smiffy? Did something fall on your head?
Smiffy – Y-yes. I did!

Policeman (to boy looking over the wall of the football stadium) – Hey, what's the game?
Bobby – Football. Rovers versus United!

Teacher (in a Glasgow school) – Do you know the population of Glasgow?
Jimmy – Not all of them. I've only been here a week!

Dad – Harold, you mustn't go fishing with the boy next door – he's just had measles.
Harold – Oh, it's all right, Dad. I never catch anything when I go fishing.

What's the longest night of the year?
A fortnight!

What is the longest word in the English language?
Smile – because there's a mile in it.

Weary Willie – Why don't you look for work?
Lazy Len – I'm afraid.
Weary Willie – Of what?
Lazy Len – Finding it!

Bill – Have you heard that they're not making lampposts any longer?
David – Why?
Bill – They're long enough already.

Freddie – My brother has taken up French, Italian, Spanish and Greek.
Old man – Goodness! What does he do?
Freddie – He's a lift boy.

Headmaster – I don't see why you're grumbling. This is splendid tea.
Teacher – Yes, sir, but Olive, the dinner lady, says it's soup!

Young girl – Please, Mother says will you give me the broom you borrowed last Thursday?
Neighbour – Yes, but don't forget to bring it back.

Sidney – How many pieces of that toffee do I get for fifty pence?
Shop assistant – Oh, two or three.
Sidney – I'll take three, please.

Danny – What do you think you're talking about?
Cuthbert – I don't think – I know.
Danny – I don't think you know either.

How's business?
I manage to keep my head above water.
Well, wood floats, you know.

'Erbert – Mother Nature is wonderful! A million years ago she didn't know we were going to wear spectacles, yet look at the way she placed our ears.

What lives under the sea and carries sixty-four people?
An octobus!

Teacher – Dennis, what do we call a person who is very talkative, yet uninteresting?
Dennis – A teacher.

An absent-minded professor went into a shop to buy a jar. Seeing one upside down, he said, "How stupid, this jar has no mouth!" Turning it over, he was more astonished. "Why, there's no bottom in it, either!"

Patient – Doctor, doctor, I think I'm shrinking!
Doctor – Well, you'll just have to be a little patient.

When did the Scottish potato change its nationality?
When it became a French fry!

Two flies were on Robinson Crusoe's head. "Goodbye for now," said one. "I'll see you on Friday!"

What do you call a man who breaks into a meat factory?
A hamburglar!

Teacher – Why have you got cotton wool in your ear? Is it infected?
Smiffy – No, sir, but you said yesterday that everything you told me went in one ear and out the other, so I'm trying to stop it.

Where do pigs play?
In a play-pork!

What kind of monkeys make the best wine?
Grey apes.

Why is a game of cricket like a pancake?
Because they both depend on a good batter.

Who tells chicken jokes?
Comedihens!

Knock! Knock!.
Who's there?
Midas.
Midas, who?
Midas well open the door!

What was the first smoke signal sent by an Indian?
HELP! My blanket's on fire!

Black – Have you ever seen wrinkles on the brow of a hill?
Brown – No, but I've seen a field furrowed with care!

Painter – Why are you hurrying?
Apprentice – I haven't much paint left and I want to finish the door before it's all gone!

Cuthbert's father (as Cuthbert entertains guests) – He will go far with his violin, don't you think?
Guest – I hope so.

Tailor – That suit fits you like a glove, sir.
Customer – So I see. The sleeves cover my hands.

Angler – Is this stream private?
Passer-by – No, sir.
Angler – Then it won't be a crime if I land any fish?
Passer-by – No, it'll be a miracle.

Visitor to jail – It must be terrible to be shut up all the time in a small room like this. What were you before you came here?
Prisoner – A lift attendant.

Teacher – Why does the earth turn round the sun?
Smiffy – Because it doesn't want to get toasted on one side.

Farmer – I haven't ploughed that field yet, but I'm thinking of doing so.
Squire – Oh, I see, you've only turned it over in your mind.

Ron – Is there any truth in the report that Mean McTavish has bought Wilson's garage?
Don – Well, I don't know for sure, but it looks like it. The free air sign has been taken down.

How do you play truant from a correspondence school?
Send them an empty envelope.

Customer – You said this parrot was worth its weight in gold and yet it won't talk!
Pet shop owner – Well, silence is golden, isn't it?

Bobby – I found a horseshoe this morning.
Mother – Do you know what that means?
Bobby – Yes, it means that some horse is running around in his bare feet.

Cuthbert – Teacher, Danny hit me with a ruler.
Teacher – Why did you hit Cuthbert with a ruler, Danny?
Danny – Because I couldn't find a stick.

Why is a banana like a pullover?
They're both easy to slip on!

Teacher – How many days of the week begin with the letter T?
Sidney – Four – Tuesday, Thursday, Today and Tomorrow.

Teacher – How many seconds in a year?
Pupil – Twelve, sir. Second of January, February, March, etc.!

What's the biggest potato in the world?
A hippopotatomus.

Man – How much do I owe you for my new hearing aid?
Shopkeeper – Forty pounds.
Man – Did you say fifty pounds?
Shopkeeper – No, sixty pounds.

Mum – Now don't eat those sweets all at once, Alistair, or you'll be ill.
Alistair – All right, Mum. I'll eat them one by one.

Terry – So your brother lost his job with the fire brigade?
Jerry – Yes. It was because of his near-sightedness.
Terry – What happened?
Jerry – He squirted water on a red-headed woman before he discovered she wasn't the fire.

Smith – So Binky told you I was a musician?
Smythe – Well, he said you blew your own trumpet a lot.

Doctor – You will only have to wear these glasses at your work.
Patient – That's impossible.
Doctor – Why?
Patient – I'm a boxer.

Owner of an old car – Someone has stolen my car.
Friend – These antique collectors will stop at nothing.

Shopper – Can I stick this wallpaper on myself?
Shopkeeper – Yes, but it would look better on the wall.

What's white when it's dirty, and black when it's clean?
A blackboard.

What biscuit flies?
A plain biscuit.

What is the chiropodists' theme song?
There's no business like toe-business …

Little boy – Would you mind moving along a bit, mister?
Fat man – Why?
Little boy – To give the wind a chance to get at my kite.

What do you get if you cross an elephant with a kangaroo?
Big holes in Australia!

What do you give a pony with a cold?
Cough stirrup!

Why did King Arthur want a round table?
He was fed up with square meals.

What's big and hairy and flies at two hundred m.p.h.?
King Kongcord!

Harry – What would you get if you crossed your teacher with a crab?
Larry – I don't know!
Harry – Snappy answers!

Housewife (seeing man pretending to eat grass in her garden) – Whatever is wrong, my man?
Man – I'm so hungry, I'm having to eat grass.
Housewife – Well, come round to the back. The grass is longer there.

Spotty – Is my back tyre completely flat, Smiffy?
Smiffy – No – only a little bit at the bottom.

Absent-minded Alfred – I seem to recollect seeing you somewhere.
Forgetful Frank – Yes, I've often been there!

Jones – What sort of fellow is Brown?
Smith – Well, if ever you see two men speaking and one looks bored to death, the other is Brown.

Guide – … and this stone is where the great General fell in the battle.
Tourist – No wonder! I almost tripped over it myself.

What key is the hardest to turn?
A donkey.

Angry customer – I've just sent my boy for eight pounds of plums and you've only sent seven pounds. I know I'm right, because I've weighed them.
Shopkeeper – What about weighing your son?

There were three mice in an airing cupboard. Which one was in the army?
The one on the tank!

What do robots eat for dinner and tea?
Micro chips!

Teacher – Anyone here quick at picking up music?
Tim – I am, sir!
Teacher – Right, boy, move that drum kit!

Bill – Can I share your sledge?
Ben – Sure, we'll go halves.
Bill – Golly, thanks!
Ben – I'll have it for downhill, and you can have it for uphill.

Knock! Knock!
Who's there?
Four eggs.
Four eggs, who?
For example!

Landlady – Why have you put your tea on a chair, Mr McTaggart?

Boarder – It's so weak that I thought it had better have a rest.

Butcher – Have you tried our sausages, madam?
Customer – Yes, and found them guilty!

Teacher – Find the lowest common denominator.
Smiffy – Is that thing lost again?!

What is the best thing to do when the brakes of one's bike give way?
Aim for something cheap.

Recruit – What's that noise, sergeant?
Sergeant – That's the Last Post.
Recruit – I'll go and see if there are any letters for me.

Visitor – You're a very small man to be a lion-tamer.
Lion-tamer – Yes, but that's the secret of my success. The lions are waiting for me to grow bigger.

Golfer (far out in rough) – Say, caddie, what are you always looking at your watch for?
Caddie – It's not a watch, it's a compass.

What is the difference between a gardener, a billiard player and a church caretaker?
The first minds his peas, the second his cues, and the third his keys and pews.

Fortune-teller (reading palm) – Your future looks very indistinct.
Customer – What do you recommend?
Fortune-teller – Soap!

Diner – Waiter, what on earth is this in my bowl?
Waiter – It's bean soup.
Diner – I don't care what it's been, what is it now?

A parachute firm advertised – No one has ever complained of one of our parachutes not opening!

Clerk – My salary is so small, sir, that I can't afford lunch.
Boss – Then from tomorrow we will cut out your lunch break.

How did Noah find his way in the flood?
He used the radars (Raiders) of the Lost Ark.

How do you raise a baby elephant?
With a crane!

Which footballers wear matches in their hair?
Strikers!

What do snake charmers feed their snakes on?
Self-raising flour!

Angler – You've been watching me for three hours. Why don't you try fishing yourself?
Smiffy – No, I don't have the patience.

Actor – Did Jones get his new play used?
Producer – Yes, the stage manager tore up the manuscript and used it in a snow-storm scene.

Simon – Did you hear the joke about the rope?
May – No.
Simon – Oh, skip it!

What did the north wind say to the south wind?
Let's play draughts.

What's a pig's favourite football team?
Queen's Pork Rangers.

Jill – Did you hear about the man who said he was listening to the match?
Jack – No, tell me.
Jill – He burned his ear!

Mum – You can't come in the house unless your feet are clean!
Minnie – They are clean, Mum. It's only my shoes that are dirty!

What did Dracula say when the dentist wanted to pull out his teeth?
No fangs!

BARMY BOOKS
The Unwelcome Visitor by Gladys Gone.
Gone Shopping by Carrie R. Bag.
Who's to Blame? by E.Z.E. Diddit.
The Invitation by Willie B. Cumming.

What did the bald man say when he got a comb?
I'll never part with you!

Knock! Knock!
Who's there?
A little old lady.
A little old lady who?
I didn't know you could yodel!

What did the orange squash say to the water?
I'm diluted to meet you!

Smith – Why are you talking to yourself?
Jones – First, because I want to talk to a sensible man and second, because I like to hear a sensible man talking to me.

Tom – I'm thinking of going to America. What will it cost me?
Travel agent – Nothing.
Tom – What do you mean?
Travel agent – Well, it doesn't cost any-thing to think.

Boxer – You're a poor publicity man. I win a fight and all you get me in the paper is four columns.
Publicity agent – What are you grum-bling for? Look at the big fights Nelson won and he only got one column.

Interviewer – Are you quick?
Job applicant – Quick? Why, I blew out the candle last night and was in bed and asleep before the room was dark.

Minnie – I want to ask you a question, Mum.
Mother – Well, go ahead.
Minnie – When a hole appears in a pair of tights, what becomes of the piece of material that was there before the hole appeared?

Tim – Don't be afraid of my dog. If he thinks you're afraid, he'll bite off your hand.
Tom – That's what I'm afraid of.

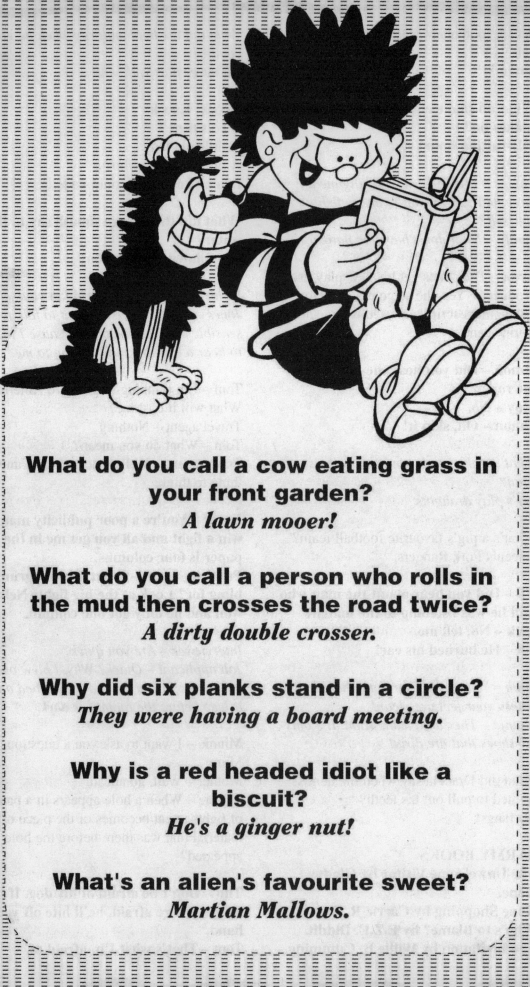

What do you call a cow eating grass in your front garden?
A lawn mooer!

What do you call a person who rolls in the mud then crosses the road twice?
A dirty double crosser.

Why did six planks stand in a circle?
They were having a board meeting.

Why is a red headed idiot like a biscuit?
He's a ginger nut!

What's an alien's favourite sweet?
Martian Mallows.

Tom – Ouch! I've scalded my hand in the hot water.
Tim – Why didn't you feel the water before you put your hand in it?

What do you get when you cross a rabbit with a spider?
A harenet!

Minnie – I woke up last night with the feeling that my watch was gone. So I got out of bed and looked everywhere for it.
Dad – And was the watch gone?
Minnie -No, but it was going!

What falls but never gets hurt?
Snow!

Knock! Knock!
Who's there?
Noah.
Noah who?
Noah good place to eat?

Patient – I keep seeing double, doctor.
Doctor – Lie down on the couch then.
Patient – Which one?

What do you get if you cross an elephant with a fish?
A pair of swimming trunks!

Fred – Did you know that Columbus was crooked?
Jack – No, he wasn't.
Fred – He was. He double-crossed the ocean.

Commanding officer (to raw recruit) – Now, my man, I want you to regard the regiment as a big band of brothers and me as the father of the regiment. Do you understand?
Recruit – Yes, Dad.

What did the pencil say to the rubber?
Take me to your ruler!

When is an artist dangerous?
When he draws a gun!

Driving instructor – Now, young man, this is the gear lever; down there is the brake; yonder is the accelerator, and over here is the clutch.
Pupil – Let's take one thing at a time – teach me to drive first.

Visitor – What's wrong with that dog of yours? Every time I take a drink of water he growls.
Tommy – Oh, he won't bother you. He's just annoyed because you're drinking out of his cup.

Prison visitor – And what brought you here?

Prisoner – Competition.
Prison visitor – Competition?
Prisoner – Yes, I made the same kind of banknotes as the Government.

Why did Smiffy take a ladder to school?
Because he wanted to go to High School!

Patient – Doctor, doctor, I feel like a pencil.
Doctor – Can we get to the point?

Why did the Gingerbread Man wear trousers?
Because he had crummy legs!

How do fish call their friends?
By tele-fin.

Which three letters of the alphabet do all the work?
N.R.G.!

Doctor – What you need is a change of occupation. Your present job seems to be making you unhappy. What do you do?
Patient – I'm a joke writer.

Comedian – The last time I was on the stage, the people were heard laughing a mile away.
Producer – Really? What was going on there?

Father – Tommy tells me you said he was a very promising pupil. Is that right?
Music teacher – Yes, that's right. He always promises to practise, but never does.

Diner – Is this a first-class restaurant?
Waiter – Yes, but we don't mind serving you!

Tourist – Is this part of the country good for rheumatism?
Old man – Yes! I got mine here.

Sandy – Jock, what can I send my brother for his birthday that'll not cost much?
Jock – Why not send him a pair of homing pigeons?

Danny – What position did your cousin play in the football team?
Wilfrid – He was a back.
Danny – Left-back?
Wilfrid – No, a drawback.

Hairdresser – Sharon, why are your hands so dirty?
Apprentice – Nobody's been in for a shampoo yet today.

Patient – Doctor, I feel like a glove.
Doctor – I think you need a hand here.

Why do witches fly on brooms?
Because they like to sweep across the sky!

What's yellow and has no brains?
Thick custard!

What do you get if you cross a jelly with a sheepdog?
The collie wobbles!

What illness do you get in China?
Kung-flu!

What do you get if you cross a baby with a U.F.O.?
An unidentified crying object!

What does a ghoul take for a bad cold?
Coffin drops.

Johnny – How did you break your arm?
Tommy – Do you see those cellar steps?
Johnny – Yes.
Tommy – Well, I didn't!

What do porcupines eat with cheese?
Prickled onions!

MacTavish – Did you hear about Sandy MacMeanie finding a box of corn plasters?
MacCulloch – No, did he?
MacTavish – Yes, so he went home and looked out his oldest, tightest shoes.

Unsuccessful actor – You know, when I'm acting, I'm carried away by my feelings. I forget everything but the part. The very audience seems to vanish.
Manager – You can't blame them.

Foreman – Look at that man carrying two loads of bricks at once, and you only carry one.
Labourer – Huh, he's just too lazy to go up the ladder twice.

Aunt – Hello, Jimmy, we don't see as much of you as we used to.
Jimmy – Well, I wear long trousers now!

Patient – Doctor, I think I'm a hi-fi system!
Doctor – Well, you certainly are a loud speaker.

What's the difference between a piano and a fish?
Anyone knows that you can't tuna fish!

Teacher – Now, Harry, tell us what you know about the Iron Age.
Harry – Er . . . I'm afraid I'm a bit rusty on that subject, sir.

Customer – What kind of bird is this, waiter?
Waiter – It's a wood pigeon, sir.
Customer – I thought so – would you bring me a saw?

What keeps the moon in place? Its beam!

Where do farmers go when they have caught a cold?
A farmacy!

Miss Screecher – I'm going away to study singing.
Neighbour – Good! How far away?

Visitor – Yes, I can see you one day stepping into your father's shoes.
Sammy – I suppose you're right. I'm wearing all his other old clothes now.

Teacher – Weight put on by overeating can be taken off by a simple reducing exercise.
Fatty – How?
Teacher – Move the head firmly from side to side when somebody suggests another helping.

Defeated boxer – I weighed in all right before the fight.
Manager – Yes, but the trouble is that you didn't wade in during the fight.

Park attendant – Excuse me, sir, but could you lend me a pencil and a piece of paper?
Visitor – Certainly. Here you are.
Park attendant – Now, give me your name and address. I saw you walking on the grass a moment ago.

Why did the egg go into the jungle?
Because it wanted to do some eggsploring!

What has three wings, three eyes and two beaks?
A canary with spare parts!

Hotel guest – Boy, dash up to room six and see if my raincoat is hanging behind the door. Hurry, because I have a train to catch.
(A few minutes later.)
Bellboy – Yes, sir. It's there as you said.

What do jelly babies wear on their feet?
Gum boots!

Teacher – First came the Ice Age, then the Stone Age. What came next?
Minnie – The sausage!

What do you call a judge with no thumbs?
Justice Fingers!

What did the mother ghost say to her child when they got into the car?
Put on your sheet belt!

What does an electric rabbit say?
Watts up, Doc!

How do you catch a squirrel up a tree? Climb up, and act like a nut!

Sheriff – Have you seen the Brown Bag Kid?
Cowboy – Nope, what does he look like?
Sheriff – He has a brown paper bag for a saddle on his horse, wears a brown paper bag hat, and a brown paper bag shirt.
Cowboy – What do you want him for?
Sheriff – Rustling!

How do you get rid of a white elephant?
Put him in a jumbo sale!

What's the easiest way to double your money?
Fold it!

Teacher – If your mum gave you nine hundred pounds, and your dad gave you eight hundred pounds, what would you have?
Janey – Rich parents!

A girl in a sweet shop is one metre and fifty centimetres tall, and wears size four shoes. What does she weigh?
Sweets!

**What is yellow and flickers?
A lemon with a loose connection.**

*Judge – Do you mean to say that a broken-down wreck such as the prisoner gave you that black eye?
Witness – He wasn't a wreck till he gave me the black eye.*

MacTavish – How did MacAndrew come to be an elephant trainer?
MacLaren – Well, he used to have a set of performing fleas then his eyesight got bad!

**Dave – So, you're a golfer? What's your favourite course?
Harry – Soup!**

*Old lady (at concert) – Is that a popular song he's singing?
Old man – It was before he sang it!*

Boastful artist – I once painted a picture of Santa Claus and it was so natural they had to take it down off the wall every month to trim his beard.

**Auntie – If your mother gave you a large apple and a small apple and told you to give one to your brother, which would you give him?
Nephew – Do you mean my big brother or my small brother?**

*Patient – Doctor, doctor, I swallowed a fairy-tale book yesterday.
Doctor – Sit down and tell me the whole story.*

Trainer – Did you find your horse well behaved?
Jockey – Yes, beautifully mannered. Every time we came to a fence he let me go first.

**What would you do if you saw three skeletons walking down the road?
Jump out of my skin and join them!**

*Who was the world's greatest thief?
Atlas, because he held up the whole world!*

What do you call a baby whale?
A little squirt!

**When is it bad luck to have a black cat following you?
When you're a mouse!**

*What did Dracula say to his wife when they were going out?
You look fangtastic!*

Diner – Waiter, look at the ends of this sausage.
Waiter – Why, there's nothing the matter with them, is there, sir?
Diner – Rather close together, aren't they?

**Burglar Bill – I am deeply indebted to you, sir. What should I have done without you?
Lawyer – Seven years' hard labour.**

*Foreman – What's all the row for?
Workman – The steamroller driver is threatening to go on strike unless they call him a chauffeur.*

Miles – The people in the flat above are very annoying. They were jumping about and banging on the floor till after midnight last night. It was very distracting for me.
Giles – You were working late, I suppose?
Miles – No, I was practising on my saxophone.

**Teacher – Name four members of the dog family, Joe.
Joe – There's Mummy dog, Daddy dog, Sister dog and Brother dog!**

Uncle – What are you looking so worried about, Jack?
Young Nephew – Well, yesterday my teacher said two and two are four, and today Dad said one and three are four, and I don't know which to believe.

Which driver never commits a traffic offence?
A screwdriver!

What can you hold without touching it?
A conversation.

Hotel manager – Rooms overlooking the sea cost £5 extra.
Miser – How much does it cost if I promise not to look?

David – If you call somebody who lives in Scotland Scottish, what do you call somebody who lives in the North Pole?
Tom – I don't know!
David – Daft!

Bill – How do you confuse a boomerang?
Ben – I don't know!
Bill – Throw it down a one-way street!

Officer – Have you cleaned your boots this morning?
Private – No.
Officer – No, what?
Private – No polish.

Dad – What's the time?
Dennis – Half past.
Dad – Half past what?
Dennis – I dunno. I've lost the hour hand of my watch!

Alec – What was your mother so angry about?
Jim – She sent me for some cold cream and I got ice-cream. It was the coldest they had.

Teacher – If you had twelve sweets, and Johnny took half, what would he have?
Tommy – A black eye!

Fireman – Hey! Come on! Can't you see your house is on fire?
Patient – Can't help it. The doctor told me not to leave my bed for two days.

Diner – There's a funny kind of film on this soup, waiter.
Waiter – Well, what do you expect for two pounds – a full-scale thriller?

Youth – Shall I have a chance of an early rise in this job?
Boss – Most certainly! Six o'clock every morning.

Boss – I want a man who is clever, hard-working and punctual.
Lazy Larry – You don't want one man, you want three.

Teacher – If you had two pounds and you asked your dad for another two pounds, how much money would you have?
Johnny – Er … two pounds, sir.

Where do old Volkswagens go?
The Old Volks' Home!

When a fly from one side of the room and a flea from the other side meet, what is the time when they pass?
Fly-past-flea!

Doctor, doctor, I keep on getting a sore throat every time I take a cup of tea.
Doctor – Have you tried taking the spoon out.

Which land do kittens like best?
Lapland!

What do you call a map-reading back-seat driver?
A nag-ivator!

Boss – What do you mean by arguing with that customer? Don't you know our rule? The customer is always right.
Assistant – I know. But he was insisting that he was wrong.

Flying instructor – If anything goes wrong, leap out of the plane and pull the cord of the parachute.
Cadet – Supposing the parachute doesn't open?
Flying instructor – Bring it back and I'll give you another.

Mother – Johnny, you ought not to eat so fast.
Johnny – But, Mum, I'm only trying to get it down before the price of food goes up again.

Smiffy – Dad, why is a sponge full of holes?
Smiffy's Dad – Er . . . well, if it wasn't for the holes, people wouldn't know it was a sponge.

Old lady – Little boy, don't pull faces at that poor bulldog!
Little boy – Well, he started it!

Knock! Knock!
Who's there?
Euripedes!
Euripedes who?
Euripedes, and you'll pay for a new pair!

Doctor – How long have you been thinking you're a ghost?
Patient – Ever since I've been walking through walls.

What is green inside and yellow outside?
A cucumber dressed up as a banana!

What would you call a Scottish cloakroom attendant?
Angus Coatup!

Doctor, doctor, I feel like a bucket!
Yes, you do look a bit pail!

Doctor – How are you coming along with your reducing diet?
Patient – Not very well. I must be one of those poor losers.

What kind of running means walking?
Running out of petrol!

Teacher – Really, Fatty, why don't you wash your face? I can see what you had for breakfast this morning.
Fatty – What was it?
Teacher – Egg.
Fatty – You're wrong. That was yesterday morning!

Spotty- My uncle was the weather forecaster in our town and he predicted sunny weather for last summer. He had to leave the town.
'Erbert – Why?
Spotty – Because the climate didn't agree with him.

Old lady – And how did those enormous rocks get there?
Guide – The glaciers brought them, madam.
Old lady – And where are the glaciers now?
Guide (fed up) – They've gone for more rocks.

'Erbert – I used to have trouble with my eyes – I saw spots in front of them.
Toots – Do your glasses help?
'Erbert – Yes. Now I can see the spots much better.

Percy – My mum hung my socks up last Christmas – and oh, did I have a headache!
Horace – How could hanging up your socks give you a headache?
Percy – She forgot to take me out of them!

Old lady (in animal shop) – What would you recommend for a flying fish – a bowl or a birdcage?

Father (enraged) – This new saw I bought is useless. It wouldn't cut butter.
Dennis – Oh, yes, it would, Dad. I cut a brick in half with it this morning.

Busy greengrocer (who has gone into next-door shop, which is a beauty parlour) – Will you massage those prunes for me, please, miss? We've run out of plums.

Tim – Do you know that boy Jones?
Jim – Oh, yes, he sleeps beside me in history.

Little brother – What's etiquette?
Slightly bigger brother – It's saying "No, thank you!" at a birthday party when you want to say "Yes, please!"

Dennis – What's the time, Walter?
Walter – Twenty-five minutes to ten.
Dennis – I'll never remember that. You'd better give me your watch.

Optician (holding up a dinner plate) – What is this?
'Erbert (getting his eyes tested) – Bring it a little nearer. I don't know whether it's a five pence or a ten pence.

Teacher (after looking at Smiffy's homework) – I didn't think it was possible for one person to make so many mistakes.
Smiffy – It wasn't only one person, Teacher. Dad helped me.

Gentleman – Are you still looking for your lost pound coin, little boy?
Boy – No, my little brother found it.
Gentleman – Then what are you looking for?
Boy – My little brother.

Mother – Why didn't you take the medicine the doctor gave you for your cold?
Minnie – Because it says on the bottle, "Keep tightly corked."

Poet – This poem of mine will make everybody's heart miss a beat.
Editor – Then it won't do. We never print anything that interferes with the circulation.

Pupil – I can't read this correction of yours, sir.
Teacher – It says, "You must write more clearly."

First weightlifter – I am stronger than Hercules.
Second weightlifter – That's nothing. I knew a man who could pick himself up by the scruff of the neck and swing himself out at arm's length.

Bill – How long did you work last week?
Ben – One day.
Bill – Gosh! I wish I could find a steady job like that.

Teacher – The people of Poland are Poles; the people of Sweden, Swedes. Can you tell me what the people of Germany are called?
Minnie – Yes, Germs.

Foreman – Look how that man's doing twice the work you are.
Workman – That's what I've been telling him, but he won't stop.

Teacher – Why are you late this morning?
Jock – Please, sir, I stopped a fight.
Teacher – That's right, always be a peacemaker. How did you stop them?
Jock – I punched them both.

Novice (hiring boat) – I've no watch so I hope I shall know when my hour is up.
Boatman – Oh, yes, you'll know by the water. The boat fills up to the seat in about an hour and a half.

Diner – I ordered a dozen oysters, and you've only given me eleven.
Waiter – I thought you wouldn't like to sit thirteen at the table, sir.

Confused judge (to noisy prisoner in court) – Quiet please! We want nothing but silence, and very little of that.

Visitor (to little boy) – If you had twelve apples, and I gave you two, how many would you have?

Little boy – I don't know. We do our sums in oranges.

Guide – Beneath that slab lies King Richard's heart; over there lies good Sir Frances Drake; and who do you think is lying here?

Tourist – Well, I don't know for sure, but I have my suspicions.

Baldheaded circus performer – Ladies and gentlemen, I offer £100 to anyone who can name anything I can't do.

Voice (from the audience) – Part your hair, in the middle!

Manager – Come here at once, John. Look at the dust on this desk. Why can't you keep it polished like the banister rails?

Office junior – Well, sir, I can't slide down your desk.

Farmer -Did you count the pigs this morning, Paddy?

Paddy – I counted nineteen, but one ran so fast that I couldn't count him at all.

Customer – You said the tortoise I bought from you would live three hundred years, and it died the day after I bought it.

Dealer – Now, isn't that too bad! The three hundred years must have been up.

Patient – How much is it to have a tooth extracted?

Dentist – Thirty pounds.

Patient – What! For three seconds' work?

Dentist – All right, I'll take it out in slow motion.

Mother – Why are you jumping up and down, Minnie?

Minnie – It's all right, Mother. I forgot to shake my medicine before I took it, so I'm doing it now.

Patient (in asylum yard, to new superintendent) – Who are you?

Superintendent – I'm the new superintendent.

Patient – Oh, it won't take them long to knock that out of you. I was Napoleon when I came here.

First gardener – What was the last card I dealt you?

Second gardener – A spade.

First gardener – I knew it.

Second gardener – How?

First gardener – You spat on your hands before you picked it up.

Teacher – Tommy, what is one-fifth of three-seventeenths?

Tommy – I don't know exactly, but it isn't enough to worry about.

Boss – What do you mean by taking the whole day off yesterday, when I gave you a half day?

Clerk – Well, you always told me never to do things by halves.

Willie – I lost a pound coin this morning, Tim.

Tim – Hole in your pocket?

Willie -No, the man who dropped it heard it fall.

Chief – We must dismiss that salesman who tells all our clients that I am an ass.

Partner – I'll speak to him, and tell him not to discuss company secrets.

Steward (to seasick passenger) – Can I fetch you anything, sir?

Seasick passenger – Yes, a small island – quick!

Angry customer – These eggs aren't fresh.

Grocer (indignantly) – Not fresh? Well, sir, the boy only brought them in from the country this morning.

Customer – Which country?

Fat man – Are you laughing at my expense?
Little boy – No, sir; I'm laughing at your expanse.

Waiter -Your coffee, sir: it's special from South America.
Diner – Oh, so that's where you've been all this time, is it?

Old man (entering office) – There is a boy, John McNab, working here. May I see him? I'm his grandfather.
Clerk – You're just too late, sir. He's gone to your funeral.

Bore – Yes, I'm very fond of birds. Yesterday one actually settled on my head.
Fed-up listener – It must have been a woodpecker.

Prospective purchaser – Is this aeroplane safe?
Manufacturer – Safest on earth.

Bailiff – Can't you read that notice, "No fishing here"?
Angler – Yes, but the man who put that up didn't know what he was talking about. I've caught twenty in ten minutes.

Mountain guide – Be careful not to fall here. It is dangerous. But if you do fall, remember to look to the left, as you get a most wonderful view.

Mother – Didn't I tell you not to jump over that tar barrel again!
Jimmy (now in the barrel of tar) – Well, I didn't.

Bill – They say there's two feet of ice on the duck pond.
Ben – Why, I had the same in bed last night.

Teacher – Henry, are you learning anything?
Henry – No, sir, I'm listening to you.

Husband – I've just swallowed a cuff-flink!
Wife – Well, at least you're sure where it is.

Boss – Peter, are you sweeping out the shop?
Peter – No, I'm sweeping out the dirt and leaving the shop.

Farmer – Do you see that pig over there? I call him Ink.
Visitor – Why?
Farmer – He keeps running out of the pen.

Builder – How is the new chap you took on this morning? Is he steady?
Foreman – If he was much steadier he'd be motionless.

Sergeant (addressing platoon) – Does any man here know anything about music?
Recruit (swiftly) – Yes, Sergeant.
Sergeant – Then go and shift the piano in the sergeants' mess room.

Gentleman – Now, what ought you to say to a gentleman who gives you fifty pence for carrying his bag?
Tim – It isn't enough these days.

Minnie – Sing for us, Dad.
Dad (pleased) – Why?
Minnie – Because we're playing at ships and we want to have a foghorn.

Diner – Waiter, what sort of pie is this?
Waiter – Cottage pie, sir.
Diner – Then this must be the foundation-stone.

A teacher caught a boy scribbling on a piece of paper which contained these words – Blow, blow, suck, blow, suck, blow, blow, suck, blow.
Teacher – What is the meaning of this?
Boy – Please, sir, it's the music for my mouth-organ.

Footballer (in black and white jersey) –
How do you like our new colours?
Supporter – What's the idea – half
mourning for the matches you've lost?

**Boxing instructor – That was a half-
hook.**
**Pupil (dreamily) – Well, just keep the
other half for yourself.**

*Mother – Where are your manners,
Dennis? You shouldn't eat your jelly with
your fingers.*
*Dennis – I've tried a spoon but the jelly's
so excited it won't stay on.*

Defeated jockey – Well, anyhow, I wasn't
last. There were two horses behind me.
Disgusted owner – Rats! Those were the
first two in the next race.

Fireman – At one fire, I saved ten lives.
Smith – And who were they?
Fireman -A child and her pet cat.

*Sergeant – Is the man seriously wound-
ed?*
*Policeman – Well, two of the wounds are
fatal, but the third doesn't amount to
much.*

Policeman (to motorist) – Why didn't
you slow down? Didn't you see the
notice – "Slow down here"?
Motorist -Yes, but I thought it was
describing your village.

**Burglar – Have you paid your dog
license?**
Brown – I haven't got a dog.
**Burglar – Have you paid your tele-
phone bill?**
Brown – I haven't got a telephone.
**Burglar – Good! I'm safe. Now open
that safe for me.**

*Fat man (to boy in railway carriage) –
Why are you looking at me?*
*Small boy -Because there's nowhere else
to look.*

Tourist – Why is there no fence at this
precipice?
Guide – Well, the more people that fall
over the more famous the place becomes.

**Perkins – Who's that chap? His face
seems familiar.**
**Jenkins – I'm not surprised. He's a
retired jailer.**

*Diner – There's only one sandwich on
that plate. I asked for a choice.*
*Waiter – Well, you've got a choice: take
it or leave it.*

Roger – Dad, give me a pound coin.
Dad – Don't you think that you're too
big to be always begging for coins?
Roger – I expect you're right, Dad. You'd
better give me a fiver.

**Teacher – Now, Smiffy, whose emblem
is the leek?**
Smiffy – Er . . . the plumber's?

*Jinks – Did the cyclone damage your
house very much?*
*Binks – I don't know. I haven't found it
yet.*

Plug – I suppose this horrible-looking
thing is what you call modern art?
Art dealer – I beg your pardon, sir, that is
a mirror!

**Auntie – Why are you eating those
cakes so quickly, Smiffy?**
**Smiffy – I'm afraid that I will lose my
appetite before I'm finished.**

*Teacher (during test) – I hope I didn't see
you look at your book, Sidney?*
Sidney – I hope you didn't, either.

Small footballer – Are you the fellow
who kicked me a few minutes ago?
Burly footballer – Yes. What are you
going to do about it?
Small footballer – Er . . . I just wanted to
tell you that I'm feeling all right now.

WHAT DOES A TEN FOOT TALL PARROT SAY?
Anything it likes!

WHAT HAPPENED WHEN TWO T.V. AERIALS GOT MARRIED?
They had a really great reception.

WHAT GOES HICK-HOCK?
A clock with hiccups!

WHAT'S WHITE ON THE OUTSIDE AND GREEN ON THE INSIDE?
A frog sandwich!

Hasn't the doctor sent that sleeping pill yet, nurse?

Not yet, sir.

Well, it'll be too late if it doesn't come soon. I can hardly keep awake.

Jim – I suppose you find skating hard to learn?

Tim – Oh, no, you soon tumble to it!

Uncle – Well, Dennis, what did you see at the museum?

Dennis – Well, nearly all the things were called "Do not touch."

Teacher – Give me a sentence with the word "gladiator".

Pupil – The lion pounced on the woman and was glad he ate her.

Inspector – Have you caught that burglar yet?

P.C. 94 – No, but I've got him so scared he won't show his face while I'm about.

Teacher – Can anyone tell me what goldfish are?

Danny – Sardines that have grown rich.

Teacher – Now, if you had five marbles and Danny said he'd give you five, how many would you have?

Sidney – Just five, miss. Danny would only be kidding. I know him.

Employer – Did you put that note where it would attract Mr Smith's attention?

Office boy – Yes, I stuck a pin through it and put it on his chair.

John (to his brother) – Where shall I put my sweets?

Brother – Put them in my mouth.

Policeman (to boy watching football match from the top of the fence) – Hi, what's the game?

Boy – No score yet.

Bus conductor (to passenger) -Why did you ring the bell at both ends of the car?

Stupid passenger – Well, don't I want both ends to stop?

Bobby – I dropped my watch in the river yesterday, and it's still running.

Billy – Your watch?

Bobby – No, the river.

Passer-by – Why are you fishing under here?

Small boy – Well, the fish will all come under the pier to shelter from the rain!

Card player (ominously) – Somebody's cheating here. Bill Jones isn't playing the hand I dealt him.

Mother – Now, Bobby you've been good all day. As a special treat you may choose something you want to do tomorrow.

Bobby – Then, may I be naughty all tomorrow?

Angus -If I gave you £100, what would you do?

Sandy – Count it!

Dentist – Don't cry. The tooth is out.

Harold – I know. I'll have to go back to school now.

Dick – Dad, would you like to save money?

Dad – Yes, of course.

Dick – Then buy me a bike, and I'll not wear out so many pairs of shoes.

Jimmy (watching tasty treats being taken into his brother's sick-room) – Please, Mummy, can I have the measles when Jack is done with them?

Plumber – Well, here we are, and we haven't forgotten a single tool.

Householder – No, but you've come to the wrong house.

Smith – Is that new watchdog of yours any good?
Brown – Very! If you hear a suspicious noise at night, you've only got to wake him, and he barks.

Prison visitor – What brought you here?
Prisoner – A mistake on my part.
Prison visitor – Really?
Prisoner – Yes, I thought I could run faster than the policeman – and I couldn't.

Railway manager – Another farmer is suing us on account of his cows.
Lawyer – Killed by trains, I suppose?
Railway manager – No. He says that the passengers have got into the habit of leaning out of the windows and milking the cows as the train goes by!

Customer – You told me that this suit will wear like iron.
Tailor – Well, it has, hasn't it?

Customer – I've had it two months and it has begun to look rusty!

Tom – If you had a wish, what would you wish?
John – If I had a wish, I'd wish that I'd get every wish I wished!

Bobby – I've been an awful good boy since I started going to Sunday school, haven't I?
Mother – Yes, dear, you've been very good indeed.
Bobby – And you don't distrust me any more, do you?
Mother – No, dear.
Bobby – Then, why do you hide the chocolate biscuits?

Teacher – Give me a sentence with the word frequent in it.
Toots – The living skeleton escaped from the circus, and nobody knew where the freak went.

Jock – Do you know how to get a hot meal without cooking or using a fire in any way?
Sandy – No, it's impossible.
Jock – Not at all. Eat bread and mustard.

Fat lady (to train attendant) – Do you mind helping me out? I cannot get out the proper way? I have already gone two stations past my town. You see, I am too stout and I have got to go out backwards and the porters, thinking I am getting in, push me back in again.

Dennis – How much is it for an empty bottle?
Pharmacist – Well, if you want the empty bottle it'll be seventy pence, but, if you have something put into it, we won't charge you anything for the bottle.
Dennis – Sure, that's fair enough. Put in a cork.

Jack (showing a photograph of himself on a donkey) – I had this taken at Margate. Isn't it like me?
Pat – Very. But who is that on your back?

Jimmy – You can take your finger off that leak now, Dad!
Dad – Why? Has the plumber come?
Jimmy – No, the house is on fire!

Uncle (telling story of the princes in the Tower) – And so they hid the two princes under the staircase, and they weren't found for a long time.
Nephew – But didn't the gasman find them when he came to look at the meter?

Gent – Hey, boy! What's the quickest way to get to the station?
Boy – Run.

Old gent (to boy fishing) – How many have you caught?
Boy – Well, when I get another, I'll have caught one.

Old lady (in a greengrocer's) – What have you in the shape of cucumbers? Nervous shop assistant – Er . . . bananas?

Boy (entering police station) – Where is the cashier, please?
Inspector – We don't have one at a police station.
Boy – Well, who counts the coppers, then?

Cavalry sergeant – Hey, you've only got one spur on! You can't ride a horse with only one spur. Where's the other?
Recruit – Well, sir, it's broken, but I thought that if I could get one side of the horse to go the other would follow.

Diner – Waiter, would you close that window?
Waiter – Is there a draught, sir?
Diner – Well, not exactly, but this is the third time my steak has blown off my plate.

Tim – Jim, do you know what I've just seen? A duck swimming on a pond and a cat sitting on its tail.
Jim – What nonsense! Why, I don't believe it.
Tim – It's a fact, honestly. Er . . . the cat was sitting on its own tail, of course!

Man – Can you tell me the nearest way to the hospital?
Little boy – I don't know, sir, but if you step in front of that car you'll get there soon enough.

Cannibal chief – What was that you served me with just now?
Cook – Motor cyclist, your majesty.
Chief – He tasted very burnt.
Cook – Yes, he was scorching when we caught him.

Mother – Hurry up, Smiffy. Have you got your shoes on yet?
Smiffy – Yes, all but one.

Jones – Your dog bit me.
Neighbour – He did not.
Jones – Then prove it.
Neighbour – First, my dog has no teeth. Second, he is not ferocious. Third, he is particular about whom he bites. Fourth, I haven't got a dog.

Smith – That's a ripping little dog of yours.
Jones – He is. He ripped up my best overcoat and slippers yesterday.

Toots – Is 'Erbert really short-sighted?
Plug – I should say so. I saw him once at the zoo, and he was looking at an elephant through a magnifying glass.

Minnie – How do you make a currant roll?
Dad (fed up answering questions, sarcastically) – Blow it up with a bicycle pump, and shove it down a hill.

Jack – When people's teeth ache they have them filled, don't they?
Mother – Yes.
Jack – Well, my stomach aches. Could I go along to the sweet shop and get it filled?

Smith – It's always dangerous to jump to conclusions. You're liable to make yourself look ridiculous.
Brown – Yes, you're right. I jumped at the conclusion of a ferryboat once, and missed!

Policeman – Can't you see that notice, "No Fishing Allowed"?
Boy – Sure, but I was fishing quietly.

Inspector – What is nothing?
Pupil – Nothing is a footless stocking without a leg.

Motorist – My tyre punctuated today.
Friend – Punctured, you mean.
Motorist – I dunno, but it came to a full stop.

Teacher – If I gave you sixteen nuts to share equally with your little brother, how many would he get?
Jimmy – Six.
Teacher – Nonsense! You can't count.
Jimmy – Oh, yes, I can, but my little brother can't.

Jimmy – Oh, Dad, there's a big black cat in the kitchen.
Dad – Oh, never mind. Black cats are lucky.
Jimmy – Yes, this one was. It's just eaten the fish for your supper.

Smith – Hello, old chap. How are you?
Jones – Not so bad. Had an accident on my bike the other day, though.
Smith – Oh, was it bad?
Jones – Fairly. I was knocked speechless, and my wheel was knocked spokeless.

Sergeant (drilling a recruit squad) – Fire at will.
New recruit (pointing his rifle among the ranks) – Which one is Will?

Angry Dad – Didn't I tell you not to have another fight with Jimmy Brown?
Son – It wasn't another fight, Dad. We were just finishing the last one.

Teacher – Now, if I gave you two apples, Bobby gave you three oranges, Tommy gave you five grapes, and Willie gave you two pears, what would you have?
Pupil – I think I'd have a pain, sir.

Billy (doing crossword puzzle) – Give me the name of a motor car that starts with "T".
Friend – Don't be an ass. You know they all start with petrol.

Lady (to weary salesman) – Can't you see the notice on the gate, "No Salesmen"? Didn't you go to school?
Salesman (sarcastic) – No, lady. I went to night school, and I can't read in the daytime.

Customer (to fishmonger) – I don't like the look of that haddock.
Fishmonger – Well, if it's looks you're after, why don't you buy a goldfish?

Where did Brown get all his money?
In the hold-up business.
Never!
Yes. He manufactures suspenders.

First Boy – My dad is so strong he can tear up a pack of cards.
Second Boy – That's nothing. My dad was late this morning, so he tore up the road.

Page – Didst thou call me, my liege?
Enraged knight – Aye, varlet. Go thou quickly and procure a tin-opener. There's a wasp in my armour.

Jim – I had a terrible fight with Bill Smasher, the boxer.
Jack – Really, did he hurt you?
Jim – Oh, no! It was a long-distance telephone call.

Dennis – Say, Billy, can you sprint very fast?
Billy – Can I? Why, yesterday I ran around a half-mile track so fast that my shadow was just starting out when I got back.

Mother – You were a tidy boy not to throw your orange peel on the floor of the bus. Where did you put it?
Dennis – In the pocket of the man sitting next to me.

Artist – Would you stand there a few moments? I want to get some local colour.
Local – You've already got it, mister. I've just painted that bench you're sitting on.

Mechanics instructor (to class) – Are there any questions?
Pupil – Yes, sir. What is the horse-power of a donkey-engine?

WHAT DO YOU GET IF YOU CROSS AN ELEPHANT WITH A SPARROW?
Broken telephone wires.

DID YOU HEAR ABOUT THE TWO DEER WHO RAN AWAY TO GET MARRIED?
They antELOPED!

WHAT'S AS BIG AS AN ELEPHANT AND WEIGHS NOTHING?
An elephant's shadow.

Shipwrecked sailor (playing noughts and crosses with his companion) – I guess we'll have to turn the raft over now, Bill!

First passenger – Pardon me, does this train stop at Paddington?
Second passenger – Yes, watch me, and get off two stations before I do.

Theatre attendant – Only stalls and boxes left, sir.
Farmer – What do you take me for – a horse?

First fireman – Where's the fire?
Second fireman – There isn't one.
First fireman – But you said the fire bell had gone.
Second fireman – So it has. Someone's pinched it.

Tommy – My father has one of Drake's flags.
Willie – That's nothing. My father has one of Adam's apples.

Cuddles – I think my drum annoys the man next door.
Dimples – How do you know?
Cuddles – Well, he gave me a penknife this morning, and asked me if I knew what was inside my drum

Jones – Honestly speaking, would you think I'd bought the car second-hand?
Smith – No, I though you'd made it yourself.

Flying instructor – And if the parachute doesn't open – well, gentlemen, that is what is known as jumping to a conclusion.

Landlady – Good morning! How do you find yourself?
Lodger – I didn't know I was lost.

Hiker – I look upon hiking as a tonic.
Tourist – Yes, and on a passing lorry as a pick-me-up, I suppose!

Tradesman (loftily) – In twenty years of business, no customer has ever complained of my work.
Neighbour – Wonderful! What are you?
Tradesman – An undertaker.

Little boy – I've asked for money, I've begged for money, and I've cried for money.
Auntie – Have you ever tried working for it?
Little boy – No, Auntie. I'm going through the alphabet and I haven't got to "W" yet.

Gent – Now, I want a really high-bred dog.
Salesman – Yes, sir. What about a Skye terrier?

Teacher – There is no difficulty in the world that we cannot overcome.
Pupil – Have you ever tried squeezing the toothpaste back into the tube, sir?

Old lady (at the zoo) – Mr Keeper, if one of the lions escaped what steps would you take?
Keeper – The biggest I could!

Smiffy's Grandad – I remember when I could walk right round the square, but now I can only walk halfway round and back.

Photographer – Do you want a large or a small photograph?
Sitter – A small one, please.
Photographer – Then close your mouth, please.

Prison visitor (to prisoner) – And why are you here, my poor man?
Prisoner -Because they've got all the doors locked.

Johnny – Pa, it's raining.
Pa (vexed at being interrupted) – Well, let it rain!
Johnny – I was going to.

Bully – Why run away? I thought you said you could fight me with one hand tied behind your back?
Small boy – So I could. I'm just running home for the string.

Actor (in the Wild West) – I'll be hanged if I act here again!
Manager – Yes, or shot!

Manager – You should have been here at nine o'clock.
Office junior – Why, what happened then?

Lady – The watch I told you about wasn't stolen. I've just found it.
Detective – Too late! We've arrested the thief.

Bailiff – Oh, most excellent majesty, this man hath stolen our sacred white elephant.
Rajah – Search him!

Bill – You've enough brass in your neck to make a kettle.
Harry – Yes, and you've enough water in your brain to fill the kettle.

Smiffy – What's the matter?
Plug – I can't get my new boots on at all.
Smiffy – Don't worry. You never can get new boots on till you've worn them once or twice.

Grocer – What are you doing here? I thought I sacked you last night.
Jimmy – I know. And don't do it again. I got an awful row when I went home.

Teacher – Has anyone a question to ask?
Wilfrid – Yes, sir. Can a short-sighted man have a faraway look in his eyes?

Victim – Wow! I thought you extracted teeth without pain?
Dentist – Correct! I assure you I felt no pain whatever.

Arctic explorer – It was so cold where we were that the candle froze and we couldn't blow it out.
Second explorer – That's nothing! Where we were the words came out of our mouths in pieces of ice, and we had to fry them to see what we were talking about.

Mike – Have you seen my boots, Pat?
Pat – Are you sure you had them on when you took them off?

Teacher – Can any lad tell me what a bison is?
Jimmy – Please, sir, a bison is what my mother cooks her puddings in.

Employer – If anyone asks for me, I'll be back in half an hour.
New office junior – Yes, sir, and how soon will you be back if no one asks for you?

Film producer – Your story is too highly coloured.
Writer – In what way?
Film producer – Why, in the very first act you make the old man turn purple with rage, the villain green with envy, the hero white with anger and the coachman blue with cold.

Man (on the telephone) – Hello, gasman, come at once! There's an awful leak in our gas-pipe!
Gasman – Have you done anything to it?
Man – Yes, I put a bucket under it.

Teacher – To what family does the whale belong?
Smiffy – Don't know, sir. No family in our neighbourhood owns a whale.

Customer – How much are these chickens?
Farmer – Three pounds.
Customer – Did you raise them yourself?
Farmer – Yes; they were two pounds fifty pence yesterday.

Toots – Smiffy is very absent-minded. The other evening he sat up till midnight trying to remember what it was he wanted to do.
Sidney – Did he remember?
Toots – Yes, he wanted to go to bed early.

Stout man – Can you tell me how to get out of this park, lad?
Jimmy – Have you tried sideways, mister?

Director – Did you have a good reception last night?
Actor – The audience pelted me with flowers.
Director – How'd you get the old black eye?
Actor – Well, they didn't take the flowers out of the pots.

Diner – Oh, goodness, waiter, I've swallowed a fly. What shall I do?
Waiter – Swallow some fly-paper, sir.

Teacher – Sidney, you were not at school yesterday afternoon. Have you any explanation to offer?
Sidney – Please, Teacher, I was going to school, and I saw a steamroller and a policeman says to me, "Mind that steamroller", and I stayed minding it all the afternoon.

Teacher – Johnny, make a sentence using the word "indisposition".
Johnny – When a boxer fights, he stands in disposition.

Dad – What is the matter now?
Small boy – I dropped the towel in the bath, and it has dried me wetter than I was before.

Policeman – What are you standing there for?
Loafer – Nothin'.
Policeman – Well, if everybody was to stand in the same place, how would the rest get past?

Road hog (recognising man he has just run over) – Why, fancy running across you, Smith! I was saying just this morning that I hadn't bumped into you for ages.

Artist (showing a blank canvas) – Look at that picture of a cow eating grass.
Friend – Where's the grass?
Artist -The cow's eaten it.
Friend – Well, where's the cow?
Artist – Oh, it went away when it saw there wasn't any more grass to eat.

Teacher – Now, Bobby, if six eggs cost sixty pence, how many would you get for twenty pence?
Bobby – None.
Teacher – What? Why would you get none?
Bobby – Because I'd buy marbles, miss.

Father – Now, Tommy, what did I say I would do if I caught you stealing the biscuits again?
Tommy – That's funny, Dad. I've forgotten, too.

Doctor (meeting patient on street) – I told you not to come out of doors.
Patient – I didn't. I came out the window.

Customer – I want to take home a small chicken.
Butcher – Do you want a pullet?
Customer – Good gracious, no! I'll carry it with me.

Charlie (to his young brother) – Mrs Dubbs sent you four apples for cutting her grass. I ate two and lost one, and Johnny pinched the other. Mind you thank her when you see her.

Old man – Ah, my poor man, you've fallen down a manhole, haven't you?
Victim (sarcastically) – Oh, no, I happened to be here when the road was being made, and they built it round me.

George – Which is farther away – America or the moon?
Harry – America, of course. You can see the moon, but you can't see America.

Small boy (to very fat uncle) – I say, uncle, what a feed someone could have if he was as roomy as you and as hungry as me.

Diner – Is there any tomato sauce on the menu, waiter?
Waiter – No, sir. I have wiped it off.

First angler – Caught anything yet, Bill?
Second angler – Well, I've caught a salmon tin, but I think the salmon must have got away.

Teacher – What are raised in damp climates?
Schoolboy – Umbrellas, sir.

Dud comedian – I'm thinking of touring South Africa next season.
Friend – Take my advice and don't. An ostrich egg weighs from two to three pounds!

Jack – Say, Dad, what is the ship's hold?
Dad – The ship's hold? Why the anchor, of course.

Absent-minded professor – You see, my dear, I've not forgotten to bring my umbrella home this time.
Wife – But you never took one with you!

First jeweller – I have had it proved to me that advertising brings results.
Second jeweller – How?
First Jeweller – Yesterday, I advertised for a night watchman, and during the night my shop was burgled.

Listener – Did you keep cool when confronted by the bear?
Explorer – Rather. I was so cool that my teeth chattered.

Smiffy – Were you a good pupil at school?
Dad – Yes! I used to say my lessons so well that the teacher made me stay behind and repeat them to her after class.

Auntie – Why don't you eat your sweets, Jimmy?
Jimmy – I'm waiting for Jack Smith to come along. Sweets taste much better if there's another boy looking on.

Terry – What does your brother work at?
Jerry – He's got a very high position in the shipping world.
Terry – A naval captain?
Jerry – No, a lighthouse-keeper.

Airman – I . . . er . . . say, you've heard that saying, "See Naples and die"?
Passenger – Yes, why?
Airman – Well, I'm sorry to say that something's gone wrong with the engine, and we're over Naples now.

Teacher – Jimmy, correct this sentence, "Our teacher am in sight."
Jimmy – Our teacher am a sight.

Zoo keeper – Have you seen my antelope?
Confused man – No, whom did your aunt elope with?

Tourist – I say, do you ever have rain here?
Texan – Say, stranger, we have ducks here that are eight years old and haven't learned to swim yet.

Uncle – You would like me to give you five pounds?
Jock – Yes.
Uncle – Yes, if you . . . what?
Jock – If you can't afford any more.

Jack – I'm head over heels in work.
Jim – What's your job?
Jack – I'm an acrobat in the circus.

Judge – You say the constable arrested you while your were minding your own business?

Prisoner – Yes. He caught me by the collar, and threatened to strike me unless I accompanied him to the station.

Judge – You were attending to your own business then?

Prisoner – I was.

Judge – What is your business?

Prisoner – I'm a burglar.

Angler – Have you any salmon?

Village storekeeper – No, but I have some excellent pork pies.

Angler – Don't be an ass! How could a fellow go home and say he's caught a couple of pork pies?

Householder (to policeman investigating burglary) – I think it must have been a cat burglar.

Policeman – Why?

Householder- Because the milk was stolen.

Mother – Dennis, have you washed your face?

Dennis – Yes, Mum. Just look at the towel, it's filthy.

Teacher – When is the best time to gather fruit?

Roger – Please, sir, when the dog is tied up.

Motorist – I had the right of way when this man ran into me and yet you say I was to blame.

Constable – You certainly were.

Motorist – Why?

Constable – Because his brother is the Lord Mayor, his father is chief of police, and I'm engaged to his sister.

Mike – Hi, Pat, what have you got your fingers in Flynn's ears for?

Pat – Well, I can't find my glasses, and Flynn's reading a letter for me, and I don't want him to hear what it's about.

Teacher (to new boy) – What's your name, my little fellow?

New boy – Jimmy Brown.

Teacher – Always say "sir" when you are speaking to a teacher. Now, what's your name?

New boy – Sir Jimmy Brown.

Flight commander – What's making the airship go so slow?

Engineer – Well, sir, we are passing along the Milky Way, and the propeller is clogged with butter.

Teacher (after a class about how a cat can see in the dark) – What can the cat do that I can't?

Danny – Please, sir, wag its tail!

Terry – My brother ran thirty miles then cleared a five-barred gate at the finish.

Jerry – That's nothing to shout about. Look at the run he took.

Aunt (as wee Jock gets third slice of cake) – I wonder if there is any kind of cake you don't like?

Wee Jock – Yes, stomachache!

Artist -What a pretty cottage. May I paint it?

Farmer – No thanks. It's just been whitewashed.

Sergeant – I wonder why everybody calls me "Zebra"?

P.C. 222 – Because you're a donkey with stripes, I suppose.

Man -What are you crying for?

Boy – I've lost a pound coin.

Man – Here's another. Oh, what are you still crying for?

Boy – Well, if I hadn't lost that pound I'd have had two pounds now.

History teacher – Where did King William die?

Pupil – On page 121, sir.

What do you get if you cross Gnasher with a rose?
Something you wouldn't want to sniff!

What happened to the man who made his dog walk in the gutter?
They both fell off the roof!

That dog bit my leg!
Did you put anything on it?
No, he liked it just the way it was!

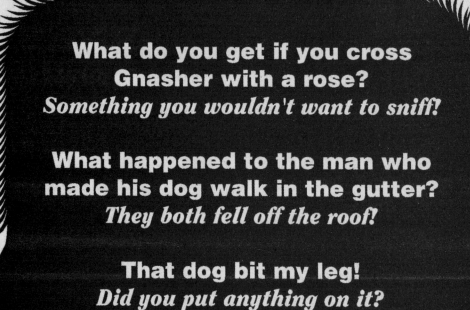

What do you get if you cross a dog with a giraffe?
An animal that barks at low flying aircraft.

Fortune-teller – Your prospects are not good, and a man stands in your way.
Client – Heaven help him. I drive a steamroller.

Tailor (to fat man) – Will you hold on to the end of this measuring tape, sir, while I run round with the other end?

Once there was a man named Berry, who owned a shop. One day a dissatisfied customer came in and said,
"You need not look blue, Berry, because I don't care a straw, Berry. Your father, the elder Berry, should not have been such a goose, Berry, so in future I will buy my goods from Logan, Berry."

Stranger – Why are you running that steam roller over the field, farmer?
Farmer – I'm trying to raise mashed potatoes.

Applicant – I came to see if you had an opening for me?
Manager – Yes, there's one behind you. Close it when you go out.

Boy (with pal at dentist's) – Please, I want a tooth out, and I don't want an anaesthetic, because I'm in a hurry.
Dentist – That's a brave boy. Which tooth is it?
Boy – Show him your tooth, Albert.

Binks – I am sorry my hen got out and scraped up your garden.
Jinks – That's all right. My dog ate your hen.
Binks -That's all right, too. I've just run over your dog.

Notice in the window of a suburban house – Piano for Sale.
Notice in the house next door – Hurrah!

Dog breeder (to man with ten children) – Why not buy a nice dachshund and let all the kids play with it at one time?

Guide – These are the ruins of one of the castles of the earliest Norman invaders.
Tourist – Yes, but I can never understand why they built them so far from the railway station.

Mother – Don't forget to pack your toothbrush, Willie.
Willie – But Mother, I thought I was going for a holiday?

Teacher – Now Johnny, what is lukewarm water?
Johnny (after a long pause) – Please, sir, it's water that looks warm but isn't.

Barber – How would you like your hair cut, my boy?
Small customer – Like Dad's, with a hole in the middle.

Customer – What's the charge for this battery?
Electrician – One and a half volts.
Customer – What's that in British money?

Jones – I see they're erecting a statue to the man who invented pneumatic tyres.
Smith – Wouldn't a bust be more appropriate?

Small boy (giving shopkeeper a five pound note for a 50p chocolate bar) – Would you give me 2 pound coins, four fifty pences, a twenty pence, two tens, and two fives as change?
Shopkeeper (sarcastically) – Are there any particular dates you want?

Uncle – Were you pleased with the drum I sent you for your birthday?
Nephew – Yes, very much, Uncle. Mother gives me five pounds every week not to use it.

Grey – If you're going to borrow money, borrow it from a pessimist.
Greene – Why?
Grey – He never expects to get it back.

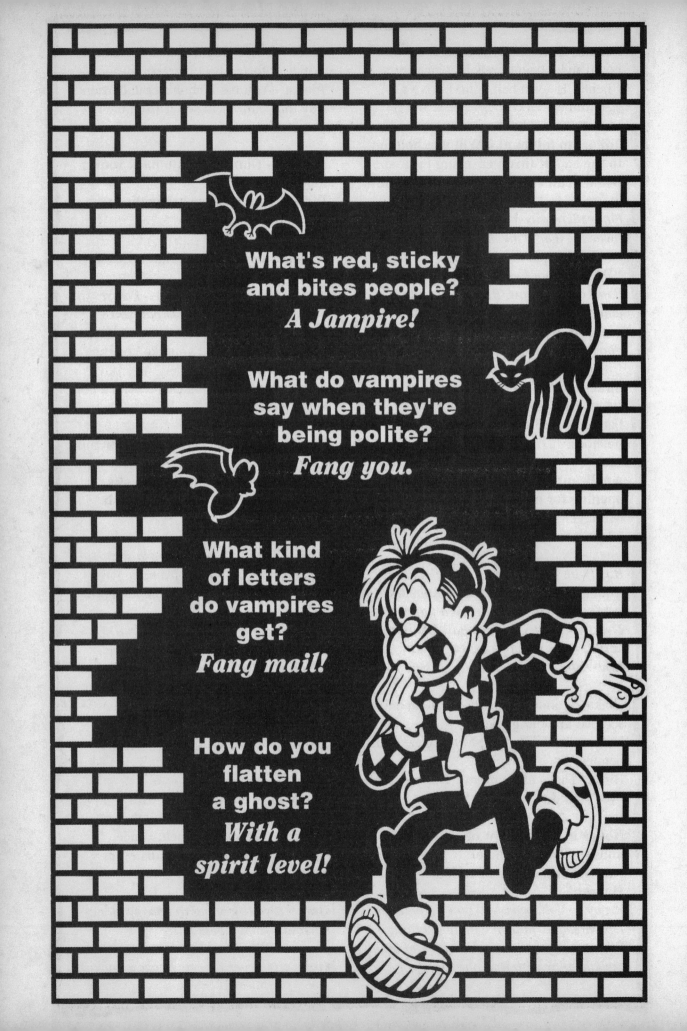

Small brother – The skateboard you left under the park seat yesterday has been found.
Big brother – Good news! Who has it?
Small brother – I don't know, but it's been found. I looked, and it isn't there now.

Auntie – Well, how did you enjoy the ride on Uncle's shoulders?
Minnie – Oh, it was quite nice, but I had a ride on a real donkey yesterday.

Manager – I'm afraid that fellow I gave a job to last week is dishonest.
Assistant – You shouldn't judge by appearances.
Manager – I'm not, I'm judging by disappearances.

Father – You ought to be ashamed of not knowing what you learned at school today. Cuthbert Cringeworthy always knows.
Danny – Yes, but he hasn't so far to go home.

Jones – I have been born unlucky.
Friend – Why?
Jones – Well, I was at a football match, and there were twenty-two players and a referee on the field, about ten thousand spectators in the ground, and the ball hit me.

Judge (to pickpocket) – Just what good have you done to humanity?
Prisoner – Well, I've kept three or four detectives working regularly.

Tommy – I had a quarrel with Pug Smith this morning, and I would have punched his head if I hadn't been held off.
Willie – Who held you off?
Tommy – Pug.

Farmer – Now, lads, you can't play cricket here.
Batsman – Oh, can't we! Why, we're 69 for no wickets already.

Interested dog buyer – Yes, he looks all right, but has he any pedigree?
Dealer – Pedigree, sir? Why, if that dog could talk he wouldn't speak to either of us.

Customer – Give me four pork sandwiches to take away.
Assistant (speaking down tube) – Dress up four grunts to go walking.

Hotel guest – Didn't I tell you to wake me at nine, and it's only eight just now?
Boy – Yes, sir, but the other lodgers want their breakfast, and you're lying on the tablecloth.

Two grubby boys go to see their doctor.
Doctor – Ah! Let me see. Vaccinations for you two, isn't it? Right arm, please.
First boy – Just our luck, Jock. We've both gone and washed the left one.

Father – Where are those chocolate bars I left on the table?
Fatty – I haven't touched one of them.
Father – But I left five, and now there's only one.
Fatty – Yes, that's the one I didn't touch.

First student – Our professor is a wonderful man. He talks like a book.
Second student – Yes, but it's a pity he doesn't shut up as easily.

Jackson – I think we met in this restaurant last month. Your coat seems familiar to me.
Johnson – But I didn't have this overcoat last month.
Jackson – No, but I did.

Doctor – How did you get here?
Patient – 'Flu!

Excited passenger – Hey, there's a bloke fallen off the bus!
Conductor – It's all right, he's paid his fare!

What's worse than an elephant on water skis?
A porcupine on a rubber life-raft.

How do hedgehogs play leapfrog?
Very, very carefully.

Why did the hedgehog say ouch?
He put his coat on inside out.

Why don't Dalmatian puppies play hide and seek?
They always get spotted.

Brown (with wire netting) – I say, Jones, do you know how to make a chicken run?
Jones – Yes, clap your hands and say "shoo"!

Dimwit – What are you doing?
Motorist (with a punctured tyre) – I'm looking for a puncture.
Dimwit – Never mind; someone will come along soon and lend you one.

Walter – Would you mind taking that yellow tie with the green spots out of the window for me?
Shopkeeper – Certainly, sir.
Walter – Thanks awfully. The beastly thing bothers me every time I pass.

Prospective tenant – Is this cottage within walking distance of the railway station?
Landlord – Well . . . er ...how far can you walk?

Friend – I could eat that fried egg, it looks so real.
Artist – Fried egg! That's a sunset I've painted.

Passenger (on board ship) – Doesn't the vessel tip a lot?
Steward – Yes, it's trying its best to set a good example to the passengers.

Passer-by (to angler) – Good river for fish?
Angler – It must be. I can't persuade any to come out.

Teacher – Who succeeded Edward VI?
Toots – Mary, sir.
Teacher – And who followed Mary?
Toots – Her little lamb?

Jones – I always feel ill the day before a journey.
Brown – Why don't you go a day earlier?

Water, waiter, there's a fly in this soup!
Don't worry, sir. It won't drink much!

Boy (to neighbour) – Father's sent me back with your ladder. He's broken it, and he hopes you'll have it mended quickly because he wants to borrow it again next week.

Teacher – What is an exit?
Pupil – An entrance you go out of.

New apprentice joiner – Please sir, I couldn't get any two-inch nails, so I brought twice as many one-inch ones.

Doctor – There's nothing wrong with you. Your pulse is regular as clockwork.
Patient – Excuse me, that's my wrist watch you've got hold of.

Father – Why were you kept in at school?
Jimmy – I didn't know where the Nile was.
Father (angrily) – In future, you must remember where you put things.

Farmer – What's the matter with you? I sent you out to brand the livestock, and you come back covered in blisters!
New farmhand – Well, I had a lot of trouble branding the bees.

Hotel manager – Are you the gentleman who wanted to be awakened to catch the early train?
Hotel guest – Yes.
Hotel manager – Then you can go back to sleep , you've missed it.

Young boy – You must be very well-travelled, Captain.
Old sailor – Travelled! There ain't many ports I haven't seen the inside of.

Hotel manager – How did you sleep last night, professor?
Professor (irritably) – Lying down.

John – Look how high that ship is floating out of the water.
Jim – Yes, it's low tide just now.

Young boy – Why, you must know a lot about geography.

Old sailor – Yes, we did put in there once but only to coal the ship. 'Tain't much of a place, what I remember of it.

Terry – Have you improved your bicycle riding lately?

Jerry – On the contrary, I would say that I have fallen off a lot.

Jimmy – My history teacher is the meanest man I know.

Father – Why is that?

Jimmy – He borrows my sharpener to sharpen his pencil to give me bad marks.

New clerk – How long has that office boy worked for you?

Manager – About four hours.

New clerk – But I though he'd been with you a long time?

Manager – So he has, but he's only worked about four hours.

Mother – It's time to wake up, Jimmy.

Jimmy – I can't wake up.

Mother – Why not?

Jimmy – Because I'm not asleep.

Teacher – Can anyone tell me what is the highest form of animal life?

'Erbert – The giraffe.

Terry – I seemed to be always twisting and turning in my sleep last night.

Jerry – Ah, sleeping like a top, I suppose!

Mother – Sandy, stop pulling the cat's tail!

Sandy – I'm not pulling it. I'm only holding. It's the cat that's pulling!

Jerry – It's a twist! It's a twist!

Terry – What's a twist?

Jerry – A corkscrew.

Teacher – In what battle was General Wolfe killed?

Danny – His last one, sir.

Mother – Will you have a little of this steak pie, Jack?

Jack – No, thank you.

Mother – What? Then what will you have?

Jack – A lot, please.

Minnie – Dad, how long will that clock go without being wound up?

Dad – Eight days.

Minnie – And how long will it go when it is wound up?

Jim – What are you digging that hole for, Jim?

Bill – It's not the hole I'm digging. I'm digging the dirt and leaving the hole.

Lady – Those apples you sold me had a fishy taste.

Greengrocer – That's all right lady – they were crab apples.

Manager – And what is your father's walk in life?

Applicant – Er . . . one foot in front of the other.

Teacher – Wilfrid, what is a semi-circle?

Wilfrid – A straight line caught bending.

Father – Who is the laziest person in your class?

Sidney – I dunno.

Father – Well, who is it that watches the other hard-working pupils instead of working himself?

Sidney – Teacher.

Man (who has been knocked down by a motor car) – Where am I?

Enterprising street hawker – Here you are, sir; map of Glasgow, three pounds.

Bill – Hey, Sam, what are you putting on all those coats for?

Sam – It's like this, Bill, I'm going to paint my fence, and it says on the tin, "To obtain good results, put on three or four coats." And that's what I'm doing.

Terry – I've just been having a tussle with the dentist.
Jerry – Who won?
Terry – It was a draw.

Which person always sticks up for his employer?
A billposter.

Street hawker – Want to buy a watch, old man?
Passer-by – What's the matter with it?
Street hawker – Nothing.
Passer-by – What are you selling it for then?
Street hawker – Nothing.
Passer-by – Righto. I'll buy it at that price.

Teacher – If ten men plough a field in six hours, how long will twenty men take to plough the same field?
Danny – They couldn't do it.
Teacher – Why not?
Danny – 'Cause the ten men have already ploughed it.

Terry – I know a man with over a thousand medals for sport.
Jerry – Some athlete!
Terry – No, but what a pawnbroker.

McTavish (victim of shipwreck) – Well, it might have been worse.
McTaggart (also a victim) – Yes, we might have bought a return ticket.

Dad – Jimmy, you are so naughty sometimes that I don't believe there's anything good in you.
Jimmy – Yes, there is, Dad. I've just eaten three mince pies, two bananas, and a chocolate bar.

Bobbie – Mother says these buns taste of soap.
Baker – Tell her they are bath buns.

Danny – A gallon of petrol, quick! The school's on fire.

Cricket fan – How many runs did you make?
Cricket player – I got twenty-four runs from one hit.
Cricket fan – How did you do that?
Cricket player – I broke a car window, and both teams and both umpires had to run for their lives.

Why is a cake like the sun?
Because it rises in the yeast and sinks beyond the vest.

Teacher – If I saw a boy beating a donkey, and I stopped him, what virtue should I be showing?
Plug – Brotherly love, sir.

Circus manager – The tent is on fire. What shall we do?
Attendant – Call the fire-eater.

Diner – Waiter, this soup isn't fit for a pig.
Waiter – Sorry, sir, I'll take it away and bring some that is.

Plug (on crowded train) – Isn't it rotten having to wait for a seat?
Fatty – You're lucky, I've to wait for two.

Polar explorer – Once we were nearly frozen to death, but we escaped.
Listener – How?
Explorer – We got into a heated argument.

Augustus Theodore d'Arcy – I want some peppah.
Store assistant – What sort? White, black or cayenne?
Augustus – Peppah, you fool, writing peppah.

Landlord (shouting upstairs) – Rent!
Tenant (shouting downstairs) – Spent!

Teacher – What is an organiser?
Minnie – The man that makes the music in church.

HOW DO YOU START . . .

... *A cockerel race?*
Ready, steady, crow!

... *A cuddly toy race?*
Ready, teddy, go!

... *A jelly race?*
On your marks. Get set!

... *An insect race?*
One-two-flea-go!

... *A glow worm race?*
Ready, steady, glow!

First author (reading) – The evening wore on.
Second author – Well, what did it wear?
First author – Oh, the close (clothes) of day, I suppose.

Boss – Have you got those tools sharpened?
Apprentice – Yes, but I can't get the nicks out of the saw.

Old lady – I thought you said this was a police dog?
Dog breeder – Yes, madam, but it's undercover.

Walter – Some powder please.
Chemist – The kind that goes off with a bang?
Walter – No, the kind that goes on with a puff.

Billy – Were you in the Ark, grandpa?
Grandpa – Of course not.
Billy – Then why weren't you drowned?

Old man -Excuse me, Mr Keeper, but does it cost very much to feed the giraffe?
Zoo keeper – Oh, no, sir. You see a little goes a long way with him.

Customer – Didn't you claim when you sold me this car that you'd replace anything that was broken or was missing?
Car salesman – Yes, sir. What is it?
Customer – Well, I want four front teeth and a collar bone!

Sharpe – Have you heard the tale of the three wells?
Smart – No, what is it?
Sharpe – Well! Well! Well!

Teacher – Can any boy give me a sentence with diploma in it?
Jimmy – Father heard a noise in the pipes, so he sent for di ploma (the plumber).

Guide – Yes, this is a marvellous echo. The people here shout out of their windows at night as they go to bed, and the echo wakes them in the morning.

Terry – Is McTavish any good at the high jump?
Jerry – No, he can hardly clear his throat.

Artist – Have you any camel hair brushes?
Village shopkeeper – No, sir, none of my customers keep camels!

Dick – I say, do you know the difference between "remember" and "recollect"?
Bob – None that I can see.
Dick – Well, I remember lending you five pounds last week, but I haven't re-collected it yet.

Pompous customer – I want two eggs, poached medium soft; toast, not too hard and buttered from edge to edge; and coffee, freshly ground Kenyan, not too strong and not too weak.
Waiter – Yes, sir, would you like any special design on the dishes?

Captain of team – Why can't you keep up with the other forwards?
Herbert – Because they didn't have to blow the ball up before we started.

Tommy had done something naughty and hid from his mother under the bed. When Tommy's father came home his mother told him what had happened. His father rushed upstairs and looked under the bed. Tommy looked at him, and then said – "Hello Dad, is she after you, too?"

Teacher -What is a niche in a church?
Boy – Well, it's just the same as an itch anywhere else – only you can't scratch it so well.

Horace – When I get old will the calves of my legs become cows?

Animal trainer – The leopard has escaped. Shoot him on the spot with the tranquilliser gun.
Circus hand – Which spot, sir?

Bandsman Bill – Our band was in a smash-up last night.
His friend – Any bones broken?
Bandsman Bill- Yes, two trombones.

Mother – What are you playing with?
Little son – A caterpillar and two little kittenpillars.

Father – I think my watch wants cleaning.
Jack – It should be really clean already. I had it in the bath yesterday.

Barber – Have I shaved you before?
Customer – No. I got these scars in the war.

Teacher – Where did King John sign the Magna Carta?
Smiffy – Please, sir, along the dotted line.

Professor Knowall is so absent-minded that he put his clothes to bed and hung himself over the back of a chair.

Billy – Why has your father such a large moustache?
Tommy – He put hair restorer on his sandwich in mistake for sauce.

Teacher – What is air?
Tommy – A balloon with the skin off.

Teacher – Smith, put what's in your mouth in the wastepaper basket!
Smith – I wish I could, sir. It's a gumboil!

Tommy – Daddy, can you sign your name with your eyes shut?
Father – Why, that's easy!
Tommy – Well would you mind shutting your eyes and signing my school report card?

Teacher – What is wasted energy?
Bright lad – Telling a hair-raising story to a bald-headed man.

Bloggs – You should think of the future.
Noggs – I can't. It's my wife's birthday, and I'm thinking of the present.

Teacher – A fool can ask questions that wise people cannot answer.
Danny – No wonder we didn't pass our examination.

Singer – I'm afraid I wasn't singing very well tonight.
Wireless announcer – Oh, that's all right. You were announced as zoo imitations.

Boy (to teacher) – How did you like my essay on electricity?
Teacher – It was shocking.

Judge – You say Prisoner 66 brutally attacked you?
Warder – Yes, sir. He kicked me in the stomach while my back was turned.

Circus owner – Have you seen an escaped elephant round here?
Dimwit – No, but I've seen a grey rubber bull eating carrots with its tail.

Boy – Have you any broken biscuits?
Grocer – Yes, boy. Why?
Boy – Then here's some glue to stick them together again.

Salesman – Good morning. My name is Sparrow.
Customer – Oh? Well hop it.

Small boy (to mother) – Mother, all the boys at school call me "big head".
Mother – Never mind, Johnny; there's nothing in it!

Tommy – John plays the piano wonderfully by ear.
Freddie – That's nothing. My Dad fiddles with his whiskers.

Patient – Doctor, shall I be able to play the piano when my hand gets better?
Doctor – Why, certainly.
Patient – That's funny. I couldn't play it before.

Uncle – Jimmy, I'm going to give you a bright pound coin.
Jimmy – I'd rather have a dirty, old five pound note.

First boy – Coming out to play football?
Second boy – Can't. I broke a window yesterday, and Dad suspended me for the rest of the season.

Stranger – Boy, where does this road go to?
Dimwit – I don't think it goes anywhere. It's here every morning.

Motorist – Is the water very deep here, sonny?
Peter – No, sir, look it only comes up to the middle of that duck.

Barber – Do you want anything on your face when I've finished?
Smith – Well, I hope you'll leave me my nose.

Teacher – Tommy, why are your hands so dirty?
Tommy – Please, sir, I thought it was Saturday.

Auntie – Why, Fatty, you appear to eat very well.
Fatty – Yes, Auntie, you see, I've been practising all my life.

Gent (to a small boy fishing) – Have you caught anything yet?
Small boy – No, I don't believe my worm's trying!

Teacher – Billy Jones, how did you get that black eye?
Billy – Please, miss, I sprained it doing my homework.

Film actor – But look here, if he's going to throw me into the rapids, how am I going to get out?
Producer – Oh, that's all right – you don't appear again.

Tommy (to father) – Dad, I'm going to be a detective. Can you tell me a good disguise?
Father – Wash your face.

Second – You're all right, Bill. The crowd's with you.
Battered boxer – Wish I was with them!

Visitor – Is your father in, Tommy?
Tommy – Yes, but he is wrapped up in his work.
Visitor – Oh, I did not know he was so studious.
Tommy – He isn't, he's papering the parlour.

Gent – Waiter, I've been waiting half an hour for my turtle soup!
Waiter – Well, sir, you know how slow turtles are!

Teacher – If I said Plug's face was handsome, what tense would that be?
Fatty – Pretence.

Bill – Did you read about that burglar who stole a mile of elastic?
Jim – No, what happened?
Bill – He got a long stretch.

Gent – This soup's very thin, waiter.
Waiter – Yes, sir. The manager likes people to admire the design on the plates.

Man – Waiter, I have only five pounds and fifty pence. What do you recommend?
Waiter – Another restaurant, sir.

Angry grocer – Why did you run away when you broke my window?
Small boy – I couldn't bear to see my ball go through all that "pane".

Teacher – What made you so late this morning?
Tommy – I fell downstairs.
Teacher – That ought not to have taken you long.

First hiker – Go easy, we've got three miles before us.
Second hiker – That's why I'm hurrying. I want to get there before I'm tired out.

Burglar – Excuse me waking you up, but does this watch keep good time?

Small boy (in sweet shop) – How much is that big stick of toffee?
Shopkeeper – Thirty pence.
Small boy – How long will you let me lick it for five pence?

Cuddles – How do ghosts get through closed doors?
Dimples – They use skeleton keys.

Circus manager – What's the matter with your hand?
New lion tamer – I put it in the lion's mouth to see how many teeth he had, and he shut it to see how many fingers I had.

Customer – How the dickens do you open this tin of sardines?
Shopkeeper – There's full instructions inside the tin, sir.

Short-sighted golfer – Why didn't you tell me I was hitting a confounded toadstool?
Caddie – I never thought you would hit it, sir.

Customer – Are those eggs fresh?
Grocer – Fresh! Why, if I hadn't torn a leaf off the calendar too soon they wouldn't have been laid till tomorrow!

Terry – Are you superstitious?
Jerry – Not at all.
Terry – Well, lend me thirteen pounds.

Stage costumier – When are you going to pay me for those wigs you bought last year?
Actor – I'm an actor, not a prophet.

Old lady – I want a nice quiet dog that doesn't bite, bark or run about.
Dealer – Will you try a china one?

Ambitious young singer – And now that you've tested my voice, Professor, what d'you think it's best suited for?
Professor of music – A market stall!

Town boy (visiting cousin in country) – This stuff's just like grass.
Cousin – It is grass.
Town boy – No, it's not, because you don't have to keep off it.

First lodger (discussing new lodger) – He's either a political speaker or an actor.
Second lodger – What makes you think that?
First lodger – Didn't you see the way he ducked at dinner yesterday when you asked him if he'd have a tomato?

Grocer (to small boy applying for job as message-boy) – You ask high wages for a boy without experience.
Small boy – Well, sir, it's harder work when you don't know anything about it.

Customer – Do you exchange unsatisfactory goods?
Salesman – Certainly, sir.
Customer – Well, this is an overcoat I got here last year. I think your new style is much better.

Smith – Let me tell you, Brown, I've forgotten more than you ever knew.
Brown – I say, that's bad. Did you ever try tying a knot in your handkerchief?

Teacher – Can you give me a long sentence?
Pupil – No, but I'd like to!

Judge – And why do you think you should be let off this time?
Prisoner – Well, this is the fiftieth time I've been brought in, so I thought we might have a fiftieth anniversary celebration.

First burglar – If I can pick this lock, we can lay our hands on ten thousand pounds.
Second burglar – Well, see you don't break the blade of my pen-knife.

Man – In my job it's impossible to get a day's work.
Woman – How's that?
Man – Well, you see, I'm a night watchman by trade!

Customer – Didn't you snip off a little of my ear just now?
Barber – Yes, sir, a little bit, but not enough to affect your hearing!

Burglar (to partner who has just knocked a flower-pot over) – That's right, Bill. Deafen 'em so they can't hear us!

Artist – I've been working like a horse all day.
Friend – How?
Artist – I've been drawing a cart!

Terry – Someone told Jimmy that he could get his trousers pressed by letting a steam roller run over them.
Jerry – Well, what about it?
Terry – Jimmy forgot to take his pants off!

Landlady – How do you like your room, as a whole?
Lodger – As a hole, it is all right, but as a room it's rotten!

Sammy – Can you telephone from a submarine?
Sailor – Of course, anybody can tell a phone from a submarine!

Teacher – If I had ten potatoes to share equally among four boys, how would I do it?
Sidney – Mash them, sir.

Willie – Boo-hoo! I've lost the apple that teacher gave for the best boy in the class.
Kind man – Here's another; but how did you lose it?
Willie – I wasn't the best boy!

Johnny – My nerves are so bad that I cannot close my eyes at night.
Percy – Try boxing. After my first lesson, I couldn't open my eyes for three days.

Farmer – Catching my fish, eh?
Angler – Yes, I've just caught one of your big eels.
Farmer – Well, now you're going to catch one of my big toes.

Policeman – I'm looking for a small boy with only one eye.
Passer-by – Well, if he's very small, you'd better use both eyes, Constable.

Pat – That ten pound note you lent me yesterday was a fake one.
Mike – Well, didn't you say you wanted it bad?

Train guard – Keep your head inside the window there.
Passenger – Why?
Train guard – Because we don't want any of our bridges damaged.

Teacher – Can any boy tell me what nothing is?
Tommy – Yes, sir, it's what you gave me yesterday for minding your car.

Caddie (to player who has let his club slip from his hands about six times) – If you go on like this, you'll soon be champion of Britain.
Amateur – At golf?
Caddie – No, throwing the hammer!

**Where do
you put a
criminal sheep?**
Behind baas.

**What do you get if you
cross a werewolf with peanut butter?**
*A monster that sticks to the roof
of your mouth!*

Which farm animals talk too much?
Blah-blah-blacksheep.

**What's got
a screen and
wobbles?**
Jellyvision.

Visitor – What are you going to do when you grow up?
Burglar's son – Follow in my father's finger-prints.

Teacher – Aren't you sorry you hit Timmy under the chin? I'm sure it was a mistake.
Jimmy – Yes, miss; I meant to bash him on the nose.

First pickpocket – Here he comes now.
Second pickpocket – All right. You keep a watch on him while I take the watch off him.

Old man – Which is the quickest way to the hospital?
Constable – Poke me in the back with that stick again, and you'll soon find yourself there.

Teacher – There's only one trustworthy lad in the class.
Jones (in whisper) – That's me.
Teacher – Did you speak Jones?
Jones – No, sir.

Teacher – Would you like your son to learn the dead languages?
Smith – Certainly; he's going to be an undertaker.

Diner – Waiter, my bill should have been thirteen pounds, and you've made it fourteen
Waiter – Yes, sir. I thought you might be superstitious.

Angry man – I'll teach you to hit our cat with stones!
Tommy – I wish you would sir. I've had ten shots, and missed each time.

Customer – What! Four pounds for a shave? And such a shave, too! Why you've cut me three times.
Barber – Yessir! Three pounds for the shave, and one pound for the sticking-plasters.

Passer-by (to owner of antique car) – Engine trouble?
Owner – Well, I can't tell till I walk back and find it.

First kid – They tell me that in New York they have buildings twenty storeys high.
Second kid – My! What a time a kid could have sliding down the banisters!

Gent – Is the horse surefooted?
Horse dealer – Very! Why, he kicked me in the same place three times last week.

Teacher – Aren't you ashamed of yourself – hitting a smaller boy?
Jimmy – I'd rather be ashamed of hitting a smaller boy than sorry I hit a bigger one.

Boss – Look here, Tommy, I wish you wouldn't whistle at work.
Tommy – I'm not working. I'm only whistling.

First mechanic – Does the boss know this plane's crashed?
Second mechanic – He ought to; he's underneath!

Diner – Waiter, a little bird told me this coffee was not filtered.
Waiter – A little bird, sir?
Diner – Yes, a swallow.

Diner – I say, waiter, there's a dead fly in the soup.
Waiter – Ah, poor thing! It's the boiling that kills them, sir.

Briggs – Did you tell Jiggs that I had the biggest feet you had ever seen?
Griggs – No, I just said that if you took off your boots you would be half-undressed.

Motorist – Someone has stolen my car.
Cynical friend – These antique collectors will stop at nothing.

What do you get if you cross a ghost with a boy scout?
Someone who frightens old ladies across the road.

What happened when the boy monster met the girl monster?
It was love at first fright!

What's a ghost's favourite game?
Hide and shriek.

Suspicious character – What am I supposed to have stolen?
Policeman – A horse and van.
Suspicious character – All right, search me.

Hobbs – I'm thinking of raising turnips next year in my allotment. What's the best way?
Bloggs – Take hold of the tops and pull.

Teacher (pointing to the map) – Now, Plug, when you stand facing the north, you have on your right hand the great continent of Asia. What have you on your left hand?
Plug – A wart, but I can't help it, Teacher.

Old man – I want you to see to my piano. My son is learning to play the thing.
Workman – But I'm a carpenter, sir.
Old man – I know. I want you to nail the lid down.

Policeman (to man in stream) – Hey, you can't swim in there.
Man in stream – I know. That's why I'm calling for help.

Old man – Why are you continually throwing that coin in the air?
Small boy – Oh, I'm flipping it to see if I shall go to school or play truant, and sixty-eight times it has come down wrong.

Jim – I met Billy just now. He says you've fallen out with him.
Tim – He called me a fool.
Jim – How tactless! Just like him to blurt out the truth.

Railway passenger (shouting out of carriage window to porter) – Hi, there's a man in this carriage gone barmy! He says he's Napoleon.
Porter – Never mind. The next stop's Waterloo.

Hotel manager – Excuse me, sir, did you take a bath this morning?
Guest – No. Is there one missing?

Teashop domino player (to shortsighted opponent) – Here, you can't cheat me. That isn't a double five; you've got a currant stuck on it.

Small boy – Is that the sun or the moon up there?
Dimwit – Sorry, I don't know. I'm a stranger to this place.

Tom – That's an awful gash you have in your forehead.
Tim – Oh, it's next to nothing, next to nothing!

Horse dealer – This donkey will go twenty miles without stopping.
Buyer – But I only stay five miles away from here.

Villager – Are you painting those trees, sir?
Artist – I am; but it's no business of yours. Get on with your work instead of interrupting mine.
Villager – Well, my work is to chop them down. So you'd better hurry up with your painting.

Visitor (to prisoner in for life) – Congratulations, Spike! You've won a world cruise in that newspaper competition you entered!

First golfer (concluding fishing story) – And I'm telling you that fish was about as long as that last drive of yours.
Second golfer – Oh, I say, really!
First golfer – Yes, so I threw him back.

Driving instructor – Well, do you understand the car now?
Beginner – Perfectly! There's only one thing I should like to know. Do you put the water and the petrol in the same hole?

Employer – Mary, you are breaking more crockery than your wages will pay for! What's going to be done about I?
Maid – I don't know, madam. Maybe you could raise my wages.

Customer – What have you got in the shape of motor tyres?
Assistant – Children's hoops, lifebelts, quoits, curtain rings, CDs, and bicycle wheels!

Host (handing guest a cigar) – Now, that's something like a cigar!
Guest (after first few puffs) – Yes, but what is it?

Bobby (on visit from city to his uncle's farm) – My word, hasn't that cow a lovely coat?
Uncle – Yes, it's a Jersey.
Bobby – Oh, is it? I thought it was its skin.

Boss (finding office boy watching football match) – So this is your uncle's funeral, Tommy?
Tommy (after some quick thinking) – Looks like it, sir. He's the referee.

Boastful explorer – And there we stood – the tiger and myself in the thick of the jungle, face to face!
Listener – How terrible it must have been for both of you!

Smith – Where did you get that suit, old man? It fits you like a glove.
Friend – That's just why I don't like it. It should fit me like a suit.

American (gazing at the Forth Bridge) – Say, what's that bit of iron protruding over the waters there?
Scotsman – I've no idea. It wasn't there yesterday.

Landlady – I don't suppose you know what it means to starve?
Lodger – No, but I'm learning.

Visitor – And how old are you, my little man?
Young Freddie (indignantly) – I'm not old at all; I'm nearly new.

Film producer – In this scene you're blown up into the air, and caught by an aeroplane.
Film star – I see. But supposing the aeroplane isn't there?
Film producer – Oh, don't wait. Just come down again.

Black – They say that Smith is a terrible grumbler.
White – Yes, he's the kind of fellow who blames his hair for needing cutting.

Green – You're getting extravagant. Why did you tip the waiter five pounds?
Brown – Hush, man! He gave me ten pounds too much in change.

Uncle (sternly) – When I was a boy I was told that if I made faces like that my face would stay like it.
Nephew – Then why didn't you stop?

Bald man (in barber's chair) – Don't you think I should get some reduction? There's very little hair to cut.
Barber – Oh no, in your case we don't charge for cutting your hair. We charge for having to search for it.

Frenchman – Ah, so you have climbed the Matterhorn! That was a foot to be proud of.
Englishman – Pardon me, sir; you mean "feat".
Frenchman – So you climb it more than once, eh?

Professor Crumb – What struck you most at my lecture last night?
Professor Noodle – A bad egg that was meant for you.

What robbery is not dangerous?
A safe robbery!

Prospective purchaser of second-hand car – What's she like on hills? Owner – Hills! Why, she's down them in a jiffy!

Tim – Say that I'm a fool again, and I'll knock your block off!
Billy – Consider it said again then!
Tim – Consider your block knocked off!

Second – Keep your eye on his left.
Battered boxer – I can't keep his left out of my eye.

Musician – Have you in stock a cylindrical flageolet?
Shop assistant – A what?
Musician – A thin whistle.

Mother – I hope your are sharing the scooter with Cyril?
Willie – Oh, yes. He has it going uphill, and I downhill.

Sergeant – When I say "one" stand to attention; at "two" jump in the air; and at "three" come down again.

Mum – Gracious me! Look at your face! Have you been fighting?
Dimples – Not me! The other boy was. I was only learning.

Professor (to student) – What are you laughing at? Me?
Student – Oh, no, sir!
Professor (absently) – Then what else is there in this room to laugh at?

Mother – I'll teach you to tie a kettle to the cat's tail!
Small boy – It wasn't our cat.
Mother – No, but it was our kettle.

Judge – You may as well just admit your guilt. This man recognises you as the burglar.
Burglar Bill – How could he recognise me? He had his head under the bedclothes all the time!

Lecturer (in village school) – Well children, what shall I talk to you about?
Small boy – About five minutes, sir.

Teacher – I've given you punishment exercises every day this week. What have you to say.
Pupil – Well, I'm glad this is Friday.

Auntie (to small boy at tea) – Why didn't you wash your hands, Harry?
Harry – I didn't think it mattered, seeing that we're having brown bread.

Father (to son) – Tom, go and fetch the old horse.
Tom – Why the old one, father?
Father – Wear out the old one first is my motto.
Tom – Well, Father, you fetch the horse.

Boss (as Jenkins comes in half an hour late) – Late again!
Jenkins – So am I!

Diner – Waiter, there's a fly at the bottom of my cup. What does it mean?
Waiter – Sorry, sir. I'm a waiter, not a fortune-teller.

First actor (speaking lines of play) – Psst! Are we alone?
Second actor – Yes, we certainly are. The last member of the audience has just gone.

First lawyer (to second lawyer) – Sir, you are the biggest ass I've ever seen.
Judge – Order, order gentlemen! You seem to forget that I am here.

Jones (to boy) – Could you direct me to the boarding-house called Pleasant View?
Boy – Yes, sir, it's just round the corner, facing the gasworks.

Courtier – Hail, O mighty King!
King – I can't. My job is to reign, and I am doing it.

Grocer – What was that woman complaining about?
Assistant – Because she had a long wait.
Grocer – Humph! Some people are never pleased. She was complaining about the short weight yesterday.

Butler – Yes, sir, Mr Smyth is at home. What name shall I give?
Visitor – Professor Gottfried von Vandersplinkenheimer.
Butler – Er . . . have you got a visiting card, sir?

Fussy diner (after altering his choice several times) – Yes, waiter, I'll have mutton chops and chip potatoes. And make the chops lean.
Fed-up waiter – Yes, sir. Which way, sir?

Mother – I am glad you are keeping quiet boys, while Dad's having his nap.
Bill – Yes, Mum, we're watching his cigar burn down to his fingers.

Centre-half – It's a coach we're needing.
Manager of the team – No! A hearse!

Falling man – Take this mirror, Joe! If I break it, I'll get seven years' bad luck!

Teacher – Now Smiffy, who discovered spots on the sun?
Smiffy – My mother!
Teacher – Really!
Smiffy – Yessir, when I had measles.

Customer – You said that this dog was fine for rats. Why, it won't even go near them!
Shopkeeper – Well, that's fine for the rats, isn't it?

Landlady (to visitor) – Good morning. Did you sleep well, sir?
Visitor – Not very well. I am not used to a three-season bed.
Landlady – Three-season?
Visitor – Yes, one that has no spring in it!

Sea cook – Ever been on a ship before?
New helper – Sure, I was a gunner in the Royal Navy.
Sea cook – Champion. Start right in and shell the peas.

Customer – You barbers always seem to have plenty of news.
Barber – Yes, sir, we always know what's in the 'air.

Newspaper editor (to visitor) – What is the best thing you have seen in my paper?
Visitor – Fish and chips.

Teacher – Your son spells atrociously.
Smiffy's dad – Splendid! That's a very difficult word to spell.

Captain – Have you cleaned the deck and burnished the brass?
Seaman – Ay, ay, sir, and I've swept the horizon with a telescope.

Pa – Failed again. You must be a wooden head.
Tommy – Yes, Pa, I'm afraid I'm a chip off the old block.

Patient (with large lump on his head) – I seem to have had a nasty blow on the head during the operation.
Nurse – Oh, that's all right; we ran short of anaesthetic, that's all.

Doctor – Now, Tommy, put your tongue out.
Tommy – No jolly fear. Ma gave me a telling off for doing that yesterday!

Stranger (pointing to cats round goalkeeper) – Are they the club's mascots?
Local supporter – No. The goalie is a fishmonger.

Diner – This lobster has only one leg.
Waiter – Yes, sir, lost it fighting.
Diner – Then take it away and bring me the winner.

DOCTOR, DOCTOR. I THINK YOU'RE A VAMPIRE!

Necks, please!

WHAT FRUIT DO VAMPIRES LIKE BEST?

Blood oranges and necktarines.

DOCTOR! I KEEP HEARING NUMBERS INSTEAD OF WORDS.

It must be something you eight!

DOCTOR, DOCTOR. I THINK I'M A BRIDGE.

What's come over you, man?

THREE BUSES, FOUR CARS AND A LORRY.

WHAT GOES ALONG THE WASHING LINE AT 100 MILES PER HOUR?

Honda pants!

Teacher – What is a zebra?
Bobby – A donkey wearing a football jersey.

Pierre- Bonjour!
Pat – What does that mean?
Pierre – Good day, in France.
Pat – Well, Hot Cross Buns.
Pierre – What does that mean?
Pat – Good Friday in England.

Barber – How shall I cut your hair, sir?
Customer – Off!

Terry – I'm awfully worried. I think I'm losing my memory.
Jerry – Oh, forget all about it!

Mother – Don't drink out of your saucer, Billy. Use your cup.
Billy – But the spoon sticks in my eye.

Visitor – Have you any brothers or sister?
Bobby – No. I'm all the children we've got.

Lady – Call your dog off! It will bite me.
Boy – Sorry but his name is Caesar (sieze her)!

Customer – Are these fish quite fresh?
Shopkeeper – Fresh? Why, they're still warm!

Passer-by – Had any bites?
Angler – Yes. One mosquito and a couple of gnats.

Jinks – Lend me a fiver for a week, old man?
Binks – Certainly. Who is the weak old man?

Brown – Take no notice of advertising slogans. I know a man who took the advice of one of them and got ten years in prison for forgery.
White – Which was that?
Brown – "Make money at home"!

Passenger – Do I take this train to Leeds?
Guard – No. Get in, and it will take you.

Tommy – Hello! What's the matter with your thumb?
Billy – I hit the wrong nail.

Cuddles – Sorry I stood on your feet.
Dimples – That's all right! I usually walk on them myself.

Teacher – So, your father is a vegetarian.
Tommy (proudly) – Yes, sir, as he has carrot red hair, a cauliflower ear, a beetroot face, and a fountain pen that leeks.

Bobby – I hear Willie is greatly troubled with noises in the head.
Nobby – Yes, it's the band on his hat.

Bill – So you've got back from your holiday. Any change?
Jim – Not a penny.

Passenger – Can you take a joke?
Taxi driver – Yes. Where do you want to go?

Teacher – Name three kinds of nuts.
Boy – Monkey nuts, chestnuts and forget-me-nots.

Dennis – What would you do if you were in my shoes?
Walter – Clean them.

Milly – Why does Arthur work as a baker?
Jilly – I suppose he kneads the dough.

Teacher – Tell me the largest island in the world.
Toots – Australia.
Teacher – Right. Now the smallest?
Toots – A brick in a puddle.

Doctor (answering call at midnight) – Well?
Caller – No, I'm ill.

Customer – A cake of soap, please.
Shopkeeper – Do you want it scented?
Customer – No, I'll take it with me now.

Hawker – Buy a paper barometer, madam; only a pound each.
Lady (after buying one) – How does it work?
Hawker – Just put it on the window-sill, and when it's wet you'll know it's raining.

Small boy (to crashed motorist) – Do it again mister; my little brother didn't see you!

Falling man – I'd like to get hold of the fool who sold me a knapsack instead of a parachute!

Sidney – Dad, what are the Russian Steppes?
Dad – Ask your sister. She knows all the new dances.

Soldier – Why do you tar your ships?
Sailor – Because you pitch your tents.

Assistant – This suit is very much worn, sir.
Mr Newrich – Well, give me something new. I don't want second-hand goods.

First lodger – I'll bet the new arrival is or has been an actor.
Second lodger – What makes you thinks so?
First lodger – Haven't you noticed the way he ducks when asked if he will have a tomato?

Customer – Waiter, this portion of roast chicken is very small.
Waiter – Yes, sir; but you wait and see how long it takes you to eat!

Doctor – What is the matter with you?
Patient – Pains in my joints. I can hardly raise my arms above my head, and it is just the same with my legs.

Doctor – Well, Mr Brown, are you feeling all right now?
Patient – Much better, doctor, but my breath is always coming in little short pants.
Doctor – Well, what do you expect it to come in – flared trousers?

Jones – I thought you hated the saxophone?
Bones – I do.
Jones – Then why did you buy your son one?
Bones – Because I hate the neighbours more.

Tourist (to policeman with extra large feet) – Can you tell me where Trafalgar Square is?
Policeman – Yes, I'm standing on it.
Tourist – No wonder I couldn't find it.

Dodgy Den – Hey, Ken, I think honesty is the best policy.
Crafty Ken – What for ?
Dodgy Den – You know that dog I pinched last night? Well, I tried to sell it, and nobody would give me more than ten pounds for it, so I took it back to the owner and got fifty pounds for it.

Artist – Yes, many a time my poor old mother implored me not to become an artist.
Critic – Don't worry, old man. You didn't.

Gent – What are you doing, barber? You're lathering my bald head.
Barber – Very sorry, sir. Force of habit. I used to whitewash ceilings before I worked here.

Artist – I'm proud of my paintings. I shall soon be able to give an exhibition of my work.
Critic – Well, take my tip and see that you don't get rheumatics through sitting on the cold pavement.

Electric company's clerk – You are not always bothered with poor light, are you?
Householder – Oh, no, not always.
Clerk – Ah, I thought not. It's only at certain times you notice it, eh?
Householder – Yes, after dark.

Diner (finally) – Anyhow, waiter, I won't eat such food. You'd better fetch the manager.
Waiter – That's no good, sir. He won't eat it.

First Cockney – Ever seen 'am growing?
Second Cockney – 'Am doesn't grow.
First Cockney – Ain't you never 'eard of an 'ambush?

Toots – Are you still looking for your dog?
Smiffy – Yes.
Toots – Why don't you put an advert in the paper?
Smiffy – What's the use? The dog can't read!

Dad – Where are you going?
Minnie – Oh, just for a stroll.
Dad – Then stroll about the lawn, and take the mower with you.

Fatty – May I have those three apples off the table?
Mother – Yes, certainly.
Fatty – Oh, that's all right, then. You see, I've already had them.

Brown – Did you go anywhere for your holiday last summer?
Jones – Yes, I went to Venice, and the beastly place was flooded.

Policeman – Lights out, no number plate, no licence, and doing sixty in a forty-mile-an-hour zone.
Motorist – While you're about it, I stole this car.

Teacher – Danny, will two go into one?
Danny – Yes, sir – two halves.

Magistrate – How is it that you managed to take the man's watch from his waistcoat pocket when it was secured by a patent safety chain?
Prisoner (with dignity) – Sorry, Your Worship, but my fee is fifty pounds for the full course of six lessons.

Manager – Henry, you wear a very old-fashioned coat in the office.
Henry – Yes, it is a bit out of date. I bought it the last time I got a rise.

Mistress – And, remember, we have breakfast at seven.
New cook – All right, madam; but if I ain't down, you needn't wait for me.

Teacher – You have a lot of history to make up now, Tommy. How long have you been absent?
Tommy – Since the French Revolution, sir.

Lady – Why didn't you come yesterday to mend my bell?
New workman – You must have been out when I called, madam. I rang three times and got no answer.

First burglar – What about the burglar alarm, Bill?
Second burglar – Oh, shove it in the sack. The bells might fetch a copper or two.

Guide – This is the battleaxe of Robert the Bruce.
Traveller – Is that so? It looks quite modern.
Guide – Well, it's had five new heads and seven new shafts since he used it.

Admiral – Captain, is there no way in which the ship may be saved?
Captain – None at all, sir. We are going to the bottom. But I would not worry about the ship, sir, if I were you, she is fully insured. You'd better find a lifebelt.

Magistrate – You are accused of stealing a chicken. Have you anything to say?
Thief – I only took it for a lark.
Magistrate – A lark! No resemblance whatever. Ten days!

Jim – Please, sir, can you change five pound note?
Old gentleman – Why, certainly.
Jim – Well, please change this one into a ten pound note.

Gordon – Gilbert's just told me I look like you.
Graham – Where is he? I'll punch his head.
Gordon – I've just punched his head.

Old man – What's the matter?
Youngster – Boo, hoo! I have lost a pound coin.
Old man- A pound does not go far nowadays.
Youngster – Mine did. It fell down the drain.

Sidney – Please, sir, Danny says he knows a baby that was fed on elephant's milk and it gained ten pounds a day.
Teacher (severely) – Danny, you should not tell lies. Whose baby was it?
Danny – The elephant's, sir.

Showman – This man can pick up a needle with his toes.
Disgusted visitor – That's nothing. I've often picked up carpet tacks with my heels.
Bystander – That's nothing. I pick up five nails every time I lift my foot.

Driver of car (going downhill) – The steering wheel's busted, the brakes won't act, but thank goodness the horn still toots.

Mike – Do you rise early?
Millie – Early? If I rose much earlier I'd meet myself going to bed.

Teacher – What is a mountain, Tommy?
Tommy – A great big lump of earth sloping straight upwards.

Mistress – Jane, I've told you over and over again I will have cleanliness; yet why is it I am always finding cobwebs on the drawing-room ceiling?
Maid – I think it must be the spiders, miss.

Jenny – Came in last night and fell against the piano.
Penny – Hurt yourself?
Jenny – No. I struck the soft pedal.

Customer (who has ordered a pancake half an hour previously) – Er . . . I say, will that pancake be long?
Waitress – No, sir, it'll be round.

Captain – Well, Private Smith, what did you have for dinner?
Private – Taters, sir.
Captain – What does he mean by taters, Sergeant?
Sergeant – It's only his ignorance; he means spuds.

Office boy – A young man called to see you, sir.
Clerk – What was he like? Tall or short?
Office boy – Both.
Clerk – What do you mean?
Office boy – Well, he was tall, and wanted to borrow fifty pounds.

Sailor – I joined the navy to see the world.
Gentleman – Did you see it?
Sailor – No, they put me in a submarine.

Teacher – Why are you so late for school this morning?
Johnny (breathless) – Please, sir, I dreamt I was at a football match that ended in a draw, and the referee ordered extra time to be played, so I stopped to see the finish.

School inspector – Can you tell me where Ben Nevis is?
Jackie – I couldn't tell you, sir. He's not at this school.

Smiffy – What have I learned today, Teacher?
Teacher – Why, that's a funny question to ask.
Smiffy – Well, they are sure to ask me when I get home.

Joe – I say, Bill, if it takes a man an hour to walk a mile, how long will it take a fly to go through a barrel of treacle?
Bill – I'm stuck.
Joe – So was the fly.

Smiffy (writing composition) – The streets of Venice are noiseless, for they are canals; boats called gorgonzolas take the place of cabs.

Delivery boy – Does Mrs Jack live here?
Lady – No, my boy. It must be a case of mistaken identity.
Delivery boy – No, Mrs; it's a case of lemonade.

Tommy (crying) – Mother, Johnny Jones hit me.
Mother – Well, don't come in here crying. Hit him back.
Tommy – I did, I hit him back first.

Jones – Did you settle with Brown about his dog barking at night?
Smith – Oh, yes.
Jones – Buried the hatchet?
Smith – No, buried the dog!

Smiffy's dad (to his son) – Don't stand there walking about. Get up and sit down.

Teacher (to class in natural history) – What kind of birds are frequently kept in captivity?
Wilfrid – Jailbirds.

Impatient passenger – How long is the next train?
Porter – About three carriages.
Impatient passenger – Smart, ain't you?
Porter – No, I'm Jenkins; Smart's gone to dinner.

Mother – Jimmy, you're a bad boy. You can just go to bed without your tea.
Jimmy – But, Mother, what about the medicine I've got to take after meals?

First prisoner – How often have you been in prison?
Second prisoner – This is the first time.
First prisoner – Huh, you're lucky.
Second prisoner – I don't know so much about that – I'm here for life.

Jones – You remember that watch I lost five years ago?
Smith – Yes.
Jones – Well, yesterday I put on a waistcoat I had not worn for years, and what do you think I found in the pocket?
Smith – Your watch – splendid.
Jones – No, I found the hole it must have dropped through.

Old man – Could you tell me where the other side of the street is, my boy?
Boy – Over there, sir.
Old man – That's funny. Another boy told me it was over here.

Old man- Oh, so you've fallen down and hurt your leg, have you, my poor little man?
Cheeky boy – Well, did you think I'd fallen up and bashed my head against a cloud?

Smith – Airmen can do anything birds can do.
Brown – I'd like to see one sleeping in a tree standing on one foot.

Teacher – What is a cannibal?
Smiffy – A thing shot out of a cannon.

Judge – Did you steal the tortoise?
Lazy Len – No, sir, it followed me home.

Professor's wife – You've got your hat on the wrong way round, dear.
Professor – Now, how do you know which way I am going?

Young boy (watching painter) – How many coats of paint do you give a door?
Painter – Two, my boy.
Young boy (brightly) – Then, if you give it three coats, it would be an overcoat.
Painter – Yes, my lad, and a waste coat.

Captain (to new sailor) – Now what is the first thing you do when you fall into the sea?
New sailor – Get wet.

Warder – Owing to economy, three of us are being sacked tonight.
Prisoner – Any chance of it spreading to our department?

Old man – I dropped a shilling. If you find it give it back to me; if you don't, keep it.

Teacher – Now, then, Dennis, what countries are on the other side of the Atlantic?
Dennis – Er . . . it all depends what side you stand on, sir.

Bill – That a nasty hole you have in your umbrella.
Tom – Oh, that? I put that hole there purposely.
Bill – Whatever for?
Tom – So that I can see when it's stopped raining.

Visitor – Are there many fools in this part of the world, my lad?
Dimwit – Not as I know of, sir. Why? Do you feel a bit lonesome like?

Teacher (giving a lesson on Norsemen) – Smiffy, what is a Norseman?
Smiffy – A man who rides an 'orse.

Examining admiral (to naval candidate) – Now mention three great admirals.
Candidate – Drake, Nelson, and – I beg your pardon, sir? I didn't quite catch your name.

Teacher – What's this? You haven't put answers to any of these sums.
Sandy – No, sir, I left that part out purposely. You see, I always get them wrong.

Teacher – What is a man called who speaks and nobody listens to him?
Dennis – A teacher, sir.

A family went away for the holidays and left a note on the door saying, "Don't leave anything."
When they came home they found a note saying. "We haven't! – Burglar Bill and Co."

Customer – Give me another half-pound of your insect powder.
Shopkeeper – I'm glad you like it, sir. Good stuff, isn't it?
Customer – Yes. I've made a cockroach very ill, and if I give him another half-pound I think he'll die.

Teacher – What are gladiators?
Minnie – Please, sir, things that give out heat.

Dad – If you want to get on, you must have push and go, my boy.
Son – I've got it. The boss gave me the push this morning, and I'm going on Saturday.

McWhirter – What do you do with your old razor blades, McHaggis?
McHaggis – I throw them on the lawn, and the grass comes up already cut.

Tom – I heard something this morning that opened my eyes.
Ted – Oh! What was it?
Tom – An alarm clock.

What games do horses like playing best?
Stable tennis!

What do you call a chicken in a shell suit?
An egg.

Which famous painter always had a cold?
Van cough.

What do you call an inquisitive pig?
A nosey porker.

Doctor, doctor! I keep seeing into the future!
When did this first happen?
Next Thursday!

When is the cheapest time to phone a friend?
When they're out.

What happened to the man who stole a calendar?
He got twelve months.

Tom – Do you see all those blackbirds up in that tree?
Johnny – Yes.
Tom – Well, my dad has a name for every one.
Johnny – What! Every one?
Tom – Yes. Crows!

Charles – My dad bought a horse and trap for ten pounds.
Bertie – You sure?
Charles – Yes. A clothes-horse and mouse-trap!

Nervous passenger – Oh, I've pulled the communication cord by mistake! What shall I do? I'll be fined £100.
Crafty Ken – Give me £50 and I'll pretend to have a fit.

Two boys were fighting in the pouring rain. They fought till one boy got the other on his back and held him there.
First boy – Will you give up?
Second boy – Never.
First boy – Then will you get on top a while; I'm getting wet through.

Airman – If you use your parachute, count ten before you pull the cord.
Passenger – B-b-but, I s-s-s-stutter w-w-when I'm afraid.

Teacher – Tommy, do you know the present tense of knew?
Tommy – No, sir.
Teacher – Correct.

Passenger (in taxi) – There's only one thing I worry about in a car, and that's the brakes.
Taxi driver – Then you've nothing to worry about, sir; this car hasn't got any.

Doctor – Well, how are you this morning, Harry?
Harry the hypochondriac (mournfully) – Oh, I'm so ill I've been looking in the papers all morning to see if my death was in.

Little boy (to capsized canoeist) – While you're there, mister, you might have a look at my hook and see if the worm's still on.

Cannibal king – What did I have for dinner?
Waiter – Grilled chauffeur.
Cannibal king – What did the servants have?
Waiter – Pneumatic tyre in oil and vinegar.

Agent – You want your office furniture insured against theft?
Manager – Yes, all except the clock; everybody watches it.

Mother – Have you given the goldfish some fresh water this morning, Smiffy?
Smiffy – No, Mum, they haven't drunk the water I gave them last week.

Kevin – What's the lump on your head for?
Colin – My father's portrait fell on my head.
Kevin – Hah! Struck by the family likeness!

Magistrate – So this is the fourth person you have knocked down this month.
Speed fiend – Excuse me, it's the third. One of them was the same person twice.

Angry grocer – What do you mean by throwing that brick at my window?
Little boy – How was I to know the wasp was on the inside?

Customer – I want a hat to suit my head.
Milliner – Try a soft one, sir.

Farmer (roused at one a.m.) – Well, what's the matter?
Tramp – Sorry to trouble you, but I'm sleeping in your barn tonight, and I want to be wakened at seven sharp.

What do you get if you cross a giant gorilla with a cement mixer?
King Koncrete.

Did you hear about the police football team?
They won the cop final.

Why was Cinderella rotten at football?
Because she kept running away from the ball.

What do you call a rich rabbit?
A million hare.

First boy – I'll bet I've got a brother bigger than yours.

Second boy – I'll bet you haven't. I've got one twelve feet high.

First boy – I don't believe you.

Second boy – Well, you see, I've two half-brothers each six feet tall.

Prospective tenant – Does the chimney always smoke like this?

Landlord – Oh, no; only when the fire's on.

Billy – My father gets a warm reception wherever he goes.

Tommy – He must be very popular.

Billy – No, it's not that. You see, he's a fireman.

Bore – Yes, cricket is a frightfully dangerous game. Why, last year I was knocked senseless while playing in bat.

Bored listener – When do you expect to recover?

Nature study teacher – Remember, you reap what you sow. If you sow poppy seed you get poppies, and grass seed you get grass, and so on.

Pupil – If I sow bird seed will I get a canary, please? I'm wanting one.

Auntie – What are you going to be when you grow up?

Nephew – I'm going to be an Arctic explorer. And now, will you give me five pounds?

Auntie – Gracious! What do you want five pounds for?

Nephew – I want to get five ice-creams and find out how much cold I can stand.

Doctor – How did you break your leg?

Patient – I threw a cigarette down a manhole and stood on it.

Shoeshine boy – My father works on a farm, sir.

Mr Jones – That's rather funny. He makes hay while the son shines!

Smiffy was reading a book, and was astounded at the description of the hero. It said he had a brass neck, a lantern jaw, his eyes flashed fire, and he had nerves of steel.

"Amazing," said Smiffy, "they must feed him on screwnails and matches."

Amateur gardener – What's the best way to grow potatoes?

Dimwit – Plant onions above them. The onion will make the potatoes' eyes water, and that'll save you a lot of work with the watering-can.

Patient – Doctor, while I was playing a game last night, spots kept coming before my eyes.

Doctor – What game were you playing?

Patient – Dominoes.

"The thing for you to do," said the doctor to the man who was suffering from nervousness, "is to stop thinking about yourself and bury yourself in your work."

"Oh dear!" exclaimed the patient. "I'm a grave digger!"

Teacher – What is torture?

Roger – Death in instalments, sir.

Lodger – Only cheese for lunch?

Landlady – Yes. The cutlets caught fire and it spread to the apple tart, so I had to use the soup to put it out.

Teacher – Tommy, give me a sentence containing the phrase "chop and change".

Tommy – The waiter brought the chop and change.

Auntie – What's that lump on your head, Georgie? Been fighting again?

Georgie – No, that was an accident.

Auntie – How?

Georgie – Well, I was sitting on Jimmy Brown's chest, and I forgot to hold his feet.

A man was being shown around a carpenter's shop. "By the way," he remarked, picking up a plank, "what are these holes in this wood?"

"Those are knot holes," explained the carpenter.

"They are holes," insisted the other angrily. "Do you think I don't know a hole when I see one?"

Danny – Does your watch tell you the time?

Smiffy – No; I have to look at it.

Man – Boy, where does your father work?

Boy – At the zoo?

Man – What doing?

Boy – Sandpapering elephants down to greyhounds.

Old man (to bricklayer) – Did your fall hurt you?

Bricklayer – No, it was the sudden stop that was most painful.

"You idiot!" said the teacher. "Write 'I have gone' fifty times on the board. Perhaps that will teach you not to use 'I have went'."

When the teacher came back some time later he found the following note: "Please, teacher, I have written 'I have gone' fifty times, and I have went home."

Old sailor – How did that new cabin boy do last trip?

His friend – Clumsy young hound! He broke all the saucers, and we had to drink out of the cups.

Customer (to barber who has accidentally clipped his ear) – Say, what do you think you're doing – fretwork?

Leader of band – Hush, man! Doesn't your music say "rest"?

New drummer – Sure! But I'm not a bit tired yet.

Nature lover (gazing at tree) – Oh, great oak tree, if you could only speak, what would you say to me?

Gardener – If you please, sir, it would say it was a sycamore, not an oak.

John – Stop rubbing your hands like that. The weather isn't cold.

Jim – I'm not trying to warm the weather – I'm trying to warm my hands.

Teacher (to Jock) – What do two and two make?

Jock (keen football fan) – Please, miss, a draw.

Prison chaplain – So you were a musician, were you? Well, I'm afraid we won't be able to give you much comfort in a musical way.

Prisoner – If you could only get me a file, sir, I think I could manage a few bars for myself.

Smith – It's going to rain, according to the radio.

Jones – I thought you didn't believe in the weather forecasts?

Smith – I didn't use to, but we've got a better set now.

Teacher – That boy of yours seems bright. He'll carve out a name for himself some day.

Father – He's done it already – on our new piano!

Stout man – You look as if there's been a famine.

Thin man – And you look as if you'd caused it.

Guest – These cakes are lovely, Mrs Brown. I don't know how many I've had.

Johnny Brown – You've had six!

Teacher – Give a sentence with the word "fascinate" in it.

Roger – My waistcoat has nine buttons, but I can only fascinate.

Polite but annoyed youngster (to man in front of him in cinema) – Please, sir, would you mind taking off your hat? I can't see the screen.
Man – Never mind, my boy; just you laugh when I do.

Locksmith – Morning, sir! I believe it was you who telephoned for the locksmith?
Smiffy's dad – Yes, that's right. Come inside, please. We've lost the key of our tin of sardines.

Burglar – Come on, let's figure up and see how much we made on that haul.
Mate – Oh, I'm tired. Let's wait and look in the morning papers.

A boastful American walked up to a British fruit seller's stall and picked up a large melon.
"Is that the largest apple you fellows can grow over here?" he asked.
"Put that grape down!" snapped the fruit seller.

Barber – And how do you find the razor?
Customer – Didn't know I was being shaved.
Barber – Very glad, I'm sure, sir.
Customer – I thought I was being sandpapered.

Optician – Weak eyes, have you? Now, sit here and tell me how many lines you can read on that chart.
'Erbert – Chart? I can't see any chart.

Admiral (testing new recruit) – What must a man be before he can be buried at sea with full naval honours?
Recruit – Dead, sir.

Mother – Sandy, take these matches back to the shop, and say they are no use. They won't light.
Sandy – But they will light, ma. I tried them all before you came in.

Motorist (with punctured tyre) – I'm looking for a puncture.
Yokel – Never mind. Someone will come along soon and lend you one.

Tim – Don't come down that ladder. I've taken it away.
Tom – Too late. I'm halfway down.

MacWhirter – These trousers seem to be rather baggy at the knees.
Tailor – Well, you see, sir, I used to make concertinas!

Optician – Has your little boy got used to his glasses?
Lady – I can't get him to wear them in the daytime, but I manage to slip them on when he goes to sleep.

Hotel guest – I tell you I won't have this room! I'm not going to pay good money for such a small room. You think that just because I am from the country ...
Bellboy – Step in, sir. This isn't your room. It's the lift.

Prisoner – Say, warder, when is the fun gonna start?
Warder – What do you mean, fun?
Prisoner – Why, the judge said that I was to be sent here for the time of my life.

Toots (to Plug with bandaged head) – What's wrong with your head, Plug?
Plug – Some water fell on it.
Toots – But surely that wouldn't hurt it?
Plug – No; but this water was in a jug.

Doctor – There's not many people live through this operation. Is there anything I can do for you before we begin?
Patient – Yes, get me my coat.

Teacher – You don't know what the word thief means? Well, if I were to put my hand in your pocket and take a pound away what would I be?
Smiffy – A conjurer, sir.

Recruit – Shall I mark time with my feet, Sergeant?

Sergeant – Did you ever hear of marking item with your hands, you idiot?

Recruit – Well, I understand that clocks do, Sergeant.

Teacher – Give me a sentence with the word "centimetre" in it.

Wilfrid – My aunt arrived yesterday, and I was centimetre.

Old man – Your father is entirely bald, isn't he, Jack?

Jack – Yes, I am the only heir he has left.

Angry customer – I can't find words to express my feelings towards you.

Smart assistant – That's all right, sir. We sell dictionaries here.

The boss – Now, James, we've forgotten to get stamps.

Office boy – There, sir, aren't we a couple of thickheads!

Teacher – I once found a fossilised fish in a rock. What could be more wonderful than that?

Quick pupil – Please, sir, a ship in a current.

Terry – You still take your morning bath, I suppose?

Jerry – Never miss it. Sometimes I take it hot, sometimes I take it cold and when I'm in a hurry I take it for granted.

Fortune-teller (to football referee) – I see you as leader of a large crowd.

Referee (worried) – Have I got a good start?

Father (angrily) – Bobbie, didn't you hear me call you?

Bobbie – Yes, Father, but you always tell me not to answer back.

Parent – My son has many original ideas.

Teacher – Yes, especially in arithmetic.

Wilfrid – Do you know Francis?

Spotty – What Francis?

Wilfrid – Francis not far from England!

Bill – I had a lot of money left me yesterday.

Bob – Really! How was that?

Bill – Well, I had a hole in my pocket, and it fell out.

First wrecked motorist – I tell you I came round that corner in my car like a tortoise.

Second wrecked motorist – So that's why my car turned turtle.

Lady – Why is your little brother crying?

Jimmy – He isn't crying – he's been playing football with an onion.

Teacher – Billy, which is the more useful – the sun or the moon?

Smiffy – The moon.

Teacher – Why?

Smiffy – Because the moon comes out at night and gives us light, and the sun comes out in the daytime when we don't need it.

Little boy – I wish I was old enough to wash my own face.

Mother – Why?

Little boy – 'Cos I wouldn't wash it at all.

Diner – Waiter, there's a fly in my soup.

Waiter – Catch it yourself. I'm not a spider.

Mother – Johnny, Auntie won't kiss you with a dirty face like that.

Johnny – That's what I thought.

Dr Dosem – One dose to be taken after each meal.

Fatty – Yes, but where do I get the meals?

HOW DO YOU GET FIVE DONKEYS ON A FIRE ENGINE?

Two in the front, two in the back and one on the roof going EE-AW-EE-AW!

What has a long neck and smells nice?
A giraffodil!

What's black and white and eats like a horse?
A zebra.

What does it mean when you find a set of horseshoes?
There's a horse going round in its socks.

WHAT DID THE FATHER BUFFALO SAY TO HIS YOUNGSTER WHEN HE WENT TO SCHOOL?
Bi, son!

First pickpocket – Why are you reading a fashion magazine, Bill?
Second pickpocket – Well, if we're to do well in our profession we must know where pockets are worn.

Jim – I took all the prizes at the racing contest the other day.
Jack – Really?
Jim – Yes, with a camera.

Lazy Len – I had a fall last night which rendered me unconscious for six hours.
Weary Willie – Really! Where did you fall?
Lazy Len – I fell asleep.

Danny (trying to buy a dog) – No, I don't care for that fox terrier. His legs are too short.
Dog dealer – You couldn't have them any longer. They reach right down to the ground!

Old gent (to policeman blocking his view of the football match) – Can you play draughts? Because it's your turn to move.
Policeman – When I move I usually take a man with me.

Boss – Now, my boy, are you boss of this business or not ?
Office boy – No, sir.
Boss – Then don't talk like an idiot!

Jones – Can you give anyone something you haven't got?
Brown – Yes, a black eye.

Passer-by – What are you digging for?
Workman – Money.
Passer-by – And when do you expect to get it?
Workman – Pay-day.

Smiffy (after being given a detention) – I knew that note Danny wrote for me wouldn't fool Teacher. He only put one "g" in excuse.

Jimmy – How are you getting on at school, Johnny?
Johnny – First rate. I can wiggle my ears now, and stand on my hands without leaning against the wall.

Fran – What's the crowd looking at?
Dan – A man tried to cross the bridge.
Fran – Well, what about it?
Dan – There isn't any bridge.

Teacher – Well, Smiffy, can you tell me what chivalry is?
Smiffy – It's when you feel cold all over.

Buyer of rather thin cow – How much do you want for this cow?
Farmer – Thirty pounds.
Buyer – I asked the price, not the weight of it.

Teacher (at swimming class) – Danny, that's not a swallow dive.
Danny – Isn't it? Why, I thought I'd swallowed the whole pool.

Teacher – Give a sentence with the word "analyse" in it.
Billy – My sister Anna lies in bed till ten o'clock.

Talkative barber (about to lather customer for a shave) – Do you mind shutting your mouth?
Tired customer – No, do you?

Mac – Are you musical, Sandy?
Sandy – Am I musical? Why at the age of two I used to play on the linoleum.

Diner – Waiter, this steak is only half the size of the one I had yesterday.
Waiter – But you're not sitting beside the window today, sir.

Man – And how are the fish biting today boy?
Small boy (fishing) – With their mouths.
Man – I mean, how are they coming out.
Small boy – Head first, sir.

Binks – I hear Brown is travelling in gas ovens.
Jinks – Why? Can't he afford a car?

Foreman – Now, then, Jock, what about carrying up some more bricks?
Jock – I am not feeling very well, boss. I'm trembling all over.
Foreman – Very well, then – get busy with the sieve.

Terry – How is it you know all about the Smiths' private affairs?
Jerry – We looked after their parrot during the summer holidays.

A man dashed onto the quayside, threw his bag aboard the boat, and jumped on. "A narrow squeak!" he said. "Nearly missed it!"
"Sorry mate, " said a passenger. "The boat's just coming in."

Sergeant – What was all that noise you were making in the dormitory last night?
Private – I was only dragging Brown's trousers about the room, sir.
Sergeant – Surely that wouldn't make all that noise?
Private – But Brown was in them, sir.

Villager – It was 'ere that Catherine of Aragon was bitten by a mad dog.
Tourist – Tudor?
Villager – Yes, chewed 'er something 'orrible.

Grocer – You want a pound of ochre? Is it red ochre for cleaning brick?
Willie – No, it's tappy ochre – the stuff Mum makes the pudding with.

Mac – What is hand painting?
Geordie – I don't know.
Mac – Two lovely black eyes!

Teacher – What is space?
Smiffy – Space is nothing. I can't explain it, but I've got it in my head all right.

McTavish – I got this cup for running.
McNab – Oh! Who did you beat?
McTavish – The owner, four policemen, and a crowd of sixty men.

Tom – What is the most useful purpose of cow's hide?
Dick – Why, to make leather, of course.
Tom – No, to keep the cow together.

Old man – What are you crying for, my little man?
Billy – My b-big b-brother d-dropped a b-big b-box on his toe.
Old man – That surely is nothing to cry about. I should have thought that you would have laughed.
Billy – I did!

Inquisitive pedestrian – What is the matter, Constable?
Constable (fed up) – Bus ran over a cat.
Pedestrian – Was the cat in the road?
Constable – Oh, no, the bus chased it up a lamppost.

Employer – I'll pay you one hundred pounds a week, starting now, and in three months I'll raise your salary to three hundred pounds a week.
Applicant – Righto! I'll look in again in three months.

Diner – Waiter, bring me a knife for the butter.
Waiter – Very good, sir.
Diner – Oh, and a revolver for the cheese.

Smiffy's mum – Did Fatty enjoy the party?
Fatty's mum – I think so. He wasn't hungry again till five o'clock next day.

Customer – Do you make life-size enlargements from photographs?
Photographer – Yes, sir. That's one of our specialities.
Customer – Well, will you do this for me? It's a snap I took of a whale.

Teacher (giving astronomy lesson) – Now, Bobby, give me the names of some stars.
Bobby (brightly) – Football or film, sir?

Jimmy – How are you getting on at your work, Jock?
Jock – Fine. I've got five men under me now.
Jimmy – Really?
Jock – Yes, I work upstairs.

Old man – Why is the railway station so far from the village?
Smiffy – I don't know, sir, unless it's so that it's near the railway line.

Old man – You mustn't say, "I ain't going"; you must say "I am not going," "he is not going," "we are not going," "they are not going."
Little boy – Ain't nobody going!?

Dud footballer – I was transferred for ten thousand, and now fifty thousand won't buy me.
Manager – And I'm one of the fifty thousand.

Aunt (listening to bird singing) – Listen, Danny! Don't you wish you were able to sing like a robin?
Danny – I'd sooner be able to squirt water through my nose like an elephant.

Doctor – Did you open both windows in your room, as I told you to?
Patient – Well, not exactly. You see, there is only one window, so I opened it twice.

Salesman – Yes, sir, this car is so economical to run that it simply pays for itself.
Buyer – Then send it along when it has.

Diner – Do you see that waiter over there? They call him "Tomorrow".
Friend – Why?
Diner – Because he never comes.

Teacher – What animals eat less than others?
Wee Jean – Moths, because they only eat holes in things.

Young man – How did you lose your hair?
Bald man – Worry.
Young man – What did you worry about?
Bald man – Losing my hair.

Sandy – Did you call me a blockhead?
Jock – No, I told you to keep your hat on; there are woodpeckers flying around!

Plug – What's the weather like, Smiffy?
Smiffy – I couldn't say yet; it's too foggy.

Prisoner (to warder) – You'd better have a key made for me. I never know what time I'll be in at night.

First salesman – Your firm can't hold a candle to mine.
Second salesman – What is your firm?
First salesman – Oh, we manufacture gunpowder.

Fussy old man (as radio announcer sneezes) – There! That's how colds spread.

Teacher (pointing to a sweet wrapper on the floor) – Wilfrid, is this yours?
Wilfrid – Not at all, sir. You saw it first.

Waiter – Eggs, sir? How will you have them cooked?
Customer – I don't mind. Any difference in the price?
Waiter – None whatever, sir.
Customer – Then have them cooked on a large rasher of ham.

Plug (sarcastically to Wilfrid) – You are so short that if you pulled up your socks you'd be blind-folded!

Weary Willie – What are you doing now?
Tired Tim – Imaginative work.
Weary Willie – What is imaginative work like?
Tired Tim – Imagining what work is like.

Youngster – Grandpa, can I ask you a question?
Grandpa – Yes. What is it?
Youngster – Did you comb your hair with a razor?

First workman – Hard lines on Jock being shortsighted, isn't it?
Second workman – Why? You don't need good eyesight for this job.
First workman – But he can't see when the foreman isn't looking, so he has to keep on working all the time.

Foreman (to workman on ladder) – Mind you don't fall.
Workman – That's all right. I'm holding on.
Foreman – I don't mean fall down; I mean fall asleep.

Benny – Hello, Roger, have you come back for something you've forgotten?
Roger – No, I've come back for something I've remembered.

Teacher – Toots, put the word "social" in a sentence.
Toots – Dennis says he'll be glad when the holidays come, and social I!

Magistrate (to offender) – The constable says you put out your left hand and turned to the right.
Offender – Yes. You see, I'm left-handed.

Snooty (at football match) – I could kick myself for missing that penalty.
Scrapper – You'd better let me do it; you might miss again.

Teacher – Tell me, Dennis, who first invented underground tunnels?
Dennis – The worms, sir.

Teacher – Now, Danny, do this subtraction mentally. Six of your friends went to the river, but two had been told not to go into the water. Now tell me how many bathed?
Danny (promptly) – Six, sir.

Foreman – What's all the arguing about down the road?
Labourer – Why, the bloke driving the steamroller wants us to call him "chauffeur".

Mum – Goodness, Minnie, where's the canary?
Minnie – I dunno, Mum. It was there when I started cleaning its cage with the vacuum cleaner.

Pedestrian – Hi, up there! You dropped a brick that nearly hit me on the head.
Workman – All right, you can keep it. I've got plenty up here.

Election candidate – Really, gentlemen. With all this uproar, I can hardly hear myself speak.
Critic – Well, cheer up! You ain't missing much!

Uncle – Are you able to keep your position in class?
Smiffy – Certainly! I started at the bottom, and no one has been able to take my place from me.

Old lady (to street musician) – Do you always play by ear?
Musician – Yes, lady, 'ere or 'ereabouts.

Merchant – Here, you told me this safe was burglar-proof, and I found it cracked and the contents stolen.
Agent – Well, isn't that proof you had burglars?

Customer – Are you sure your milk is pure?
Milkman – Oh, yes. Every drop of water we put in is filtered.

Roger – How much will it cost to take me and my luggage right to my door?
Taxi driver – Five pounds. The luggage goes for nothing.
Roger – Right! Take my luggage and I'll walk.

Teacher (to Toots who is laughing) – What are you laughing at?
Toots – Nothing, sir.
Teacher – Then why are you laughing?
Toots – I can't help it sir. I've got on a new shirt, and it tickles me.

Diner (who has had a long wait) – I suppose I will sit here till I starve?
Waiter – Hardly that sir. We close at eleven.

Tobacconist – Try these cigars, sir. You can't get better.
Customer – I know. I had one last week, and I'm still ill.

Jimmy – Who cut your hair, Jock?
Jock – Father did, but he couldn't find the scissors, and the bread knife was a bit blunt.

Sidney – That kid lives in a sweet shop. Isn't he lucky?
Wilfrid – Rather! That's what you call "Home, sweet home".

First shipwrecked sailor – I say, where are we?
Second shipwrecked sailor – I don't know. I'm a stranger here myself.

Roger (in butcher's shop) – I suppose you have joints to suit everybody's pocket?
Butcher – Yes, my man, I have.
Roger – Well, what have you got to suit an empty pocket.
Butcher – The cold shoulder.

Teacher – Now Smiffy, what do we get from India?
Smiffy – I know: India-gestion!

Traveller (on spotting a bad-tempered-looking dog) – What's the matter with that dog?
Rustic – Laziness.
Traveller – How's that?
Rustic – He's sitting on a thistle, and he's too lazy to get off.

Waiter – Thank you very much, sir.
Gent – What do you mean? I haven't given you anything.
Waiter – No, sir, but I had bet a fiver with another man that you wouldn't.

Old man – What are you digging for, Johnny?
Johnny – Lemonade. Teacher says that minerals are found in the earth.

Spotty – I know something that doesn't weigh an ounce yet I'm certain you couldn't hold it for ten minutes.
'Erbert – What's that?
Spotty – Your breath.

Judge – Have you anything to say before I sentence you?
Prisoner – No. Get it over quickly, guv'nor, or I won't be at the jail by dinner time.

Visitor (to local) – It's been glorious weather here since I came. Doesn't it ever rain here?
Boastful local – Rain? Why, there's frogs in this town over five years old that ain't learned to swim yet.

Stage manager – You handle millions of pounds in this play. Try to look as if you were used to it.
Hard-up actor – I see. Could you let me have fifty pounds to rehearse with?

Customer (to shoemaker) – What I complain of in these boots is that the soles are too thick.
Shoemaker – Oh, just put on the boots and the objection will gradually wear away.

Stage manager – You received a tremendous ovation. They're still clapping. What did you say?
Actor – I told them I would not go on with my act until they quietened down.

New tenant – The roof is so bad that it rains on my head. How long is this going to continue?
Landlord – What do you think I am – a weather prophet?

Roger – Look, the man behind has been looking for a pound coin for ages.
Dennis – How do you know it was a pound coin?
Roger – I picked it up.

Jock – I have an awful cold in my head.
Tom – Well, that's better than nothing.

Scene-shifter (called in at the last moment to take the place of an actor who has not turned up) – The police have discovered everything, my lord, and are at the gate.
The wicked earl – 'Tis false, knave! 'Tis false!
Scene-shifter – All right, go and ask the manager yourself. 'E told me to say it.

Gamekeeper – Now, you young rascal, I've caught you. You weren't fishing with a permit, I bet.
Roger – No, sir. I was fishing with a worm.

Professor – Now, Jenkins, what is your opinion on this point?
Jenkins (nervously) – The same as yours, sir.

Customer – Let me see. How much do you want for that dog?
Dealer – Forty pounds.
Customer – I thought you said thirty yesterday?
Dealer – Yes, but he swallowed a ten pound note last night.

Doctor (to patient) – It's nothing to worry about. Just a little boil on the back of your neck. But you must keep your eye on it.

Manager – Why do you keep saying "Bah!" while you're acting?
Villain – Well, you see, I'm the black sheep of the family.

Sam – I caught a snake forty-eight inches long this morning.
Joe – Why do you always measure snakes by inches?
Sam – Because they haven't any feet.

Visitor – So they call this the Black Mountain? Is there any legend about it?
Guide (bored stiff) – Yes, sir. Two men went up it and never returned.
Visitor – Awful! Wonder what happened to them.
Guide – Oh, they went down the other side.

Teacher – Smiffy, how many letters are in "blackbird"?
Smiffy – Four letters?
Teacher – What?! You silly boy. Spell it please.
Smiffy – C-R-O-W?

Doctor – Can you tell me how you felt when you first took ill?
Dennis – Yes. Very pleased because I didn't have to go to school.

Actor – Did you see the audience cry when I played the death scene?
Critic – Yes, they knew you weren't really dead.

Jock – I once had a parrot for five years, and it never said a word.
Sandy – It must have been tongue-tied.
Jock – No, it was stuffed.

Old man – So you are an exporter?
Young man – Yes, the railway company sacked me.

Visitor – How is your new man getting on?
Farmer – Well, he broke two spade handles yesterday.
Visitor – Working hard?
Farmer – No, leaning on them.

Wilfrid – How would you like to drop two hundred feet with a parachute?
Plug – I'd hate to drop that far without one.

Teacher – What's wrong with your brother?
Pupil – Please, sir, he's broken his leg, and the doctor says it's one of those compound fractions.

Optician (testing Smiffy's eyesight) – Can you read that?
Smiffy – Yes, but I can't pronounce it!

District nurse – Do your twins make much noise?
New mum (stressed) – Not really. One makes so much racket that you can't hear the other.

Sergeant – You've only one shot out of ten on the target.
Recruit – It isn't my fault. The bullets left this end all right.

Teacher – Anybody know anything about alabaster?
Sidney – Yes, sir. He was the chap who outfoxed the forty thieves.

Fortune-teller – Do not worry, the dark clouds will soon roll by.
Old gent – Look here, I want to know my fortune, not the weather forecast.

Gent (who has fallen) – Help! Help! I've broken my leg.
Shop assistant – Walking stick department, third floor, sir.

Motorist – My car will do ninety.
Friend – Per hour, per litre, or perhaps?

Foreman – I see you are coming earlier of late. You used to be behind before, now you're first at last.

Old lady (at first football match) – Why have they had that player framed?
Spectator – That's not a frame; that's the goal.

Sergeant – If you could only shoot as well as you can eat you'd be OK.
Recruit – Well, I've been practising eating for twenty-six years, but I've only had this gun a fortnight.

Teacher – Strange as it may seem, quite a number of flowers have the prefix "dog". For instance, the dog-rose and the dog-violet. Can you name any more, 'Erbert?
'Erbert – Yes, Teacher, the collie-flower.

Host (to guest) – Would you like to sit on my right hand at supper?
Guest – I don't mind at all. But can you eat all right with your left?

Indignant householder (holding up a dead cat) – Here, constable, look what I found in my garden. What are you going to do about it?
Constable – Well, you know the law. If it's not claimed in six months it's yours.

Sandy – Lend me ten pounds.
Jock – Can't. I've only got eight pounds.
Sandy – Well, lend me that, and owe me two pounds.

Chairman (at concert) – Miss Screecher will now sing, "Had I the wings of a dove I'd flee."
Jimmy (nudging his dad) – Dad, what kind of a thing is a dove-eyed flea?

Salesman – These shoes are the finest quality. They will last a lifetime.
Smiffy – Then I'll have two pairs.

Country greyhound (as hare runs past) –
That's a big hare.
Town greyhound – That's not a real hare.
A real one has wheels and runs on a line.

**Two motorists met in a narrow lane,
which was too narrow to allow two
cars to pass at the same time. Neither
would go back until one shouted, "I
never go back for a fool!"
The other said, "I do!" and he backed
his car.**

*Professor – What is the result when a
patient's temperature gets dangerously
low?
Student doctor – Why . . . er . . . he gets
cold feet!*

Teacher – It is well known that heat
expands and cold contracts. Give me an
example of this.
Danny – Please, sir, holidays. In summer
they last six weeks, but in winter only
two.

**Teacher – Tell me, Dennis, what is
silence?
Dennis – Something you don't hear
when you listen.**

*Dad – Minnie, if you eat too much pud-
ding you will be ill.
Minnie – All right, Dad, give me a piece
more and send for the doctor.*

Teacher – What is a primeval forest?
Tommy – A place where the hand of man
has never set foot.

**First motorist – How did you get on at
the police court?
Second motorist – Fine.**

*Doctor – How did you get your nose
smashed up like that?
Patient – Well, I had a terribly red nose,
and when I put it through a hole in the
boiler for a sniff of fresh air the man with
the hammer mistook it for a red-hot rivet.*

Toots – Where are you going, Sidney?
Sidney – I'm not going anywhere, Toots
Toots – Yes, you are.
Sidney – No, I'm not. I'm coming back.

**Teacher – Give me a sentence using the
word "miniature".
Dennis – The miniature asleep you
begin snoring.**

*Teacher – Now I have an impression in
my head. Can any of you children tell me
what an impression is?
Dennis – Yes, sir. An impression is a dent
in a soft place.*

Traveller (with hours to wait at small
country station) – Any cinema here, or
billiards hall, or library?
Railway porter – No, nothing like that
here.
Traveller – Well, how do you spend the
evenings?
Railway porter – We go down to the village store. They've just got a new bacon
slicer – it's wonderful!

**Father – If you want a thing done well
you must do it yourself.
Wee Jock – How about a hair-cut?**

*Tim – Look there's Giles Miles the actor.
Jim – Does he act tragedy or comedy?
Tim – Both. He's tragic in comedy, and
comic in tragedy.*

Sandy – I work in a shirt factory.
Mac – Well, why are you not working
today?
Sandy – Because we are making night-
shirts.

**Teacher – What king is said to have
never smiled again?
Sidney – Charles I. After his execution.**

*Jim – Did you ever feel that the whole
world was against you?
Tim – Yes, this morning when I slipped
and fell on the pavement.*

Bill (in new car) – I passed a car going at ninety miles an hour the other day.
Bob – You must have been going fast.
Bill – I wasn't. I was going the other way.

Young boy – Dad, what's a family tie?
Dad – Mine. Every time I want it one of your brothers is wearing it.

Theatre producer – Couldn't the villain shoot himself instead of taking poison?
Writer – Why?
Theatre producer – Well, the bang would wake the audience up.

Diner – Hey, waiter, there's a fly in my soup.
Waiter – Well, you don't want me to jump in and rescue it, do you?

Clarke – You say your business is picking up. What is your job?
Sparke – Picking up wastepaper in the public park.

Landlady – Mary, the new lodger is a sword-swallower at the circus. Be sure to count the knives when you clear the table.

Drummer – I'm the fastest man in the world.
Runner – How do you make that out?
Drummer – Time flies, doesn't it?
Runner – So they say.
Drummer – Well, I beat time.

Policeman – Now then, what's your name?
Culprit – John Smith.
Policeman – I want your proper name!
Culprit – William Shakespeare.
Policeman – That's better. You can't pull that "Smith'" stuff on me!

Warder – There's talk of us getting our wages reduced.
Prisoner – Any chance of it spreading to our sentences?

Teacher – And now I have told you the uses of measures of length, Tommy, can you tell me anything which we buy by the metre?
Tommy – Yes, miss. Gas.

Mum – Our little Smiffy shows great determination.
Dad (proudly) – Yes?
Mum – Yes, indeed! He spent the whole day making soap bubbles and trying to pin one to the wall.

Teacher – Danny, you mustn't laugh like that in the classroom.
Danny – I didn't mean to do it. I was smiling, and all of a sudden the smile burst.

Terry – What did you give me that nasty look for?
Jerry – Well, you have a nasty look, but I didn't give it to you.

Teacher – Aren't you ashamed of yourself, being at the bottom of the class?
Smiffy – No, it's warmer near the radiator.

First boy – My dog went to the dog show, and got two firsts and a second and was highly commended.
Second boy – Well, my dog stayed at home and got two fights and a feed and was highly delighted.

Dougal – Sorry I'm late, sir. I slipped and sprained my ankle.
Teacher – Another lame excuse!

Teacher – Do you know, Billy, that a grasshopper is so strong that it can jump a hundred times its own length?
Billy – Why, that's nothing. I once saw a wasp lift a twelve-stone man two feet into the air.

Visitor to hospital – Have you been under an operation?
Patient – No, under a car.

Terry (during a quarrel) – Well, I'm not two-faced.
Jerry – No; if you were you wouldn't be wearing that one.

Captain – What is strategy in war?
Sergeant – Well, strategy is when you don't let the enemy discover you are out of ammunition, but keep firing on.

Barber – You say you've been here before for a shave? I don't remember your face.
Victim – Probably not. It's all healed up now.

Voice from radio – Will Mr John Brown, who is believed to be on a pleasure cruise, return home at once?

Mother – Dennis, didn't I tell you to count fifty before fighting with Walter?
Dennis – I am counting, mother. I'm just sitting on him to make sure he's here when I've finished.

Teacher – Name a popular general?
Pupil – General holiday.

Man (with very big feet) – I should like to see some boots that would fit me.
Assistant – So would I, sir.

Magistrate – Didn't I tell you I didn't want to see you here again?
Prisoner – Yes, but the policeman wouldn't believe that.

Maid – When shall I waken you, sir?
Absent-minded master – I'll ring when I want wakened.

Tourist – And is the chin-strap to keep the helmet on?
Policeman – No, mister, it's to rest the jaw after answering foolish questions.

Roger – I always do my hardest work before breakfast.
Dad – What's that?
Roger – Getting up.

Mother – Why don't you give your brother a bite of your apple?
Sandy – I've given him the seeds. He can plant them, and have a whole orchard to himself.

Teacher – Putting a tin tack in a teacher's chair is a stupid old joke.
Dennis – Yes, but it hasn't lost its point yet, sir.

Dad – Roger, I hear you had detention at school today. Why was that?
Roger – Teacher told us to write an essay on laziness, and I sent in a blank sheet.

Spectator – I'll be mighty surprised if that referee doesn't get into hot water after the match.
Country chap – Then you'll be surprised. He's going in the horse trough.

McHaggis – That new florist certainly believes in the slogan, "Say it with flowers".
McTaggart – Why?
McHaggis – Well, he sent me a bunch of forget-me-nots with my bill last week.

Sam – I thought my rich uncle would leave me some money, but all I got was a rotten old flowerpot.
Jim – That must have been a nasty jar.

Jones – Who was that man you just raised your hat to?
Bones – Oh, that was my barber. He sold me a bottle of hair restorer a month ago, and whenever I meet him I let him see what a fraud he is.

Dentist – Have you seen any small boys ring my bell and run away?
Policeman – They weren't small boys – they were grown-ups.

Sailor (on sinking ship) – Say, mate, give us a read of that book on How to Swim when you've finished with it!

Porter (cheerfully) – Miss the train, sir?
Passenger (sarcastically) – No. I didn't like the look of it, so I chased it out of the station.

Jim – I've got the sack, Tom. I dropped a brick, and it broke.
Tom – That's nothing to get the sack for.
Jim – But it broke on the foreman's head.

Teacher (explaining a hard sum to class) – Now, watch the board carefully, boys, and I'll run through it again.

Old man – Where did you catch that nice string of fish, my boy?
Boy – You go down that lane marked "Trespassers Will be Prosecuted", keep right on till you come to a field with the notice, "Beware of the Bull", go right across till you come to a stream where there's another notice saying "Fishing Forbidden", and there you are!

Dud golfer – Notice any improvements since last year?
Caddie – You've had your clubs cleaned, haven't you?

Joe (from the top of a high building) – How do I get down?
Bill – Same way as you went up.
Joe – No fear! I came up head first!

Diner – Waiter, take away this egg.
Waiter – What shall I do with it, sir?
Diner – Wring its neck!

Teacher – Stand up, John. Did you give Jack this black eye?
John – No sir; he had the eye – I simply blackened it for him.

Workman (after digging hole in ground) – Where shall I put this pile of earth I have left?
Foreman – Use your sense, man – dig another hole and put it in.

Teacher – What is the difference between "goose" and "geese"?
Minnie – Why, one "geese" is a "goose" and a whole lot of "gooses" are a "geese".

Shopkeeper (to boy assistant) – Now look what you've done. You've knocked the arm off the Duke of Wellington's statue.
Boy assistant – It doesn't matter. Knock his eye out too, and call him Nelson.

Roger – Those eggs I bought is no good.
Shopkeeper – Why, what's the matter with it?
Roger – I've dropped them on your step.

Office boy (about to ask for increase in wages) – I tell you I'm going to get a rise or know the reason why.
Friend (later) – Well, did you get your rise?
Office boy – N-no, but I know the reason why.

Judge – You tell me you have no present occupation. What did you do last?
Prisoner – Six months, your Honour.

Father – So you are president of your bicycle club. That's nice. Why did they choose you?
Jimmy – Well, you see, Dad, I'm the only one that has a bicycle.

Smiffy's dad – Would you be good enough to look after my car, please?
Mayor – Sir, I'm the mayor of the town!
Smiffy – That doesn't matter. You look honest enough.

Gunfighter – See that fellow? He's the best gunman in town, and he's never killed a man yet.
Stranger – How's that?
Gunfighter – Well, he shoots so fast the second bullet catches up with the first and pushes it out of the way.

Bill – How long did it take you to learn to roller-skate?
Bob – Oh, about a dozen sittings.

Old man (to small youngster fishing) – Did you catch all those fish by yourself?
Youngster – No, sir. I had a worm to help me.

Angry gentleman – Porter, call me a taxi!
Porter – Yes, sir, you're a taxi.

Walter – Say, Dennis, I can trace my ancestry way back through my family tree.
Dennis – Well, there are only two things that live in trees, birds and monkeys, and I don't see any feathers on you.

Jock – What sort of a boat would you take to shoot rapids?
Sandy – A gunboat.

Sergeant (on rifle range) – This new bullet will penetrate nearly two feet of solid wood, so remember to keep your heads down.

Mrs Green – Did the burglars waken you last night?
Mrs Brown – Oh, no! They took things very quietly.

Teacher – Why are you boys arguing?
Sidney – There's no argument, sir. We're in agreement. Fatty thinks I'm not going to give him half this chocolate bar – and I think the same.

Prisoner – What are you doing?
Reporter – I'm taking notes.
Prisoner – Umph! That's what brought me here.

Jack – Brown fell asleep in his bath this morning with the water running.
Jock – Did the bath overflow?
Jack – No; fortunately he sleeps with his mouth open.

Minnie – Dad, are you still growing?
Dad – No, my girl. What makes you ask?
Minnie – Because the top of your head is coming through your hair.

Old man – Can you direct me to the Bank of England?
Little boy – I'll tell you for a fiver.
Old man – Isn't that rather a lot?
Little boy – Well, bank directors are always well paid.

Visitor (listening to an old sailor's tall tales) – You say you killed a whale, how inhumane. What did you do with it?
Old sailor – Why, miss, we ate him.
Visitor – Really, how horrible! And what did you do with the bones?
Old sailor – We left them on the sides of our plates.

Father (to young son) – Where are you going, Jock?
Son – I'm going fishing, Dad.
Father – But what about school?
Son – There! I knew I'd forgotten something!

Prisoner 99 – I say, mate, when is your time up?
Prisoner 66 – In ten years' time.
Prisoner 99 – Well, I'm in for twenty. Will you post this letter for me when you get out?

First burglar – Any luck lately, mate?
Second burglar – None! Worked all night on a butcher's safe, and when I got it open I found it was a refrigerator.

Caller – Are you sure the manager is not in?
Dignified office boy – Do you doubt his word, sir?

Terry – You say your brother is a leading light in the cinema?
Jerry – Yes; he shows the people to their seats.

Prison visitor – And what sort of man will you be when you leave prison?
Prisoner – An old one!

Barber – Haircut, sir?
Sarcastic old man – No, part it in the middle, then do it up in a bun on top, and tie it with pink ribbons.

Mum – Eat your rice up, Minnie.
Minnie – Don't like rice.
Mum – Well, eat it and pretend you like it.
Minnie – Ah, I know! I'll pretend I've eaten it.

Mum – Dennis! Don't you dare shoot that arrow at Walter's stomach!
Dennis – But we're playing at William Tell, and he's swallowed the apple.

Dad – Who gave you that black eye, Dennis?
Dennis – Nobody. I had to fight for it.

Trainer (to boxer who is being continually hit) – Why don't you stop them lefts, Bill?
Bill – Well, none have passed me yet, have they?

Prospective employer – I advertised for a strong office boy. Do you think you'll suit?
Applicant – I guess so. To get here first I knocked twenty-four applicants down the stairs.

Terry (in café, examining bill) – What? Five pounds fifty! Look here, waiter, I had sardines on toast, not goldfish.

Diner – Waiter, I want some chicken. The younger it is the better.
Waiter – How about an egg, sir.

Terry – My uncle died of music on the brain.
Jerry – How's that?
Terry – A piano fell on his head.

A passenger in an aeroplane was far up in the sky when the pilot began to laugh hysterically.
Passenger – What's the joke?
Pilot – I'm thinking what they'll say at the asylum when they find out I have escaped!

Acrobat (on flying trapeze, to partner who is flying towards him with outstretched hands) – You'll have to excuse me a minute, old man; my back feels itchy.

Explorer (speaking on advance of civilisation) – In the past, the Eskimos used to eat candles.
Old lady (seriously) – And now I suppose they eat electric bulbs?

Film director – The lion will pursue you for a hundred yards; no farther, understand?
Actor – Yes, I do, but does the lion?

Officer (to new recruit during manoeuvres) – Hi! Do you realise you're exposing yourself to an imaginary enemy five hundred yards away?
Recruit – Yes, sir. But I'm standing behind an imaginary rock thirty feet high.

The village team were getting severely beaten on their own ground.
Visitor – Do you ever score any goals?
Local – Dunno. I've only watched them for two seasons.

Binks – I've a pair of golf socks.
Jinks – Golf socks?
Binks – Yes. There's eighteen holes in them.

Poet – So you think I ought to give up writing poetry?
Editor – No, you ought to begin.

Bill – What fish can't live in water?
Harry – I dunno.
Bill – Dead ones, of course.

Customer – Can you recommend this hair restorer?
Barber – Yes, I know a man who pulled out the cork with his teeth, and in twenty-four hours he had a moustache.

**First cannibal – And what makes our Royal Highness so full of laughter?
Second cannibal – Oh, he must have swallowed that last gent's funny-bone.**

*Judge (to witness, for fifth time) – Did the bus run over the man?
Weary witness – No, the conductor leaned out and bit him as the bus passed by.*

Visitor – So you own a pet store? Do you have any trouble in selling parrots?
Store owner – Oh no, they speak for themselves.

**Why did you give up your position in the choir?
I was ill last Sunday, and didn't go, and after the service someone asked if the organ had been mended.**

*Mr White – Excuse me, sir, are you Mr Green?
Mr Brown – No, sir. I'm Mr Brown.
Mr White – A thousand pardons! You see, I'm colour-blind.*

Boss – Has the foreman told you what to do?
New watchman – Yes; I've to wake him up when the boss comes.

**Freddie – My father is a mounted policeman.
Visitor – Is that better than being a foot policeman?
Freddie – Course it is. If there is any trouble he can get away quicker.**

*Fireman – Hi, what are you going back for?
Rescued person – I just love sliding down this chute.*

Pat – I'd sooner be in a collision than an explosion.
Mike – How's that?
Pat – Because in a collision there you are, but in an explosion, where the dickens are you?

**Uncle – What's etiquette, Bobby?
Bobby – Oh, that's the noise you mustn't swallow your tea with when there's company.**

*Teacher – Tommy, why did the boy stand on the burning deck?
Tommy – Because it was too hot to sit down.*

Plumber (to applicant) – Got any references?
Boy – Yes, but I left them at home.
Plumber – You'll do.

**Jack – I've never seen a dog marked like yours before, Bobby!
Bobby – Well, Dad is an artist, and he never looks where he wipes his brush.**

*Doctor – What you need is an iron tonic to sharpen your appetite. By the way, what is your profession?
Patient – I'm a sword-swallower at a circus.*

Politician (at a party rally) – My friends, if we were to turn and look ourselves squarely in the face, what should we find we needed most?
Voice from the crowd – A rubber neck!

**Mr Smith – Your son threw a potato at me.
Mr Jones – Did it hit you?
Mr Smith – No.
Mr Jones – Then it wasn't my son.**

*Teacher – What are weights and measures?
Smart boy – Waits are people who sing carols round this time, and measures are what father takes to stop them.*

Brown – Where have I seen your face before?
Stranger – Same place as you see it now.

Teacher – Johnny, your mouth is open.
Johnny – Yes, I know; I opened it.

Boss (to office boy) – Why is it that every time I come into the office I find you reading a book?
Office boy – Because you wear rubber soles.

Office boy (to employer) – Can I take a day off, sir?
Employer – Yes; off that calendar.

Damaged boxer – Am I doing him any damage?
Second – No, but swing your arms and make a draught. It might give him a cold.

Jim (to Bill who has already been asked the question fifteen times) – Who gave you that black eye?
Bill – No one. I was looking at a football match through a hole and my eye got sunburnt.

Jim – Gracious me! Look at your face! Have you been fighting?
Bill – Not me. The other bloke was; I was only learning.

Mother – Billy, why is the baby crying like that?
Billy – There was a naughty fly biting him on the head, so I killed it with my spade.

Foreman – There goes Mr Twister. He twists so much that if he swallowed a nail it would become a corkscrew.

Jimmy (as his mother dishes out the Christmas pudding) – Is that big bit of pudding for Mary?
Mother – No, it's for you.
Jimmy – Crumbs, what a tiny bit!

Mother – If you eat any more plum pudding, Billy you'll burst.
Billy – Pass over the dish then, and stand out of the way.

Two boys were passing a ruined castle on Christmas Eve.
Darren – They s-say them castles a-are haunted. A-are you s-scared of g-ghosts?
Derek – N-n-no.
Darren – N-n-neither am I.

Teacher – What are weights and measures?
Smart boy – Waits are people who sing carols round this time, and measures are what father takes to stop them.

Burglar (caught in cupboard) – If you p-please, sir, I've called for my Christmas box.
Bashem Billy (drawing on his boxing gloves) – Righto! Come out here and get it!

Kevin (to uncle who has just been thrown from his horse) – Uncle Dave, has your horse thrown you?
Uncle Dave – No. Just as he kicked up his hind legs, I gently dismounted over his head.

Passenger – Hi, captain, one of the nails on your seat has torn my trousers.
Captain – Well, that's what we advertise. Cheap sea trips (seat rips).

Teacher – Now, the cow is a very useful animal. Can anyone tell me what is made from its horns?
Danny – Yes, sir – hornaments.

Uncle – How can you eat so much?
Nephew – I don't know; but I'm always empty when the table's full.

Billy – Didn't you tell me that if I ate the rest of the turkey it would make me ill?
Mother – Yes. Why?
Billy – Well, er, it hasn't.

Terry – How did you get on at the skating rink?
Jerry – All right.
Terry – Did you fall?
Jerry – No, but my neck changed places with my feet several times.

Youngster (calling in at shop door) – Please, sir, your wife sent me to tell you that the chimney of your house is on fire, the dinner is all spoilt, the baby's having a screaming fit, and the water pipe's busted, and before I forget, sir, allow me to wish you a merry Christmas!

Policeman – Come on, now, you must not stand there singing.
Carol singer – Thanks! You're the first one to admit that I can sing.

Teacher – Well, my boy, what are you going to give your little brother for his Christmas?
Jimmy – I don't know. I gave him measles last year.

Terry – What kind of Christmas did you have?
Jerry – Same as last year, twenty minutes of turkey and mince pies, and a week in bed.

It was the day after Christmas, and the two chums were comparing how they spent Christmas:
Jock – I bet you didn't have a good time yesterday.
Wullie (angrily) – I bet I did.
Jock – Then why aren't you ill to-day?

Mother – Surely you're not hanging a stocking up with a large hole in it?
Willie – Oh, that's all right, Mum. I'm going to put your largest clothes basket under it.

What did the baby light bulb say to its mother?
"I love you watts and watts!"

Jimmy – Did you get many Christmas presents?
Johnny – You bet I did. More than my brothers and sisters.
Jimmy – Did you? You're lucky.
Johnny – Yes, you see I got up two hours before them.

Minister – You like going to Sunday school, don't you, John?
John – Yes, sir.
Minister – What do you expect to learn there today?
John – The date of the Christmas party, sir.

Father – Did you hear Father Christmas this year, Sandy?
Sandy – No, it was too dark to see him, but I heard what he said when he knocked his toes against the bedpost.

Is a graveyard like a herring because it's full of bones?

"How time flies!" as the husband said when his wife threw the clock at him.

"Drop me a line," remarked the sailor as he fell overboard.

When the storm is brewing, what does it brew?

Can a drink be got from a tap on the door?

Is an angle a triangle with only two sides?

Smiffy wrote in his history exam: Boney Prince Charlie got his name because he was so thin. Another famous thin man was Napoleon, who was nicknamed Boney Pat.

Wilfrid wrote in his history exam: The Romans made their roads straight so that the Britons could not hide round the corners.

Is a quack doctor one who looks after ducks?

Father – Well, Alfie, what were your end-of-term marks like?
Alfie – Underwater!
Father – What do you mean?
Alfie – Below "C" level!

Busy man – I really can't see you today.
Salesman (eagerly) – Well, I'm the very man you want to see, sir. I'm selling spectacles.

Aunt – Do you know what toffee does to your teeth, Tommy?
Tommy – No, Auntie. But I know what my teeth do to toffee.

Andrew – My brother's so thin he looks just like a garden rake.
Bobby – That's nothing. My brother's so thin that if you see a door open and nothing comes in, that's him.

Teacher – Are you sure your father didn't do these sums for you, Alex?
Alec – Quite sure, sir. He did have a try, but he got into such a muddle that Grandad had to do them all over again.

Fred – Do you know, when I was young I couldn't walk for a whole year?
Old lady – Oh, you poor boy. Why was that?
Fred – I wasn't old enough!

What's a barbecue?
A line of people waiting for a hair cut!

What kind of job did the lazy man get?
He stood around for so long, he became a dust collector!

Did you hear about the werewolf's party?
It was a howling success!

Jane – Why was the farmer hopping mad?
Jill – Someone stepped on his corn!

Bill – What do hedgehogs eat?
Bob – Prickled onions!

What do birds eat between meals?
Tweets!

Ship's officer – Oh, there goes eight bells. Excuse me, it's my watch below.
Old lady – Gracious! Fancy your watch striking as loudly as that!

Angry diner – Look here, waiter, there's a button in my salad!
Waiter – Yes, sir, that's part of the dressing.

Salesman – This bicycle is a very sound model.
Customer – I know that. I heard that when I tried it.

Lazy man – I dreamed last night that I was working.
Workmate – I thought you looked tired this morning.

Sergeant – How did the prisoner get away from you?
Policeman – Well, you see, on the way to the police station we were chased by an angry bull, and the prisoner stood still.

Teacher – Now, tell me the names of any wild animals found in this country – beginning with Danny.

How do you send a baby astronaut to sleep?
Sing him a luna-by!

If you cross a dog with a cat, what do you get?
An animal that chases itself!

What goes fast around castles?
Moat-a-boats!

Patient – Doctor, doctor, I keep stealing things.
Doctor – Have you taken anything for it?

Bill – What kind of make-up do ghosts use?
John – Vanishing cream!

What's black when it's clean, and white when it's dirty?
A blackboard!

What nail should you never hit with a hammer?
Your fingernail!

What lives under the water and wears a cowboy hat?
Billy the squid!

Teacher – Sidney, you give me a sentence using the word "gruesome".
Sidney – Er, my mum's plants grew some in the past two weeks!

First workman – Poor Bill. He's working himself to death.
Second workman – How's that?
First workman – He's so short-sighted he can't see when the boss isn't looking.

Host (absent-mindedly, to singer) – Will you sing your song now, or shall we let the guests enjoy themselves for another half-hour?

Visitor (in deserted Scottish village) – Where are all the people today?
Grocer – The laird's out shooting.
Visitor – Ah – everyone has gone to watch, then?
Grocer – Not likely! They're all indoors out of his way.

Uncle – Did you have measles worse than Pete Smith?
Jimmy – Much worse. I had them during my holidays.

Bill (at Scout camp) – Is Jack a good cook?
Sam – I don't think so. The last time I saw him he was trying to open an egg with a tin-opener!

What did the alien say to the petrol pump?
Take your finger out of your ear when I'm talking!

What do you get when you cross an insect and a rabbit?
Bugs Bunny!

Girl – A packet of helicopter flavoured crisps, please.
Shopkeeper – We have no helicopter flavour left, only plane (plain)!

Why do bees buzz?
Because they can't whistle!

Customer – I want three lawnmowers.
Assistant – You must have a large lawn, sir.
Customer – No, no. I have two borrowing neighbours.

Local – Hello! Caught anything yet?
Angler – No, not yet.
Local – I thought not. There was no water in the pond till it rained last night.

Seaside visitor (whose wig has blown into the sea) – Lifeguard! Lifeguard! Get my wig!
Lifeguard – Excuse me, sir, but I'm a lifeguard, not a hair-restorer.

Smiffy – Fancy going to bed with shoes on!
Toots – Who does?
Smiffy – A horse.

What happened to the snake with a cold?
She adder viper nose!

What happened to the boy who ran away with the circus?
His parents made him bring it back!

Man (waiting for change) – You don't seem very quick at giving change.
Waiter – I'm a bit out of practice, sir. Most folk tell me to keep it.

Did you hear about the scientist who crossed a parrot with a crocodile?
It bit off his leg and said, "Who's a pretty boy, then!"

Customer – Will the band play anything I ask?
Waiter – Yes, sir.
Customer – Well, ask them to play cards!

Boy – Dad, I can't eat this hamburger. It's awful!
Dad – Shall I call the waiter?
Boy – No, I don't think even he'll be able to eat it!

Motorist (stopped for careless driving) – What I know about driving would fill a book.
Constable – And what you don't know will fill mine.

Patient – Doctor, doctor, I feel like a bell.
Doctor – Take some of these pills, and if they don't work, give me a ring.

Ian – When I'm grown up, everybody will be scared of me.
Pa – What'll you be – a boxer or a wrestler?
Ian – None of them. I'm going to be a dentist!

Teacher – Give me a sentence using the word "pasture".
Bobby – On the way to school yesterday, I pasture house!

Son – Mum, can I get 50p?
Mum – Do you think money grows on trees?
Son – 'Course it does. Otherwise why would banks have so many branches?

Customer – I ordered a dozen oranges and you only sent eleven.
Grocer – Well, sir, one was bad so I didn't send it.

How do you stop a cold going to your chest?
Tie a knot in your neck!

Where do sheep like to do their shopping?
Woolworths, of course!

Why did the boy not hurt himself when he fell on a pin?
Because it was a safety pin!

Where can you find a rubber trumpet?
In an elastic band.

Dennis – How do you cure a cold?
Minnie – Drink a glass of orange after a hot bath.
Dennis – Does it work?
Minnie – I don't know. I haven't finished drinking the bath yet!

Jim – Do you like the dentist?
James – No, he's a real bore!

The Dachshund is so long and thin,
You pat its head on Sunday.
And though the message travels fast,
Its tail won't wag till Monday.

Dennis – I want to thank you for that woolly vest you sent me.
Auntie – Were you pleased with it?
Dennis – Pleased? I was tickled to death!

Tim – Funny, isn't it?
Jim – What's funny?
Tim – Well, this year will be last year next year.

Mum – Jack, why are you buttering both sides of your bread?
Jack – I'm going to eat both sides, Mum.

Householder (to burglar) – Put all that stuff back in the safe at once. Do you hear?
Burglar – Gosh, not all of it! Half of it belongs to next door.

What do you call a man covered in beef, vegetables and gravy?
Stu?

Why didn't the monkey hurt himself when he jumped from 1,000 metres into a glass of lemonade?
Because it was a soft drink!

Man – You've been working in your garden for ages. What are you growing?
Gardener – Tired!

Why is a lion in the desert like Father Christmas?
Because it has Sandy Claws!

What do you get if you mix the white of an egg with a pound of gunpowder?
A boom-meringue!

Captain – Haven't you got that rope untangled yet, my man?
Sailor – No, sir.
Captain – You're very slow.
Sailor – Not really, sir, I'm doing thirty knots an hour.

First cricket captain – Our best batsman can't play, he has measles.
Second cricket captain – That's no excuse, our fast bowler would have knocked spots off him!

Diner – I want a dozen oysters – not too large, not too small. Don't bring me any that are not plump and fresh. Choose them carefully.
Waiter – Er – with or without pearls, sir?

Very lazy, slow plumber – Yes, I remember your little boy, ma'am. When I was working at the school, he was in the infant class.
Woman – And what class was he in when you finished?

What wears shoes, but has no feet?
The pavement!

Gent – So you have a cottage for sale. Is it within walking distance of the railway station?
Landlord – Well, it all depends on how far you can walk!

What do you get if you cross a horse with a football player?
A centaur-forward!

Teacher – What comes before seven, boy?
Sidney – Er, the milkman!

What is it that lives in winter, dies in summer, and grows with its roots upwards?
An icicle!

Patient – Doctor, I've got a sore stomach.
Doctor – What have you been eating?
Patient – Yesterday I had three black snooker balls. Today for breakfast, I had two white snooker balls, and for dinner, I had five reds!
Doctor – Ah, yes, I see the problem. Not enough greens!

Doctor – Why have you got a fried egg on your head?
Patient – Because a boiled one keeps rolling off!

Manager – I want to post a notice where all the men will see it.
Foreman – That's easy. Paste it up on the face of the clock!

Dad – Your teacher has written to me saying it's impossible to teach you anything.
Dennis – There you are, I always said he was no good.

Dennis – Dad says will you lend him your gardening tools?
Polite man – Haven't you forgotten something, young man?
Dennis – Oh yes, he said if the old miser refuses, try next door.

Foreman – Look here, that man's doing twice the work you are!
Lazy workman – That's what I keep telling him, but he'll not slow down.

Customer (to baker) – Are you sure this loaf is today's – because yesterday's wasn't.

Dave – Jimmy told me you told him that secret I told you not to tell him.
Andy – He's the limit! I'll have to talk to him about it.
Dave – All right, but don't tell him I told you because he told me you told him what I told you!

Teacher – Dennis! You can't sleep in my class.
Dennis – Please, sir, if you didn't talk so loudly I could.

Doctor (to patient) – Did you take your two-mile walk every day last week?
Patient – Yes, but I was very giddy after it.
Doctor – Giddy? Why?
Patient – Well, I'm a lighthouse keeper.

Why was the clock nervous?
Because it was all wound up!

Doctor, doctor, I feel like a car!
Stop driving me round the bend!

What is flat as a pancake, round as a berry, has the head of a woman, and the tail of a lion?
A ten pence piece!

What must you do if you break your leg?
Limp!

Heard about the two peanuts walking down the road?
One was a salted!

What do you call a man who can chop down twenty trees a day?
A good feller!

When does it rain money?
When there's a change in the weather!

What gets dirty by washing?
Water!

My brother gets a warm reception wherever he goes.
He must be very popular.
No, he's a fireman!

Lecturer – Will the members of the audience who keep on interrupting please be quiet. I can hardly hear myself speak.
Voice – Cheer up – you're not missing much.

McAndrew – It's no use. I can't talk to a fool.
McPherson – Well, I can. Listen ...

Jock – Hector and Hamish had a terrible row last night.
Alec – I thought they were inseparable friends?
Jock – That's right. It took six of us to separate them.

Doctor – What's this? You've sent a letter saying you had smallpox, and I find you have rheumatism.
Patient – Well, doctor, no one in the house could spell rheumatism.

Tommy – My father can write with both hands at the same time.
Hamish – How does he manage that?
Tommy – He uses a typewriter.

What has six legs and would kill you if it jumped out of a tree on top of you?
A snooker table!

Teacher – If there were ten sheep in a field and two got out through a hole in the hedge, how many would be left?
Angus – None, miss.
Teacher – Nonsense! The answer is eight.
Angus – You may know arithmetic, miss, but you don't know sheep.

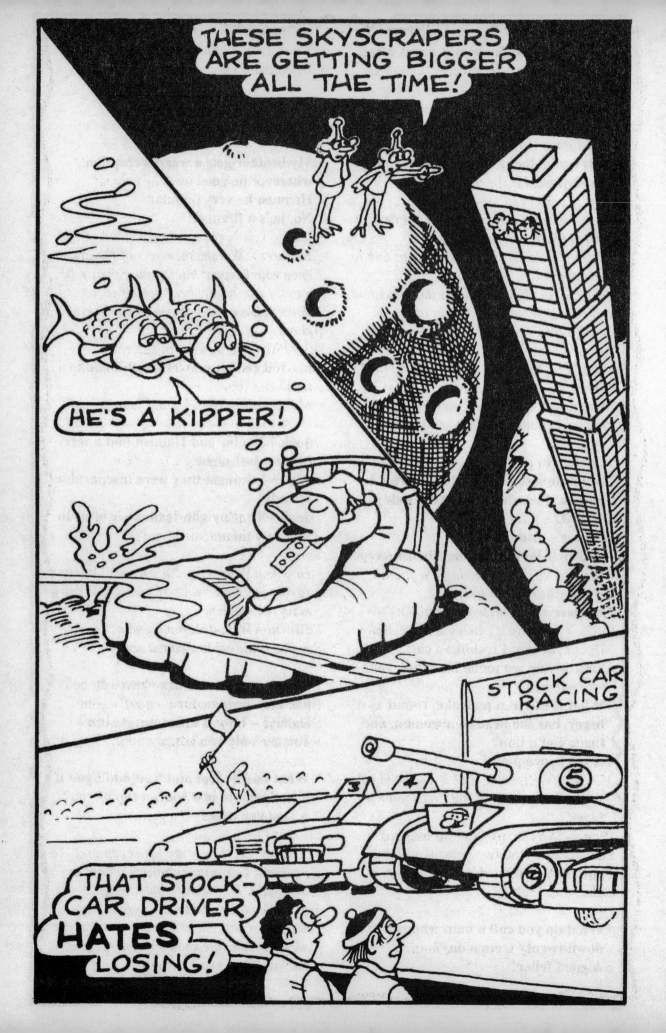

Jack – Did you hear about the man who knocked down a house with one blow of his hammer?
Jill – No.
Jack – Yes, he was the auctioneer!

Terry – A man was walking down the road stealing all the garden gates.
Jerry – What did you do
Terry – I didn't say anything, in case he took offence!

Customer – Can I have my milk bill?
Shopkeeper – Excuse me, sir, my name isn't Bill, it's Colin.

Dennis – I fell off a sixty-foot ladder yesterday.
Minnie – It's a wonder you weren't killed.
Dennis – Not really. I fell off the first rung.

Smiffy (in bed) – Gosh! It's quarter to eight! If Mum doesn't wake me up soon I'll be late for school!

Teacher – Now look at the map, Harry. Which is the warmest side of Scotland?
Harry – The east.
Teacher – And why do you say that?
Harry – Because it's nearest the radiator.

Alistair – Ma, am I rude if I speak with my mouth full?
Ma – Yes, Alistair.
Alistair – And am I polite when I say, "Thank you"?
Ma – Why, yes.
Alistair – Well, what am I if I say "Thank you" with my mouth full?

Diner – Why is my food all mashed up?
Waiter – You did ask me to step on it, sir!

Jim – Do fish sing?
Tim – Only when they have musical scales!

What does an invisible baby drink?
Evaporated milk!

What kind of an ant can count?
An accountant!

Why should you never trust a shepherd? Because he's always walking around with a crook!

What do you get if you cross a load of diamonds with a road?
A jewel carriageway!

Jill – I bumped into an old friend today.
Bill – Was she pleased to see you?
Jill – Not really; we were both in our cars at the time!

Jock – Jamie's not such a big fool as he used to be.
Alistair – Is he getting wiser, then?
Jock – No – thinner.

Dad – How many sums did you have wrong in your arithmetic test?
Smiffy – One.
Dad – And how many did you have to do?
Smiffy – Twelve.
Dad – So you had eleven right?
Smiffy – No, I didn't do the rest.

Officer – Sergeant, where have all these silly asses in our company gone?
Sergeant – I don't know, sir. It seems we're the only two left.

Tommy – I'll bet you won't go into that haunted room alone, Andy.
Andy – Oh, won't I? You just come with me and I'll show you.

Boatman – Come in, number 91, your time is up!
Boss – Hang on! We haven't got a number 91!
Boatman – Oh, sorry! Are you in trouble, number 16?

Jim – Nick was very confused yesterday.
Joe – What happened?
Jim – The foreman gave him five shovels, and told him to take his pick!

Piano tuner – I've come to tune your piano.
Man – But I didn't send for you.
Piano tuner – No, but your neighbour did!

What would be worse than finding a maggot in an apple you're eating?
Finding half a maggot!

How do you make a bandstand?
Take away their chairs!

Sword swallower – I'm off my food.
Pal – Really?
Sword swallower – Yes, I can only eat razor blades!

Zoo keeper – Now then, keep away from that lion, sonny.
Smiffy – I'm not hurting him!

Absent-minded professor (caught in revolving doors) – I can't remember if I'm going out or coming in!

Cuddles – I saw a funny thing the other day.
Dimples – You shouldn't go looking in mirrors!

Slow barber – Your hair is turning very grey, sir.
Customer – Quite possibly, but do you think you could finish cutting it before it becomes white!

Old man – Where's your brother, Charlie?
Charlie – He's in the house playing a duet on the piano with me, but I finished my part first.

What is a frog's favourite flower?
A croak-us!

First farmer – Do you own a lot of land?
Second farmer – Not really, my farm's so small, the cows give condensed milk!

Susan – Everything ends in "ing".
Annie – Don't be silly – of course it doesn't!
Susan – Yes it does – everything!

Judge – You've been up before this bench seven times – I fine you £200!
Prisoner – Can I get a discount for being a regular customer?

Jill – Have you heard the joke about the eggs?
June – No!
Jill – Two bad!

Why did Mickey Mouse go on a journey to Outer Space?
He wanted to find Pluto!

Boss – Everything in this office is worked by electricity.
Office boy – I know, sir. Even the wages give you a shock!

Old lady (visiting prison) – How long are you in for, my man?
Prisoner – Two years.
Old lady – What is the charge?
Prisoner – Oh, there's no charge. Everything's free.

Jockey – That horse you sold me dropped dead this morning.
Dealer – That's strange. He never did that before.

Chief of village fire brigade – I want a shave, Joe. And make it fast. I'm on my way to a fire.

What do you get if you cross a bee with a giant ape?
Sting Kong!

Why do lions eat raw meat?
Because they can't cook!

Old man – Which way do you go from here to see the football match?
Billy – Straight up.
Old man – Straight up this road?
Billy – No, straight up this tree.

Ma – Goodness, Jimmy, how can you eat so much?
Jimmy – I don't know, I suppose it's just my good luck!

Waiter – Wasn't your egg cooked long enough, sir?
Diner – Oh, yes – but not soon enough.

What do you get if you cross a parrot with an elephant?
Something that tells everything that it remembers!

Patient – Doctor, doctor, my legs feel like jelly.
Doctor – Don't worry, they'll be better in a trifle!

What do you get if you cross an elephant with a goldfish?
Swimming trunks!

What is the speed limit in Egypt?
Six Niles an hour!

Mum – Where have you been?
Charlie – Helping Mr McKay to look for a five pound note he'd lost.
Mum – Did you have any luck?
Charlie – No – he found it himself.

Shopkeeper – That man tried to cheat me with a dud pound coin yesterday.
Friend – Did you give it back to him?
Shopkeeper – Yes, I mixed it up with his change today.

Patient – Doctor, doctor, I feel like a thermostat.
Doctor – Oh control yourself, man!

What do bees do with their honey?
They cell it!

Customer – Can you give me a really good shave?
Barber – Yes, sir. Satisfaction guaranteed or whiskers returned.

Archie – That's a very short coat you're wearing.
Angus – Maybe so, but it'll be long enough before I get another.

What is the best cure for a splitting headache?
Glue and an aspirin!

What do you call a monkey born on 1st April?
An Aperil fool!

What is a snake's favourite football team?
Slitherpool!

Which members of an orchestra are most untrustworthy?
The fiddlers!

How does a robot stand?
Bolt upright!

MacDonald – Why are you pulling the wallpaper off the walls? Are you spring-cleaning?
MacDougal – No, we're moving house!

Mum – Do you know your alphabet yet, Angus?
Angus – Yes, Mum.
Mum – Well, what comes after T?
Angus – Supper.

Poet – What do you think of my last poem?
Editor – Well, I'm glad to hear it's your last.

Gamekeeper – Fishing is not allowed in this steam, sir. I'm afraid you must give me what you've caught.
Angler – Well, I've caught the cold so far; you're welcome to it.

Smiffy – Do you always walk as fast as this, Uncle?
Uncle – No – I walk a lot faster when I'm by myself.
Smiffy – Gosh! I wouldn't like to be with you when you're by yourself.

Colonel (inspecting barracks) – If the barracks caught fire, Sergeant, what order would you give?
Sergeant – Cease fire, sir!

What is rhubarb?
Celery with a high temperature!

Teacher – Why were you so late for school this morning?
Danny – I squeezed too much toothpaste onto my brush, and it took me ages to get it back into the tube.

What did the rake say to the hoe?
"Hi, hoe!"

What nut has no shell?
A dough-nut!

Mum – I thought I told you to watch when the milk boiled over.
Dennis – I did. It was exactly two o'clock!

Where do monsters travel?
From ghost to ghost!

Which king of England first introduced wine into the country?
Alfred the Grape!

What do Martians eat for breakfast?
Unidentified frying objects!

Prison visitor – It must be terrible to be shut up all the time in a small room like this. What were you before you came here?
Prisoner – A lift attendant.

Sergeant – What are fortifications?
Recruit – Two lots of twentifications!

Mum – My pastry brush is very stiff today!
Dennis – That's funny – it was OK yesterday when I varnished Gnasher's kennel with it.

Butler – There's a man wanting to see you, sir.
Absent-minded professor – Tell him I'm not in.
Butler – I told him, but he won't go away, sir.
Absent-minded professor – Oh well, I'd better go and tell him myself!

Passer-by – What's that lamp on top of these stones for?
Workman – So that no one will tumble over them.
Passer-by – But what are the stones for?
Workman – Why, to hold the lamp up, silly.

Dentist – Which is the sore tooth?
Patient (who is cinema attendant) – Balcony, third from the left in the front row.

Why couldn't the little boy go to his friend's birthday party?
Because the invitation said for 3 to 5, and he was 7!

What kind of animals can jump higher than a house?
All animals – houses can't jump!

What's a frog's favourite television programme?
Top of the Hops!

What has one horn and gives milk?
A milk delivery van!

Joe – My uncle's very absent-minded.
Moe – Is he?
Joe – Yes. He thought he had left his watch at home yesterday, and then he took it out of his pocket to see if he had time to run back and get it.

Visitor – When I saw your circus last year you had a very good ventriloquist. What has become of him?
Attendant – He's left us. He found he could make more money selling parrots!

Andy – Will you please come at once, doctor? Our door's jammed.
Doctor – It's a joiner you want then, sonny, not a doctor.
Andy – But Dad's fingers are in it!

Doctor – I don't like that cold of yours.
Dennis – I'm sorry, but it's the only one I've got.

Lift boy – There you are, son – the fourth floor.
Old man – Who are you calling "son"?
Lift boy – Well, I brought you up, didn't I?

Employer – The man who can't make himself understood is a fool. Do you understand?
Clerk – No, sir.

What did the mummy bee say to the naughty baby bee?
"Go home and behive yourself!"

What do you get if you cross a sheep with a thunderstorm?
A wet blanket!

First naturalist in jungle – I've just spotted a leopard!
Second naturalist – You can't fool me! They're born that way!

Where do sick gnomes go to be cured?
A national elf service hospital!

Terry – Why are you eating all these cheese biscuits?
Jerry – Because I'm crackers about them!

What is easy to get into, but hard to get out of?
Trouble!

Judge – The next person who raises his voice in this court will be thrown out!
Prisoner – Hip, hip, hooray!

Diner – Look here, waiter, first I found a splinter in this pie, then I found a button.
Waiter – I suppose you haven't seen anything of a fork, have you? One went missing the other night.

Teacher – What is 1314?
Toots – The Battle of Bannockburn.
Teacher – What is 1066?
Cuthbert – The Battle of Hastings.
Teacher – Good. Now, Smiffy, what is 1215?
Smiffy – Quarter past twelve!

Slow waiter – How did you order your steak, sir?
Weary customer – I ordered it by word of mouth, but I suppose I ought to have sent you a postcard two weeks in advance!

Why was a shellfish driving a getaway car?
It was a smash and crab raid!

Doctor – Have you been taking that medicine I prescribed?
Patient – No, I tried it, but I decided I'd rather cough!

Doctor – Please breathe out three times.
Patient – Is that so you can check my lungs?
Doctor – No, it's so I can clean my glasses!

Did you hear about the man who crossed a snail with a dog?
He sent it down to the newsagent's, and it came back with last week's papers!

What do you get if you cross an octopus with a sheep?
A jumper with eight arms!

Which monkeys like eating sweet cakes?
Meringue-utans!

Teacher – Now, Danny, can you tell me how many days there are in a year?
Danny – Seven, sir.
Teacher – I said a year, not a week
Danny – It's still seven, sir. Monday, Tuesday, Wednesday, Thursday, Friday, Saturday and Sunday. If there are any others, I've never heard of them!

Where do you go to get a stopper for your bottle?
Cork!

First mother – My daughter is only two, and she can spell her name backwards.
Second mother – Really? What is her name?
First mother – Anna.

Comic artist – Has the editor seen the joke I left last week?
Office boy – Not yet, sir, but he's trying hard.

Pa – Do you know what's happened to my shaving brush?
Bobby – No, Pa, but Jimmy's wooden horse has a new tail.

Andy – Dad, I've just saved you a pound!
Father – How?
Andy – Remember you said you'd give me a pound if I behaved at Billy Martin's birthday party?
Father – Yes.
Andy – Well, I didn't.

Danny – Smiffy, you've got your trousers on inside out.
Smiffy – Yes, I'm saving the outside for Sundays!

Old man – I take a walk every morning to get an appetite for my breakfast.
Poacher – I take one every morning to get a breakfast for my appetite!

What do you call a man in between two houses?
Alley!

How does a skeleton eat his dinner?
Off bone china!

What makes Donald Duck fall over?
Disney spells!

First farmer – I've just bought a piece of land ten miles long and an inch wide.
Second farmer – What are you going to grow on it?
First farmer – Spaghetti!

Film actor – But look here, if I'm to be thrown into the rapids, how am I going to get out?
Producer – Don't you worry about that – you don't appear again in the film!

Customer – Hey, waiter, there's a caterpillar on my plate.
Waiter – Oh, no, sir – that's a sausage.

Diner (suspiciously) – Why do you call this "enthusiastic" stew?
Waiter – Because the cook put everything he had into it.

Brown – I say, old man, will you push me or give me a kick.
Jones – What on earth for?
Brown – Well, I've just bought this dog, and I want to see if he's fierce.

Showman – Two pounds to see the acrobats. Come along, sonny – only two pounds.
Davie – I've only got one pound, mister – but if you let me in, I'll only open one eye.

What is oval and wears a kilt?
A Scotch egg!

First postman – Why don't you go in, Sam? The dog's wagging his tail.
Second postman – Yes, and he's growling too. I don't know which end to believe.

What flower spreads?
A buttercup!

Why are opticians such nice people? They see eye to eye with all their patients!

What's the difference between an elephant and a banana? Try picking them both up!

What's a volcano? A mountain with hiccups!

Farmer – Gosh, you must be brave to come down by parachute in a gale like this.
Stranger – I didn't come down by parachute. I went up with a tent.

Lady (to train conductor) – I'm afraid my little dog has eaten the ticket. Conductor – Well, lady, you'll have to buy him a second helping.

First man – Why do you sleep with a parrot beside your bed? Second man – Because I want to know what I say in my sleep.

Angry passenger – Here, what's happened to my clothes?
Ship's steward – Where did you put them last night?
Passenger – In that cupboard.
Steward – That's not a cupboard – that's a port hole.

Patient – Doctor, doctor, I keep thinking I'm a dog! Doctor – Just lie on the couch! Patient – I'm not allowed up on the furniture!

Why was the dentist thrown out of the army? Because he didn't know how to drill!

Why did the horsebox? Because it saw the wire fence!

When is a car not a car? When it turns into a garage!

What is the best day for cooking bacon and eggs?
Fry-day!

Cat – When are you going on holiday, mousey? Mouse – Next squeak!

Andy – What kind of car have you got now, Sandy? Sandy – Oh, a runabout. You know, it'll run about a mile then stop.

Old lady (on ship) – What's the matter, Captain?
Captain – The rudder's broken.
Old lady – But that won't matter, will it? It's always under the water and no one will notice it.

Conductor – A lady has left a pint of milk in the bus. Inspector – Take it to the office, and if nobody claims it in six months you can have it.

Patient – Doctor, doctor, what will you give me for my sore throat? Doctor – Nothing, I don't want one!

King to Queen – What's that rabbit doing in there?
Queen to King – That's not a rabbit – it's the "hare" to the throne!

First boy – Do you know the difference between an elephant and a Post Office? Second boy – No. First boy – Well, I won't send you to buy a stamp!

Who tells jokes about knitting? A nitwit!

Lazy Len – Can I have a shave please?
Barber – You'll have to hold your head up if you want a shave, sir.
Lazy Len – Will I? Oh well, make it a haircut.

Dad – How did that window get broken?
Dennis – I was cleaning my catapult, and it went off!

Father (to Tommy) – You're going to take your medicine like a man, aren't you, Tommy?
Tommy – No fear! It says double dose for adults!

Prospective house buyer – Yes, it's a good house, but why are all the windows broken?
Landlord – That's nothing serious. I was only convincing a few inquirers that it was a stone's thrown from the beach.

Why did the Romans always build straight roads?
Because they didn't want to drive their soldiers round the bend!

What is the difference between an angry rabbit and a counterfeit £10 note?
One's a mad bunny, and the other's bad money!

What walks on its head all day?
A drawing pin stuck in your shoe!

Gas man – What's this Irish coin doing in your meter, madam?
Lady – Oh, I was cooking Irish Stew!

What did one cucumber say to the other cucumber?
"If you had kept your big mouth shut, we wouldn't be in this pickle!"

Thief – Pardon me, sir, but have you seen a policeman around here?
Pedestrian – No, I'm sorry.
Thief – Thank you. Now will you kindly hand over your watch and wallet?

Teacher – Now, what's wrong with this sentence, "The toast was drank"?
Smiffy – It should be "The toast was eaten"!

Bill and Bert paid a visit to a court while a trial was in progress.
Bert – I've no doubt about this case. One glance at that fellow over there tells me he's guilty.
Bill – Sssh! That's the judge!

Dramatist – In the third act there is an earthquake.
Manager – Well, that ought to bring down the house!

Visitor (speaking of little boy) – He has his mother's eyes.
Mother – And his father's mouth.
Boy – And his brother's trousers.

What does a winner lose in a race?
His breath!

What would you get if you crossed a gorilla with a skunk?
I don't know what you would call it, but it'd have no trouble getting a seat on the bus!

Car salesman – This car has had one careful owner.
Customer – But it's all smashed up.
Car salesman – The others weren't so careful!

Teacher – If you add 387, and 769, then double it and divide by 5, what do you get?
Smiffy – The wrong answer!

What do you get when you cross a carrier pigeon with a woodpecker?
A bird who knocks before he delivers his message!

Teacher – Now, boys, if I drop this pound coin into this chemical, will it dissolve?
Boy – Not likely, sir, or you wouldn't risk it.

What's worse than a crocodile with the toothache?
A centipede with bunions!

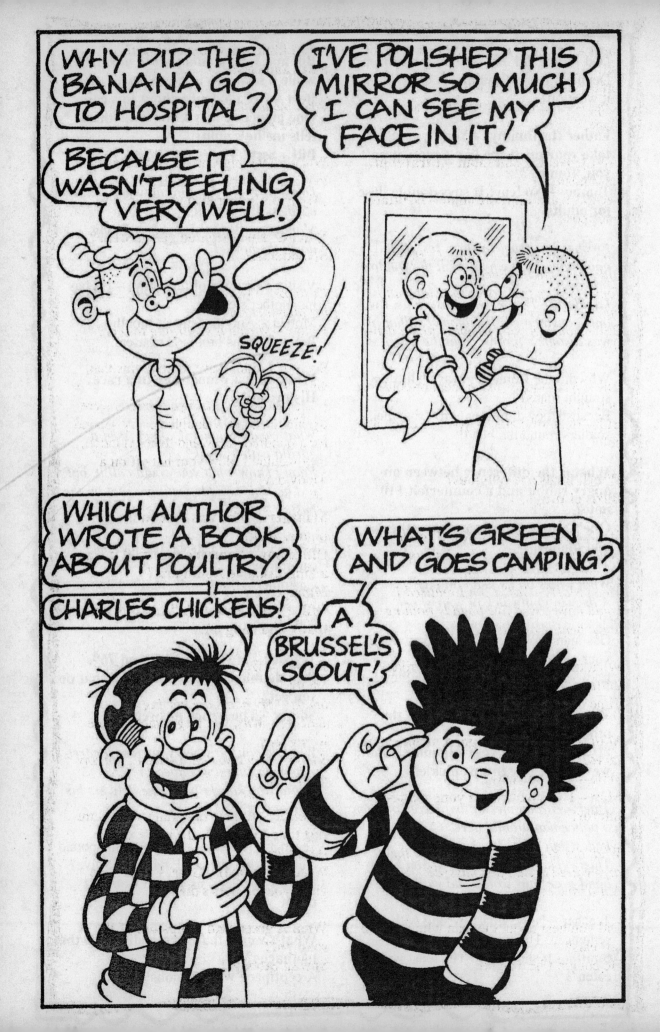

Jones – Once I was glad to be down and out!
Green – When was that?
Jones – After my first trip in an aeroplane!

First travelling salesman – I travel in toothpaste.
Second travelling salesman – By tube, I suppose?

Tom – Why are you walking so slowly?
Bill – I've got toothache.
Tom – What's that got to do with walking?
Bill – Nothing, but I'm going to the dentist.

Bill – What moves faster, heat or cold?
Ben – I don't know.
Bill – Heat, of course – you can catch a cold!

Which birds are religious?
Birds of pray!

Mean Marty – I've just saved seventy pence running home behind a bus.
Friend – Really, how daft!
Mean Marty – Yes! Then I realised I could have saved five pounds running home behind a taxi!

What time is it when the clock strikes thirteen?
Time the clock was fixed!

Man – Do you have a good memory for faces?
Wife – Yes, but why?
Man – I've just broken your make-up mirror!

What did Robin Hood have when the arrow fired at him just missed?
A n-arrow escape!

Did you hear about the man who had two left ears?
He couldn't hear right!

What kind of fish make shoes?
Soles and eels!

What makes the Tower of Pisa lean?
It never eats!

What did the big Christmas cracker say to the little Christmas cracker?
"My pop's bigger than your pop!"

What do short-sighted ghosts wear?
Spooktacles!

Customer – Waiter, waiter, there's a fly in my alphabet soup!
Waiter – Maybe it's learning to read!

Son – If I didn't have more brains than you, I'd –
Father – Listen, lad, if your brains were dynamite and they doubled every second for a hundred years, and then exploded, they wouldn't blow your hat off on a windy day!

Manager – Who was that on the phone, Jock?
Office boy – Someone who said it was a long-distance from Paris?
Manager – Yes?
Office boy – So I said, "Any fool knows that", and rang off.

Teacher – What are you crying for, Smiffy?
Smiffy – My boots are hurting me.
Teacher – Why, you've got them on the wrong feet.
Smiffy – Don't be daft, I haven't got any other feet.

Customer – I must say, waiter, this is the first time I've ever had a really tender steak here.
Waiter (horrified) – Gosh, I must have given you the boss's dinner!

What is green and jumps out of the soup pot?
Spring cabbage!

Teacher – What is your favourite subject Danny?
Danny – Latin.
Teacher – But you're not learning that.
Danny – I know, that's why it's my favourite.

Haughty lady – Can you tell me where I can find my son, Algernon Fitzgerald Popplethwaite Fitzroy?
Schoolboy – Hey, Butch, your mother wants you.

Old gent (to small boy) – Well, sonny, what are you crying for?
Small boy – I haven't a pond to sail my boat on.
Old gent – Keep on crying and you'll soon have one.

What bird does a happy dog represent?
A wag-tail.

The pianist thumped and pounded his way through his piece at the concert.
First music lover – Wonderful! Wonderful!
Second music lover – How he plays, you mean?
First music lover – No. How the piano stands it.

Boastful man (telling the story of an accident in his car) – There I was on a lonely road, miles from anywhere, with a blazing car. What do you think I did?
Bored listener – Took a deep breath and blew it out.

Diner – Look here, this will never do. That man over there has got much more to eat than me. Where's the manager?
Waiter – That man is the manager.

Mother – Danny, how was the test?
Danny – Oh, fine.
Mother – Then why did Teacher send this note home with you?
Danny – I said the test was fine, I said nothing about the answers.

There are two flies in the airing cupboard. Which one is in the army?
The one on the tank!

First man – Five of my friends went fishing and fell in the river, but only one got his hair wet.
Second man – That's amazing!
First man – Not really – four of them were completely bald!

What is a minimum?
A little mother!

How do chickens communicate?
They use fowl language!

Doctor – What seems to be the trouble?
Patient – I swallowed a clock last week.
Doctor – Good grief! Why didn't you come to see me before?
Patient – I didn't want to alarm anyone!

Why did the boy push his father into the fridge?
Because he wanted ice-cold fizzy pop!

What fish sings?
A tuna fish!

What do you call a foreign body in a chip pan?
An unidentified frying object!

What do musicians like to wear best?
Cords!

Sergeant (in army camp) – Why haven't you shaved this morning?
Private – Well, there were eight of us using the same mirror, and I must have shaved the wrong face.

Teacher – Give me an example of a collective noun.
Danny – Vacuum cleaner, sir.

What do you call a class of university students on the underground?
A tube of smarties!

Absent-minded professor – Who's there?
Burglar – No one.
Absent-minded professor – That's funny, I was certain I heard something.

Customer – If this is an all-wool jersey, why is it marked "cotton"?
Shopkeeper – That's to deceive the moths, sir.

Jerry – How did you get on when you asked the boss for a rise?
Terry – Aw, he was like a lamb.
Jerry – What did he say?
Terry – Bah!

Passenger – Why are we late, porter?
Railway porter – The train ahead is behind and we were behind before besides.

Wilfrid – I wonder what time it is?
Smiffy – Well, it can't be four o'clock yet because my mum said I was to be home then, and I'm not!

Dud singer – I will now sing "On The Banks of Allan Water".
Voice from audience – Thank goodness! We thought you were going to sing here.

Teacher – Sidney, spell "wrong".
Sidney – R-O-N-G.
Teacher – That's wrong.
Sidney – Well, that's what you asked me to spell.

Bill – You know, Tom, I sent a shirt to the laundry and it came back with the wrong buttons on.
Tom – I sent one as well, but the buttons came back with the wrong shirt on.

Teacher – What is a worm?
Sidney – A caterpillar that has been shaved, sir.

How does an octopus go to war?
Well armed!

Old lady (in museum) – Don't be afraid sonny. That lion is stuffed.
Little boy – But maybe he's not stuffed so full that he can't make room for a little boy like me!

Bald man – I'd like to buy that wig, please.
Shopkeeper – That will be £50 with tax, sir.
Bald man – It's all right. I'll glue it on!

Where do cows go in the evening?
To the moovies!

Fatty – They say that travel broadens a man.
Plug – Oh, my goodness, you must have been round the world!

Patient – Doctor! Doctor! I feel like a ladder!
Doctor – Keep calm, and let me take this one step at a time!

Diner – Waiter, this fish is awful! Why did you tell me to try it?
Waiter – Well, if you hadn't taken it, sir, it would have been served to us in the kitchen!

Teacher (on a winter morning) – Smiffy, correct the following sentence. "It am very hot."
Smiffy – It am very cold.

Barney – I was born in New York, but I went to school in Scotland.
Jock – Gosh, what a long way you had to go every day!

Businessman – If you want to get on, you must wrap yourself in your business.
Listener – That doesn't suit me. I'm a manufacturer of sticky tape.

Spotty – Why do you sleep with your spectacles on?
'Erbert – I'm so short-sighted I can't recognise the people I dream about.

John – Joe's feeling sore today.
Dick – Why? What happened to him?
John – He was in a restaurant with Bill, who found a fly in his soup. Bill called the waiter and said – "Waiter, please remove this insect!" and the waiter threw Joe out on his bottom in the street.

Police sergeant – How do you account for having all this silverware in your pockets?
Suspect – Well, you see, we've got no sideboard at home.

A diner at a restaurant saw at another table a man whom he thought he had met before and went across to speak to him.
"Excuse me, but are you Dunn?" he asked.
"Done?" he said, "No, I've only just started!"

George – I made two trips from London to New York and didn't even have time to take a bath.
Jim – You dirty double-crosser!

Visitor to new housing estate – I didn't expect to hear mice in a new house like this.
Tenant – That's not mice. That's the man next door eating celery.

What would you call a mischievous egg? A practical yolker!

Terry – What hand do you stir your tea with?
Jerry – I stir mine with a spoon!

Why did the weight-lifter eat bricks? To build himself up!

Why did the snake walk out of his maths lesson?
Because he'd adder-nough!

Patient – I snore so loudly, I keep myself awake.
Doctor – Sleep in another room, then!

Ghoul – My goodness, hasn't your little ghoul grown!
Ghoul mother – Yes, I must say she's certainly gruesome!

Smith – Jones is going to retire from business for five years.
Brown – Oh, I've heard him say that before.
Smith – This time the judge said it.

Customer – That bacon I bought from you last week was bad.
Shopkeeper – Impossible, madam. Why, it was only cured last week.
Customer – Then it must have had a relapse.

Speaker (after a very boring lecture) – Now is there anybody who has a further question to ask about the railways of Great Britain?
Angus – Yes. What time does your train leave?

Dad was talking to little Bobby when they were out for a walk.
Dad – Just fancy, Bobby, at one time these fields were covered by the sea, and fish were swimming about on the very spot where we stand.
Bobby – Yes, Dad. Look! Here's an empty salmon tin!

Prison Governor – We must set you to work. What can you do?
Forger – Give me a week's practice and I'll sign your cheques for you.

Farmer (to carpenter) – I want this ladder mended. It needs new sides and new rungs, but the same holes will do.

Where do frogs hang their coats?
In the croakroom!

Winston the cat (visiting sick pal) – Did you eat your dinner today?
Sick moggy – No, I could only manage a little swallow!

How do you start a jelly race?
Just say, "Get set!"

First boy – Why do you call your lizard Tiny?
Second boy – Because he's my newt (minute)!

Daddy Bear, Mummy Bear and Baby Bear all came back from their walk.
"Who's been eating my porridge?" asked Daddy Bear.
"And who's been eating my porridge?" said Mummy Bear
"Never mind about that!" said Baby Bear. "Somebody's stolen the video!"

Son – I am sure Dad gets more absent-minded every day.
Mother – What makes you think that?
Son – Well, when I met him today, he shook hands with me and said: "Pleased to meet you, my boy. And how's your father?"

Golfing beginner – I always seem to strike the ball on the top. How can I put that right?
Caddie – What about turning the ball upside down?

Tom – You don't look well, Tim. Why don't you take a holiday?
Tim – I should very much like to, but I couldn't stay away from the office.
Tom – Couldn't the firm do without you for a week?
Tim – Quite easily. That's the trouble. I don't want them to find out.

Naturalist – There I was, face-to-face with a lion and only five feet between us.
Friend – How unusual! A three-legged lion!

Why can't a car play football?
Because it's only got one boot!

What date is a command to go forward?
March 4th!

Petshop owner – Would you like to buy a budgie? They're only £12 apiece.
Customer – How much is it for a whole one?

Teacher – Sarah, what was the first thing James did on coming to the throne?
Sarah – He sat down!

What do you call a polite spy?
A-gent!

Teacher – A biped is anything that goes on two feet. Toots, can you give me an example?
Toots – Yes, Teacher, a pair of shoes.

Uncle – Good gracious, Minnie, that's your third helping of pudding! You do eat a lot for a little girl!
Minnie – Oh, I'm not as little as I look from the outside!

Footballer (to spectator) – Do you know enough about football to referee?
Spectator – I know enough about football not to.

Jones – My son wants to be a racing driver. What shall I do?
Smith – Whatever you do, don't stand in his way.

Two insurance agents were boasting of their quickness.
"Why," said the first, "one man had an accident and we handed the insurance money to him within an hour."
"That's nothing," said the second. "A man fell from the top storey of our building, and I handed him his money as he passed my window."

How do you know if there's an elephant in your bed?
He has an E on his pyjamas!

What has 45 heads, but can't think?
A box of matches!

What is the definition of an archaeologist?
A man whose career is in ruins!

**What do you call a Stone Age cowboy?
Flint Eastwood!**

Teacher – Gary, did your sister help you with your homework?
Gary – No, miss. She did it all.

Tourist – How many sheep do you have here?
Shepherd – I can't say exactly. Every time I start to count them, I fall asleep.

**Injured man (to workman who had dropped a hod of bricks) – Confound you! One of those bricks hit me on the head.
Workman – My word! You're lucky. Look at all the bricks that didn't!**

Doctor – Stop smoking, and you will live to be eighty.
Old man – It'll be too late.
Doctor – It's never too late to mend.
Old man – But I'm eighty-eighty now!

Crystal-gazer – I'm afraid someone very near to you is going to be very disappointed.
Client – You're right. I've forgotten to bring my money.

**First student – I wonder if Professor Smart meant anything.
Second student – What about?
First student – He advertised a lecture on "Fools", and when I bought a ticket it said "Admit one".**

What is round and red and goes up and down?
A tomato in a lift!

Bad golfer – Why has that man with the tin been following us all afternoon?
Caddie – Oh, he's after worms to go fishing, sir.

Diner – Hey, waiter!
Waiter – Yes, sir!
Diner – Bring me a saw for this pudding and an axe for this meat.
Waiter – Anything else, sir?
Diner – Oh, yes. A hammer to mash the potatoes!

**Mother – Why don't you sing to the baby when it cries?
Father – I did, but the neighbours said they'd sooner hear the baby cry!**

If King Kong went to Hong Kong to play ping-pong and have a sing-song and then died, what would they put on his coffin? A lid!

Shall I tell you the story about the red-hot poker?
No, I'd never be able to grasp it!

**What's long and thin and goes "hith, hith"?
A snake with a lisp!**

If I cut three bananas and four oranges into ten pieces each, what would I have? A fruit salad!

Is your new car fast?
Fast? Why, when I want to go from Dundee to Glasgow I have to start putting on the brakes halfway.

**Gipsy – Tell your fortune, mister.
McWalter – How much?
Gipsy – A pound!
McWalter – Quite correct.**

Teacher – I was very angry yesterday when I heard a boy snoring during my lesson.
Pupil – Yes, so was I. The noise woke me up!

Danny – Why are you running?
Sidney – To stop two boys fighting.
Danny – What two boys?
Sidney – Billy Smith and me!

Jack – Would you please open the gate for me?
Old man (opening the gate) – Yes, but why don't you open it yourself?
Jack – Because it's just been painted!

Angry diner – You're not fit to serve a pig.
Waiter – I'm doing my best, sir!

Terry – Have you heard the joke about the empty house?
Jerry – No.
Terry – There's nothing in it to tell!

Why is your heart like a policeman?
It follows a regular beat!

What happened to the wasp that got run over?
It was taken to waspital!

"Tough luck," said the egg in the monastery. "It's out of the frying pan, and into the friar!"

What part of a clock is always old?
The second hand!

What did the Spanish farmer say to his hens?
"Olé!"

Landlord – You aren't always bothered with poor light, are you?
Tenant – Oh, no, not always.
Landlord – I thought not. It's only at certain times you notice it, eh?
Tenant – Yes, after dark!

Teacher – If I said a man was creating a stir, what would he be doing, Hamish?
Hamish – Making porridge, miss.

What does a kettle suffer from?
Boils!

What did the bell say when it fell in the water?
I'm wringing wet!

Mum – Quick, Garry, run for the doctor! Baby's swallowed one of your marbles!
Garry – That's all right. I've got plenty more!

Guide – This, ladies and gentlemen, is the room where Sir Walter Scott wrote Ivanhoe.
Tourist – But last year you said it was written in the room over there.
Guide – Yes! But we can't get in there just now. It's being cleaned.

Dud actor – You know, when I'm acting I'm carried away by my feelings. I forget everything but the part – the very audience seems to vanish.
Manager – You can't blame them.

Judge – After the prisoner put his fist through the window did you observe anything?
Witness – Yes. There was a hole in the glass.

Inspector – You're late. Don't you have a watch?
Detective – No – One of the pickpockets I was after pinched it from me!

If Shakespeare were alive today he'd be looked upon as a very wonderful man. Yes, he'd be over 300 years old!

Terry – Briggs says he's the big noise at the factory.
Jerry – So he is. He's the fellow who blows the hooter at stopping time.

Applicant for a job in a music shop – I've a marvellous ear for music. I can pick up anything musical.
Boss – All right. Help me shift this piano.

Jenny – I believe Freddie was caught cheating at an examination?
Penny – Yes, he went in for the botany exam with twenty-four flowers in his buttonhole.

What happened to the first chair made for the king?
It was throne out!

What did the ground say to the rain?
If you keep this up, my name will be mud!

What does a geometry teacher like when he's hungry?
A square meal!

Why did the tea bag go to hospital?
Because it was under a strain!

Why was the crab arrested?
He kept pinching things!

Teacher – Toots, say something beginning with "I".
Toots – I is . . .
Teacher – No, "I am" not "I is".
Toots – Right, I am the ninth letter of the alphabet!

What is a sick crocodile called?
An illigator!

One day I saw a man pouring a bowl of broth into the radiator of his car.
"What are you doing?" I asked.
He said, "I'm trying to soup it up!"

Boss – Did you put those circulars in the post?
Secretary – No, sir, I couldn't find any round envelopes for them.

Bore – Talking about Africa makes me think of the time –
Friend – Good gracious you're quite right. I had no idea it was so late. Goodbye!

Why do people laugh at fish?
Because they think they are finny!

What do you get if you cross a quarter pound of mince with a bee?
A humburger!

Variety agent – You say you're a magician?
Applicant – Yes.
Variety agent – Well, vanish!

Teacher – Don't bother me now Dennis, I have a good deal on my hands.
Dennis – So I notice. Why not try soap and water?

Farmer Jones – That's the third time in six months you've gone and cut off your whiskers.
Farmer Brown – Yes. My wife is stuffing the sofa!

Stranger – Have you had much rain?
Farmer – Yes, but my neighbour had more.
Stranger – How was that?
Farmer – He has more land than me.

What do you call a flying pig?
Piggles!

What do you get if you cross a kangaroo with a chicken?
Pouched egg!

Barry – Why do you call your dog "Locksmith"?
Garry – Because every time I open the door he makes a bolt for it.

Who makes a success loafing at his job?
A baker!

Terry – Did you buy that second-hand car, or do you still have to walk to and from your work?
Jerry – The answer to both of your questions is, yes.

Algernon – Your father's a cobbler, yet your boots are full of holes.
Albert – That's nothing. Your father's a dentist, yet your little brother has no teeth!

Clerk – I can't read this letter. The writing is too bad.
Employer – Nonsense! Any fool can read it. Pass it over here!

Dougal – I'm thinking of raising turnips next year. What's the best way?
Donald – Take hold of the tops and pull.

Would-be comedian – Well, you've seen my act. What sort of clothes should I wear on the stage?
Stage manager – Armour!

Policeman – Now then, what's your name?
Speeding motorist – Demetrius Aloysius Fortescue.
Policeman – None of that, now. It's your name I want, not your family motto.

Actor – On my first appearance, the people stormed the box office.
Friend – And did they get their money back?

Sid – Bill, there's a hole in the boat, and water's coming in.
Bill – Never mind. I'll drill another hole to let the water go back out!

Customer – I wish to return this cricket bat. It's useless.
Shopkeeper – What's wrong with it?
Customer – Every time I've been in to bat with it, I've been out first ball!

A dog and a porcupine had a boxing match. The porcupine won on points!

Boy – Do you like baked apples, Mr Bloggs?
Farmer – Yes, boy, I love them! Why?
Boy – Your orchard is on fire!

What would you do if you're alone in a jungle and an elephant charges you?
Pay it!

How do porcupines kiss?
Very carefully!

Patient – Doctor, I'm afraid my wife mistook that medicine you gave me for furniture polish.
Doctor – So you want me to give you some more?
Patient – No, I want you to come and shake our table!

New neighbour – Have you a large family to support, Mr Green?
Mr Green – Yes, and if they didn't earn their own livings I don't know how I'd do it.

Patient – My head is like a lump of lead, my neck is as stiff as a poker and I feel as if I have bands of iron round my chest.
Doctor – It's not a doctor you want, it's a blacksmith!

First lodger – This cheese is so strong it could walk over and say "Hello" to the coffee.
Second lodger – Yes, and the coffee is too weak to answer it.

Angry customer – Look here, that honey you sold me was full of hairs.
Shopkeeper – Well, it came straight from the comb!

Mum – Now, then, take your dinner and grow up big like Dad.
Dennis – Has Dad stopped growing?
Mum – Yes.
Dennis – Well, why do you still feed him?

Salesman – I am working for the support of literature.
Customer – Oh, what are you doing?
Salesman – Selling bookcases.

Did you hear about the man who always wore sunglasses?
He took a very dim view of things!

Did you hear about the pharaoh who had Egyptian 'flu?
He caught it from his mummy!

What sits at the bottom of the sea and laughs?
A merrymaid!

What runs around a house, but never moves an inch?
A fence!

Why do you forget a tooth when the dentist pulls it out?
It goes right out of your head!

What did people wear at the time of the Great Fire of London?
Blazers!

Jock – How much are these handkerchiefs?
Shopkeeper – Four pounds a pair, sir.
Jock – How much for one?
Shopkeeper – Two pounds fifty.
Jock – Right, I'll take the other one!

For a long time the visitor to the museum stood gazing at the Egyptian mummy, swathed in bandages.
"Tell me one thing," he ventured.
"What is it, sir?" asked the guide.
"Was he in a car accident?"

Inquisitive man – How much do you get paid for banging that hammer down?
Workman – Nothing. It goes down itself. I get paid for lifting it up.

Bobby – Pa, does a cup of coffee do any harm?
Pa – No, Bobby.
Bobby – That's lucky! I've just spilled one over your new suit.

Barber (giving bald customer hair restorer) – Now don't go putting any on until you get home. You don't want your hair to push your hat off in the street.

Old man – How old are you sonny?
Little boy – Eight, sir.
Old man – Eight? And you're not as big as my umbrella!
Little boy – How old is your umbrella?

First boy – Here's a bull coming.
Second boy – Well, don't just stand there! Help me to climb this tree.

Teacher – Can you give me the name of an underground creature?
Boy – A worm.
Teacher – Another underground creature?
Boy – Another worm!

What has sixty keys, but can't open a door?
A piano!

What do you get two of in every corner?
The letter R.

What do you get if you cross a mouse and a bar of soap?
Bubble and squeak!

Teacher – What is the meaning of this, Minnie? I told you to write an essay on the funniest thing you've ever seen and you handed me a blank page.
Minnie – Well, sir, the funniest thing I've ever seen was too funny for words.

Absent-minded professor – I say, Mary, bring my hat.
Maid – It's on your head, sir.
Absent-minded professor – Don't bother, then. I'll look for it myself.

Landlady – How did you like my cake? I took great pains with it.
Lodger – So did I!

Teacher – Walter, what do two tens make?
Walter – Twenty, sir.
Teacher – Correct. Now, Dennis, what do two elevens make?
Dennis – A football match, sir.

Willie – There was a fly in that currant bun you sold me yesterday.
Grocer – Well, sonny, you bring the fly back and I'll give you a currant for it.

Policemen – Lost your way, sonny?
Little boy – No, but I've found a street I don't know.

What is a vampire's favourite game?
Bat-minton!

Why is it hard to talk when a goat is around?
Because it always butts in!

How can you tell the difference between a stoat and a weasel?
A weasel is weasily recognised because a stoat is stoatally different!

What do you call a man with a spade?
Doug.
And what do you call a man without a spade?
Douglas!

Why is the letter "A" like a sweet-smelling flower?
Because a bee always comes after it.

Passenger – Porter, porter, I've lost my luggage.
Porter – Well, you won't need me then, will you?

Teacher – Can you give me a proverb?
Harry – Yes, miss. A sock on the foot is worth two on the nose!

Bob – Who do you think you're pushing?
Bully – Dunno. What's your name?

Visitor – Is this place good for rheumatism?
Local inhabitant – I think so. I got mine here!

How do you make anti-freeze?
Hide her coat!

Boxing instructor – Well, now that your first lesson is over, have you any questions?
Dazed novice – Er . . . how much is your postal course?

Terry – Did your grandfather remember you when he made his will?
Jerry – He must have – he left me out!

Patient – Doctor, doctor, I feel like a snooker ball.
Doctor – Go to the end of the cue!

First golfer – How long have you been playing golf?
Second golfer – Two months!
First golfer – You're terrific for someone who's only been playing for two months!
Second golfer – Yes, but I've been learning for ten years!

Diner – Waiter, waiter, what kind of soup is this? I ordered pea soup – this tastes like soap!
Waiter – My mistake, sir. That's tomato soup. The pea tastes like petrol!

Dennis – Please, Mum, may I have two pieces of cake?
Mum – Certainly. Cut the piece you have in half.

Bus driver – I don't have much time for meals, so I generally have a bite at the wheel.
Passenger – That's a bit tough, isn't it?

Father – What can you do that no other boy at school can do?
David – Read my writing!

Sandy (in shop) – Mum wants a tape measure.
Assistant – Certainly. How long does she want it?
Sandy – She wants to keep it.

What do you call a sleeping bull?
A bulldozer!

Why is a clock a shy piece of furniture?
Because it covers its face with its hands!

Mary – How come you never passed the maths exam? I thought you had all the answers written on your sleeve!
Julie – I did, but I put on my biology blouse by mistake!

Patient – Doctor, doctor, I keep thinking I'm a bee!
Doctor – Well, go home, and if it gets worse, give me a buzz!

Which cheese is made backwards!
Edam!

Cabbie – Where to, sir?
Customer – Waterloo, please, driver.
Cabbie – Is that the station?
Customer – Well, I'm too late for the battle!

Who played at Hampden Park and didn't get a kick at the ball?
The pipe band!

What is never seen, but often changes?
Your mind!

Who wrote Great Eggspectations?
Charles Chickens!

What did the rolled-up piece of string with fuzzy hair say when it was asked if it was a piece of elastic?
"No, I'm a frayed knot!"

How can you get out of a locked music room?
Play the piano until you find the right key!

Man – What's your cat called?
Boy – Felt-tip.
Man – Is that his real name?
Boy – No, just his pen name!

Where do pilots keep their money?
In air pockets!

Terry – What's your idea of an optimist?
Jerry – A fellow without any money going into a restaurant and ordering oysters in the hope he can pay for his dinner with a pearl.

Dave – That's a very mean boss I'm working for.
Dan – Oh, why is that?
Dave – He's cut the legs off the wheelbarrow so I can't put it down and have a rest.

What do you get if you cross an ocean with a crook?
A crime wave!

What colour is the wind?
Blew, of course!

What is the perfect cure for dandruff?
Baldness!

What do you get if you cross a rag with a skeleton?
A rag and boneman!

What is small, brown and carries a suitcase?
A handle!

If a magician brought you a cup of tea, what would you have?
A cuppa and a sorcerer!

Traveller – I say, can you tell me where I am? I'm lost.
Local – Is there a reward out for you?
Traveller – No.
Local – Then you're still lost.

Old gent – How old are you, my boy?
Billy – Six
Old Gent – And what are you going to be?
Billy – Seven

Teacher – Now, Wilfrid, tell me what a grape is.
Wilfrid – A bald gooseberry.

Cabin boy – Is a thing lost if you know where it is?
Captain – Of course not.
Cabin boy – Well, I've dropped your gold watch to the bottom of the sea!

Pat – So you're distantly related to the Jones family, are you?
Tim – Yes. Their dog is our dog's brother.

Stranger – Are there any clever crooks in this town?
Local – Clever crooks? Why, someone stole my trousers and hung weights on my braces so that I wouldn't miss them.

Mother – Was the conjurer good at the party last night?
Dick – Rather! I gave him a dud pound coin to do a trick and he gave me a good one back!

Why did the chewing gum go across the road?
It was stuck to the chicken's foot!

Teacher – Late again! What's the excuse this time?
Minnie – Sorry, miss the bus said "Dogs must be carried", and I couldn't find one anywhere!

What has no legs and runs down hills?
Water!

What do you call a policeman ghost?
Chief-in-spectre!

What did the flour say when it fell off the table?
"Don't pick me up, I'm self-raising!"

Teacher – What were you saying, Tommy?
Tommy – Nothing, miss.
Teacher – But I saw you speaking to Johnny.
Tommy – Yes, miss. He asked me what I had in my pocket, so I said "Nothing".

What do you get if you dial 666?
A policeman standing on his hands!

Father – Why didn't you tell me the truth when I asked who broke the window?
Son – I thought my story was more interesting.

What can make a cow fly?
The letter "R" because it makes a cow into a crow!

Woodwork teacher – What are you making John?
John – It's a collapsible, sir.
Teacher – A collapsible what?
John – I don't know. I've only got as far as the handle!

What flies under water?
A bird in a submarine!

What is the most common illness amongst spies?
A code in the nose!

McDuff – Did you have much trouble with your French when you went to Paris?
Mcleod – No, But the Parisians did!

Ted – How did you get that bump on the head?
Fred – Playing a saxophone.
Ted – I don't understand.
Fred – Well, you see, I was sitting in front of the trombone player.

What did the mouse do when the other mouse fell in the river?
Gave him mouse-to-mouse resuscitation.

Dick – I'm positively finished with gambling.
Chick – For ever? I don't believe it.
Dick – Oh, no? I'll bet you fifty pence I stop.

When does a doctor get angry?
When he loses his patients!

Brown – I hear that Green's in hospital suffering from shock. His business partner let him down.
Smith – What was his profession?
Brown – A trapeze artiste.

Teacher – Now, Smiffy, will five go into one?
Smiffy – Yes, Teacher.
Teacher – How do you make that out, you stupid boy?
Smiffy – Well, I put five toes into one sock every morning.

Did you hear about the man arrested for stealing luggage?
He asked for forty other cases to be taken into consideration!

What did the cobbler say to the flock of geese that walked in?
Shoo! Shoo!

Dan – My girlfriend's one of twins.
Dave – How can you tell them apart?
Dan – Her brother's got a beard!

What do you get if you cross a sheep with six radiators?
Central bleating!

Sid – My feet are always frozen when I wake up in the morning.
Billy – If they're so cold, why don't you try a hot water bottle?
Sid – I tried that.
Billy – Didn't it work?
Sid – No, I couldn't get my feet in the neck of the bottle.

Waiter – Don't you like our college pudding' sir?
Diner – No, there's an egg in it that should have been expelled.

Toots – I hear your father is a very smart man.
Smiffy – Yes. He walks in his sleep, so he can get rest and exercise at the same time.

Hector – Who are we playing next week, Hamish?
Hamish – Auchentogle Gasworks Football Club.
Hector – Are they good?
Hamish – Not half. They've got a football!

Patient – Doctor, Doctor, I've been stung by a bee. Shall I put some cream on it?
Doctor – Don't be silly. It'll be miles away by now.

What are pupils at ghost schools called?
Ghoulboys and Ghoulgirls!

Why did the dinosaur cross the road?
Because there were no chickens in those days!

Where does a king go to buy a new house?
Newcastle!

What never asks questions, but usually gets an answer?
A telephone!

Knock, Knock!
Who's there?
Alison.
Alison who?
Alison to my radio in the morning!

Cuthbert – Smiffy, why do you not put your hand in front of your mouth when you yawn?
Smiffy – No fear! I bit myself last time.

Visitor – What's the name of that river?
Local – Wye, sir.
Visitor – Because I want to know.

Fat uncle – Alex, take the cat out of the room. I can't stand the noise it's making.
Alex – No wonder. You're sitting on it.

Teacher – Can you read French?
Minnie – Yes, if it's written in English.

Patient – I have a terrible corn on the bottom of my foot.
Doctor – That's a good place to have it. Nobody can step on it but you.

Mother – Oh, dear! Did you fall down the stairs?
Bertie – Yes, but it didn't matter – I was on the way down anyway.

Uncle – How did you like your first day at school, David?
David – Oh, it wasn't bad, but there was a big man in front who kept spoiling all the fun.

Policeman – This man is charged with stealing an elephant, sir.
Judge – Search him!

Naturalist – How did you make fifty lions run?
Explorer – Well, I ran, and they all ran after me!

Old lady – What sort of man will you be when you come out of prison?
Prisoner – An old one, madam.

Sandy – That star up there is larger than the earth.
James – Then why doesn't it keep off the rain?

Boaster – I've got the most wonderful family tree.
Fed-up listener – And what are you – the sap?

Ma – You shouldn't make faces at the bulldog, Bertie.
Bertie – Well, he started it.

Diner – These oatcakes are terrible.
Waiter – They're not oatcakes, they're cork tablemats.

Judge – You say the stone was as big as my head?
Constable – Yes, but not so thick.

Joe – Do your glasses magnify, Mum?
Mum – Yes, Joe.
Joe – Well, please take them off when you cut me my piece of tart.

Judge – Why did you put your hand in the man's watch pocket?
Prisoner – I wanted to know the time, your honour.
Judge – Well, it's six months!

Excited maid – Oh, sir, there's a burglar in the kitchen.
Absent-minded professor – Tell him I can't see him.

Uncle – Well, Tommy, what did you get on your birthday?
Tommy (tired of answering questions) – A year older.

Tim – Coming out to play football?
Tom – I can't. I broke a window yesterday, and Dad's suspended me for the rest of the season.

Diner – Waiter, I can't eat this food. Fetch the manager.
Waiter – That's no use, sir. You can't eat him either.

Teacher – Why are you always late for school?
Danny – Because you always ring the bell before I get here.

Teacher – You used to be as good at sums as Cuthbert.
Danny – Yes, but I don't sit beside him now!

Sandy – If a farmer raises wheat in dry weather, what will he raise in wet weather?
Hector – I don't know!
Sandy – His umbrella!

Teacher – How many seasons are there in the year?
Sandy – Two, sir: football and cricket.

Lady (at lunch) – This isn't a clean knife, Jennie.
Maid – Well, it ought to be, because the last thing it cut was soap.

McDonald – I know a man who shaves more than twenty times a day.
McDougall – Who?
McDonald – A barber.

Policeman (after accident) – This man says you used your right indicator then turned left.
Motorist – Ah, well, you see, I'm left-handed.

Waiter – What? No tip! Why, the champion miser of the world once gave me a five-pence tip!
Diner – Then gaze upon the new champion.

Jones (showing off new suit) – I've got a suit for every day of the week now.
Smith – Really!
Jones – Yes, this is it.

Salesman – Ladies and gentlemen, I'm selling a wonderful comb that will stand any amount of rough handling. You can bend it, hit it with a hammer, twist it, bite it, and you can . . .
Listener (interrupting) – Can you comb your hair with it?

Magistrate – You say the defendant struck you? Have you any witnesses to prove it?
Plaintiff (pointing to black eye) – I have an eye-witness, your honour.

Old man – Haven't I seen your face somewhere else, sonny?
Donald – No, it's always here, between my ears.

Diner – Give me something to eat, and make it snappy.
Waiter – Will a crocodile sandwich do, sir?

Foreman – Why do you always pull your barrow instead of pushing it?
Workman – Because I hate the sight of it.

Danny – I dreamed last night that I was talking to the wisest man in the world.
Cuthbert – What did I say?

Old lady in department store – I want to buy enough wool to knit a sweater for my dog.
Saleswoman – How big is he?
Old lady – Oh, dear! It's hard to say exactly.
Saleswoman – Why not bring him in, and I'll be able to see how big he is, and tell you how much wool you will need.
Old lady – I couldn't do that – it's meant to be a surprise for him!

Why were the flies playing football on the saucer?
Because they were playing for the cup!

Diner – This restaurant must have a very clean kitchen.
Owner – Thank you, sir, but how did you know?
Diner – Everything tastes of washing-up liquid!

What is the best way to light a fire with two sticks?
Make sure one's a match!

What did the big tooth say to the small tooth?
"Get your coat on, the dentist is taking us out!"

Did you hear about the sheepdog trials?
Three of the dogs were found guilty!

Dennis – You should keep your eyes open this afternoon, mister.
Man – Why, sonny?
Dennis – You won't be able to see if you don't.

Terry – Why does that man keep staring at every garage and car park he passes?
Jerry – Because he's a nosey parker!

Teacher – Now, if I have ten tennis balls in one hand and eight in the other, what do I have?
David – Big hands, sir!

Sister – How did Mum find out you hadn't washed yourself?
Brother – I forgot to wet the soap!

One thousand bars of soap have been stolen from a warehouse.
Police say the thieves made a clean get-away.

Chris – I'm glad I wasn't born in France.
Louise – Why?
Chris – I don't speak French!

How do you get rid of a boomerang?
Throw it up a one-way street!

What happened to the hyena who ate a box of beef cubes?
He became the laughing stock!

Mum – Well, Jane, how does your teacher like your work?
Jane – I think she likes it. She puts little kisses beside all my sums.

Weary mother (to a group of wild children at a birthday party) – There is a special prize for the one who goes home first!

What does a skeleton serve his food on?
Bone china!

What do snowmen sing at parties?
"Freeze a jolly good fellow!"

New bricklayer (working on scaffolding) – How can I get down?
Foreman – Shut your eyes and walk about.

What sort of a boat would you take to shoot rapids?
A gunboat!

Minnie – Why are you going bald, Dad?
Dad – Oh, that's because my mother used to pat me on the head so much for being a good boy.

Doctor (to midnight visitor) – Well?
Visitor – Of course not – I'm ill!

Teacher – Now, Hamish, can you tell me why swans have long necks?
Hamish – To keep them from drowning at high tide.

Big brother – What's the idea of wearing my raincoat?
Little brother – Well, you don't want your shirt to get wet in the rain, do you?

Minnie – Please, Mum, may I have two pieces of cake?
Mum – Certainly. Cut the piece you have in half!

Plug – Let's see who can make the funniest face.
Wilfrid – No fear!
Plug – Why?
Wilfrid – Well, look at the start you've got.

What fish terrorises other fish?
Jack the Kipper!

Jenny – What is the most common parting gift?
Jill – A comb!

Why is a duck always in debt?
Because it always has a bill in front of it.

Farmer – Do you know it takes three sheep to make a sweater?
City man – Goodness! I didn't even know sheep could knit!

What do rabbits do when they get married?
They live hoppily ever after!

Knock! Knock!
Who's there?
Yvonne.
Yvonne who?
Yvonne though it is cold, I'm not wearing gloves!

Mum – Would you like a duck's egg for tea?
Billy – Only if you quack it for me!

Woman – I bought a carpet that was in mint condition.
Neighbour – What do you mean?
Woman – It had a hole in middle of it!

Teacher – Give me the name of an underground creature.
Smiffy – A worm.
Teacher – Any other creature?
Smiffy – Another worm!

Maggie – B-Bert! There's a cow in the garden!
Bert – Well, don't stand there stammering, lass! Get a pail and milk it before it runs away!

Spectator at a football match – Go on! Shoot, Bill!
Second spectator – Why pick on Bill?

Passenger (in train) – I wish I had my piano with me!
Ticket collector – What for?
Passenger – I've left my ticket on it!

Teacher – You mean to tell me you don't know where your tonsils are?
Danny – That's right. You see, they were taken out over a year ago!

Teacher – Give me a sentence with the word "omnivorous"!
Fatty – Omnivorous happy as when I'm eating toffee apples!

Cuddles – Why are you washing your feet with your socks on?
Dimples – The water's cold!

Guide – I'm sorry I can't show you round the castle just now. Food and drink aren't allowed inside.
Visitor – But I'm not eating anything.
Guide – No, but I am.

Why do bees have sticky hair?
Because they use honey combs!

Manager – We want you to leave on medical grounds.
Player – But I'm fully fit.
Manager – I know, but we're sick of you!

How does a sparrow land safely when it has engine failure?
By sparachute!

Which musical instrument could be used for fishing?
A cast-a-net!

Which animals on Noah's ark did not come in pairs?
Worms! They came in apples!

Garry – My nerves are so very bad that I can't close my eyes at night.
Barry – Try boxing. After my first lesson I couldn't open my eyes for days.

Customer (in store) – May I see some of your pipes?
Assistant – Gas, water, drain, or bag, sir?

Garry – I was troubled with rheumatism in school today!
Mum – Nonsense! You're too young to have rheumatism.
Garry – It wasn't that, Mum! I couldn't spell it!

Patient – I haven't slept for days!
Doctor – What's the matter?
Patient – Nothing. I sleep at nights!

Manager – So you want a job as a sardine packer? Have you had any experience in this line?
Applicant – Well, I've been a bus conductor for two years.

Smith – Hello, bought a saxophone?
Jones – No, I borrowed it from the man next door.
Smith – But you can't play it.
Jones – Neither can he while I've got it.

Mum – Did you go and see if the butcher had pigs' feet?
Dennis – Yes, but I couldn't see! He had his shoes on!

Mrs Meanie – I want you to paint my house, but I won't be able to pay you until next year. When can you start?
Painter – Next year!

Boss – What would you do with two thousand pounds?
Office boy – Gosh, I wasn't expecting a wage increase, sir!

Teacher – An epidemic is something that spreads rapidly. Now, Smiffy, can you name an epidemic?
Smiffy – Margarine?

What's worse than being with a fool?
Fooling with a bee!

When is a Scotsman like a donkey?
When he stands on the banks and brays!

Why did the burglar cut the legs off his bed?
Because he wanted to lie low for a while!

A man bought a parrot for £25 at an auction. When he went to pay for the bird he asked if it was a good talker.
The auctioneer replied: "You should know – he was the only one bidding against you!"

Charity collector – Can I have a donation for the new swimming pool?
Mrs Meanie – Certainly! Here's a bucket of water!

What runs around the forest making the other animals yawn?
A wild bore!

Man – Do you have any camouflage jackets?
Shopkeeper – Yes, we have hundreds of them, but I can't find them!

Teacher – What does the world 'asset' mean?
Charlie – It's a young donkey, sir!

Boss (to boy applying for job) – I want someone who's good at book-keeping!
Forgetful Fred – That's me! I've had six reminders from the library about the book I borrowed months ago!

Toots – Why do you wear only one glove? Lost the other?
'Erbert – No! I found this one!

Ma – There's some apple-pie left. Have you had all you want?
Tommy – No, but I've had all I can eat!

An engineering student went went to visit a factory.

"Have you any experience of working in this industry?" the foreman asked.
"Not much," the student replied.
"Well, what do you know about gas regulations?"
"I know it's mark 5 for a sponge," said the student.

Brown – I once knew a man who was so small that his shirt was only the size of a handkerchief.
Green – That's nothing!
Brown – I knew a man who was so small that when his corns hurt, he thought it was toothache!

Boy – Do you notice any change in me?
Mum – No, why?
Boy – I've just swallowed twenty-five pence!

Angry man – I'll teach you to throw stones at my greenhouse!
Boy – I wish you would! I've had ten shots and haven't hit it yet!

Customer – Is this a pedigree dog?
Dealer – Pedigree? Why, if this dog could speak, it wouldn't talk to either of us!

Patient – I keep seeing insects and creepy crawlies in front of my eyes.
Doctor – Don't worry, it's just a bug going about.

Garry – Mum, can I have fifty pence for an old man crying in the street?
Mum – Yes, of course. What's he crying about?
Garry – Toffee apples: fifty pence each.

What did the Judge say to the dentist?
"Do you swear to pull a tooth, a whole tooth, and nothing but the tooth?"

Plug – Once, I was surrounded by lions and tigers!
Toots – What did you do?
Plug – Nothing much, I just got off the roundabout at the end of the ride.

Patient – I am not feeling well.
Doctor – Well, go and stand at the window and stick your tongue out.
Patient – Why should I do that?
Doctor – Because I don't like the man on the other side of the road!

What does a monster do in the summer?
Goes on its horrordays!

Customer – Waiter, this soup is poisonous.
Waiter – Who told you?
Customer – A little swallow!

Dad – What's wrong, son?
Jamie – Tommy hurt my hand!
Dad – The big bully! How did it happen?
Jamie – I was going to punch him on the nose, but he ducked and I hurt my hand on the wall behind him!

Farmer Spriggs – I hear that you're giving your hens hot water to drink.
Farmer McKay – That's right! I want them to lay boiled eggs!

Teacher – John, your essay on your dog is word for word the same as your brother's.
John – Well, sir, it's the same dog.

Walter – Gnasher just chased an old lady on a bike.
Dennis – You must be mistaken, Gnasher hasn't got a bike.

Jo – My baby sister has been walking for four months.
Sue – Goodness, she must be tired.

A farmer had no chickens, nobody ever gave him any, he never bought, borrowed, begged or stole any, yet he had two eggs for breakfast every morning. How?
He kept ducks!

Visitor – How many people work in this office?
Office junior – Oh, about half of them!

Tim – Here's the money back that you gave me for a stamp!
Mum – Didn't you post my letter?
Tim – Yes, I posted it, but it didn't cost anything. I slipped it into the letterbox when nobody was looking.

Sailor Bob – Is that a good telescope you have?
Sailor Bill – I'll say it is. It brings that ship so close that you can hear the passengers drinking tea!

Why is a bird sitting on a fence like a penny?
Because there's a head on one side and a tail on the other!

Newsflash – A pet shop in Liverpool was broken into last night and thirty-five dogs taken. Police are looking for the culprits, but so far they haven't come up with any leads.

Collector – We are collecting for 'Save The Children Fund', can you help, madam?
Tired mother – Certainly, you can have my nine to start with!

Teacher – What do you call an American Indian's wife?
Sammy – A squaw!
Teacher – What do you call an American Indian's baby?
Sammy – A squawker!

Plumber – I'm sorry I'm late, but I just couldn't get here sooner.
Man of the house – Well, time hasn't been wasted. While we were waiting for you, I taught my wife how to swim.

Why didn't the little pig listen to his father?
He was just an old boar!

Dad – What was that noise I heard in your room last night?
Jock – That was me falling asleep!

Canoing instructor (in canoe) – Careful now, one move and the canoe will capsize!
Smiffy – Er . . . will it be all right if I move my chewing gum to the other side of my mouth?

First farmer – I had a bad time last year. My wheat was only an inch high!
Second farmer – You should worry! My wheat was so small, the sparrows had to kneel to eat it!

Teacher – I thought I told you to write an essay on "chees"?
Smiffy – Have you tried it? Your pen gets all clogged up!

In a bank, a little boy suddenly called out, "Did anyone drop a pile of money with a rubber band round it?" Several people at different tellers' windows answered, "I did."
"Well, I just found the rubber band," said the little boy.

What sort of lighting did Noah use on his Ark?
Flood lighting!

Auntie – Would you like me to give you fifty pence?
Hamish – Yes.
Auntie – Yes what?
Hamish – Yes, if you can't afford any more!

Nosey visitor – Why does that stork stand on one leg?
Zoo keeper – Because if he lifted it, he'd fall down!

Diner – If this is chicken, I'm a fool!
Waiter – Quite correct, sir. It is chicken!

Sidney – I wish Napoleon had been Russian!
Toots – Why?
Sidney – Because that's what I've written on my exam paper!

Joe – Want to buy a pen-knife?
John – What's wrong with it?
Joe – Nothing!
John – Then what are you selling it for?
Joe – Nothing!
John – Right! I'll have it at that price!

City gent – What's that noise, guide?
Country guide – That's an owl, sir!
City gent – I know that! But who's howling!

Office junior – I think you're wanted on the phone, sir.
Boss – You think? Why don't you know, boy?
Office junior – Well, the voice on the phone only said, "Is that you, you old fool?"

Henry – This watch you sold me is always slow!
Jeweller – Well, sir, you did ask for the latest type!

First camper – Isn't that drain-pipe rather hard for a pillow?
Second camper – No, I've stuffed it with straw!

Plug – It's funny how the biggest fools have the most sensible pals!
Smiffy – Stop the flattery, now!

New footman – In my last place I took things easy!
Butler – It's different here. We lock everything up!

Bookseller – This excellent book will do half your work.
Schoolboy – Good! I'll take two!

First cat – How did you get on in the milk-drinking competition?
Second cat – Oh, I won by six laps!

Quiz master – Who was the first woman in the world?
Jack – Give me a clue.

Quiz master – Apple . . .
Jack – I've got it! Granny Smith!

What can't you eat for your lunch or dinner!
Your breakfast!

Plug – I heard something this morning that opened my eyes!
Danny – What was it?
Plug – An alarm clock!

Teacher – Why are you late, Danny?
Danny – Because of a sign down the road.
Teacher – What has a sign got to do with you being late?
Danny – The sign said – "School Ahead, Go Slow".

Pharmacist (preparing lotion) – Boy, bring me a blue bottle!
New assistant – I can't see one. Will an ordinary fly do?

Smith – How do you like your new gas fire?
Jones – Great! I lit it a fortnight ago and it hasn't gone out once!

Office boy – Have you an opening for a bright young boy?
Boss – Yes, but don't slam it as you go out!

Joe – I don't like cheese with holes in it!
Mum – Stop being fussy! Eat the cheese and leave the holes at the side of your plate!

Teacher – Where does sugar come from?
Mary – From Mrs Smith next door!

Boss – That new office boy is lazy!
Clerk – Yes, slow in everything.
Boss – No – not everything! He gets tired very quickly!

What has ten legs but can't walk?
Five pairs of trousers!

Joe – I'm thirteen now!
Jim – Thirteen? But you were only six last year!
Joe – That's right! Six last year and seven this year! That makes thirteen!

Mum – Where's the sponge I told you to buy?
Smiffy – I couldn't see a good one. They all had holes in them!

Teacher – Tell me what a clean sweep is, Danny?
Danny – One that's had a bath.

Lady – Can I try on that dress that's in the window?
Assistant – Yes, but I think it would be better if you tried it on in a changing room!

Patient – Doctor, doctor, I swallowed a plank yesterday.
Doctor – How do you feel?
Patient – Board stiff.

Teacher – I hear the school fencing team lost last night.
Pupil – Yes, foiled again!

Auctioneer – Now, gentlemen, how much for this valuable cup? Someone give me a start?
Voice – Four pence!
Auctioneer (horrified) – What?
Voice – Ah, I thought that would give you a start!

Dad – What's your new teacher like?
Minnie – She's so sour-faced, that if she put face-cream on, it would curdle!

Archie – There was a burglar in our house last night!
P.C. Murdoch – What did your father do under the circumstances?
Archie – He wasn't under the circumstances – he was under the bed!

Cuddles – Do you know what Italians do with banana skins?
Dimples – No.
Cuddles – Throw them away!

Doctor – Take three tablespoons of this medicine a day.
Man – Then I'll have to borrow another tablespoon. I've only got two at home!

Teacher – What is a snail?
Sidney – A worm with a crash helmet on.

Teacher – Why do polar bears have fur coats?
Wilfrid – Well . . . er . . . oh, I suppose they'd look funny in tweed ones!

Dad – Did you break the window this morning?
Minnie – No.
Dad – Are you sure?
Minnie – Positive! I broke it last night!

The doctor stood by the bedside, and looked down at the sick man. "I cannot hide from you the fact that you are gravely ill," he said. "Is there anyone you would like to see?"

"Yes," replied the patient faintly. "Another doctor."

Girl – How much is that budgie?
Shop owner – Twenty pounds.
Girl – Fine, send me the bill.
Shop owner – Sorry, madam, but you have got to take the whole bird.

Teacher – Have you heard of Julius Caesar?
Danny – Yes, sir.
Teacher – What do you think he would be doing now if he were alive?
Danny – Drawing the old-age pension.

Teacher (explaining arithmetic problem) – Now watch the board while I run through it once more.

Terry – Where are you going?
Jerry – To collect strawberries.
Terry – In those horrible-looking trousers?
Jerry – No. In this basket.

Why did the sword-swallower start eating pins and needles?
Because he was on a diet!

Where's the best place to hold a party on a ship?
Where the funnel (fun will) be!

Teacher – Where are elephants usually found?
Danny – They're so big they aren't often lost.

Teacher – An anonymous person is one who wishes to remain unknown and . . . who is that laughing?
Pupil – Please, sir, an anonymous person.

Millionaire – I came to this country without a shirt on my back and now I've gathered two million.
Awed voice – Gosh, mister, you'll never wear them all out!

First postman – I am not going to that house again.
Second postman – Afraid on account of the dog?
First postman – Yes, my trousers are.
Second postman – Your trousers are what?
First postman – Frayed on account of the dog.

Jim – Are you superstitious?
Jack – No.
Jim – Good! You won't mind lending me thirteen pounds, then!

Diner – What kind of bird is this, waiter?
Waiter – It's a wood pigeon, sir.
Diner – I thought so. Bring me a saw!

Patient – Doctor, doctor. I keep thinking that I'm a goat.
Doctor – Have you had this feeling long?
Patient – Ever since I was a kid.

News flash – Last night a lorry carrying glue turned over on the M1. Police are asking motorists to stick to the "A" roads.

Teacher – What is the plural of hippopotamus?
Toots – The plural is . . . oh, well, er, well, who'd want more than one anyway?

Boastful man – There I was on a lonely road, miles from anywhere, with a blazing car. What do you think I did?
Bored listener – Took a deep breath and blew it out.

Dennis – Dad, what do you do at the office all day?
Dad (fed up answering questions) – Oh, nothing.
Dennis – Then how do you know when you're finished?

Customer – Have you a horse that won't jump or rear or run away, and will trot along peacefully.
Dealer – Do you want a clothes horse or a rocking horse, sir?

Lady MacDonald – Why are you cleaning the inside of the windows but not the outside?
Maid – That way, madam, you can look out, but the people outside can't look in.

Diner _ Waiter, I haven't been given a teaspoon
Waiter – There are none left, sir. But I'll tell the orchestra to play something stirring!

Tom – What goes dot, dash, croak, dot, dash, croak?
Jim – I don't know. What goes dot, dash, croak, dot, dash, croak?
Tom – Morse toad!

Customer – Waiter, I can't eat this soup!
Waiter – I'll get the manager, sir!
Customer – Manager, I can't eat this soup!
Manager – Sorry sir, I'll get the chef.
Chef – What's wrong with the soup?
Customer – Nothing. I haven't got a spoon!

Where do spacemen park their spaceships?
At space meteors!

Sam – What is white and hairy with green spots?
Tom – I don't know.
Sam – Neither do I, but there's one crawling up your leg.

Teacher – You ought to be ashamed of yourself. A boy of your age, who can only count to ten. What are you going to be when you grow up?
Micky – A boxing referee.

Mike (to an old enemy) – I'm living in a house across the river. I'd really be pleased if you'd drop in some day!

Uncle – You're awfully quiet, Tommy!
Tommy – Well, Mum gave me five pounds not to say anything about your bald head and your big red hose!

Manager – I hope you have been carefully brought up, my boy.
Office boy – Yes, sir. I came up in the lift

Have you heard of the car that runs out and in?
Out of petrol and into lamp-posts!

Charlie – Have you see a man-eating tiger?
Jimmy – No, but I've seen a man eating haddock.

Jack – Please, sir, Dad's upset a bottle of the hair-restorer over his trousers.
Barber – Then I presume he wants another bottle.
Jack – No, sir, he wants you to come and shave his trousers.

Kindly old man – Will you two boys stop fighting if I give you a pound each?
Young scamp – Make it two pounds for the winner, sir.

Why did the girl keep a loaf of bread in her comic?
She liked crummy jokes!

What is a waste of time?
Telling a hair-raising story to a bald man!

Jack – I wanted to go water skiing for my holiday, but I couldn't manage.
Jill – Oh, why not?
Jack – I couldn't find a lake with a slope!

Why did the needle start to cry?
Because it had something in its eye.

Auntie – What are you making with your chemistry set, Cuthbert?
Cuthbert – A liquid that will dissolve anything!
Auntie – How clever! What are you going to keep it in?

Footballer – This ointment makes my arm smart!
Trainer – You should rub some into your head then!

Comedian – I was insulted last night!
Friend – What happened?
Comedian – The manager put me on stage after a performing monkey act, and the audience thought it was an encore!

How do you speak to a fish?
Drop it a line!

Plug – Did you know that the most handsome person in the world was going deaf?
Teacher – Really, who is it?
Plug – Pardon?

A woman with six children was trying to get on to a crowded bus.
"You should have left half your children at home," said the conductor.
"I did," said the woman wearily.

Knock! Knock.
Who's there?
Nobel.
Nobel who?
Nobel, so I knock, knock!

Minnie and her dad are out fishing.
Minnie – Is it true that fish go about in schools, Dad?
Dad – Yes, Minnie.
Minnie – Well, these ones you've caught must have been in the infant class!

When is water musical?
When it's piping hot.

New office boy – I've added up the figures ten times, sir!
Boss – Good lad!
Office boy – Here are the ten answers!

Teacher – What is a mirror?
Smiffy – I don't know!
Teacher – You don't know? What do you look at to see if you're clean when you have washed?
Smiffy – A towel, sir.

Why is a snake clever?
Because you can't pull its leg!

Diner – Hey waiter! You've given me a wet plate!
Waiter – That's your soup, sir!

Judge – Have you anything to say?
Accused – I've plenty to say, sir if you'll just give me time to say it.
Judge – Certainly. You can have three months!

Jim – What does your father do for a living?
Joe – Chops trees down!
Jim – What does he do when he has chopped them down?
Joe – Chops them up!

Why was the 14th century known as the dark age?
Because there were so many knights!

James – I've fallen into the bad habit of talking to myself!
Jones – I wondered why you were looking so bored!

Teacher – The school orchestra played Beethoven last night.
Smiffy – Who won?

Why did the boy's granny knit him three socks for Christmas?
Because he had written to say he had grown another foot!

What do gorillas sing at Christmas?
Jungle Bells, Jungle Bells . . .

Mrs Jones to station porter – Which way to platform four, please?
Porter – Turn left and you'll be right!
Mrs Jones – I'm sure you're wrong!
Porter – Okay, turn right and you'll be left!

Patrick – I've just been out riding.
Peter – Horseback?
Patrick – Yes, the horse got back hours before me!

Landlord – I'm glad you've stopped complaining about the plaster falling!
Tenant – Yes, it's all down now!

Teacher – You'd be a good dancer if it weren't for two things.
Plug – What are they?
Teacher – Your feet!

Customer – Do you make life-size enlargements?
Chemist – Yes.
Customer – Well, here's a snapshot of Mount Everest!

Railway traveller – Congratulations! I've travelled on this railway for thirty years and this is the first time I've known the train to arrive on time. Have a cigar!
Driver – Keep your cigar! This is yesterday's train!

Mother – John, what is the cause of all that racket coming from the pantry?
John – Me! I'm busy fighting temptation, Mum!

Tom – Jack, there was a dog and a hedgehog fighting in the road a minute ago.
Jack – Who won?
Tom – The hedgehog of course, on points!

Girl – I'd like two ounces of bird seed please.
Pet shop owner – How many birds have you, dear?
Girl – None, that's why I want the seed to grow some!

Knock! Knock!
Who's there?
Felix.
Felix who?
Felix my ice cream, I'll lick his!

Patient – Doctor, doctor, I keep on dreaming I'm being followed by a snow-man!
Doctor – Just stand beside a fire and your dreams will melt away.

Teacher (to pupil) – What happens to a body when it is immersed in water?
Pupil – Please, miss, the phone rings!

Judge – Why did you steal the woman's purse?
Prisoner – I wasn't feeling well, Your Honour, and I thought the change would do me good!

Actor – I can't possibly play the three parts you've given me in the play.
Producer – Why not?
Actor – Well, in the first act I have to fight with myself and then rush in and separate the two of us!

House buyer – I want a house out in the country, at least five miles away from any other house!
Estate agent – Ah, you want to practise the simple life?
House buyer – No, I want to practise the bagpipes!

Fatty – I'm a mind reader, you know!
Smiffy – Really? Can you read my mind?
Fatty – No! I've left my magnifying glass at home!

What happened to the man who kept throwing his pudding into the street? He was held in custardy for six days!

Patient – Doctor, doctor, I feel like an ice cream.
Doctor – Here's twenty pence. Get me one too!

Jill – Why are you running?
Jack – To stop a fight.
Jill – Who's fighting?
Jack – Me and another fellow.

Lady – Could I have a bath bun, please?
Baker – Certainly, madam! Would you like a sponge to go with it?

Teacher – In Great Britain, where are kings and queens crowned?
Smiffy – On the head!

Tourist – Where does this road go to?
Local – Nowhere. It's here every day!

Bob – What's the idea of calling your dog "Swindler"?
Bill – Just for fun. You should see half the people jump when I call him in the street.

Fred – My grandfather's clock is one hundred years old.
Ted – That's nothing. My grandfather's clock is so old that the shadow of the pendulum has worn a hole in the back.

I know a dog who eats garlic . . . his bark is much worse than his bite!

Son – Dad, can I have another glass of water?
Dad – Another? This is your tenth!
Son – I know, but my room's on fire!

Street hawker – Do you want any laces, studs, buckles, ribbons, ties . . .?
Mrs Jones – Go away or I'll call the police.
Street hawker – Here you are, madam: whistles, five pounds each!

How did the man feel when he was run over by a steamroller?
Flattered!

Mr Jones – Excuse me, officer, I've lost my dog.
Policeman – Come back tomorrow, sir, we might have a lead on him.

Teacher – I told you to do five hundred lines for bad English, and you've only done fifteen!
Danny – Yes sir, I'm no good at maths either!

First salesman – What do you sell?
Second salesman – Salt!
First salesman – Why, I'm a salt seller too.
Second salesman – Shake!

One morning Ed saw Bob running along the road pushing his bike.
Ed – What's wrong with your bike, Bob?
Bob – It's not the bike, it's me! I got up late and haven't had time to get on it!

Diner – I've found a cuff-link in my soup!
Waiter – Thank you, sir. I've looked everywhere for it!

Dennis – Quick! Dad's being chased by a bull!
Chemist – What do you want?
Bandages? Splints? Ointment?
Dennis – No! A film for my camera!

First boy – My dad's a film star.
Second boy – My dad's connected with the movies, too.
First boy – I know, I saw him driving a furniture van yesterday.

McTavish – I've been swindled! I answered an advertisement that said, "Send a pound for an instrument that will halve your bills".
McLaren – And what did you get?
McTavish – A pair of scissors.

Why is a banana like a sweater?
You slip on both!

What do you call two spiders who have just got married?
Newlywebs!

Who invented the sword dance?
Someone who wanted to dance and cut his toe-nails at the same time!

What do you get if you cross a football team with some ice-cream?
Aston Vanilla.

Teacher – What happens to sailors who don't eat their vegetables?
Toots – They don't get any pudding!

Two mice were sitting eating a reel of film.
First mouse – I don't think much of this film.
Second mouse – No, the book wasn't much good either.

Customer – Have you any invisible paint?
Painter – Yes. What colour would you like?

Diner – Boil my eggs for four minutes, please!
Waiter – Yes, sir. Be ready in half a second!

Servant – The doctor's here, sir!
Absent-minded professor – Tell him to go away. I'm too ill to see him!

Teacher – If I have forty apples, and eat twenty of them, what have I got?
Plug – A stomach ache!

Where do rabbits go when they marry?
On a bunnymoon!

Patient – Doctor, doctor, I feel like a ten pound note.
Doctor – Then go and buy something, the change will do you good.

Small ghost – Mum, how did you meet Dad?
Mummy ghost – Oh, it was love at first fright.

Sue – Where do tadpoles change to frogs?
Sandra – Croakrooms!

Patient – Doctor, you know those strengthening tablets you gave me?
Doctor – Yes . . .
Patient – Well, I can't get the lid off!

How does a pixie eat?
By goblin!

Mum – What are you doing, Sammy?
Sammy – I'm writing a letter to Cousin Bobby.
Mum – But you haven't learned to write yet.
Sammy – That's all right. Bobby can't read yet.

Ticket inspector – Here, you can't use this ticket. It says London to Glasgow, not Glasgow to London.
Smiffy – That's all right, I'm sitting with my back to the engine!

Mrs Gow – If you want work, Farmer McNab is looking for a right-hand man!
Lazy Len – What a pity. I'm left-handed!

What's a ghost's favourite sport?
Spooker!

What surprising things happen every day?
Day breaks, but doesn't fall – Night falls, but doesn't break!

Smiffy – These shoes you sold me don't fit.
Shoemaker – But you've got them on the wrong feet.
Smiffy – They're the only feet I've got, aren't they?

Mechanic – See how much petrol is in the tank.
Apprentice – It says 'half' on the indicator, but I don't know whether it's half-full or half-empty.

First snake – Are we supposed to be poisonous?
Second snake – Why?
First snake – Because I've just bitten my lip!

Teacher – You are fifteen minutes late for school, girl!
Toots – No, I'm actually only five minutes late. I was outside thinking of an excuse for ten minutes!

Doctor – You need new glasses!
'Erbert – How on earth do you know that?
Doctor – I could tell as soon as you walked staright through the door!

Joe – When I grow up, I'm going to be a policeman and follow in my father's footsteps.
Jack – I didn't know your father was a policeman.
Joe – He's not. He's a burglar!

Which two words have thousands of letters in them?
Post Office!

Auntie Flo – What brings you to the city, Sidney?
Sidney – I came to see the sights, so I thought I'd call on you first!

Which famous chiropodist conquered England?
William the Corn Curer!

Jack – Why is Dad singing?
Mum – He's singing baby to sleep.
Jack – If I were baby I'd pretend to be asleep.

Car dealer – This car has had one careful owner.
Customer – But it's all smashed up.
Car dealer – The other owners weren't so careful.

What do you call an elephant at the North Pole?
Lost!

Teacher – What is concrete made of?
Danny – Ooh, that's a hard question!

What swings through the jungle playing rock 'n' roll?
Guitarzan!

What can you serve, but not eat?
A tennis ball.

Terry – You say this fellow is crooked?
Jerry – Crooked? Even the wool he pulls over your eyes is half cotton.

Actor – What? You want me to jump off that cliff into the water? I won't. The water's only a foot deep.
Producer – Naturally. We don't want you to drown.

Customer – Are those eggs fresh?
Grocer (to assistant) – Feel the eggs, George, and see if they're cool enough to sell yet!

Mr Meanie – I want a cheap coat-hanger.
Shopkeeper – This one is twenty pence, sir.
Mr Meanie – Have you nothing cheaper?
Shopkeeper – Only a nail, sir.

Passenger – Does this bus stop at the Ritz Hotel?
Conductor – No we leave it in the garage at night.

Boaster – After I'd sung my encore, I heard a gentleman in the audience call out, "Fine! Fine!"
Bored friend – Dear me – and did you have to pay it?

Smiffy – There are three things I can't remember. I can't remember names. I can't remember faces and . . .
Danny – What's the third thing?
Smiffy – I can't remember.

What do you call a ghost in a doctor's surgery?
A surgical spirit!

Alan – What kind of fish can't swim?
Keith – I don't know.
Alan – Dead ones!

What is the difference between an elephant and a biscuit?
You can't dip an elephant in your tea!

Motorist – I'm terribly sorry I've just run over one of your pigs. But don't worry, I'll replace it.
Farmer – Impossible. You're not fat enough.

Boaster – I throw myself whole-heartedly into everything I undertake.
Bored listener – Have you tried digging a well?

Mum – There are two cream buns in the cupboard this morning and now there's only one. Why is that?
Fatty – It must've been so dark I didn't see the other one!

Judge – Do you mean to say such a physical wreck as the accused gave you that black eye?
Plaintiff (indignantly) – He wasn't a physical wreck till after he gave me the black eye!

Who invented the fraction?
Henry the 1/8!

Boastful Benny – I've just got back from a trip round the world.
Lenny – Did you visit Egypt?
Benny – Yeah!
Lenny – Go up the Nile?
Benny – Sure. Great view from the top.

What dance do tin-openers do?
The can-can!

Patient – Doctor, doctor, I feel like a banana.
Doctor – Come back tomorrow and I will try to slip you in.

Gentleman – Waiter, waiter! What is this fly doing in my soup?
Waiter – Well it needed a bath after falling in the flour, sir!

Why did the electrician eat electric bulbs at noon?
Because he wanted a light lunch.

How do ghosts travel?
By British scareways!

Johnny – Jimmy McDougal said his father could wipe up the floor with you.
Dad – You didn't let him get away with that, did you?
Johnny – Of course not! I asked him to bring his father round tomorrow night to prove it!

Poet – I'm going to publish a book of poems under the pen name of John Smith.
Critic – That's unfair! Think of all the innocent people who will be suspected!

Auctioneer – I am offering this splendid sofa at a bargain price. Who will take it away for twenty pounds?
Voice from the crowd – Show me the money!

Doctor – Have you been waiting long?
Patient – Well, did you know that there are 291,474 spots in your wallpaper?

Employer (to new typist) – I hope you thoroughly understand the importance of punctuation.
Typist – Don't you worry, sir. I always get to work on time.

Terry – How do you like your new gas fire?
Jerry – It's wonderful. I lit it a fortnight ago, and it hasn't gone out since!

Salesman – This car is so economical that it soon pays for itself.
McSporran – Let me know when it does and I'll take it.

Toots – What do you get if you cross soap with some toothpaste?
Sidney – I don't know, what?
Toots – A bubbling smile!

First sportsman – I've got a terrible cold. I won't be able to make the high hump.
Second sportsman – Why not?
First sportsman – I can't even clear my throat!

Teacher – Smiffy, spell weather.
Smiffy – W-E-V-V-E-R.
Teacher – That's the worst spell of weather we've had for some time.

What lies on the ground, a hundred feet up in the air?
A centipede!

How do you catch a squirrel?
Climb up a tree, and act like a nut.

What do you call Chinese spies?
Peking Toms.

Wilfrid (seeing Smiffy cutting his clothes with scissors) – What are you doing, Smiffy?
Smiffy – I'm taking all the wool labels off my clothes and putting on cotton labels.
Wilfrid – Goodness! Why?
Smiffy – I want to fool the moths!

Motorist – We've got a puncture!
Friend – You should have been more careful. You knew there was a fork in the road near here!

Landlady – I don't suppose you know what it is to starve?
Lodger – No, but I'm learning!

Smith – Jones is so conceited!
Smythe – Isn't he! On his last birthday he sent a telegram of congratulations to his mother!

Visitor – When I was here before, there were two windmills.
Farmer – We took one down to leave more wind for the other!

Jock – You're just a typical hen-pecked husband!
Jake – You wouldn't dare say that if my wife was here!

Diner – I find that I have just enough money to pay for the dinner, but I have nothing in the way of a tip for yourself.
Waiter – Let me add up that bill again, sir.

Crossword puzzle fan – I've been trying to think of a word for two weeks.
Pal – How about "fortnight"?

McBoast – I played Jones at golf the other day. He's a superb player – tremendous hitter of a ball – perfect putter.
McDonald – How much were you beaten by?
McBoast – Oh, I won.

Smith – I passed by your place yesterday!
Jones – Thanks awfully!

Olive the dinner lady – Goodness! What a noise you make when you eat! Didn't you ever learn to eat politely?
Fatty – Olive, I've had so few meals it's a wonder I've learned to eat!

Who invented fire?
Some bright spark!

What time is it when an elephant sits on your fence?
Time to get a new one!

Teacher – Order, children, order!
Pupil – I'll have an ice-cream and jelly, please.

Cuddles – What is the opposite of "cock-a-doodle-do"?
Dimples – Cock-a-doodle-don't!

Sidney – What's the similarity between a pork chop and an old radio?
Fatty – Don't know.
Sidney – You get crackling off both!

Boy – If there's a referee in football, and an umpire in cricket, what is there in bowls?
Teacher – I don't know.
Boy – Goldfish.

Uncle Jim – Don't give in to bullies Johnny. I always believe in fighting an enemy with his own weapons!
Johnny – But, Uncle Jim, have you ever tried stinging a wasp?

Guest – This is a boring party! I'm going to leave right now!
Mrs Green – I would, too, but I've got to stay. I'm the hostess.

First man – I'm a man of few words.
Second man – I know what it's like – I'm married too.

Mr Green – Mr Brown, this is Mr White!
Mr Brown – Ah, Mr White! I've heard a great deal about you!
Mr White – You'll never prove it!

Old lady (seeing tug-of-war for the first time) – Why don't they take a knife, and cut it?

Boss – Why didn't you deliver that message as I instructed?
Terry – I did the best I could, sir!
Boss – The best you could? Why, if I had known I was going to send a fool, I would have gone myself!

Jack – How do you make a skeleton laugh?
Jill – I don't know.
Jack – You tickle its funny-bone!

Here's the bad news! My friend swallowed twenty five pence.
Here's the good news! It's all right, because it was his dinner money!

Customer – If I go on holiday to the Isle of Man, can I swim there?
Travel agent – Certainly, sir, but it's easier to take the ferry.

Why did the bird sleep on the chandelier?
Because he was a light sleeper.

Dennis – You must be an awfully clean lady, Mrs Jones!
Mrs Jones – Thank you, Dennis!
Dennis – Yes, my Dad says you're always sponging!

Cuthbert – Here, Toots, I've been told you've been calling me a bookworm!
Toots – Who said anything about books?

Jack – How is your father getting on with his diet?
John – Fine! The battleship he had tattooed on his chest is now a rowing boat!

Lady – No, thank you, I never buy anything at the door.
Salesman – Then I've just the thing for you, madam: "No Salesman" notices.

Nice old lady – And what are you going to do when you get as big as your father?
Little boy – Go on a diet!

Doctor – Did you follow my advice and count sheep till you fell asleep?
Patient – I counted up to 18,000.
Doctor – And then you fell asleep!
Patient – No, then it was time to get up.

First man – I don't think anyone will ever give us work!
Second man – Oh, I could work for anyone I please!
First man – Why don't you, then?
Second man – I don't seem to please anyone!

Smart – What are you doing with that bandage around your arm?
Simple – I fell on my face.
Smart – Then why bandage your arm?
Simple – I wouldn't be able to see where I was gong if I bandaged my face.

A little centipede came home crying.
"Mummy, mummy, I've sprained my foot."
"Which foot have you sprained, dear?" said the mum.
"I can't tell you, I can only count to ten," replied the baby.

What is a meatball?
A dance in a butcher's shop!

Teacher – What is the capital of Iceland?
Pupil – "I" sir.

Peter – Would you like two fifty pence tickets?
Sandy – What for?
Pete – A pound!

Boy – How do you keep a boy in suspense?
Friend – I don't know. How?
Boy – I'll tell you tomorrow!

Traveller – Can I catch the express for London?
Porter – That depends on how fast you can run, sir. It left five minutes ago!

How does a bear forecast the weather?
With a bearometer!

**Customer – A mousetrap! Quickly! I
want to catch a bus!
Assistant – I don't think we've got one
big enough for that!**

*Sergeant – Now then, I want some volunteers for railway work.
Private – Put me down as a sleeper, sir!*

Pat – That barber's the meanest man I
know!
Mike – Why?
Pat – He puts hair-restorer in the shaving-cream!

**First diner – Don't you find eating
rather difficult with that large moustache hanging over your lips?
Second diner – Yes, it's rather a strain!**

*Patient – Doctor, doctor, I've just swallowed a sheep!
Doctor – How do you feel?
Patient – Very ba-a-a-a-ad!*

Dodgy Dan – I always admire people
who sleep with their windows open.
Crafty Ken – Why, are you a doctor?
Dodgy Dan – No, a burglar!

**Mary – Mum, please may I play the
piano?
Mum – No, you can't. Your hands are
dirty.
Mary – I will only play the black notes.**

*Garry – Your dad's car is like a baby!
Barry – Why do you say that?
Garry – 'Cause it doesn't go anywhere
without a rattle!*

Judge – Thirty days!
Cheerful prisoner – Hath September,
April, June and November . . .

**Bill – What do you call a hippy's wife?
Ben – Mississippi.**

*Mrs McTavish – When does the nine
o'clock train leave?
Porter – Sixty minutes past eight, ma'am.*

Car driver – It's great speeding along like
this. Don't you feel glad to be alive?
Passenger – Glad isn't the word. I'm
amazed!

**Boss – What made you so late?
Lorry driver – I ran into a garage on
the way!
Boss – Did you need repairs?
Driver – No, but the garage will!**

*Diner – Call the manager! I've never
seen anything so tough as this stead.
Waiter – Wait till you see the manager!*

Horse owner – Why didn't you keep up
with the others?
Jockey – What? And leave the horse
behind?

**Diner – Waiter, there's a funny film in
my soup.
Waiter – Well, what do you expect for
two pounds? Star Wars?**

*What do you call a musical insect?
A humbug!*

How do you make a poisonous snake
cry?
Take away its rattle!

**What do you get if you cross a turkey
with an octopus?
Something with a leg for everyone at
Christmas!**

*Manager – Look at the dust on my desk!
Why can't you keep it polished like the
banister rails?
Office boy – I can't slide down your
desk!*

How do you find out if a flea has bitten
you?
Start from scratch!

Beryl – You know Fatty Johnson, the butcher? What do you suppose he weighs?
Cynthia – I don't know. What does he weigh?
Beryl – Meat!

Jack – A big beer keg fell on my head yesterday.
Bill – I bet it hurt.
Jack – No, it was light ale!

What do monkeys clean their bikes with?
Gorilo pads!

What happens when you throw a green rock into the red sea?
It gets wet!

Did you hear about the teenage boy who ran away with the circus?
The police made him bring it back!

What do you get if you cross a sheepdog with a jelly?
The collie wobbles?

American – The ceiling in my house is so high that I have to go up in a balloon to whitewash it.
Scotsman – That's nothing. In my house, the ceiling is so low that all we can eat is flat fish and pancakes.

Johnny – I'm going to be a teacher when I grow up, Dad.
Dad – But you don't know enough to be a teacher, my boy.
Johnny – Oh, that doesn't matter. You only have to ask questions.

Diner – Waiter, I have only one piece of steak today instead of the usual two.
Waiter – Sorry, sir. The cook must have forgotten to cut it in half.

Why was Goliath surprised when David hit him with a stone?
Because such a thing had never entered his head before!

Kevin – How are you doing these days?
Terry – Oh, I'm just managing to keep my head above water.
Kevin – I can see that by the colour of your neck!

Teacher – Can you tell me what happened in 1066, Smiffy?
Smiffy – Me? No. I can't even remember what happened last week!

Why is it cheap to feed a giraffe?
Because a little goes a long way!

Why do dragons sleep in the daytime?
Because they like to hunt knights!

Where do wasps come from?
Stingapore!

Jack – Your face is like a million dollars.
Jill – Why, thank you, Jack.
Jack – It's all green and wrinkled!

Mad scientist – I've just crossed a kookaburra with a man-eating tiger.
Assistant – What did you get?
Mad scientist – I don't know, but when it laughs, you'd better join in.

Teacher – Any more questions?
Smiffy – Please, sir, how many crumbs are there in a loaf of bread?

Mother – And do you really feel ill, Bobby?
Bobby – Well, Mum, I'm too ill to go to school, but I'm not ill enough for that yucky medicine.

Newsflash – There has been a theft in Disneyland. A crook was charged with taking the Mickey?

When does a bed change its size?
At night, when two feet are added to it!

Small boy – If I wash my face, will I be clean?
Mother – Let's soap for the best!

A doctor had just given a boy a vaccination, and was about to put a bandage on his arm.

"Would you put it on the other arm, please, doctor?" asked the boy.

"What's the point of that?" said the doctor. "I'll put it over your vaccination so that the other boys will know not to bang into it."

"You don't know the boys at my school!" said the boy sadly.

Doctor – You need glasses.
'Erbert – But I'm already wearing glasses!
Doctor – In that case, I need glasses!

How can you tell which end of a worm is it's head?
Tickle his tummy, and see which end smiles!

Teacher – If you had five apples on your desk, and the boy next to you took three, what would you have?
Boy – A fight, miss!

Little boy – Mister, why is your dog wearing black boots?
Old man – Because his brown ones are in the cobblers.

Manager – You let in thirteen goals, today.
Goalie – That's all right, I'm not super-stitious!

Smiffy's dad – You know that music stool you sold me?
Shopkeeper – Yes.
Smiffy's dad – Well, I've twisted and turned it in all directions, and I can't get a single tune out of it.

When is it dangerous to enter a flower shop?
When the bulbs are shooting!

What do you call an interfering pig?
A nosy porker!

Diner – Waiter, there are two flies fighting my soup.
Waiter – Well, what do you expect for three pounds, a bull-fight?

Old lady – You say you were sent to prison for telling the truth?
Convict – Yes, lady. The judge asked me if I was guilty and I said "yes".

Mum – Come along, Danny, it's past time to get up.
Danny – Huh! It's no pastime for me – it's very hard work.

Teacher – How is it that you can never answer any of my questions?
Smiffy – Well, if I could, what would be the use of coming here?

First scout – I failed my first aid test.
Second scout – Why?
First scout – I tried to put a plaster on a hiccup!

Patient – Doctor, doctor, I feel like a pound note!
Doctor – Go shopping. The change will do you good.

What has feathers, fangs and goes quack-quack?
Count Duckula!

Dad – Didn't you promise not be naughty again?
Tommy – Yes, Dad!
Dad – Well, didn't I promise to punish you if you were?
Tommy – Yes, Dad, but since I didn't keep my part of the bargain you needn't keep yours!

Diner – Waiter, why are the flies so thick around here?
Waiter – Well, sir, we just can't keep them thin. The food is too good.

Teacher – What is memory?
Smiffy – The thing you forget with.

Uncle – You look rather puzzled, Freddie.
Freddie – Yes, uncle, I was just wondering if a wasp settled on a nettle, would the wasp sting the nettle or would the nettle sting the wasp?

Teacher – Make a sentence, using the word "politics" in it.
Jack – Our parrot swallowed a wrist watch, and now Polly ticks!

Friend – Why are you putting up your wallpaper with tacks?
Miser – You don't think I'm staying here all my life, do you?

Sandy – May I have an extra day's pay this week, sir?
Boss – Whatever for?
Sandy – I dreamt about my work all last night!

First workman – Does the foreman know that the trench has fallen in?
Second workman – No, but we're just digging him out to tell him!

Teacher – Can you give me an example of a collective noun?
Sidney – A vacuum cleaner, sir.

Teacher – Now Bobby, if your father could save thirty pounds a week for two years, what would he have?
Bobby – A new car, miss!

Did you hear about the cat who joined the Red Cross?
He wanted to be a first aid kit!

Jo – Flo, if a red house is made of red bricks, a blue house made of blue bricks and a yellow house made of yellow bricks, what's a green house made of?
Flo – Green bricks!
Jo – No, glass, stupid!

What did one ear say to the other?
"I didn't know we lived in the same block!"

Man to friend – How do you know I live in a small flat?
Friend – Your dog is wagging his tail up and down!

Why do people laugh up their sleeves? Because that's where their funny bones are!

Bert – That's a fine dog you've got. Is he faithful?
Bob – He is that! I've sold him five times and he always comes back!

Teacher – What is an optimist?
Danny – An optimist is someone who doesn't care what happens as long as it happens to somebody else!

Boss – So you want a job, eh? Do you ever tell lies?
Applicant – No, sir – but I could learn if I had to.

Terry – My brother has a new job.
Jerry – He's connected with the police department.
Terry – Police department. How?
Jerry – By a pair of handcuffs.

Boy – Why did the hedgehog cross the road?
Girl – Don't know.
Boy – To get a chocolate bar. Did you get it?
Girl – No.
Boy – Neither did he, he only had twelve pence!

Why is it against the law to whisper? Because it isn't aloud.

What do you put in a currant cake?
Your teeth!

George – The lion-tamer at the circus was attacked by his lions last night.
Dave – Was he clawed?
George – I don't know what his name was.

Where do flies go in the winter time?
To the glassworks to make bluebottles!

**Lord Posh – My last butler left me without any warning.
Lord Posher – You're lucky, mine left me without any silver!**

*Freddie – Mum, what happens to a car when it's too old to go any more?
Mother – Somebody sells it to your dad!*

Hector – I've seen ants so big that they could uproot a tree.
Hamish – What kind of ants.
Hector – Elephants!

**Sandy – Mum, I dreamed last night that I fell into the sea.
Mum – Well?
Sandy – Well . . . er . . . I won't need to wash my face this morning, will I?**

*What exams do farmers have to take?
Hay levels!*

Jean – Why did Cinderella get put out of the football team?
Joan – She ran away from the ball!

**What do you call a Roman Emperor with hay-fever?
Julius Sneezer.**

*Why did the biscuit cry?
Because its mother was a wafer too long!*

Who did Dracula marry?
His necks door neighbour!

**What do you do at a clock factory?
Sit down and make faces.**

Patient – Doctor, doctor, I've lost my memory.

Hugh – You don't mean to tell me that fish are musicians?
Charlie – Certainly. Have you never heard of the piano tuna?

**Doctor – When did this happen?
Patient – When did what happen?**

*One mouse collapsed. What did the other mouse do?
He used mouse-to-mouse resuscitation!*

What do misers do in cold weather?
Sit around a candle!
What do misers do in exceptionally cold weather?
Light the candle!

**What's grey and flies out of a burrow at 200 mph?
A hareoplane.**

*What is white and furry, and smells of peppermints?
A polo bear!*

What's the difference between a mouldy lettuce and a dismal song.
One's a bad salad, and the other's a sad ballad!

**Terry – This neighbourhood seems a bit noisy.
Jerry – Yes, the only time it's quiet here is when a train goes by and drowns outthe noise.**

*Boastful singer – I just can't help breaking into song.
Bored listener – If you got the right key, you wouldn't have to break in.*

Joe – So you're good at conundrums, eh? Well, try this one. Take away my first letter, then my second, then all my letters, and I'm still the same. What am I?
Moe – I give in.
Joe – A postman.

**Fatty – I'm putting on weight, doctor. What can I do about it?
Doctor – Take regular exercise.
Fatty – What kind of exercise?
Doctor – Push yourself away from the table three times a day!**

What's it called when a policeman goes to bed?
Laying down the law!

Penny – Do you know what the dragon said when he saw St George, in shining armour, bearing down on him?
Jenny – What?
Penny – Oh, no, not more tinned food!

What would you do if you saw two skeletons crossing the road?
Jump out of your skin and join them!

What is the opposite of minimum?
Minidad!

What is green and sings in the garden.
Elvis Parsley.

Teacher – Name four animals that live in the jungle.
Smiffy – Three lions and a tiger!

Syd – Does the giraffe get a sore throat if it gets its feet wet?
Fred – Yes, but not until the following week.

Teacher – How many ribs have you got, Jenny?
Jenny – I don't know, miss. I'm so tickly I can never finish counting them.

Diner – Waiter! This soup is cold. Bring me some that's hot.
Waiter – What? And scald my thumb?

Teacher – What was the former ruler of Russia called?
Toots – Tsar.
Teacher – Correct. And what was his wife called?
Toots – Tsarina.
Teacher – Right. What were the Tsar's children called?
Toots – Tsardines!

What are dog biscuits made of?
Collie-flour!

Erbert – I didn't know they played tennis in biblical times.
Teacher – They didn't, why?
'Erbert – Well, it says here that Joseph served in Pharaoh's Court!

Patient – Doctor, doctor what's that axe in the wall for?
Doctor – That's for splitting headaches!

What kind of fish do you find in a bird's cage?
A perch!

What birds fly in formation, and let off red, white and blue smoke?
The Red Sparrows!

Gent – Do you have any trouble in selling parrots?
Pet shop owner – Oh, no! They do their own sales talk!

Waiter – How did you find the steak, sir?
Diner – Quite easily. I just looked under a pea.

Foreman – You're not one of those men who drop their tools as soon as the whistle goes, are you!
New hand – No. I sometimes have to wait about five minutes after I've put my tools away before the whistle goes.

Hamish – What's the difference between a barber in Rome and an angry circus owner?
Donald – One is a shaving Roman and the other is a raving showman!

Donald – You couldn't lend me fifty pence, could you?
John – No, but how did you know?

Aunt – Is you mother in, Donald?
Donald – Of course she's in. Do you think I'd be standing here cleaning windows on a Saturday afternoon if she was out?

Dad – You get more pocket money in a week than I used to get in a month!
Minnie – Well, don't grumble at me about it, go and complain to Grandpa!

What do you call a gentle, kind, loving, careful, shy monster?
A failure!

Why did the boy clean up the spilt coffee with cake?
Because it was sponge cake!

Who are the strongest people in the world, men or women?
Women, because they can carry ladders in their tights!

What do you all an unmarried mer-maid?
A single fish!

Why don't elephants ride bicycles?
They haven't got a thumb to ring the bell!

What do you call a flying policeman?
A heli-copper!

Danny – Did your father punish you when you went home last night?
Sidney – Yes, he made me stay in the room where my sister was doing her singing practice.

Johnny – What's up, Davie? Been fighting again?
Davie (face covered in plasters) – No. We've been moving house, and I had to carry the cactus plants!

Chairman – When you have finished your lecture, sir, bow gracefully and leave the platform on tiptoe!
Lecturer – Why on tiptoe?
Chairman – So as not to wake the audience!

What do you call Dracula?
A pain in the neck!

Athlete – What's my temperature, doctor?
Doctor – A hundred and one.
Athlete – What's the world record?

Small car owner – Half a pint of petrol, please and two spoonfuls of oil.
Garage attendant – Would you like me to sneeze into the tyres, too?

Customer – I haven't come to any ham in this sandwich yet.
Waiter – Try another bite.
Customer – (taking a mouthful) – Nope, none yet.
Waiter – Hmm! You must have gone right past it.

What do you call a vampire's favourite dance?
A fang-dango!

Knock! Knock!
Who's there?
Butcher.
Butcher who?
You butcher left leg in, you butcher left leg out.

Newsflash – A thousand mattresses have been stolen from a warehouse in the city. Police are springing into action.

Cinema attendant – That's the sixth ticket you've bought, sir.
Customer – Yes, I know. There's a girl in there who keeps ripping them up.

Sandy – Did you hear about the man who was listening to the match?
Andy – No, what about him?
Sandy – He burnt his ear!

Teacher – Did you have much trouble with your French when you were in Paris?
Dennis – No, but the Parisians did!

Why is a railway line like a blanket?
Because it lies on sleepers.

Diner – Hey, waiter! This steak's so tough, I can't get my fork into it.
Waiter – That's not so bad, sir. At the place across the road, you can't get your fork into the gravy!

Alf – What's the difference between a jeweller and jailer?
Dick – I don't know. What is the difference?
Alf – One sells watches and one watches cells?

Bob – I never wear a coat or a hat when it rains.
Bert – You must get soaked.
Bob – No. I just don't go out when it rains.

Uncle Jack – How are you getting on at school, Tommy?
Tommy – Oh, fine! The teacher said that if all the boys were like me, he would shut the school tomorrow.

Patient – Doctor, doctor! I feel like a pop star!
Doctor – Nurse, get his records.

What did the mouse say when he chipped his tooth?
Hard cheese!

First candle – What shall we do tonight then?
Second candle – Well, I was thinking of going out!

Bill – Did you hear about the man who got employed as a dustman?
Bob – No.
Bill – He said he would pick it up as he went along.

Why did the scout feel dizzy?
Because he did so many good turns!

What do you call a seven-foot gorilla with a machine gun?
Sir.

What do you get if you cross an owl with a skunk?
A bird that smells horrible but doesn't give a hoot!

When is an operation funny?
When it leaves the patient in stitches!

Teacher – What is a yokel?
Pupil – The centre of an eggle!

Bill – Why did the Manx cat cross the road?
Ben – To get to the tail-ors!

Hamish – I went horseback riding today.
Duncan – Well, sit down and tell me about it.
Hamish – I can't.
Duncan – You mean you can't tell me about it?
Hamish – No, I can't sit down.

John – Did you hear about the silly photographer?
Peter – No.
John – He saved burnt-out light bulbs to use in his darkroom!

What do you get if you put duck eggs in a cement mixer?
Quacks in the wall!

What do you get if you cross a palm tree with a toad?
A croakanut.

How did Luke Skywalker shave his beard?
With a laser blade!

Old man – When does the last train leave for Auchentogle.
Porter – Ten-thirty, sir.
Old man – All the clocks in the station are at different times, so which one am I going to go by?
Porter – Well, sir, you can go by any clock you like, but you can't go by the last train. It has already gone!

WHY DID TOMMY THROW THE CLOCK OUT OF THE WINDOW?
BECAUSE HE WANTED TO SEE TIME FLY!
CHUCKLE CHUCKLE!
THREE PEOPLE WERE STANDING UNDER AN UMBRELLA . . . WHICH ONE GOT WET?
NONE OF THEM, IT WASN'T RAINING!

McKenzie – My wife dreamed last night she was married to a millionaire.
Campbell – You're lucky! My wife dreams that in the daytime.

Harry – You know, the other night at the theatre a man fell out of the balcony, and everybody laughed but me.
Larry – Why didn't you laugh?
Harry – I was the man.

Customer – I want a pair of spec-rimmed hornicles . . . I mean sporn-rimmed hectacles . . . confound it . . . I mean heck-rimmed spornacles . . . I . . .
Optician – I know what you mean, sir. Mr Peck, show this gentleman a pair of rim-sporned hectacles. Oh, no! Now you've got me doing it!
Customer – Never mind, fit me with some contact lenses.

Harry – What do you think of your new teacher?
Tom – He's the kind of a fellow who, when you first meet him, you don't like him. But when you get to know him, you hate him.

Where do frogs borrow money?
From the river bank!

Why did the man go up the mountain with only one wellington boot on?
Because the forecast had said there was only one foot of snow!

Where does Tarzan buy his clothes?
At the Jungle Sale!

Which tree would you make a deck chair from?
A beech tree!

Terry – Have you had an accident?
Jerry – No.
Terry – Then why are you limping?
Jerry – A bull pitched me over a fence.
Terry – Well, wasn't that an accident?
Jerry – No, that bull did it on purpose.

Waiter – How would you like your steak, sir?
Diner (tired of waiting) – Very much.

Mother – What are you looking for?
Tommy – A fifty pence piece.
Mother – Where did you lose it?
Tommy – I didn't lose it, I'm just looking for one!

Teacher – I asked for a two-page composition about milk. Your paper is only half a page long.
Tommy – That's right. I wrote about condensed milk!

Mum – I think Dad's going to take us to the pictures, Danny. You'd better wash your face and hands.
Danny – I'd rather make sure he's going to take us before I do that, Mum.

Ian – Auntie, what do caterpillars taste like?
Auntie – How should I know, Ian?
Ian – Well, there was one in that piece of lettuce you just ate!

Sam – I know everything about football.
Geordie – Is that so?
Sam – Yes.
Geordie – Well, how many holes are there in a goal net?

How do you make an apple puff?
Chase it around the garden!

Patient – Doctor, will I be able to play the piano when my fingers get better?
Doctor – Yes, certainly!
Patient – That's good! I never could play it before!

Man – Doctor, doctor I keep seeing the future!
Doctor – When did this happen?
Man – Next Wednesday!

Why is it crazy to break into a bank?
'Cos it's full of coppers!

TEE-HEE!
WHO STOLE THE SOAP?
THE ROBBER DUCK!
WHAT IS BIG, RED AND EATS ROCKS?
A BIG RED ROCK EATER!
TEE-HEE!
WHAT HAS FOUR LEGS BUT DOESN'T MOVE?
A TABLE!
HEE-HEE!
WHO WAS BIGGER, MR. BIGGER OR HIS SON?
HIS SON . . . HE WAS A LITTLE BIGGER!
WHAT IS H2O4?
DRINKING!

What do policemen have in their sandwiches?
Truncheon meat!

Why do they put telephone wires so high?
To keep up the conversation!

Daisy – Dad, Jack's just broken my new doll.
Dad – How did he do that?
Daisy – I hit him with it.

Mad scientist – I have just successfully crossed a giraffe with a hedgehog?
Assistant – Brilliant, master. What have you created?
Mad scientist – An eight-foot toothbrush.

Where do nomads of the desert get married?
At a mirage bureau!

Why did the man fail his driving test?
He opened the door to let the clutch out!

What is caught but never thrown?
A cold.

Why did the boy take a car to school?
Because he wanted to drive the teacher round the bend!

Man – Can I cut your grass for my dinner?
Lady – Certainly, and I hope you enjoy eating it!

Margaret – You said you wouldn't give away that secret I told you.
Jean – I didn't give it away! I exchanged it for another!

Boss – What do you mean by going for a haircut in the firm's time?
Office boy – Well, it grows in the firm's time, doesn't it?

Why is it fun to work in a clock factory?
Because you're making faces all day!

Jimmy – Dad, was Robinson Crusoe a contortionist?
Dad – No, why?
Jimmy – Well, it says here he sat down on his chest!

Chef – How would you make a sausage roll?
Apprentice – Push it!

Post Office assistant – There we are, miss, one first class stamp.
Young girl – Do I have to stick it on myself?
Post Office assistant – No, miss, on the envelope.

Biology teacher – Name two crustaceans.
Mike – Kings crustacean and Charing crustacean.

Teacher – To do anything in life, you must start at the bottom and work up.
Danny – What about learning to swim, sir?

Patient – Doctor, doctor, I keep seeing spotted horses.
Doctor – Have you seen a psychiatrist?
Patient – No, I just keep seeing spotted horses.

Teacher – Name a collective noun.
Eric – Dustman.

Commuter – I want to catch a late train to London.
Porter – Take the 9.30 train – it's usually as late as any!

Charlie – Why does this radio whistle when I turn the dials?
Mick – That means you're coming to the station!

Smith – I've certainly outfoxed the railway company this time.
Jones – How?
Smith – I've bought this return ticket and I'm not going back!

Teacher – What is a distant relative?
Sandy – My brother Andy is one.
Teacher – How can your brother be a distant relative?
Sandy – Because he lives in New Zealand.

Terry – I'm looking for someone to lend me five pounds.
Jerry – Let me know if you find anyone. Perhaps he'll lend me some money, too.

Why did the computer cross the road?
Because it was programmed by a chicken!

Why was the sheep arrested on the M1?
It made a ewe turn!

Patient – Doctor, doctor, my wife keeps thinking she's a hen.
Doctor – Why didn't you tell me earlier?
Patient – We needed the eggs.

Why do leopards never escape from the zoo?
Because they are always spotted.

Bill – How do you make antifreeze?
Ben – Don't know.
Bill – Hide her woolly socks!

Old man – Why are you crying, my boy?
Boy – Harry hit me!
Old man – Why don't you hit him back?
Boy – Because then it would be his turn again.

Crook – Look at that car. Let's pinch it.
Mate – We can't do that, we don't have driving licences!

Patient – Doctor, doctor can you help me out?
Doctor – Yes, which way did you come in?

Holiday maker – What are your weekly rates?
Receptionist – Well, that's rather difficult, I don't know anyone who's stayed for a week!

Speaker – There are so many interruptions I can't hear myself speak.
Voice – Don't worry, mate! You're not missing much.

Customer – I'd like some buttered bop corn . . . that is . . . poppered butt corn . . . I mean corn buttered pop . . . or rather cuttered pot born . . . I mean – oh, give me a hot dog.

Fortune-teller – I'll tell you your fortune for two pounds!
McTavish – If you were a real fortune-teller you'd know I don't have two pounds.

Golfer – How do you like my game?
Caddy – I suppose it's okay, but I still prefer golf!

Danny – Mum, does an apple a day keep the doctor away?
Mum – Yes.
Danny – Well, you'd better give me one now. I've broken the doctor's window with a cricket ball.

What's green, covered in custard, and miserable?
Apple grumble!

What monster only rings the doorbell when he comes to visit?
The knock-less monster!

What do you get if you cross a centipede with a parrot?
A walkie-talkie!

Old man – What is you dog's name?
Boy – Ginger, sir.
Old man – Does Ginger bite?
Boy – No, sir, but Ginger snaps.

Actor (playing a detective) – There has been foul play. What shall I do?
Voice from the audience – Give yourself a free kick.

Visitor to Wild West – How can you tell a poisonous snake from a non-poisonous one?
Bronco Bill – Just let it bite you. If you die, it's poisonous. If you live, it ain't!

Mum – Keep that dog out of the house, it's full of fleas.
Son – Rover, don't go in the house. Mum says it's full of fleas!

What do you call a magician from outer space?
A flying sorcerer!

Girl – Mum, what do you think I should wear with my pink and green spotted ankle socks?
Mum – Knee length boots!

Which two animals keep you company wherever you go?
Your calves, of course!

What is round, yellow, flies, and is made of egg?
An unidentified flying omelette!

Archie – Have you forgotten about the five pounds you owe me?
Alistair – Not yet. Give me time

Mum – Now, lads, stop quarrelling. Can't you ever agree?
Dave – We've agreed this time, Mum. Andy and I both want the biggest piece of cake.

Teacher – Any questions?
Smart Alec – Yes. How many full stops are there in a bottle of ink?

Did you hear about the Scotsman who washed his kilt?
He couldn't do a "fling" with it!

Donald – Well, Dad, I've got better news from school this time.
Dad – Have you passed your exams at last?
Donald – Well, I didn't exactly pass, but I was top of those who failed.

Ian – What sort of a boat would you use to shoot the rapids?
Charlie – A gunboat.

Jones – Were you relieved when the thief went away?
Smith – I'll say! He relieved me of fifty pounds!

Jimmy – Dad, can I ask you something?
Dad – Sure son, go ahead.
Jimmy – I've just asked it!

What did the hungry lion do?
Kept walking until he was fed up!

Bill – What travels around the world, but stays in a corner?
Ben – I don't know.
Bill – A stamp!

What does a monster eat after he's had a tooth out?
The dentist!

Describe, in one word, 962 little cakes dancing.
Abundance!

Auntie Jean – Danny, why is your baby brother crying?
Danny – He doesn't want to learn anything, Auntie. I took his piece of cake and showed him how to eat it.

Terry – Did you hear of the man who invented something for looking through brick walls?
Jerry – No, what did he call it?
Terry – A window.

What's green and miles and miles long!
The Grape Wall of China!

What do you get if you cross a policeman with a dog?
A copper spaniel.

What do you do if you find an eight-foot ape in your bed?
Sleep somewhere else!

Actor – I once acted in a play called Breakfast in Bed!
Interviewer – Did you have a big role?
Actor – No, just toast and marmalade!

First artist – Why have you got your face bandaged?
Second artist – I drew a pop bottle yesterday, and it was so real that the cork flew out and hit me in the eye!

Cinema manager – Hello! Where's the queue tonight?
Door attendant – It started fighting, and a policeman came round and arrested both of them, sir.

Policeman – What's the matter, laddie?
Little boy – Please sir, have you seen a lady without a little boy that looks like me?

Dad – I hear you and Garry nearly had a fight yesterday.
Andy – Yes, we were going to fight, but there was nobody there to hold us back.

Diner – Waiter, bring me a jug of water.
Waiter – For drinking, sir?
Diner – No, I'm going to give a high-diving display!

Tommy – Mum sent me back with this steak. She says it's so tough she could almost sole her shoes with it.
Butcher – Why didn't she?
Tommy – The nails wouldn't go through it.

What do sea-monsters live on?
Fish and ships!

What do you call a parrot with a machine gun?
A parrot trooper!

What is a ghost's favourite music?
Haunting melodies!

What does a mouse eat for breakfast?
Mice Krispies.

Kevin – Garry Thomson told me that I'm like you.
Ashley – And what did you say to that?
Kevin – Nothing. He's bigger than me!

Impatient customer – Haven't you finished mending those boots yet?
Cobbler – Not quite. I'm doing the second one now!
Impatient customer – Well, where's the first one?
Cobbler – I'll do it when I've finished the second.

McKay – This cornflour is no good.
Grocer – What's wrong with it?
McKay – Well, I've used it on my corns for a fortnight now, and they're just as bad as ever.

Dennis – A bottle of cod liver oil.
Chemist – Wouldn't you prefer the tasteless capsules?
Dennis – Nah! It's for my Dad!

Smith – Do you think you could lend me your CD player for tonight?
Jones (his neighbour) – Certainly. Are you giving a party?
Smith – Oh, no. We just want to get some sleep.

What's small, round, white and giggles?
A tickled onion!

Peter – Would you rather a crocodile attacked you or an elephant?
Tom – I'd rather he attacked the elephant!

What is the difference between China and Japan?
You can't eat off Japan!

Tim – They're not going to grow bananas any longer.
Tom – Really, why not?
Tim – Because they're long enough already!

Why do devils and ghosts get on so well together?
Because demon's are a ghoul's best friend!

Lady – I would like a pair of crocodile shoes, please.
Assistant – Certainly, madam. What size is your crocodile?

Inventor – I've only two more difficulties to overcome and my new aeroplane will be a great success.
Friend – What are they?
Inventor – Getting it into the air and making it say there.

Dad – You've taken a long time to blacken these boots.
Smiffy – Yes, but some of them were brown when I started.

What sits in the garden and rings?
A telegnome!

What question can never be answered "yes"?
Are you asleep?

What do elephants have that other animals don't?
Baby elephants!

May – Is this hand-knitted?
Jay – No, it came with the arm!

Alistair – Why does a giraffe have such a long neck?
Archie – Because its head is so far from its body.

How do you tell that a kangaroo is annoyed?
He goes hopping mad!

What looks after a haunted stretch of beach?
The ghost guard!

Did you hear about the man who was told to dress in white when going out at night, so he could be seen in the dark?
He was run over by a snowplough!

Baker – Try these cakes, sir. You can't get better.
Customer – I know. I had one last week, and I don't feel well yet.

Why did the taxi driver give up his job?
Because people kept talking behind his back.

What do you find in a haunted cellar?
Whines and spirits!

First farmer – What did the baby ear of corn say to the mummy ear of corn?
Second farmer – I don't know, what did the baby ear of corn say to the mummy ear of corn?
First farmer – Where's pop corn?

Where is Felixstowe?
On the end of Felix's foot!

Policeman – How did you get up that tree?
Sarcastic young man – I sat on it when it was an acorn.

What would you have if you owned a cow and two ducks?
Milk and quackers.

Grandpa – Well, Jimmy, and what do you want to be when you grow up?
Jimmy – I want to be an old man like you, with nothing to do all day but sit about and ask questions.

Doctor (to stuntman in hospital) – How did you get these injuries?
Stuntman – I tried to jump over twenty-five cars in a bus.
Doctor – What happened?
Stuntman – Someone rang the bell!

Why will television never take the place of a newspaper?
Have you ever tried swatting a fly with a television?

What do ghosts watch at the theatre?
A phantomime.

If you were surrounded by Dracula, Frankenstein's monster, a ghost and a werewolf, what would you be hoping?
That it was at a fancy dress party!

Cuthbert – Can you telephone from an aeroplane?
Fed-up airman – Of course I can tell a phone from an aeroplane!

Policeman – What are you crying for, sonny?
Bobby – Ma's giving me a party today.
Policeman – Well, that's nothing to cry about.
Bobby – Aye, it is. I can't find my way home.

What do you call a Scottish kangaroo locked in a cage?
A kana gar oot!

Jack – Yesterday my dog started chewing up my dictionary.
Jill – What did you do?
Jack – I took the words right out of his mouth!

What do you call an egg that loves playing tricks?
A practical yolker!

What do sheiks use to hide from their enemies?
Camelflage!

First fortune teller – Lovely weather we're having at the moment.
First fortune teller – Yes, reminds me of the summer of 2040!

First boaster – Where I come from we had rain one year that flooded the streets to the height of the lamp-posts.
Second boaster – Huh! When we had our last rainstorm we had to go down in submarines to milk the cows!

Moe – What side of a chicken has the most feathers?
Joe – I don't know.
Moe – The outside!

What did the pencil say to the sharpener?
"Stop going round in circles and get to the point!"

Did you hear about the man who gave a party for his chickens?
He had to cancel it because he couldn't make hens meet!

Teacher – Name of famous designer of coats.
Pupil – Anna Rack.

Teacher – If you had three eyes, where would you like the third one to be?
Jock – On the point of my finger.
Teacher – Why?
Jock – So that I could stick it through a hole in the fence to see the football match every week!

Jimmy – Please, may I have a pair of rubber gloves?
Auntie Jean – What for?
Jimmy – So I can wash my hands without getting them wet!

Hector – Have you ever seen an elephant's skin?
Hamish – Yes.
Hector – Where?
Hamish – On an elephant of course.

Landlady – How do you like your eggs boiled?
Lodger – Three at a time.

Jack – What's wrong with your head, Jock?
Jock – Some water fell on it.
Jack – But surely that wouldn't hurt it?
Jock – Yes, but the water was in a jug!

Jim – I've got a terrible cold. I won't be able to do the high jump.
PE Teacher – Why not?
Jim – I can't even clear my throat!

Lodger – I don't like all these mice in my room.
Landlord – Point out those you do like and I'll get rid of the rest!

What makes a chess player happy?
Taking a knight off!

Why are sardines stupid?
They lock themselves inside the tin and leave the key outside!

Boy – Mum, my torch is not working.
Mum – Maybe the batteries have run out.
Boy – No, they're still inside it!

How do you keep cool at a football match?
Sit next to a fan!

Henry – My cat took first prize at the bird show.
Harry – How was that?
Henry – He ate the prize canary.

Lord Toff – You know that horse you sold me yesterday? He died this morning.
Stable man – That's funny. He never did that before.

McNab – Do you think it's unlucky to have thirteen people at the table?
McKay – No – unless there's only food for twelve.

Boss – Stop whistling while you're working.
Office boy – Who's working?

Yes, this is the lost property office.
Well, I'm lost!

What's black, furry and knocks down buildings?
A de-mole-ition gang!

When is a pound note like a bridge?
When it goes from bank to bank!

What did the artist do when he was stopped by a robber?
He drew a gun!

What does a ball do when it stops rolling?
Looks round!

Frank – I am glad my parents named me Frank.
Jack – Why?
Frank – Because that's what everyone calls me!

Shop manager – Smith! Fetch in those waterproof overcoats. It's raining!

Waiter – Excuse me, sir, but I think I've seen you before. Are you a brother or relative of Major Brown?
Major Brown – No, I am Major Brown.
Waiter – Ah, then that accounts for the remarkable resemblance, sir.

Alan – Hello, Pat! Seen Mike lately?
Pat – Well, I thought I saw him across the street the other day, and he thought he saw me, but when we got up close to each other, it was neither of us!

Jim – My brother is a cashier in a police station.
Tim – What does he do?
Jim – He counts the coppers as they come in.

Optician – Here are your new glasses. Remember, you will only wear them when you are working.
Patient – That might be difficult.
Optician – Why, what do you do for a living?
Patient – I'm a boxer.

Diner – Waiter, waiter, this soup tastes funny!
Waiter – Then why aren't you laughing, sir?

What did one rock pool say to another rock pool?
"Show us your mussels!"

Two flies were on a cornflakes packet.
"Why are we running so fast?" asked one.
"Because," said the second, "it says 'tear along dotted line'!"

Servant – Your bath is ready, sir!
Absent-minded professor – Oh! I'm too busy. You take it for me.

Lady – What is the best way to cover a cushion?
Fed-up assistant – Sit on it!

Andy – How long have you been working for the boss you have now?
Barry – Ever since he threatened to fire me.

Customer – I won't buy this hat. It makes me look like an idiot.
Salesman – But that's the one you were wearing when you came in, sir.

Green – Have you heard of the tragedy that happened in the library last week?
Brown – No, what was it?
Green – A man was found buried in a book.

How did the glow-worm feel when it wouldn't glow.
De-lighted!

Why did the boy go to night school?
To learn to read in the dark!

Stranger – Do these steps take you to the station?
Local – Course not! Steps can't walk!

What is the best thing to take to the desert?
A thirst-aid kit!

What do you get if you cross a zebra with a pig?
Striped sausages!

Where are there no fat people?
In Finland!

Teacher – How do you spell "inconsequentially"?
Smiffy – Always wrong!

What do you get if you cross grass seeds with a cow?
A lawnmooer!

Moe – Hey, Jock, what's a black pudding?
Joe – A sausage in mourning.

Teacher – What grows on palms?
Sidney – Four fingers and a thumb!

Who was the first underwater spy?
James pond!

What are chiropodists' favourite crisps?
Cheese and bunion!

What can cut waves?
A sea-saw!

First-aid teacher – What would you do if you broke your arm in two places?
Boy – I'd never go to either place again!

How can you avoid starving on a desert island?
Eat the sand-which is there!

Teacher – You all know, I suppose, that it is the law of gravity that keeps us from falling off the earth.
Smiffy – Please, sir, what kept people on the earth before the law was passed?

Mother – Dennis, how many more times will I have to tell you to leave the chocolate spread alone?
Dennis – No more, Mum, the jar's empty now!

Mother – I hope the boys at school don't give you nasty nicknames?
Sammy – They call me "Toe Nails" because I'm at the foot of the class.

Diner – Waiter, there's a button in my lunch!
Waiter – Well, sir, you did ask for a jacket potato!

Where does a gardener play snooker? The potting shed!

Why are giraffes slow to apologise? Because it takes a long time for them to swallow their pride!

Boy – Doctor, doctor, my knees won't stop shaking! What can I do about it?
Doctor – Tie a pair of cymbals to them and join the school band!

What does a vicar fly in? A holycopter!

How do you post a rabbit? Hare mail!

What goes whistling up the aisle at a wedding?
The bride's train!

Why was the envelope on the roof? Because it wanted ceiling!

Did you hear about the man with five legs? – His trousers fitted him like a glove!

Dad (pointing to a statue) – That is Sir Thomas Rich, my boy. He gave big sums to the school.
Jimmy – Is that so? Couldn't he do them himself?

Michael – You don't seem to be growing any taller.
Bobby – I know. It's all my mother's fault. She washes me so often that I shrink.

Teacher – A fool can ask questions that a wise man can't answer.
Plug – No wonder we didn't pass our exam.

Actor – When I played my last part on the stage, the audience were glued to their seats.
Critic – Well, that was certainly a good way to keep them there.

Teacher – Dear me, Jack, how dirty you are! What would you say if I came to school as dirty as that?
Jack – Please, sir, I'd be too polite to mention it.

Drowning man – Help, help! I can't swim!
Passer-by – I can't play the piano, but I don't shout about it!

Girl – My teacher does bird impressions.
Mother – Really?
Girl – Yes, she watches me like a hawk!

Teacher – Tommy, can you tell me how iron was discovered?
Tommy – Yes, sir, I heard Dad say the other day that they smelt it!

What do you get if you cross a cocker spaniel, a poodle and a rooster? A cockapoodledoo!

Music teacher – Is there anything special you'd like to be able to play?
Pupil – Yes, miss, truant!

Father – Why didn't you tell me the truth when I asked you who broke the window?
Son – I thought my story was more interesting.

Customer – Waiter! Waiter! There's a fly in my soup!
Waiter – Don't worry, sir. There's a spider on your bread!

Patient – Doctor, doctor, I keep thinking I'm a needle!
Doctor – Yes, I can see your point!

Why did the boy want to become a chimney sweep?
Because he thought it would soot him!

Why did the man have to repair the horn of his car?
Because it didn't give a hoot!

Sam – Why are you going upstairs with the piano, Bill?
Bill – I'm going to mend it.
Sam – But why take it upstairs?
Bill – Well, the hammer's up there.

Town boy (in country for first time) – Why doesn't that cow have horns?
Country friend – Well, the chief reason is that it's a horse, not a cow.

Teacher – Now, children, I hope you have a nice weekend, and come back to school with a little sense in your heads.
Class (in unison) – Same to you, sir!

Judge – Didn't I say when you were here before that I never wanted to see you again?
Prisoner – Yes, but I couldn't make the policeman believe me.

Why do birds in a nest always agree?
Because they don't want to fall out!

What do computers eat?
Fish and microchips!

What do you do when a kangaroo has appendicitis?
You hoperate on him!

Jones – Smith wants to borrow five pounds. Do you think I should give it to him?
Brown – Yes, of course.
Jones – Why?
Brown – Well, if you don't let him have it, he'll come to me for it.

Why couldn't the sailors play cards?
The captain was standing on the deck!

Teacher – Why did Robin Hood only rob the rich?
Wilfrid – Because the poor people didn't have any money?

Moe – My big sister uses lemon juice for her complexion.
Joe – No wonder she always looks so sour!

"This is the worst essay I've ever read," complained teacher. "I shall tell your father about it."
"I wouldn't if I were you," grinned Sammy. "He wrote it for me!"

Bill – Why have you put that bit of looking-glass in the foot of your dog's dish, Sandy?
Sandy – Don't you see that Rover thinks he's getting two bones instead of one?

Mum – I don't like the boy next door, so I want you to keep away from him as much as possible at school.
Pete – Oh, that's easy. He's usually at the top of the class!

Teacher – Can anyone tell me something of great importance that didn't exist one hundred years ago?
Small girl – Yes, miss, me!

Judge – Did you get hurt in the riot?
Witness – No, in the eye.

Postman – Is this letter for you? The name is illegible.
Man – No, it can't be mine. My name is Brown.

Canvasser (to little boy standing by house door) – Is your mother in?
Boy – Yes.
Canvasser (after knocking about a dozen times) – I thought you told me your mother was in.
Boy – So she is, but we don't live here.

Harry – Give me fifty pence to go to the zoo to see the snakes, Dad.
Dad – What a waste of money! Take this magnifying glass and go and look at the worms in the garden.

Don – Why are you putting your hand in the dog's mouth?
John – Putting it in? I'm trying to get it out!

Bobby – I can fight anybody.
Henry – You can't fight my brother!
Bobby – Yes, I can.
Henry – No, you can't – 'cause I don't have a brother!

What do you get if you cross a cow with a duck?
A milk float!

Mum – Why did you not do your decimals homework?
Son – I couldn't see the point!

Son – How much am I worth, Mum?
Mum – To me, you're worth a million pounds, son.
Son – Well, could you lend me five of them?

What do you get if you cross an elephant with a swallow?
A lot of broken telephone wires!

Teacher – What do we make from horns?
Dunce – Please, sir, hornaments!

Patient – Doctor, doctor, for ages now, I've thought I'm a bit of string.
Doctor – Why didn't you come to me earlier?
Patient – Because I was tied up for a while.

Daisy (sobbing) – A man ran over my hula hoop with his motor cycle.
Dad – The scoundrel! I'll teach him! Where is he?
Daisy – In the infirmary.

Brainy – Why are you putting all those patches on your inner tube?
Dopey – Well, it's like this, if I get a puncture it will be mended already!

Patient – I keep thinking I'm covered in gold paint.
Doctor – Don't worry, it's just a gilt complex!

Where does a dog go when he loses his tail?
To a retailer!

Why was the tennis ball deaf?
Because it put up with too much racket!

Zoo keeper – We've lost a giraffe and a mouse.
Visitor – What are you going to do about it?
Zoo keeper – Search high and low!

Mother – No, Fatty, no more cake tonight. Don't you know you can't sleep on a full stomach?
Fatty – Well, I can sleep on my back.

Copper – Well, sonny, are you lost?
Ken (tearfully) – No, but I've found a street I don't know!

James – They tell me they have buildings more than eighty storeys high in New York.
John – Oh, boy! What a time we could have sliding down the banisters!

Variety agent – You say you are a magician?
Applicant – Yes.
Variety agent – Well, vanish!

Joe – Ever seen sausages hanging up in the shop?
Len – Course I have.
Joe – That's funny. I always thought they hung down!

Mum – You mustn't play the piano when Dad is sleeping.
Jess – But, Mum, I can put thick gloves on.

Lou – How many seconds are there in a year?
Sue – I don't know.
Lou – There are twelve seconds in a year!
Sue – How do you make that out?
Lou – For example, January 2nd, February 2nd . . .!?

What did the dog say to the bone?
It was nice gnawing you!

What always weighs the same, no matter how big it gets?
A hole!

Son – Do you remember you said that if I got a good report you would give me five pounds?
Dad – Yes, why do you ask?
Son – Well, I've just saved you the expense!

General (to sergeant) – You idiot! Instead of addressing this despatch to the "Intelligence Office" you've addressed it to the "Intelligent Officer". Don't you know there's no such officer in the Army?

Diner – Waiter, there's a dead fly swimming in my soup.
Waiter – That's impossible, sir, dead flies can't swim.

Inquisitive boy – Have you ever had any narrow escapes all the time you've been a sailor?
Old sailor – Yes, I was nearly drowned once.
Boy – How did it happen? Did your ship hit a rock?
Old sailor – No, no! I went to sleep in my bath and left the water running!

Passenger – Here, driver, why is the taxi jumping about like this? Have you lost your head?
Driver – No, sir. I've lost the steering wheel.

Shopkeeper (to assistant) – How many new-laid eggs have we in stock?
Assistant – Oh, about enough to last us six weeks.

Why is your nose in the middle of your face?
Because it is the scenter!

Mother – Billy, why did you put this frog in your aunt's bed?
Billy – Because I couldn't find a mouse!

What did the wig say when it was blowing along the street?
"I'm off my head!"

Teacher – Johnny, why are you doing your sums on the floor?
Johnny – But miss, you told me to try them without using tables!

Boy to dentist – How much would it be to have three teeth out?
Dentist – Ten pounds.
Boy – Huh, forget it! I'll pick a fight on the way home!

Master – You might get my bath ready for me.
Butler – I'm sorry, sir, it's being used by the goldfish. The mistress said it was to have a treat on its birthday.

Knock! Knock!
Who's there?
Mavis.
Mavis who?
Mavis be the last time I knock on this door!

Car salesman – Our cars no good? Why, we're selling them by the dozen. Prospective buyer – I'm not surprised. How much are they a dozen?

Teacher – Dear me, you haven't put any answers to these sums.
Smiffy – No, sir, I left those out. I always get that part wrong.

Jamie – Is it true, Ma, that you shouldn't put off until tomorrow what can be done today?
Ma – Yes, James.
Jamie – Well, in that case I'd better finish off that cake in the cupboard.

Teacher – Would it be correct to say, "You can learn me nothing"?
Danny – Yes, sir.
Teacher – Why?
Danny – 'Cos you can't.

First golfer – That fool Brown crossed my tee as I drove off.
Second golfer – Well, if he crossed your tee, you should have dotted his eye.

How do you spell "dried grass" in three letters?
H-A-Y!

What happened to the cricketer who opened Dracula's coffin?
He got a bat in the mouth!

Tom – I've just got a job at the Eagle Laundry.
Tim – That sounds dangerous!

Boy – Farmer, do you like baked apples?
Farmer – Yes, why?
Boy – Because your orchard is on fire!

Benny – What time is it, please?
Kenny – Three o'clock.
Benny – Oh, no, not again!
Kenny – Why, what's the matter?
Benny – I've been asking people the time all day, and everyone tells me something different!

Who rides a camel and carries a lamp?
Florence of Arabia!

Teacher – Have you learned anything today, Sidney?
Sidney – No, sir! I've been listening to you all the time.

Golfer – I'll stay here until I hit his ball!
Caddie – You'll need a new caddie, then. I'm going on holiday next week.

"Just think of it," said Johnny. "My mum was born in Iceland, and my dad was born in Cuba. I must be an ice-cube!"

How can you tell a miser's house?
There's a padlock on the dustbin, a fork in the sugar bowl and tea bags on the washing line.

Smiffy – What do you mean, telling everybody I'm an idiot?
Toots – Oh, I'm sorry. I didn't know it was meant to be a secret.

Doctor – Nurse, where's the next patient?
Nurse – She didn't look very well, so I sent her home.

What goes black, white, green, black, white, green, black, white, green?
A zebra rolling down a hill!

Brown – What's an optimist?
Green – A man who looks in a cuckoo clock for an egg!

What would you do if you saw two snails fighting?
Let them "slug" it out!

Chemist – The meat you sold me yesterday didn't taste very good.
Butcher – Then we're quits. The medicine you sold me last week tasted awful.

Dad – I promised you a bicycle if you passed your exams, but you've failed in everything. What have you been doing with your time?
Sidney – Learning to ride a bicycle!

How do you make gold soup?
Put 14 carats in it!

Patient – Doctor, doctor, everyone thinks I'm a liar.
Doctor – Come now, I don't believe that for a minute!

What did one ear say to the other ear? Between you and me we need a haircut.

Why is it unwise to buy a cheap violin?
Because it might be a fiddle!

What party game did Doctor Jekyll like best?
Hyde and seek.

Where do ghosts like to swim?
The Dead Sea!

Patient – Doctor, there's a mist before my eyes. What can it be?
Doctor – I haven't the foggiest idea!

Teacher – Now, Plug, what do you know about the Dead Sea?
Plug – I never even knew it was ill, sir!

Young singer – And now that you've tested my voice, Professor, what do you think it is best suited for?
Professor – Selling papers.

Patient – Will my measles be better next week, doctor?
Doctor – Well, I hate to make rash promises!

Judge (to prisoner) – How did you manage to pick the lock after it was fitted with a safety catch?
Prisoner – Sorry, guv'nor, but it's a pound a lesson!

Nephew – That 20p you gave me dropped through a hole in my pocket.
Uncle – Well, here's another.
Nephew – Wouldn't a bigger coin be safer?
Uncle – Quite right – here's 2p!

Slow barber – Your hair is getting grey, sir.
Customer – No wonder. Hurry up!

When does an astronaut have his main meal of the day?
At launch time!

Why are mother cats tidy?
Because they always pick up their litter!

What has the teacher got that we haven't got?
The answers!

How do you cut the material for a Roman toga?
With a pair of Caesars!

Baker (in shop) – What is the best thing to put in pies?
Fatty – Teeth!

Gent (to policeman directing traffic) – Where shall I get the bus for King's Cross?
Policeman – Right in the back, sir, if you stand there much longer.

What's the cheapest way to see the world?
Buy an atlas!

What do you call a happy can that lives in the United States?
A-merry-can!

Maid (to absent-minded professor) – What are you looking for?
Professor – My hat.
Maid – Why, it's on your head.
Professor – It's a good job you told me or I'd have gone away without it.

Why did the Cyclops have to close his school?
Because he only had one pupil!

Who chews gum and chases spies?
Bubble-oh-seven!

How does a flea get from one place to another?
By itch-hiking!

What do cats read every morning?
Mewspapers!

Why is it hot in a beehive?
Because the bees make it s'warm!

Patient – Doctor, doctor, I'm at death's door!
Doctor – Don't worry, I'll pull you through!

Freddie – My brother has taken up French, Italian, German, Spanish and Greek.
Old man – Goodness! What does he do?
Freddie – He's a lift boy.

Friend (to farming student) – What's the hardest thing to learn about farming?
Student – Getting up at four o'clock in the morning!

Teacher – Robert, I told you to do 1,000 lines on this paper!
Robert – Well, sir, I didn't bother, because there were already a lot of lines on the paper.

Why did the composer stay all day in bed?
He wrote sheet music!

How are dog catchers paid?
By the pound!

Patient – Doctor, doctor, I feel like a dishcloth!
Doctor – Take these tablets, and I'll give you a wring in the morning!

Patient – Doctor, doctor, I keep seeing double!
Doctor – Sit on the couch, please.
Patient – Which one?

Why did the bald man put his head out of the window?
To get some fresh (h)air!

Gent – Goodness, why are you putting that muzzle on your brother?
Jimmy – I'm sending him to get some sweets and I'm taking no risks!

Mother (to small son who is going to party) – Now, dear, what are you going to do when you've had enough to eat?
Small son – Come home.

Teacher – Why weren't you at school this morning?
John – I was coming, sir, but I saw a road-roller, and a policeman said to me, 'Mind that roller' and I stayed and minded it all morning.

First lady – Our Jack slept in a field of cows last night.
Second lady – Wasn't he cold?
First lady – No, it was a field of Jerseys!

What do you call electric bulbs made in Israel?
Israel-lites!

What would you say to a German barber?
Good morning, Herr Dresser!

Sue – What do you call a boomerang that doesn't come back?
Lou – A stick!

John – My grandad was still alive at the age of 102!
Jim – That's nothing! My grandad is still living at 133!
John – What? 133?
Jim – Yes – 133 High Street!

Teacher – In Greek mythology, what was half man and half animal?
Smiffy – Buffalo Bill?

Why did the bee go to the bank?
Because it wanted some 'oney.

Patient – Doctor, doctor, I feel like a tub of butter.
Doctor – Well, spread yourself out on the couch!

Why was the ghost arrested?
Because he hadn't got a haunting licence!

What do scientists' children swim in?
Microwaves!

Hard-up householder – Hey, what are you looking for?
Burglar – Money!
Householder – Wait a minute. I'll put on the light and we'll both look!

Joe (from top of a high tree) – How do I get down?
Bill – Same way as you got up.
Joe – No fear! I came up head first.

Teacher (to latecomer) – Where have you been, Tom?
Tom – I slept late, dreaming I was going to America.
Teacher (to another latecomer) – And where have you been, Sam?
Sam – I was seeing him off, miss.

Joe – I've had my nose broken in three places!
Pete – Oh, really?
Joe – Yes, in London, in Liverpool and in Manchester!

Teacher – Boy, when I was your age I could do problems twice as hard as that.
Fatty – Yes, sir, but perhaps you had a better teacher.

What do you say to a flying dog that thinks it's a vehicle?
"Land Rover!"

Patient – Doctor, doctor, one minute I think I'm a wigwam, the next minute I think I'm a teepee.
Doctor – You're too tense (two tents)!

What tools de we use in arithmetic?
Multipliers!

Sally – You certainly hammer those nails in like lightning!
Paul – You mean I'm fast?
Sally – No, you never strike in the same place twice!

Stranger – Will this road take me to the village?
Farmer – No, sir. You'll have to walk.

Old lady – And what are you in prison for, my good man?
Prisoner – Well, the Government and me had a competition to see who could make the best pound notes, and the Government won.

Singer's mother – What a good singer. His voice really filled the hall.
Critic – Yes, I noticed several people had to leave to make room for it!

Which animal needs oil?
A mouse, because it squeaks!

Teacher – If you had £4 in one pocket, and £3 in the other pocket, what would you have?
Pupil – The wrong trousers!

Barber – Do you want a haircut?
Customer – I want them all cut.

What do you get if you cross a camel with a cow?
Lumpy milk!

What did one lift say to the other lift? "I think I'm going down with something!"

Teacher – Do you like Beethoven's works, William?
William – I've never visited them. What does he make?

What does the Statue of Liberty stand for?
Because it would look funny lying down!

Mean boss – No, I don't need an office boy. I do all the work round here myself.
Applicant for job – Gosh, sir, that would suit me fine.

Patient – Doctor, doctor, skin trouble has given me a broken arm.
Doctor – How could skin trouble give you a broken arm?
Patient – It was a banana skin.

How does a frog cross the English Channel?
By Hoppercraft!

Boy – Dad, what did Tarzan say when he saw five elephants coming over the hill wearing dark sunglasses?
Dad – I don't know. What did Tarzan say?
Boy – Nothing! He didn't recognise them!

What doesn't get any wetter no matter how much it rains?
The xcean!

Teacher – Tony, point to America on the map. (Tony does it). That's right, well done. Now then, children, who found America?
John – Tony, sir!

What do you call an area where ghosts live?
A terrortory!

Diana – Did you hear about the silly girl who goes around saying "no" to everything she hears?
Jane – No.
Diana – Oh, it's you, is it?

What do cannibals have for breakfast?
Beings on toast!

Customer – Waiter, do you have frogs' legs?
Waiter – Of course, sir.
Customer – Then leap over the counter and get me a drink!

Customer – Could I please have an old television set?
Assistant – Why an old one?
Customer – I want to see a programme I missed.

What do you call a plastic king?
A ruler!

Nan – How did you make this cake?
Jan – Here's the recipe. I cut it from a magazine.
Nan – Are you sure you read the right side? The other side tells you how to make a rock garden!

What kind of shoes do frogs wear?
Open-toad!

Mum – Where do you think you're going?
Minnie – To school.
Mum – What with dirt all over your face?
Minnie – No, with Sue from next door!

John – I am going to fail my English exam through illness.
David – Why, what's wrong with you?
John – The boy I copy from is off with the mumps!

CHORTLE!
WHAT HAPPENS IF YOU EAT YEAST AND SHOE POLISH?
EVERY MORNING YOU'LL RISE AND SHINE!
SNIGGER-SNIGGER!
HOW MANY BOOKS CAN YOU PUT IN AN EMPTY SCHOOL BAG?
ONE! AFTER THAT IT'S NOT EMPTY!
HA-HA-HA!
HEE-HEE!
WHAT WASHES UP ON VERY SMALL BEACHES?
MICROWAVES!

Why did the wasp dance on top of the jam jar lid?
Because it said "twist to open"!

Nurse – Can I take your pulse now?
Patient – Why, haven't you got one of your own?

Teacher – Here is a biblical question. What was Noah's profession?
Pupil – Please, sir, he was an arkitect!

Why did the dragon enter the Grand National?
Because he was a hot favourite!

Teacher – And what are you going to be when you leave school?
George – Sixteen, sir!

Who wrote music for feet?
Shoe Burt!

Why did the boy wear his shirt in his bath?
Because the label said wash and wear!

Why do men get paid extra for working on top of Big Ben?
Because they are working overtime!

When do elephants have sixteen feet?
When there are four of them!

Who always goes to bed wearing shoes?
A horse!

Jean – Did you hear about the leek in the Clyde Tunnel?
Betty – No.
Jean – It fell off the back of a vegetable cart!

Willie – What is the best way to prevent infections caused by biting insects?
Millie – Don't bite any insects!

What is the most important part of a horse?
The mane part!

Why is a football park cold?
Because it has so many fans!

Roger – Dad, will you play at zoos with me?
Dad – All right, lad, but how do you play it?
Roger – I'll be a bear and you'll be the kind gentleman who feeds me with buns and sweets.

Bob – I suppose you were relieved when you found that the ghost had stopped following you?
Norman – I'll say! I was so relieved, I slowed down to a sprint.

Girl – What do you get if you cross an Alsatian with a giraffe?
Mum – I don't know.
Girl – A dog who barks at aeroplanes!

Patient – Doctor, doctor, my brother thinks he's an orange.
Doctor – Tell him to come in and see me.
Patient – Oh, that's all right, I've got him here in my pocket!

What's the cure for water on the knee?
Drainpipe trousers!

Billy – What's blue and swings through the trees?
Fred – I don't know!
Billy – Tarzan with the cold!

Teacher – I asked you to draw a horse and cart, John, and you've only drawn the horse. Why?
John – I thought the horse would draw the cart itself, sir.

Uncle – Are you saving 20p pieces?
Nephew – Yes.
Uncle – There's one for you. How many have you got now?
Nephew – One!

What grows up as it grows down?
A baby duckling!

Diner – Waiter, there's a twig in my soup.
Waiter – Wait a moment, sir, while I fetch the branch manager!

What trees do fingers and thumbs grow on?
Palm trees!

Patient – Doctor, doctor, I feel like a pin!
Doctor – I see your point!

Why is a paper boy never cold?
Because selling papers increases circulation!

What do you get if you cross bubble bath with a famous detective?
Sherlock Foams!

Optician – What made you need glasses?
Customer – I strained my eyes reading your book on how to avoid eye strain and strengthen the eyes.

Boxing promoter – How good is this new heavyweight you're training?
Manager – Why, he's so good that when he's shadow-boxing, his own shadow gets scared and runs away.

Diner – This pea soup is full of sugar.
Waiter – It must have been made with sweet peas.

Terry – I've had to ask you five times for that money you owe me.
Jerry – What if you have? I had to ask you eight times before you'd lend it to me.

Billy – How much are those guinea pigs?
Pet shop owner – A pound apiece.
Billy – How much for a whole one?

Doctor (to patient who has just rushed in) – Don't you know my hours are between two and five?
Patient – Yes, but the dog that bit me didn't.

Schoolmaster – Can anyone tell me the name of something that shrinks when it is washed?
Bright pupil – A piece of soap!

Gardener – Is that your ball in my garden?
Sandy – Are there any windows broken, or anything that the lad who owns the ball will have to pay for?
Gardener – No.
Sandy – Well, it's my ball, then!

Doctor – Did you drink that water an hour before breakfast, as I told you to?
Patient – I tried, Doctor, but I couldn't keep it up for more than five minutes.

Mrs Brown (at party) – Have another piece of cake, Fatty.
Fatty – I'm full up!
Mrs Brown – Well, put some in your pockets.
Fatty – They're full up, too, Mrs Brown!

Bald boss (to the office boy) – What untidy hair you have! When I was a boy, I used to brush my hair every morning.
Office boy – And look what you've done. You've swept it all away.

Theatre doorkeeper – You're too late, sir. The show has begun.
Gent – But I can slip in without making a sound.
Doorkeeper – It ain't that, sir. If I open the door, the audience will slip out!

Patient – Doctor, doctor, I keep thinking I'm a packet of biscuits!
Doctor – Are they square ones? Have they got writing on them?
Patient – Yes!
Doctor – You must be crackers!

Why do goldfish always seem so well travelled?
Because they go round and round the globe!

First little girl – I want to marry a Dutchman.
Second little girl – Why?
First little girl – I want to be a Duchess!

Jane – Why do bears have fur coats?
John – I don't know!
Jane – Because they would look stupid in plastic macs!

Kay – Do you know what happened to the lady who turned up her nose at everything?
Fay – No, what happened?
Kay – She sneezed and blew her hat off!

Bore – Below us yawned the chasm.
Listener – Why, were you talking to it?

Bobby – Dad, I've got a pain today.
Dad – Where do you feel it worst?
Bobby – At school!

McTavish – I want to buy a hundred tons of sand.
McDonald – Whatever for?
McTavish – I won a camel in a raffle!

Teacher – Smiffy, what comes after G?
Smiffy – Whizz!
Teacher – Let's try again. What comes after U?
Smiffy – The bogey-man!
Teacher – Last chance. What comes after T?
Smiffy – Supper!

Why did the ball become deaf!
Because of the racket!

Why was the banker bored?
Because he lost interest in everything!

What's a frog's favourite sweet?
A lollihop!

Arab – This palm tree is over 3,000 years old.
Tourist – How do you know?
Arab – It's got a date on it!

Doctor, doctor, I feel like a crystal ball!
Sit down and I'll look into this!

Why are robots never afraid?
Because they have nerves of steel!

I've lost my budgie!
Well, notify the flying squad!

First builder (on tall building) – There's an ambulance and a big crowd down below.
Second builder – That's quick work. It's only five seconds since I dropped my hammer.

Johnny – You know, Dad, you're a very lucky man.
Father – Why?
Johnny – Well, you won't need to buy me any new school books next year because I'm going to be kept in the same class!

First plumber – You remind me of Henry the Eighth!
Second plumber – But he didn't know anything about plumbing.
First plumber – That's why!

Uncle – Do you have much trouble when you are doing your lessons in school?
Harold – Yes, Uncle!
Uncle – What troubles you most?
Harold – The teacher.

Diner – Waiter, is this a lamb or pork chop?
Waiter – Can't you tell by the taste?
Diner – No, I can't.
Waiter – Then what does it matter?

Why is a retired carpenter like a lecturer?
He is an ex-planer.

Black – Every man should sing at his work.
Brown – I can't.
Black – Why?
Brown – I'm a trombone player.

Did you hear the story about the bed?
It hasn't been made up yet!

What did the father ghost say to his son?
Spook when you're spooken to!

Why did the lady put her bed in the fire?
She wanted to sleep like a log!

Newsflash – 1,000 mattresses have been stolen. Police are springing into action!

Patient – Doctor, doctor, I feel like a dustbin!
Doctor – Don't talk rubbish!

Manager (to office boy) – Now, Harry, if you and I were to change places, what would be the first thing you'd do?
Harry – Sack the office boy.

Father – Tommy! This is awful writing!
This 3 looks like a 5.
Tommy – It is a 5.
Father – Then why does it look like a 3?

What sort of mistakes do ghosts make?
Boo-boos!

What is a comedian's favourite motor-bike?
A Yama-ha-ha!

Do robots have any brothers?
No, only tran-sisters!

Why was the apple tree crying?
Because people are always picking on him!

What is the simplest way to increase your bank balance?
Look at it through a magnifying glass!

Reporter (to circus owner) – Whatever happened to the lady you used to saw in half?
Circus owner – Oh, she's now living in London and Cardiff!

Sam – What was your last job?
Bill – I was a bank cashier.
Sam – Why were you fired?
Bill – I took home some samples of my work!

Foreman – What are you doing, Bob?
Bob – Helping Jim.
Foreman – What's Jim doing?
Bob – Nothing.

Smith – Where did James get all his money?
Brown – Oh, he's in the hold-up business.
Smith – What!?
Brown – Yes, he manufactures braces.

Sleepy Sam – Any chance of work in this town?
Passer-by – No!
Sleepy Sam – Good! I'll spend the summer here!

Pete – Why are you carrying all that steel wool around?
Steve – Because my mum's going to knit me a car!

What has a head like a cat, feet like a cat, a tail like a cat, but isn't a cat?
A kitten!

Harry – I swallowed a wishbone yesterday.
Horace – What did you wish?
Harry – I wished I hadn't!

Patient – Doctor, doctor, I feel like a spoon.
Doctor – Well, sit down, and don't stir!

What has six legs and is furry?
An ant wearing a fur coat!

Scot – Are your buildings high?
American – Why, they're so high that once I was told to take a tulip bulb to the top storey and when I got to the top it was in full bloom.

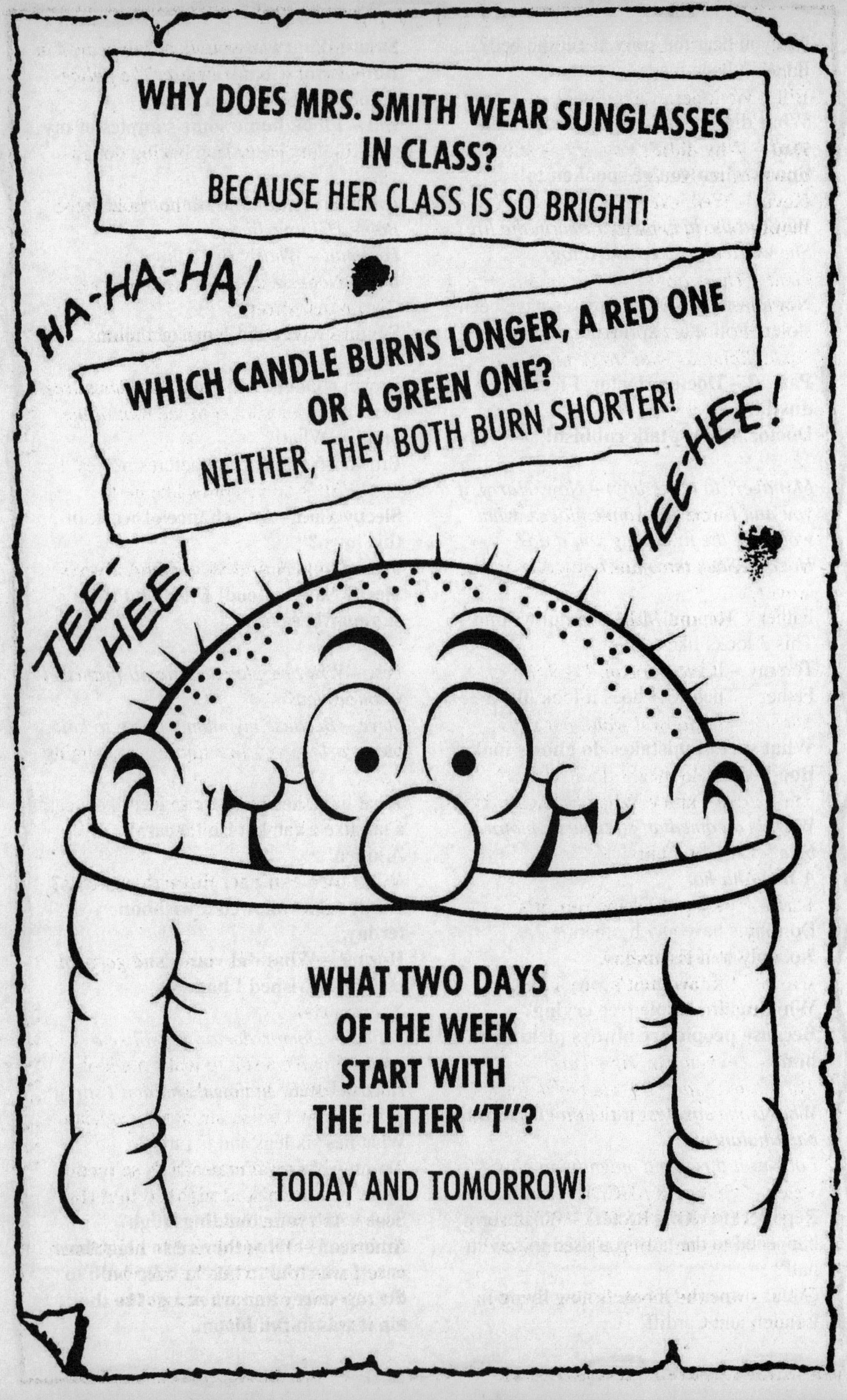
WHY DOES MRS. SMITH WEAR SUNGLASSES IN CLASS?
BECAUSE HER CLASS IS SO BRIGHT!
HA-HA-HA!
WHICH CANDLE BURNS LONGER, A RED ONE OR A GREEN ONE?
NEITHER, THEY BOTH BURN SHORTER!
HEE-HEE!
TEE-HEE!
WHAT TWO DAYS OF THE WEEK START WITH THE LETTER "T"?
TODAY AND TOMORROW!

Jack – I like to read something with a punch in it.
Bill – Well, here's a train ticket.

Dad – Why didn't you cry as you fell downstairs, Kevin?
Kevin – Well, every time I opened my mouth to cry, another step shut it.

Gent – These aren't very good bananas. I can hardly peel them.
Fruiterer – What do you expect for 15p each? Bananas with zip fasteners?

Knock! Knock!
Who's there?
Mr.
Mr Who?
Mr Bus Home. That's why I'm late!

Who are the two smallest ladies in the world?
Molly Cule and Milli Metre!

Patient – Doctor, doctor, I feel like an apple.
Doctor – Sit down, I won't eat you!

Ben – What do raisins do at school?
Jen – I don't know. What do raisins do at school?
Ben – Currant affairs!

Carla – I keep thinking that it's Sunday.
Lisa – But it is Sunday.
Carla – I know, that's why I keep thinking it!

Mike – Do you like tripe, Pat?
Pat – I don't, and I'm glad of it, for if I did I'd be eating it all the time and I hate the rotten stuff.

Peter – What goes ABCDEFGHIJKLMNOPQRSTUVWXYZ slurp?
Kay – Someone eating alphabet soup!

What stops the moon falling down?
Moonbeams.

Newsflash – A large hole has appeared in the fence of a nudist centre. The police are looking into it!

Why did the baker stop baking doughnuts?
Because he was tired of the "hole" business!

Why do white sheep eat more grass than black sheep?
Because there are more of them!

Patient – Doctor, doctor, I feel like a tree!
Doctor – We must get to the root of the matter!

Which fruit do vampires like best?
Neck-tarines!

What is black and yellow and always moans?
A grumble bee!

What is big, purple and near to France?
Grape Britain!

George – Do you like my new swimming pool?
Rose – There's no water in it!
George – I know! I can't swim!

What bird can't get through customs?
An ill-eagle!

What lives under the water and goes dit, dit, da, dit?
A morse cod!

Plug – I'd like a suit to make me look slim, debonair and handsome.
Tailor – I'm a tailor, sir, not a magician.

Jones – I know a man who's so mean he stops his clock at night so that the cogs won't wear out.
Smith – That's nothing. My neighbour is so mean, that when he found a French coin he swam across the Channel to spend it!

Wife – You're always complaining. I wish you would make allowances for my mother's little shortcomings.
Husband – I'm not complaining about her shortcomings, it's her long stayings I object to.

First clerk – Well, and how are you getting on with your requests for a rise?
Second clerk – Not so bad. I'm getting some encouragement now.
First clerk – Really, has the boss said yes?
Second clerk – Not exactly, but today he told me he's said no for the last time.

New shop assistant – Ah, good morning, Mr Right.
Customer – My name's Brown.
Assistant – That's funny. I've just been told the customer's always right.

Ringmaster – What's become of the contortionist?
Clown – Oh, he's doing a stretch in prison.

What language do twins speak in Holland?
Double Dutch!

Customer – Are you sure this fish was fully cooked?
Chip shop manager – Yes, why?
Customer – Because it ate all my chips!

What kind of warmth do sheep like in cold weather?
Central bleating!

Doctor to man – You've broken your arm in three different places.
Man – But that's impossible! I've only been in one place!

Dick – So you're a golfer, eh? What's your favourite course?
Harry – Soup!

Bobby – Are you ready for the fancy dress party?
Tommy – Yes.
Bobby – Why are you wearing two suits?
Tommy – I'm going as twins!

Sammy – Hey, Sandy, where are you going?
Sandy – Can't you see? The dog's taking me for a walk!

Jack – Have you seen a chap with one leg named Johnson about here?
Jim – What was the name of the other leg?

Brown – I say, didn't you say your dog's bark was worse than his bite?
Smith – Yes.
Brown – Then please don't let him bark. He's just bit me.

Maid – You know, ma'am, how you've been trying to get a vase to match that one in the living room?
Lady – Yes.
Maid – Well, madam, I've solved your problem – I've broken it.

Boss – Why are you late for work?
McLaren – When I got up this morning I looked in the mirror and I couldn't see myself, so I thought I'd gone to work. Two hours later I found that the mirror glass had fallen out of the frame.

Diner – Waiter, the tea has a soupy taste.
Waiter – Yes, sir, that's to wash your meal down.

Teacher – Now, Benny, what letter in the alphabet comes before "J"?
Benny – I don't know, sir.
Teacher – Think, boy, think! What have I got on both sides of my nose?
Benny – Freckles.

Guest – Is this a quiet room?
Hotel manager – It's never been known to make a sound, sir!

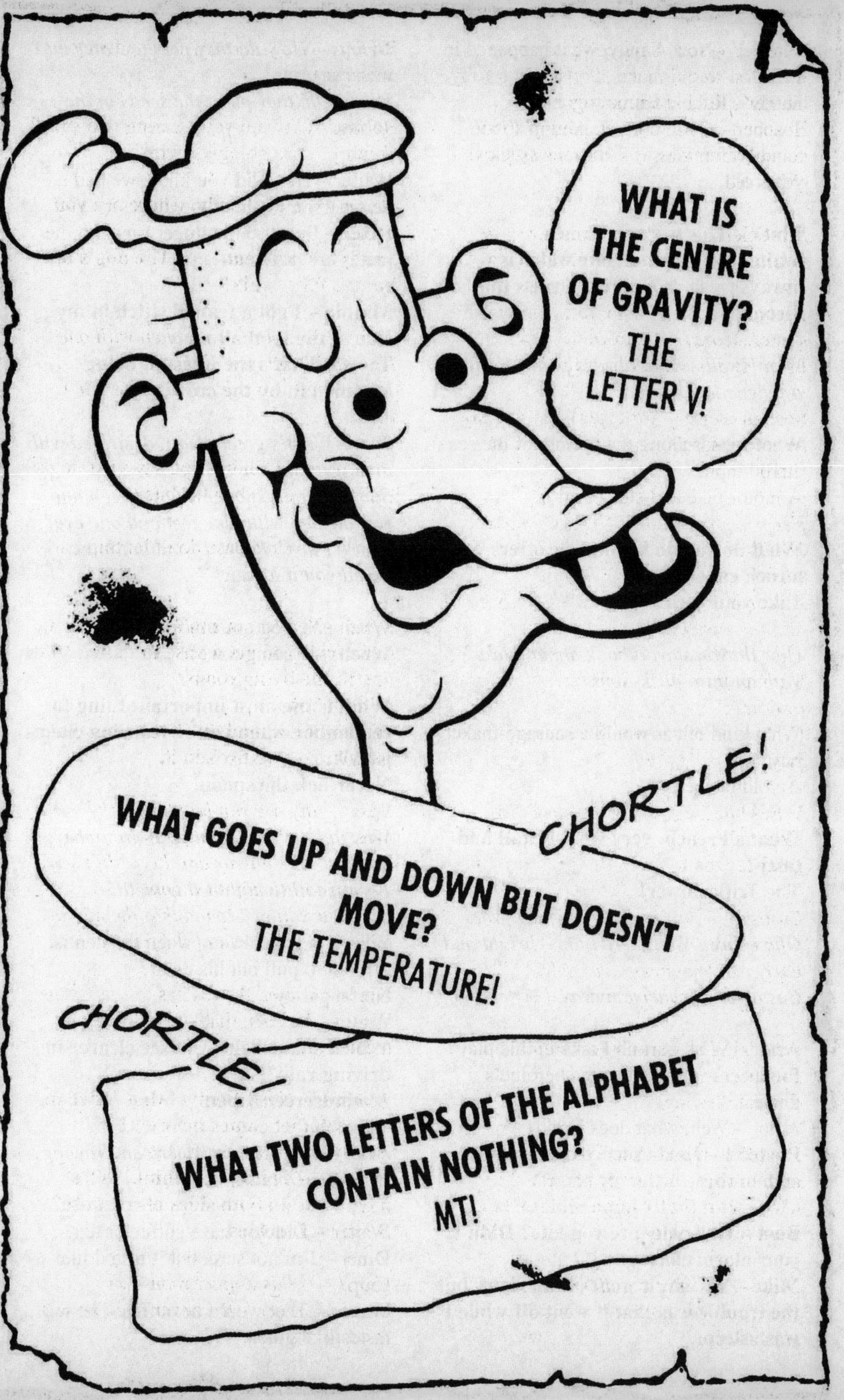
WHAT IS THE CENTRE OF GRAVITY? THE LETTER V!
WHAT GOES UP AND DOWN BUT DOESN'T MOVE? THE TEMPERATURE!
CHORTLE!
CHORTLE!
WHAT TWO LETTERS OF THE ALPHABET CONTAIN NOTHING? MT!

Teacher – Now, Sandy, what happened in 1759?
Sandy – Rabbie Burns was born.
Teacher – Quite correct. And in 1765?
Sandy (after pause) – Burns was six years old.

Diner – This water is cloudy.
Waiter – No, no, sir, our water is always fresh. It's only the glass that's dirty.

What's yellow and always points north?
A magnetic banana.

What speeds along the bottom of the sea at 100 mph?
A motor pike and side carp!

What do you do if someone offers you a rock cake?
Take your pick!

How do you start a book about ducks?
With an intro-duck-tion!

What kind of car would a sausage-maker buy?
An old banger!

What's French, very wobbly, tall and tasty?
The Trifle Tower!

Office boy – Well, here I am – bright and early.
Boss – You're early anyway.

Actor – What part do I take in this play?
Producer – The part of the heroine's uncle.
Actor – Well, what does he do?
Producer – He dies ten years before the curtain rises.

Boss – Well, why are you late? Didn't your alarm clock go off?
Mike – Yes, sir, it went off all right, but the trouble was that it went off while I was asleep.

Dennis – How do they get the water into water melons?
Dad – Oh, they plant the seeds in the spring.

Waiter – How did you know we had a new person washing the dishes?
Diner – Because the fingerprints on the plates are different.

Minnie – I got a fearful stitch in my side at the football match.
Toots – That's the worst of being hemmed in by the crowd.

Tam – What's green and red, striped with nine feet and one eye?
Sam – I don't know. What is green and red, striped with nine feet and one eye?
Tam – I don't know. I wouldn't have asked you if I knew!

When is a frog not a frog?
When it is being towed!

What is the most important thing to remember when you're learning chemistry?
Never lick the spoon!

Why did the orange have to go to the doctor?
Because it wasn't peeling well!

What did Dracula say when the dentist offered to pull out his teeth?
No fangs!

Which snake helps you see clearer in driving rain?
A windscreen viper.

What do you call an American drawing?
A Yankee Doodle!

Waiter – Did you have coffee or tea?
Diner – I'm not sure, but it tasted like soup.
Waiter – That would be coffee. The tea tastes like glue.

WHY IS IT DANGEROUS TO PUT THE LETTER "M" INTO THE REFRIGERATOR?
BECAUSE IT CHANGES ICE INTO MICE!
CHORTLE! CHORTLE!
WHAT STARTS WITH A T, ENDS WITH A T, AND IS FULL OF T?
A TEAPOT!
TEE-HEE!

What's the height of stupidity?
Measure yourself and find out!

Brown – Have you spoken to your little boy about imitating me?
Jones – Yes, I told him not to act like a fool!

Mad scientist – With my new invention, train accidents will be impossible.
Assistant – How's that?
Mad scientist – Well, instead of moving the trains I move the stations.

Tourist – Why don't you buy a bicycle?
Farmer – I'd rather buy a cow.
Tourist – You'd look funny riding a cow.
Farmer – Not half as funny as I'd look trying to milk a bicycle.

Second – What did you think of his right?
Boxer – I was very much struck by it.

Millionaire – I didn't always have a limousine. When I started life I had to walk.
Young man – You were lucky! When I started life I couldn't even crawl.

Where do bees wait for transport?
At a buzz stop!

Where do fish wash?
In a river basin.

What's the best way to count cows?
On a cow-culator.

What does the American Indian ghost live in?
A creepy teepee!

What happens when you sleep under the car?
You wake up oily in the morning!

Publisher – Your story is quite well written, but this firm only publishes work by writers with well-known names.
Writer – Splendid! My name's Smith.

What is a Laplander?
A clumsy man on a bus!

Doctor – You should take a bath before you retire.
Patient – But, doctor, I don't expect to retire for another twenty years.

Judge – Describe what passed between you and the prison officer during your quarrel.
Prisoner – The plates were regular dinner size, your honour, and the teapot had a broken spout.

First angler – What's the bone for?
Second angler – I'm fishing for dog fish stupid!

Waiter in a new French restaurant – We are famous for our snails!
Bored diner – Yes, I know. I've been served by one already.

Why was Adam known as a good runner?
Because he was first in the human race!

Boy – Ouch! A crab just bit my toe.
Mother – Which one?
Boy – I don't know, all crabs look alike to me!

What's a monster's favourite soup?
Scream of tomato!

What is blue and yellow and has a wing span of 14 metres?
A 21/2 ton budgie!

What's the definition of a milk shake?
A nervous cow!

First snail – I'm exhausted.
Second snail – Yes, me too. We seem to have been walking for centimetres.

Little boy to golfer – You're lucky!
Golfer – Why?
Little boy – I just managed to stop your ball before it went down that little hole!

Why did the jester wear diamonds and rubies?
He thought they were the clown jewels!

Toots – Smiffy really is stupid!
Plug – What makes you say that?
Toots – He broke a washing-machine trying to wash the steps!

What would you see at a chicken show?
Hentertainment!

Why are people tired on 1st April?
Because they have just been on a 31-day March!

Worried brother – Doctor, doctor, my sister feels like a lift!
Doctor – Well, tell her to come in!
Worried brother – I can't. She doesn't stop at this floor!

What is the odd one out between a fork, a knife and a potato?
The fork is the odd one out. You can make chips with the other two.

Doctor – Your throat is in a bad way. Have you ever tried gargling with salt water?
Old sailor – Yes, I've been shipwrecked six times.

Doctor – You're looking a lot better.
Patient – Yes, I followed the instructions on the bottle you gave me.
Doctor – Let me see, what were they?
Patient – "Keep tightly corked."

Proud new father (holding his baby son) – He's the living image of me!
Mother-in-law – Why worry, so long as he's strong and healthy?

Grandson – Why do you have three pairs of specs, Grandpa?
Grandpa – One pair is for reading, one pair is for long distance and the third pair is for when I'm looking for the other two!

Helen – Mum, do you know what I'm going to give you for your birthday?
Mum – No, dear, what?
Helen – A nice tea pot.
Mum – But I've got a nice tea pot.
Helen – No you haven't. I've just dropped it!

PE teacher – I made twenty boys run, yet I didn't even have to ask them.
Maths teacher – How did you manage it?
PE teacher – Er . . . well, I ran and they ran after me!

Plug – If two's company and three's a crowd, what's four and five?
Smiffy – Nine.

What did the ivy plant say to the holly bush?
Stop being so spikeful!

What's the difference between an Indian elephant and an African elephant?
About 3,000 miles!

A man walked into a shop and stole a packet of salt and a packet of batteries. The police caught him and charged him for a salt and battery!

Jim – There's one thing I can never do without putting my foot in it.
Joe – What's that?
Jim – Put on my shoe.

Patient – Doctor, can you help me? My name is Bertha Higginbottom.
Doctor – I'm sorry, I can't do anything about that.

Office boy – Can I go to lunch now, sir?
Boss – Lunch? What do you want lunch for? You've been licking stamps all morning!

Mrs Green – Did you scold your little girl for mimicking me?
Mrs Brown – Yes, I told her not to act like a fool!

Shopkeeper – What made that customer walk out of the shop in such a temper?
Assistant – I don't know. He asked me for a hat to suit his head and I said, "Try this soft one!"

Kevin – Mum, may I go out to play with Bobby Brown?
Mum – No, you know I don't like Bobby.
Kevin – Then may I go out and fight with him?

Dentist (to patient) – Remember how you used to wallop me when we were at school, Bob . . . ?

What do you get when you cross a cockerel with a poodle?
A cock-a-poodle-doo!

Did you hear about the man who bought a sleeping bag?
He spent two months trying to wake it up!

What's as big as an elephant but weighs nothing?
It's shadow!

What do you call a deer with no eyes?
No-eye-deer!

Policeman – Stop! You were doing fifty miles an hour!
Speeding driver – Nonsense, I haven't been out for an hour yet!

How does a Zombie speak?
In a grave voice of corpse!

What do snakes do after a fight?
Hiss and make up!

What did the father ghost tell his son?
Spook only when you are spooken to.

What lives under the sea and carries a lot of people around?
An octobus!

What do you get if you cross the Atlantic with the Titantic?
Halfway!

Landlord – If you won't pay your rent, I want your room!
Tenant – Aw, you wouldn't like to live here!

Boarder – Look here, I haven't got a decent towel, sponge or piece of soap!
Landlady – Well, you have a tongue, haven't you?
Boarder – Yes, but I'm not a cat!

Customer – Well, what happens now that your opening sale has closed?
Shopkeeper – Our closing sale opens!

What do pixies eat at parties?
Fairy cakes!

What do young elves do after school?
Gnome work!

What has to be done by Friday?
Robinson Crusoe's washing!

What did the man say when he broke into the glue factory?
This is a stick-up!

Why are your hands shaking?
I suppose they must be glad to see each other!

Smiffy – What does the x-ray of my head show?
Doctor – Nothing.

What's yellow and holds up stage-coaches?
Dick Turnip!

Minnie – Dad, why are you going bald?
Dad – I am not bald! I just have a very tall forehead.

What goes cluck, cluck, click?
A hen in a seat-belt!

Weary diner – Are you the waiter who took my order?
Waiter – Yes, sir.
Diner – My, how you've grown!

Lady – How much are these chickens?
Butcher – Three pounds.
Lady – Did you raise them yourself?
Butcher – Yes, they were two pounds yesterday.

Dave – Why are you looking so puzzled?
Dan – Someone's stolen my car.
Dave – That's no reason to look puzzled.
Dan – Yes, it is. I wonder how he got it started.

Artist – I have been working like a horse all morning.
Farmer – What have you been doing?
Artist – Drawing a cart.

Customer – I'd like to see a really reliable second-hand car.
Salesman – So would I, sir!

Fred – Do insects cry, Sam?
Sam – Haven't you ever seen a moth bawl?

Peter – Are the people next door poor?
Mike – I don't think so.
Peter – Then why did they make a big fuss when their baby swallowed a penny?

What do you get if you cross a motorway with a wheelbarrow?
Knocked down!

What did the baby ghost say when he wanted his favourite food?
I scream!

Fatty – I feel as fit as a fiddle!
Plug – You look more like a bass drum to me!

Hiker – What a splendid sunset!
Villager – Yes, not bad for a little place like this, is it?

Johnson – I do spring cleaning in all seasons of the year.
Jackson – How's that?
Johnson – I'm a clock maker.

Jim – Look at these big oranges, John.
John – Yes, I'm sure you wouldn't get many of them for a dozen!

Aunt – Tommy, when will you come round to tea again?
Tommy (hungrily) – Now, if you like.

Tom – My father's got the softest job in town.
Bill – What is it?
Tom – He's a tester in the feather bed factory.

The miser's wife had a birthday coming up so he asked her what she wanted.
"Something with lots of diamonds in it," came the reply.
He bought her a pack of cards!

Ringmaster – I will give five pounds to anyone who steps in the lion's cage.
Man – I'll do it, under one condition.
Ringmaster – Very well, what is your condition?
Man – You take the lions out first.

Girl – Did you hear about the telephone that fell in the river?
Boy – No, tell me.
Girl – It came out wringing!

How do you get a baby to sleep in space?
You rocket!

Do you need training to be a litter collector?
No, you just pick it up as you go along.

Mr Jackson – Are you using your mower this afternoon?
Mr Smith – Yes.
Mr Jackson – Fine. Then I can borrow your tennis racket as you won't be needing it!

First ghost – I see "The Phantom Killer" is on the telly tonight.
Second ghost – Yes, I saw it last week, and it nearly frightened the life into me!

Waiter – Did you say you wanted your eggs turned over, sir?
Diner – Yes, to the Museum of Natural History!

Chauffeur – Shall I pump up the tyres, sir?
Lord Toff – Wait until we get out into the country. My doctor tells me the air there is very good.

Caller – Who's the responsible man here?
Office boy – If you mean the chap who always gets the blame, it's me.

Librarian – I suppose you read Shakespeare?
Trainee librarian – Oh, yes, sir, I read all of his stuff, just as soon as it's published!

Teacher – Did your father punish you when you went home last night?
Tommy – Yes, sir.
Teacher – How did he do it?
Tommy – He made me stay in and help him with my homework.

Tom – I was so hungry, that the moment I got home, I began eating the tables.
Tim – Do you expect me to believe that?
Tom – Yes- they were vegetables!

Passenger (to captain of sinking ship) – How far are we from land?
Captain – About 200 metres.
Passenger – In which direction?
Captain – Straight down!

Which King of England was a milkman? Alfred the Crate!

Why did the boy take sugar and milk to the cinema?
Because they were showing a serial!

Adult ghost – What are you going to do when you're grown up?
Young ghost – I like the seaside, so I'm going to join as a ghost guard.

Owner – I'm very proud of my horse. He only lost one race the whole of last season.
Friend – My word, that's good! How many times was he entered?
Owner – Once.

Corporal – Hey! You're not paying the slightest attention. What is your head for?
Recruit – To prevent my collar slipping off?

Friend – Aren't you afraid sometimes when you look down at the road?
Steeplejack – Yes, I once felt sure that a man I saw was going to be run over.

American – I come from the greatest country in the world.
Scotsman – Oh, aye – I see you've lost your Scottish accent, then.

First boy – My father's got an upright piano.
Boy next door – And my father say it's a downright nuisance.

Fatty – Is dinner ready yet?
Mother – No, it'll be an hour yet.
Fatty – Huh! My tummy must be fast!

Policeman – It would be best if you could provide an alibi. Did anyone see you at the time of the crime?
Criminal – Fortunately, no!

Man – Could I have a dog for my son, please?
Pet shop owner – I'm sorry, sir. We don't do swops!

Teacher – Andy, I hope I didn't see you copying from Nicola's work.
Andy – I hope you didn't either!

Olive (the dinner lady) – Why is Cuthbert crying?
Fatty – He's crying because I'm eating my cake and I won't give him any.
Olive – Is his own cake all gone?
Fatty – Yes, and he cried all the time I was eating that as well!

Where do astronauts leave their space-ships?
On parking meteors!

Dad – Did your watch stop when it fell on the floor?
Roger – Of course, did you expect it to go right through?

Colonel – How is the new recruit getting on, sergeant?
Sergeant – Terrible, sir. I've taught him all I know and he still knows nothing.

Boarder – What's for breakfast? I hope it isn't bacon and eggs again.
Landlady – No, sir, not bacon and eggs again.
Boarder – Thank goodness. What is it?
Landlady – Bacon.

First hiker – Only six miles to home.
Second hiker – Good! That's three miles each!

Manager – Have you ever been on Government work?
Applicant – Nearly.
Manager – What do you mean?
Applicant – They hadn't enough evidence.

Mountain guide – Have you ever seen such a great sight as that volcano?
American tourist – Oh, your volcano's all right, but we've got a waterfall that could put it out in five minutes!

How do you know that carrots are good for your eyes?
Because you never see a rabbit with glasses!

Handyman – I would like a job as a handyman.
Employer – Can you mend a fuse, paint, do joinery work?
Handyman – No, I can't.
Employer – What's so handy about you, then?
Handyman – I live right next door!

Sue – Why is your dog wearing green wellingtons?
Jamie – Because his red ones are being repaired.

A cabbage, a tap and a tomato had a race.
The cabbage was head, the tap was running and the tomato tried to ketchup!

Patient – Doctor, doctor, I feel like a book.
Doctor – Well, sit down and tell me the story.

Cricketer – There's not much grass on this pitch, is there?
Umpire – Well, you haven't come here to graze, have you?

Did you hear about the plant in the maths class?
It grew square roots!

Why can't you depend on a parachute?
Because it always lets you down.

What do animals read in zoos?
Gnus-papers!

What do you call a Dutchman who gets "A"s in all of his exams?
Clever clogs.

What do you get if you cross a footballer with a smoked fish?
A goal-kipper.

Why did the girl keep her violin in the freezer?
Because she wanted to play it cool!

Teacher – Why did you kick Julie?
Jane – Because she failed her exams!
Teacher – That's no reason to kick her!
Jane – Yes, it is. I was copying her!

Gamekeeper – Oi! There's no fishing allowed here!
Johnny – I'm not fishing, I'm just washing my pet maggot!

Why did the farmer feed his cow on money?
To get rich milk!

Knock! Knock!
Who's there?
Cook
Cook who?
Oh, that's the first one I've heard this year.

What happened to the couple who met in a revolving door?
They're still going round together!

There was a man who sat up all night wondering where the sun had gone to. Next morning, it dawned on him!

Why did the witches call off the cricket match?
They couldn't find the bats.

Why don't bananas worry when people say bad things about them?
Bananas are noted for their thick skins!

Why don't centipedes play football?
The game's over by the time they get their boots on!

If you have ducks in cricket, birdies in golf, what do you have in bowls?
Soup!

Grant – What's yellow and good at sums?
Bruce – A plate of custard with a calculator in it!

Boss – What we prize most in this office is neatness.
New boy – Shall I straighten your tie, sir?

Playwright – In the third act there is an earthquake.
Manager – Ah, well, that should bring the house down.

Jim – Did you hear the thunder last night?
John – Eh? Why didn't you waken me? You know I can't sleep during a thunderstorm!

Diner – Waiter, what is your name?
Waiter – John Smith, but everyone calls me "billiard cue".
Diner – Why?
Waiter – Because I work much better with a tip.

First angler – Caught anything yet?
Second angler – Not yet. I don't think the silly worm is trying!

Teacher – What is your name, boy?
Boy – Tom, miss.
Teacher – Tom, is short for Thomas. In this class I want you to call everyone by their proper names. For example, what is Jack's proper name?
Boy – Er . . . Jackass?

Jones – I caught a pickpocket in the act of stealing my watch.
Smith – What did you say?
Jones – I told him I'd no time to spare.

Mrs Smith – Can I borrow your record player this weekend?
Neighbour – Having a party?
Mrs Smith – No, we just want some sleep.

Molly – Why is that squirrel tied to the back of your car?
Mandy – To gather up the nuts, of course!

Why does that man always shut his eyes when he sings?
Because he hates to see us suffer!

Clueless car owner – Have you got my car started?
Mechanic – No, sir, your battery's flat.
Clueless car owner – What shape should it be?

Mother owl – I'm worried about our son.
Father owl – Oh, why's that?
Mother owl – He just doesn't seem to give a hoot about anything.

What begins with T, ends with T and has T in it?
A teapot!

Teacher – When they take out an appendix, it's called an appendectomy; when they remove your tonsils, it's a tonsillectomy. What is it when they remove a growth from your head?
Danny – A haircut!

What is copper nitrate?
Police overtime.

Diner – Do you charge extra for bread in this restaurant?
Waiter – No, sir.
Diner – Then bring me a loaf.

Why can't you fool a snake?
Because he hasn't a leg to pull!

Timid clerk – Please, sir, my wife said I was to ask you for a rise.
Boss – Very well. I'll ask my wife if it's all right.

Mean father – What did I give you for your birthday last year?
Son – A balloon.
Father – Right, I'll blow it up for you this year!

Why did the teabag go into hospital?
Because he was under a strain!

First angler – How are the fish today?
Second angler – Dunno! I dropped a line but they haven't answered yet.

What is bigger when it is upside down?
The number 6.

Why is an elephant large, grey and wrinkled?
Because if he was small, round and white, he would be an aspirin!

Doctor – You need more exercise. You should try walking.
Patient – But, doctor, I'm a postman!

Accused (in court for speeding) – But, Judge, it's simply my nature to do everything fast!
Judge – Right! Let's see how quickly you can do thirty days!

Waiter – What did you think of the cottage pie?
Diner – Let's just say I could almost taste the thatched roof.

Boss – You've been with the firm for sixty years, but you'll have to leave.
Bob – Huh! If I'd known it wasn't to be a steady job I'd never have joined!

Office boy – The boss is beginning to take notice of me.
Clerk – How's that?
Office boy – This morning he asked me if I worked here.

Teacher – Aha! So I've caught you eating sweets, have I?
Tam – No, sir. They're so sticky that I keep them in my mouth instead of my pocket!

Why do witches fly on broomsticks?
Because a vacuum cleaner is too heavy!

First mum – What's your son going to be when he passes all his exams?
Second mum – A pensioner!

Boastful farmer – I can reap, plough and mow. Can anyone tell me something I can't do on a farm?
Friend – Can you lay an egg?

Tim – Think of those Spaniards going 2000 miles on a galleon.
Jack – Forget it! You can't believe all you hear about those foreign cars.

Waitress – But, sir, you asked me to bring you weak tea!
Diner – Weak, yes, but this stuff is help-less!

Angus – I've had to sell my Dachshund.
Geordie – Why?
Angus – It took him so long to get in and out of the door that we froze every winter.

Bill – You would believe anything a fool told you.
George – Not always, but you are most convincing!

Mum – I don't like the boy next door, so I want you to keep away from him as much as possible at school.
David – Oh, that's easy. He's usually at the top of the class.

Teacher – And what are you going to be if you can only count up to ten?
Jim – A boxing referee, miss!

Detective – Can you give me a description of your missing teller?
Bank manager – He's about five feet eight inches tall and £70,000 short.

Teacher – When was the Magna Carta signed, Toots?
Toots – At a quarter past twelve.
Teacher – At a quarter past twelve?
Toots – Yes, 12.15!

What are private detectives called in fairyland?
Sherlock Gnomes.

Billy – Mum, I came top in arithmetic today. Teacher asked what 5 x 12 was and I said 58.
Mum – But that's not right. 5 x 12 is 60.
Billy – I know, but I was closer than anyone else!

What happened to the schoolboy who did his homework with sticky hands?
He got stuck in the middle of a sum!

Why did Father Christmas get himself a garden?
So he could Ho, Ho, Ho!

Brown – Smith is an old miser.
Grant – Why?
Brown – He jumps over his gate to save wear and tear on the hinges!

Big Bill – Why are you so small?
Small Sam – I was raised on shortbread and condensed milk!

Prison governor – Any complaints?
Prisoner – Yes, there aren't enough exits!

Bore – And then the burglar threatened to blow my brains out!
Listener – And did he?

Dad – Did you get my boots soled?
Son – Yes! I got 20p for them!

Constable – You are accused of stealing a motorcar!
Prisoner – Well, search me!

Who invented spaghetti?
An Italian man who used his noodle!

What happened to the ship that crossed the Pacific with 25 tons of yo-yos on board?
It sank 42 times!

If horses wear horseshoes, what do camels wear?
Sandshoes

Tom – One of my ancestors fell at Waterloo.
Jim – Really!
Tom – Yes, he fell off platform five!

Why did the boy take his bicycle to bed?
He was too lazy to sleepwalk.

What did the mother worm say to her baby when he was late for breakfast?
"Where in earth have you been?"

What game do horses like best?
Stable tennis!

Football manager – I've found the very man for us: eyes like a hawk, strong as an ox, speed of a racehorse and a kick like a mule.
Director – It's a forward we want, not a farmyard!

Dud golfer – I suppose you get a good many weekenders on this course, caddie?
Caddie – Yes, also a few weak beginners.

Teacher – How many sexes are there?
Smiffy – Three.
Teacher -What are they?
Smiffy – The male sex, the female sex, and the insects.

Jim – What rent do you pay?
Bill – I don't pay it.
Jim – What would it be if you did pay it?
Bill – A miracle.

Boy – Are you offering ten pounds for finding your dog?
Lady – Yes. Have you found him?
Boy – No, but I'm going out to look, and I wondered if you'd like to advance me some of the money?

Old man – When do you go back to school, Tommy?
Tommy – When Dad finds out I'm playing truant.

Fat man – I've travelled all over the world and there's nothing I haven't seen in the past few years.
Voice from audience – What about your own feet?

Driver in racing car (to companion) – We are doing ninety miles an hour. Are you game for another ten?
Companion (swallowing another mouthful of dust) – Yes, I'm full of grit.

Teacher – Your essay is very good, Plug, but it is word for word the same as Cuthbert's. What shall I conclude from that?
Plug – That Cuthbert's is very good, too?

Eric – Can you tell me the weakest part of a steam engine?
Alec – That's easy. The tender!

Teacher – What is Australia bounded by, Peter?
Peter – Kangaroos, miss.

Suspicious PC – Hey, didn't I hear a window smash?
Dennis – Oh, no, sir. It was me breaking the glass of my watch.

Bus diver – You ought to be driving a pram.
Lorry driver – And you ought to be in it.

First prisoner – What are you in for?
Second prisoner – I just picked up a rope I found on the road.
First prisoner – What? Is that all?
Second prisoner -Well, there happened to be a cow on the end of it.

Bruiser – Hullo, Bill, you look annoyed. What's the matter?
Burglar – Matter! Do you see this bill in the police window? They're only offering a hundred pounds for my arrest, and it used to be two hundred pounds.
Disgusting, that's what it is.

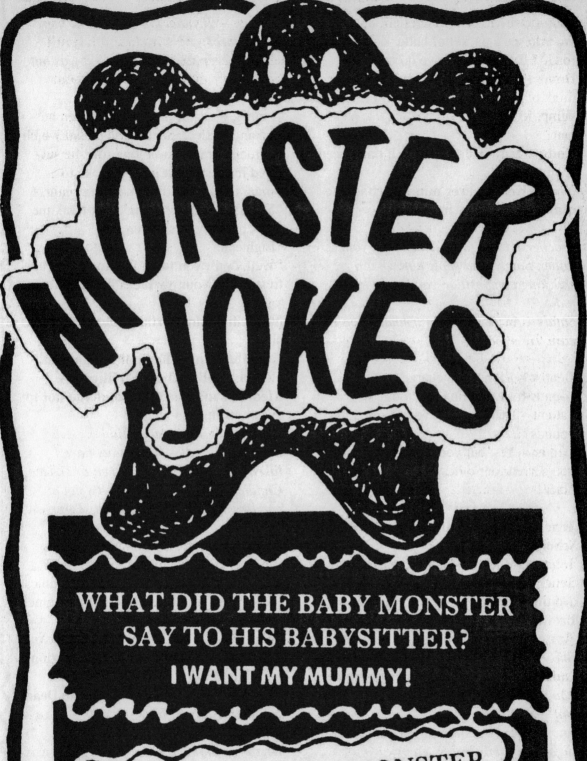

MONSTER JOKES

WHAT DID THE BABY MONSTER
SAY TO HIS BABYSITTER?

I WANT MY MUMMY!

WHY DID THE SEA MONSTER
EAT 5 SHIPS THAT WERE
CARRYING POTATOES?

NOBODY CAN EAT JUST ONE
POTATO SHIP!

Lady (to driver of steam roller) – Driver, did you see a packet of butter down the road? I think I must have dropped it.
Driver (scratching his head) – Come to think of it, miss, I did feel a bit of a bump.

Dodgy Dan – He called me a barefaced scoundrel.
Crafty Ken – Never mind, perhaps he didn't notice your moustache.

Teacher – I am going to send for your father, Sandy, and show him what a shocking composition you handed in today.
Sandy – All right, send for him. I don't care. He wrote it.

Dentist – I'll have to charge you fifty pounds for extracting that tooth.
Patient – But I thought you charged ten pounds?
Dentist – Yes, but you yelled so loudly you scared four other patients out of the place!

Teacher – Johnny, take your cap off in school.
Johnny – I haven't got my cap on, sir.
Teacher – Yes, you have.
Johnny – No, I haven't. This is my brother's.

Shopkeeper – Aren't you the boy who came last week and asked me to employ you?
Boy – Yes, sir.
Shopkeeper -But didn't I tell you I wanted an older boy?
Boy – Yes, sir, but I'm older now.

First golfer – Oh I meant to tell you where that bunker was.
Second golfer – It's quite all right, thanks. I found it for myself.

Sandy -Troubled with toothache, Jock?
Jock – You don't suppose I'm pleased with it, do you?

Farmer – Why did you not tell me there was a hare?
Pat – I never saw the hare till it was out of sight!

A quiet, patient little man had been hustled and jostled about in the crowd which boarded a train. For a long time he suffered in silence. At last he spoke to a young fellow standing in front of him.
"Young man, I hope you don't think me rude, but may I ask your age?"
"Eighteen."
"Well, don't you think you're old enough to stand on your own feet?"

Medicine man – What's the matter, sire?
Cannibal king – I've got indigestion. I've just polished off a millionaire.
Medicine man – Well, I told you not to eat anything too rich.

Beginner at golf – How many have I taken to that hole? Is it fifteen or sixteen?
Caddie – Oh, I don't know. It's not a caddie you need, it's a cricket scorer.

Globetrotter – Yes, while we were in Egypt visiting the pyramids we found them literally covered with hieroglyphics.
Lady – Oh, and weren't you afraid some of them would bite you?

Know-all – I can answer any question you like to ask.
Bored friend – Well what did the Dead Sea die of?

Bertie – I took the piece of cake that was in the cupboard to give to a poor boy.
Mother – Oh, that was very good of you. And did he thank you for it?
Bertie – Well, I waited for a long time and no poor boy came, so I ate it myself.

Guide – Look at that half-ruined castle. It might be at least eight hundred years old. Believe me, folks, they don't build such ancient castles nowadays.

Doctor – Have you been anywhere else?

Patient – I went to the chemist first.

Doctor – And what idiotic advice did he give you?

Patient – He told me to come and see you.

Teacher – Now, boys, it's quite common to speak of two things together. For instance, health and happiness, gold and silver. Tommy, give me another example.

Tommy – Liver and onions, miss.

First thief – You know that lantern I pinched?

Second thief – Yes.

First thief – Well, some dirty thief's been and gone and stole it.

Doctor – What's wrong with you?

Smiffy – Oh, I've got a splinter in my finger.

Doctor – You should have more sense than scratch your head.

Minnie – Where are you going?

Dennis – Nowhere.

Minnie – Wait a minute. I'll come, too.

Voice from the river – Help! Help! I've fallen in and cannot swim!

Voice from the bank – Now's your chance to learn, mister.

Father – Don't ask so many questions, child. Curiosity killed the cat.

Little boy – What did the cat want to know, Dad?

Smith (to man who is standing in front of him at football match) – Do you know how to play draughts?

Man – Yes.

Smith – Well, it's your move.

Housekeeper – There's no bread in the house, sir. What shall I do?

Absent-minded professor – Oh, don't bother about that. Just make some toast.

Servant – Sire, there is a messenger without.

King – Without what, fool?

Servant – Without the gate.

King – Then give it to him.

A cyclist was travelling along a lonely road on a dark night and came to a very tall signpost. The sign was so tall and the night was so dark that he could not make out what the sign said. With difficulty he struggled to the top and read "Wet Paint"!

Teacher (setting problem) – A train leaves Perth travelling at thirty miles an hour. Half an hour later another train leaves the same station, travelling at fifty miles an hour. Where will the second train run into the first?

Curly – At the back, miss.

Ship's engineer (to new assistant) – Say, I thought you said you knew something about engines?

Assistant – So I do, sir, but on a smaller scale.

Ship's engineer – What's your regular job?

Assistant – Watchmaker, sir.

Old lady (visiting prison) – Have you any plans for when you leave prison?

Prisoner – Yes, lady. A bank, two mansions, three jeweller shops, and a post office.

Counsel – How far from the door were you?

Witness – Four yards, two feet, three and a half inches.

Counsel – How can you be so sure?

Witness – Because I expected some fool would ask me, and so I measured it.

Moe – When the tourist arrived home he fell on his face and kissed the pavement of his native city.

Joe – Emotion?

Moe – No. Banana skin.

Freddie – Do you know what keeps the moon in place, Charlie?
Charlie – I think it must be the beams.

Mother – Your face is fairly clean, Wilfrid, but how did you get your hands so dirty.
Wilfrid – Washing my face, mother!

Customer (looking at socks) – Aren't they rather loud?
Shop assistant – Yes, sir. They are specially made for people whose feet are in the habit of going to sleep.

Policeman – You say you were held up by a robber with a revolver this morning. At what time?
Shop assistant – Five minutes to one.
Policeman – How can you fix the time so precisely?
Shop assistant – Because I could see the church clock, and I noticed the hands were in the same position as mine.

First footballer – I once took a penalty kick and broke the net.
Second footballer – That's nothing. Once I hit the crossbar with a penalty kick. The next day walking round the ground I noticed the bar was still shaking.

Diner -Waiter, this chicken has no wishbone.
Waiter – He was a happy and contented chicken, sir, and had nothing to wish for.

Conceited Colin is so used to getting his own way that he writes up his diary for a week ahead.

Thug – Can't you help a poor, lonely man who hasn't got anything in the world except his loaded revolver?

Angry producer – What do you mean by smiling in that death scene?
Actor – With the salary you pay, death seems a pleasant relief.

Passenger (on board ocean liner) – Doesn't the ship tip frightfully?
Dignified steward – The vessel, madam, is trying to set a good example to the passengers.

"Mind that step," said the young policeman to the very old offender as he led the way to the cells.
The hardened thug growled. "I knew that there step afore you was born."

Robbie – What does "knows no bounds" mean, Dad? Explain it.
Dad (buried in newspaper) – Kangaroo with rheumatism.

Land owner – Don't you see this notice, "No Fishing Allowed in these Grounds"?
Angler – But I'm not fishing in the grounds. I'm fishing in the river!

Lodger – This steak is like a cold day in June, Mrs Bordem – very rare.
Landlady – And your board bill is like March weather – always unsettled.

Sergeant – Now, then! Line up alphabetically. What's your name, my lad?
Private – Philips, sergeant.
Sergeant – Well, what are you doing up here? Get amongst the "F"s at once.

Private – The tallest chap in our company is six feet nine inches.
Corporal – That's nothing. In our barracks we have a sergeant who has to kneel when he wants to scratch his head.

Lady – Are you sure this salmon in fresh?
Salesman – Fresh! Why, madam, I've just had to cut him up to keep him from jumping at the flies!

Moe – I don't like that fellow Brown.
Joe – Why not?
Moe – He is the sort of man who pats you on the back to your face, and smacks you in the eye behind your back!

Businessman – I am a self-made man, sir. I began life as a barefoot boy.
Shop assistant – Well, I wasn't born with shoes on either.

Footballer – I'm sorry, but you'll have to clear out.
Angler – Indeed I won't. I've permission to fish in this river.
Footballer – River? This is our football pitch!

Notice outside football ground – There are two kinds of kick-offs. One is seen, the other is felt. To see one and avoid the other, please pay at the gate.

Lady – Are you sure these field glasses are powerful?
Salesman – Powerful? Why, when you use these glasses, anything less than ten miles away looks as if it's behind you!

Sailor (shouting) – Man overboard!
Seasick passenger (with a groan) – Lucky dog!

Teacher – What is a cannibal?
Sandy – I don't know, miss.
Teacher – If you ate your father and mother what would you be?
Sandy – An orphan.

Teacher – Now if I subtract 29 from 87, what's the difference?
Smiffy – That's what I say. Who cares?

Diner (to waiter) – The man who killed this chicken must have had a very kind heart.
Waiter -What makes you think that, sir?
Diner – He must have hesitated six or seven years before doing it!

Mother (to music teacher) – Do you think my son will be able to do anything with his voice?
Teacher – Well, it might come in handy in the event of a fire!

Teacher – What is a volcano?
Danny – A mountain that keeps on interrupting.

Witness (entering box) – Good gracious! They've caught a pretty tough bunch, I must say!
Policeman – Those aren't the prisoners, sir. You're looking at the jury!

Manager of restaurant (haughtily) – I'm very sorry you don't like our cakes, sir, but I can assure you this business has been built up almost entirely on our cookery!
Diner – Yes, and with a few more buns like these you could build a fortress!

Teacher – How many bones have you in your body, Tommy?
Tommy – Thousands of them. We had kippers for breakfast.

Clerk – If the boss doesn't take back what he said, I'm leaving.
Office boy – What did he say?
Clerk – "You're sacked."

Old-fashioned lady (at concert) – Is that a popular song that man is singing?
Nephew – It was before he sang it.

Terry – Do you ever hear of the money you lent your neighbour?
Jerry – I should think I do! He bought a CD player with it.

Teacher – Why, when I was your age I could repeat the names of kings and Queens of England backwards and forwards.
Pupil – Yes, but when you were my age there weren't so many kings and queens.

Mother – Your teacher complains that you're always late for school. Why is that?
Tommy – It's not my fault, mother. They always ring the bell before I get there.

Tim – I've fallen into the bad habit of talking to myself lately.
Bob – I wondered why you were looking so bored.

Motorist – Robert is going mad over his new car.
Friend – Strange, the last time I saw him he was going mad underneath it.

Contractor – Does the foreman know that the trench has fallen in?
Labourer – Well, sir, we're digging him out to tell him.

Small boy (to fallen man) – You big bully. Look what you've done to Tommy's banana.

Contortionist – Too bad about the lion-tamer, isn't it?
Sword-swallower – What happened to him?
Contortionist – He's got such a swelled head through being praised so much that he can't get it into the lion's mouth.

Motorist (telephoning after he has had an accident) – Send assistance at once, I've turned turtle.
Voice from the other end of telephone – This is a garage, not a pet shop.

Visitor to circus – What's wrong?
Dejected circus hand – The elephant's dead.
Visitor – Were you very fond of it?
Circus hand – Well, yes . . . but, you see, I've been given the job of digging its grave.

Reporter – To what do you attribute your long life?
Oldest inhabitant of village – Well, you see, I was born long ago.

Foreman (to workman entwined in rope) – What do you think you're doing, snake charming?

Judge – After you saw the prisoner put his fist through the window, did you observe anything?
PC Sapp – Yes, I observed a hole in the glass.

Village shopkeeper – Well, that's three hot-water bottles, a dozen lemons, a jar of honey, a packet of paracetamol, a large bottle of cough medicine and three boxes of tissues. I'll send them right away. All well at home, sir?

Workman – Can you give me a job, mate?
Foreman – I've got a man here today who hasn't come, and if he doesn't turn up tomorrow I'll send him away and take you on.

Golf instructor – Swing the club, man. Swing it! Don't chop at the ball as if you were a butcher.
Beginner – Why, that's just what I am.

New resident – This village boasts a choral society, doesn't it?
Old resident – Well, we don't boast about it; we put up with it.

Boss – You're an idiot! Why my last office boy was worth twice as much as you.
Office boy – I bet he didn't get it.

Visitor – I don't know how you can work here. Your office is as hot as an oven.
Boss – Well, I make my daily bread here, you know.

Customer (buying a dog) – Is this dog fond of children?
Assistant – Oh, yes, but I would advise you to give him biscuits, they're better for his digestion.

Diner -Waiter, what kind of meat is this?
Waiter – It's spring lamb, sir.
Diner – Ah, then it must have been a spring that I've been chewing this last half-hour.

WHAT DOES A GHOST DO WHEN HE GETS IN A CAR?
PUTS HIS SHEET BELT ON!

WHAT DO SEA MONSTERS EAT FOR LUNCH?
POTATO SHIPS!

WHAT DID ONE GHOST SAY TO THE OTHER?
DON'T SPOOK UNTIL YOU'RE SPOOKEN TO!

WHO DID THE MONSTER TAKE TO THE HALLOWEEN DANCE?
HIS GHOUL FRIEND!

WHAT DO YOU CALL A 10 FOOT TALL MONSTER?
SHORTY!

Old man – You're rather a young chap to be left in charge of a chemist's shop. Have you a diploma?
Assistant – Why . . . er . . . no, sir; but we have a preparation of our own that's just as good.

Judge – What passed between you?
Defendant – One turnip, seven rocks, and a lump of mud.

Gardener – What are you tying those onions down for?
Assistant – Well, they're spring onions, aren't they?

Teacher – Now, boys what do we get out of the earth besides coal and iron?
Pupil (after a long pause) – Please, sir, worms.

Magistrate (discharging prisoner) – Now, then, I would advise you to keep away from bad company.
Prisoner – Thank you, sir. You won't see me here again.

First scout – Are there any matches left?
Second scout – Yes, there's one.
First scout – Only one? What if it doesn't light?
Second scout – No fear, it won't do that. I've tried it already.

Professor (lecturing on the rhinoceros) – I must beg you to give me your undivided attention. It's absolutely impossible that you can form a true idea of this hideous animal unless you keep your eyes fixed on me.

Football captain – If we win you'll be richer by fifty quid.
Referee – And if you lose?
Captain – You leave on a stretcher.

Artist – I hope you don't mind if I sketch in your field?
Farmer – Oh, no. You'll help keep the birds off the peas.

Moe – What's the matter?
Joe – I've just lost a hundred pounds.
Moe – Oh cheer up, and take things as they come.
Joe – That's far easier than parting with things as they go.

First workman – That chap's really lazy. He's been sitting doing nothing for two hours.
Second workman – How do you know?
First workman -I've been sitting here watching him.

Terry – That's a bad cold you've got. You'll have to take care of it.
Jerry – Take care of it! Gracious, I want to lose it.

Peter – I say, Dad, when I had toothache you took me to the dentist to have my tooth filled.
Dad – Yes, what about it?
Pete – Well, I've got a stomach ache. What about going into that tuckshop?

Diner – I believe it is improper to speak disrespectfully of one's elders.
Waiter – Yes, sir, it is.
Diner – Well, then I shan't say anything about this chicken.

Boss (to boy applying for job) – This reference from your last employer seems pretty black.
Boy – Yes, sir. You see, he licked his pencil before writing it.

Boss – On the way to the bank you'll pass the football ground.
Office boy (expectantly) – Yes, sir?
Boss – Well, pass it.

Waiter – Tea or coffee, sir?
Diner – Don't tell me. Let me try to guess for myself.

Teacher – How is sawdust produced?
Pupil – Why . . . er-
Teacher – Come, come, use your head!

WHAT IS DRACULA'S FAVOURITE FRUIT?
NECKTARINES!

WHY DIDN'T DRACULA HAVE MANY FRIENDS?
HE WAS A PAIN IN THE NECK!

WHAT DID THE VAMPIRE SAY WHEN HE WAS DONE BITING SOMEONE?
ITS BEEN NICE GNAWING YOU!

WHAT IS A VAMPIRE'S FAVOURITE TYPE OF BOAT?
BLOOD VESSELS!

WHAT IS DRACULA'S FAVOURITE PLACE IN NEW YORK?
THE VAMPIRE STATE BUILDING!

Inspector – So this is the bloke who stole the barrow-load of turnips. Did you get the turnips?
Constable – No, sir.
Inspector – Well, search him!

Teacher – Why can't you repeat your history lesson, Sandy? Didn't you learn it?
Sandy – No, sir. You see, I thought history always repeated itself.

Diner (holding up fork with meat on it) – Do you call this pork, this stuff on the end of my fork?
Waiter – Which end, sir?

First golfer – That ass Green crossed my tee when I was driving.
Second golfer -Well, if he crossed your tee you should have dotted his eye.

Tourist – Is it healthy in this part of the country?
Local – Sure it is, guv'nor. Why, we had to shoot people to start a cemetery.

Officer – Right face!
New recruit – What?
Officer – Right face, I said.
New Recruit – Yes, this is my right face.

Clerk (making excuse) – But, sir, man isn't a machine. He can't go on forever.
Boss – Yes, he can. You're going forever at the end of this week.

Recruit – What's the password tonight?
Sentry – Metempsychosis.
Recruit – Thanks; but I think I'll stay in camp tonight.

Photographer (to foreman) – Can I take a photograph of your men at work?
Foreman – Yes, if you get a chance.

Castaway (as he sees a passing ship) – Just my luck. It would be going in the direction I don't want to go.

Visitor (at museum) -Where are those Oliver Cromwell relics that were here last week?
Attendant – I don't know, sir. I fancy they must have been returned to Mr Cromwell.

Young Bob was thrilled by a succession of wonders on his first train journey. The train rushed into a tunnel, then came out into the open.
"Gosh!" said young Bob. "It's tomorrow!"

Teacher – Today the school breaks up for the holidays. What could be more glorious than spending the following week's holiday in the country?
Pupil – Spending the following two weeks in the country, sir!

First footballer – Why do you call your manager "sulphur"?
Second footballer – Because he flares up at the end of every match!

Boarder (on arriving at lodgings to find them burnt down) – Oh, Mrs Cater, did you save anything that belonged to me?
Landlady – Yes, sir, your bill. Here it is.

Merchant (to salesman) – What's wrong with your nose? Somebody hit it?
Salesman – No. You said I wasn't to show it in here again, so I've tied it up!

Farmer – Let me tell you, my friend, that that horse knows as much as I do.
Friend – Well, don't tell anybody else; you might want to sell him some day.

Burglar Bill – My opinion is that you can't get too much of anything.
Housebreaking Horace – What about "time"?

Mr Jones – You've made a rotten job of painting this fence.
Handyman – Well, you said it wanted painting badly.

Stranger (as gun fires from castle) – What's that noise?
Local inhabitant – Why, don't you know? It's sunset.
Stranger – Well, I've been in a lot of towns, but this is the only one where the sun went down with a bang like that!

Mr Screecher (about to sing) – What's your favourite air?
Friend (making for door) – Fresh, and plenty of it!

Doctor – What's the matter this time?
Patient – I've got pains in my back, sir.
Doctor (handing him a bottle) – Take a dose of this a quarter of an hour before you feel the pains coming on.

Customer – I've brought back those shoes. I've changed my mind, and I don't like them.
Shopkeeper – Sorry, I can't take them back. You'll just have to change your mind again.

Actor – I must insist on real food in this banquet scene.
Manager – Yes, and I think you should have real poison in the death scene.

Dad – The last time I gave you £2 you said you wouldn't walk into the nearest shop and spend it.
Danny – Yes, Dad.
Dad – But I saw you do it.
Danny – Don't you know the difference between a walk and a sprint, Dad?

Boss (to office boy who is late, as usual) – Don't you know what time we start?
Office boy – No, sir. You're always started when I come in.

Visitor – Does Mr Murphy live here?
Neighbour – He used to, but he's dead.
Visitor – How long has he been dead?
Neighbour – Well, if he had lived till tomorrow, he'd have been dead a fortnight.

Judge – You still say you're innocent, though six witnesses saw you steal the hen?
Prisoner – Your Honour, I could produce six thousand people who didn't see me.

Diner – I want some meat without bone, gristle or fat.
Waiter – How would an egg do, madam?

Small boy (to pal pursued by bull) – Run round in circles, Sandy, and make him giddy.

Pickpocket (visiting pal in jail) – I hired a lawyer for you this morning, Slim, but I had to leave my watch with him as part payment.
Pal – And did he keep it?
Pickpocket – He thinks he did.

Pupil (at boxing class) – I want my money back. It says on the notice outside, "Boxing taught first floor," and I've been floored half a dozen times, and I don't know any more about it than I did when I first started.

Terry – I see they have stopped running the 7 a.m. train. Do you miss it?
Jerry – Not so often as I used to.

Nervous speaker (before large audience) – Ladies and g-gentlemen, when I c-c-came here tonight, only t-two people knew my speech: my father and myself. N-now only F-f-father knows it!

Mother (at table) – Will you have some bread, Tommy?
Tommy – No, I don't want bread.
Mother – Where are your manners, Tommy? No what?
Tommy – No fear. Not when there's cake on the table.

McTavish – I always do my hardest work before breakfast.
McHaggart – What's that?
McTavish – Getting up.

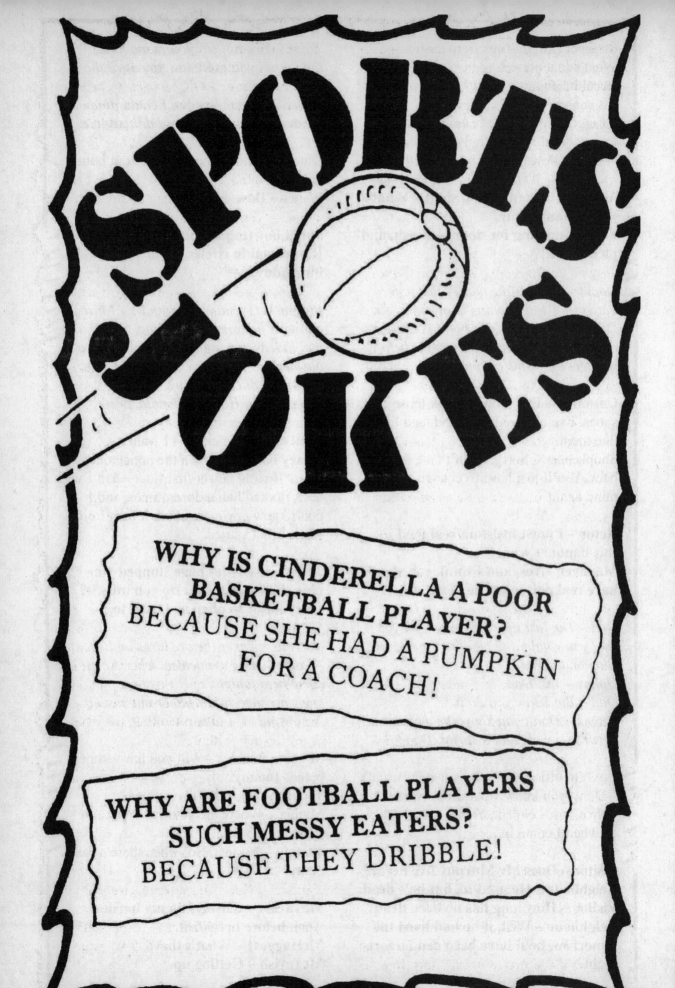

SPORTS JOKES

WHY IS CINDERELLA A POOR
BASKETBALL PLAYER?
BECAUSE SHE HAD A PUMPKIN
FOR A COACH!

WHY ARE FOOTBALL PLAYERS
SUCH MESSY EATERS?
BECAUSE THEY DRIBBLE!

Diner – Quick, give me two eggs and six pieces of toast before the big fight starts.
Waiter (after diner has finished eating) – And where is the big fight, sir?
Diner – Right here! I haven't any money!

Judge – Prisoner, the jury finds you did not steal the watch. You may go.
Prisoner – And can I keep the watch, your worship?

Terry – Nothing is impossible.
Jerry – Try lighting a match on a bar of soap.

Youthful football captain – Bit of luck getting Bill Bashem to play for us.
Youthful club secretary – Yes, but it cost us £3-worth of toffees, and that's the biggest transfer fee we've paid yet.

Visitor to the Wild West – Does Mr Jones live here?
Rancher – No.
Visitor – But he said he lived within gunshot of you.
Rancher – That's why he ain't here.

Billy – How big is your roller-skating rink?
Bobby – It seats two thousand people.

Terry – It's hard to beat!
Jerry – What is?
Terry – A drum with a hole in it.

Danny – Is a zebra a white animal with black stripes or a black animal with white stripes?

Old lady (seeing boy carrying bale of hay on his head) – My goodness! That lad's needing a haircut!

Farmer (to yokel up tree) – Come down, George. Don't you see that tree's going to be cut down?
George – Yes, I know it is; but the last time a tree was cut down it fell on top of me, so I'm going to be safe this time!

First farmer – What became of the new man you got from the city?
Second farmer – Oh, he used to be a chauffeur and one day he crawled under a mule to see why it wouldn't go.

Teacher – Danny, don't you know it's bad for little boys to fight?
Danny – Yes, but I'm teaching Cuthbert; he doesn't know.

Domestic tips: The best way to deal with a stain on a tablecloth is to cover it with a plate before anyone spots it.

Sergeant (at camp) – Hey, come away from there; you can't go into the general's tent.
Private Jones – But it says "Private" over the door.

Plug – What are you doing up there on that horse?
Smiffy – Well, teacher told us to write an essay on a horse and that's what I'm doing.

Butcher – Did the roast I sold you do for the whole family?
Customer – Very nearly. The doctor's still calling!

Hatter – Would you like a straw hat or a felt one, sir?
Old farmer – I'll have a straw one; it might be a mouthful for the cow when I'm finished with it.

Butler (outside study door) – Please, sir, here's a letter for you.
Professor – All right. Just slip it under the door.
Butler – Please, sir, I can't. it's on a tray.

Second – What! You want to give up? Why, you're not half licked yet.
Battered boxer – Well, if the other half is like what I've already had, I don't want it.

Danny – Does ppnneeuummoonniiaa spells double pneumonia?

Father (to son picking himself up at bottom of stairs) – Did you miss a step?
Son -Well, I missed one, but I hit all the rest.

Prison warder – Ain't you asleep yet?
Burglar – No, it seems so funny to be lying in bed in the middle of the night.

Father – What are you grumbling about?
Tommy – Well, me and Sandy Brown were arguing about our favourite football teams, and teacher made us write them out 100 times after school.
Father – Well, that's fair enough.
Tommy – But his is Ayr, and mine is Inverness Caledonian Thistle!

Doctor – Well, you are certainly looking much better than I expected to find you.
Patient – I think that is because I followed the directions on your medicine bottle.
Doctor – Very likely. What were they?
Patient (grimly) – Keep the bottle tightly corked!

Small boy – Daddy, what do you call a man who drives a car?
Father – It all depends on how close he comes to me.

Reporter – Good morning, Mrs Brown. Is that prize-fighter husband of yours in?
Boxer's wife – He's in, but not up. Since he's been a boxer, he never gets up before the stroke of ten.

What would a football team be without a goalie?
A man short, of course.

Optician – Can you read the chart?
Jimmy – Yes, I can read it, but I'm wondering how to pronounce the word!

Teddy (at boat race, pointing to cox) – That man at the back of that boat doesn't seem to be doing much.
Eddy – Perhaps he's a stowaway.

Native – These tiger tracks lead north.
Nervous explorer -Then we go south?

Pupil – Please, sir, did you ever hear a rabbit bark?
Teacher – Rabbits do not bark.
Pupil – But my natural history book says that rabbits eat cabbage and bark.

Town boy (at country farm for first time) – What are the hens making such a noise for?
Farmer – I expect they want something to eat.
Town boy – Well, if they're hungry, they should lay themselves some eggs!

Mike – Get up, Sandy, the ship's on fire!
Sandy (dreamily) – That's all right, Mike; it's on water too.

First farmer – Did the gale damage your barn?
Second farmer – I don't know. I haven't found it yet.

Auntie – Would you like some bread and butter, Willie?
Willie – No.
Auntie – No what?
Willie – You shouldn't say "what" auntie; you should say "I beg your pardon".

Johnny – I wish father hadn't invented that new soap of his.
Mother – Why?
Johnny – Well, every time a customer comes in, I'm washed as a sample.

Old lady – Why has the ship stopped?
Sailor – Can't get along for the fog.
Old lady – But can't you go by the stars?
Sailor – We ain't going that way unless the boiler bursts.

Sidney – Dad, there's a black cat in the kitchen.

Father – That's good. Black cats are lucky.

Sidney – This one is . . . it's eating the fish you were going to have for dinner.

Officer – Kit all complete?
Private – Yes, sir.
Officer – Buttons on everything?
Private – No, sir.
Officer – What's without buttons?
Private – My socks sir.

Angry pedestrian (who has been knocked down by man carrying grandfather clock) – Why don't you wear a wristwatch?

Teacher – Read the first sentence, Harry.
Harry – See that horse runnin'.
Teacher – Don't forget the "g" Harry.
Harry – Gee! See that horse runnin'.

Seasick passenger – How far are we from land?
Captain – About a mile.
Passenger – Thank goodness! Which direction is it?
Captain – Straight down!

Butler – You should be proud to be in the service of such a famous General.
Page boy – General? Huh, I thought he was a gangster.

Customer – Hey! You're giving me a piece of bone.
Butcher – Oh, no, I'm not, you're paying for it!

Mother – A little bird told me that you've been stealing biscuits out of the pantry.
Johnny (under his breath) – I'll wring that blinking parrot's neck.

PC Dobbs – You'll have to accompany me, my man.
Street musician – Splendid! What'll you sing?

New lodger – And what's the food like here?
Old lodger – Oh, we get chicken every morning.
New lodger -That's great. Roasted?
Old lodger – No, in its shell!

Lady – Oh, so you've been in touch with royalty, have you?
Boy – Yes, lady. I was once stung by a queen bee!

Jimmy – If I had been offered the plate first I would have taken the smallest apple.
Tommy – Well, you've got it! What are you grumbling about?

Motorist (in court) – My speed was nothing like fifty miles an hour, sir, nor forty, nor thirty-
Magistrate – Careful now, young man, or you'll be backing into something!

Lord Posh – How did you puncture the tyre so badly?
Chauffeur – Ran over a bottle, sir.
Lord Posh – Didn't you see it in time?
Chauffeur – No, sir. You see, the man had it in his pocket.

Hostess – And where is your brother?
Bobby – Only one of us could come, so we tossed for it.
Hostess – And you won?
Bobby – No, I lost!

Tim – I say, old chap, will you be using your fishing line this afternoon?
Henry (who is rather mean) – Er . . . y-yes, I think so.
Tim – Righto! Then you can lend me your football boots.

City chap (pointing to haystack) – What kind of a house is that?
Country chap – That's not a house, that's hay.
City chap – Go on, you can't fool me. Hay doesn't grow in a lump like that.

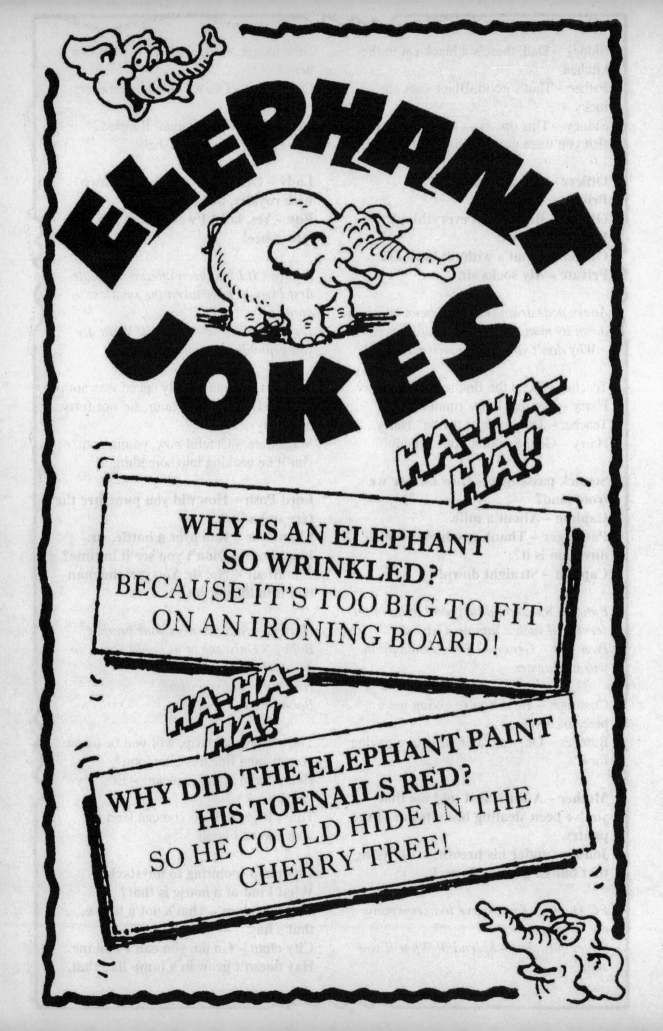

Scout – Father, I shall have to lie down.
Father – Why, are you ill?
Scout – No; I have done so many good turns that I feel giddy.

Bill (holding up two fingers) – My old uncle can't use these two fingers.
Jack – That's strange. Why can't he?
Bill – Because they're mine.

Teacher (without looking up) – Tommy, did you do your homework?
(Tommy shakes his head, but teacher does not see him.)
Teacher – Answer me!
Tommy – Please sir, I shook my head.
Teacher – Well, I can't hear it rattle from here, can I?

Visitor – And what is your new little brother's name?
Sandy – He can't speak yet, so he hasn't told us.

Very fat golfer – When I stand where I can see the ball I can't reach it, and when I stand where I can reach it I can't see it.

Dad – When I was young, I thought nothing of walking thirty miles.
Jimmy – Well, I don't think much of it myself.

Sandy – Is it right, mother, that you shouldn't put off till tomorrow what you can do today?
Mother – Yes. Why?
Sandy – Well, I was thinking I'd better finish up that cake in the cupboard.

Mrs Jinks – Now, then Johnny, what's Teddy up to?
Johnny – Up to the ears, Mrs Jinks. He's just fallen into the river.

Old man (to little boy) – Are you lost, sonny?
Little boy – No, but my mother and father are.

Airman (to only passenger, after doing a daring dive) – I bet half of the people down there thought we were going to crash.
Passenger – And I bet half up here did, too!

Producer – Now, I want you to walk across that narrow log.
Film star – But supposing it breaks?
Producer – Gee, that's an idea.

First traveller – London is the foggiest place in the world.
Second traveller – Oh, no, it's not. I've been in a place much foggier than London.
First traveller – Where was that?
Second traveller – I don't know where it was, it was so foggy.

Art teacher – Suppose you were in the National Gallery when it caught fire, which three pictures would you save?
Phil – Please, sir, the three nearest the door.

Dr Dobbs – Did you take my advice and sleep with all the windows open?
Patient – I did, doctor.
Doctor – Good! And I suppose you have pretty well lost that cold you had?
Patient – No, doctor. Only my best suit and my watch and chain.

Teacher – Well, Billy, what is the difference between mouse and mice?
Billy (after thinking hard) – Well, one mice is a mouse, and a lot of mouses are mice.

Tom – Can I go and play with Jim Brown?
Mum – He isn't a nice boy to play with.
Tom – Then can I go and fight with him?

Officer – What call would you blow if the barracks were on fire?
Bugler – The cease fire, sir!

Mother – Harry, who broke this window?
Harry – Joe! He ducked when I threw a stone at him.

Diner – Is it customary to tip the waiter in this restaurant?
Waiter – Why, yes, sir.
Diner – Then hand me the tip. I've waited three-quarters of an hour for the steak I ordered.

Diner – This is a very small portion of ice cream.
Waiter – Well, do you expect to be able to ski on it for two pounds?

Lady Posh – Are you the plumber?
Plumber – Yes, madam.
Lady Posh – Well, be very careful while you are doing your work. All my floors are highly polished.
Plumber – Oh, don't worry, about me madam, I won't slip. I've got nails in my boots.

Tim – Snakes are wise creatures.
Tom – Why?
Tim – Ever heard of a snake getting its leg pulled?

Shopkeeper – Has anyone given any orders while I've been away?
Assistant – Yes, sir. A man came and ordered me to put up my hands while he emptied the till.

Teacher – Now, Sandy, can you tell me why swans have long necks?
Sandy – To keep them from drowning at high tide, miss!

Tom – There's one thing, Jack, that everyone shuts his eyes to.
Jack – What's that, Tom?
Tom – Soap.

Lady – Do you know that jam I bought was full of twigs?
Shopkeeper – I know. It said on the jar, "Branches Everywhere".

Bob – You know that old vase you said had been handed down from generation to generation?
Mother – Yes.
Bob -Well, this generation has dropped it!

A large crowd had gathered round an overturned car.
"Hello, Bill!" came the voice of a new arrival. "Car turned turtle?"
"Oh, no, old chap," said Bill sarcastically. "These kids wanted to see how the car worked, so I turned it over for them."

Traveller (to old villager) – Have you lived in this village all your life?
Old villager – Oh, no, not yet.

Infuriated motorist (in car up to the mudguards in water after being informed by a local that it was not deep) – Idiot! You said this wasn't very deep!
Local – I can't understand it, mister; the water only comes halfway up our ducks!

Mother – Every time you are naughty I get another grey hair.
Bobby – You must have been a terror. Look at grandpa!

Diner – Waiter, my bill comes to thirteen pounds, and you have made it fourteen.
Waiter – Sorry, sir, but I heard you tell your friend you were superstitious.

Father – An apple a day keeps the doctor away.
Sandy – Well, I must have kept eleven doctors away from the Hallowe'en party, but there's a feeling in my tummy that tells me one will be coming soon.

Joiner – Have you measured the length of that piece of wood?
Apprentice – Yes, it was the length of my foot and two thumbs over with this piece of brick, the length of my arm from here to there, bar two fingers!

Diner – Have you any wild duck?
Waiter – No, sir, but we can get a tame one and irritate it for you!

Sandy – Gosh! I've cut down the tree and here's Dad coming. Now, what am I going to climb up to get out of his reach?

Teacher – I heard that you stayed off school yesterday to play at football.
Tommy – That's not true, and I've got a string of fish to prove it!

Charlie -What's the time, old chap? I've an invitation to a party at six, and my watch isn't going.
Sammy – Why? Wasn't your watch invited, too?

Lady – You naughty boy. You should give and take.
Boy – Well, lady, I gave him a black eye and took his sweets.

Professor – Give me the names of the bones that form the human skull.
Student – I've got them all in my head, but I can't remember them.

First workman – Where's Joe gone for his dinner?
Second workman – Having it in his steam roller. He says with so many car thieves about he's not taking any chances.

Soldier (indicating his heart) – I was shot round about here.
Old lady visitor – Oh no, that's impossible; you would have been killed outright.
Soldier – But my heart was in my mouth at the time!

Explorer – The lion was nearly on me. I could feel its breath on my neck. What do you think I did?
Bored listener – Turned up your coat collar?

Jock – If you can guess how many nuts I have in my hand, I'll give you them.
Jack – Don't be silly. How can you give me your hands?

First traveller (watching train steam out of station) – If you hadn't wasted so much time at home we shouldn't have missed the train.
Second traveller – Yes, and if you hadn't made me run so quickly, we shouldn't have had so long to wait for the next one.

Jones – I don't need a speedometer on my car. I can easily tell the speed.
Brown – How do you do it?
Jones – When I go twenty miles an hour my headlights rattle, at thirty miles an hour my mudguards rattle, and at forty miles an hour my teeth rattle!

Prison visitor – Don't any of your relatives come to see you, my poor man?
Prisoner – They don't have to; they're all in here.

The speaker was getting tired of being interrupted.
"We seem to have a great many fools here tonight," he said. "Wouldn't it be advisable to hear one at a time?"
"Yes," said a voice. "Get on with your speech."

Toots – What's that bump on your forehead?
Smiffy – Oh, that's where a thought struck me!

Airman (explaining crash) – I just happened to get into an air pocket.
Sympathetic old lady – Oh dear, and I suppose there was a hole in it?

Asylum doctor – This room is for motor maniacs.
Visitor – I don't see any.
Asylum doctor – They are all under their beds making repairs.

Landowner (angrily) – What's the idea of fishing in my pond?
Angler – That's what I'm beginning to wonder. I can't get a bite.

George (to his pal, Bill, who is about to fight a man three times his size) – Don't get windy, Bill. Keep on saying you will beat him.
Bill (gloomily) – That's no good, George; you know what a liar I am.

"My teacher has never seen a horse, Dad," said Bobby.
"Oh, and what makes you think that?" said his father.
"Well, I did a drawing of a horse at school today and my teacher asked me what it was."

General – A brave soldier is always found where the bullets are thickest. Where would you be, Smith?
Smith – In the ammunition waggon, sir.

Doctor – I'm afraid your stomach is out of order. You must diet.
Patient – What colour?

Absent-minded professor – I believe my wallet has been stolen.
Wife – Didn't you feel a hand in your pocket?
Absent-minded Professor – Yes, but I thought it was my own.

Baker – I want a lad who is not afraid of early hours.
Boy – That's me, sir. I don't mind how early you close.

McTavish – Hey, that cold remedy you sold me turned out to be a laxative.
Chemist – Gosh! I ought to have charged you another pound.

Old lady (regarding perspiring football player) – You seem hot, my good man. Why don't you use one of those football fans I've heard so much about?

Friend – What did the editor think of your drawings?
Artist – When he looked at them he clapped his hands.
Friend – Splendid!
Artist – Er . . . over his eyes!

Doctor – Well, and how are your broken ribs this morning?
Patient – Quite well, but I've had a stitch in my side all day.
Doctor – Excellent! That shows that the bones are knitting.

Policeman – You can't go down that street. It's one-way traffic along there.
Motorist – Well, I'm not going two ways, am I?

Tourist – That church clock is all wrong.
Old inhabitant – Well, you see, when the little hand points to five and the big hand points to nine, and it strikes six, all the folks in these parts know it's two o'clock!

Ticket collector – Tickets, please!
Old man (first time on train) – No fear. You go and buy one for yourself like I had to.

Patient – How can I cure myself of sleep-walking?
Doctor – Sprinkle tacks on the floor!

Teacher – What was Lord Nelson famous for?
Toots – His memory.
Teacher – What makes you think that?
Toots – Why, they erected a monument to it!

Resident – The young student upstairs has a lot of correspondence, postman. You always have something for him.
Postman – Yes. I quarrelled with him once, and ever since he has sent himself a postcard every day because I have to climb five flights of stairs to deliver it.

A teacher set his class to write a composition of one hundred words.
One boy wrote:
"My uncle went for a trip in his car. After a few miles it broke down, and he had to walk home. The other eighty words are what he said on the way home."

Passenger – This train is very slow, guard.
Guard – Yes, madam, it's those sleeping carriages behind.

Judge – Have you any concrete evidence to show that you were attacked?
Prisoner – No, your worship. I was hit by a brick.

Motorist – Constable, my car has been stolen.
Constable – You're lucky! I was going to summon you for parking here without permission.

Wife (to absent-minded professor) – Have you seen this? There's a report in the paper about your death.
Professor – Is that so? We must send a wreath.

Busker – I say, sir, you've given me a fake pound coin.
Gent – Keep it for your honesty.

Tenant (paying bill) – Well, I'm square now.
Landlord – Yes, sir and I hope you'll soon be round again.

First neighbour – Do you know that your hens are always coming into my garden?
Second neighbour – Yes.
First neighbour – How did you know?
Second neighbour – Because they never come back!

Schoolmaster – What can a canary do that I can't do?
Scholar – Take a bath in a saucer.

Sidney (who has been trying to get to the chocolate biscuit tin hidden on the top shelf of the larder, deliberately out of his reach) – It's no use, Tom, mother's hidden it too well.
Tommy – Well, then, all we can do now is to wait until mother comes home and ask her for something for being good boys.

Golfer – Where's the caddie I went round with yesterday, boy?
Caddie – Gone fishing with the worms you dug up, sir!

A teacher was reading a story to his class.
"'The weary soldier leaned upon his rifle, and stole a few minutes' sleep.' Where did he steal it from?"
"Please, sir, I know," said Tommy. "From someone's knap-sack."

White – My car has wonderful brakes. No matter how fast I'm going I always stop dead. Would you like to try them?
Brown – No, I'd much rather stop alive.

Landlord (to stoney-broke tenant) – Look here, I'll meet you halfway. I'm ready to forget half of what you owe.
Tenant – Right! I'll meet you. I'll forget the other half.

Master – Before I start the next lesson, has anyone a question to ask about thermometers?
Wullie – If I swallowed a thermometer, would I die by degrees?

Master – What is an engineer?
Sandy – A man who works an engine.
Master – Correct. Now tell me what a pioneer is?
Sandy – A man who works a piano.

Uncle – Yes, my boy, for fifty years I had my nose to the grindstone.
Nephew – Gosh uncle, it must have been a big one to start with.

Man (in ironmonger's) – I'm going to a fancy-dress ball as Father Time. Could you sell me a scythe?
Ironmonger – We've no scythes, sir. Would a lawnmower do?

Domestic tips: When driving a nail into wood you can avoid hitting your thumb by getting a friend to hold the nail.

Dad – Now, children, don't quarrel. What's the matter?
Jimmy – We're playing shipwreck, and Peter won't get in the bath and drown himself.

Villager – Yes, sir, I always go to church when you preach.
Parson – But why not go every Sunday?
Villager – Because I get a good seat when you're preaching.

The professor had a very bad memory. One day he was at a dinner party when he suddenly exclaimed: "Dash it, I didn't want to come tonight. I meant to forget to come, but I forgot to forget."

Seasick passenger – Captain, is it true that Britannia rules the waves?
Captain – Yes sir.
Passenger – Well, I wish she would rule them straight.

Pat recently received the following letter from his friend Tim:
Dear Pat,
I am sending you my old coat by parcel post. I have cut off the buttons, because it will make it lighter. You will find them in the breast pocket.
Yours,
Tim

Boastful farmer – I can reap, sow, plough and mow. Can anyone tell me anything I can't do about the farm?
Small voice – Can you lay an egg?

Irish farmer (to friend) – My neighbours are a bad lot.
Friend – Why do you think that about them?
Farmer – Well, every night some of my sheep come home missing.

Mean man (to bald-headed barber) – Have you any hair restorer?
Barber – Yes, we have some that makes hair grow in twenty-four hours.
Mean man – Well, put some on your head, and I'll come back in twenty-four hours to see if you're telling the truth.

Professor's wife – Septimus, baby has swallowed the ink. Whatever shall I do?
Absent-minded professor – Oh, write with a pencil!

Smart guy (to angler who has just landed a two-pounder) – Is that fish for sale?
Angler – I'm a sportsman, not a saleman. I fish for the pleasure of catching them.
Smart guy (kicking fish back into water) – Well, you can have the pleasure of catching that one again.

Captain (to newly-recruited sailor) – I suppose it's the same old story: the fool of the family sent to sea?
Newly-recruited sailor – Oh, no, sir. That's all changed since your day.

Rick – Uncle, how is it that no hair grows on your head?
Uncle – What a silly question. Why doesn't grass grow on a busy street?
Rick – Oh, you mean it can't get up through the concrete?

Little boy – Say, mister, can I help you?
Porter (struggling with crate) – You help me! What could you do?
Little boy – Why, I could grunt while you lift.

Prison governor – Any complaint?
Prisoner – Yes, there ain't enough exits.

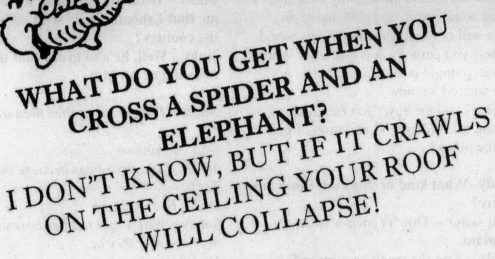

WHAT DO YOU GET WHEN YOU CROSS A SPIDER AND AN ELEPHANT? I DON'T KNOW, BUT IF IT CRAWLS ON THE CEILING YOUR ROOF WILL COLLAPSE!

WHAT IS GREY AND HAS A TRUNK?
AN ELEPHANT ON HOLIDAY!

"Here, boy," said the wealthy motorist, "I want some petrol, and get a move on. You will never do anything in this world unless you push. Push is essential. When I was young, I pushed and that has got me where I am now."

"Well," said the boy, "you can push again, for we haven't got a drop of petrol in the place."

Lady – What kind of ships are those out there?
Old sailor – They're men-o'-war, madam.
Lady – And the small ones round about them?
Old sailor – They're tugs, madam.
Lady – Oh, yes, they will be the tugs-of-war I've heard about.

Boy – I've been sent to buy a small mirror.
Shop assistant – A hand mirror?
Boy – No, one that you can see your face in.

First shipwrecked sailor – Why does that big cannibal look at us so strangely?
Second shipwrecked sailor – Perhaps he's the food inspector!

An explorer was wandering round an island with a cannibal chief. They came upon a spot strewn with bones. "Ah," said the explorer, "a cemetery, I suppose?" "No," replied the chief, smacking his lips, "a restaurant."

Mrs Brown – Tommy, go over and ask how old Mrs Moore is.
Tommy (returning) – Mrs Moore says it's none business of yours how old she is.

Two mean men were held up by a robber. Realising that they were both going to be robbed, one of the victims turned to the other and said:
"Here, Jock, take this. It's the ten pounds I owe you."

Binks – What do you mean by telling me that I should never send my son to the country?
Jinks – Well, he's so green that the cows might eat him.

Smiffy – Dad, are flies flies because they fly?
Dad – I think so.
Smiffy – And fleas fleas because they flee?
Dad – Er . . . maybe.
Smiffy – Well, I told teacher bees were bees because they be.
Dad – Er . . . well done.

Foreman (as bricklayer lets brick fall on his head) – Now, then, you clumsy fool!
Bricklayer – What are you grumbling at? It didn't stop on your head for more than half a second.

Man (after 20 minutes' hard work trying to deliver trunk) – We'll never get this trunk in through the doorway!
Helper – In? I thought you were trying to get it out!

Mother – That was very greedy of you, Tommy, to eat your little sister's share of the pie.
Tommy – But you told me, mother, I was always to take her part.

Sergeant (to sentry) – If anything moves, you shoot.
Sentry – Yes, sir, and if anything shoots, I move.

Jimmy – Do fish grow very fast?
Sammy – I should think so? Father caught one, and it grows ten centimetres every time he mentions it!

Old lady (to boy writing on a wall) – What would your mother say if she knew you were vandalising a wall?
Small boy – What would your husband say if he knew you were talking to a strange man in the street?

Angry man (whose car is in the garage for repairs, to manager) – Do you hear? Everything I say goes.
Youthful mechanic – Then ask him to say "Engine".

A weary-looking fellow who had been looking for a job for months happened to see a police poster headed "Theif Wanted".
"Well," he said, "it's better than nothing, anyway. I'm going to ask for the job."

A great woman singer was singing a solo.
Tommy – Why is that man hitting at the lady with his stick?
Father – He's not hitting at her. He's the conductor.
Tommy – Then what's she yelling for?

Old lady – Did you fall?
Sarcastic man – Oh, no! I'm trying to break a bar of chocolate in my back pocket.

Father – I hope you aren't at the foot of the class.
Johnny – No, father; I'm about at the ankle!

Golfer – This can't be our ball. It's a very old one.
Caddie – Still, it is a long time since we started.

"Isn't it hard," said the kind-hearted landlady, "to think this poor lamb was cut down in its youth to satisfy our appetites?"
"Yes," admitted the sour-faced lodger, struggling with his portion, "it is tough."

"Is my son getting well grounded in languages?" asked the millionaire.
"I would put it even stronger than that," replied the private tutor. "I could say that he is actually stranded on them."

Teacher – If your father and your uncle separately could do the same piece of work in six days, how long would your father and uncle take together?
Tommy – They'd never get it done. They'd sit down and talk about golf.

Teacher – What are the four words most used by schoolboys?
Smiffy – I do not know.
Teacher – Quite correct.

Boastful person – My hens lay double-yolked eggs twice the size of yours.
Smart – That's nothing. Last week my uncle laid a foundation stone.

Minnie – I say, mother, you remember you said the dentist was painless?
Mother – Yes, what about it?
Minnie – He isn't, because when I bit his finger he yelled like mad.

New maid – Was it at seven or eight you wanted your breakfast, madam?
Lady Posh – Er . . . what time is it now?
New maid – Twenty to nine, madam.

"Come out here and I'll lick the lot of you," said the bold little boy to the big sticks of candy in the shop window.

Moe – Why do you call your car "Fishy"?
Joe – Because I've got to kipper look out that it doesn't bloater pieces!

Dad – You know that unbreakable toy you gave Danny for this Christmas?
Mum – Yes, he hasn't broken it, has he?
Dad – No, but he's broken nearly everything else in the house with it!

Scout – Dad, I've done my good deed for today.
Father – Well, what was it?
Scout – I saw Mr Smart running for the train this morning, and he was almost sure to have missed it, so I set the bulldog after him.

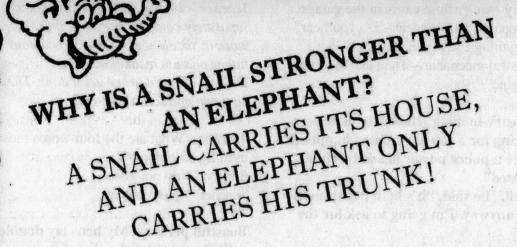

WHY IS A SNAIL STRONGER THAN AN ELEPHANT?
A SNAIL CARRIES ITS HOUSE, AND AN ELEPHANT ONLY CARRIES HIS TRUNK!

WHY IS AN ELEPHANT LARGE, GREY AND WRINKLED?
BECAUSE IF IT WAS SMALL, WHITE AND SMOOTH IT WOULD BE AN ASPIRIN!

Jimmy – Scientists have discovered that our feet are growing bigger.
Johnnie – Never mind. Just think how much more our Christmas stockings will hold!

Janey – We had chicken-pox at Christmas!
Minnie – That's nothing. We had turkey.

Postmaster – This Christmas parcel's so heavy you'll need another stamp on it.
Irishman – Gosh, if I put another stamp on it, that'll make it heavier still!

McHaggis – Look at the snowflakes dancing!
McTaggart – Yes, they're practising for the snow-ball!

First clown – Have you ever seen an apple turn over?
Second clown – No, but I've seen a Christmas pudding look round.

Johnny – Do your glasses make things smaller, Auntie?
Auntie – Yes.
Johnny – Well, take them off while you give me my Christmas pudding.

Teacher (practising Christmas carols) – You must sing louder than that.
Johnny – But I'm singing as loud as I can.
Teacher – Well, let yourself go. Open your mouth and throw yourself into it.

Diner – I can tell a turkey's age by the teeth.
Waiter – Turkeys have not teeth.
Diner – No, but I have!

A cabbage head, a hose and a bottle of ketchup had a race.
How did it go?
The cabbage was ahead, the hose was still running, and the bottle of sauce was trying to ketchup!

Patient -What is your favourite winter sport, doctor?
Doctor – Sleighing.
Patient – No, I mean apart from business.

Country man (in London for Christmas) – Is this Piccadilly Circus?
Policeman – Yes.
Country man – What time does it start?

Andy – Why does Santa come down the chimney?
Sandy – Because it "soots" him.

Billy – I wish you had the toothache instead of me.
Granny – Oh Billy, that's most unkind!
Billy – Well, you can take your teeth out, I can't.

Uncle – It was nice of you to lend your little brother your skates, Sandy.
Sandy – Oh, I only wanted to see if the ice was thick enough!

Doctor – You should take a walk every morning on an empty stomach.
Patient – Whose?

Tommy entered a shop and said that he wanted a Christmas present for his grandfather.
"A tie?" suggested the assistant.
"No, he has a long beard."
"Well, a fancy waistcoat?"
"No, it's a very long beard."
"Well, how would carpet slippers do?"

PC 99 – Now, then, where are going with that sack?
Christmas burglar – Ssh! Don't tell anyone. I'm Santa Claus.

Why is a coach trip like a tree?
They both branch off in different directions!

What did the sea say to the sand?
Nothing, it just waved!

"Daddy," said young Eddy, "I dreamed last night that you gave me a hundred pounds for Christmas."
"Well, as you've been a good boy lately, you may keep it."

Bertie – Will this Christmas card reach London if I post it now?
Postman – Certainly.
Bertie – Well, that's funny. It's addressed to Glasgow.

What did the policeman say to the three-headed monster?
Hello, hello, hello!

How does an Eskimo dress?
As quickly as possible!

What did the polite vampire say?
Fang you very much!

Diner – Waiter, waiter, there's a bug in my soup. I want the manager here at once!
Waiter – Sorry, sir, he's scared of them as well!

What's brown and sneaks around the kitchen?
Mince spies!

What do you get if you cross two banana skins and a bottle of tomato sauce?
A pair of red slippers!

Tommy (to his big sister) – Does it hurt when you stand on the scales?
Big sister – No, why?
Tommy – Oh, because when you stand on them you always cry!

Which floats best, tin or stainless steel?
Tin, because you always find stainless steel sinks!

How do you stop a dog from barking in the back seat of a car?
Make him sit in the front!

Knock, knock!
Who's there?
A little boy who can't reach the doorbell!

Why did the rooster cross the road?
To prove he wasn't chicken!

Did you hear about the man who listened to the match?
Yes, he burnt his ear!

What's yellow and goes click, click?
A ball-point banana!

Sidney – What did the sand say when the tide came in?
Toots – Long time no sea!

Bob – I went fishing yesterday, and caught a fish, but it hit me in the face!
Bert – Oh, that's a load of codswallop!

How do you make a Mexican chilli?
Take him to the North Pole!

Why is a fish so easy to weigh?
Because it has its own scales!

What gunfighter lives at the bottom of the sea?
Billy the Squid!

Teacher – Name five things that contain milk.
Toots – Butter, cheese, cream and two cows!

Nurse – I bet your wife misses you a lot.
Patient – No, her aim's very good. That's why I'm here.

Why do we dress baby girls in pink, and baby boys in blue?
Because they can't dress themselves!

What's the difference between a cat and a comma?
A cat has claws at the end of its paws, and a comma has a pause at the end of its clause!

Teacher – Now, Danny, tell us what you know about the Iron Age.
Danny – Er . . . I'm afraid I'm a bit rusty on that subject, sir.

Diner – I say, waiter, why is my food all mashed up?
Waiter – Well, you did ask me to step on it, sir!

Why are so many people fishermen?
Because it's an easy sport to get hooked on!

What did one ghost say to the other?
"Do you believe in people?"

Did you hear about the demons who went on a protest march?
They were having a demon-stration!

Why are potatoes good detectives?
Because they keep their eyes peeled!

What goes put-putt-putt?
A bad golfer!

Plug – (waving left hand) Why doesn't the Queen wave with this hand?
Danny – I don't know, why doesn't the Queen wave that hand
Plug – Because it's mine!

Why is the letter "E" lazy?
Because it is always in bed!

When vampires go to jail, where are they kept?
In blood cells!

What do snowmen use for money?
Ice lolly!

Patient – Doctor, doctor, I feel like the moon!
Doctor – I can't see you now, come back tonight!

Why is the moon like a hole in the roof?
Because it is a skylight!

Why do hairdressers always get home early?
They know the short cuts!

What did the dentist say when his wife baked a cake?
"Can I do the filling?"

Old woman – Come out of that puddle at once, young man!
Boy – No way. I saw it first!

Did you hear about the frog who became a secret agent?
He wanted to be a croak and dagger man!

Why did the magician include a football boot in the spell?
To give it a little kick!

What did the trampoline champion say?
Life has its ups and downs, but I keep bouncing back!

Bobby – Why did Slim Tim eat a brick?
Tommy – Because he wanted to build himself up!

Diner – Waiter, waiter, what's that fly doing in my ice-cream?
Waiter – Learning to ski, sir!

Why don't bananas snore?
They don't want to waken the rest of the bunch!

What is the difference between a nail and a bad boxer?
One gets knocked in and the other gets knocked out!

Pupil – Would you like to buy a pocket calculator, sir?
Teacher – No, thanks. I already know how many pockets I have!

Where do ghosts do their shopping?
In a spooker market!

CHUCKLE CHUCKLE!

WHAT HAPPENED TO
THE CAT THAT
SUCKED A LEMON?
IT WAS A SOUR-PUSS.

TEE-HEE!

How did Vikings keep in touch with each other?
They used Norse Code!

Boy – How do ghosts get through locked doors?
Pal – They use skeleton keys!

What's worse than an elephant in a china shop?
A hedgehog in a balloon factory!

Moe – Every time the door bell rings my dog goes in a corner.
Joe – Why is that?
Moe – Because he's a boxer!

Why do tall people sleep better?
Because they're longer in bed!

What do you get if you cross a stereo with a fridge?
Cool music!

Girl to her mum – If teachers are so clever, why do they always ask us questions?

What happened to the man who crossed an electric blanket with a toaster?
He kept popping out of bed all night!

What happens to a man who doesn't know toothpaste from putty?
All his windows fall out!

What does an octopus wear on a cold day?
A coat of arms!

What's a monster's game?
Snap!

What do you get if you cross a pig and a flea?
Pork scratchings!

What's round, white, and laughs a lot?
A tickled onion!

What do you get if you cross a parrot and a caterpillar?
A walkie-talkie!

What do you call a short vampire?
A pain in the knee!

How do you start an onion race?
"Onion marks! Get set! Go!"

What do horses like to watch on television?
Neighbours!

Why do astronauts wear bullet-proof vests?
To protect themselves from shooting stars!

Did you hear about the Arab who bought a herd of cows?
He became a milk sheikh!

Why did the chicken cross the road and come back again quickly?
Because his braces got caught in the lamppost!

What do you get if you cross a crocodile and a camera?
A snap shot!

What do you call a cat who ate a duck?
A duck-filled-fatty-puss!

What kind of cat has eight legs, and can stay underwater?
An octo-puss!

What do you call a sneezing sweet?
A chew!

Which month of the year has twenty-eight days?
All of them!

Jimmy – Would it hurt your feelings if I called you a fathead?
Johnny – No, but it would hurt my knuckles!

Did you hear about the boy who put sugar under his pillow?
He wanted to have sweet dreams!

What did the duck say to the waiter? "Why have you put this lunch on my bill?"

What have 18th-century scientists got in common?
They're all dead!

When is a river like a bird cage?
When there is a perch in it!

What is made of chocolate and lies on the seabed?
An oyster egg!

What's yellow, brown and hairy?
Cheese on toast that's fallen on the carpet!

Shall I tell you a story about a brick wall? No, perhaps not – you might never get over it!

Knock, knock!
Who's there?
Toby.
Toby who?
Toby or not Toby, that is the question!

Why is an astronaut like an American footballer? They both want to make safe touch-downs!

Moe – Why do you have a bag of manure in your garden?
Joe – To put on our rhubarb, silly!
Moe – What a daft idea. We put custard on ours!

Why did the astronomer hit himself on the head?
Because he wanted to see stars!

What is 18 feet tall, and sings Scotland the Brave?
The Loch Ness Songster!

How does a broom act?
With sweeping gestures!

In which month do people sleep the least?
February. It's the shortest month!

What do you call a cow that eats grass?
A lawn mooer!

Did you hear about the stupid ghost?
He's learning to climb walls!

What kind of motorbike can cook eggs?
A scrambler!

What's the speed limit in Egypt?
60 Niles an hour!

Did you hear about the shark who swallowed a bunch of keys!
He got lockjaw!

What do you call a dog that is on a lead and likes managing footballers?
Kenny Dogleash!

What did the wool say to the trampoline?
"I would make a good jumper!"

What has four legs, a back, and a body?
A chair!

What vitamins do fish take?
Vitamin sea!

Why did the liquorice sweet go swimming and play football and tennis?
Because it was a liquorice all-sport!

Two Martians landed beside a flashing traffic light.
"I saw her first," said one.
"So what?" the other said. "I'm the one she winked at!"

What kind of cat do you always find in a library?
A catalogue!

What trees are deck chairs made from?
Beech trees!

Sign in shop – "For sale – Space ship. One owner, only 6,750,000 miles!"

What do pandas play on in the park?
Bamboo shoots!

What's worse than raining cats and dogs?
Hailing taxis!

Where do cows dance?
A disc-cow-theque!

First angler – Did you get many bites today?
Second angler – Yes, forty-four.
First angler – That's amazing. What were they?
Second angler – Four fish and forty mosquitoes!

What did the buffalo say to his son when he left on a long journey?
"Bison!"

What do you get if you cross a radiator and six sheep?
Central bleating!

What is a lobster's attorney called?
His clawyer!

What jewels do ghosts wear?
Tomb stones!

What do people say when there's a terrible orchestra on board a boat?
"A-band-on ship!"

What animals need oiling all the time?
Mice, because they squeak!

What did the fishmonger say to the rotten fish?
Long time no sea!

Why can snowmen see very well?
Because they have good ice sight!

First rabbit – I bought a new gold watch yesterday.
Second rabbit – Was it very expensive?
First rabbit – Oh, yes! 24 carrots!

Knock, knock!
Who's there?
Ivor.
Ivor who?
Ivor sore hand from knocking on your door.

What kind of driver never gets a parking ticket?
A screwdriver!

Did you hear about the witch who was top of the class?
She was the best speller!

What do they call robberies in china?
Chinese takeaways!

Teacher – What family does the rhinoceros belong to?
Boy – I don't know, miss, nobody in our street has one!

Why do giraffes have long necks?
Because they can't stand the smell of their feet!

Did you hear about the duck that lost its voice?
He had to visit the quack!

First monster – Arg!
Second monster – Arg, Urg!
First monster – Don't change the subject!

What did one tree say to another tree that was annoying it?
"Please leaf me alone!"

A man went to the doctor and asked how he could prevent himself from ever dying.
"Make sure you never leave the living room!" said the doctor.

Did you hear about the lady who was knocked down by horses?
She's in a stable condition!

Producer – Have you ever been in a play before?
Actor – Well, my leg has been in a cast!

Why did the man wear two pairs of glasses?
Someone told him that he had second sight!

What is a millionaire's favourite soup?
Moneystronie!

Man (in plumbers) – Can I have a sink, please?
Plumber – Certainly, sir. Do you want a plug with it?
Man – Gosh, I didn't realise they were electric!

What has eleven heads and runs around screaming?
A school hockey team!

What is the smallest ant in the world?
An infant!

What do you get if you cross a TV with a TV?
A television repeat!

Why should you never tell peacocks any secrets?
Because they always spread their tales!

What do you call a farmer who used to like farm machinery?
An ex-tractor fan!

How do you get freckles?
Sunbathe under a collander!

A man whose car had broken down asked a motorist to help.
"I'm not a mechanic, I'm a chiropodist,"
said the man.

What do you call the overweight ghost who haunts the theatre?
The Fat Tum of the Opera!

Waiter – What's the new chef like?
Manager – Oh, he's really violent. You should see how he whips the cream!

What does Frankenstein do if he can't get to sleep?
Count Dracula!

Loudspeaker – Will passengers who took the train from platform six to Dundee, please put it back!

What kind of time did the two walnuts have on holiday?
A cracking good time!

Where do farmers leave their pigs when they go to market?
At porking meters!

What do you get if you cross a snowman with a shark?
Frostbite!

"Well," said the other man, "you can give me a tow!"

What is a beetroot?
A potato with high blood pressure!

What do you get if you cross a frog with a chair?
A toadstool!

How do Martians drink tea?
Out of flying saucers!

What has six legs, four ears and a tail?
A man on a horse!

What can a whole orange do that half an orange can't?
Look round!

Why is a rifle like a worker?
Because they can both be fired!

Why is the sky so high?
So the birds don't bump their heads.

Boy (at dentist) – Oh, I wish we were born without teeth!
Dentist – We usually are!

Man – My doctor has told me to give up golf.
Friend – Why? Because of your health?
Man – No. He looked at my score card!

What vegetable do plumbers fix?
Leeks!

What is a ghost's favourite biscuit?
A custard scream!

What do you call a motor-bike with a sense of humour?
A yamaha-ha-ha!

When things go wrong, what can you always count on?
Your fingers!

Diner – Excuse me please, waiter, may I have a pie?
Waiter – Anything with it, sir?
Diner – If it's anything like last time, I'd better have a hammer and chisel!

How far can a pirate ship go?
Fifteen miles to the galleon!

When is a green book not a green book?
When it is read!

What happened to the jellyfish?
It set!

What do you call a four-foot disc jockey?
A compact disc player!

What's a boxer's favourite drink?
Punch!

Terry – Why did your brother give up his job in the biscuit factory?
Jerry – He went crackers!

Do you know who invented spaghetti?
Someone who used his noodle!

Did you hear about the cat who ate a pound of cheese?
It waited for a mouse with baited breath!

Don – I've just had my appendix removed.
Ron – Do you have a scar?
Don – No, I don't smoke.

Jimmy – Why did the boy call his dog "Sandwich"?
Ned – Because it was half-bred!

First explorer – Take my advice – never play cards in the jungle!
Second explorer – Why?
First explorer – It's full of cheetahs!

Snake charmer – Be careful with that trunk, porter, there's a ten-foot snake in there.
Porter – You can't kid me. Snakes don't have any feet!

Which part of your body tells lies?
Your fibula!

What's yellow and stupid?
Thick custard!

What makes a boxer laugh?
A punchline!

First audience member – Why does that man always shut his eyes when he sings?
Second audience member – Because he hates to see us suffer!

Passer-by – Training for a race?
Athlete – No, racing for a train.

Instructor (to pupil) – Tomorrow you will fly solo.
Pupil – How low?

Why did the elephants leave the circus?
They were tired of working for peanuts.

Where do bees come from?
Stingapore!

Where do you take injured wasps?
To the waspital.

**Why did the pear go out with
the plum?**
*Because he couldn't
find a date.*

**What's a
wasp's
favourite ice
cream?**
A hornetto.

**What's the
difference between
a hippo with
measles and a dead
bee?**
*One's a seedy beast and
the other's a bee
deceased.*

Teacher – Did you write, "Teacher is a fool" on the blackboard?
Danny – Yes, sir.
Teacher – Well, I'm glad you told the truth.

Lord Posh – You might get my bath ready for me.
Butler – I'm sorry, sir, it's being used by the goldfish. Lady Posh said it was to have a treat on its birthday.

Curly – See that picture over there? It's hand painted!
Walter – That's nothing! So is our hen-house!

Uncle – And how do you like going to school, Alfie?
Alfie – Oh, I don't mind going, but I don't like having to stay!

Smart Alec – Dad, I can do something you can't do.
Dad – What's that?
Smart Alec – Grow!

Mum – Now remember, Davie, there's a ghost in that cupboard where I keep the cake.
Davie – It's a funny thing, but you never blame the ghost when there's any cake missing.

Businessman – You should never worry. I pay a man two hundred pounds a week to worry for me.
Employee – Where do you get the two hundred pounds to pay him?
Businessman – That's his first worry.

Battered motorist (regaining consciousness) – Where am I?
Nurse – This is number seven.
Motorist – Ward or cell?

MacDuff – I hear your son is getting a to be big chap.
McDonald – Yes! Two years ago he wore my old coat – now I wear his.

Guest – There's something wrong with that clock in my room.
Landlady – Oh, you have to get used to it. When it strikes seven and shows a quarter to eleven, it's about ten past two.

Optician – Now, which line of the chart can you read.
'Erbert – What chart?

Boxing instructor – You say you've been here before? I don't remember your face.
Pupil – No, it's healed up now.

Why should you never shave a man with an umbrella?
It's much better to use a razor!

Moe – My sister is getting married to an Irishman.
Joe – Oh, really?
Moe – No. O'Brien.

What did the fireman's wife get for Christmas?
A ladder in her stocking.

Street artist (to lady) – Excuse me, but will you keep your cat in the house? Every time I draw a fish, the cat licks it away.

Teacher – If you had £10 and multiplied it by 20, what would you get?
Danny – A bicycle.

McTavish (rescued from drowning) – You've saved my life. I must give you a reward.
Rescuer (modestly) – Oh, no, I don't want any reward.
McTavish – Oh, you must take something! Have you change of a pound?

Customer – You know those chickens you sent me? Well, they escaped, and after searching the district I only found ten.
Farmer – Well, you should be satisfied. I only sent you six!

Old lady – That was very kind of you to take the small apple to yourself and give your little brother the big one.
Garry – Oh, it wasn't that. The big one is rotten.

Customer – Is your gorgonzola good?
Grocer – Good? It's unapproachable.

Mother – So you had dates to eat in the cinema? I hope you didn't throw the stones on the floor?
Jimmy – Of course not. I put them in the pocket of the gentleman beside me.

Teacher – You will always find birds where there are trees, and worms where there is earth. What would you expect to find where there are fish?
Bob – Chips, miss

Dad – No, Jimmy, you can't have the hammer to play with. You'll hurt your fingers.
Jimmy – No, I won't. Andy is going to hold the nails.

Teacher (to lazy Danny) – If you answer me one question, I won't ask you another today.
Danny – Very good, sir.
Teacher – How many hairs have you got on your head?
Danny – 107,005,679.
Teacher – How do you know?
Danny – Aha, that's another question.

Customer (in big store) – Why do you have the complaints department on the sixth floor?
Manager – Well, by the time the customers have climbed six flights of stairs they're too breathless to complain!

Plumber – Did you want a plumber, lady?
Lady – Yes, I phoned you in January.
Plumber (to mate) – Wrong house, Harry. The lady we're looking for phoned last December!

Teacher – How do you know when winter is approaching?
Davie – It begins to get late earlier.

Boaster – There's nothing I can't do if I set my mind to it.
Friend – Oh, no? Have you ever tried to slam a revolving door?

Judge – You are sentenced to fifteen years in prison.
Prisoner – But, Your Honour, I will never live to serve it all.
Judge – Never mind. Just you do as much of it as you can.

Customer – A pound of your strongest cheese, please.
Grocer – Willie, unchain No. 21!

Guest – This room is just like a prison cell.
Hotel manager – Well, it's all a matter of what one is used to, sir!

Archie – Dad . . .
Dad – What is it, Archie?
Archie – Where does a snake begin when it wags its tail?

What's the difference between a lion with a toothache and a rainy day?
One roars with pain and the other pours with rain!

Jim – Angus hasn't had a haircut for ten years.
Bob – He must be daft.
Jim – He isn't. He's bald.

Actor – It's not fair. I've got to die in the first act.
Producer – You should think yourself lucky! If I let you into the second act the audience would murder you.

Lady Posh – If you want eggs to keep fresh, they must be laid in a cool place.
Maid – All right, ma'am, I'll go and tell the hens straight away.

Waiter— "Would you like to try some of our bullet salad sir?"
Diner— "I've never heard of such a thing before. Why do you call it that?"
Waiter— "Because there are slugs in it, sir."

Diner— "Waiter! There are two flies splashing about in my coffee!"
Waiter— "Not splashing about, sir— they're swimming for the cup!"

Diner — "Waiter! My teeth are stuck in a bit of steak!"
Waiter — "Don't you mean a bit of steak has got stuck in your teeth?"
Diner — "No—my false teeth stuck in the steak—look, there they are on the plate, beside the lettuce!"

Diner — "Waiter, bring me a plate of spaghetti, and step on it!"
Waiter — "Oh, no, sir, I'll spoil my new shoes!"

Diner — "Do you play tennis?"
Waiter — "Yes, sir!"
Diner — "Then get some coaching on your service—it's rotten!"
Diner — "I'll have the steak pie, please!"
Waiter — "Anything else?"
Diner — "A hammer and chisel to eat it with!"

Diner — "Look out of the window! See how the sun is slowly sinking and the hills are tipped with gold!"
Waiter — "At times like this, sir, I wish I was a hill!"

Diner — "Waiter! There's a tooth in my cream!"
Waiter — "There's a dentist at the next table— I'll ask him to whip it out!"

Diner — "You've brought me a glass full of muddy brown liquid—I asked for still water!"
Waiter — "It may be muddy and brown, but I can assure you, it's still water, sir!"

Waiter — "What? MORE salt and pepper, sir?"
Diner — "Yes, please—they're the only things that are keeping me from starving in this place!"

1st Waiter — "I hate New Year's Eve!"
2nd Waiter — "I know—all those tablecoths to change!"

Diner — "I'll have the fish—no, make it a steak!"
Waiter — "I'm not a magician, sir!"

Diner — "May I use your telephone, please?"
Waiter — "Is it urgent?"
Diner — "I'll say it is—I'm calling the Missing Portions Bureau!"
Diner — "I asked for a game bird, but this is just chicken!"
Waiter — "But that chicken's a game bird too, sir—it was playing snakes and ladders when it died!"

1st Diner — "I'll have the steak and chips, and a glass of water, please!"
2nd Diner — "I'll have the same—and make sure my glass is clean!"
Later . . .
Waiter — "Here is your order, gentlemen . . . now, which one of you wanted the clean glass?"

Waiter — "Can I take your order, sir?"
Diner — "Certainly not! I'm paying for it, and I'm eating it!"

Diner — "Why is my cake soaking wet?"
Waiter — "It's a bath bun!"

Waiter — "I'm sorry, sir, but there's nothing left in the kitchens!"
Diner — "But you're carrying a trayful of food—what do you call that?"
Waiter — "My dinner!"

French Diner — "The dishes we have in France are far superior to your English ones!"
Waiter — "Why? Are they unbreakable!"

Diner — "You say the ham is home-cured?"
Waiter — "Yes, sir!"
Diner — "Well, the cure didn't work— it still doesn't look at all well!"

Diner — "Can I have a doggy bag, please?"
Waiter — "Certainly, sir!"
Diner's son — "Gosh, Dad—have we got a dog?"

Diner — "I've been waiting here for half-an hour! It's disgraceful!"
Waiter — "I've been waiting here for seven years, and you don't hear me complaining!"

Diner — "Do you do fast-food here?"
Waiter — "Well, we have a nice rocket salad on the menu!"

Diner — "Waiter! There are no currants in this currant bun!"
Waiter — "So what? There are no angels in the angel cake!"

Diner — "Waiter! There's no beef in my beefburger!"
Waiter — "Correct, sir—and there's no horse in your horseradish!"

Diner — "Waiter! I have a complaint!"
Waiter — "In that case, sir, you'll have to leave—it might be infectious and we're very strict about health regulations here!"

Diner — "Last time I ate here, the steak made me sick for a week!"
Waiter — "Please don't bring that up again, sir!"

Diner — "Waiter! There's a bluebottle in my ice-cream!"
Waiter — "Poor little thing! He must be frozen!"

Diner — "Why is that dog staring at me like that?"
Waiter — "I don't know sir—perhaps he doesn't like you using his plate!"

Diner — "I'm afraid that once I've paid this bill, I'll have no money left for a tip for you!"
Waiter — "Hang on, sir, and I'll see if I can take something off the total!"

Diner — "I see the portions are getting more generous at last!"
Waiter — "How can you tell, sir?"
Diner — "Yesterday, there was a fly paddling in my soup. Today, it's having to swim!"

Waiter— "Do you like tagliatelli, sir?"
Diner— "I haven't come here to discuss opera. I want something to eat!"

Diner — "I'm so hungry I could eat a horse!"
Waiter — "Sorry sir, horse is off tonight!"

Waiter — So you're an actor, sir? Then perhaps you'd like a Shakespearean steak!"
Diner — "Shakespearean steak? What's that?"
Waiter — "It's cooked 'As You Like It', sir!"

Why is a waiter like an athlete?
Because he runs for cups and plates!

Diner — "Come here, young man—I've a tip for you!"
Waiter — "Sir?"
Diner — "Yes, here it is — don't bring your girlfriend here—the food's terrible and the service is worse!"

Headless ghost — "I'm so hungry, my stomach think's my throat's been cut!"
Waiter — "I-I-I h-h-hate to tell you this, sir, b-b-ut it has!"

Waiter — "One pound for a cup of coffee, sir and the refills are free!"
Diner — "I'll just have a refill, then!"

Diner — "Waiter! The water in my glass is cloudy!"
Waiter — "Don't worry sir—the water's perfectly fine. It's just a dirty glass, that's all!

Waiter — "Would you like to try some of our special two-handed cheese, sir?"
Diner — "Two-handed cheese?"
Waiter — "Yes—hold the cheese with one hand and your nose with the other!"

Waiter — "Just one egg, sir?"
French Diner — "Yes, please. One egg is un oeuf!"

Diner — "Waiter! There's a splinter of wood in my ice cream!"
Waiter — "That pesky fly must have left its snowboard behind, sir!"

Waiter — "Before you order, sir, I should tell you that the steak's off, the fish is off, the vegetarian dish is off and the chef's off!"
Diner — "I'm off as well, then!"

Diner — "Is that onion soup I smell?"
Waiter — "It is and you do, sir."

Diner — "I'll have the ploughman's lunch, please!"
Waiter — "Sorry, sir, but the ploughman got here before you!"

A boy is watching in admiration as a waiter comes out of the kitchen, carrying four plates on each arm and whistling.
"That's very clever! How do you manage to do it?" he says.

The Waiter replies — "Easily! I just pucker up my lips and blow!"

Diner — "I'd like four scoops of ice cream, two slices of apple pie, a piece of chocolate cake and lots of whipped cream!"
Waiter — "And a cherry on top?"
Diner — "Oh, no! I'm watching my weight!"

Diner — "Waiter! This egg is bad!"
Waiter — "Don't blame me, sir, I only laid the table!"

Waiter— "Is there a problem with your food, sir?"
Diner— "The food looks delicious, but I'm afraid I can't eat it!"
Waiter— "Why is that sir?"
Diner— "Because you haven't brought me a knife and fork!"

Diner — "Waiter! There's a worm on my plate!"
Waiter — "That's not a worm, sir, that's your sausage!"

Diner — "I'll have the chef's salad, please!"
Waiter — "That's hardly fair, sir—chef hasn't had a thing to eat since breakfast time!"

Waiter— "Enjoying your coffee, sir?"
Diner— "No! It tastes just like mud!"
Waiter— "Well, sir, it was fresh ground this morning!"

Diner — "Just look at the state of your shirt! It's covered in jelly and custard!"
Waiter — "Yes, sir, one does get a trifle messy in this line of work!"

Diner — "Waiter! There's a cockroach in my soup!"
Waiter — "Don't worry, sir. There isn't enough in your plate to drown him!"

Diner — "Waiter, can you describe to me exactly what it is that I have just eaten?"
Waiter — "Why, sir?"
Diner — "They'll want to know when I reach hospital!"

Diner — "Waiter! Do you have frog's legs?"
Waiter — "Yes, sir!"
Diner — "Well, hop off to the kitchen to get my order, then!"

Diner— "Waiter! There's a caterpillar in this lettuce! What have you got to say about it?"
Waiter— "Well, sir, it's green, hairy, about an inch long . . ."

Waiter — "You haven't touched your custard, sir—is there a problem?"
Diner — "I'll say there is! It's so rubbery that there's a fly on it using it as a trampoline!"

Diner — "Waiter! I've bitten my tongue!"
Waiter — "And did it taste any better than the steak, sir?"

Waiter — "I don't see why you're complaining, sir. There's nothing wrong with your food."
Diner — "Nothing wrong with it? Even the flies are turning away from my plate!"

Diner — "Waiter, I can't eat this! The steak is too tough, the fries are burnt to a crisp and the peas are as hard as marbles! Have you got anything that's a little easier to swallow?
Waiter — "How about a glass of water, sir?"

Diner — "Waiter! There's a dead insect in this bottle of wine!"
Waiter — "Well, sir, you did ask for something with a little body in it!"

Jim — "I've just had dinner at that new restaurant in town."
Joe — "What was it like?"
Jim — "The food was fine, but the bill was a bit hard to swallow!"

An orange that peels itself.

Doctor, doctor. I think I'm a pencil. *Draw up a chair and we'll talk about it.*

Diner — "Waiter! There's a bluebottle in my stew!"
Waiter — "Yes, sir, it's the rotten meat that attracts them!"

Diner — "Waiter! There's a flea in my custard!
Waiter — "Just tell him to hop it, sir!"

Diner — "What's today's special?"
Waiter — "Yesterday's leftovers, sir!"

Diner — "Waiter! There's a fly in my starter!"
Waiter — "Hold on, sir, and I'll ask him if he's ready for your main course yet!"

Diner — "Waiter! There are TWO flies in my soup!"
Waiter — "Yes, sir. I'm afraid neither of them liked the look of what your friend was having!"

Diner — "Waiter! What's this spider doing in my alphabet soup?"
Waiter — "Looks like he's trying to spell 'help', sir!"

Waiter — "What's the matter, sir— curry a little too spicy?"
Diner (Sarcastically) — "Naw! I always have smoke coming out of my ears!"

Diner — "Waiter! There's a slug in my salad! I can't eat it"
Waiter — "Why not, sir? Are you a vegetarian?"

Bill — "I couldn't get what I wanted at the fry bar!"
Will — "What was that?"
Bill — "Chocolate chips!"

Prison visitor— "I hear you let the prisoners borrow classical CD's from the prison library."
Prison governor — " Yes, but only one Purcell."

What kind of music can you play on a lemonade bottle?
Pop!

Notice on music shop's door "Gone for lunch. Bach in fifteen minuets."

Many years ago, a man went to see his old friend, who was a composer. He knocked on the door, but there was no answer. "Come on out," he shouted. "I know you're Haydn in there somewhere!"

What musical instrument do l umberjacks play?
The TIMBER!-ine!

What did the fat musician write on his refrigerator door?
"Sibelius too round—Schumann!"

Little boy (home from music lesson) —
"I played Bach today!"
Mum — "That's nice dear—did you win?"

"I used to play the drums when I lived in the Outback in Australia
—then I stopped beating around the bush!"

What kind of music do blacksmiths like?
Heavy metal!

Who are the most untrustworthy members of the orchestra?
The fiddlers!

Do musicians give each other presents on their birthdays?
No—they just exchange chords!

How did the musician get locked out?
Because he'd got the wrong key!

What musical instrument did they play in Ancient Britain?
The Anglo-saxophone!

What musical instrument to fishermen play?
The cast-a-net!

"I used to play the triangle, but now I want to do some ting else."

"I used to play the piano, but now I'm having a bash at the drums."

"I used to play the bagpipes, but I became disenchantered."

"I used to play the trombone, but my playing began to slide."

"*My brother plays the harp—he's a plucky little fellow!*"

What kind of music do ghosts like? Boo-gie woo-gie!

"**My sister's just smashed her violin to smithereens!**"
"**What did she say when she did it?**"
"**Fiddlesticks!**"

"*What's that rabbit doing on your violin?*"
"*That's not a rabbit—that's my hare on a G string!*"

"I used to play percussion, but I couldn't drum up any enthusiasm for it."

"**Did you ever own a musical instrument?**"
"**Well, I used to have some drumsticks. . .**
—but I cooked them and ate them!"

What do you call five boulders with guitars?
A rock band!

"Are you nervous about your singing solo tonight, Madame Bellows?"
"Nervous? I'm up to high doh!"

Q What kind of music do woodcutters listen to when they're relaxing?
A Chopin.

Notice on musician's front door
"Handel not working. Please use Bach door."

Visitor to musician's house— "What's this on your fridge? (reads) 'Peas, piano, bread, violins. . .'
Musician— "That's my Chopin Liszt!"

Teacher — "For your geography lesson today, I want you to draw me a map of the school!"
Pupil — "Don't you know your way around yet?"

Pupil — "Miss! Miss! Joey's swallowed a bottle of ink!"
Teacher — "Incredible!"
Joey — "No—indelible!"

Teacher — "What comes after 'O'?"
Pupil — "Yeah!"

Teacher — "name four animals from the cat family!"
Pupil — "Mummy Cat, Daddy Cat and two kittens!"

Teacher— Name the Scottish engineer who invented a steam engine.
Pupil— What, sir?
Teacher— Well done! Watt!

Teacher— "The principal, Mr Smith is going to be retiring at the end of this year, children!"
Pupil— "So he decided to quit while he was a head, did he!"

Teacher — "Are you chewing gum?"
Pupil — "No miss—I'm Billy Smith!"

Teacher — "Well done, Watkins. You're in good time for the English essay exam but what's that bit of wood for?
Watkins — "Well, sir, that's my writer's block!"

Teacher —"What is the least used bone in your body?"
Pupil — "My head!"

Teacher (in chemistry class) — "Whatever is the matter, Simpkins? You're trembling all over!
Pupil — "I'm following the instructions for this experiment, sir. It says 'Add liquid to test tube, then shake for two minutes!'"

Teacher — "Can anyone give me an example of something you take for granted, but which didn't exist 200 years ago?"
Pupil — "My mum!"

Teacher — "What does 'N-E-W' spell?"
Pupil — "New!"
Teacher — "and if we add a 'K'?"
Pupil — "Canoe!"

Billy — "Our teacher's like a bird of prey—she's eagle-eyed and watches us like a hawk!"

Teacher — "Annie, you're pretty dirty, aren't you?"
Annie — "Yes—and I'm even prettier when I'm clean!"

Teacher — "Why are you late, George?"
George — "I had to say goodbye to my pets!"
Teacher — "It doesn't take long to say goodbye to a couple of rabbits or a dog!"
George — "No— but I've got an ant farm!"

Teacher — "What is a fortification?"
Pupil — "Two times a twentyfication!"

Teacher — "Can anyone name a deadly poison?"
Pupil — "Aviation—one drop and you're dead!"

Teacher — "What have you got in your pockets, Smithers?"
Smithers — "Holes!"

Teacher — "Who's that girl walking across the playground? She looks like Helen Brown!"
Pupil — "She doesn't look much better in red, Miss!"

Pupil — "I'm glad I wasn't born in Spain, Miss!"
Teacher — "Why is that, Jimmy?"
Pupil — "because I can't speak Spanish!"

Teacher — "What family does the whale belong to?"
Pupil — "Can't be any family round here, miss—no-one's got a bath big enough to keep one!"

Teacher — "And now Annie's going to play something for us on her violin. Are you going to play by ear, Annie?"
Annie — "No— I'm going to play over there!"

Teacher — "Which month has twenty-eight days?"
Pupil — "All of them—and some have a few extras!"

Teacher — "If b = 10, a = b + 6 and c = b - a, what is c?
Pupil — "It's a whole lot of salty water surrounded by beaches, sir!"

Teacher — "Can you give me two examples of pronouns, Jimmy?"
Jimmy — "Who, me?"
Teacher — "Correct!"

Teacher — "Can anyone give me a sentence starting with 'I'?"
Pupil — "I is—"
Teacher — "I am, I AM!"
Pupil — "I AM the ninth letter of the alphabet!"

Teacher — "Mrs Jones, your son has a perfect attendance record, so I've decided to give him a week off school!"
Mrs Jones (proudly) — "Ah, so he deserves a break!"
Teacher — "No, Mrs Jones—I do!"

Teacher — "How are you enjoying your singing lessons, Ray?"
Pupil — "Me? Ray? Hum . . . soh-fah, so good!"

Teacher — "What do John F. Kennedy, Abraham Lincoln and George Washington have in common?"
Pupil — "Well, sir, they're all people I have never heard of!"

Teacher — "What are two two's?"
Pupil — "Frilly dresses for ballet dancers, miss!"

Teacher— "Derek, do you think you're the person in charge of this class?"
Derek— "No, miss."
Teacher — "Then stop acting the goat!"

Teacher — "You have all heard of the Ice Age, and the Stone Age—what age do you live in today?"
Annie — "My mum says I'm at a difficult age!"

Teacher — "What is a quart?"
Pupil — "A place where a judge works!"

Teacher — "What did Charles II do when he came to the throne?"
Pupil — "He sat down!"

Pupil (to friend) — "What will I do? I can't see the blackboard!"
Friend — "Don't worry—there's nothing interesting on it at the moment!"

Teacher — "Can anybody tell me where Cleopatra's needle is?"
Pupil — "In her sewing box!"

Teacher — "What is one twentieth of a half?"
Pupil — "Not big enough to bother about!"

Teacher — *"Why did you fail your maths exam, Billy? You did so well last time!"*
Pupil — *"This time my mother washed my shirt and the answers came off my cuff!"*

Teacher — "Why aren't you facing the front, like the rest of the class, Jimmy?"
Jimmy — "Because you said you'd be glad to see the back of me!"

Teacher — "I'm sorry, Mrs Smith, but your son is way behind in his maths lessons!"
Mrs Smith — "But he told me that he sat at the front of the class!"

Teacher — *"You got all your maths homework wrong last night, Annie. I can't understand it!"*
Annie — *"Neither could I!"*

Teacher — "If I took a cake and sliced it in four, and then cut each quarter into ten pieces, what would I have?"
Pupil — "Crumbs!"

Teacher — "Why do you want to become an astronaut, Bobby?"
Bobby — "Because I can't think what on earth to do when I grow up!"

Teacher — *"Who discovered the atom?"*
Pupil — *"Eve!"*

Teacher — "Can anyone give me a sentence using the word 'centimetre'?"
Pupil — "My grandma got the train up from London, and my Dad was centimetre at the station!"

Teacher — "Jimmy—can you spell the other word for bucket? Is it p-a-i-l with an i or
p-a-l-e with an e?
Jimmy — "No idea!"
Teacher — "Wrong!—And don't call me dear!"

Teacher — *"Why are you biting your pencil, Annie?"*
Annie — *"I can't find my sharpener!"*

Teacher — "What makes you think that Adam and Eve lived on cheese?"
Pupil — "You told us they lived in the Garden of Edam!"

Teacher — "Mrs Brown, I'm afraid your son's rather wet!"
Mrs Brown — "That's a terrible thing for a teacher to say about any pupil!"
Teacher — "But it's true!—He fell in the school swimming pool five minutes ago!"

Teacher — *"Now, children, you should never be afraid to ask questions. Asking questions helps you get along!"*
Billy — *"In that case, can I get along home now?"*

Teacher — "Now, children, I want you all to be very quiet, for I'm not feeling very well today!"
Johnny — "You should do what my mum does when she's not feeling very well, miss!"
Teacher — "And what does your mummy do, Johnny?"
Johnny — "She sends us outside to play!"

Teacher — "Do you know your grammar, Sadie?"
Sadie — "Of course I do—she lives with my gramper just along the road from us!"

Teacher — *"I'm afraid your behaviour goes against the spirit of this school, Billy!"*
Billy — *"Aren't you too old to believe in ghosts, miss?"*

Teacher — "Can anyone tell me anything about the Arctic Circle?"
Pupil — "It's like my dad's head—a great white bare place!"

Teacher — "Who invented fractions?"
Pupil — "Henry the eighth, Miss!"

Teacher — *"Can anyone give me a sentence using the word 'coincide'?"*
Pupil — *"If it starts raining during the lunch break the headmaster tells us to coincide."*

Teacher — "What's wrong with Joe, Tom?"
Tom — "He's bashful, that's all."
Teacher — "Bashful?"
Tom — "Yes, Miss. We were fighting at playtime, and now he's bash-full!"

What do you call a baker with red hair? *A ginger bread man.*

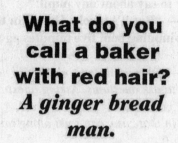

Doctor, doctor. I've just eaten five red snooker balls, four browns, three yellows, a pink, two blacks and a blue and I don't feel well. *No wonder, you're not eating your greens!*

Doctor, doctor. I feel like a packet of biscuits. *You must be crackers!*

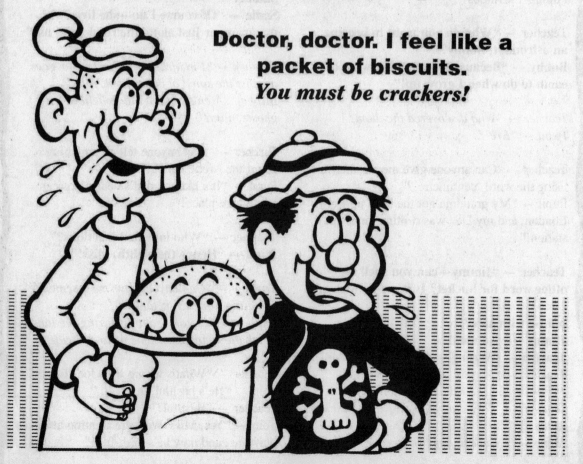

Teacher — "You were sick and missed school yesterday, didn't you, Billy?"
Billy — "Yes and No, sir."
Teacher — "What do you mean— yes and no?"
Billy — "Yes, I was sick. No, I didn't miss school one little bit!"

Teacher — "Can anyone tell me the name of the first woman on earth?"
SILENCE
Teacher — "Come along children, someone must know—think of an apple!"
Billy — "Granny Smith!"

Teacher — "Now, children, in this picture you will see a kangaroo. A kangaroo is a native of Australia. . . What's the matter, Freddy?"
Freddy — "My auntie's married to one of those!"

Teacher — "Can anyone tell me what the word 'adult' means?"
Pupil — "An adult is a person who has stopped growing at both ends and has started growing round the middle!"

Teacher — "Why are you the only one in class today, Katie?"
Katie — "Because I'm the only one who didn't eat school dinner yesterday!"

Teacher — "Can anyone here name three famous Poles?"
Pupil — "North, South and tad, sir!"

Teacher — "The exam will take one hour; that's ten minutes for each question."
Pupil — "But that doesn't leave any time for the answers!"

Teacher — "Why haven't you done your Geography homework?"
Pupil — "My Dad says the world is changing, so I decided to wait until it was finished."

Teacher — "What are the Great Plains?"
Pupil — "Concorde, and the jumbo jets!"

Teacher — "Where is Hadrian's Wall?"
Pupil — "Round Hadrian's garden, sir!"

Teacher — "When was Rome built?"
Jimmy — "At night, sir!"

Teacher — "Why do you say that?"
Jimmy — "Because my mother's always saying that Rome wasn't built in a day!"

Teacher — "What do you know about the Dead Sea, Annie?"
Annie — "Not much, Miss—I didn't even know it had been ill!"

Teacher — "Billy! I'm not going to tell you to stop talking again!"
Billy — "Thank goodness for that! I can't think what I'm saying with all these interruptions!"

Teacher — "Harry, please don't whistle while you're working."
Harry — "It's all right, Miss, I'm not working, just whistling!"

Teacher — "Is there any wildlife in the Amazonian jungle?"
Pupil — "The parrots can get quite angry, sir!"

Teacher — "What is an island, Jimmy?"
Jimmy — "It's a bit of land, surrounded by water, except on one side!"
Teacher — "Except on one side?"
Jimmy — "Yes, sir—the top!"

Teacher — "What's the matter, Joe?"
Joe — "When I try to do maths, I feel like a ship!"
Teacher — "What do you mean?"
Joe — "I'm all at sea!"

Teacher — "Can anyone give me a sentence using the word 'defence'?"
Pupil — "Our dog keeps escaping from the back garden, so Dad's going to mend defence!"

Teacher — "Where is the English Channel?"
Pupil — Press the right button on your TV remote and you'll find it, sir!"

Teacher — "Is there any wildlife in the Arctic?"
Pupil — "No, Miss, it's too cold for parties!"

Teacher — "What do we do with crude oil?"
Billy — "We could teach it some manners, sir!"

Teacher — "How do we know that the world is round?"
Pupil — "Because my mum and dad say it is!"

Teacher — "What's five times five?"
Annie — "That's the third time you've asked us that, Miss. Can't you remember the answer?"

Teacher — "Can anyone tell me anything about Robinson Crusoe?"
Billy — "Yes, miss—he lived on a desert island and turned red!"
Teacher — "Turned red?"
Billy — "Yes— it said in my book that he was marooned!"

Teacher — "Why didn't you do your homework, Billy?"
Billy — "You were looking so, tired, Miss, that I didn't want to give you any more problems!"

Teacher — "If you multiplied 15 by 20 and divided the answer by 5, what would you get?"
Pupil — "The wrong answer, probably, sir!"

Teacher — "If I had five oranges in one hand and six in the other, what would I have?"
Pupil — "Very big hands!"

Teacher — "If you had five pounds and you asked your father for another two, how many pounds would you have?"
Pupil — "Five, sir!"
Teacher — "You don't know your arithmetic, my lad!"
Pupil — "You don't know my father, sir!"

Teacher — "What time do you wake up in the morning, Johnny?"
Johnny — "About two hours after I get to school, Miss!"

Pupil — "Can you send my exam results to my parents by e-mail, please, miss?"
Teacher — "But you don't have a computer at home, Jimmy!"
Pupil — "That's right, miss!"

Teacher — "What is half of eight?"
Pupil — "Sideways, it's three, and up and down it's zero!"

Teacher — "How are you getting on with the novel I asked you to read, Jimmy?"
Jimmy — "I got stuck at page ten, miss."
Teacher — "How is that?"
Jimmy — "My brother glued my hand to the paper!"

Teacher — "How are you getting on with your science project, Freddy?"
Freddy — "It's inspiring, sir!"
Teacher — "Inspiring?"
Freddy — "Yes sir, it's inspiring me to forget all about it and go out and play football!"

Teacher — "Did anyone see who wrote this rude word on the blackboard?"
Dim Tim — "I hope not, miss, or I'll be in big trouble!"

Teacher — "Tommy, how do you spell your name backwards?"
Tommy — "e-m-a-n-r-u-o-y!"

Teacher — "Now, can anyone find the lowest common denominator in this problem?"
Pupil — "Have you still not found that pesky thing?"

Teacher — "What's 4+4, Katie?"
Katie — "8, Miss"
Teacher — "Good!"
Katie — "Good? It's perfect!"

Teacher — "Do you have a pet, Jimmy?"
Jimmy — "Yes, miss. I keep him in the pond and I call him Tiny."
Teacher — "Tiny? Why do you call him that?"
Jimmy — "Because he's my newt!"

Teacher — "Come on Tommy, it's not a difficult sum—a five year-old could do it!"
Tommy — "But I'm nine!"

Teacher — "Bobby, you haven't answered any of the questions in this maths test!"
Pupil — "I know, miss I wanted to be able to go home and tell my parents that I got nothing wrong!"

Teacher — "Why are you picking your nose in class, Jimmy?"
Jimmy — "Because I'm not allowed to do it at home!"

Teacher — "Billy, can you count to ten?"
Billy — "One two, three four, five, six, seven, eight, nine, ten."
Teacher — "Well done! Can you go on from there?"
Billy — "Jack, Queen, King, Ace!"

Teacher — "Annie, can you count from one to five?"
Annie — "One, two, three, four, five!"
Teacher — "Any higher?"
Annie (stands on chair) "One two, three, four, five!"

Bill— "I hear Lee won the Chinese cookery competition"
Will— "Yes, in fact you could say it was a wok-over!"

Fred— "I've signed up for Chinese cookery classes."
Ted— "Chinese cookery? That sounds difficult!"
Fred— "Not really, as long as you use your noodle."

Bill — "I could never eat goat meat!"
Will — "Why not?"
Bill — "Because my mother always said that butter wouldn't melt in my mouth!"

Where were lemons first found?
In a lemon tree!

What can a whole orange do that half an orange can't do?
Look round!

How do people eat cheese in Wales?
Caerphilly!

What kind of vegetables do drummers like best?
Beets!

Will — "I've invented a truth drink—would you like a taste?"
Bill — "Ugh! That tastes terrible!"
Will — "Ain't that the truth!"

How do you put your hair in a bun?
Stick your nose in a beefburger!

What's the difference between chili and chilli?
One 'l' of a difference!

What is small, green and hangs around?
A drip-dry gooseberry!

A sausage is lying on the refrigerator shelf, next to a fillet of salmon. The sausage tries to strike up a conversation with the fillet, but the fillet says nothing. After several minutes, chatting to the salmon fillet and getting no response, the sausage turns to the butter on his other side.
"See him over there?" he says, "He's a bit of a cold fish, isn't he?"

What did the fish-finger say to the tomato?
"That's enough of your sauce!"

What cheese is made back to front?
Edam!

What kind of fruit begins with the letter 'N'?
'Nana!

What's green and full of bounce?
Spring cabbage!

What did one potato say to the other potato?
"This is a fine mash you've got us into!"

When is cheese like a nose with a cold?
When it's blue, smells and is runny!

How can you tell a dishonest sandwich?
It's full of baloney!

Why was the lemonade bottle crying?
It had lost its pop!

How do you please a piece of toast?
Butter it up a bit!

When is the pantry generous?
When it has a treat in store for you!

Why did the coffee mug crack?
The spoon made it stir-crazy!

Why did the strawberry call for help?
It was in a jam!

Why did the cucumber call for help?
It got into a pickle!

Why did no-one love the shrimp?
Because he was shellfish!

What kind of food do furniture-makers like best?
Veggie-tables!

What has no beginning, no end, and nothing in the middle?
A doughnut!

What is the most expensive food in the world?
The fortune cookie!

When is an apple pie like a headmaster?
When it's crusty and old!

What do card-players like to eat?
Ginger snaps!

What do choristers eat?
Hum-burgers and doh-nuts!

What do chickens eat on special occasions?
Layer cake!

Which kind of meringues always come back?
Boo-meringues!

Turkey — "Brr—December's such a cold month, isn't it? I could do with something warm over me!"
Farmer — "How about some gravy?"

Why are Wimbledon players difficult customers in a restaurant?
Because whatever is served, it's sure to be returned!

What does Superman like to eat?
A hero sandwich!

What wobbles and flies?
A jellycopter!

What did the goalkeeper have for lunch?
Beans on post!

What kind of food is never ready for dinner parties?
Mayonnaise—it's always dressing!

What do gymnasts have for breakfast?
A few rolls!

What do bus drivers eat?
Cheap fare!

How do you stop fish from smelling?
Cut their noses off!

What lies under a tree with its tongue hanging out, covered in mustard?
A hot dog!

Why did the orange stop rolling downhill?
It ran out of juice!

What is green, edible and makes holes in trees?
Woody Woodpickle!

Why was the fruit shop assistant confused?
Because his boss told him to arrange the apples in pairs!

Two turkeys are sitting in the butcher's shop.
1st Turkey — "I'm never going to listen to another human being again!"
2nd Turkey — "Why not?"
1st Turkey —"The farmer said 'Trust me!'
—then he trussed ME!"

Why do the strawberries go out in couples?
They don't like playing gooseberry!

Why is a sofa like a roast chicken?
They're both full of stuffing!

What is a doughnut?
A mad millionaire!

What two things can you never have for breakfast?
Lunch and dinner!

Why could the apple not get through to the orange on the telephone?
Because the lime was engaged!

Why are apples cheeky?
Because they give us plenty of sauce!

What did the orange say to its friend as they sat by the juice extractor?
"Squeezed to see you!"

What kind of fish is illegal?
Poached salmon!

What do karate experts like to eat best?
Chops!

What do lady race-drivers like to eat?
Pasta!

What do hippies like to eat?
Peas, man!

Who was the most popular artist in the police force?
Constable!

What do shoemakers like to eat?
Sole!

What do policemen have in their sandwiches?
Truncheon meat!

Sergeant — "Who's been using my notebook?"
Police officer — "Must have been PC Simpkins, Sarge. I'd know his prints anywhere!"
Sergeant — "Fingerprints?"
Police officer — "No, misprints! His spelling's terrible!"

What do reporters have in their sandwiches?
Front-page spread!

What do road menders like to eat?
Chips!

What did the policeman say to his stomach?
"You're under a vest!"

Newspaper headline — Mystery thief steals lightbulbs from police station. Police are still in the dark.

Newspaper headline —Dog food stolen from pet shop. Police are looking for a man with strong teeth and a healthy coat.

Newspaper headline —River floods Police station. Police officers rescued by Tosh Smith, in Mack Black's boat. Police say Mack and Tosh kept them dry.

Newspaper headline — Model's arm washed up on beach. Police say this one's a bit of a poser.

News headline — Army drill sergeant goes missing. Police say they're giving it swift attentions.

Newspaper headline — Missing dogs— Police say they are following a number of leads.

Newsflash — Rhubarb thefts—Police say suspects are in custardy!

News headline — Five campers charged with loitering within tent!

News headline —Dog has nine pups— Police have charged her with littering!

Newspaper headline — Thefts from underwear store. Police in-vest-igating.

News headline — Planks stolen from builder's yard. Police hope to nail the culprit.

Newspaper headline — Theft from babywear shop—Police have found the bootee!

Newsflash —Fireworks thefts—suspect banged up!

Newsflash —Sheepdog trials—sheepdogs plead not guilty!

Newsflash —Phantom wig thief—Police say they have him locked up!

Newsflash —Javelins stolen from stadium—Inspector spearheads enquiry.

Newsflash —Dogfood thefts—Police say they've collared a suspect.

Newspaper headline —Missing crosswords— Police looking for clues.

Newspaper headline —China Thefts— Police studying mugshots.

Newsflash —Man has all holiday clothes stolen —Police are looking into the case.

Newspaper headline —Shirt thief—Police have got him in cuffs.

Newspaper headline —Broken window mystery—Police have cracked it!

Newspaper headline —Constable steals hair bleach—Police say it's a fair cop!

Newspaper headline —Demolition man charged with home-icide!

Newspaper headline — Holiday snaps stolen—Police have identified prints.

Newspaper headline — Theft of gold paint and balloons—Police have found gilty party.

Newspaper headline — Police station gets new lawn—Criminals say who grassed?

Newspaper headline —Holes appear in garden of MI6 building. Police suspect a mole.

Newspaper headline —Policeman learning semaphore causes havoc at road junction.

Newspaper headline —Earth tremor hits police headquarters. Police are shaken.

Newspaper headline —Government secrets sold to enemy agents by man in violet suit. Police are looking for the purpletraitor.

Newspaper headline —Thefts from Municipal Dump— Police have received a tip-off.

Newsflash — Singing burglars—Police continue with enchoiries.

Newsflash —Stable hand murdered— Police are making horse-to-horse enquiries.

Newsflash —Cat found dead in mysterious circumstances—Police are making mouse-to-mouse enquiries.

Newsflash — Bo Peep's sheep taken—police have arrested crook!

Newspaper headline —Ten tons of soap missing from factory. Police say burglars made a clean getaway.

Newsflash — Two hundred blankets stolen from hotel. Police say there's been a cover-up.

Newsflash — Pig farm robbery. Perpetrators caught. Crooks ask 'Who squealed?'

Newsflash — 100 pairs of curling tongs stolen from factory. Police say it's a crime wave.

PC Plod — "I'm off on the beat now, sergeant."
Sergeant — "And may the force be with you!"

Criminal — "How did you know I was lying?"
Police officer — "Easy—your lips moved!"

Police officer — "And how did the intruder get in?"
Home owner — "Intruder window, of course!"

Did you hear about the police officer who caught a falling star?
He charged it with glittering!

Sergeant — "And does the suspect have a record?"
Police officer — "No, sergeant, but he has quite a large CD collection!"

Police officer — "I'm afraid your son has been run over by a steamroller, Mrs Bloggs!"
Mrs Bloggs — "How is he feeling?
Police Officer — "Rather flat!"

Police officer — "I'm afraid your husband has been run over by a steamroller, Mrs Smith!"
Mrs Smith — "Slide him into an envelope and send him home!"

Police officer — "I've had reports that your son has been throwing stones at the next door neighbour, Mr Jones!"
Mr Jones — "No need to worry, officer, he's got a rotten aim!"

Car driver — "Excuse me, officer, but can you tell me if my indicator light is working?"
Police officer — "It is—it isn't —it is—it isn't —it is. . ."

What do policemen in Hawaii say when they see someone acting suspiciously?
"Alo-ha, alo-ha, alo-ha, what have we got here, then"!

Policeman (to driver of crashed vehicle) —
"Now then, can you tell me what happened?"
Driver — "No, officer, I can't—my eyes were
shut at the time!"

Why do police cars have radios?
So that the officers don't have to listen to
each other!

Man — "How do you know it was my car that
knocked over the lamppost, officer?"
PC Plod — "I found the 'eavy dents on your
vehicle, sir!"

What did the policeman say when he cut
himself shaving?
"I'm nicked!"

Newsflash — Burglary in lingerie store —
Police say robbers gave them the slip.

Policeman — "I'm putting you in the cells for
the night, mate!"
Criminal — "What's the charge?"
Policeman — "No charge—it's absolutely
free!"

Criminal — "I've spent four years making the
Queen happy!"
Friend — "What do you mean?"
Criminal — "I've been serving her Majesty's
pleasure!"

Former prisoner — "I could see the lock of
the cell door was easy to pick, so I put my
little finger in the keyhole and twisted. . ."
Friend — "And then?"
Former prisoner — "I broke my fingernail!"

Newsflash —Lorry with load of strawberries
and sugar has overturned on the motorway.
Police are dealing with the jam.

Why was the police officer not allowed to
search the rabbit hole
Because he didn't have a warren-t!

PC Bloggs waved down a car one day,
because the driver was continually
sounding the horn.
"As keeper of the peace, I order your
peeper to cease!" he said.

Notice on toy-shop window "Bicycle horns
for sale. Come in and take a peep!"

Notice on roofing contractor's office door
"Gone for lunch. Slater!"

Notice on Italian restaurant's door
"Closed. It's pasta our bedtime!"

Notice on computer shop window "Back in
five minutes. Gone for chips!"

Notice on plumber's window "Doorbell not
working. Tap on door."

Notice on baker's shop window. "Taking a
nap. Doughnut disturb."

Notice on fridge door from maths teacher to
his wife "Add sum π for lunch.
Do you minus having take-away for supper?"

Notice on bank window Closed today.
If you have any enquiries, please leave
a note.

Notice on lawyer's office door "Gone for
lunch. Back suin'!"

Notice on beautician's window "Unsightly
blemishes? On-the spot-treatment available!"

Notice on hairdresser's window "Sorry,
we're closed. Comb back tomorrow!"

Notice on barber's window "Closed.
Urgent appointment elsewhere.
Moustache!"

Notice on chip-shop window "Closed for
holidays. Open again next Fry day!"

Notice on door of nuclear power station
"Gone fission!"

Knock-knock!
Who's there?
Sacha!
Sacha who?
Sacha lot of questions! Just let me in,
will you!

Knock-knock!
Who's there?
Buster!
Buster who?
Buster London, broken down outside in
the street!

Knock-knock!
Who's there?
Barbara!
Barbara who?
Barbara Black Sheep!

Knock-knock!
Who's there?
Europe!
Europe who?
Europe early today!

Knock-knock!
Who's there?
Arthur!
Arthur who?
Arthur got what I came for!

Knock-knock!
Toby!
Toby who?
Toby or not Toby, that is the question. . ."

Knock-knock!
Who's there?
Ida!
Ida who
Ida feeling I might find you here!

Knock-knock!
Who's there?
Jamaica!
Jamaica who?
Jamaica habit of leaving your visitors
standing out here in the cold like this?

Knock-knock!
Who's there?
Rupert!
Rupert who?
Rupert your left leg in, your left
leg out. . ."

Knock-knock!
Who's there?
Martin!
Martini who?
Martini hand is frozen!

Knock-knock!
Who's there?
Owl!
Owl who?
Owl you know unless you open
the door?

Knock-knock!
Who's there?
Watt!
Watt who?
Watt the Dickens are you doing in my
house?

Knock-knock!
Who's there?
Sibelius!
Sibelius who?
Sibelius broken again!

Knock-knock!
Who's there?
Juno!
Juno who?
Juno my name? I've forgotten!

Knock-knock!
Who's there?
Alice!
Alice who?
Alice-ened at the door, so I knew
you were in!

Knock-knock!
Who's there?
Red!
Red who?
Red the sign that says your doorbell's broken!

Knock-knock!
Who's there?
Carob!
Carob who?
Yes, deer!

Knock-knock!
Who's there?
Howard!
Howard who?
Howard de wife and kids?

Knock-knock!
Who's there?
Blue!
Blue who?
Blue my tyres up—here's the pump back!

Knock-knock!
Who's there?
Yule!
Yule who?
Yule never find out unless you open the door!

Knock-knock!
Who's there?
Thatcher!
Thatcher who?
Thatcher dog I hear barking in
the back?

Knock-knock!
Who's there?
Lena
Lena who?
Lena little closer to the door and see
if you can recognise my voice!

Knock-knock!
Who's there?
Ammonia!
Ammonia who?
Ammonia little boy, and I can't reach
the handle!

Knock-knock!
Who's there?
Sindy!
Sindy who?
Sindy payment for your new doorknocker
to my house!

Knock-knock!
Who's there?
Few!
Few who?
Few were me you wouldn't be happy being
left out here in the cold!

Knock-knock!
Who's there?
M. Brown!
M. Brown who?
M. Brown and fit after my foreign
holiday!

Knock-knock!
Who's there?
Jupiter!
Jupiter who?
Jupiter hurry or you'll be late for your
meeting!

Knock-knock!
Who's there?
Phil!
Phil who?
Philthy weather out here—open
the door!

Knock-knock!
Who's there?
Candy!
Candy who?
Candy owner of the red car outside please
move it?

Knock-knock!
Who's there?
Mima!
Mima who?
Mima fingers! They're shut in the door!

Knock-knock!
Who's there?
Lefty!
Lefty who?
Lefty iron on—gotta go back home!

Knock-knock!
Who's there?
Rick!
Rick who?
Rickon you'll need a new doorbell!

Knock-knock!
Who's there?
Alexander!
Alexander who?
Alexander 'usband!

Knock-knock!
Who's there?
Sawyer!
Sawyer who?
Sawyer light was on—thought I'd pop in!

Knock-knock!
Who's there?
Althea!
Althea who?
Althea out-thide!

Knock-knock!
Who's there?
Shaw!
Shaw who?
Shaw you don't won't to come out?

Knock-knock!
Who's there?
Y!
Y who?
Y-ping my fingerprints off the
doorknocker!

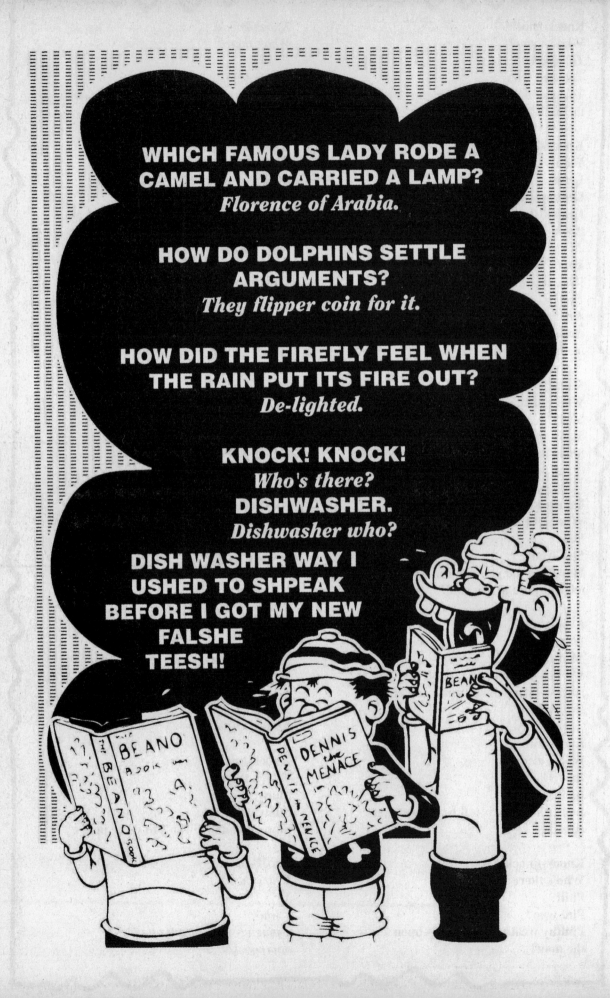

Knock-knock!
Who's there?
A.King!
A.King who?
A.King feet—let me come in for a seat!"

Knock-knock!
Who's there?
C.
C.Who?
C. me outside!

Knock-knock!
Who's there?
P.!
P. who?
P.King through the keyhole!

Knock-knock!
Who's there?
Annie!
Annie who?
Annie one gonna answer this door?

Knock-knock!
Who's there?
F.!
F. who?
F. you don't hurry up, I'll freeze
out here!

Knock-knock!
Who's there?
H.!
H. who?
H. your sandwiches while I was waiting!

Knock-knock!
Who's there?
Q.!
Q. who?
Q.-cumber sandwiches, fresh to
your door!

Knock-knock!
Who's there?
M.!
M. who?
M. freytfully sorry to disturb you!

Knock-knock!
Who's there?
R.!
R. who?
R. you ever going to answer?

Knock-knock!
Who's there?
N.!
N. who?
N.-chanted to meet you!

Knock-knock!
Who's there?
O.!
O. who?
O.-ping you'll open the door!

Knock-knock!
Who's there?
Z.!
Z. who?
Z. I was coming round, didn't I?

Knock-knock!
Who's there?
Betty
Betty who
Betty lot of people tell you to get
a doorbell!

Knock-knock!
Who's there?
Freezer!
Freezer who?
Freezer jolly good fellow!

Knock-knock!
Who's there?
Adair
Adair who?
Adair when I was young, but now I'm bald!

Knock-knock!
Who's there?
Hippo!
Hippo who?
Hippo-ray! You're in!

Knock-knock!
Who's there?
Doug!
Doug who?
Dougle Blazing - oops - I mean Double
Glazing Salesman!

Knock-knock!
Who's there?
Colin!
Colin who?
Colin round to see if you want to come out!

Knock-knock!
Who's there?
School!
School who?
School out here! Is it warmer inside?

Knock-knock!
Who's there?
Wayne!
Wayne who?
Wayne are you going to open the door?

Knock-knock!
Who's there?
William!
William who?
Williamake an effort and answer the door!

Knock-knock!
Who's there?
Spain!
Spain who?
Spainful knocking on the door for so long!

Knock-knock!
Who's there?
Fred!
Fred who?
Fred I've broken your doorbell!

Knock-knock!
Who's there?
Ivor!
Ivor who?
Ivor good idea what's wrong with your doorbell!

Knock-knock!
Who's there?
Drat!
Drat who?
Drat-a-tat-tat! It makes a change from knock-knock!

Knock-knock!
Who's there?
Joanna!
Joanna who?
Joanna buy a doorbell?

Knock-knock!
Who's there?
Hilda!
Hilda who?
Hilda handle, turn it, and open the door!

Knock-knock!
Who's there?
Walter!
Walter who?
Walter Wall carpeting—bargain prices!

Knock-knock!
Who's there?
Orange!
Orange who?
Orange-ya glad to see me?

Knock-knock!
Who's there?
Herbert!
Herbert who?
Herbert opening the door and letting me in?

Knock-knock!
Who's there?
Cilla!
Cilla who?
Cilla old me! I forgot my key again!

Knock-knock!
Who's there?
I'm a fridge!
I'm a fridge who?
I'm a fridge-yer house is fallin' down!

Knock-knock!
Who's there?
Who!
Who who?
I'm not coming in if there are ghosts in the place!

Knock-knock!
Who's there?
Alaska!
Alaska who?
Alaska man I know to fix your doorbell!

Knock-knock!
Who's there?
Toodle!
Toodle who?
But I've only just got here!

Knock-knock!
Who's there?
Celia!
Celia who?
Celia later! I'm fed up waiting for you to answer the door!

Knock-knock!
Who's there?
Aesop Esau!
Aesop Esau who?
Aesop Esau a puddy tat!

Knock-knock!
Who's there?
Adder!
Adder who?
Adder you get in here?

Knock-knock!
Who's there?
Abba!
Abba who?
Abba banana!

Knock-knock!
Who's there?
Aeron!
Aeron who?
Aeron the side of caution!

Knock-knock!
Who's there?
Humphrey!
Humphrey who?
Humphrey Bonnie Scotland!

Knock-knock!
Who's there?
Len!
Len who?
Len me a raincoat, willya, it's pouring
down out here!

Knock-knock!
Who's there?
Agnew!
Agnew who?
Agnew if I just kept on trying, you'd
answer the door at last!

Kn-kn!
Kn-kn? Don't you mean 'Knock-knock?'
Not any more, mate! I've broken your
knocker!

Knock-knock!
Who's there?
Annie!
Annie who?
Annie more knocking and my hand's going to
fall off!

Knock-knock!
Who's there?
Adore!
Adore who?
Adore stands between us—why don't you
open it?

Knock-knock!
Who's there?
Justin!
Justin who?
Justin case you didn't know, your doorbell's
broken!

Knock-knock!
Who's there?
Agatha!
Agatha who?
Agatha therrible thore thongue, tho I canth
thpeak plperly!

Knock-knock!
Who's there?
Bally!
Bally who?
Well, if you're just going to talk nonsense,
I might as well go back home!

Knock-knock!
Who's there?
Eammon!
Eammon who?
Eammon a bicycle and ey can't get orff!

Did you hear about the burglar who
was caught breaking into a tailor's
shop?
He was stitched up good and proper!

Did you hear about the lorry that
overturned with a load of margarine?
It was spread all over town!

Did you hear about the new bank in the
high street?
They're closing it because of lack of
interest!

Did you hear about the man who painted a
purple stripe on his hair?
It was headline news!

Did you hear about the man who swam all
the way from Dover to Calais?
He didn't believe in ferries!

**How can you tell when Smiffy's
in a car wash?**
He's the one on the bike.

**Why did Smiffy take a watering can
when he went diving?**
To water the seabed!

**Why did Smiffy
park his bike by his bed?**
He was fed up sleepwalking!

How do you sink Smiffy's submarine?
Knock on the door!

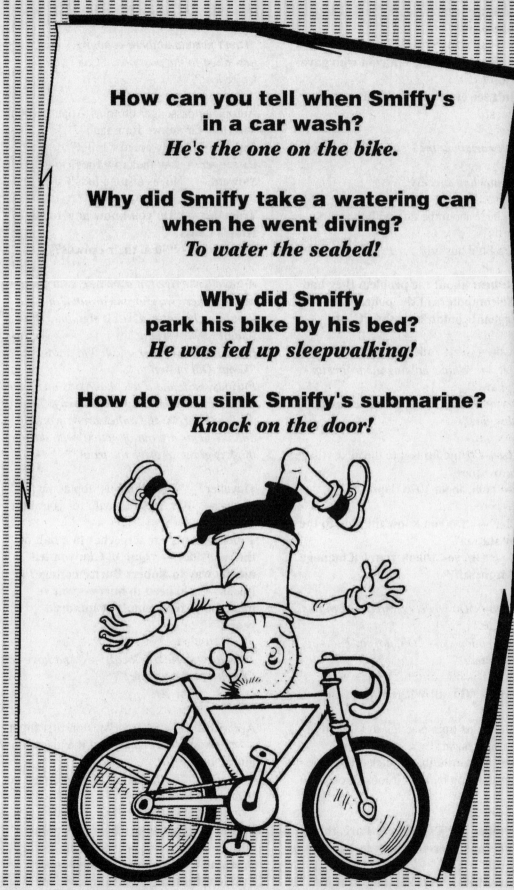

Did you hear about the electrician who wanted to advertise his business?
He phoned the local radio station and asked for a plug!

Did you hear about the optician who gave up his job?
He didn't see eye-to-eye with his customers!

Did you hear about the werewolf's party last night?
It was a howling success!

Did you hear about the dog with the sore throat?
He was a little husky!

Did you hear about the problem they had with the computers at the police station?
The sergeant couldn't get the PC's to work!

Traveller — "What's holding the trains up today, guard?"
Guard — "Wheels and axles, same as any other day, sir!"

Traveller — "How far is it to the next village, as the crow flies?"
Local — "Oh, about 1076 flaps, sir!"

Traveller — "Do you know the way to the railway station?"
Local — "Oh, yes, thank you. I'll manage to find it myself!"

Traveller — "Do you serve breakfast in this hotel?"
Hotel Receptionist — "Oh, no, sir. The waiters do that!"

Traveller — "Guard! Where is this train going to?"
Guard — "This train is going to London in twenty minutes, sir!"
Traveller — "Gosh, that's quick—last time I went to London by train it took three hours!"

1st Traveller — "I've been in Paris three days now, and I haven't been to the Louvre yet!"
2nd Traveller — "You should eat more fruit!"

Two aliens, landing in Great Britain for the first time, walked up to a post box and asked it the way to London. Naturally, it did not reply.
"Don't just stand there grinning," said the first alien to the post box. "Can't you see we're lost?"

Aeroplane passenger on trans-Atlantic flight — "How far are we from land?"
Steward — "Only about a mile!"
Passenger — "As the crow flies?"
Steward — "No, as a stone falls!"

Traveller — "Do you know how to get to King's Cross?"
Little boy — "Steal their crowns?"

A traveller arrived at a small country railway station. There was no-one around, and the first thing he noticed was a sign on a door "Ladies Not Working".
He turned the corner and found another sign "Gents Out of Action".
Furious, he found a telephone box and called the director of the railway company. "Tell me," he said, "if the ladies aren't working and the gents are out of action, who do you think is going to drive the train?"

Traveller — "Does this bus stop at the pier?"
Driver — "If it doesn't, swim for your life!"

Tourist (as his car screeches to a halt at the roadside) — "Quick! Can you tell me the way to Robert Burns' cottage?"
Local — "No need to hurry—you've missed him by a couple of hundred years!"

Traveller (to elderly local) — "And have you lived here all your life?"
Local — "Not yet!"

Aeroplane passenger, nervous on first flight — "Steward, what happens if the plane runs out of fuel?"
Steward — "Then, sir, we all have to get out and push!"

Steward (to passenger boarding plane with enormous hat — "Welcome aboard, madame—I see you've brought your own overhead luggage compartment with you!"

Traveller (to local, working in his front garden) — "Can you tell me where this road leads to?"
Local — "Nope!"
Traveller — "In that case, do you know where THAT road leads to?"
Local — "Nope!"
Traveller — "You don't know much, do you?"
Local — "Nope— but at least I'm not lost!"

Traveller — "I'd like a room for the night please—and could you make sure that I have a good shower!"
Receptionist — "I think you're old enough to wash properly by yourself, sir!"

Station announcement — "Would those taking the London train please put it back—some people want to ride on it!"

Guard — "That's your train over there, sir!"
Traveller — "Cor! I don't get much for my money, do I!"

Traveller — "Is this my train?"
Guard — "No, sir, it's the property of the railway company!"

Station announcement — "The train standing at platforms 1,2,3 and 4 has just come in sideways!"

What happened when the DJ got a job on the railways?
He mixed the tracks!

Traveller — "I love riding the surf!"
Friend — "Does the horse like it too?"

Traveller — "Can I take that train to London?"
Guard — "I suppose you can, sir, but the driver might be a little upset when he comes out and finds it has gone!"

Traveller (to hotel receptionist) — "Do you have a single bedroom with shower?"
Receptionist — "Oh, yes, I do, sir. The staff quarters are excellent here!"

Traveller (phoning airport enquiries) — "How long does it take to get to New York from London?"
Telephonist — "Just a minute, sir... "
Traveller — "Thank you very much!"

An elderly lady is sitting on a bus, opposite a boy who is chewing gum. The old lady looks at the boy, then says — "You can say what you like, young man, but I won't answer—I'm as deaf as a post!"

Traveller — "This room stinks of fish!"
Landlady — "But you said you wanted a sea phew, sir!"

What do you call a man with a rucksack, and salt and pepper all over his head?
A seasoned traveller!

Guard — "Whatever's the matter, sir? You seem terribly angry!"
Traveller — "You bet I'm angry! I just missed my connection by one minute!"
Guard — "Only one minute, sir? I thought by the fuss you were making you must have missed it by an hour at least!"

Traveller — "How do I get to London in this car?"
Local — "Well, you've got the engine going, so you're off to a good start, sir!"

Traveller — "Do you serve Earl Grey tea in your dining room?"
Hotel Receptionist — "We'll serve anyone tea, provided they're prepared to pay for it, sir!"

Traveller — "Porter! Can I please have a luggage trolley for my wife?"
Porter — "I'm sorry, sir, but wives don't count as luggage!"

Traveller — "How long will the next bus to Glasgow be?"
Local — "Oh, about the same length as the last one, I should think!"

Traveller — "This rail ticket you just sold me is out of date!"
Ticket officer — "That's all right sir; so is the train!"

Airline official — "I'm afraid that your child can't travel on this plane, sir—she hasn't got a ticket!"
Traveller — "But when I booked my ticket, I was told that a little baggage goes free!"

Traveller — *"Have you rooms to spare for two tired travellers, footsore and weary?"*
Hotel receptionist — *"Certainly Mr Footsore. If you and Mr Weary would care to sign the register . . ."*

Traveller — "Guard! Why is my train disappearing out of the station? It's five minutes early!"
Railway guard — "Sorry, sir. I think it's my fault. I was just blowing some grit out of my whistle. . ."

Traveller — "I've just returned from Switzerland!"
Friend — "Really? What did you see?"
Traveller — "Not much at all—all these mountains were in the way!"

What's large and grey and wears a flower behind its ear?
A hippy-potamus!

What is the difference between an wolf and a flea?
One howls on the prairie and the other prowls on the hairy!

What did the slug say when it slipped off the wall?
"How slime flies!"

What do worms leave round the bath?
The scum of the earth!

Two flies are sitting on a piece of meat. One fly starts pushing the other.
"Stop!" cries the fly who is being pushed.
"You'll put me off my dinner!"

What happened when the cat ate a ball of wool?
She had mittens!

What do you call a dog with a flat nose?
A blunthound!

What kind of dogs do plumbers like?
P(l)ugs!

What kind of dogs do mountaineers like?
Pekes!

What kind of dogs do landladies like?
Boarder collies!

What did the trumpet player call his dog?
Blew!

What kind of dogs do mechanics like?
Spannerels!

What kind of dogs do scientists like best?
Lab-radors!

What kind of dog lives on cream?
The whippet!

What kind of dog did the robber have?
A Doberman pincher!

Did you hear about the film about lots of dogs with no spots?
They called it 101 Dullmations!

What kind of dog do sprinters like best?
The daschund!

Why was the dog crying?
Because it was a tear-rier!

Why was the other dog crying?
Because it was a chi-wah-wah!

What kind of dog does a pessimist have?
A disa-pointer!

What did the cleaner call his dog?
Dusty!

What did the electrician call his dog?
Sparky!

What did the dentist call his dog?
Floss!

What did the demolition man call his dog?
Rex!

What did the doctor call his dog?
Spot!

What did the gardener call his dog?
Bud!

What did the car mechanic call his dog?
Rusty!

What did the yachtsman call his dog?
Bob!

What did the musician call his dog?
Hi-doh!

What did the wine merchant call his dog?
Corky!

What did the boatman call his dog?
Row-ver!

What kind of dogs do they keep in
monasteries?
Monkrels!

What did the optician call his dog?
Glassie!

What kind of dog do crossword compilers like
best?
The setter!

What did the road mender call his dog?
Digger!

What did the photographer call his dog?
Flash!

What did the cricketer call his dog?
Stumpy!

What did the baker call his dog?
The baker didn't have a dog—he had a
bunny!

What kind of dog do cattle farmers
like best?
Bull terriers!

What kind of dogs always live on farms?
St Barnyards!

What kind of dogs do gymnasts like best?
Springer spaniels!

What kind of dogs do teachers like best?
Ssh-now!-zers!

What did the fireman do with his cat?
He put it out at night!

What do you do with a ghost dog?
Exorcise it daily!

What did the dog say when it sat on some
sandpaper?
"Ruff, ruff!"

Two fleas are sitting by the roadside when a
man comes along with five dogs on leads.
One flea sighs, and says to his friend—
"Wouldn't you know it, you wait all day for
one of these things and then several come
along at once!"

What happened when the dog swallowed a
tropical fish?
It had guppies!

Where did the banker get his dog?
From the pound!

What do you give a dog with a cold?
A chew!

What kind of dogs do skinflints like best?
Cheapdogs!

What kind of dogs do electricians like best?
Wire-haired terriers!

What kind of dogs do office managers like
best?
Chairman shepherds!

When is a dog like an archeologist?
When it digs up old bones!

When is a dog like a piano player?
When he gives you a good chewin'!

How do you clean up after a ghost dog?
Use a whoo-oo-per scooper!

When is a detective like a dog?
When he's on a lead!

How does a dog ask for a share in its
owner's ice cream?
It says "Arf! arf!"

Bill — "My dog's a sniffer dog!"
Will — "Well, train it to use a handkerchief!"

Where does the squirrel keep his dog?
In a kernel out the back!

What did the greedy man say to his dog?
Wolf down!

What did the dog say when it saw the
firework go off?
"WOOF!"

Fred — "I think my dog's a gun-dog!"
Ted — "What do you mean by that?"
Fred — "Every time I call him, he shoots off!"

What's bouncy and playful and wears a dog collar?
A puppy, of course!
Anything else?
The minister on his day off!

Why did the butcher put ten canaries in the mincer?
To make cheep sausage meat!

What's black and white and goes round and round?
A rolled-up newspaper!

What else is black and white and goes round and round?
A zebra in a revolving door!

What else is black and white and goes round and round?
A zebra in a cement mixer!

What else is black and white and goes round and round?
A zebra on the waltzers!

Maisie — "My poodle cost £500!"
Mo — "I wouldn't call that a poodle—I'd call it a dearhound!"

Why do dogs smell?
Because they never change their coats!

Have you ever wondered why zebras do so many silly things?
Yes—I asked them, but I didn't get an answer!
Why?
Zebras can't talk!

Daddy Bear — "Who's been eating my porridge?"
Baby Bear — "Who's been eating my porridge?"
Mummy Bear — "Calm down! I haven't made it yet!"

"I'm calling my dog Carpenter!"
"Why?"
"Because he does odd jobs around the house!"

Jimmy — "I got a goldfish for my birthday!"
Joe — "That's nice!"
Jimmy — "Yes—it's a pity I have to wait till next birthday for the bowl!"

What do you get if you cross a model with a cat?
A glamour puss!

Baby Bear — "Who's been eating my porridge?"
Daddy Bear — "Burp!"

What do you call a donkey in a playground?
Ee-aw, Marjorie Daw!

Did you hear the joke about the slippery eel?
You wouldn't grasp it!

Did you hear the story about the peacock?
It's a wonderful tale!

What creature can see just as well from either end?
A hippopotamus with its eyes shut!

The lion is walking through the jungle, asking every animal he meets, "Who is king of the jungle?"
He asks the monkey, he asks the crocodile, he asks the parrot, "Who is king of the jungle?" and without exception, they all give the same answer; "You, your majesty, you are king of the jungle!"
Then he comes to the elephant. "Who is king of the jungle?" he asks the elephant. The elephant says nothing, but picks the lion up with his trunk and flings him against a nearby tree. The lion winces with pain.
"All right," he says to the elephant. "So you don't know the answer—but did you have to get so cross about it?"

What happens when the cows get mixed up at the dairy?
Udder chaos!

How do you get a set of teeth put in for free?
Annoy a guard dog!

What kind of poultry do you get in sport?
Ducks in cricket and fowls in football—and there's always some old grouse among the spectators!

Why were no frogs born in 2001?
Because it wasn't a Leap Year!

Why did the pigeon go to the race track?
For a flutter on the horses!

Why did the whale let Jonah go?
He couldn't stomach him!

Why can the leopard never escape from the zoo?
Because he's always spotted!

How do you stop a dog from barking in the back of the car?
Put it in the front!

What did one racehorse say to the other?
"Your pace is familiar—have we met before?"

Two ants are running along the top of a packet of biscuits. one says to the other, "What's the rush?" The other replies, "Can't you read? It says 'Tear along the dotted line'!"

What did one sardine say to the other sardine when they saw a submarine?
"Fancy opening a can of people?"

How did the chihuahua kill the alsatian?
It got stuck in its throat and choked it!

What do you get if you cross a rabbit with a shallot?
Bunions!

What's small, black, and stars in Kung Fu movies?
Bruce Flea!

Why are goldfish like cartoon characters?
Because they speak in bubbles!

Why did the horse go to school?
He wanted hay-grades!

Where do squid go camping?
In their tentacles!

What's got six eyes but can't see?
Three blind mice!

Why did the chicken go fishing?
She wanted a perch for dinner!

What did the parrot say to the float?
"Who's a pretty buoy, then?"!

What did the mother kangaroo say when her baby was snatched from her pouch?
"Stop! Pickpocket!"

Why did the rabbit go to the beauty parlour?"
Because it was having a bad hare day!

How can you move a really heavy pig?
With a pork-lift truck!

What do you call a thieving rooster?
A cock robbin'!

Why did the scientists refuse to clone the parrot?
Because it repeated itself already!

What's large and hairy and can break the sound barrier?
King Kongcorde!

Where do limpets go camping?
They don't have tentacles, so they sleep in barnacles!

How did the chicken pay for her groceries?
She put them on her egg-spense account!

Did you hear about the sheep's choir?
They all sang in ewe-nison!

Never eat in a bull's restaurant.
—They charge for seconds!

Newsflash —"Disaster in the jungle. Elephants are sending a special tuskforce to deal with it."

Did you hear about the absent-minded chicken?
She mislaid her eggs!

Did you hear about the pigeon who wanted to buy New York?
He put a deposit on the Statue of Liberty!

1st fly — "I hear poor Freddy was squashed inside an atlas!"
2nd fly — "Yes—but he always wanted to put himself on the map!"

Doctor, doctor. I think I'm a dog.
Lie on the couch.
I can't. I'm not allowed up on the furniture.

Doctor, doctor. My wife thinks she's a lift.
Send her in.
I can't. She doesn't stop at this floor.

Doctor, doctor. I keep seeing double.
Sit on this chair.
Which one?

Maisie — "My new puppy has a pedigree!"
Mo — "Do you have papers for it?"
Maisie — "Not any more—it's house-trained now!"

What do you call a line of cats?
A purrade!

How do you get your dishes squeaky clean?
Put a mouse in your dishwasher!

What do camels take in their tea?
One hump or two!

What did the skunk take to read on holiday?
A best-smeller!

Why did the bear drive round in circles?
Every time he came to a junction, he saw a sign saying 'Bear Left'!

How do you teach a duck new words?
Buy it a duck-tionary!

How fast can a duck go?
At a quacking pace!

Why do people throw bits of bread to the ducks?
Because they've eaten all the cakes!

What did the duck say when she bought a tube of lipstick at the drugstore?
"Just put that on my bill, will you?"

Why did the chicken cross the road?
For a joke!

Why did the breadcrumbs cross the road?
They were stuck to the chicken legs!

Why did the musician cross the road?
For a new set of drumsticks!

Why did the crow get an enormous telephone bill?
He made too many caw-lls!

Why did the jackdaw cross the road?
To crow about his success!

Why did the dalmation disappear?
His owner used spot remover!

Why did the farmer cross the road?
To find his wandering poultry!

How can you tell if a chicken likes you?
It gives you a peck on the cheek!

Man in pet-shop — "You've got a talking dog advertised for sale. Can I hear it speak?"
Pet-shop owner — "Sure! Come here, Barney, and tell the man something about yourself!"
Dog — "Hi! I'm Barney! I'm a world-champion long-distance runner, and I've climbed Everest three times!"
Customer — "That's incredible! (To pet-shop owner) Why would you want to part with such an incredible dog?"
Pet-shop owner — "I'm sick of his lies!"

How did the baby chicken manage to cross the road safely?
Beginner's cluck!

What do you get if you cross a dog with a cheetah?
A dog that chases cars-then overtakes them!

Why should you never trust a nanny-goat?
Because she might be kidding!

Why did the duck cross the road?
To prove he wasn't chicken!

What happened to the chicken who was left out of the henhouse in winter?
He became a brr-rd!

Why did the bird fall out of the sky?
It was dead, silly!

What do you call a canary on roller blades?
A cheepskate!

Bertie Bear calls round at Willy Wolf's house. He rings the bell, but gets no answer. So he checks his watch and says, "What's the time? Missed the wolf!"

What do you get if you cross a dog with a giraffe?
An animal that barks at low-flying aircraft!

Why do bears wear fur coats?
Because their raincoats are at the cleaners!

Teacher — "The pheasant is a game bird . . ."
Pupil — "What game does it like best?"

WHAT DO CATS EAT FOR BREAKFAST?
Mice Krispies or mewsli.

**WHAT HAPPENED
TO THE MOUSE THAT FELL INTO THE
WASHING MACHINE?**
It came out squeaky clean.

**WHAT DO YOU
CALL A COW THAT LIVES
IN GREENLAND?**
An eskimoo!

**WHAT DO
YOU GET IF YOU
CROSS A SOLDIER
WITH A BIRD?**
A parrot-trooper.

What do crabs do when they run out of food?
They nip down to the shops for some more!

What did the frog say on the golf course?
Divot!

Golfer — "Where's my golf ball, Fido?"
Dog — "Rough! Rough!"

1st fly — "I hurt my feet tap-dancing!"
2nd fly — "How did you manage that?"
1st fly — "I burnt them—it was the hot tap!"

Farmer —"Sorry sir, we have no eggs—the batteries have run down!"

Who won the obstacle race in the jungle?
The cheetah was first over the lion!

Why did the bear get his head shaved?
Because he wanted a de-fur-ent hairstyle!

What do you call a male parrot?
Polly-fella!

Why can chickens never tell their children apart?
Because they all look eggsactly the same!

What did the maths teacher say when his parrot went missing?
"Polygon!"

What did the snake do when he had a headache?
He took some asp-irin!

Why did the chicken go to the theatre?
To see its favourite comedy-hen!

What did the sow give her husband for his birthday?
A pig's tie!

Where does the captain exercise his dog on board ship?
The poop deck!

1st rabbit — "I've got an idea!"
2nd rabbit — "Not another of your hair-brained schemes!"

Did you hear about the worm that lived to be 100?
He always got up before the early bird!

What's a flea's favourite song?
"Home on the mange!"

Why did the zoo-keeper end up in hospital?
The boa constrictor had a crush on him!

Mum — "Where on earth did you get that elephant, Johnny?"
Johnny — "At the Jumbo Sale!"

Why was the buffalo smiling?
Because it was laugh-a-bull!

Why did the hare's friend's think he was boring?
He just kept rabbiting on an on . . .

What do you call a pigeon in uniform?
A military coo!

How do hens dance?
Chick-to-chick!

Why did the chickens leave the dance floor?
Because they heard the foxtrot!

What ballet do pigs most enjoy?
Swine Lake!

Why did the cow cough?
It had a bullfrog in its throat!

Which animal goes to bed with its shoes on?
The horse!

Why did the sheep fail its driving test?
Because it couldn't do a ewe-turn!

Why are mosquitoes good at arithmetic?
Because they add to your misery and subtract from your pleasure!

Why are rabbits good at arithmetic?
Because they multiply faster than most other animals!

What's the easiest way to count cattle?
With a cow-culator!

What do you call a shrimp with a machine gun?
Al Caprawn!

What do you get if you cross a shark with a dog?
An animal that barks at submarines!

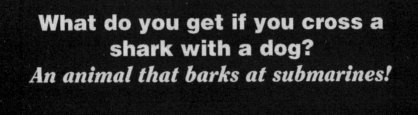

What happens if you eat caterpillars?

You get butterflies in your stomach.

Why did the pig learn karate?
So he could do pork chops.

What has fifty legs but can't walk?
Half a centipede.

What happens when chickens drink whisky?
They lay Scotch eggs!

Why did the cows all sit down at once?
They were playing moo-sical bumps!

What is the difference between a diving duck and a lost dog?
A diving duck up-ends in the pond, and a lost dog ends up in the pound!

What did the chicken say when its mother sat on an orange?
"Look at the egg mamma-laid!"

What do you get if you cross a dog with a chicken?
Pooched eggs!

What do you give a horse with a chest infection?
Cough stirrup!

Why did the cat wear a turtle-neck sweater?
To hide his flea-collar!

How do dogs cook their eggs?
They pooch them!

Why did Mr and Mrs Skunk sit at opposite sides of the church?
They refused to share the same pew!

What do you call an ant which has come from abroad?
Important!

What do you call an ant with a high voice?
Descant!

Why do cats make bad sailors!
Every time they set sail, there's a mew-tiny!

What do you call an ant that has fallen in the paint pot?
A colourant!

What happens when a firefly becomes confused?
It doesn't know if it's coming or glowing!

What do you call a sweetly smelling ant?
Fragrant!

What do you call a helpful ant?
Assistant!

What do you get when you send two rockets full of toads into space?
Star Warts!

Why do frogs have webbed feet?
To stamp out forest fires!

Why do elephants have singed feet?
From stamping on smoking frogs!

Why do frogs wear tin helmets?
To protect them from stamping elephants!

Why did the frog break off his engagement?
His girlfriend spawned his affections!

What's green, covered in ketchup and mustard, and rolls?
Hot frogs!

What happens if you eat a poisoned frog?
You croak!

Why did the frog go to the doctor?
He had a troublesome person in his throat!

Two cats had a milk-drinking race
The first one won by a lap!

What do you call an ant that can swim?
An ant-phibian!

What did one vulture say to the other vulture?
"I've got a bone to pick with you!"

How do American cats get around town?
In catillacs!

1st maggot — "What's the matter?"
2nd maggot — "I'm in despair!"
1st maggot — "Well try dis apple instead, it might cheer you up!"

Why did the horse go to the theatre?
It wanted a stall for Saturday night!

When is it unlucky to see a black cat?
When you're a mouse!

What lies on the ground, 100 feet up in the air, and smells?
A dead centipede!

Mummy centipede — "What's the matter, son?"
Little centipede — "I've hurt my foot!"
Mummy centipede — "Which one?"
Little centipede — "Hang on—I'm still counting!"

What's speckled and travels at 100 miles an hour?
A trout on a motor bike!

How do you get milk from a cat?
Steal her saucer!

What do you do if you find a bookworm eating your book?
Take the words right out of its mouth!

Why did the cat cry over her maths homework?
Because the sums were im-puss-able!

What do you do with a hyperactive dog?
Press paws!

What did one flea say to the other flea after a night out?
"Shall we walk home or catch a dog?"

What did Wild Bill Hickock call his cat?
Posse!

1st golfer — "What's that little grey creature holding up your golf ball?"
2nd golfer — "That's my-tee mouse!

What do you do with a dog that chases everything on a bike?
Take the air out of its tyres!

1st man — "My dog loves children!"
2nd man — "Does he?"
1st man — "Yes, but he has to make do with dog meat instead!"

Did you hear about the cat that kept thinking it was Mickey Mouse?
It was having Disney spells!

What do you call a rich frog?
A gold-blooded reptile!

What do you do if a frog turns up at your party uninvited?
Tell him to hop it!

What do you call a frog spy?
A croak-and-dagger agent!

Do mice give each other Christmas presents?
No—they just exchange Chris-mouse cards!

What do you call a homeless snail?
A slug!

How do sheep record special family events?
They make videos with their lambcorder!

What do you call a nervous flea?
A jitterbug!

When is an amphibian like a car?
When it's being toad!

What do you call a hen that is covered in oil?
A slick chick!

What happened to the wolf who swallowed a sheep whole?
He felt very baa-aa-aa-d!

Why did the sheep choose the most expensive washing machine?
Because it was easiest to ewes!

What kind of birds are found in Portugal?
Portu-geese!

Bill — "My dog can count!"
Will — "Prove it!"
Bill — "Okay! Rover, what is four minus four?"
Will — "But he's saying nothing!"
Bill — "Exactly! That's the right answer!"

What did the dog say to the bone?
"It's been nice gnawing you!"

Did you hear the joke about the egg?
Never mind—it was rotten anyway!

Café owner to little boy — "You can't bring your dog in here—it's smelly and full of germs!"
Little boy — "If it's as bad as that, then I don't want to come in, either!"

What's the difference between lions and whales when they're upset?
Lions roar, but whales blubber!

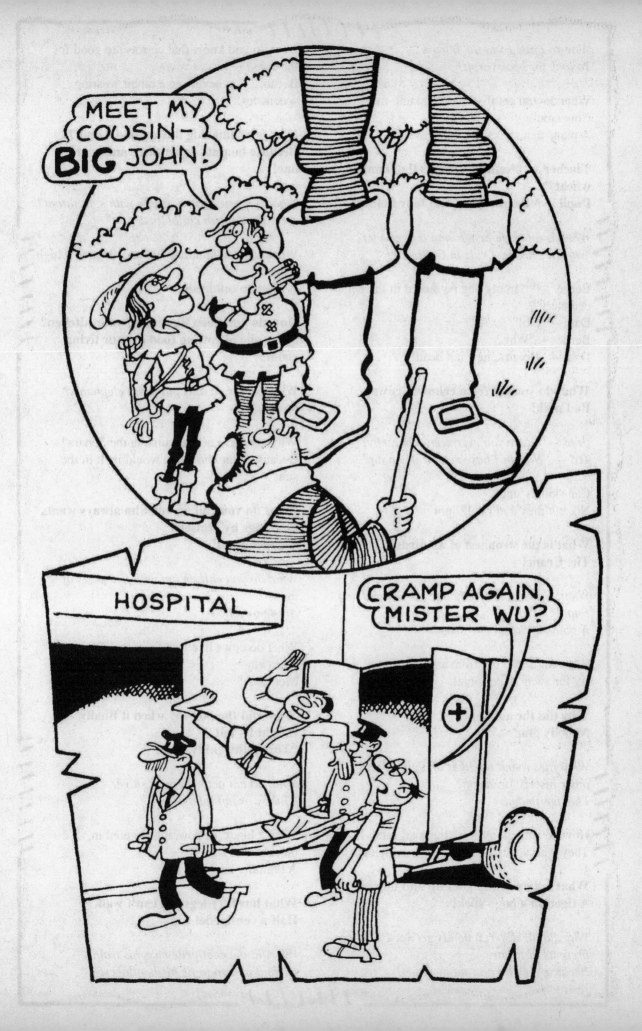

Why do birds go to the library?
To look for bookworms!

What do you get if you put a skunk in Concorde?
A plane that stinks to high heaven!

Teacher — "Name six things that contain wheat."
Pupil — "Bread, cakes and four fields."

When is an eagle faster than a jumbo jet?
When it's taking a ride in Concorde!

Bertie — "Can my dog be buried in the pet's cemetery?"
Dad; — "No!"
Bertie — "Why?"
Dad — "Because he's not dead!"

What do you get from criminal cows?
Bad milk!

Fred — "Have you ever seen a horsefly?"
Ted — "No, but I have seen a sheep dip!"

Can skunks sing?
No, but they don't half hum!

What is the strongest of all birds?
The Crane!

What's warm and smelly and goes round and round?
A skunk in the tumble drier!

What fur do we get from a grizzly bear?
As fur away as possible!

Why did the antelope?
Nobody gnu!

What flies round the light at night, biting other insects' heads off?
The tiger moth!

How do baby lions cross the road safely?
They wait until they see a zebra crossing!

What's stripey and goes up and down?
A tiger on a pogo stick!

Why did the desert animals get not Christmas presents last year?
Because the lion had sandy claws!

How do you know that carrots are good for the eyes?
Because you never see a rabbit wearing spectacles!

Why is a lame dog like adding 6 and 7?
Because he puts down three and carries one!

What is worse than a giraffe with sore throat?
A centipede with chilblains!

What has one hundred feet and sings in a high voice?
A soprano centipede!

How do you keep flies out of your kitchen?
Put a pile of rotting food in your living room!

What games do ants play with elephants?
Squash!

Why are there no penguins in the Sahara?
Because their chocolate would melt in the sun!

What do you call an ant who always wants do things by himself?
Independ-ant!

What do you call an ant with five pairs of eyes?
Ant-ten-eye!

What do cows like best from the Chinese takeaway?
Moo-dles!

What did the dog say when it finally caught its tail?
"This is the giddy limit!"

What do cat actors say on stage?
"Tabby or not tabby!"

What's black, yellow and covered in blackberries?
A bramble bee!

What has fifty legs but can't walk?
Half a centipede!

Why did the centipede miss his train?
He had to stop to tie his bootlaces!

What do you call a centipede on guard duty?
A sentrypede!

**What goes ninety nine, clickety, ninety nine, clickety splosh?
A centipede in River Dance!**

*Why are cats the funniest animals?
Because they are most a-mews-ing!*

What does a queen bee do when she burps?
She issues a royal pardon!

**What do you call an ant who cannot sing in tune?
Discord-ant!**

*What do you call a maggot who becomes an ace pilot?
Buggles!*

Why did the ladybird go to the doctor?
Because she had spots!

**What kind of medicine do you give a sick ant?
Ant-ibiotics!**

*What do baby mice look like after their baths?
Squeaky clean!*

Where do flies meet before they go into town?
At the buzz stop!

**What has six legs, and can work out your dad's income tax?
An account-ant!**

*Where do caterpillars lay their heads at night?
On their caterpillows!*

Why did Mr and Mrs Spider keep a money box under their mattress?
They were saving for their golden webbing!

**Why did the hedgehog cross the road?
To see his flat mate!**

*What would you get if you gave lemon juice to a cat?
A sour puss!*

Why do elephants wear green shoes?
So they can hide in the grass!

**What kind of bears like rainy weather?
Drizzly bears!**

*What kind of maths do owls like best?
Owlgebra!*

What do you call a camel with three humps?
Humphrey!

**How do you stop two snakes from having an argument?
Tell them to hiss and make up!**

*What do you say to a bald porcupine?
Anything you like—he's too spineless to do anything about it!*

Did you hear about the tiger who swallowed a comedian?
He felt very funny!

**What did the man-eating tiger cook for lunch?
Baked beings!**

*What do you call a woodpecker with no beak?
A headbanger!*

How does a bird with a broken wing manage to land safely?
With its sparrowchute!

**Why was the snake kept in at school?
Because his writhing was bad!**

*What did one firefly say to the other?
Got to glow now!*

Where do spiders play football?
Webley!

**What did the spider say when it got a hole in its web?
"Darn it!"**

*Why should you never go to a shop owned by elephants?
Because they charge too much!*

Why was the chicken sent off the football pitch?
Because it was a fowl!

WHAT DO YOU CALL
A BOY WITH LEAVES ON HIS HEAD?
Russell.

WHAT SWEETS
DO FROGS LIKE?
Lollyhops!

WHAT DO YOU CALL A
LOST MONSTER?
A where wolf.

WHAT'S GREEN AND
SCALEY AND RED AT
THE BOTTOM?
*A dragon with
nappy rash!*

Why are spiders computer wizards?
Check out their websites for more
information!

What is black and white and red all over?
A zebra with an allergy!

1st glow worm — "I'm delighted!"
2nd glow worm — "But you look miserable!"
1st glow worm — "I am. Someone cut off my
tail and I'm de-lighted!"

**What do you get if you cross a skunk with
a bat?**
A smell that hangs around all day!

*What did the mouse say when he was leaving
his friend's house?*
See you next squeak!

Why did the rhinoceros buy a bicycle bell?
Because his horn wasn't working!

**Why did the chicken cross the adventure
playground?**
To get to the other slide!

*What is black and white and green, black and
white and green?*
A zebra wrestling with a gooseberry!

Why was Charlie glow worm always top of
the class?
Because he was the brightest!

How did the owls get into Noah's Ark?
Two-hoo by two-hoo!

What happens when flies become cold?
They turn into bluebottles!

Why did the two maggots in an apple get
turned away from Noah's Ark?
Because the animals were supposed to be in
pairs!

**Why did the lame chicken go to the music
shop?**
To get another drumstick!

How do you find where a flea has bitten you?
Start from scratch!

What do you call a Russian flea?
A Moscow-ito!

**What do you get if you cross a skunk with
a boomerang?**
A bad smell that keeps coming back.

*What is worse than finding a maggot when
you bite into an apple?*
Finding half a maggot!

Which side of a hen has the most feathers?
The outside!

**If there were six cats in a boat and one
jumped out, how many would be left?**
None! All the rest were copy cats!

*What do you get if you cross a young goat
with a maggot?*
A grubby kid!

What do sea monsters eat?
Fish and ships!

1st cat — "I'm feeling down in the mouth!"
2nd cat — "Why is that?"
**1st cat — "I caught a duck earlier on
today!"**

What is a French cat's favourite pudding?
Chocolate mousse!

A dog in a cowboy hat, with a bandage on his
foot, limped into a Wild West Saloon. "What
are you doin' here, stranger?" asked the
barman. The dog growled and replied, "I'm
lookin' for the man who shot ma paw!"

Why was the centipede late?
**Because he was playing "This little piggy"
with his baby sister.**

What do you get if you cross a centipede with
a minah bird?
A walkie-talkie!

**What do you get if you cross a centipede
with a chicken?**
Enough drumsticks to feed an army!

*What is worse than a crocodile with
toothache?*
A centipede with athlete's foot!

What do you get if you cross a dog with a
gorilla?
An animal that won't let you up on the couch!

What did Mr Dopey do to the flea in his ear?
He shot it!

What do you get if you cross a glow-worm with a glass of beer?
Light ale!

How do you know when a spider's angry?
He goes up the wall!

What goes "snap, crackle, pop"?
A firefly with a short circuit!

What is the name of the most famous insect movie producer?
Stephen Spielbug!

A man goes into the riding supplies shop and asks the first man he sees for a new bridle for his horse. "I'm sorry, but I can't help you, sir," says the man. "I'm a saddle sewer." "Look here," says the first man, "I've been riding for three days to get here, and I'm pretty saddle sore myself, but do you hear me complaining about it?"

What do you get if you cross a bee with a skunk?
A bee with a nasty stink in its tail!

What kind of dog makes a good hairdresser?
A shampoodle!

What is a vampire's favourite kind of dog?
A bloodhound!

How do you catch a runaway dog?
Hide behind a tree and make a noise like a bone!

What do you call a happy sheepdog?
A jolly collie!

What did the cowboy say when a bear ate his dog?
"Well, doggone!"

What kind of dog loves the smell of flowers?
A budhound!

What do you get if you cross a sheepdog with a daisy?
A collie-flower!

Why did the poor dog chase its tail?
He was trying to make both ends meet!

Bob — "Why did you call your dog 'Discovery'?"
Joe — "Because I've never seen anything like him before!"

Annie — "Why did you call your dog 'germ'?"
Betty — "Because I got him from a friend!"

Where does a Rottweiler sit in the cinema?
Anywhere it wants to!

What kind of meat do you give a stupid dog?
Chump chops!

Why did the dachshund bite the woman's ankle?
Because that was the only part of her he could reach!

Bill — "Why do you call your dog Frost?"
Will — "Because Frost bites!"

Why do dogs wag their tails?
Because no-one else will do it for them!

Bill — "Have you heard about the dog that ate twelve cloves of garlic?"
Will — "No—what about him?"
Bill — "His bark was much worse than his bite!"

What do you call a meditating dog?
A paws for thought!

Why do dogs bury their bones in the earth?
Because they can't dig a hole in the pavement!

Bill — "My dog's so clever, he can answer the telephone!"
Will — "What kind of dog is he?"
Bill — "A golden receiver!"

What do you get if you cross an aeroplane and a dog?
A jet setter!

What can you do if your dog eats your shoes?
Wear your boots instead!

What's the difference between a bear and a hot dog?
A bear wears a fur coat, a hot dog just pants!

What do you get if you cross a teddy bear with a skunk?
Winnie the Poo-ee!

How can you tell if it's been raining cats and dogs?
There are poodles on the streets!

What is the name of the bear who wears wellington boots and steps in puddles?
Paddlington!

Why are bears bad at dancing?
They have two left feet!

What do you get if you cross a skunk with a faithful dog?
A bad smell that follows you around!

What do you get if you cross a kangaroo with a dog?
A pooch with a pouch!

How can you find a dog in the woods?
Put your ear to a tree a listen for its bark!

What is grey, has big ears and a trunk?
A mouse going on holidays!

What sport do flies play with humans?
Squash!

1st furniture polisher— "So you're pleased with your new puppy, then?
2nd furniture polisher— "Oh, yes, I've taken quite a shine to him!"

1st weather forecaster— "What's your new baby like?"
2nd weather forecaster— "Oh, you know the sort of thing fair, windy, occasionally wet!"

Friend — "Why did you give up your job as a fishmonger?"
Fishmonger — "It was making me sell-fish!"

What kind of football do bankers play?
Fiver side!

What's a hairdresser's favourite sport?
Curling!

Did you hear about the butcher who joined the union?
He wanted to become chop steward!

Salesman — "So you want a career in sales, do you—do you ever tell lies?"
Job applicant — "No, but I'll learn quickly!"

Why did the baker stop making doughnuts?
because he was tired of the hole business!

Why did the traffic cop arrest the sheep?
Because it did a ewe-turn on a dual carriageway!

Why did the banker fall off his bike?
He lost his balance!

Did you hear about the footballer who became a pilot?
He was sacked for playing on the wing!

Why did the farmer feed his cows five-pound notes?
To make the milk richer!

Why did the farmer build the cattle-shed squint?
To get lean beef!

Why did the farmer daub stripes on his pigs?
To get streaky bacon!

1st fisherman — "I caught five mackerel yesterday, all of them weighing more than three pounds!"
2nd fisherman — "So what? I caught six jellyfish—all of them different flavours!"

What team do car mechanics support?
The Oil Stars!

Why did the chef get a job in a roof-top restaurant?
He wanted to be a high-fryer!

Did you hear about the lift attendant who got a job as an airline steward?
As the passengers boarded the plane, he asked them, "Going up?"

What did the movie star call out to his adoring fans?
"See you swoon!"

How do hens dance?
Chick to chick.

What happened to
the hen that fell
into the cement mixer.
It turned into a brick layer.

What do
you give a sick bird?
Tweetment!

What's yellow and
white and goes at one
hundred and fifty miles per hour?
*A train driver's egg
sandwich.*

What is the difference between a night watchman and a butcher?
One stays awake and the other weighs a steak!

Why do inventors make useless cooks?
Because most of their ideas are half-baked!

Did you hear about the submarine captain who got a job driving a subway train?
Every time he stopped at a station, he shouted "Up periscope!"

Why did they call in the glazier to the atomic power plant?
They wanted new clear (nuclear) windows!

What part of the police force can bacon join?
The Special Brunch!

Why was the writer kept in prison?
He hadn't finished his sentence!

Why did the lawyer go to the skating-rink?
Too see just-ice!

Did you hear about the chef that burnt through all his saucepans?
The manager told him he would make a good potholer!

Take up astronomy—it's a heavenly job!

Take up astrology—there's a future in it!

Take up aromatherapy—you'll soon get the massage!

Take up a litter collection—you'll pick it up as you go along!

Work in a casino—spin the roulette wheel and watch things take a turn for the better!

What do they sing when someone retires from the frozen foods factory?
"Freezer jolly good fellow!"

What did the supermarket manager say to the late employee?
There's trouble in store for you!

Why was the weatherman depressed?
Because there were too many clouds on his horizon!

What's the difference between a baker and a cricketer?
One makes buns and rolls and the other makes runs and bowls!

What did the weatherman say when he had beans for supper?
"Gale force wind predicted later on tonight!"

What did the miserly weatherman write on his bathroom door?
"Brief showers only!"

Musician — "Do you know 'Madame Butterfly'?"
Man — "Know her? She's been my friend since she was a cocoon!"

1st archeologist — "I'm sorry we quarrelled. Can we be friends again, and forget about our little argument?
2nd archeologist — "Certainly. I've always said there's nothing to be gained from digging up the past."

Did you hear about the card-player who bought a double-decker bus?
He tried to drive under a low bridge, and cut the top deck!

Optometrist — "How many fingers am I holding up Mr Smith?"
Mr Smith — "Goodness—you're even more short-sighted than I am!"

Man (to barber) — "Would you shave a man with a wooden leg?"
Barber — "No— with a razor!"

1st Farmer — "I haven't had enough rain for my crops this year!"
2nd farmer — "You've had more than I have!"
1st farmer — "How can that be?"
2nd farmer — "You've got more land!"

Tex jumped onto his saddle and galloped out of town into the desert in a cloud of dust. Two minutes later, he was back.
He had forgotten his horse!

What did the banker say when the butcher's safe blew up?
"It wasn't my vault!"

Friend — "So you've given up your job as host on the TV show, have you?"
TV personality — "Yes—I came, I saw, I compered!"

What was written on the magician's gravestone?
"I came, I sawed, I conjured!"

Man — *"I make a lot of money in my new job!"*
Friend — *"What's that?"*
Man — *"I work at the mint!"*

A farmer is standing in a field with forty pigs—how many feet are there?
Two—the pigs have trotters!

What did the electrician say to his teenage son?
"Wire you insulate?"!

Why is a telephone engineer like an explorer?
Because his work takes him from pole to pole!

Window cleaner — "I fell off a fifty-foot ladder yesterday!"
Friend — "Did you hurt yourself?"
Window cleaner — "No—I was only on the second rung!"

Did you hear about the comedian who took up chicken farming?
The chickens got plenty of corn!

What about the eggs?
Oh—they kept cracking up!

Ted — "I started at the bottom in my career!"
Fred — "Did you?"
Ted — "Yes—I got a job in a toilet paper factory!"

How did the beautician remember her clients' names?
She kept them all on file!

Why was the sword-swallower arrested?
Because he hiccuped and stabbed a member of the audience!

What is the difference between a film star and an enormous sweater?
One's a crowd-drawer, the other's a drawer-crowder!

"Did it hurt when you fell of the piano stool?"
"No—I hit the soft pedal!"

Why did the little boy trip up the waiter?
He wanted to see a flying saucer!

When is a bus-driver not a bus-driver?
When he turns into a side-street!

Why was the shoemaker relieved?
Because he had found his hammer at last!

Did you hear about the man whose wife bought a whisky firm?
He loved her still!

They stopped using string at the packaging plant. It was tape for the parcels or nothing. Every day, bits of string would queue up at the door, looking for a job, only to be turned away. Then one day, a tassel turned up at the door. The man at the door looked at him and said, "Are you a bit of string?"
"No," said the tassel. "I'm a frayed knot."

Why did the nurse put a band-aid on her pay check?
Because she got a cut in her salary!

Why did the person with second-sight get depressed?
Because nothing surprised him any more!

What is the difference between a dentist and an artist?
One draws teeth, the other just draws!

Why did the barber go to the bank?
To open a shaving account!

Why did the public speaker go to the bank?
To open a say-things account!

Why did the duck farmer go out of business?
Because profits were down!

Why was the prize-fighter house-proud?
Because he wiped the floor with his opponent!

At the grand parade this afternoon, most of the crowd were waving flags.
The hairdresser didn't have a flag, so she waved her hair instead!

What does a comedian do when he's going out on his motorcycle?
He puts on a helmet and giggles!

Friend — "Why did you lose your job as a pilot?"
Ex-pilot — "My work went into a decline!"

Fisherman — "I've worked on the trawlers all my life, hauling up one net after another, day after day. . ."
Friend — "Life's a drag, isn't it!"

Friend — "So you gave up your job running the carousel?"
Fairground attendant — "Yes—things took a turn for the worse!"

Farmer — "My horse does impressions!"
Friend — "Really?"
Farmer — "Yes! He gave me an impression of his shoe on my backside!"

Rob — "Why did you lose your job as a dog-catcher, Bob?"
Bob — "Inflation!"
Rob — "Inflation?"
Bob — "Yes—I couldn't get many dogs to the pound any more!"

Friend— "So how's the window cleaning business going?"
Window cleaner— "It's a bit of a pane!"

Molly — "My sister works for an ironing service."
Maisie — "Does she earn much?"
Molly — "No, just a flat rate—but she's hoping for a pay in-crease soon!"

Why did the carpenter go to the doctor's?
Because he had a saw finger!

What happens when cows won't give milk?
The dairyman doesn't see the pint!

"What do you do for a living?"
"I sell salt!"
"Really? I'm a salt sellar too!"
"Shake!"

Friend — "Well, Gladys, how's your slimming club going?"
Gladys — "Very well!—for every pound my members lose, I gain two!"

1st man — "And what do you earn at the frozen foods factory?"
2nd man — "Ice lolly!"

How much do chicken farmers earn?
A poultry amount!

How did the ringmaster pay the strongman?
Weakly!

How did King Arthur pay the knights in his castle?
Fort-knightly!

What did the doctor say to his dog?
"Heal!"

Do anglers make any money?
Not much, but they sometimes get a couple of squid!

Why did the pianist refuse his salary cheque?
Because he wanted to be paid in notes!

Do hairdressers make a lot of money?
No—but there are plenty of fringe benefits!

Friend — "How is your new job as a lifeguard going?"
Lifeguard — "Oh, swimmingly, thanks!"

Farmhand to friend — "I used to have a job collecting eggs on a chicken farm, but I was laid off."

Friend — "Why on earth did you choose to be a rodeo rider?"
Rodeo rider — "I wanted lots of bucks!"

What do you call two lawyers in an underwear shop?
A pair of briefs!

What did the undertaker say when he knocked on the coffin lid?
"Is there any body in?"

Man to police officer — "Officer! Someone's dug an enormous hole in my front garden!"
Police officer — "We'll look into it right away, sir!"

Friend— "What's life like on the oil rigs?"
Oil rig worker— "Boring!"

Friend — "So you've given up Scottish country dancing— why is that?"
Dancer — "Problems, problems—it was just one fling after another!"

What does the detective carry to work with him?
An open-and-shut case!

Friend— "How exciting! Twin boys! Congratulations! How did the birth go?"
Musician— "Not bad at all of course, they arrived one sonata time!"

Friend— "How's the fireworks business?"
Fireworks manufacturer— "Business is booming!"

Friend— "How are you getting on in your new job as a bus driver?"
Bus driver— "Oh, not bad, but it's a bit stop-and-go!"

Friend— "So why did you give up your career as a sword swallower?"
Sword swallower— "I just couldn't see the point any more!"

Friend— "You're retiring from sprinting, are you? Why is that?"
Athlete— "I was getting too far behind!"

Friend — "Why did you give up swimming?"
Swimmer — "I threw in the towel!"

Friend— "So what are you going to do after you retire?"
Gardener— "Grow older!"

Friend— "Why did you give up your job on the farm?"
Farm worker— "It was the hay baling — that was just the last straw!"

Friend— "So you're retiring, are you? Why is that?"
Butcher— "I didn't retire —I was given the chop!"

Friend— "Why did you give up your job as a waiter?"
Waiter— "I had too much on my plate."

Dairyman to farmer— "I'm sick of this job! I'm going to look for an udder one!"

Friend— "Why did you give up your job as a tailor?"
Tailor— "The job didn't suit me!"

Friend— "Why did you leave the orchestra?"
Musician— "It all went rather flat!"

Friend — "So you've given up DIY—why is that?
DIY enthusiast — "I just didn't know what to do with my shelf any more!"

1st fisherman — "I hear you've got a great new job — how did you find it?
2nd fisherman — "It was advertised on the Net!"

Why was the photographer depressed?
He kept seeing the negative side of things!

Friend— "I hear you're giving up your job as a train driver —what are you going to do next?"
Train driver— "I'll be looking for something else along the same lines!"

Did you hear about the absent-minded train-driver?
He lost track!

Why did the novelist go mad?
He lost the plot!

Dry-cleaner to customer— "Sorry, madam, I can't clean your curtains today. I have a pressing appointment elsewhere!"

Friend— "So you're giving up your dreams of being a writer —what will you do next?"
Writer — "One chapter closes, another one opens. . ."

Friend— "Why did you give up your job in the duvet factory?"
Duvet stuffer— "The job was getting me down."

Why did the sandwich-maker go to the dentist?
His fillings kept coming out!

Friend— "So you've given up your haggis-making business. Why is that?
Butcher— "I didn't have the guts for it any more!"

What did the architect's children say to him at bedtime?
"Give us another storey, Dad!"

Why did the theatre manager give up his job?
He wanted a change of scenery!

Why did the orange give up acting?
He didn't like the limelight!

Why did the miner give up his job?
It was the pits!

Why did the casino worker give up his job?
Someone offered him a better deal!

Will — "I was fired from my job, because they said I was slow at everything. But it's just not true!"
Bill — "Why not?"
Will — "Because I'm not slow at everything—I tire quickly!"

Friend — "What made you become an exorcist?"
Exorcist — "I don't know—I can't think what possessed me!"

Patient — "Can you recommend some cough mixture for me?"
Pharmacist — "This stuff's great—you won't get any better!"

Friend — "So you're not cutting grass any longer?"
Greenkeeper — "No—I'm cutting it shorter!"

Manager — "If you don't keep up with your work, I'm going to have to get another man!"
Worker — "Thank goodness! I could do with an assistant!"

Why is a tree surgeon like an actor?
Because he takes boughs!

Interior designer — "The room's nearly finished, but I think you should get a chandelier!"
Client — "What would be the point? No-one in our family plays one!"

Notice outside dry-cleaners "We'll clean for you, we'll press for you—we'll even dye for you!"

Instructor — "You're ready to fly solo today!"
Trainee pilot — "How low?"

Friend — "Why did you get a job at the bank?"
Bank clerk — "Because there's money in it!"

Will — "My brother's an exporter!"
Bill — "Does he send goods abroad?"
Will — "No—he used to work at the railway station!"

Book title — "Punctuality Pays" by Justin Time

Book title — "The Dangers of Coastal Cliffs" by Eileen Dover

Book title — "Success in the Christmas Sales" by Jocelyn Ann Grabbin

Book title — "The Key to Happiness" by Eve R. Smylie

Book title — "Fishing is Fun" by Rod N. Lyne

Book title — "1000 funny stories" by Owen Lee Joe King

Book title — "Writing a Bestseller" by Will U. Buyatt

Book title — "Laundry Tips" by Crispin White

Book title — "My life as a prize-fighter" by K.O.D. Best

Book title — "Archery for Beginners" by Pierce Stallover

Book title — "Notes from a Desert Island" by I. Malone

Book title — "Life on the Beach" by Sandy Shaw

Book title — "Living discreetly" by Annette Curtain

Book title — "Amazing ball tricks" by C. Lyon

Book title — "Successful partnerships" by Mary A. Richman

Book title — *"How a Steamroller Changed My Life" by I.M. Flatman*

Book title — "How to avoid sunburn" by C.U. Redden

Book title — "1000 Questions and Answers" by Noah Lotte

Book title — "My life as a lion tamer" by Claude B. Hind

Book title — "How to Get Rich" by Mary A. Tycoon

Book title — "Successful Orienteering" by Ivor Mappe

Book title — "Deep-sea Fishing for Women" by Netta Shark

Book title — "Gem-hunting" by Williamina Ruby

Holiday reading for gardeners "Ivanhoe"!

Holiday reading for welders anything riveting!

Holiday reading for furniture sales staff "A Tale of Two Settees"!

Holiday reading for electricians "The Vital Spark"!

Holiday reading for firefighters The Complete Works of Burns!

Holiday reading for goat-keepers — "Kidnapped"!

Holiday reading for musicians — "Murder on the High C's"!

Holiday reading for genealogists — "Goldilocks and the Forebears"!

Holiday reading for magicians — "Tom Saw-yer"!

Holiday reading for indecisive people — "Maybe Dick"!

Holiday reading for mothers-to-be — "Great Expectations"!

Holiday reading for acrobats — some magazines to flip through!

Holiday reading for monsters — The Tales of Grimm

Holiday reading for hairdressers — "Tess of the Barbervilles"!

Holiday reading for knights — "David Coppershield"!

Holiday reading for bakers — anything by Agatha Crusty!

Holiday reading for dog-lovers — "The Beagle has Landed"!

Honeymoon reading for nits — "Brideshead Revisited"!

Holiday reading for florists — "How to Twine Fronds and Influence People".

Holiday Reading for skiers — "Slithering Heights"!

Holiday reading for ballroom dancers — "The Thirty-nine Steps"!

Holiday reading for herbalists — "A Brief History of Thyme"!

Holiday reading for grasshoppers — "What Katydid"!

Holiday reading for fortune-tellers — "The Foresight Saga"!

Reading for sleeping under the stars — "The Wind in the Pillows"!

Reading for orbiting astronauts — "Around the World for Eighty Days"!

Why do surgeons wear gloves? Because their patients are out cold!

What do an anaesthetist and a baked bean have in common? They both give you gas!

Which sweet moans?
Whine gums!

Why is a pea small and green?
*Because if it was long and yellow it would be
a banana.*

**Where does the cleaner go to have her
eyes tested?**
To the mopticians.

What do you call a singing herb?
Elvis Parsley.

Why do you call your fish "Explorer"?
*Because he's been round the globe
thousands of times.*

Why did the surgeon x-ray his stomach? He wanted to be on bellyvision!

Patient;— "Doctor, doctor, I'm all fingers and thumbs!"
Doctor — "In that case, can you lend me a hand?"

Patient — "Well, doctor, what do you think is wrong with me— measles or chickenpox?"
Doctor — "To be honest, I can't spot the difference!"

Patient — "Doctor, doctor, I've swallowed the ring I was going to give my wife!"
Doctor — "There's nothing I can do —but wrap up carefully for the present!"

Patient — "Doctor, doctor! I've been bitten by a dog!"
Doctor — "Name?"
Patient — "Rover!"

Nurse — "I drove into the hospital today!"
Patient — "Did you?"
Nurse — "So don't worry about the noise—they're just repairing the wall!"

Patient — "Doctor, doctor, I've swallowed a fly—should I take something for it?"
Doctor — "No—just let it starve!"

Patient — "Doctor, doctor! I feel like an aeroplane!"
Doctor — "Give me a wing tomorrow!"

Patient — "Doctor, doctor, everybody treats me like a cricket ball!"
Doctor — "How's that?"
Patient — "See what I mean?"

Doctor — "Drink plenty of fluids, and keep away from draughts!"
Patient — "I can't stand that game anyway!"

Patient — "Doctor, doctor, I'm locked out!"
Doctor — "That's no concern of mine!"
Patient — "Yes it is—my son's swallowed the key!"

Patient — "Doctor, doctor, I'm a terrible liar!"
Doctor — "I don't believe a word you're saying!"

Nurse — "Have you found the golf ball the patient swallowed?"
Surgeon — "Yes—here it is!"
Nurse — "Right, I'll call in the other man to take his next shot, then!"

Doctor — "This is a very strange problem, Mrs Green! Have you had it before?"
Mrs Green — "Yes, doctor!"
Doctor — "Well—you've got it again!"

Patient — "Doctor, doctor, can you recommend something for my liver?"
Doctor — "Onions, gravy and some creamed potatoes!"

Patient — "Doctor, doctor, I've put my back out!"
Doctor — "Shouldn't have done that—you need it to hold your neck up!"

Patient — "Doctor, doctor! I still feel like an aeroplane!"
Doctor — "Wait one moment please!"
Patient — "Sorry—can't stop—must fly!"

Patient — "Doctor, doctor, can you treat me?"
Doctor — "Certainly not! Pay at the desk as you go out!"

Patient — "Doctor, doctor, I think I'm a ladder!"
Doctor — "Have you rung me about this before?"

Patient — "I'm very nervous—this is my first operation!"
Surgeon — "That makes two of us!"

Nurse — "Doctor, doctor, what have you done to my book?"
Doctor — "Nothing to worry about, nurse—I just removed its appendix!"

Patient — ". . . and I think that's all, doctor!"
Doctor — "I certainly hope so! Now, excuse me one moment while I write out something for you!"
Patient — "A prescription?"
Doctor — "With all your complaints a prescription wouldn't do the trick at all. . .No, I'm writing you a letter of introduction to the undertaker!"

What happens when a banana hits a strawberry?
You get fruit punch.

What do you call a two year old grape?
Mouldy.

What did the shy pebble say?
I wish I was a little boulder.

What grows in a field and makes music?
Popcorn.

WHAT WOULD YOU GET HANGING FROM A CHRISTMAS TREE?
Tired arms!

Patient — "Will you give me something for my legs, doctor?"
Doctor — "How about a decent pair of trousers?"

Patient — "Doctor, doctor, I've got an enormous pimple!"
Doctor — "That zit, is it?"

Patient — "Doctor, doctor, I've got a headache, my joints are painful and I'm running a fever!"
Doctor — "Flu?"
Patient — "No, I came by taxi!"

Doctor (calling at patient's house) — "This is serious! Have you got a hammer and chisel?"
Patient — "You're not going to use them on me, are you doctor?"
Doctor — "No—I've locked myself out of my car again!"

What did the surgeon say to the patient on the operating table?
"Right—that's quite enough out of you!"

Doctor — "Well, Mr Smith, I've got good news and bad news!"
Mr Smith — "What's the bad news?"
Doctor — "You're seriously ill!"
Mr Smith — "And the good?"
Doctor — "I've won the surgery sweepstake!"

Patient — "Doctor, doctor, my last doctor thought I was a dog!"
Doctor — "Why do you say that?"
Patient — "Well, he told me I had a terrible bark and gave me some 'ruff' treatment!"

Patient — "Doctor! Doctor! I don't feel so hot!"
Doctor —No wonder! You have a cold!"

Patient — "Doctor, doctor, can I tell you something about this germ I've caught?"
Doctor — "No! No! You mustn't spread it around!"

Receptionist — "I'm sorry, but the doctor can't see you just now!"
Patient — "Why not?"
Receptionist — "Because he's in the other room, silly!"

When is a hat like an injection?
When it's felt!

Patient — "Doctor, doctor, I was walking barefoot in the park and I cut my foot!"
Doctor — "Must have been a sharp blade of grass!"

Patient — "Doctor, doctor, my ears keep ringing!"
Doctor — "Have your number changed!"

Patient — "Doctor, doctor, I've just been attacked by a giant ladybird!"
Doctor — "That'll be one of these superbugs they're always talking about!"

Lady in phone box — "Emergency services? A man has just been knocked down by a car outside his house!"
Operator — "Keep calm, and try to tell us how to get to you!"
Lady — "Haven't you got an ambulance or something?"

Will — "I was on the way to the doctor's and I met three women, two children and six men!"
Bill — "So how many people went to the doctor's with you?"
Will — "None! They were all coming back!"

Will — "My doctor carries a cat in the back of his car!"
Bill;— "Really?"
Will;— "Yes—it's the first-aid kit!"

Patient — "Doctor, doctor! My left side is crumbling away!"
Doctor — "Don't worry—you'll soon be all right!"

Patient — "Doctor, doctor, my sheets keep falling off the bed!"
Doctor — "Don't worry, the nurses will help with your recovery!"

Doctor — "Well, Mr Smith, I've got good news and bad news!"
Hospital patient — "What's the good news?"
Doctor — "We're sending you home today!"
Patient — "And the bad?"
Doctor — "Your house burned down last night!"

What's 300 metres high and wobbles?
The Trifle Tower.

What exams do horses take?
Hay levels.

What has six legs and always does its homework?
A fly swot.

What cuts and waves?
A sea-saw!

Who lives in the desert and invents flavoured crisps?
Sultan vinegar!

Patient — *"This dressing you've given me is playing a tune!"*
Nurse — *"Yes—it's a band-aid!"*

Nurse — "Well, Mr Brown, you may have a broken leg, but with my help you can still jump over two men!"
Patient — "What do you mean?"
Nurse — "I've brought you a game of checkers!"

Doctor — "You are going to need an operation, but I'm afraid you'll have to wait for a hospital bed!"
Patient — "As long as it gets there before I come round, I don't mind!"

Doctor — *"So you thought you were a werewolf, did you, Mr Jones?"*
Patient — *"Yes, Doctor, but I'm all right Now-oo-oooh!"*

Patient — "Doctor, doctor, I've got insomnia!"
Doctor — "Never mind that—why are you late for your appointment?"
Patient — "I overslept!"

Patient — "Doctor, doctor, I fell down the stairs!"
Doctor — "And where did you hurt yourself?"
Patient — "From top to bottom!"

Doctor — *"Don't worry, Mr Jones, the injection won't hurt a bit!"*
Mr Jones — *"OW! I thought you said it wouldn't hurt!"*
Doctor — *"It didn't—I hardly felt a thing!"*

Doctor — "Nurse! What is your weedy boyfriend doing in my hospital?"
Nurse — "You told me to bring you a drip!"

Patient — "Doctor, Doctor, my mother thinks she's a goose!"
Doctor — "I'd better look at her at once!"
Patient — "You can't see her, I'm afraid— she's flown south for the winter!"

Patient — *"Doctor, doctor, I'll lay odds of five to one that you don't know what's wrong with me!"*
Doctor — *"Ah, better already, I see!"*

Witch — "Doctor, doctor, my friend here thinks she's invisible!"
Doctor — "NURSE! NURSE! There's a woman here who thinks she's got an invisible friend!"

Patient — "Doctor, doctor, I think I'm a horse!"
Doctor — "Take these pills to make you stable!"

Patient — *"Doctor, doctor, I feel as if there's a great black cloud hanging over me!"*
Doctor — *"Don't worry, you're just under the weather!"*

Patient — "Doctor, you must make me better—I'm taking part in the Olympics next week!"
Doctor — "Dear, oh, dear—you have a temperature of 105 degrees!"
Patient — "That's my personal best!"

Patient — "Doctor, doctor, I've got hives!"
Doctor — "Thought of taking up bee-keeping?"

Doctor — *"I gave you a repeat prescription last week, Mrs Smith—how are you now?"*
Mrs Smith — *"I'm all right now, I'm all right now, I'm all right now, I'm all right now!"*

Patient — "Doctor, doctor, I've drilled a hole in my finger!"
Doctor — "Which part?"
Patient — "This bit here!"

Doctor — "So you lose your temper every time someone calls you a name? Surely that can't be true!"
Patient — "DON'T CALL ME SHIRLEY!"

Patient — *"Doctor, doctor, I think I'm a cat!"*
Doctor — *"Don't worry, Mr Jones, I'm an ex-purr-t!"*

Patient — "Doctor, doctor, I think I'm an insect!"
Doctor — "Beetle off and fetch the next patient, will you?"

Patient — "Doctor, doctor, I feel really funny!"
Doctor — "Tell us a joke, then!"

IF YOU HAVE A REFEREE IN FOOTBALL, WHAT DO YOU HAVE IN BOWLS?
Goldfish!

HOW DO YOU KNOW OWLS ARE MORE CLEVER THAN FISH?
Have you ever had owl and chips?

WHAT DO BABY APES SLEEP IN?
APEricots!

WHAT DO YOU GIVE A PONY WITH A COLD?
Cough stirrup!

WHAT EXAMS DO GARDENERS TAKE?
Hoe levels!

Patient — "Doctor, doctor, I've got pins and needles!"
Doctor — "Here's material and some thread;—make me some new curtains for the waiting room!"

Doctor — "This is very serious! I'm calling an ambulance!"
Patient — "What is it, doctor?"
Doctor — "It's a van with a flashing blue light that will get you to hospital quickly!"

Patient — "Doctor, doctor, I've got carrots growing from my ears!"
Doctor — "I can't understand it!"
Patient — "Nor can I— I planted potatoes!"

Patient — "Doctor, doctor, I've got insomnia!"
Doctor — "Well, you mustn't lose any sleep over it!"

Patient — "Doctor, doctor, I think I'm changing into a fish!"
Doctor — "Oh, you poor sole!"

Patient — "Doctor, doctor, I feel like a caterpillar!"
Doctor — "You little creep!"

Patient — "Doctor, doctor, I think my wife is a ghost!"
Doctor — "Why do you say that?"
Patient — "Because she looks a fright!"

Patient — "Doctor, doctor, my wife thinks she's the Queen!"
Doctor — "And how does she feel?
Patient — "Grand!"

Patient — "Doctor, doctor, I keep hearing music in my head!"
Doctor — "Just one moment, while I read your notes. . ."

Patient — "Doctor, doctor, I've got my head stuck in this piece of luggage!"
Doctor — "Come into the surgery and I'll take a look at you —just in case!"

Doctor — "What seems to be the trouble, Mrs Smith?"
Mrs Smith — "You tell me—you're the doctor!"

Doctor — "I tell you, nurse, I've never lost a patient!"
Nurse — "But all your patients are dead and buried!"
Doctor — "Yes—and I know exactly where each one of them can be found!"

Patient — "Doctor, doctor, I make a mewing sound whenever I breathe through my nose!"
Doctor — "Nothing to worry about, Mr Brown; it's just cat-arrh!"

Patient — "Doctor, doctor, it's me bloomin' back again!"
Doctor — "Yes it's you, bloomin' back again— but what's the bloomin' matter?"

Patient — "Doctor, doctor, my shoulders keep jerking up and down. Is it serious?"
Doctor — "Don't worry— you'll soon shrug it off!"

Patient — "Doctor, doctor, I've just swallowed a roll of camera film!"
Doctor — "We'll have to wait a few days for developments."

Patient — "Doctor, doctor, I feel like a baby!"
Doctor — "Don't come crawling to me!"

Patient — "Doctor, doctor, I've become a terrible thief!"
Doctor — "You'll have to take something for that!"

Patient — "Doctor, doctor, look at all these insects buzzing about my head!"
Doctor — "Don't worry, there are a lot of bugs going round at this time of year!"

Patient — "Doctor, doctor, what did you see when you X-rayed my head?"
Doctor — "Absolutely nothing!"

Doctor — "Now, Mrs Jones, say Aaa-aah!"
Mrs Jones — "Aaa-aah!"
Doctor — "Oh, dear, oh dear!—Now, Mrs Jones, cough!. . . and again. . . and again. . . and again. . . and again. . ."
Mrs Jones — "For heaven's sake, doctor, whatever is the matter with me?"
Doctor — "Nothing—I dropped a contact lens down your throat, and I'm trying to get it back!"

Doctor — "Don't worry, Mrs Jones, I've been practising medicine for seventeen years?"
Mrs Jones — "If you've been practising for seventeen years, how come you still can't do it right?"

Patient — "Doctor, doctor, I think I'm a bear!"
Doctor — "And how long have you been feeling this way?"
Patient — "Ever since I was a cub!"

Patient — "Doctor, doctor, I was drinking tea last night when I suddenly got a terrible pain in my eye!"
Doctor — "You left the spoon in the mug again!"

Patient — "Doctor, doctor, my ears have dropped off!"
Doctor — "Let's face it, sir you're not all there any more!"

Patient — "Doctor, doctor, I swallowed a bone!"
Doctor — "You're choking!"
Patient — "No, honestly, I really did!"

Patient — "Doctor, doctor, can you give me something for wind?"
Doctor — "How about a kite?"

Patient — "Doctor, doctor, I think I'm a mountain!"
Doctor;— "Well, you do look peaky!"

Patient — "Doctor, doctor, my wife ironed my clothes while I was still wearing them!"
Doctor — "And how do you feel?"
Patient — "Rather flat!"

Doctor — "Back again, Mrs Smith? You were only here yesterday! What can I do for you?"
Mrs Smith — "I've come back for a second opinion!"

What did the doctor say when Dracula came to see him?
"Necks, please!"

Patient — "Doctor, doctor, I think I'm a pop star!"
Doctor — "Don't worry, you're getting on famously!"

Patient — "Doctor, doctor, my skin's turning gold!"
Doctor — "Looks like a gilt complex to me!"

Why did the banker go to the doctor's?
For a cheque-up!

Why is a doctor like a comedian?
They both have people in stitches!

Patient — "Doctor, doctor, I think I'm a snail!"
Doctor — "Don't worry, you'll soon come out of your shell!"

Patient — "Doctor, doctor, I took the medicine you gave me and I still feel like ten-pound note!"
Doctor — "No change yet, then!"

Patient — "Doctor, doctor, I've got a stitch in my side!"
Doctor — "So what? I've got hundreds in my jumper!"

Mrs McTavish — "Well, ye see, doctor, I've got a wee cough. . ."
Doctor — "A whole week? I haven't even had a day off all year!"

Patient — "Doctor, doctor, I think I'm a moth!
Doctor — "But why did you come round here so late at night?"
Patient — "Well, I saw the light at your window. . ."

Mr and Mrs Bloggs — "Doctor, doctor, our new baby doesn't look like us at all!"
Doctor — "I know. Lucky little thing, isn't he?"

Patient — "Doctor, doctor, can you help me out, please?"
Doctor — "Certainly. The door's just over there!"

Patient — "Doctor, doctor, I think I'm a duck!"
Doctor — "You're quackers!"

Patient — "Doctor, doctor, what can you recommend for food poisoning?"
Doctor — "Well, eating half-cooked chicken might do it. . ."

Patient — "Doctor, doctor, I feel like a bridge!"
Doctor — "Like a bridge? What's come over you?"
Patient — "Two cars, a bus and a lorry so far. . ."

Patient — "Doctor, doctor, I've hurt my leg!"
Doctor — "Where does it hurt?"
Patient — "Everywhere I walk!"

Patient — "Doctor, doctor, I think I've got chickenpox!"
Doctor — "What are you complaining about? Every time I look at you I get spots before my eyes!"

Patient — "Doctor, doctor, I've got blurred vision!"
Doctor — "Have you tried cleaning your spectacles?"

Patient — "Doctor, doctor, I can't hear properly!"
Doctor — "Take your earmuffs off, Mrs Jones!"

Patient — "Doctor, doctor, I don't feel well!"
Doctor — "Take your mittens off, Mrs Green!"

Patient — "Doctor, doctor, I've got hot flushes!"
Doctor — "I told you that plumber was useless!"

Patient — "Doctor, doctor, it's my foot—it's just not right!"
Doctor — "That's because it's your left foot, Mr Brown!"

Patient — "Doctor, doctor, I've got a tight feeling round my chest!"
Doctor — "Your vest's too small, Mr Bloggs!"

Patient — "Doctor, doctor, I'm choking!"
Doctor — "No you're not—your scarf has caught on the door!"

Fred — "When's your birthday?"
Ted — "10th June!"
Fred — "What year?"
Ted — "Every year!"

Daisy — "Dad's spent all morning doing something impossible!"
Dora — "What's that?"
Daisy — "He's been looking round for a pencil behind his ear!"

How can you ask a blunt knife to do the impossible?
Tell it to look sharp!

What happened when the astronaut tried to read a book in zero gravity?
He couldn't put it down!

Sergeant — "How did the thief escape? I told you to cover all exits!"
P.C — "He got out the entrance, sir!"

Will — "Has your girlfriend gone off in a huff again?"
Bill — "No—she's taken the bus!"

What's black and white and noisy?
A zebra with a drum kit!

"Have you ever chased elephants on horseback?"
"Don't be silly—elephants don't ride horses!"

Mum — "Are you sweeping out the lounge, as I asked?"
Son;— "No—just the dust!"

Man (to singer) — "Can you sing 'Over the Hills and Far Away?"
Singer — "Yes, I can!"
Man — "Well, off you go, then!"

Man — "Do you know 'Loch Lomond'?"
Singer — "Yes, I do!"
Man — "Well go and jump in it!"

"Are you hungry?"
"Yes, Siam!"
"Come on then, I'll Fiji!"

Man — "Is this river good for fish?"
Angler — "It must be—they refuse to come out!"

Two lorries crashed at a junction One was carrying purple paint, the other red, The drivers are marooned on the island in the middle of the road!

Bill — "Dark, isn't it?"
Will — "Dunno—can't see to tell!"

Bill — "Am I handsome or ugly?"
Will — Both—you're pretty ugly!"

"Open Seasme!"
"Open says-a who?"

"I didn't come here to be insulted!"
"Where do you usually go?"

"A donkey wants to cross a river, but there's no bridge, no boat, the water's very deep and the donkey can't swim. What does he do?"
"I give up!"
"So did the donkey!"

Why did the teddy bears leave the building site today?
Because today's the day the teddy bears have their picks nicked!

"My girlfriend's one of twins!"
"How can you tell them apart?"
"Her brother has a beard!"

Fred — "my dog's really lazy—I was watering the garden and he wouldn't lift a leg to help me!"

"My bird can talk and it lays square eggs!"
"What does it say?"
"Ouch!"

Why did the mummy kangaroo have a sore tummy?
Because her baby was bouncing in bed!

What did the germ say to its friend?
"Keep away! I've got a dose of antibiotics!"

Where does Thursday come before Wednesday?
In a dictionary!

When is a car like a golfer?
When it goes 'Putt, putt, putt!"

Three crows sitting on the wall. A man shoots one. How many are left?
None—the others fly away!

What colour is a hiccup?
Burple!

A family of tortoises are eating in a café. Baby tortoise is sent to wash his hands before they have their ice cream. The ice cream arrives and the baby tortoise still isn't back. "Perhaps we'd better eat his ice cream, before it melts," says Mummy.
"If you do that," says a voice from the edge of the room, "I won't even go!"

What do men do standing, ladies do sitting, and dogs do on three legs?
Shake hands!

"Is that your black dog?"
"No—I've got a greyhound!"

What is the shortest job?
An astronaut—they are hired—then they're fired!

Did you hear about the unfortunate archeologist?
He got buried in his work!

What is the name of the woman in charge of the space programme?
Kate Canaveral!

What is open when it's shut and shut when it's open?
A level crossing!

What happens if you swallow uranium?
You get atomic-ache!

What do you get if you cross some chocolate with a sheep?
A Hershey Baa-aa!

What's yellow and dangerous?
A herd of thundering bananas!

What are nitrates?
More expensive than day rates!

Have you heard the joke about the rope?
Oh—skip it!

Customer — "But you said my car was rust-free!"
Car salesman — "Exactly—we don't charge a penny for the rust!"

Bill — "What do you think of monogamy?"
Will — "It's not bad—but I prefer pine!"

WHY DID THE LION SPIT OUT THE CLOWN?
BECAUSE HE TASTED FUNNY!
CHORTLE! CHORTLE!
WHAT'S THE DIFFERENCE BETWEEN A TV AND A NEWSPAPER?
EVER TRIED SWATTING A FLY WITH A TV!
HEE-HEE!

How do you make a lamb stew?
Keep it waiting!

Why was Humpty-Dumpty a disappointment?
He wasn't All he was cracked up to be!

Don't swim in the river in Paris—
It's in Seine!

Butcher — "I've got liver, kidneys,
heart. . ."
Customer — "I came here for meat—not
an organ recital!"

Bill —My friend's so mean that he bought a
house with tiny rooms so that he could use
smaller lightbulbs!
Will —My friend's so mean that he goes
visiting whenever it gets dark, so he doesn't
have to use lightbulbs at all!

Fred — My friend's always exaggerating—he
told me he was rolling in dough, but he
hardly has two pennies to rub together!
Ted — My friend told me he was rolling in
dough as well—when he got a job at the
bakery!

Why was the butcher a bully?
Because he made mincemeat of the steak!

Little boy — "Why do bulls wear rings
through their noses?"
Dad — "Because they don't have fingers,
son!"

What do hitch-hikers carry for emergencies?
A truck-sack!

Why did the hitch-hiker stay at home?
Because he felt like doing thumb-thing
different for a change!

Maisie — "That hitch-hiker looks familiar!"
Mo — "That's because we've seen him at
least five times before!"
Maisie — "How's that?"
Mo — "Because you're driving round in
circles!"

Why did the criminal drive past the prison?
He was taking the see-nick route home!

What is small, blue, and eats mud?
A small blue mud-eater!

Minister — "Envy is a sin—you must not be
jealous of other people's possessions."
Burglar — "Oh, I never do that!"
Minister — "Really?"
Burglar — "No! I'm never envious of other
people's possessions—I just take them!"

Mum — "George! I keep telling you not to be
greedy, but you're eating enough for two!"
George — "It's not because I'm greedy,
Mum—it's because I'm twice as hungry as
anyone else!"

Mum — "Billy? Did you break the
window?"
Billy — "Well, Mum, I would be lying if I
said I didn't, but I would be a fool if I said
that I did!"

Mum — "What race are you taking part in on
Sports Day, Jimmy?"
Jimmy — "The race to the ice-cream tent!"

Little boy — "Help! Help! I can't swim!"
Lazy Lifeguard — "Stand up! Stand up!
You're in the shallow end!"

Teacher — "Does anyone know what
eidelweiss is?"
Pupil — "It's a vice, miss—there's greed,
there's envy, and then there's sloth—the
eidelweiss!"

Boastful —"I lost my aeroplane in the
Bermuda Triangle!"
Forgetful —"I lost my car in Trafalgar
Square!"
Cheerful —"I lost my bike, but it's somewhere
a-round!"

Boastful —"I left my old life far behind me."
Romantic —"I left my heart in San
Francisco."
Surprised —"I left my socks on in bed last
night!"

Achiever —"I've come a long way to get
where I am!"
Traveller —"I've come far from my roots
to settle in this place!"
Sponger —"I've come from next door to
borrow some milk!

Why did the library book cry?
Because it didn't like being a-loan!

Nasty Nora — "Are you in a hurry?"
Nice Nancy — "No—why?"
Nasty Nora — "Because your make-up's been running all the way here!"

What did the parking attendant say to his friend?
"Wanna come and play on my pay-station?"

Rude Ron — "You've got a Roman nose!"
Polite Pete — "Have I?"
Rude Ron — "Yes—it's roamin' all over your face!"

Bill — "Do you know the sun burns?"
Will — "No— but I could sing you a couple of verses of 'Moon River'!"

Fred — "How did you learn that quicksand was dangerous?"
Ted — Oh—it didn't take long to sink in!"

Maisie — "Mo—your eyes look awfully far apart today—what's wrong with them?"
Maisie — "Nothing—my plaits are too tight, that's all!"

Man in chemist's shop — "Why are you tip-toeing?"
Pharmacist — "I'm trying not to wake the sleeping pills!"

Why is Europe like a frying pan?
Because it has Greece at the bottom!

Mr Dopey — "There's something wrong with this television—it will only show a picture of a revolving potato!"
Repair man — "That's not the television—that's your lunch in the microwave!"

Molly — "Will you join me in a pot of tea?"
Mo — "Not likely! The water's far too hot in there!"

What did the alien say to the petrol pump?
"Don't pick your nose while I'm talking to you!"

Bill — "I was riding the rollercoaster at the fair the other day, and my watch slipped off my wrist!"
Will — "Time flies when you're enjoying yourself!"

Bill — "Your sister certainly likes peanuts!"
Will — "Yes—elephants usually do!"

Will — "I'm in love with Mrs Mopp, the cleaner!"
Bill — "Did she sweep you off your feet, then?"

Will — "I'm in love with Miss Briggs, the optician!"
Bill — "Was it love at short sight, then?"

Will — "Where might you find dandruff?"
Bill — "Ask Mrs Druff—she might know where he is!"

How can you recognise Mr Dopey at the car wash?
He's the one on the motorbike!

Bill — "Why have you got a bandage on your ear?"
Will — "I burnt it!"
Bill — "How?"
Will — "Someone phoned me while I was doing the ironing!"

What's the difference between leather and bananas?
Leather makes shoes, but bananas make slippers!

Did you hear the joke about time?
It's not worth telling!

What has ten feet and sings?
A quintet!

Man passing chip shop with friend —
"What's that terrible smell?"
Friend — "That's the UFO's!"
Man — "UFO's?"
Friend — "Unidentified Frying Objects!"

What do you get if you take a hand-held vacuum cleaner out on a windy day?
A dust-guster!

Why did Mr Dopey iron his face?
Someone told him he had wrinkles!

Did you hear about the soldier who got a job in the cookhouse?
The chef asked him to shell the eggs and he blew the kitchen wall down!

How can you recognise a worried farmer? His eyebrows are furrowed!

Did you hear about the butler who raced his lordship?
He took the silver!

Fred — "Do you know any animals that are peculiar to Great Britain?"
Ted — "A duck-billed platypus!"
Fred — "But there are no duck-billed platypuses in Great Britain!"
Ted — "And that's what makes it peculiar!"

1st man — "Why are you carrying that chest of drawers along the street?"
2nd man — "Because it refuses to walk!"

Bill — "I just saw a bus driver go straight past the traffic lights and into a shop!"
Will — "And what happened next?"
Bill — "He bought a newspaper, came out, and went back to where he had parked the bus!

Mum — "What's that noise in the kitchen?"
Son — "I'm just clearing away the dishes!—Where are the brush and shovel kept?"

Why was the bridesmaid arrested? Because she held up a train!

Bill — "My, this fog is thick! I can't see my hands in front of my face!"
Will — "That's because they're in your pockets!"

Did you hear about the dopey man who wanted to start a chicken farm?
He went out and bought fifty eggplants!

Ike — "My car was run into by a lorry yesterday—you have no idea what I went through!"
Mike — "From the look of you I can guess—it was the windscreen!"

Man in boat — "Here—take my hand! The current's too strong for swimming!"
Man in water — "I'm not swimming—I'm riding my bike!"

Bill — "I keep racing pigeons!"
Will — "And if you keep racing them long enough, you might win!"

Major — "Who's that, playing the 'Last Post' so badly?"
Sergeant — "Corporal Jones, sir—we call him the Lone Bungler!"

Man to friend — "I need your advice. My son's just told me he wants to be a racing driver!"
Friend — "Whatever you do, don't stand in his way!"

Did you hear about the lighthouse keeper's accident?
He ran up the spiral staircase so fast that he screwed himself into the roof!

Save money—take up boxing and live on scraps!

"Romeo—Romeo! Wherefore art thou, Romeo?"
Romeo appears from the bushes and stares up at his sweetheart on the balcony.
"I've made you some dinner, Romeo," she calls, "A nice piece of steak!"
"Yummy!" says Romeo, and catches the tasty morsel that is thrown down to him. He tries to take a bite. It's rather tough, but he sets to work with his strong white teeth. . .
Some years later, a young man called Will sits down at his desk with his pen. Carefully, he writes out the title of his new play
"Romeo Ain't Chewed it Yet"!

Sherlock — "I can tell you're wearing your winter underwear, Watson!"
Watson — "Incredible, Holmes! How did you deduce that?"
Sherlock — "Because you've forgotten to put your trousers on!"

First aid instructor — "Now, let's suppose someone picked up a very hot pan without wearing oven gloves, and burnt their hands. What would you do?"
Pupil — "Tell them to drop the pan, double-quick!"

Why was the prisoner's wife not allowed to see him on visiting day?
Because she had a ladder in her stocking!

Prison warder — "Why do you never get any letters from your friends, Wiggins?"
Prisoner — "Because they're all in here too!"

Lady (to charity collector on doorstep) — "No, I'm sorry, but I never give money to people at the door."
Charity collector — "Shall I knock at the window, then?"

Owner of country hotel — "We used to be haunted by a ghost who kept walking up and down the stairs all night. But things are a lot quieter since we had the place modernised!"
Visitor — "Why? Has he gone"
Owner — "No—he uses the lift!"

Two dogs are sitting watching the washing going round in the washing machine.
"What's on?" asks one.
"Soap!" says the other.

Railway station announcement — "The train on platform four will be back on the rails as soon as possible."!

Ted — "People who gamble are foolish!"
Fred — "But I don't gamble!"
Ted — "Then you're no better!"

Why are cameramen dangerous in the cinema?
Because they shoot films!

Driving instructor — "Right, Mrs Jones, release your clutch!"
—so Mrs Jones let go of the steering wheel!

A writer was very short of money, so he sent a letter to his friend, asking for a loan.
"I am penniless and I hope you will be kind enough to help me out," he wrote, "for I can't write on an empty stomach!"
His friend wrote back — "Indeed, you can't write on an empty stomach. Please find enclosed a pad of notepaper."

Absent-minded professor — "Don't I know you? Aren't you Mr Jones?"
Man — "No—I'm Mr Jones' twin brother!"
Absent-minded professor — "And the name is. . .?"

Fred — "How did you get that puncture, Ted?"
Ted — "I drove over a milk bottle!"
Fred — "What was a milk bottle doing in the middle of the road?"
Ted — "The milkman was carrying it!"

Bill — "Go straight along this road and you'll come to a sign for the village. You can't miss it!"
Five minutes later. . . "CRUMP!"
Will — "You were right!"

Fred — "My body is like a temple!"
Ted — "I know—an ancient ruin!"

A businessman travelling from King's Cross to Waterloo settled himself on his seat in the train, dumped his briefcase beside him and went to sleep.
After a while he woke up, and realised the train was not moving.
"Are we in the station?" he asked the guard sleepily.
"Yes," said the guard.
So the businessman got off the train and the train moved away.
It was only then that he realised he was still in King's Cross!

Mum — "And what did the coach say when you scored a goal, son?"
Son — "He said next time I was to get it into the other team's net!"

Farmer — "My cow's grown a lot!"
Friend — "And I thought all cows went 'moo'!"

Explorer — "I've travelled all over South America!"
Bob — "So what? My goldfish travels round the globe several times a day!"

Ship's captain — "My, my, a singing whale! How do you think that has happened?"
Sailor — "I dropped my portable CD player overboard, sir!"

Stunt Pilot — "Looping-the-loop takes a lot of courage and skill, you know!"
Little boy — "Well, my granny taught me how to loop-the-loop when I was five, and it wasn't so bad!"
Stunt Pilot — "What do you mean by that?"
Little boy — "The knitting needles weren't nearly as sharp as I expected!"

Mail man — "Is this letter for you? The name on the envelope is smudged!"
Man — "Can't be for me, then—my name's Smith!"

Will — "It's quite possible to live on vegetables alone!"
Bill — "But it must get a little soggy underfoot when they go rotten!"

What is the latest letter in the alphabet?
'Y'—because it comes at the end of day!

Bill — "I just met a tall man with a black beard who said he went to school with you!"
Will — "There was no-one with a beard in my class at school!"

Burglar to accomplice — "I hear sirens—quick! Jump out of the window!"
Accomplice — "But we're on the thirteenth floor!"
Burglar — "Look, this is no time to be superstitious!"

Referee at football match — "Now, I want to see fair play and good sportsmanship in this match!"
Ape-like centre-forward — "Any more last wishes?"

How did the jester get promoted to royal puppeteer?
He pulled a few strings!

Maisie — "Have you noticed that ignorant people are often the loudest talkers?"
Mo — "Yes—and you don't have to shout!"

When is elastic like a microwave?
When it goes 'ping'!

Mr Dopey went ice-fishing
He caught twenty-five tons of ice!

Schoolboy's essay — "The Lone Ranger needed help fast, so he called for his friend Pronto!"

Two burglars are looting the home of a very wealthy tycoon. One of them is about to stand on a chair to reach a painting hanging on the wall. "Take your filthy shoes off first!" says his accomplice. "Have some respect for other people's property!"

Will — "Quite a small place, isn't it?"
Bill — "Yes—I had to remove the wallpaper to get the furniture in!"

A plane crashes on the border between France and Spain. Where are the survivors buried?
Nowhere! The survivors were still alive!

What happened to the shy stone?
It grew to become a little boulder!

Johnny — "I'm going out, Mum!"
Mum — "With that dirty face?"
Johnny — "No—with Bobby next door!"

Bill — "I once knew a man with very long arms. When he went up steps, he trod on them!"
Will — "His arms?"
Bill;— "No— the steps!"

Why did the woman jump overboard?
Because the captain invited her to launch!

Ted — Which is right—nine and five is thirteen or nine and five are thirteen?"
Fred — "Neither—nine and five are fourteen!"

Maisie — "What is a buttress?"
Mo — "A female goat!"

Betty — "What is a water otter?"
Kitty — "A kettle!"

If it takes ten men three hours to dig a hole, how long does it take five men to dig half a hole?
They can't—there's no such thing as half a hole!

Billy — "Mum's given us two apples to share, but one's much bigger than the other!"
Bobby — "Do I get the choice?"
Billy — "Yes—you choose the smaller one or nothing!"

Two old men are sitting on a bench outside the old folk's home. The weather is breezy.
1st man — "Windy!"
2nd man — "Same here—must have been the beans!"

If you get hiccups, hold your breath for thirty seconds and they might go away.
—If that doesn't work, hold your breath for three hundred and thirty seconds, and you will never be troubled by hiccups again!

Later that same day. . .
1st man — "Still windy!"
2nd man — "No-Thursday!"
1st man — "Let's go for a drink then!"

A policeman noticed a little girl with a suitcase trudging along the road. He was concerned to see a small child setting out on a journey all on her own, so he followed her to make sure she got to her destination safely. He followed her round one corner, round another corner and round another corner, and realised that they were now back where they started. He stopped the little girl and asked her what she was doing.
"I'm running away from home," she said.
"But all you are doing is walking round the block!" said the policeman.
"I know, said the little girl. "But I'm not allowed to cross the road!"

Burglar's son — "Dad, may I leave the table?"
Father — "Certainly not! We'll take it in the van with the rest of the loot!"

Owner of country mansion — "In the blue bedroom, you will see a plaque on the wall, telling you that Nelson once slept there!"
Visitor — "Why did he not use the bed?"

Bill — "I'm exhausted!"
Will — "Why?"
Bill — "I hurt my leg and the doctor said I wasn't to climb the stairs for a week—you have no idea how difficult it is getting up the drainpipe every night!"

What did the robber call his horse?
Black Booty!

Billy — "There was a hold-up at the bank yesterday!"
bobby — "So what? There was a hold-up in our garden today!"
Billy — "Really?"
Bobby — "Yes—ten pegs held up five shirts on the washing-line!"

What word can no-one spell?
I'm sorry—I can't write it down—as I said, no-one can spell it!

What word is always spelt badly?
Badly!

Did you hear about the new superhero who cleans up after dogs?
They've called him Scooperman!

Why is a ship's rudder like a policeman?
Because it has a stern duty to perform!

What is the sneakiest way to catch fish?
Swallow some worms, then wait by the side of the river with baited breath!

Helicopter passenger — "Pilot, it's rather cold up here! Do you think you could switch that fan off above our heads?"

What's the definition of a pyromaniac?
Someone with burning ambition!

Percy, the would-be pop star, rubbed the lamp in his dressing room one night, and a genie appeared.
"What is your desire, sir?" asked the genie.
Percy did not hesitate. "I would like to be surrounded by clamouring babes!" he said. The next thing he knew, he was in the middle of the nursery in the maternity hospital!

What is the difference between a forged five-dollar note and an angry rabbit?
One is bad money, the other is a mad bunny!

Why did King Kong climb the Empire State Building?
He wanted to catch a plane!

"What does it feel like when you're half-way down the chimney, Santa?"
"Claus-trophobic!"

Tuneless singer — "I have to take care of my throat, doing what I do!"
Friend — "I expect you do, with all those people out there longing to throttle you!"

What do Nellie the Elephant and Alexander the Great have in common?
Their middle name!

Little boy — "I'd like a pound of bird seed for my cat, please!"
Pet-shop owner — "Why do you want bird-seed for your cat?"
Little boy — "how else am I going to feed the canary he swallowed?"

"I've bought a new hammer!"
"Watch out for the nail!"
"What nail?"
"The one on the end of your thumb!"

Will — "Do you realise that every time I breathe out, a person dies?"
Bill — "You should think about using mouthwash, then!"

Little girl — "I don't know what to do with myself!"
Old Lady — "Why not?"
Little girl — "I've just found out that I'm the sort of child my mother doesn't want me to play with!"

Will — "What is the longest word you can think of?"
Bill — "Eternity!"

Father — "I taught my son everything I know!"
Friend — "He'll be ready for junior school soon, then!"

Zookeeper to young zoo visitor — "Have you come to see my long-eared antelope?"
Visitor — "Who is your long-eared aunt going to elope with?

Dad — "Come on, Shirley, get on with your homework. Homework never killed anyone yet!"
Shirley — "And I don't want to be the first to die!"

Old Lady — "What do you want to be when you grow up, young man?"
Little boy — "I'd like to follow in my father's footsteps, ma'am!"
Old Lady — "So you want to be a doctor, too?"
Little boy — "No—I'll be the undertaker!"

Practise DIY in safety —
get someone else to hold the nails while you hammer them!

Can you think of a container which has no lid, and which contains a golden secret?
An egg!

Bill — "Do you think it might rain today?"
Fred — "It depends on the weather!"

What is green, hairy and goes 'clickety-click?'
A ball-point gooseberry!

Why did the bald man stick his head out of the window?
He needed some fresh 'air!

The sheriff spent three weeks riding in the desert, looking for the rustlers. Finally, he had to admit defeat. He turned his horse around and headed back into town. Four days later, he rode into Dodge city. What did he say to his horse when he got back?
"Whoah!"

If a gallon of milk had a race with a litre of milk, which one would win?
The gallon would get the pints!

What is the difference between a needlewoman and a horse doctor?
One mends tears and the other tends mares!

What's black and white and bounces?
A zebra on a trampoline!

Anything else?
A nun on a pogo stick!

Anything else?
A rubber penguin

Molly — "My car is just like a baby"
Mo;— "Why?"
Molly — "It never goes anywhere without a rattle!"

Bill — "Will, Will, we've got a gas leak in here!"
Will — "Don't panic—just put a bucket under it!"

What's the most popular place in town?
The cemetery—people are dying to get there!

Vet — "That's it, Mr Brown—your dog won't chase cars any more. I've cured him!"
Mr Brown — "How did you do that?"
Vet — "I tied his back legs together!"

What is the difference between a big black cloud and a child with toothache?
One pours with rain and the other roars with pain!

Have you heard the joke about the Eiffel Tower?
I don't think it's up your street!

Bill — "I'm selling my carpet. It's in mint condition!"
Will — "Yes—it's got a hole in the middle of it!"

Fred — "Your dog has been chasing me on my bicycle!"
Ted — "When did he learn to ride it?"

Who wears the biggest hat in the American navy?
The sailor with the biggest head!

Why did the dragon divorce his wife?
She kept smoking in bed!

Bill — "My dog's really stupid!"
Will — "What makes you say that?"
Bill;— "He spent all afternoon chewing a bone, and when he got up, he only had three legs!"

Why did the scientist clone the trifle?
He wanted second helpings!

How can you hide in the desert?
Use camelflage!

Maisie —"My husband's in hospital. He was cutting down a tree in the garden the other day, when the chainsaw slipped and he cut off his leg!"
Annie —"Goodness. What did you do?"
Maisie —"I found someone else to cut the tree down!"

"I'm a little boy now, but when I was born, I was a little bare!"

What happened when the scientist cloned his girlfriend?
He fell in love with her all over again!

Did you hear about the man who wrote a poem first thing every morning, as soon as he got up?
He went from bed to verse!

What do you get if you cross a toaster with a hand-held vacuum cleaner?
A dust-cruster!

What happens if you put a brush in the fridge?
You get a br-rr-oom!

Friend — "How are you getting on with the book you're writing?"
Writer — "I've written the end!"
Friend — "So you've finished?"
Writer — "No—I've written 'the end', and now I'm trying to think up the rest of the story!"

Did you hear about the egg in the monastery?
It went out of the frying pan into the friar!

What do you need if your toaster breaks down?
You need the bread to pop out for a new one!

Will — "My hamster got stuck in the tumble drier, and his name changed!"
Bill — "What do you mean?"
Will — "He went in Silky and he came out Fluffy!"

Lord and Lady Muck were holding a grand ball and they asked their chef to prepare some canapés to serve to their guests when they arrived. The great day dawned and Lord and Lady Muck went round the castle, checking that the servants had everything ready for the big night. Last of all they went into the kitchen, and found, to their surprise, that the cook was busily emptying packets of chewing gum into an enormous pan of hot oil.
"What are you doing? Have you gone mad?" screamed Lady Muck.
"No, ma'am," answered the cook. "I'm just making a little something for the guests. Haven't you heard the old saying? 'FRIED GUMS BEFORE A BALL'!"

Will — "Why are you covered in bruises, Bill?
Bill — "A ladder took a dislike to me!"
Will — "What do you mean by that?"
Bill — "It couldn't bear me!"

Will — "Why are you black and blue, Bill?"
Bill — "I was hit by a balloon!"
Will — "How could a balloon do so much damage?"
Bill — "It was stuck on the bonnet of a ten-ton truck!"

Mo (outside cemetery) — "I wouldn't like to be buried there!"
Maisie — "Why not?
Mo — "Because I'm still alive!"

Did you hear about the criminal who took up German sausage-making?
He went from bad to wurst!

Sailor — "There's something wrong with the boat, captain!"
Captain — "We'll have to take it to the dock!"

Dentist — "Looks like your lucky day!"
Golfer — "Why?"
Dentist — "You've got a hole in one!"

What day does the landlord collect the rent?
Duesday!

Where do Americans get their laundry done?
Washington!

Joe — "Can I stay over with Jimmy tonight, Mum?"
Mum — "But you don't have a sleeping bag!"
Joe — "It's all right—I'll take my knapsack!"

Why did the sheikh not let his brother meet his wives?
He wanted to keep him out of harem's way!

What happened to the maths teacher in the jungle?
He added four and four, and got ate!

Did you hear about the vain nomad?
He spent too much time gazing into the mirage!

Little girl — "I know a man who can go out in the rain without getting his hair wet!"
Friend — "Who's that?"
Little girl — "My Dad—he's bald!"

When is a window like a star?
When it's a skylight!

Did you hear about the mad astronaut?
He went into space in a loony module!

What stays hot in the refrigerator?
Chilli!

"I was once glad to be down-and-out!"
"When was that?"
"After a really bumpy plane ride!"

Why is honey scarce in Boston?
Because there's only one 'B' in Boston!

Did you hear about the wooden car?
It wooden go!

What did the balloon say to the pin?
"Hi, Buster!"

Why is a pair of handcuffs like a guide book?
Because it's for two-wrists!

Why is the letter 'D' like a naughty boy?
Because it makes ma mad!

What did the envelope say to the stamp?
"Stick with me, and you'll go places!"

Did you hear about the latest invention to see through the thickest of walls?
It's called a window!

Why was the tin of beans happy?
Because it was A-merry-can!

Did you hear about the smallest sailor?
He fell asleep on his watch!

"What's five Q and five Q?"
"Ten Q!"
"You're welcome!"

What's round and dangerous?
A vicious circle.

Annie — "What's the difference between a packet of cookies and a packet of fertilizer?"
Al — "I don't know!"
Annie — "I'm not coming round to your house for a snack, then!"

What colours should you paint the sun and the wind?
The sun rose, and the wind blew!

Ted — "My wife's gone on holiday to the West Indies!"
Fred — "Jamaica?"
Ted — "Certainly not—but I gave her plenty of encouragement!"

Where can you find letters that are not in the alphabet?
In a letterbox!

What walks on its head all day long?
A tack in your shoe!

Bill — "I'm glad you called me Bill!"
Bill's mum — "Why?"
Bill;— "Because that's my name!"

What do you call a couple of french fries, flying past each other in the darkness?
Chips that pass in the night!

What's the hardest thing about learning to ride a bike?
The ground!

If two's company and three's a crowd, what are one and four?
Five!

Why did the old man put wheels on his rocking chair?
To rock n' roll!

A man is standing at a bus stop, eating a hot dog. Beside him is a lady with a dog, and the dog is whining at the man. The man turns to the lady and says, "Do you mind if I throw him a bit?" and the lady says, "That would be very kind of you!"
So the man picks up the dog and throws him over the wall behind them!

"Which one of your sisters plays the mouth organ?"
"Oh—that'll be our Monica!"

"I've just seen two kangaroos tickling each other!"
"Don't be silly—it's just a hop-tockle illusion!"

What kind of bus crossed the ocean?
Columbus!

Will — "Do you have any distant relatives?"
Bill — "No—they all live nearby!"

Will — "Old George is really mean!"
Bill;— "How mean?"
Will — "So mean that when he pays you a compliment, he asks for a receipt!"

Coach — "Your career as football player is like a plane parked on the runway!"
Football player — "You mean it's ready to take off?"
Coach — "No—it's going nowhere!"

Will — "Why are you going barefoot, Bill?"
Bill — "Because the road wears my shoes out!"

Mo — "I went out without my umbrella last night!"
Molly — "You must have got very wet!"
Mo — "No—it wasn't raining!"

What did the trousers say to the very short belt?
"Don't get around much, do you?"

Politician's wife — "How did the crowd like your election speech?"
Politician — "Terrible—they threw eggs, tomatoes and potatoes at me!"
Politician's wife — "They really made a meal of you, didn't they!"

Mum — "A penny for your thoughts, Billy!"
Billy — "Have you never heard of inflation?"

What has three heads and three tails?
Three coins!

Bill — "Where are you going, Will?"
Will — "I'm going out to water the flowers!"
Bill — "But it's raining!"
Will — "That's all right—I'll take my umbrella!"

Bill — "I can tell you're enjoying your hot-dog!"
Will — "Really—how?"
Bill — "Because you're eating it with relish!"

Jack — "My dog's like a grandfather clock!"
Mack — "Why's that?"
Jack — "Because he has a round face and ticks!"

Len — "My brother didn't say a word until he was five years old!"
Larry — "Then what happened?"
Len — "He picked up a wheel and spoke!"

Molly — "I fancy a great big doughnut!"
Mo — "You never had good taste in boyfriends!"

Park-keeper — *"Why have you stopped your car on the grass, sir? Don't you know it isn't allowed?"*
Driver — *"Why not? The sign says 'Park'!"*

Annie — "Mum, what's the difference between a matador and a matadeer?"
Mum — "What's a matadeer?"
Annie — "Nothing! What's the matter with you?"

Jill — "What happened to your nose?"
Joe — "I hurt it smelling a brose!"
Jill — "There's no B in rose!"
Joe — "There was in this one!"

When is a car like a piece of music?
When it has four flats!

Maisie — "I met my first boyfriend in a revolving door!"
Mo — "Really?"
Maisie — "Yes—we went around together for ages!"

President — "Jackson! You can be my right-hand man!"
Jackson — "Sorry, Mr President, but I'm left handed!"

Traveller — *"I've seen some spectacles in my time!"*
Optician — *"Not as many as I have, I'll bet!"*

How do robots make their cars go faster?
They put the metal to the pedal!

Bill — "I wrote a letter to myself today!"
Will — "What did it say?"
Bill — "I don't know—it hasn't arrived yet!"

Monkey in safari park, watching visiting cars — "Look, they've brought more humans round to see us!"
Lion — "I know—but don't you think it's cruel keeping them caged up like that?"

Did you hear about the man who slept in just his underpants?
He had a vestless night!

Maisie — "I put on lots of cream last thing every night!"
Mo — "So why are you covered in lumps and bumps?"
Maisie — "I keep slipping out of bed!"

Bill — "Your cooking's terrible!"
Mo — "How do you know?"
Bill — "A little bird told me!"
Mo — "What little bird?"
Bill — "A swallow!"

Farmer — "I've only got Fresian cows on my farm!"
Friend — "Why don't you ask your wife to knit you a Jersey?"

Fisherman (to fish) "I'm taking you home for dinner!"
Fish — "I've already had dinner—can we go to the movies instead?"

Bill;— "I can do the impossible!"
Will;— "What's that?"
Bill — "I can walk a mile and only move two feet!"

Maisie — "My husband's got no manners— when he drinks a cup of tea, he holds the cup with his little finger sticking out!"
Mo — "Some people consider that to be good manners!"
Maisie — "Not when the teabag's dangling from it!"

Why did the axe go to the doctor's?
It had a splitting headache!

Why did Mr Dopey somersault down the hill? He wanted to turn something over in his mind!

Ted — "Why are you dancing with that jam jar?"
Fred — "Because it says on the label 'Twist to open'!"

Mum — "Why can't you amuse yourself for a few minutes, Bobby?"
Bobby — "Because I've heard all my jokes before!"

Have you heard about the dance called the elevator?
It has no steps!

Witch — "I can go into the street and turn a passer-by into a frog!"
Little boy — "I can go into the street and turn into an alley!"

What did one diamond say to the other?
"It's a hard life!"

What did the other diamond say back?
"I think you're brilliant!"

What did one taxi say to the other?
"It's a hired life!"

What did one poet say to the other?
"It's a bard life!"

What did one prisoner say to the other?
"It's a barred life!"

1st comedian — "Your routine should be in a book!"
2nd comedian — "Really?"
1st comedian — "Yes—then I could shut it up!"

Annie — "I wish I were in your shoes!"
Betty — "Why?"
Annie — "Because they're much nicer than mine!"

What does an artist do to relax?
She draws a bath and paints her nails!

Bill — "This looks like a bargain!"
Will — "What?"
Bill — "Violin—two pounds-fifty. No strings attached."

Why did the tailor go to the doctor's?
He had terrible pins and needles!

Politician — "I want my speech to reach thousands of ears!"
Farmer — "Then make it in my cornfield!"

Mother goat, to kid — "Butt me no butts, young man!"

Little boy — "Thank you very much for the dictionary you gave me, Auntie!"
Auntie — "It's a pleasure!"
Little boy — "Not exactly, but I'm sure it'll come in useful when I do my homework!"

Maisie — "I've been on a chicken diet!"
Mo — "How do you feel?"
Maisie — "Terrible—do you know how little chickens eat?"

Annie — "Are you coming to the fire-sale, Betty?"
Betty — "No—I don't need any fires!"

Why did Mr Dopey take his dog to the watchmaker?
Because it had ticks!

What did the jumper say to the shirt?
"Want to hang out for a while?"

Maisie — "They say the world's getting smaller every day!"
Mo — "That'll make the postal service a bit quicker, then!"

Little boy — "I'm going to camp this summer!"
Friend — "Do you need a holiday?"
Little boy — "No—my parents do!"

Little boy — "Thank you very much for the present, Auntie!"
Auntie — "Don't mention it!"
Little boy — "Okay—it can be a secret, just between you and me!"

Optician — "There now, son; with these glasses you'll be able to read everything!"
Little boy — "Does that mean I don't have to go to school any more?"

Billy — "Were you nervous about being presented with your prize, Jimmy?"
Jimmy — "No—I was calm and collected!"

Bill — "I've just had twelve rides on the carousel!"
Will — "You really do get around, don't you?"

Old man — "I had my first bath when I was sixty five years old!"
Friend — "Why?"
Old man — "Because the best time to have a bath is before retiring!"

Mum — "What are you making all that noise for in the larder, Billy?"
Billy — "I'm fighting off temptation!"

A cyclist was on a country road trying to fix a puncture. Suddenly a horse poked its head over the wall and said; "You'll have to take the wheel nuts off first!" The man was astonished.

Not long after that, the farmer came to feed the horse. The cyclist said to him; "Your horse just spoke to me!"

"What did it say?"

"It told me to take the wheel nuts off—can you believe it!"

"Well," said the farmer, "it knows a lot more about bikes than I do!"

Psychiatrist — "Why are you taking all those biscuits, son?"
Psychiatrist's son — "Oh, they're not for me—they're for my personal demons!"

Mum — "Why do you think your teacher is stupid, Sam?"
Sam — "Because she had to ask me how to spell my name!"

Little boy to farmhand milking cow — "I don't think the farmer likes you!"
Farmhand — "Why not?"
Little boy — "Because I asked him how to milk a cow and he told me a little jerk does it!"

Mum — "Why can't you go to Lucy's party, Annie?"
Annie — "Because the invitation says from three to six—and I'm seven!"

Fred — "My mother's sister gets great TV reception!"
Ted — "What's her name?"
Fred — "Aunt Enna!"

Why did everybody feel sorry for the demolition worker's children?
They came from a broken home!

Bill — "Our house is really small!"
Will — "Not as small as ours—why, our house is so small that even the mice have round shoulders!"

Maisie — "I feel great on Saturdays and Sundays, but I can hardly get out of bed on Mondays, Tuesdays, Wednesdays, Thursdays or Fridays—why is that?"
Mo — "That's because they're weakdays!"

Why did the man throw the thermometer out of the window?
He wanted to make the temperature drop!

Maisie — "Someone jumped out from an alley at me last night and I fell into a faint!"
Mo — "Very careless of someone to leave the cover off the faint!"

What hand does an ambidextrous chef use to stir the soup?
Neither! He uses a spoon!

Mo — "Your hair looks lifeless today!"
Maisie — "Yes—it's dyed!"

Why did the martial arts expert go to the doctor?
Because he had Kung flu!

When is a hippie invisible?
When he's outta sight, man!

How do you beat the bus home?
Step on some glass, and find a short cut on foot!

Why did the lifeguard have to save the hippie?
Because he was too far out, man!

Why did Batman buy a pound of worms?
They weren't for him—they were for Robin!

What did the big teddy say to the little teddy?
"One more word, and I'll knock the stuffing out of you!"

What did the eggs say when they saw the saucepan?
"Scramble!"

What did one telephone say to the other telephone?
"Who knows what the future might brr-rring!"

Why do cows use vanishing cream?
Because vanishing cream helps the cowhide!

Billy — "I've got something I can give to my friends and still keep myself!"
Bob — "What's that?"
Billy;— "A cold!"

Two burglars broke into a bed shop.
They were caught napping!

*There was an archery contest today, but there was no outright winner.
The referee said it was a bow tie!*

What did the priest say to the sprig of mint?
"Go in peas!"

**Why do mothers dress their baby girls in pink and their little boys in blue?
Because babies can't dress themselves!**

*Why was the Scotsman unhappy?
He had just washed his kilt and couldn't do a fling with it!*

What is the difference between Mount Everest and a school dinner?
Mount Everest is hard to get up, and a school dinner is hard to get down!

**Bill — "Where's yesterday's paper?"
Betty — "I put it out in the bin!"
Bill — "But there was something in it that I wanted to look at?"
Betty — "Why would you want to look at a pile of potato peelings?"**

*What is over seventy years old, rides out on the prairie and knits?
The Crone Ranger!*

What rides out on the prairie going "bring, bring"?
The phone ranger!

**Optician — "Tell me what's written on the chart in front of you, please."
Client — "Are you having trouble with your eyesight too?"**

*Customer in pet shop — "I'd like to buy this parrot please. Will you send me the bill?"
Pet shop owner — "Not likely! Take the whole parrot, or nothing at all!"*

Bill — "It's all over the building!"
Will — "What is?"
Bill — "The roof!"

**What do you get if you cross a sheep with a chocolate bar?
A Mars baa-aa!**

*What did the saucer say to the cup?
"None of your lip!"*

Bill — "Why are you crying, Betty?"
Betty — "I baked a special cake just for you, but the dog has eaten it!"
Bill — "Don't worry, he's a tough little thing—he'll soon recover!"

**Fred — "I've been playing the piano on and off for years now!"
Ted — "On and off?"
Fred — "Yes—the stool's rather slippy!"**

*What do American footballers eat their chowder from?
A soup-erbowl!*

What do you call a skeleton who rides a horse and wears a mask?
The Bone Ranger!

**Teacher — "Where did King John sign the Magna Carta?"
Pupil — "At the bottom, Miss!"**

*Did you hear the joke about the bed?
It hasn't been made yet!*

Did you hear the joke about the very thin insect?
There's not much to it!

**Did you hear the joke about the dime?
It's not worth it!**

*Man (to street singer) — "Do you know your voice drives me mad?"
Singer — "No, but if you hum the first few bars, I'll join in!"*

What is the difference between a weightlifter and a sick person?
A weightlifter finds it hard to keep things up, and a sick person finds it hard to keep things down!

**Did you hear the joke about the aeroplane?
It'll go over your head!**

*"My grandma is still alive at 102!"
"That's nothing—my grandpa's still alive at 115!"
"115?"
"Yes! 115 Cherry Tree Avenue!"*

SNIGGER–
SNIGGER!
WHY CAN'T YOUR NOSE BE 12 INCHES LONG?
BECAUSE THEN IT WOULD BE A FOOT!
DOES YOUR SHIRT
HAVE HOLES IN IT?
NO,
THEN HOW DID
YOU PUT IT ON?

Bill — "What do you think of my home-made toffee?"
Will — "Mmmmmmmmmmmm!"

Why did the musician's son take a lump of toffee out to play conkers with?
It was his Nutcracker Sweet!

Did you hear the joke about the birthday present?
You won't get it!

Did you hear the joke about the invisible needle?
You won't see the point!

Did you hear the joke about the guffaw?
It's a laugh!

Did you hear the joke about the dentist?
Aa-aah!

What is the name of the character that appears in every book?
Chap one!

The vicar had a bonfire today.
—Holy smoke!

Bill — "Why did you call both your sons Edward?"
Fred — "Because two Eds are better than one!"

Why does superman wear enormous shoes?
Because of his astounding feats!

Criminal — "I was sent to prison for the rest of my life!"
Prison officer — "So?"
Criminal — "You won't let me rest at all!"

"I'm a good speaker—people say I have the gift of the gab!"
"I'm a successful pickpocket—people say I have the gift of the grab!"

Who shopped the bank robbers?
It was the teller!

What do careful criminals do?
Practise safe robbery!

Why are canals burglar-proof?
Because they have so many locks!

What do you call a cannibal who eats his parents?
An orphan!

Barber — "This hair restorer is so good, it makes hair grow on a bowling ball!"
Man — "But that's no good—I want hair on my head!"

Why do flies walk on the walls?
Because if they walked on the floor, they would be stood on!

Why did the elephant wear size ten hiking boots?
Because it had size ten feet!

Annie was visiting her grandmother.
"Would you like to see the cuckoo come out of the cuckoo clock?" her grandmother asked.
"I suppose so," said Susie, "But I'd prefer to see Grandpa come out of the grandfather clock!"

Father — "I took my son to the zoo yesterday!"
Friend — "And did they accept him?"

Lady to paper-boy — "What's your name, my lad?"
Boy — "Bill Clinton, ma'am!"
Lady — "That's a well-known name!"
Boy — "I should think so—I've been delivering the papers around here for over a year now!"

Fred — "Last week my mother-in-law hit me on the back with a frying pan, and she cried for the rest of the day!"
Ted — "With remorse?"
Fred — "No—with disappointment—she was aiming for my head!"

Did you hear about the man who broke into the bank and put £3,000 in the safe?
He was generous to a vault!

What is the penalty for bigamy?
Two sets of in-laws!

1st sailor — "The barometer's falling!"
2nd sailor — "Rotten weather ahead?"
1st sailor — "No—rotten nail that was holding it on the wall!"

Why did the bus go mad?
It was driven to distraction!

Mother — "If you found a five-pound note on the street, would you keep it?"
Billy — "Of course not!"
Mother — "What a good boy! What would you do with it?"
Billy — "I'd spend it!"

Betty — "I've just come from the beauty salon!"
Barbara — "What a pity it was shut!"

Old gentleman — "And what does your father do, sonny?"
Little boy — "He drives other people's cars!"
Old gentleman — "So he's a chauffeur, is he?"
Little boy — "No—he's a car thief!"

Mother — "Jimmy, do you think your little brother can tell me what nationality was Napoleon?"
Jimmy — "Corsican!"

Notice outside head teacher's office —
"There is no such thing as a free education. All pupils must pay attention or pay the penalty!"

Molly — "How can I make a sculpture of myself out of this bit of clay?"
Mo — "Easy! Just take away all the bits that don't look like you!"

Two burglars broke into a theatre during a performance.
They were caught in the act!

Woman in newsagent's shop — "Do you keep stationery?"
Newsagent — "No, ma'am, I move about a bit, otherwise I get terribly stiff!"

Bobby — "Can you fight?"
Bertie — "No!"
Bobby — "Right—take that!"

What is the first step you must take towards a divorce?
Get married!

What did one plank say to the other one?
Are you coming to the board meeting?

Woman in dress-shop — "Can I try on that pink dress in the window?"
Assistant — "Oh, no, ma'am, you'll have to use the changing-rooms!"

The politician finished addressing the crowd outside the shopping centre, but before he stepped down, he asked if there were any questions.
"Yes," said a small boy in the front of the crowd, "can I have the box you're standing on when you've finished with it?"

What can catch runaway burglars from ten feet away?
The long arm of the law!

Bill — "I keep seeing spots before my eyes?"
Will — "Have you seen an ophthalmologist"
Bill — "No—just spots!"

What do you say when you hear a ghost on the other side of your bedroom wall?
"Just come on through!"

"Guard! Guard! The carriage is on fire!"
"That's all right sir—it's a smoking carriage!"

Golfer (to caddie) "What should I take for my next shot?"
Caddie — "Golf lessons!"

What was the name of the legendary Spanish detective?
El C.I.D!

A king of a far-off country went out and bought a bottle of perfume and a bottle of poison. The perfume was for his future queen and the poison was for his deadliest enemy. He wrapped them up and put the same note in with each parcel — "A little drop of something to sweep you off your feet. . . "

Walt — "So how was the food on the channel crossing?"
Ike — "It went down quickly—but it came up really fast!"

Bill — "You remind me of Lord Neilson!"
Will — "Don't you mean Lord Nelson?"
Bill — "No—you remind me of Neilson—before he lost his i!"

Did you hear about the geologist who married a gardener?
They built a rock garden together!

"This is a picture of Benjamin Franklin!"
"You're kidding me—he's not franklin'—he's just standin' there!"

"Do you like Kipling?"
"Don't know—never kippled in my life!"

"My wife's in hospital!"
"What's wrong with her?"
"She was in a road accident—someone bumped into her car and her rear end was damaged!"

Did you hear about the sick sprinter?
His nose ran all the way to the finishing line!

Bill — "My brother gave me chickenpox! —He said it was better to give than to receive!"

How do you keep Mr Dopey busy?
Give him a piece of paper with P.T.O. written on both sides!

Fred — "I can read you like a book!"
Ted — "Oh? Do I have a happy ending?"

What do you do when a raging elephant steps on your foot?
Wait quietly until it steps off again!

What time is it when an elephant stands on your foot?
Time to call the doctor!

An astronaut walks into Al the butcher's shop.
Al — "What are you doing here?"
Astronaut — "N.A.S.S.A.!"
Al — "So you're from space headquarters!"
Astronaut — "No— Need Another String of Sausages, Al!"

Joiner — "That's the job done, sir!"
Chess player — "Great! Will you take a check, mate?"

What is the difference between a doormat and a bottle of medicine?
One is taken up and shaken and the other is shaken up and taken!

Two robots are sitting on a park bench, munching on a couple of cans of beans.
1st robot — "Crust's nice and crunchy!"
2nd robot — "Yes, but I don't think much of the filling!"

Mum — "How's school?"
Son — "On the up!"
Mum — "On the up?"
Son — "Yes—sit up, stand up, own up, speak up and shut up!"

Fred — "There was a fire in the cobblers' premises today, and the cobblers sent up an S.O.S."
Ted — "What does S.O.S. stand for?"
Fred — "Save Our Soles!"

What is the difference between a married man and a single man?
One kisses the missus and the other misses the kisses!

Little girl at dentist — "I wish we were born without teeth!"
Dentist — "We are!"

Maisie — "I can see right through you!"
Mo — "Oh, yeh? Then you can tell me what I had for breakfast today!"

Dogs have puppies.
Mad dogs have rabies!

What the daddy rabbit tell his friends when his wife had more babies?
"Fresh buns today!"

1st boy — "I don't feel very well—I've got butterflies in my stomach!"
2nd boy — "Huh! You're lucky! I've got a school dinner in mine!"

Billy — "I can't wind my watch!"
Bob — "Why not?"
Billy — "I lost it a week ago!"

Bill — "I fell in the river today!"
Will — "Wearing your smart new suit?"
Bill — "I'm afraid so—there was no time to change!"

Joe — "I can't put on my socks!"
Mum — "Why not?"
Joe — "Because the dog's just eaten them!"

Brown — "I'm a builder and I'm going to make a name for myself!"
Hamish McShoogle — "Ah'm a builder—an' ah'm goin' tae make a hame for my sel'!"

Billy — "I sat next to a very pretty girl in class today!"
Mum — "Did you ask her what her name was?"
Billy — "No—I didn't like to wake her!"

Why did the writer write quickly?
Because his pen was running out!

Bobby — "Billy? Are you awake?"
Billy — "Not telling you!"

What happened when the cat got its head chopped off?
It didn't live to tell the tail!

Few people know this, but when Anne Hathaway met William Shakespeare, it was love at first sight for both of them. Their first date was very romantic, and Will walked Anne home, hand in hand, through the woods. Halfway home, Anne stopped, dived into a thicket, and started to make a noise like an owl.
"Why hootest thou thus, my sweet?" asked Shakespeare.
"Because, my love," replied Anne, "A bard in the hand is worth 'two-hoo' in the bush!"

Old lady (to husband, who is one hundred years old today) — "Look—the Queen's sent you a birthday message—isn't that nice?"
Old man — "Huh! She never remembered before!"

When is a general like a ballet dancer?
When he is graceful in defeat (feet)!

Why is becoming an MP like being on a crowded bus?
Because you have to stand before you can get a seat!

Why did the doctor go to the bingo hall?
He wanted to make a house call!

Bob — "I used to be a child criminal!"
Batty — "And you changed your ways?"
Bob — "No—I grew up!"

Four monsters were out hunting for frogs for their evening soup. Three of the monsters dribbled slime and goo constantly as they shuffled along, but the fourth waited until he came to a frog, then he would drop a couple of bits of slime on the frog—killing it, splitch, splotch, splash— just like that. At the end of the hunt, the first three monsters had run dry, and had only five frogs each. The fourth monster had killed ten frogs and still had plenty of slime to spare. The moral of the story? A splitch in time saves slime!

1st spider — "I'm famous now!"
2nd spider — "Why do you say that?"
1st spider — "Didn't you see me on the television last night?"

Bill — "I tried to swat a fly that was crawling on the television last night!"
Will — "Did you hit it?"
Bill — "No—but I got it on video!"

Midwife — "Well, Mr Jones, your wife has had a healthy baby!"
Mr Jones — "Is it a boy? I wanted a boy!"
Midwife — "Sorry, it's a girl!"
Mr Jones — "Never mind—that was my second choice!"

When is a fly like a bank robber?
When it's caught on camera!

Little boy — "Mister, have you seen yesterday's newspaper?"
Man — "No—why?"
Little boy — "Because my fish and chips are in it!"

Mr Dopey really doesn't know much— He thought Hertz Van Rental was a Dutch painter!

Fred — "People always 'phone me when I'm in the bath!"
Ted — "There's not much you can do about that!"
Fred — "Yes, there is—I've stopped taking baths!"

"My father's given up his knife-throwing act!"
"What does he do now?"
"He's head of the Missing Persons Bureau!"

TEE-HEE!

WHAT HAS
FOUR EYES
BUT CAN'T SEE?
MISSISSIPPI!

WHAT LETTER IS FOUND IN A CUP?
T!

WHAT OCCURS ONCE IN A MINUTE, TWICE IN
A MOMENT, BUT NEVER IN A DAY?
THE LETTER M!

What's a snorkeller's favourite night out?
A dive-in movie!

Interviewer — "And have you any children, Mrs Dobbs?"
Mrs Dobbs — "I had three girls—but now I've got two!"
Interviewer — "What happened to the third girl?"
Mrs Dobbs — "She grew up!"

Bob — "I could marry anyone I pleased!"
Bill — "So why are you still single?"
Bob — "I haven't pleased anyone yet!"

Man in fish and chip shop — "I hope you're not going to wrap my fish in that newspaper!"
Shop assistant — "Why not?"
Man — "Because I've already read that one!"

What dance do Scotsmen do at parties?
The Hochaye Cokey!

When is a lawyer like a Wimbledon player?
When he's serving in court!

Why is there a pile of letters at the end of the race track?
It's the finishing post!

Maisie — "Where's my new lipstick?
Mo — "It's on your mouth—right under your nose!"

Mike — "Your watchdog's very quiet!"
Ike — "Yes—he's digital!"

How do you train your child to be a tightrope walker?
Feed him a balanced diet!

"The vicar's gone missing!"
"Quick—phone the Missing Parsons Bureau!"

Bill — "I'm off to the bottle bank!"
Will — "No need—I'll give you some of my bottles!"

Bank robber to bank manager's wife — "I'm sorry madam, your husband can't come to the phone— he's tied up at the moment!"

Old Lady — "I'm 85 and I've got a perfect set of teeth!"
Neighbour — "My, that's wonderful! How have you managed that?"
Old Lady — "The dentist fitted them yesterday!"

How do you make an antidote?
Be very polite when she comes to visit!

The hairdresser lost his keys to the salon. Luckily, he were able to change his own locks.

Why did Freddy become a fireman?
He wanted to join the jet set!

Why did the doctor go to work when he was sick?
He wanted to get better at his job!

What did the farmer say when he turned up at the publishers of the Guinness Book of Records with a giant vegetable?
"Here's a turnip for the books!"

Did you hear about the bad-tempered sailor?
He had a ship on his shoulder!

Billy — "Can I have a milk-shake and two straws, please?"
Waitress — "Are you going to share with your friend?"
Billy — "No—I just like to fill both sides of my mouth at the same time!"

Molly — "My husband's a lighting engineer!"
Mo — "A bright young man?"
Molly — "No—a shady character!"

Scrawled on a toilet wall — "Don't just sit there—do something!"

Why did the soldier open the walnut?
He wanted to see the kernel!

Minister — "Well, Ted, what do you know about reincarnation?"
Ted the gardener — "Just about everythin', sir! Oi've been rearin' carnations since I were nowt but a lad!"

Why are camping enthusiasts good singers?
Because they always find the right pitch!

WHY WERE THE TEACHER'S EYES CROSSED?
SHE COULDN'T CONTROL HER PUPILS!
HEE-HEE!
WHY DID THE CYCLOPS STOP TEACHING?
BECAUSE HE ONLY HAD ONE PUPIL!
HA-HA-HA!
WHAT OCCURS 4 TIMES IN EVERY WEEK,
2 TIMES IN EVERY MONTH, AND ONCE IN A YEAR?
THE LETTER E!
CHUCKLE CHUCKLE!

Did you hear about the spy who slept out in a gale?
His cover was blown!

What was Percy Pig's favourite nursery rhyme?
The Grand Old Duke of Pork!

How do you get to know a golfer?
Invite him for tee!

Did you hear about the photographer's near-death experience?
He saw his life flash before him!

Scrawled on a wall in Washington "When the Clintons moved out of the White House, Hilary was left with the Bill!"

What's the difference between Richard Cross and Tony Blair?
You can make Richard Cross but you can't make Tony Blair!
Yes you can!
How?
Turn up his microphone!

Mum — "What are you doing with your little brother's bike, Jimmy?"
Jimmy — "We're studying care of the environment at school, and Miss Smith asked us to take something in for wee-cycling!"

Two maggots are sitting in the middle of an apple when they hear the sound of chomping teeth approaching.
"Remember," says one to the other, "We're in this thing together!"

Bill — "Do you like cartoons, Ted?"
Ted — "Oh, yes, I always listen to music when I go for a drive!"

What subject do keep-fit fanatics do best in at school?
Jog-raphy!

What did one champagne cork say to the other champagne cork?
Let's pop out for a celebration!

Woman —"Five pounds for one question—that's rather a lot to charge, isn't it?"
Fortune-teller — "Next!"

Mrs Jones — "Did you get fitted for your new trousers and jacket?"
Mr Jones — "No. They took my measurements and said I was unsuitable!"

Molly — "My mum's got a new dishwasher!"
Mo — "I wish my mum would get one too!"
Molly — "What's wrong with the one she's got?"
Mo — "I'm tired!"

Scrawled on seaside wall — "School sucks."
Scrawled underneath — "So
does
qui
ck
sa
n
d!"

Mum — "So how was camp?"
Billy — "Great! But the food was terrible, I got bitten all over by mosquitoes, I fell out of a tree and hurt my arm, and the other kids were horrible!"
Mum — "So what was so great about it?"
Billy — "I didn't have to have a bath for a whole week!"

Will — "When my wife left me, all the light went out of my life!"
Bill — "Is that because you miss her so much?"
Will — "No—it's because she stole all the lightbulbs!"

Golfer — "New to the game are you? I don't suppose you have a handicap yet!"
Novice — "Handicap? I thought it was a golfing glove!"

Kindly lady — "Can I help you, little girl?"
Little girl — "I can't reach this doorbell—can you ring it for me, please?"
Kindly lady — "There—is that it?"
Little girl — "Thanks—now, run for your life!"

Did you hear about the man who always wore white when out walking at night so that the cars would see him?
He was knocked down by a snow-plough!

Ted — "I really miss my home comforts!"
Fred — "Are you staying somewhere else, then?"
Ted — "No—some burglars stole my bed and sofa!"

Scrawled on the bike-shed wall "Manners maketh man. Never crumble your bread or roll in the soup."

Why did the bellringer stop practice early? The vicar tolled him to shut up!

Prisoner — "I've gone on hunger strike, you know!"
Visitor — "That's a pity—I put a file in this cake I made for you!"

Bob — "I call my girlfriend 'Peach'!"
Bill — "Why—because her skin is soft?"
Bob — "No—because she has a heart of stone!"

Molly and Mo are eating apples.
Molly — "Watch out for maggots!"
Mo — "Why? The maggots can look after themselves!"

Billy — "My granny's teeth are like stars!"
Bobby — "Really?"
Billy — "Yes, they come out at night!"

Scrawled on the bike shed wall "Some girls who are the picture of health are just painted that way."

Why was the young pharaoh confused? Because his daddy was a mummy!

Fred — "My Dad's so bald, we have to take an extra bottle of sun-tan lotion on holiday with us, just for his head!"
Ted — "My mum talks so much that we need an extra bottle of lotion, just for her tongue!"

Billy — "What are you putting that stuff on your face for, Mum?"
Mum — "To make me beautiful!"
Billy — "I'd take it back to the shop and ask for my money back, if I were you!"

Bill — "I'm going to get one of those new water-bed things!"
Will — "Oh, don't do that, Bill—you can't swim!"

Fred — "I've just been to America with Dave. It was great, but when we took our first look at the Grand Canyon, Dave's face dropped a mile!"
Ted — "Did he not like it?"
Fred — "No—he fell into it!"

Why are there no kings in the desert? Because there is no rain (reign)!

Maisie — "Don't go swimming there! There are sharks in the water!"
Mo — "It's all right—they're man-eaters!"

Fred — "Does your dog bite?"
Ted — "No. He's got no teeth left. But don't go too close—he'll give you a nasty suck!"

Old Lady — "And what does your father do, Annie?"
Annie — "He's a magician."
Old Lady — "And what trick does he do best?"
Annie — "He makes people vanish!"
Old Lady — "And have you any brothers and sisters?"
Annie — "I used to have a brother, but he went into my Dad's wardrobe one day and disappeared!"

"My father is a pilot in the air force. He distinguished himself in the war."
"My father is a fireman. He extinguished himself when his helmet caught fire!"

Annie — "So, do you think I should take up the violin as a hobby?"
Mo — "No, I think you should put it down as a favour!"

Fred — "I'm on a seafood diet!"
Ted — "What's that like, then?"
Ted — "Great—I see food, and I eat it!"

Annie — "It was test day at school today!"
Mum — "Really?"
Annie — "Yes. The teacher tested our English, and we tested her patience!"

Mum — "Davie, why are you crying?"
Davie — "I've got six peanuts stuck up my nose!"
Mum — "And why's your brother crying?"
Davie — "He wants the rest of his snack back!"

Bill — "Mr Dopey, I would like to ask for your daughter's hand in marriage."
Mr Dopey — "But what will I do with the rest of her?

Bill — *"What I meant was that I would like to take your daughter for my wife!"*
Mr Dopey — *"But why does your wife want her?"*

Bill — "No—what I meant was that I would like to marry your daughter!
Mr Dopey —"But you've got a wife already—you just told me!"

Bill — "What happened to you?"
Will — "I fell while I was out riding!"
Bill — "Horseback?"
Will — "I don't know—I haven't checked the stables yet!"

What is the best way to rise and shine?
Eat yeast and shoe polish!

What's the difference between a mirage and a mirror?
A mirage shows you what you long for and a mirror shows what you fear!

Bill — "Do you have a girlfriend?"
Will — "I have a lovely redhead!"
Bill — "I know you have a red head—but have you got a girlfriend?"

Mum — "So, how was your second day at school, Jimmy?"
Jimmy — "Great—the teacher didn't shout at us once today!"
Mum — "You must have been very good, then!"
Jimmy — "No—after all her shouting yesterday, the teacher had lost her voice!"

Why did the man take a net to bed?
To catch forty winks!

Bill — *"I love baked beans!"*
Will — *"So do I!"*
Bill — *"Great—do you want to see my collection?"*

1st man — "What's wrong with you?"
2nd man — "I forgot my girlfriend's birthday, so she gave me something to remember her by!"

Bill — "Mr Drone is a little bit dreary till you get to know him!"
Will — "And then?"
Bill — "And then you find out that he's a complete bore!"

Ted — *"My girlfriend says I'm a great wit!"*
Fred — *"My girlfriend called me a great twit too!"*

Molly — "My boyfriend said my legs were very striking!"
Maisie — "Did he?"
Molly — "Well, not exactly—he said they were like matchsticks!"

Jim — "I call my dog 'Treasure'!"
George — "Why is that?"
Jim — "Because the first time I took him home, my wife said 'Where did you dig that up?' "

Mum — *"Quiet please, Johnny—your father can't read his paper!"*
Johnny — *"That's terrible—I learnt to read when I was five!"*

What did the girl's leg say to her hip?
"What's a joint like you doing in a girl like this?"

Fred — "My brother's job really gets him down."
Ted — "What does he do?"
Fred — "He's a miner!"

Did you hear about the artist who became an actor?
He drew a large crowd at the theatre!

Why did the football disappear?
It was fed to the wing!

Old Lady — "That's a very old teddy bear! What do you call him?
Little girl — "Fred Bear!"

How do you hire a car?
Lift it with a crane!

Fred — "What's your sister like, Ted?"
Ted — "She's a swot!"
Fred — "Huh! Top in every subject. I suppose!"
Ted — "No, but she kills a lot of flies!"

What is the national drink of Australia?
Koka-Koala!

Mother (searching through old photographs)
— "Freddy, do you remember what I did with
the prints of Spain?"
Freddy — "I didn't even know you had met
him!"

Where can you get pig food in a casino?
At the slop-machines!

Pandas live on bamboo shoots. What do polar
bears live on?
Ice!

Why did the knight cross the chess board?
To see his checkmate!

1st man — "Does your baby cry much?"
2nd man — "Cry? We call him the Prince of
Wails!"

Fred — "I was woken by a terrible noise this
morning!"
Ted — "What was it?"
Fred — "The crack of dawn!"

How did King Arthur get his men to
dismount?
He waited for knightfall!

"My father went to war and was rewarded for
gallantry."
"My father went to the filling station and was
awarded a gallon free!"

Bill — "I've got some money to spend and
I'm going to share it fifty-fifty with you!"
Will — "How much do we get?"
Bill — "I get fifty dollars and you get fifty
cents!"

Billy — "I got you some perfume for your
birthday, Mum—it's called 'Angel.'
Mum — "How nice! Why did they call it
'Angel' I wonder?"
Billy — "Probably because it smells to high
heaven!"

Bill — "I've just found £20— what should I
do with it?"
Will — "Buy something nice with half and
give me the rest—the change will do me
good!"

What did the executioner say to Charles I?
"You're history!"

"Help, help, my jacket's on fire!"
That's a fine blazer you've got there, sir!"

Gamekeeper (seeing man with fishing rod
over his shoulder) — "Oi! You can't go
fishing round here!"
Man — "I'm not going fishing—I'm going
home!"

1st boy — "I've seen a man-eating tiger!"
2nd boy — "So what? I've seen a man eating
chicken!"

1st boy — "I was named after my father."
2nd boy — "So what do they call you?"
1st boy — "Dad!"

1st man — "My clients are always late for
their appointments!"
2nd man — "What do you do?"
1st man — "I'm an undertaker!"

Maisie — "You haven't lost much weight—
what happened to your four-week diet?"
Mo — "I finished it in two days!"

A little boy and his mother are going to the
subway.
Little boy — "We can't go down there,
mum!"
Mum — "Why not?"
Little boy — "Can't you read the sign? It
says 'Dogs must be carried on the
escalator'—and we haven't got one!"

Where do company directors go when they
have nothing to do?
The bored room!

Why did the bar on the high jump break?
An accident—nobody's vault!

What goes 'peck-bang-peck-bang'?
Two chickens playing with balloons!

Why did the musician hold a shoe to his ear?
He was listening to sole music!

Simpering Sadie — "Our new baby fills the
house with laughter and joy!"
Cheeky Charlie — "Our new baby fills the
house with the smell of his nappies!"

What do sheep do straight after opening their Christmas presents?
They write their 'thank-ewe' letters!

What does the sheepdog say when he guides the flock into the pen?
"After ewe!"

Simpering Sadie — "My father is a saint. His home is filled with kindness and his life is spent doing good deeds."
Suspicious Sid — "My father is a burglar. His home is filled with stolen property and his life is spent doing time!"

Simpering Sadie — "I have lived my life surrounded by love."
Nautical Ned — "I have lived my life surrounded by water!"

Suspicious Sid — "My life is a life of crime."
Dustbin Dan — "My life is a life of grime!"

Simpering Sadie — "I take great pleasure from other people's happiness."
Suspicious Sid — "I take great treasure from other people's houses!"

Billy (in the cinema) — "Dad? Can I have some money to give to the woman crying down at the front?"
Dad — "What woman crying?"
Billy — "The woman crying 'Ices! Popcorn!' "

Old lady — "Why are you crying, son?"
Little boy — "I've lost 50p!"
Old lady — "Never mind—here's another 50p. . . .but why are you still crying?"
Little boy — "Because now I wish I had lost £1!"

Dad — "Johnny, how many times have I told you not to come down the stairs like that; it makes such a racket. Go upstairs again and come down quietly!"
Two minutes later. . .
"That's better. I didn't hear a thing that time!"
Johnny — "That's because I slid down the banister!"

Why did the snake fail his exams?
The examiner couldn't read his writhing!

What's the difference between a crossword solver and a man eating dessert?
One's a good puzzler and the other's a pud guzzler!

Dr Watson — "So, Holmes, it was the elephant who had been fiddling the books all along. How was he doing it?"
Sherlock Holmes — "Elly-mentally, my dear Watson!"

Watson — "Holmes, where did you learn to become such a great detective?"
Holmes — "At the elementary, my dear Watson!"

What's the difference between glue and sticky tape?
You've got me stuck there!

Boy genius — "There are sixty thousand ants in this anthill!"
Teacher — "How did you work that out?"
Boy genius — "Easy! I counted the legs and divided by six!"

Billy — "I'm glad I'm not a bird!"
Bobby — "Why?"
Billy — "Because I can't fly!"

Lifeguard — "Don't dive into that pool! There's no water in it!"
Man on diving board — "That's all right! I can't swim!"

Gamekeeper — "I hope you're not going to fish here, sir!"
Fisherman — "I was, but I've just lost my watch and now I haven't the time any more!"

Mike — "I'm not going to school today, Mum—the children hate me and the teachers are mean!"
Mike's mum _ " You've got to go to school, son—you're the headmaster!"

Mo — "What have you got there, Molly?"
Molly — "It's a letter from a distant relative—my sister!"
Mo — "But your sister's not a distant relative!"
Molly — "Yes she is—she lives in Australia!"

Why was the gardener kept behind at school?
Because he needed help with his weeding!

What happened to the man who put his foot through a sieve?
He strained his ankle!

Neighbour — "Your son is dreadfully spoiled, Mrs Bloggs!"
Mrs Bloggs — "What a terrible thing to say—you know it isn't true!"
Neighbour — "Oh, but it is—he's just been run over by a steamroller!"

Fred — "I found six frogs today!"
Ted — "Where are you going to keep them?"
Fred — "In the bath!"
Ted — "But what will you do when you want to have a bath?"
Fred — "I'll blindfold them!"

Bill — "Is this plastic, or wood?"
Will — "It's wood!"
Bill — "Well, wooden you know it!"

Johnny's dad has taken away his pocket money for bad behaviour this week and Johnny is not speaking to him. When Dad comes home from work at night, Johnny calls to his mother; "Mum! That man you call your husband has come back again!"

Annie (in video store) — "Have you seen 'The Invisible Man', Mo?"
Mo — "Don't be stupid!"

Angry man — "Come here! I'll teach you to throw stones at my greenhouse!"
Little boy — "Thanks, mister! I'm needing a few tips!"

Maisie — "My friend's ambidextrous"
Mo — "I'd give my right hand to be like that!"

Fred asked his mum how old she was. Mum wouldn't tell him exactly how old she was, so Fred asked her if she was the same age as the mother and father of his best friend, Bill Hill. Mum said that she was. Next day, Fred had to write an essay on his mother.
"My mother," he wrote, "is as old as the Hills. . ."

Why did the boy fall out of the plane?
He was annoying the other passengers and one of them told him to go outside and play!

Mum — "Tommy—you're bursting out of that jumper. We'll have to get you a new one!"
Tommy — "It must be the growing season for this family, Mum. Look at Dad—his head's bursting out of his hair!"

Bobby has been having dinner at his friend's house. A terrible storm comes. His friend's mum looks out at the wind and rain and says to Bobby "You can't go out in this terrible weather. You'd better just stay the night here."
"Righto," says Bobby. "I'll just run home and get my pyjamas and toothbrush!"

Scrawled on bike shed wall — "James Bond rules—OOK!

Scrawled on bike shed wall "One good turn deserves another. . .keep it up and you'll get dizzy."

Betsy — "My dad's stronger than your dad!"
Annie — "Huh! That's rubbish. Do you know the Atlantic Ocean? My dad dug the hole!"
Betsy — "So what! Do you know the Dead Sea? My dad killed it!"

Why did the ghost go to the doctor?
To get something for his eerie-ache!

What is stretchy and musical?
An elastic band!

Santa Claus — "Rudolf says it's raining outside!"
Mrs Claus — "What makes you think he's right?"
Santa Clause — "Because Rudolf the Red knows rain, dear!"

Maisie had earned a lot of money trick-or-treating. She went to the shop to spend it. "If I had all that money," said the shopkeeper, "I would give it all to charity." "Righto," said Maisie, "I'll give it to you for these sweets and then you can give it all to charity."

Why did the boy take a clock and a bird out on Hallowe'en?
Tick or tweet!

What does a duck do when you tell it a joke?
It quacks a smile!

**WHY DID THE BOY CLOSE THE
REFRIGERATOR DOOR?**
HE DIDN'T WANT TO SEE THE
SALAD DRESSING!

CHUCKLE
CHUCKLE!

**WHAT DO YOU CALL TWO
BANANA PEELS?**
A PAIR OF SLIPPERS!

**WHY DID THE TOMATO TURN
RED?**
BECAUSE HE SAW THE SALAD
DRESSING!

Why when is a Frenchman like a ballet dance?
When he's a pa de deux!

A little boy arrives at a neighbour's house on Hallowe'en, with a sheet over his head.
"Are you a ghost?" asks the neighbour.
"No," says the little boy. "I'm just airing the bedlinen for my mother!"

Annie and her mum are sitting on the bus, behind their next-door neighbour Mrs Smith. Annie whispers something in her mother's ear.
"Don't whisper, Annie," says her mother. "you know it's not polite. Now tell me what it is you wanted to say in a nice clear voice."
"Okay," says Annie, "I was just wanting to know why you think Mrs Brown is an old so-and-so!"

Why is painting such hot work?
Because two coats are necessary!

Mum — "Why are you listening to the radio and your CD player at the same time?"
Little Mo — "I like to keep both ears occupied!"

Why did the taxi driver give up his job?
Someone kept driving away his customers!

Why did the witch make her friend leave the table?
Because he was goblin!

Billy(to sister) — "You're stupid and ugly!"
Dad — "That's quite enough! Say sorry to your sister!"
Billy — "Okay—I'm sorry that you're stupid and ugly!"

What's the difference between a person who can't mind his own business and a person who has just got out of the bath?
One's rude and nosey and the other's nude and rosy!

Billy falls down the stairs. "Ouch! **** ****** *****" His language is shocking!**
"Billy," says his mum, "you mustn't use language like that!"
"Shakespeare does," says Billy.
"Right," says his mum, "you're not playing with him any more!"

Mother ship to alien visiting earth — "So—is there intelligent life on the planet?"
Alien — "Yes, but I'm only here for a short while!"

How do you stop a head cold from going to your chest?
Tie a knot in your neck!

Ted — "I used to be so forgetful!"
Fred — "And are you any better now?"
Ted — "What were we talking about?"

Ted — "I've just bought a pig!"
Fred — "Where are you going to keep him?"
Ted — "Under the bed!"
Fred — "But what about the mess?"
Ted — "I'm sure he won't mind!"

Bill — "I bumped into an old friend the other day!"
Will — "Really? Was it good to see him?"
Bill — "I didn't see him—that's why I bumped into him!"

Bill — "I bumped into an old friend yesterday!"
Will — "Was your car badly dented?"

Wife — "Shall I put the kettle on, dear?"
Husband (not really listening) — "Whatever you like my love—you look wonderful in everything!"

Molly — "I've just bought the latest thing in dresses!"
Mo — "Really—what is it?"
Molly — "A nightdress!"

What gets bigger by half when you turn it on its head?
The number 6!

Newspaper headline — "Basketweaving! Reed all about it!"

Will — "Are those two thin men very good friends?"
Bill — "No—they're just slight acquaintances!"

Auntie Doris — "My, my, you've grown another foot since I last saw you!"
Little boy — "I have not! I've got two feet, just as I always had!"

What is green and can jump a mile a minute?
A grasshopper with hiccups!

Ted — "Why are you swimming on your back?
Fred — "I've just eaten, and I don't want to swim on a full stomach!"

Ted — "Is it dangerous to swim on a full stomach?"
Fred — "Dunno—I always swim in water!"

Which two letters spell rotten teeth?
D.K.!

What do you do with a haunted bicycle?
Take the spooks out of the wheels!

How did the gardener get lost?
He took the wrong root!

Two burglars in a music shop hear the sound of police sirens approaching. "Quick!" says one of them, "Grab the lute and run!"

What did the headless ghost say when his friend gave him a comb?
"I'll never part with this!"

Can you drop an egg ten feet without breaking it?
Yes—Drop it from eleven feet and it won't break for the first ten!

What did one lump of earth say to the other when they bumped into each other?
"Watch where you're going, you stupid clod!"

1st woman — "My husband's a romantic. He was attracted to me by the smell of my perfume!"
2nd woman — "My husband's a banker. He was attracted to me by the smell of my money!"

What do you call a vampire dentist?
An extractor fang!

What did the grumpy gardener say to his friend?
"Go away and leave me a-lawn!"

What do ghostly parrots say?
"Whoo-oo's a pretty boy, then!"

How do gardeners get paid?
They get their celery once a month!

What do you do when you can't find the bathplug?
Look for the robber duck!

What did the burglar do in the supermarket?
He took what was on offer!

Did you hear about the robbery in the fishmongers?
It was a smash-and-crab raid!

What do you call a millionaire who never washes?
Filthy rich!

Did you hear about the honest bowler?
He never did anything underhand!

Why are there no chairs in the prison concert hall?
Because on opening night, the audience took their seats!

Where do you find garden snails?
On the end of Gordon's fingers!

Why do robots never wash their hands?
They don't want to get rusty nails!

What do ghosts wear on their feet in wet weather?
Wail-ington boo-oots!

Owl — "To-whoo! to-whoo!"
Teacher — "To WHOM! To WHOM!"

Bill — "Our pet pig's just like one of the family."
Will — "Yes, I can see the resemblance!"

What did the bus driver say to the man with the broken leg?
"Hop on!"

What is the difference between a bottle of perfume and a parcel?
One goes wherever it is sent, the other is scent wherever it goes!

What did the mole say when he met the worm?
"What in earth are you doing here?"

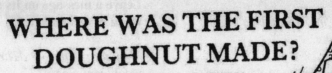

WHERE WAS THE FIRST DOUGHNUT MADE?
IN GREASE!

WHAT KIND OF BEAN DOESN'T GROW IN A GARDEN?
A HUMAN BEAN!

CHORTLE!

CHORTLE!

WHAT IS RED AND GOES UP AND DOWN?
A TOMATO IN A LIFT!

What has two wheels and flies?
A wheelie bin!

What do ghosts do in the woods at night?
They go fox-haunting!

Why did the rodeo rider go to the doctor's?
Because he had bronco-itis!

What has fangs and says "ten, nine, eight, seven. . . ?"
Count Backula!

Will — "There are two caterpillars in camouflage outfits and tin helmets in the middle of this apple!"
Bill — "Don't worry—that's just the apple corps!"

How much do bakers get paid?
Lots of dough!

Gamekeeper — "Oi! you're not allowed to fish here!"
Fisherman — "I'm not fishing—I'm teaching this worm to bungee-jump!

Prisoner (newly released from jail) — "I'm free! I'm free!"
Small boy — "You're very tall for your age, aren't you?"

Bill — "Do you file your nails, Will?"
Will — "No, I just throw them away!"

1st fish — "Percy the pike was caught today!"
2nd fish — "What? after all those years? I bet he was fed up!"
1st fish — "Fed up? He was gutted!"

Customer — "I cleaned my watch yesterday, and now it won't work!"
Jeweller — "What did you clean it with, sir?"
Customer — "Soap powder and water, of course!"
Jeweller — "Soap powder and water? No wonder it won't work now!"
Customer — "Oh, I don't think the washing was the problem, actually. It just all went horribly wrong in the spin-drier!"

Bill — "Where does your wife come from?"
Will — "Alaska!"
Bill — "Don't worry, I'll ask her myself!"

How can you speak to the sea when the tide's out?
Leave a message on its answer-foam for when it gets back in!

Man in fish shop — "Throw me that salmon, would you please?"
Fishmonger — "Why?"
Man — "So I won't be lying when I tell my wife I caught it!"

What do you call a dentist in the army?
A drill sergeant!

Chef — "Can you lay five eggs over there by the cooker for me?"
Assistant — "What do you think I am? A chicken?"

What is the difference between a bus driver and a bad cold?
One knows the stops and the other stops the nose!

Did you hear about the judge who had his wig stolen from his head?
It was a hair raising experience!

Did you hear about the burglar who was arrested for breaking into a writer's home? He got a long sentence!

"My name is Mackintosh and I work in the clothing industry."
"My name is Hiram and I'm in the rental business."
"My name is Player and I'm a sportsman."
"My name is Idle and I don't do anything!"

"My name is Walker and I'm a driver."
"My name is Thrower and I'm a batsman."
"My name is Joiner and I work in the demolition business."
"My name is Keen, and I'm just not interested!"

"My name is Frantz, and I come from Belgium."
"My name is Scott, and I'm American."
"My name is Isla and I come from the mainland."
"My name is Mappin and I'm lost!"

Where did the secret agent go shopping?
At the snooper-market!

TEE-HEE!

WHAT DO YOU CALL ARTIFICIAL SPAGHETTI?
MOCKARONI!

SNIGGER-SNIGGER!

WHY DID THE MAN AT THE ORANGE JUICE FACTORY LOSE HIS JOB?
HE COULDN'T CONCENTRATE!

CHUCKLE!

HAR! HAR!

HAW! HAW!

"My name is Rich and I haven't got a penny."
"My name is Rider and I haven't got a horse."
"My name is Carpenter and I haven't got a saw."
"My name is Smart and I haven't got a clue!"

"My name is Cross and I never lose my temper."
"My name is Watt and I never ask questions."
"My name is Cook and I never go near the kitchen."
"My name is Herd and I never listen!"

Shop assistant — "I must say, sir, I'm surprised to see any customers on a day like this. It must be the wettest day in history!"
Customer — "I know, but my wife said I should splash out and buy a new suit!"

Why did the history teacher go to the grocer's shop?
He wanted some dates!

Customer in grocer's shop — "Do you have asparagus?"
Assistant — "No—we don't have sparrows, and my name's not Gus!"

Customer in hardware store — "Have you got two-inch nails?"
Assistant — "Yes, sir!"
Customer — "Scratch my back, then, will you?"

For sale —Rubber gloves in handy packs!

For sale —Playing cards with eight aces—it's a great deal!

For sale —Second-hand buses—not to be missed!

For sale —Skittles—knock-down prices!

For sale —Coffins—a once-in-a-lifetime offer!

Unbeatable offer—drum with hole in it!

Cars for sale —Quick—they're going fast!

How do you choose a lawyer?
Ask for a free trial!

"Coming to the car boot sale?"
No thanks—I wear sneakers when I'm driving!

Fire sale!—Red-hot deals!

"How did you get on at the garage sale?"
"They didn't have any garages I liked!"

A woman went into a shop, looking for a new bedroom mirror. She caught sight of one that looked quite nice, and went over for a closer inspection.
"Do you like that one madam?" enquired the assistant.
The woman looked into the mirror and frowned.
"On reflection," she said, "No, I don't!"

An actor went into a shop looking for a new shirt. They didn't have one that fitted him on the shelves, but he saw one in the window that he thought might be in his size, so he asked if he could try it on.
"I'm sorry, sir," said the assistant, "but that shirt's for display only."
"Oh," said the actor, "and what play might that be?"

Assistant — "Still here, sir?"
Robber — "Yes—just looting!"

What kind of shop is full of unpleasant people?
The shoe-shop—you'll always find loafers and sneakers there!

Customer — "Do your eggs come from a local farmer?
Shop assistant — "No, sir— they all come from hens!"

A shoplifter is heading out of the door of a department store when the alarm goes off. The store detective is there in a flash.
"May I look in that bag, sir?" he asks sternly.
"Of course," says the shoplifter, relieved.
"Just don't ask what I have in my pockets, whatever you do!"

Assistant — "Can I help you, sir?"
Robber — "No thanks—just lurking!"

A man goes into an electrical goods store to buy a washing machine. "I want a nice quiet machine," he says. "The one I have at the moment is very noisy." The assistant is very reassuring. "All our machines are very quiet," he says. "Why don't you take this one? It doesn't make a sound!"
The man buys the washing machine and has it delivered to his home, but two days later, he's back. "That washing machine is just as noisy as my old one!" he complains. "You said it didn't make a sound!"
"It doesn't," says the shop assistant, "unless you switch it on!"

Newsagent — "Good morning son. Can I help you?"
Little boy — "Can you lend me some money to buy a bar of chocolate?"

Customer — "This knife you sold me is blunt!"
Assistant — "Yes, sir, it's the new safety feature!"

What do you call a clapped-out vacuum cleaner?
A poor old sucker!

Customer — "Could I have that loaf of raisin bread on the shelf over there?"
Assistant — "That's not raisin bread. We're just having a bit of a problem with flies at the moment!"

Customer — "Do you carry 20lb sacks of potatoes in this shop?"
Grocer — "No sir, I get my assistant to do all the heavy lifting!"

Customer — "Do you have an ox tail?"
Butcher — "No, sir, it's just the strings of my apron hanging down at the back!"

Shop assistant— "You're quite right sir; you do need some new glasses!"
Customer— "You haven't tested my eyes yet! How do you know I need new glasses?"
Shop assistant— "Because this isn't the optician's— it's the fruit shop!"

Customer — "Are these chillis very hot?"
Grocer's assistant — "I don't think so, sir; they're sitting right by the doorway, and there's quite a draught!"

Customer — "Do you have any sweet potatoes?"
Grocer — "These ones are quite cute!"

Manager — "Did you count the takings?"
Assistant — "Yes, sir—they took half the contents of the shop!"

Customer — "Do you have crab's legs?"
Fishmonger — "I can assure you, sir; I walk forwards, just like you!"
Customer — "Do you have zucchini?"
Grocer — "never heard of him, sir!"

What did one keyboard say to the other keyboard?
"Sorry, but you're not my type!"

What does the sign on the door to the Internet Café say?
"Press 'Enter' "!

How do you get a choice at the Internet café?
Press 'Option'!

Which bit of a computer do astronauts like best?
The space bar!

Why did the sheep kick in the computer screen?
They were looking for the ram!

What did the computer do when it went out on the motorway?
It crashed!

What do chickens put in their computers?
Flappy disks!

Why did Mr Dopey wear a helmet whenever he used his computer?
Because he was afraid it might crash!

Why did the martian storm out of the Internet café?
The microchips tasted terrible!

How do archeologists select their options from the computer screen?
They press the Dead Sea Scrollbar!

Why is it so bright in the Internet Café?
Because of all the Windows!

What do you get if you cross a toad with a computer?
A wart processor!

Why was the school computer keyboard upset?
Because it wanted to be a monitor!

Why could Mr Dopey not get his computer to work?
He couldn't find his keys!

What do you do if your computer overheats?
Open all the Windows!

Why did the Internet Café close down?
Because it couldn't be saved!

Why did the elephant get rid of its computer?
It was afraid of the mouse!

Why could the computer whizz not bend his knees?
He'd left his Caps Lock on!

Which ballet was first to be shown on the Internet?
The Netcracker!

How do you get a drink at the Internet Café?
Ask at the scrollbar!

Why did the minister want to change his word processing package?
There was no Baptismal font!

Bill — "Do you want to buy a pocket calculator?"
Will — "No thanks, I already know how many pockets I have."

Two martians are sitting at a table, with a computer between them.
1st martian — "Well, what do you think?"
2nd martian — "Not bad—but it could do with a little more seasoning!"

What's a hiker's favourite computer game?
Pack-Man!

Bill — "If you don't stop tapping away at that computer I think I'll go nuts!"
Will — "You've gone nuts already—I stopped half an hour ago!"

What did one mouse say to the other mouse?
"I get a click out of you!"

Why don't ponies send e-mails?
Because they prefer to use horse code!

Bill — "I've just bought a really sophisticated computer."
Will — "Really?"
Bill — "Yes—it's so sophisticated, even a child can't work it!"

What do you get if you cross a computer with a mosquito?
100,000 mega-mega bites!

Dim Jim — "I've got a great new printer for the computer!"
Friend — "How on earth could you afford that?"
Dim Jim — "I sold the computer to raise the money!"

Bill — "Would you like to buy a second-hand computer?"
Will — "No, thanks, I need both hands for the one I've got already!"

What do you get if you cross a dog with a computer?
A dog that fetches joysticks!

I think there's a problem with my computer's memory—
I asked it what 1+1 was and 'Sorry, I forget!' flashed up on the screen!

What do you get if you cross a computer with a skunk?
A niff-ty machine!

Man in computer shop — "No, I'm sorry, but I don't want a Japanese computer. I don't understand a word of Japanese!"

Why was the doctor's computer out of order?
Because it had a slipped disk!

Where do you go for spare connections for your PC?
Leeds!

Where is the computer capital of America?
Washington CD!

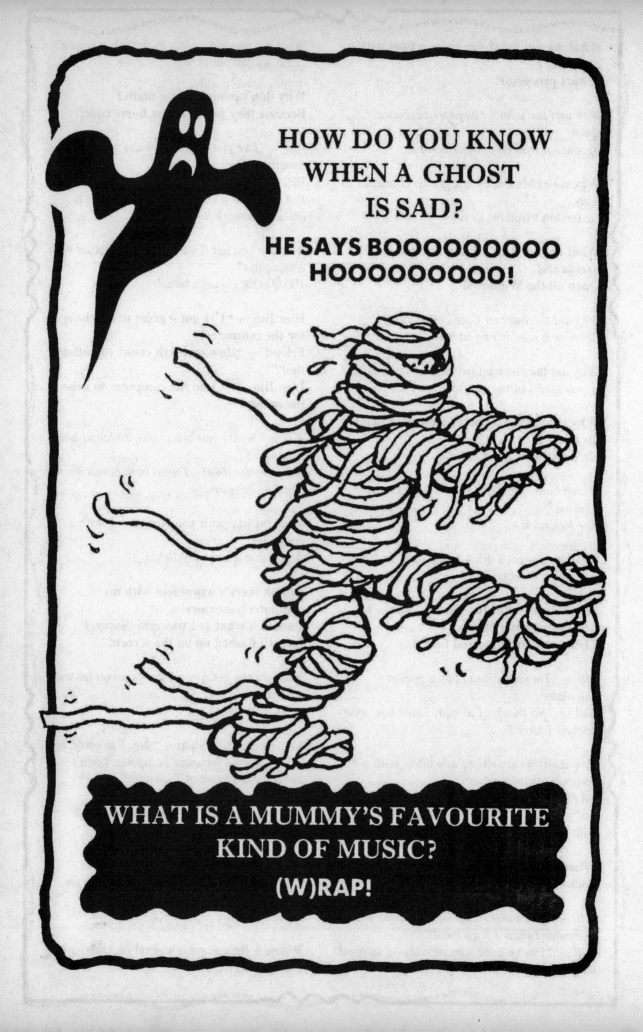

What did the orthodontist do with his computer?
He fixed its byte!

Why did Mr Dopey take his computer to the optician's?
Because the screen was blinking!

Why did the prison governor ban computers?
Because the prisoners kept using the Escape key!

Bill — "What's the difference between a finger and a drill?"
Will — "I don't know!"
Bill — "In that case, you're not going to get a shot of my computer keyboard!"

What do you get when you key in ytprowiwksjfugnbvmc8295760s,wlfknmhgogitj fuehdgst0h. com on your computer?
Cramp!

Who holds up stagecoaches and steals computers?
Click Turpin!

Why couldn't the alligator send e-mails in its PC?
Because it was an old croc!

How did the violinist break his computer?
He kept fiddling with the keyboard!

Why do doorbells never send e-mails?
They prefer to give each other a ring!

Why don't Vikings send e-mails?
They prefer to use Norse Code!

How do athletes send e-mails?
On the Intersweat!

How do whales send messages by computer?
By sea-mail!

How do footballers send messages on their computers?
By referee-mail!

How do skunks like their e-mails?
Scent!

How do spots send e-mails?
On the Skinternet!

How do referees send messages on their computers?
By penalt-ee mail!

How do ghosts and ghouls use computers?
They type in instructions on a skeleton keyboard!

How do horses send messages on their computers?
By gee-gee-mail!

How do comedians send messages by computer?
By hee-hee-mail!

Teacher — "Jimmy Smith, why have you been e-mailing all the other children, telling them that I'm stupid?
Jimmy — "Oh, I'm sorry, miss. I didn't know that you wanted it kept a secret!

How do skunks look up information on the Internet?
They turn on their com-phew-ters!

What do robots put at the bottom of their e-mails?
Yours tin-cerely!

What do werewolves put at the bottom of their e-mails?
Beast wishes!

What do sheep put at the bottom of their e-mails?
Ewes sincerely!

How do athletes send e-mails?
On the Sprinternet!

How do you get rid of internettles?
Weed your e-mails properly!

How does Old Macdonald send messages on his computer?
By e-i-e-i-o mail!

How did the postman break his computer?
He tried to stamp his e-mails, and his foot went right through the screen!

How does James Bond type in e-mails?
With his Goldfinger!

How do writers send e-mails?
On the Inkernet!

How do milkmen send e-mails?
On the Pinta-net!

How do wasps send messages on their computers?
By bee-mail!

How do snowmen read their e-mails?
With an icy glare!

Why did the disk drive go to the doctor's?
It felt a little floppy inside!

How do golfers send messages on their computers?
By tee-mail!

What should you do if carrots appear all over your computer screen?
Check for Bugs in your system!

Mike — "You're spending far too much time playing computer games, Ernie. You should get your eyes checked."
Ernie — "Oh, no. I like them blue, just as they are."

How do cod type their e-mails?
With their fish fingers!

How do tiny creatures send computer messages?
By wee-mail!

How do squirrels send e-mails?
On the Internut!

How do sweets send e-mails?
On the Mintynet!

Why do composers not send e-mails?
They prefer to write notes!

Why do knights in armour never communicate by computer?
Because they have their own chain-mail!

Why did the witch buy a computer?
She wanted a spellchecker!

How can you send a bill by computer?
Use fee-mail!

How do cheeses send messages on their computers?
By brie-mail!

How do orthopedic surgeons send messages on their computers?
By knee-mail!

Where did the jockey go on his holidays?
To Gallup in New Mexico!

Where do small dogs go for their holidays?
New Yorkie!

Where do baby birds go for their holidays?
Chickago!

Where do cats go on their holidays?
Miaowmi or Mew Zealand!

Where do dalmatians go on their holidays?
Spotland!

Where do mathematicians go on their holidays?
To see the Great Divide!

Why did the lawyer get upset on holiday?
Because he lost his case!

Where do shipbuilders go on holiday?
Hull!

Where do sheep go on their holidays?
Jersey!

Where do chip shop owners go on holiday?
Greece!

Where do computers go on holiday?
IT-aly!

Where does sickly Cedric the cissy go on his holidays?
Cissy-ly!

Where do sharks go on holiday?
Finland!

Where do criminals go on holiday?
Barred-cell-ona!

Where does Dennis the Menace go on holiday?
Menace-ota!

Where do sardines go on holiday?
Cannes!

Where do drivers go on holiday?
Rhodes!

Where do bakers go on holiday?
Flourida!

Where do financiers go on holiday?
The Costa Banka!

Where do mobile phone addicts go on holiday?
Text-us!

Where did the 100m sprint champion go on holiday?
Iran!

Where did the brown buffalo go on holiday?
Istanbul!

Where do shopping addicts go on holiday?
Mall-ta!

Where do turnips go on holiday?
Swede-n!

How did the joiner reach his holiday destination?
He went by plane!

How did the cleaner reach her holiday destination?
She went in a hoovercraft!

How did the crows reach their holiday destination?
They went by caw-er!

How did the chimneys reach their holiday destination?
They flue!

How do bees travel on holiday?
By buzz!

How do students go on holiday?
On Uni-cycles!

Why did the postman go to Spain on holiday?
He didn't really want to go there, but he chose it as a last re-sort!

How do plumbers travel on holiday?
They go by drain!

How do police officers travel on holiday?
By 'copter!

How do baby bees travel on holiday?
They go by minibuzz!

What kind of holidays do postmen prefer?
Package tours!

What kind of holiday do tailors enjoy?
Sew-faris!

How do cows reach their hotel?
Straight down the moo-torway!

How did the waiter reach his holiday island?
He found a chip to take him!

Why did the shop assistant choose a cruise for his holiday?
He got it cheap in the Summer Sails!

How do elephants fly to India?
They go by jumbo jet!

Where do cats like to go on holiday?
To a-mews-ment parks!

Where do dogs like to go on holiday?
Barking!

Where do fishermen go on holiday?
Any plaice will do!

Where do pilots go on holiday?
Eire!

Where do comedians go on holiday?
The Silly Isles!

Where do grumpy people go on holiday?
Girnsey!

Where do mathematicians go on holiday?
Anglesea!

How do postmen travel when they fly?
First class!

How did the bridesmaids get to go on the honeymoon?

They rode on the bride's train!

Where do spooks go on holiday?
They travel from ghost to ghost!

What do librarians do before they go on holiday?
They book them!

Where do ghosts like to go swimming?
Mali-boo beach!

How do dogs get about when they're on holiday?
On muttorcycles!

How do flat fish get about on holiday?
On skateboards!

What do skunks ask for when they check into their holiday hotel?
A room with a phew!

What is a vulture's favourite part of a meal?
The s-w-oup!

Why do sprinters always have a two-course meal?
Because they have to have a starter!

What's a skunk's favourite part of a meal?
The pooh!-dding!

What do moths like to eat best?
Something light!

What did the policeman order for lunch?
Irish stew in the name of the law!

What did the weather man say when he opened his lunchbox?
"It's chilli again!"

Why do fairies eat alphabet soup?
To help them with their spelling!

What do actors like for breakfast?
A big role!

Why are golfers healthy eaters?
Because they like getting to the greens!

What do undertakers drink at 10am every day?
Mourning coffee!

What do grumpy people drink with their dinner?
Whine!

Do vampires go to restaurants?
Yes, but they steer clear of stakehouses!

When do astronauts eat?
At launch time!

What did the computer have for dinner?
Just a byte!

What would happen if you took the school bus home?
The police would make you take it back!

Mum — "How was your first day at school, Jimmy?
Jimmy — "Rotten! The teacher told me to sit down and be quiet for the present. . . and I didn't get one!"

Dad — "Well, Annie, how did you find school today?"
Annie — "Mum showed me the way!"

Mike — "My teacher's like rice pudding!"
Mum — "Aah!—is she sweet, and warm, and comforting?"
Mike — "No! She makes me sick!"

Why is sand in the eyes like the school caretaker's cat?
Because it scratches the pupils!

Mum — "How many prizes did you take at the sports day, son?"
Son — "I took first, second and third in the 100 metres—then the headmaster caught me!"

Mary — "I only made ten mistakes in my English essay toady, Mum!"
Mum — "That's much better! How did you manage it?"
Mary — "I only wrote one sentence!"

Pupil to English teacher — "I'll pass this spelling test, you mark my words!"
English teacher — "If I mark your words, you'll fail!"

Why was the history teacher depressed?
He couldn't face the future!

How can you cheer up a maths book?
Solve its problems!

Weatherman — "How was your test today, son?"
Son — "It was a breeze!"

What did the cannibal do when he went to school?
He tried to butter up the teacher!

How did the maths teacher get to school?
On his pi-cycle!

How does an English teacher scratch his head?
With his subjective clause!

How did the science teacher get to school?
He came by test tube!

Why was the PE teacher sacked?
He wasn't fit for the job!

Why was the drama teacher depressed?
The pupils were always acting up!

Why did the children run out of the cookery class?
Because the teacher said "Take one egg and beat it!"

Why was the cookery teacher terrified?
Because the pupils found the recipe for disaster!

1st pupil — "I'm on playground litter duty today!"
2nd pupil — "Things are picking up, then!"

1st pupil — "Someone threw a stink bomb into the school toilets today!"
2nd pupil — "So what does it smell like in there?"
1st pupil — "A lot better!"

Why did the computer teacher call in sick?
An Apple fell on his head!

Did you hear about the cannibal teacher?
She grilled the pupils!

What do you call a pupil who can't add?
A total failure!

Why was the history teacher always out at night?
She had plenty of dates!

Why did Susie put on lipstick and eyeshadow before she went to school?
Because she had been absent and the teacher told her she'd have to make up for lost time!

How do you get rid of a geography teacher?
Tell him he's history!

Joe — "The teacher changed my English mark from a B to a C today!"
Mum — "How do you feel about that?"
Joe — "Degraded!"

Why did the pupils have nothing to lean on in the English class?
Because all the tables were in the maths room!

The teacher was angry, because some pupils had scrawled rude messages all over the blackboard.
"Would all those guilty of scrawling rubbish all over the blackboard please stand up!"
There was silence for a while and then a little girl stood up.
"Did you write something stupid on the blackboard?" asked the teacher.
"No, said the little girl. "But I didn't want you to have to take all the blame!"

It was their first day of school and the little children looked very nervous.
"If anyone needs to go to the bathroom," said the teacher, "please raise your hand."
"Please Miss," called out a little girl, "what difference will that make?"

Teacher — "Have you ever cheated in a test, Jimmy?"
Jimmy — "No!"
Teacher — "Do you ever chew gum in class?"
Jimmy — "No!"
Teacher — "Do you ever run in the corridors?"
Jimmy — "No!"
Teacher — "Do you never do anything wrong, Jimmy?"
Jimmy — "I tell dreadful lies!"

Headmaster — "What do you think of this school, young man?"

Little boy — "It's not bad, but the headmaster's a real pain in the neck!"

Headmaster — "Do you know who I am?"

Boy — "No!"

Headmaster — "I'm the headmaster!"

Boy — "Oh, really? Do you know who I am?"

Headmaster — "No!"

Boy — "That's all right, then!"

Teacher — "Can anyone make a sentence for me, using the words 'defeat' and 'deduct'?"

Pupil — "Defeat of deduct are webbed, to help it swim!"

Mum — "Tommy, why are you taking a fish to school?"

Tommy — "It's flounder's day today!"

Mum (reading school report) — "What are all these F's for, Jimmy?"

Jimmy — "Fantastic!"

Johnny — "I think I might get an 'A' for effort in my report this year, Mum!"

Mum — "Why do you think that?"

Johnny — "The teacher said I was very trying!"

What did one school dinner-lady say to the other school dinner-lady?

"Only sixty slopping days left till Christmas!"

Mo — "I hate my needlework lessons!"

Maisie — "Why?"

Mo — "The teacher is just an old sew-and-sew!"

Dad — "What's all this, Billy? 'E' for English, 'F' for French. . . "

Billy — "That's just the teacher showing that she knows her alphabet, Dad!"

Dad — "Detention? Huh! You're lucky! In my day, we had corporal punishment at school!"

Jimmy — "Was he very fierce?"

Dad — "Jimmy—why are you crying? It's the first day of the summer holidays!"

Jimmy — "I know Dad—and now I've only five weeks and four days until I'm back at school!"

Jamie — "Cows eat fish, don't they Miss?"

Teacher — "Of course they don't, Jamie. They eat grass!"

Jamie — "That's the last time I listen to my Dad! He told me that cows chew the cod!"

Headmaster — "I have no problem children in my school!"

Parent — "How do you manage that?"

Headmaster — "I expel them!"

Sam — "My best friend at school has enough brains for two people!"

Mum — "Stick with him, then!"

Sam — "My teacher thinks I'm a miracle child!"

Mum — "Why is that?"

Sam — "She says it's a miracle I learn anything!"

Freddy — "Before I go to school, Mum, can I just check with you how to spell my name?"

Mum — "F-R-E-D-D-Y—but why are you asking me?"

Freddy — "I just want to make sure I get something right in our English test today!"

Teacher to mother (watching pupils playing in playground) — "That boy over there drives me round the bend!"

Mother — "That's my son!"

Teacher — "Oh, I'm sorry!"

Mother — "YOU'RE sorry?"

Mum — "How was your first day at school, Johnny?

Johnny — "School, huh! I'm not going back there!"

Mum — "Why not?"

Jimmy — "I've been there a whole day, and I still can't read, I can't write, and I'm not allowed to talk!"

Note from Jimmy's mum — "I'm sorry Jimmy wasn't able to come to school yesterday. His computer had a virus and he caught it."

Dad — "Bobby, why does your History exam have a great big zero at the bottom of the page?"

Bobby — "That's not a zero, Dad. The teacher ran out of stars, so she gave me a moon instead!"

Mum — "What's your new teacher like, Annie?"
Annie — "She's very nice, and she just loves me!"
Mum — "How do you know that?"
Annie — "Look at all the X's she put at the bottom of my paper!"

What kind of tree is best at maths?
Geometry!

Mum — "George, this note from the teacher says that all your homework sums were wrong!"
George — "I know; but don't tell Dad. He thought he'd done them quite well!"

How do you get full marks in a geometry exam?
It's easy, if you know all the angles!

Bobby — "Dad, can't you think of anything good to say about my report?"
Dad — "Well, son, with marks like that at least we know that you haven't been cheating!"

Dad — "What? It says on this paper you got only 26 for maths!"
Jimmy — "Oh, no, Dad, that's not my mark. That's the number of people in the class!"

What kind of tools are best at arithmetic?
Multipliers!

What makes a miser a good maths teacher?
He knows how to make every penny count!

Why was the Maths book depressed?
It had nothing but problems!

Billy — "I got 80 in school today, Dad!"
Dad — "80? What for?"
Billy — "20 for geography, 20 for English, 20 for History and 2 for Maths!"
Dad — "That's terrible! And it doesn't make 80— it only makes 62!"
Billy — "That's why I only got 2 for Maths!"

Dad — "What were your exam results like, son?"
Son — "Underwater, Dad."
Dad — "Underwater?"
Son — "Yep, well below C-level!"

Johnny — "I got 100 in an arithmetic test today, and I still didn't pass!"
Dad — "Why is that, son?"
Johnny — "Because the answer was 150!"

What makes arithmetic such hard work? You have to carry an awful lot of tens and hundreds!

Annie — "I got 45 for Maths and 51 for English, but I knocked them all cold with my geography today!"
Mum — "What did you get?"
Annie — "Zero!"

What is the other name for the school canteen?
The mush-room!

What kind of meals do maths teachers eat? Square meals!

What is the worst thing you can find in the school canteen?
The school dinners!

Little Monster — "I hate my teacher!"
Mummy monster — "Well, put him to the side of your plate and eat up your vegetables, dear!"

Mother — "Off you go, now Johnny —oh, and here's some money for your lunch!"
Johnny — "Can't I have food like everybody else?"

Dad — "Do you get a choice for school dinner?"
Son — "Yes, Dad, we do— we can take it or leave it!"

What do French children say when they are given their school dinners?
Mercy!

Where is the best place to put the sickroom at school?
Next to the dining room!

What's the difference between school tapioca and frogspawn?
There is no difference!

What was King Arthur's favourite game?
Knights and crosses!

Where do tiny insects go to learn to read and write?
Miniscule!

Why did the knight go to sleep in his armour?
He couldn't find the tin opener in the dark!

What was Camelot famous for?
Its knight life!

Did you hear about the comedian who tried to conquer the world?
His name was Atilla the Pun!

And then there was the chicken who tried to do the same thing!
His name was Atilla the Hen!

What did the leader of the Vikings say when his longboat landed in Scotland?
"Right, men, take your Pict. . ."!

Why did the Vikings power their longboats with oars?
Because they couldn't af-fjord motors!

Why were the Arabian knights homeless?
A nasty boy knocked down their sandcastle!

Why did Julius Caesar buy felt pens?
To Mark Anthony!

Why do dragons sleep all day?
Because they fight knights!

Which centurion in the Roman legion was best at climbing?
iv!

Why did the lord of the manor arm his knights with soap and buckets of water?
Because the peasants were revolting!

1st Dragon — "Looks like they're eating beans for supper!"
2nd Dragon — "I'm staying in and reading my book, then!"
1st Dragon — "Why?"
2nd Dragon — "I'm scared of windy knights!"

Why did King Arthur's men need new suits of armour every summer?"
Because in summer the knights grew longer!

Why did King Arthur have a round table?
He wanted to invite a circle of friends to dinner!

What was the name of the first mouse to become emperor of Rome?
Julius Cheeser!

Why was the Norse god of war called Thor?
Becauth hith thaddle wathn't thoft enough!

Who was the most revolting emperor of Rome?
Disgustus!

What was the name of the first rodent to become a dictator in Italy?
Mouse-olini!

Who succeeded the first prime minister of Great Britain?
The second one!

Which King of England invented the apple box?
Alfred the Crate!

Why does history repeat itself?
Because no-one was listening the first time!

Who helped Noah design his boat?
An Arkitect!

Who was the first woman in New York?
Eve—she fell for the Big Apple!

Where did the explorers land when they reached America?
On their feet!

Notice on a knight's grave — "Here lies sir Killalot, buried in his armour where he fell in battle. RUST IN PEACE."

Why were King Arthur's army tired?
They had too many late knights!

Which king was a champion rally-driver?
William the Cornerer!

Which king was a chiropodist?
William the Corn-cutter.

Why did the Romans build straight roads?
So that the soldiers didn't go round the bend!

WHY CAN'T AN ELEPHANT RIDE A TRICYCLE? BECAUSE THEY DON'T HAVE THUMBS TO RING THE BELL!

WHY DON'T ELEPHANTS LIKE PLAYING CARDS IN THE JUNGLE? BECAUSE OF ALL THE CHEETAHS!

Which king of England invented the fireplace?
Alfred the Grate!

Why were the early ages of history called the Dark Ages?
Because there were so many knights!

Roman commander — "Right men—number off from right to left!"
Roman centurions — "i, ii, iii, iv, v. . ."

Which Roman emperor is associated with bad weather?
Julius Caesar—everywhere he went, people called out 'hail!'

Roman soldier —"What's the time, citizen?"
Roman citizen — "XX to XII!"

Why did King Arthur have a round table?
So that no-one could corner him.

Why did King Arthur's knights have nowhere to park their horses?
Because there was no horse park—only a Camelot!

Who invented King Arthur's round table?
Sir Cumference!

The young prince of Bloggsnia was having a boiled egg for breakfast, but when his nanny brought it in to him, he wasn't at all pleased. "Where are the soldiers?" he said. "Why, your majesty," the nanny replied, "they're marching up and down in front of the castle as usual!"

What do cannibals do at weddings?
They toast the bride and groom?

Gavin Ghost — "My girlfriend is a magazine model—and this week she's the cover ghoul!"

Why did the cannibal get sick?
He ate someone who disagreed with him!

What do vegetarian cannibals eat?
Swedes!

What do you call a man who's taken home from lunch by a cannibal?
Stu!

1st cannibal — "We had burglars last night!"
2nd cannibal — "Fried or boiled?"

What do cannibals play at birthday parties?
Swallow my leader!

1st cannibal — "I've got three nice men in the fridge called Hamish, Angus and Fergus!"
2nd cannibal — "Great! Let's make Scotch broth!"

Did you hear about the cannibal's new convenience food?
Boil-in-the-body-bag!

1st cannibal — "Two helicopter pilots have just landed slap-bang in the middle of our village. What do you make of that?"
2nd cannibal — "A nice hot-pot, don't you think?"

1st cannibal— "Am I late for dinner?"
2nd cannibal— "Yes—everybody's eaten!"

Why do cannibals never eat fashion models?
Because the pickings are too slim!

What did the cannibal make for dessert?
Baked Alaskan!

1st monster — "What's your new girlfriend like?"
2nd monster — "She's smelly, hairy, ugly and scary—but she has some bad points too!"

Did you hear about the monster comedian? Every time he told a joke, the other monsters laughed their heads off!

Little monster — "Mum! I've brought someone home for lunch!
Mummy monster — "Put him in the fridge son, and we'll eat him later!"

What kind of trees do zombies like best?
Ceme-trees!

How do you keep vampires out of your home?
Fang-shoo-i!

What do ghosts wear in the rain?
Ca-ghouls!

WHY DID THE TWIN ELEPHANTS GET KICKED OFF THE BEACH? BECAUSE THEY ONLY HAD ONE PAIR OF "TRUNKS"!

WHAT DO A GRAPE AND AN ELEPHANT HAVE IN COMMON? THEY'RE BOTH PURPLE, EXCEPT FOR THE ELEPHANT!

1st monster — "You look like a million dollars!"
2nd monster — "Do I?"
1st monster — "Yes—all green and wrinkled!"

Did you hear about the ghost who haunted the sheikh's wives?
It was a harem-scarem creature!

Two nuns were driving along the road in their car, when a vampire leaped out into the road in front of them.
"What'll we do, Sister Mary?" asked Sister Benedict.
"Show him your cross!" said Sister Mary.
So Sister Benedict rolled down the window and shouted; "Get lost, you horrible blood-sucking little monster. I'm really cross with you!"

Why did the monster go to church?
To get a gargoyle for his sore throat!

What did Dracula have for pudding?
Leeches and scream!

Newsflash — "Strange ghostly noises were heard on the roof of the multi-storey flats last night. Police say it was high spirits!"

Did you hear about the ghost hospital?
It was full of surgical spirits!

Mummy ghost — "So you think you can walk through the wall now?"
Little ghost — "I'm not quite sure yet—will you go through it with me one more time?"

How do you keep a ghost down?
With a spirit level!

Why do werewolves need a new coat each spring?
Because of the were and tear on the old one!

Did you hear about the one-eyed monster who took up teaching?
He had a vacancy for a pupil!

What ghostly bird haunts the ocean shores by night?
The seaghoul!

What do you call an unmarried vampire?
A bat-chelor!

Why does the Abominable Snowman never wander from the Himalayas?
Because there's snow place like home!

How can you tell when a vampire is old?
It gets long in the tooth!

What did one vampire say to the other vampire at the tea-table?
"Pass the jugular, please!"

Why did the scientist clone Dracula?
Someone demanded a re-count!

Why do ghosts make good parents?
Because they go to all their babyscare classes!

What do you do if you find a ghost in your linen cupboard?
Give him some clean sheets!

What happens when you can't pay an exorcist?
You get re-possessed!

What do lorry-drivers do on Hallowe'en?
They go truck-or-treating!

1st monster — "Have you had dinner yet?"
2nd monster — "Yes—I was hungry by seven-thirty, so I eight o'clock!"

Can you trust a mummy to keep a secret?
Of course—mummies keep everything under wraps!

What do bad card-players do on Hallowe'en?
They go trick-or-cheating!

Why did the mummy go on holiday?
It needed to unwind!

What do watchmakers do on Hallowe'en?
They go ticker-treating!

Why did the two three-eyed monsters fall out?
Because they didn't see eye-to-eye-to-eye!

What trails around the Himalayas at a speed of two miles a year?
The abominably slow-man!

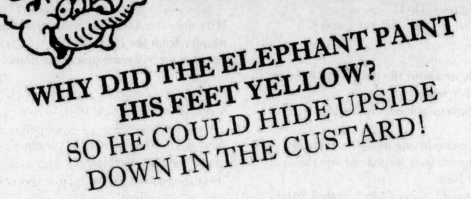

WHY DID THE ELEPHANT PAINT HIS FEET YELLOW?
SO HE COULD HIDE UPSIDE DOWN IN THE CUSTARD!

WHAT DO YOU DO WHEN AN ELEPHANT STUBS HIS TOE?
CALL A TOE TRUCK!

WHAT TIME IS IT WHEN AN ELEPHANT SITS ON YOUR FENCE?
TIME TO FIX THE FENCE!

What lives in the Himalayas, sings songs
and lives on buns and champagne?
The a-bun-and-bubbly showman!

What do ghosts do when they get in the car?
They fasten their sheet belts!

What kind of monster is easy to care for?
A wash'n werewolf!

What do you call a vampire comedian?
Crack-ula!

What do you call a cute vampire?
Draculaaah!

Ghost's saying — Remember the folks back
home—let them know you scare!

Why do ghosts wear sheets over their
heads?
Because their clothes are in the overnight
laundry!

Little monster — "Mummy, can I eat my pie
with my fingers?"
Mummy monster — "No, dear, save your
fingers for later!"

How did the monster come up with a great
idea?
He put his heads together!

Newspaper advert — "Friendly monster
for sale. House trained. Will eat anything.
Loves children"!

Newspaper advert — "Friendly monster for
sale. Will eat off you hand"!

Why was the invisible man upset?
He went away for two weeks and no-one
noticed he was gone!

Mr Monster — "Can you hurry up with
the dinner? I'm starving!"
Mrs Monster — "Give me a chance! I've
only got two pairs of hands, you know!"

1st monster — "Have you been to the Dead
Sea?"
2nd monster — "Been there? I killed it!"

Angler — "I haven't had a bite for hours!"
Vampire — "Perhaps I can help!"

What did the martian say to his
girlfriend?
"I love you with one of my hearts!"

What do you call a monster with good looks,
a kind heart and a gentle nature?
A failure!

A monster is standing in the middle of a
department store, dripping gooey slime all
over the floor.
"Can I help you sir?" the assistant asks.
"No thank you," says the monster politely,
"I'm just glooping!"

What do monster like to drink?
Slime gore-dial!

Mummy monster — "Remember, I've got my
eye on you!"
Little monster — "How can I forget,
when you've stuck it on the end of my nose!"

1st monster — "I'm going to be a teacher
when I grow up!"
2nd monster — "What makes you think
you'll be good at it?"
1st monster — "I've got eyes in the back of
my head!"

Why was the little ghost fed-up with
school?
Because the teacher gave him a
punishment exorcise!

Bill — "Mum! That monster's rolling her eyes
at me!"
Mum — "Well, I'll tell her to stop—she might
knock you over with one of them!"

Bill — "I saw a film about an ice monster last
night!"
Will — "Was it good?"
Bill — "No—it left me cold!"

Mummy monster — "Hurry up, dear!
Come and get your boiled legs before they
get goosepimples!"

What does a one-fanged vampire do?
Grin and bear it!

Monster — "Your eyes are startling!"
Girlfriend — "Thank you—they're my spare
pair, you know!"

What's the difference between a deer being chased, and a very small witch?
One is a hunted stag and the other is a stunted hag!

What do you call someone who tries to thumb a lift on a broomstick?
A witchhiker!

Why was the two headed monster always short of money?
He had an extra mouth to feed!

What do you get if you cross a mummy with a vampire?
A blood-sucking bandage!

What do you call a one-eyed monster on a bicycle?
A cycle-ops!

What is huge and hairy and can break the sound barrier?
King Concorde!

What do you call a blood-sucking pig?
A hampire!

What do you call a blood-sucking bee?
A hum-pire!

What do you call a blood-sucking sheep?
A rampire!

What do you call a blood-sucking shellfish?
A clampire!

Why did the cyclops teaches have an easy time of it?
He only had one pupil!

1st monster — "Your daughter has certainly got bigger since I last saw her!"
2nd monster — "Yes, she's gruesome all right!"

1st monster — "Mrs Bloggs makes great stew!"
2nd monster — "Delicious—but we'll miss her!"

What do you get if you cross a vampire with a snail?
A vampire that's too slow to catch its victims!

Two aliens from outer space landed in the middle of London. They were walking along the street, when they came to a set of traffic lights. One of the aliens looked at the lights and then blushed.
"What's the matter?" asked his friend.
"She winked at me!" he said.

1st monster — "I've just been on a crash diet!"
2nd monster — "No wonder you look like a wreck!"

1st monster — "Great new drink, this!"
2nd monster — "Yes—gore-juice, isn't it?"

Jimmy — "Why are you looking so cross, Joe?"
Joe — "I won a prize for ugliest monster at the fancy dress party!"
Jimmy — "What's wrong with that?"
Joe — "I was just calling in to collect my little brother!"

What happens if you cross a vampire with a cow?
If you milk it, it'll be your loss!

What do you call a mummy that eats biscuits?
A crummy mummy!

What do you call a musical mummy?
A hummy mummy!

Why do zombies speak Latin?
Because Latin is a dead language!

What do you call a zombie who plays the drums?
A dead-beat!

Mummy monster — "Where's your little brother and what are you eating?"
Little monster — "He's my half-brother now—and I'm eating the other half!"

Why did the ghost marry the skeleton?
Because he liked no-body better!

Why did Dracula's girlfriend leave him?
Because he was a pain in the neck!

Why did the monster refuse to eat the knight in armour?
He was sick of tinned food!

What did Dracula say to his girlfriend when she left him?
"That's right, off you go—find some other sucker!"

Why did the head haunt alone?
Because he couldn't find any body he liked!

Little monster — "Mum! There's someone at the door with a really ugly face!"
Mummy monster — "Tell him I've already got one!"

1st monster — "I can do farmyard impressions!"
2nd monster? — "Really"
1st monster — "Name a smell, and I'll make it!"

What's shiny and scares monsters?
A mirror!

Why do witches ride broomsticks?
Because they can't work vacuum cleaners!

What did mummy monster say to little monster when he chased a human being round the garden?
"Stop playing with your food!"

Little monster is in trouble for being cheeky.
His dad is giving him a row.
"And you can take that slime off your face right now!"

Why was the mummy vampire happy?
Because her daughter was dating the boy necks door!

1st zombie — "Who are you taking to the dance, then?"
2nd zombie — "Any old girl I can dig up!"

Why did the witch fail her driving test?
She steered left and turned into a tree!

Why could the monster not sleep at night?
His brother kept telling him human stories!

Why is it always cold in a witch's house?
Witches always have brr-rooms!

Did you hear about the witch who turned herself into an insect?
She beetled off!

1st monster — "My, aren't you ugly!"
2nd monster — "Why, thank you!"

A little boy is startled when a monster comes and sits beside him in the cinema.
"What are you doing here?" he asks.
"Well," says the monster, "I liked the book. . ."

A boy is walking down the road with his pet monster when he is stopped by a policemen.
"You should take him to the zoo," says the policeman.
"I took him there yesterday," says the little boy; "we're going to the cinema today!"

Why was the werewolf's mother cross with him?
He didn't comb his face before he went to school!

Mummy monster — "I'm so proud of my son. He's at medical school!"
Friend — "What is he studying at the moment?"
Mummy monster — "Oh, HE's not studying anything—THEY'RE studying HIM!"

Ghost — "Ooh—I'm tired! I've been trailing round this castle for two hundred years!"
Tourist — "In that case, can you tell me where the tea-room is?"

Monster at filling station — "Fill me up, please!"
Attendant — "But you don't have a car!"
Monster — "I had a car for breakfast!"

Mummy monster — "Stop fighting you two—what's the matter?"
Little monster — "He called me BEAUTIFUL!"

Why do monsters never have candles on their birthday cakes?
Because the candles melt when they blow them out!

Why are demons and ghouls so chummy?
Because demons are a ghoul's best friend!

Why did the monster go fishing on Loch Ness?
He wanted to catch Nessie's eye!

Little monster — "Mum, I haven't any friends left!"
Mummy monster — "I told you to save some for later!"

What did the grave-digger say to the hole?
"I'll fill you in later!"

Why did the debating champion sharpen his pencil?
To make a point!

What did the digital clock say to the grandfather clock?
"Look, old timer—no hands!"

Why was the diver depressed?
Because he had hit rock bottom!

When does a boxer think of America?
When he sees stars and swipes!

Why did the sailor's trousers fall down?
Because he spliced the main brace!

What did the sailor do at the village pond?
He swabbed the ducks!

What do you call a ship full of hairdressers?
A hair-craft carrier!

What do you call an aircraft in a knitted top?
A jumper-jet!

What kind of aeroplane do the Waltons travel in?
A Jim-Bob jet!

What do you call a group of helicopters?
A Rotor-y club!

What kind of can is impossible to open?
A peli-can!

What do you call a broken helicopter?
A heli-flopter!

Why did the train driver sing along to the radio?
They were playing his favourite track!

Why was the baker rushed to hospital, covered in pastry and jam?
He'd had a tart attack!

When is a musician like a footballer?
When he makes the perfect score!

When is a sweet like make-up?
When it makes your lips-stick!

Why is a make-up artist like a builder?
They both need a good foundation to work on!

What has a neck but no head?
A bottle!

What did one karate black belt say to the other?
"Only 60 chopping days left till Christmas!"

What's yellow and white and travels at 90 miles an hour?
A train driver's egg sandwich!

When are your eyes not eyes?
When the wind makes them water!

What is sometimes right but can never wrong?
An angle!

What stands on one leg and has its heart in its head?
A cabbage!

What has a bed but does not sleep?
A river!

What are the most powerful letters in the alphabet?
NRG!

What becomes more stupid as it grows older?
A forest—the more it grows, the denser it gets!

How do boxers catch fish?
With a right hook!

What do you call a small water pistol?
A little squirt!

Why do motor mechanics never wash before bed?
Because they like to get up oily in the morning!

What did Little Boy Blue's mother say when she had run his bath?
"Indigo!"

What do a round-the world yachtsman and a bargain hunter have in common?
They'll both go a long way for a sail (sale)!

How did the hunter find the railway station?
He followed the tracks!

Why did the lobster blush?
Because the seaweed!

Why are Scout camps so serious?
Because they are always intents (intense)!

When is a footballer like a magician?
When he does a hat trick!

Why are germs good at maths?
Because they can multiply faster than anything!

Why is the Mississippi such an unusual river?
Because it has four eyes but can't see!

What are the small rivers that flow into the Nile known as?
Juve-Niles!

What do a pair of frilly bloomers and a cartoonist have in common?
They're both fancy drawers!

What did the mountaineer say when he met his friend on Everest?
High there!

What is the strongest creature on the seabed?
The mussel!

How did the baker get an electric shock?
He stepped on a bun and a currant went between his toes!

Where does the Queen go when she goes for a drive in her royal coach?
Along the jewelled carriageway!

Why did the army private refuse to go to the dentist?
He wasn't allowed a general anaesthetic!

When are cars like senior citizens?
When they are re-tyred!

When are hairdressers like racing drivers?
When they make the hairpin bend!

When are racing drivers like ships?
When they're going along the strait!

When is a tennis player like a lazy waiter?
When his service is poor!

How do tennis players tip waiters?
They give them a backhander!

Why did the powder puff?
Because the mascara ran!

Why is the number 9 like a peacock?
Because it is nothing (0) without its tail!

What has got thousands of ears but can't hear?
A field of corn!

What has got three feet but can't walk?
A yard!

What has no hands but can still clap?
Thunder!

How do you find where the sun goes at night?
Stay up all night and it'll dawn on you in the morning!

Which letter of the alphabet is most like a frying pan?
'B'—because it makes oil boil!

What is used one day and made the next?
A bed!

What is the easiest thing to break?
Silence!

What has a mouth but does not speak?
A river!

What can you put in your left hand but not in your right?
Your right elbow!

What can you catch but never hold?
A cold!

Which American state is high in the middle and round at both ends?
Ohio!

Why is a germ like a passing remark?
You never see them, but you often catch them!

What is the most warlike nation?
Vaccination—it's always up in arms!

What do you do if you laugh until you split your sides?
Run till you get a stitch in them!

When is a farmhand yellow?
When he is a cowherd!

What is it that a poor man has, a spendthrift saves and a miser spends?
Nothing!

What did one seedling say to the other?
"Shoot!"

Which animals can go without food the longest?
Stuffed ones!

What did the window say when it was arrested for burglary?
"I was framed!"

What did the egg say to the whisk?
"I know when I'm beaten!"

When is an aircraft hangar like a water-pistol?
When a jet comes out of it!

Who likes to see their work worn out and destroyed?
A shoemaker!

What flies but stays in the same place?
A flag!

Why did the auctioneer go to school?
Because he had lots to learn!

Where can you get satisfaction?
A satis-factory!

What is the most frightening letter of the alphabet?
'V'—because it always comes after 'U'!

What can you return but never borrow?
Thanks!

Which letter of the alphabet is like a pig's tail?
'K'—it's found at the end of pork!

What did the auctioneer do when he was taken prisoner in the war?
He made an escape bid!

What part of your body is the most musical?
Your nose—you can pick it, or blow it!

What did the calculator say to the schoolboy?
"You can count on me!"

What did the man say when he dropped his watch?
"I've had a smashing time!"

What does a traffic cop put on his bread?
Traffic jam!

What did the auctioneer say to his wife when he left for work in the morning?
"Goodbye, dear—I'm going...going...gone!"

What did the judge's wife do when she moved into a new house?
She ordered the curtains to be hung!

What did the big hand on the clock say to the little hand on the clock?
"I'll be round in an hour!"

What person has more than one mummy?
The caretaker of the Egyptian collection at the museum!

What did the astronaut's wife say when he brought her some moon rock?
"I knew you were coming down with something!"

What did the astronaut's wife say to him when they had an argument?
"Don't just take off like that!"

What's green and travels at 90 mph?
An MG pea GT!

What do you call a Scottish chef?
Dinner Ken!

What did the mosquito say to the insect spray?
"You're a repellent little squirt!"

What did the auctioneer say when he asked for a pay rise?
"Any advance on £50?"

How do you kill a miser?
Throw a cent under a bus!

What can go round the world and still stay in a corner?
A stamp on an envelope!

Why do white sheep eat more than black sheep?
Because there are more of them!

What did the ribbon say to the hat?
"You go on ahead and I'll hang around hair!"

Why is a rag doll like a sore leg?
Because it's limp!

Why did the astronaut's wife throw him out?
He was just taking up space!

What's yellow and swings from cake to cake?
Tarzipan!

What did the mummy say when he invited his friends round to his pyramid?
"Don't wait for me to answer the door—just Toot n' come in!"

What do you call a train full of toffee?
A chew-chew!

What do you do when a boxer injures himself?
Give him fist-aid!

Why are teddy-bears stupid?
Because they're soft in the head!

What did the mother bell say to the baby bell?
"Don't make a sound until you're tolled!"

Why was Robinson Crusoe delighted when an old window washed up on his desert island?
Because he would have something to open on his birthday!

Why did the rope go to school?
To be taut!

What happens if you walk under a flying cow?
You get a pat on the head!

Why did the stupid mailman get the sack?
To put his stupid letters in!

Why is the sea restless?
Because it has stones in its bed!

Why can the world never come to an end?
Because it is round!

Why did the car not get chosen for the football team?
Because it only had one boot!

"Where were you when the lights went out?"
"In the dark!"

What makes the Tower of Pisa lean?
Lack of food!

How did Noah light the ark?
With floodlights!

What do you call a tell-tale whale?
A blubber-mouth!

Why was the athlete never cold?
Because he was a long jumper!

What do meanies do when it's cold?
They sit round a candle!

What do meanies do when it gets really cold?
They light the candle!

Why did the Ken doll melt?
He sat too close to the Barbie!

What made the marathon runner collapse?
He did a lap of honour!

What did the black cat say on the zebra crossing?
"Now you see me, now you don't, now you see me. . ."

What did the father clock say to the naughty baby clock?
Nothing—he just gave him a ticking-off!

What's red and green and yellow and black?
A burnt parrot!

Why did Mr Dopey take a car door into the desert?
So that when it got too hot, he could roll down the window!

Why did red turn purple?
Because it was a little bit blue!

Why did the clock get out of bed?
Because time was up!

Why was the table afraid of the chair?
Because the chair was armed!

What did the burglar do when he stole the table top?
He legged it!

How can you get four suits with one week's allowance?
Buy a pack of cards!

What did the 8 say to the 0?
"Why have you taken your belt off?"

What do you get if you cross a ball of wool with a comedian?
A knit-wit!

How can you make pimples look more attractive?
Turn off the light—then they'll become dimples!

Why do robots have no brothers?
Because they just have trans-sisters!

What does the scientist do when he's stuck with the crossword?
He looks for the solution in his lab!

When is a tree like a book?
When its leaves are turning!

Why do comedians never go skating?
Because the ice might crack up!

Why are cards like foxhounds?
They belong in a pack!

Why did the bread go to school?
To butter itself!

What can be driven into a wall without causing any damage?
A screw!

Why did Mr Dopey cut four inches off his bed?
He didn't want to sleep long!

What will you always overlook, no latter how organised you are?
Your nose!

How did the ice feel when the soda rejected it?
It was crushed!

How do you know when you've got a useless car?
When you lose the key and the garage offers you a can-opener!

What did one plate say to the other plate?
"Dinner's on me tonight!"

Why do women carry babies?
Because babies can't walk!

How did the astronaut hold up his trousers?
With an asteroid belt!

How does the man in the moon cut his toenails?
Eclipse them!

Where do spacemen play football?
On the astroturf!

What do you call a potato in outer space?
A spudnik!

What did the martian say when he walked into court?
"Take me to your pleader!"

What's white and pink and flies around in outer space?
A Mars-mallow!

What did the martian say to the book?
"Take me to your reader!"

What is the most unfriendly colour in the spectrum?
G'way!

When is a darts player cruel?
When he hits the bullseye!

When is a gardener like a novelist?
When he's working on his plot!

Why did the cannibal become vegetarian?
He was fed-up with people!

How did the grocer fix the burst tomato?
With tomato paste!

What did the short man say to the tall man?
"I've always looked up to you!"

Why is the dentist's drill painless?
Because drilling a tooth doesn't hurt a bit!

Bill — "I'm never going to leave my car parked out in the street any more!"
Will — "Why not?"
Bill — "Because the last time I did it, the neighbours thought it was a skip and filled it up with rubbish!"

What letter of the alphabet is just like noon?
A—because it's in the middle of 'day'!

What is the longest word in the English language?
Smiles—there's a mile between the first letter and the last!

How can you tell if a ship is haunted?
It has a skeleton crew!

What did the trout say to the fisherman?
"You won't get me falling for that line again!"

What do you call a sick crocodile?
An illigator!

What do you call a crocodile with a stiff neck?
A crick-o-dile!

What does it mean when the cattle are lying down?
The farmer is raising ground beef!

What do you call a very old grape?
A raisin!

What do you call a man who stands out in the storm, waving a baton?
A lightning conductor!

What do you call a friendly crocodile?
A pal-igator!

What do you call a crocodile out shopping?
A mall-igator!

What do you call an impassable crocodile?
A wall-igator!

Why was the banana lonely?
Because he'd been separated from the rest of the bunch!

What becomes darker when it's brighter?
A shadow!

Why is the sun like a cowboy?
Because it settles in the West!

What do you get if you cross a frog with a sieve?
A leakfrog!

When is a river like a gossip?
When it has a big mouth!

Why did the man stand on the piano keys?
He wanted to make sole music!

Why did the corpse fail art?
Because it couldn't even draw breath!

Why can't you go river-fishing on a Sunday?
Because the banks are closed!

Why did the car mechanic cry?
Because the engine died!

What did the broken cup say to the glue?
"Will you join me at the table?"

Why was the plumber out of breath?
Because the water was running everywhere!

Why was the broken compass tired?
Because it wanted a west!

What's the difference between an oak tree and a tight shoe?
One makes acorns, the other makes corns ache!

What do you see when your house falls into the sea?
Your kitchen sink!

Why can't you lift an elephant with one finger?
Because elephants don't have fingers!

Why did Mr Dopey stick his hand down his throat?
He was trying to hold his breath!

What do historians do when they get together?
They talk about old times!

Why was the sailor afraid of woodworm?
Because he had a wooden chest!

What do you call a clumsy nurse?
A medicine dropper!

Why did the pharmacist go to sleep?
Because she wanted a little dose!

Why did the nurse buy a barometer?
To take its temperature!

What do you get if you put a whistle in a jar of peanut butter?
A jar that can blow its top off!

What did the guitar say to the guitar player?
"Stop picking on me!"

How can you make a slowcoach fast?
Don't give him any food!

Why did the gardener turn his central heating up?
Because he heard that flowers grew better in hothouses!

What's harder to catch the caster you run?
Your breath!

What can speak every language but has never learned any?
An echo!

When is a horse like a motor car?
When it is stalled!

When is a fashion model like a car?
When she is in the wrong gear!

What letter is nine inches long?
'Y'—it's a quarter of a yard.

What's green and sounds like a bell?
Dung!

How can you escape from a room with no windows and no doors?
Through the doorWAY! (No doors, remember?)

What did the hairdresser get when she left her job at the salon?
They gave her a parting gift!

Why did the boy not get dressed after his shower?
Because his shampoo said 'Wash and go'!

Why did the computer get arrested?
Because it was robbing the memory bank!

Why did the match factory close?
Because all the matches went out on strike!

Why could the mountain climber not call for help?
Because he was hanging by his teeth!

Why did the spy hide under the bedclothes?
He was an undercover agent!

What kind of horse wakes you up shaking?
A nightmare!

When is a rotten tooth like a big space?
When it's an acher!

What is the best way to track bear?
With your clothes off!

What kind of musical group stretches the law?
A robber band!

What is the best way to win a race?
Run faster than anyone else!

Why did the astronaut become stupid?
Zero gravity made him witless!

What do you get if you cross a boy scout with a monster?
A boy that scares old ladies across the street!

How did the invisible boy upset his mother?
He kept appearing!

What's the difference between a hungry man and a greedy man?
A hungry man longs to eat and a greedy man eats too long!

How do you stop a rooster from crowing in the morning?
Eat him the night before!

What's the difference between a church bell and a thief?
One peals from the steeple and the other steals from the people!

Why did the boy take his bicycle to bed?
Because he was tired of walking in his sleep!

Why did the girl sit on the cream cake?
She had been asked to write an essay on her favourite food!

What happened when Pinnochio scratched his head?
He got splinters in his fingers!

What should you keep because no-one else wants it?
Your temper!

Where do ponies go when they're sick?
Horse-pital!

What do you get if you cross a polar bear with a harp?
A bear-faced lyre!

What do pigs sleep in?
Hammocks!

Why did Tolstoy's wife tell him to slow down?
Because he was Russian!

How do you make Victoria sponge?
Send her to the neighbour's to ask for a cup of sugar!

Why did the mouthless monster go to Holland?
To get two lips from Amsterdam!

How do you make a Viennese whirl?
Play his favourite waltz!

How do you make bread rise?
Put it in the elevator!

How do you make an apple crumble?
Hit it with a sledgehammer!

What do actors do when they break their legs?
They go to the casting agency!

What do actors do when they lose there temper?
They make a scene!

How does the fairy on top of the Christmas tree keep clean?
She takes a bauble bath!

How was Santa Claus killed?
He was sleighn!

What vegetable makes us think of Christmas?
Peas on earth!

Why did the cowboy pile bricks on the stove?
He was building a home on the range!

Why don't dinosaurs smell?
Because they're ex-stink-t!

What do you call a small rodent that eats flesh?
A carni-vole!

How do skeletons communicate?
By telebone!

When is a cheetah like a bad snooker player?
When it tears across the veldt (felt)!

Why did the pencils get angry?
Because their box was rattled!

Why are tame horses like cold germs?
Because they are easy to catch!

Why was the fossil afraid?
Because it was petrified!

Why did the hermit eat a box of grass seed?
He wanted to be a-lawn!

What did the footballer say when his head got stuck in the trellis?
"I'm in de-fence!"

What did the general say when he found a nail in his helmet?
"A tack! A tack!"

What do you call a prison officer on duty during the festive season?
A Christmas turnkey!

And did the soldiers attack?
No—they weren't going to listen to a pinhead!

When is a cake like an unhappy bride?
When it's in tiers!

Why is a startled squirrel like a robot?
Because it eats nuts and bolts!

Why is a panda dangerous?
Because it eats bamboo leaves and shoots!

When is a man on a fishing boat like a fish?
When he's (s)kipper!

Why was the ice cream lonely?
Because the banana split!

Why did the chocolate dance?
Because it saw the hazelnut whirl!

What did the naughty boy say to his friend when they visited the gallery of modern art for the first time?
"Quick! Let's get out of here, or they'll think we did it!"

What happened when the actor fell from the top of the skyscraper?
He made an impression on Broadway!

What happened when the undertaker took a one-man show on tour?
He got grave reviews!

What do you get if you cross a car with a bottle of bath foam?
A BM Bubble-you!

Why are there no baseball stadiums in outer space?
Because there is no atmosphere!

Why is an ice cream like a hopeless boxer?
They both take a lot of licking!

When is a dog like a mountain?
When it's a peke!

Why did the boy take hay to bed?
To feed his nightmare!

Where was Solomon's Temple?
At the side of his head!

How do you make a chocolate drop?
Let go of it!

Have you ever had chicken-in-a-basket?
No, but I've had breakfast in bed!

How can you tell if a ghost's on the building site?
He's the one driving the screamroller!

What did the old lady say when she crashed her mini into a flashy big car?
"So that's the way the Mercedes Benz!"

What kind of car does a chemist drive?
A formula one!

What kind of car does a railway porter drive?
A station wagon!

What kind of car does a cowboy drive?
An Audi, partner!

What kind of vehicle does a refuse collector drive?
A pick-up truck!

What kind of car does a chicken farmer drive?
A hatchback!

What kind of car do anglers like best?
Hot-rods!

What is the most flexible car?
The Mercedes Benz!

What kind of car does a flea drive?
A mange-rover!

What kind of car does a fast-food outlet owner drive?
A hamburg-ini!

**What kind of car does a skeleton drive?
A boneshaker!**

What kind of car does a librarian drive?
A Boo-ic-k!

What kind of car does a duchess drive?
A dame-ler!

**What kind of boar does a Wild West
bartender drive?
A saloon!**

What kind of car does a weatherman drive?
A rain-ault!

What kind of car does a shepherd drive?
A lamb-drover!

**What kind of car does a penny-pinching
man drive?
Just a-f-ford!**

What kind of car does a sewer worker drive?
A poo-geot!

What kind of vehicle does a hunter drive?
A track-tor and trailer!

**What kind of car does a lemon-grower
drive?
A citron!**

*What kind of vehicle does an aquarium owner
drive?*
A tank!

What kind of car do dolphins like?
A multi-porpoise vehicle!

**What kind of car do whales like?
Four-whale drive!**

What kind of vehicle does a lifeguard drive?
A float!

What kind of car does an electrician drive?
A voltswagon!

**What kind of car does an orthopedic
surgeon drive?
A limb-ousine!**

What kind of cars do bakers drive?
Rolls!

What kind of car does a nurse drive?
A jag-you-aargh!

**What kind of car does a wine merchant
drive?
A vintage car!**

*Signs above two garages in the undertaker's
yard — "HIS"... "HEARSE".*

Why did the minister take his car to church?
He was putting it in for a service!

**Why did the engine stutter?
Because it saw the oil change!**

Why are car mechanics cruel?
Because they bleed the brakes!

Driving instructor — "Hit the brake!"
Pupil — "What with?"

**Driving instructor — "Change gear!"
Pupil — "But I only brought one set of
clothes with me!"**

Why did the car have a breakdown?
Because the clutch was depressed!

Driving instructor — "And are you confident
about the reverse manoeuvre?"
Pupil — "Confident? I know it backwards!"

**What do frogs have to learn before they're
allowed to drive a car?
The highway toad!**

Why did the spy fail his driving test?
He couldn't decipher the highway code!

Driving instructor — "Foot off the
accelerator, Mrs Jones—you don't want your
picture on speed camera, do you?"
Mrs Jones — "Are you saying I'm ugly?"

**What's black and white and travels at
eighty miles an hour?
A speeding ticket!**

*How do you take a photograph of a racing
car going at 200 mph?*
Use a zoom lens!

Who will play James Bond as a bald man?
Shorn Connery!

"Dad, the car won't work. The engine's flooded."
"How do you know that, son?"
"Because I just reversed into the swimming pool!"

Bill — "Of course, the Vikings didn't have cars. They had longships!"
Will — "How were they powered?"
Bill — "Twelve men sat on each side of the ship and rowed."
Will — "Ah! Twenty-four Norse power, eh!"

Which computer heroine wins prizes at dog shows?
Lara Crufts!

Which film actor is like an orange?
Brad Pith!

Who is the most houseproud film star?
Dustin' Hoffman!

Film about an awful lot of swear words — 101 Damnations.

Film about a man in the desert who got a jumper knitted by his absent-minded grandmother — Ali Baba and the Forty Sleeves.

Which film actor gives in too easily?
You-win McGregor!

What's a toad's favourite film?
"Star Warts"!

When is a film actor like a cat's holiday?
When he's Tom Cruise!

What is the name of the most famous horse in film?
Sylvester Stallion!

What is the name of the most famous pig in film?
Hugh Grunt!

Which film star cuts lawns in her spare time?
Demi Mower!

Which is the strongest cartoon character of all time?
Bart Samson!

Film about the short life of a gardener — Four Weedings and a Funeral.

Film about a heroic Chinese chef — Wokky.

Film about hard potatoes — Mashin' Impossible.

Film about a bunch of crazy pigs — The Madhams Family.

Film about a dishonest monarch — The Lyin' King.

Film about an elf on a desert island — Gnome Alone.

Film about an army barber — Shaving Private Ryan.

What's Bert the baker's favourite film?
"The Buns of Navarone"!

What's Superman's favourite film?
"The Great 'S' Cape"!

"I hear you sat on a drawing pin!"
"That's a sore point!"

"How do you manage to carry so many plates at once?"
"It's a trayed secret!"

"I've just been in a sword-fight!"
"And are you feeling cut-up about it?"

"I can't get my teeth into this sandwich!"
"Hard cheese!"

"This just can't go on, I tell you!"
"What?"
"This dress—it's far too small!"

"I have had quite enough of this!"
"What?"
"This ice cream—d'you want the rest?"

"I have had it up to here!"
"What?"
"The bathwater!"

"I was once a dry cleaner!"
"And then?"
"And then I had a drink of water!"

"It's a blooming nuisance, that's what it is!"
"What?"
"A weed!"

It's gone for ever!
What?
Yesterday!

"I don't think I'm cut out for teaching. Time passes, but the children still don't!"

"I can't get this calculation to work out at all!"
"Why tell me? It's not my problem!"

"Are you going to France this year?"
"No—the ferry makes me cross!"

"My fridge is broken!"
"What happened—did it lose its cool?"

"I used to make paper dolls
—but I wasn't cut out for it!"

"Since my wife's taken up gardening, she's really gone to seed!"

"Since my wife's taken up tapestry, she's been in stitches every night!"

"Since my husband's taken up greyhound racing, he's really gone to the dogs!"

"I'm the teacher's latest pet!"
"Why? Did her budgie die?"

"Since my friend took up gymnastics, she's really flipped!"

"Since I started dieting, I've really lost a lot—my temper, my sense of humour, my friends. . ."

"Ever since my husband saw a flea circus, he's been itching to have a go at it!"

"I'm going home in a tick!"
"I'm taking the bus as usual!"

"I can't stand this vase!"
"Lay it on its side then!"

"How do you get rid of excess dirt and grime in your home?"
"I keep the children in the garage!"

"I can't stand the stress!"
"Wear these trousers instead!"

"I just can't take any more!"
"End of a life of crime, eh?"

"I'm sinking! I'm sinking!"
"Stop sat noise! I'm trying to sink too!"

"Rod! Rod!"
"Yes?"
"Take me fishing Rod!"

"You're a witch!"
"Charming!"

"Are jumpers ever worn in the Tropics?"
"No—they're all in very good condition!"

"I exchanged names with a Frenchman today."
"Really"
"Yes—he gave me a bill and I gave him a franc!"

"And were you angry when he dropped the brick on your foot?"
"Angry? I was hopping mad!"

"When my children are naughty, my husband acts like Nelson!"
"Does he take command?"
"No—he turns a blind eye!"

"In my job, I'm known as electricity Bill!"
"Because you're a bright spark?"
"No— because no-one wants to pay me!"

"Look at the planet today and you will see the effects of man's over-consumption."
"Look at my husband's stomach and you will see the same thing!"

"The children at this school are raised on good books"
"Are they too small to reach their desks?"

"I'm giving my mother a pet canary!"
"That's nice—she deserves a tweet!"

When is the best time to buy a new mattress?
In the spring sales!

So you had your cat shaved—why?
It was a special off-fur at the pet shop!

**I'm bored stupid!
Don't call me stupid!**

"*Rubbish!*"
"*What?*"
"*Nothing—that was just a throw-away remark!*"

"Peg, Peg!"
"What?"
"Find me a tent Peg!"

"So you got your cow from Scotland?"
"Yes!"
"What do you call it?"
"Ochaye the moo!"

What do you call a Scottish owl?
Hoots Mon!

"Bill! Bill!"
"What?"
"Pay me shopping Bill!"

"Doug! Doug!"
"What?"
"I need my garden Doug!"

"*Ron! Ron!*"
"*What?*"
Got my homework Ron!"

"Will! Will!"
"Me?"
"Yes, you Will!"

"Dan! Dan!"
"What?"
"Write this Dan!"

Jack and Jill went up the hill—
Oh, dear! How they puffed and they panted!
Why didn't they think of the tap at the sink
If water was all that they wanted?

Little Miss Muffet sat on her tuffet
Eating her curds and whey—
Then she stopped and said "Ooh! This is horrible goo!
I'm going out to get take-away!"

Jack Spratt would eat no fat
His wife would eat no lean—
So they both became vegetarian
And lived on potatoes and beans!

There was an old woman who lived in a shoe—
But she had to move out rather quickly
For the soles let in wet—she isn't dry yet—
And the foot odour made her feel sickly!

Hickory-dickory dock,
The mouse is running amok—
It just doesn't know when to come or to go—
For it can't read a digital clock!

Half a pound of tuppeny rice—
My mother's making a curry—
Some chutney too—that's £1.52
And some poppadums—thanks—bye—
must hurry!

If you go down to the woods today, you're in for a big surprise
They've chopped all of the trees down and built a new high-rise!

The owl and the pussy cat went to sea—
The cat was a terrible moan!
"You call this a boat? Why it's hardly afloat!"
The owl ditched him and sailed on alone.

Mary, Mary, Quite Contrary—
Why do you always say 'no'?
'Cos Mary Agreeable doesn't sound right,
And one lives up to one's name, you know!

Mary had a little lamb—
It was black, so she christened it Inky—
She bathed it one night and its fleece turned to white
And the soap made it lovely and stinky!

Little Bo-Peep—
Had twenty-four sheep,
And she loved them all to pieces;
She fed them on chocs
From a big purple box
And sewed names on the backs of their fleeces!

Twinkle, twinkle, little star—
How we wonder where you are.
Put the lights on, then we'll see
Where you fell off the Christmas tree!

Pussy cat, pussy cat, where have you been?
I've been in the bath—now I'm all nice and clean!
Pussy cat, pussy cat, what did you there?
I used all your bubble bath washing my hair!

Bob — "Will you love me when I'm old and fat, ugly and smelly?"
Bob's girlfriend — "of course I do!"

Annie — **"That boy over there is really annoying me."**
Kate — **"But he's not even looking at you!"**
Annie — **"That's why he's really annoying me!"**

Betsy — *"I've broken up with my boyfriend!"*
Bella — *"But I thought it was love at first sight!"*
Betsy — *"It was—but then I saw him again—and the second time, I didn't like him!"*

Why did the owl cancel his date?
Because it was too wet to woo!

Did you hear about the two octopuses who fell in love?
They went everywhere arm in arm in arm in arm in arm in arm in arm in arm!

Shady Sadie — "wow, Sid! Is this really a mink stole you got me?"
Suspicious Sid — "Well, it might not be mink, but it was certainly stole!"

Posh Patsy — "I fell in love with Arthur at second sight!"
Humble Hannah — "Really—why is that?"
Posh Patsy — "When I first met him, I didn't know how rich he was!"

Desperate Davy (on phone) — "I had to call you—to ask you—to ask—I mean—will you marry me, please?"
Dopey Dinah — "Certainly! Who's calling?"

1st bull — "Got a girlfriend then?"
2nd bull — "Not yet—but when I fall in love, it will be for heifer!"

Susie — "I ask for very little in life. . ."
Mack the Meanie — "In that case, will you marry me?"

Molly — "Today, my boyfriend whispered that he loves me!"
Mo — "Well, he wouldn't want to admit it out loud, would he?"

How did the gymnast ask his girlfriend to marry him?
He bent over backwards to persuade her!

How did the telephone engineer ask his girlfriend to marry him?
He gave her a ring!

How did the toilet attendant react when his girlfriend proposed?
He flushed!

Why did the magician marry his assistant?
Because he loved her as soon as he sawed her!

How did the lawyer persuade his girlfriend to marry him?
He courted her!

Why did the arctic explorer refuse to marry at the last minute?
He got cold feet!

Why did the bat never get married?
You can never trust these fly-by-night characters!

Why did the martian fall in love?
Because his girlfriend was out of this world!

Who did the fireman marry?
An old flame from his past!

How did the fireman's girlfriend feel when he left her?
She was quite put out!

Why did the judge's wife leave him?
Because he was trying!

Why did the perfume sales assistant never get married?
Because she had the good scents to stay single!

Why did the squirrels fall in love?
They were nuts about each other!

How did the grubby man propose to his girlfriend?
He left a ring round her bathtub!"

How did the florist meet her boyfriend?
She made an arrangement with him!

Why did the astronaut split up with his girlfriend?
He needed more space!·

How did the arctic explorer split up with his girlfriend?
He gave her the cold shoulder!

How did the carpenter pluck up the courage to propose?
Whittle by whittle!

Why did the prisoner split up with his secretary girlfriend?
She put the wrong kind of file in his cake!

Why did the printer's girlfriend refuse to marry him?
Because he wasn't her type!

How did the sprinter know he was in love?
His girlfriend kept running through his mind all day!

How did the synchronised swimmer meet her boyfriend?
It was a stroke of luck!

What makes bachelors so clever?
They are never miss-taken!

How did the manager of the slimming club propose to her boyfriend?
She promised to love him for allweighs and for heavier!

Why did the cow fallout with her boyfriend?
Because he was too moo-dy!

How did the secretary get her boss to marry her?
She put an engagement in his diary!

What did the cook say when he made his wedding vows?
He promised to take her for batter or wurst!

How did the magician persuade his girlfriend to marry him?
He charmed her!

How did the rugby player meet his wife?
He made a try for her!

How did the hypnotist's girlfriend feel when he proposed to her?
She was entranced!

Why did the boxer's wife fall in love with him?
He was a knock-out!

Why did the two tennis players get married?
It was a love match!

Why did the gardener's girlfriend fall in love with him?
He grew on her!

Why did the soldier's girlfriend fall in love with him?
He gave her lots of attention!

How did the shopkeeper persuade his wife to marry him?
He sold himself to her!

What happens when two swimmers get married?
They take the plunge!

Why did the mountaineer fall in love with his girlfriend?
He fell for her charms!

How do butchers split up with their girlfriends?
They give them the chop!

Why did the two photographers get married?
They clicked in a flash!

Why did the butcher's girlfriend fall in love with him?
He saved her bacon one day!

Why did the surveyor never get married?
He couldn't find anyone to measure up to him!

What did the lemon do when the orange proposed to her?
She gave him an affectionate squeeze!

How did the burglar ask his girlfriend to marry him?
Ask? Don't be silly! He just took her for his wife!

Why did the fisherman fall in love?
He was hooked!

How do sailors split up with their girlfriends?
They give them the old heave-ho!

How did the footballer meet his girlfriend?
He made a pass at her!

How do shop assistants split up with their girlfriends?
They leave them on the shelf!

Why do models get married so often?
Because they're pro-posers!

How did the road mender choose his wife?
He took his pick!

How does a golfer cut his wedding cake?
He slices it!

What did no-one eat the mathematician's wedding cake?
Because it was in-add-ible!

How does a gardener cut his wedding cake?
With a fork!

And how does he eat his wedding cake?
He shovels it all in!

What did the footballer say to his wife after their wedding?
"We're a team now!"

And what did his wife say?
"Yes, we're United!"

When is it legal to marry two people at the same time?
When you're the minister!

Why did the refuse collector's wife agree to marry him?
She got carried away!

What did the horse say when the mare asked him to out with her?
Neigh!

Mrs Frog — "What is it that keeps us two together, Freddy?"
Freddy Frog — "Rivet!"

Why did the builder get married?
He wanted to cement the relationship!

Why did the bus driver's girlfriend fall in love with him?
Because he was just the ticket!

How did the mechanic feel when his wife left him?
It was quite a wrench!

How did the balloon seller ask his girlfriend to marry him?
He popped the question!

Was the musician's girlfriend excited when he asked her out?
No—she was perfectly composed!

What happened when the two cooks announced their engagement?
There was quite a stir!

Why did the fisherman's girlfriend agree to marry him?
He was quite a catch!

Why did the two orthopedic surgeons go to the bank on their wedding day?
To open a joint account!

Why did the waiter say no when his girlfriend proposed?
Because he had reservations!

Why did the accountant's girlfriend leave him?
Because she took no account of his feelings!

What did the hotel manager say when he proposed to his girlfriend?
"I'll join you in reception!"

What did the prime minister do when he took his wife home for the first time?
He put her in the cabinet!

Mo — "If we're going to be married, you should give me a ring."
Bill — "Certainly. What's your number?"

Joe — "My wife has a wonderful sense of humour."
Jim — "She must have—to marry a joke like you!"

How does a cricketer get a girlfriend?
He bowls a maiden over!

What did the gardener give his wife on their wedding anniversary?
Some lovely bloomers!

What does the baker do on his wedding anniversary?
He gives his wife flours!

Bill — "I gave my girlfriend some sweets, because she's sweet."
Will — "And did she give you anything in return?"
Bill — "Yes—a bag of nuts!"

Maisie — "Why, Molly, you've turned a peculiar shade of blue!"
Molly — "Yes—I told my boyfriend if he didn't want to marry me, I'd dye!"

Why did the candy fall in love with the chocolate?
Because he thought she had good taste!

What did the yolk say to the white?
"Darling, we will never be separated!"

What is the horse's favourite part of the wedding cake?
The mare-zipan!

What did the postage stamp say to the envelope?
"Darling, I'm stuck on you!"

Why did the grandfather clock fall in love with the grandmother clock?
Because she was striking!

What did one pimple say to the other pimple?
"You're swell!"

What did one pastry say to the other pastry?
"Will you be my sweet-tart?"

What did one sand-dune say to the other sand-dune?
"I will never desert you!"

How does a refuse collector split up with his girlfriend?
He dumps her!

Why was the banker's wife so proud of him?
He was a credit to her!

What does a banana say when he wants to break up with his girlfriend?
Nothing! He just splits!

How did the anteater propose to his girlfriend?
He promised to love her for all eat-termite-y!

How do bankers split up with their girlfriends?
They make a quick withdrawal!

How did the doctor discover how her boyfriend felt about her?
She sounded him out carefully!

How did the painter celebrate his anniversary?
He gave his wife a new coat!

How did the dishwasher persuade his girlfriend to marry him?
He asked her to be his wipe!

Why did the electrician fall in love with his girlfriend?
Something sparked between them!

Was the mountaineer's girlfriend surprised when he proposed?
No—she knew he was up to something!

Why was the shoe shop assistant not surprised when his girlfriend proposed?
He thought something was afoot!

"Darling! Your mouth is a perfect Cupid's bow —
and when you open it to speak, I hear a little twang!"

What did the ghost give his wife for their wedding anniversary?
A see-through nightdress!

What did the monster give his wife for their wedding anniversary?
Shock-olates!

Why did the chiropodist say when her boyfriend asked her to marry him?
"How corny!"

Why did the dishwasher miss his wedding?
Sud's law!

Why did the comedian's girlfriend refuse to
marry him?
She thought he was joking!

How did the miner win his girlfriend's love?
He made a claim on her!

Was the surgeon upset when his girlfriend left
him?
Yes—he was very cut-up about it!

There once was a lady from Delhi
Who wanted to be on the telly
So she painted her nose
In a deep shade of rose
And stuck five daffodils in each welly.

There was an old man from Peru
Had a secret that no-one else knew;
For Paddington Bear
Wasn't really born there
But came from a cottage near Crewe.

There was a young lady called Tish
Who was ever so fond of her fish
She took it to bed
Where it slept by her head
And she pandered to its every wish.

There was a young lady from Wales
Who saved rainwater in silver pails
At the end of the week
The pails started to leak
And she drowned several innocent snails.

There once was an old man called Fred
Who slept on the edge of his bed.
He fell off one night
Got a terrible fright
And slept on the carpet instead.

There was a young woman from Hove
Who fell ever so deeply in love
With a young man called Benny,
Who took her last penny—
Then heartlessly gave her the shove.

There was a young woman from Malta
So perfect that no-one could fault her;
Then she started to sing
Which spoiled everything
And she sailed off in shame to Gibraltar.

The was a young fellow from Wick
Who tried to guzzle a stick;
But at the first chew
His tonsils turned blue,
And the sap made him terribly sick.

There was a young fellow called Clive
Who wanted to twist and to jive;
He wriggled and jiggled
And squirmled and squiggled
Then the jitterbug ate him alive.

There was an old woman from Poole
Decided to go back to school;
She came top in geometry
And loved trigonometry
But skived off PE as a rule.

There was an old man from Nepal
Whose stories were known to enthral;
Some were sad, some were thrilling
Some were truly spine-chilling
But the rude ones were best of them all.

A young lady called Maureen o'Hara
Bought a very expensive tiara;
But it didn't fit right,
It was painfully tight;
So she wept, and blotched all her mascara.

There once was a man from Bulgaria
Who said humbly, "I don't want to
scare ya
But my wife's got the 'flu
And my face has turned blue—
And my dog's coming down with malaria!"

There was an old man from New York
Who was frightened of bacon and pork
Said he, "does it bite?—
I think that it might!"
And he gave it a poke with his fork.

There was an old woman from Troon
Who knitted a hot-air balloon;
When she landed her invention
At a Star Wars convention
She thought she'd set foot on the moon!

What happens when tennis players get
together for a party?
They make a terrible racket!

Did you hear about the hair stylists' party?
It was fancy tress!

What kind of party did the gardener have?
A hoe-down!

Did you hear about the undertakers' party?
It was a g-rave!

Did you hear about the party on the ocean liner?
It was a high-prow affair!

What kind of party did the king of mice hold?
A grand mousequerade ball!

Why did the dalmatians lose the game of hide-and-seek?
Because they were spotted!

What's a chicken's favourite party game?
The Grand Old Chook of York!

What do you wear to a party at the pond?
A ducks-edo!

Did you hear about the florists' party?
It was blooming marvellous!

What is a camel's favourite party game?
Musical humps!

What game do they play when there's a party at the filling station?
Musical pumps!

What is a musician's favourite party game?
Pass the Purcell!

What did Bertie Bull do to celebrate his birthday?
He invited his friends to a dis-cow!

The cows and the pigs are having a party next week.
Dress in-farm-al!

What does RSVP stand for on a skunk's party invitation?
Re-pong-dez s'il vous plait!

Do sick hamsters go to parties?
No, but they might go to a small vet-together!

What kind of party do dollies have?
A Barbie-Q!

How do comedians entertain their friends?
They hold a tee-hee party!

Did you hear about the chickens' party?
It was most hen-tertaining!

What do geologists drink at parties?
Mineral water!

What do tailors drink at parties?
Sew-da!

Why are parties in the jungle so smart?
The animals all wear tails!

What kind of meal did they have at the ghost's annual dance?
A boo-fet!

Do librarians ever have parties?
Yes, but they're always hush-hush affairs!

Did Harry the Horse have many guests at his party?
Yes—he invited all the neigh-bours!

How did the insect celebrate his birthday?
He invited his friends to a gn-at-home!

What kind of party do photographers prefer?
Wine and "Cheese!"

What kind of parties do Mathematicians prefer?
Square dances!

Why did Broken-leg Bill get all dressed up on Saturday night?
He was going to the hop!

Did you hear about the pastry chefs' party?
It was a light-tarted affair!

Did you hear about the fisherman's party?
He invited his friends round to his plaice!

Did you hear about the birds' fancy dress party?
They all came as flappers!

How do train drivers have a good time?
They go line-dancing!

Why are police officers good dancers?
Because they keep to the beat!

What is a banker's favourite party game?
Musical Shares!

What do tennis players drink at parties?
Deuce!

How did the sentry celebrate his birthday?
He held a guardin' party!

What kind of music do gardeners like?
Mow-town!

What kind of music do mechanics like?
Garage!

Have a dance in the playground
—Make your party go with a swing!

At your party, hang a torch from the ceiling
—It'll be the highlight of the occasion!

Why couldn't the footballer have his party
at home?
Because he had no ball-room!

Why couldn't the tennis player have a party in
her home?
Because her mother wouldn't "let!" her!

Do astronauts have parties?
Yes—they invite their friends to launch from
time to time!

Did you hear about the anaesthetist's
party?
It was a gas!

What did the decorator do to celebrate his
birthday?
He painted the town red!

What was the most popular dance at the
fishermen's ball?
The reel!

What kind of music is played at the
travelling salesman's convention?
Rap. . rap. . rap. . .

What is the most popular dance at the engine
stoker's party?
The Pokey-Cokey!

What do coalminers drink at parties?
Coke!

Did you hear about the soft-drinks
manufacturer's party?
It was a cordial affair!

Did you hear about the campanologists'
party?
It was a ding-dong affair!

Did you hear about the pirates' party?
It was a rum do!

What do sailors drink at parties?
Port!

What do chefs drink at parties?
Whisk-y!

What do athletes drink at parties?
Sprintzers!

What do archeologists drink at parties?
Carbon-dated water!

What do spacemen drink at parties?
Mars-tini!

What do police officers drink at parties?
Coptails!

What do Arctic explorers drink at parties?
Brrr-bon!

What do mermaids drink at parties?
Anything on the rocks!

What did BYOB stand for on the fly's party
invitation?
Bring your own bluebottle!

What do baseball players drink at parties?
Highballs!

There was a terrible fight at the actors'
party—
They all wanted the sausage role!

What is a sculptor's favourite party game?
Musical statues!

What do you give a chess-player for his
birthday?
Send him a check!

What is a postman's favourite party game?
Pass the parcel!

What is a fisherman's favourite party game?
Sardines!

What is a secret agent's favourite game?
I-spy!

What is an engineer's favourite card game?
Bridge!

What is a donkey's favourite party game?
Pin the tail on the human!

What game do parrots play?
Mono-polly!

What game do ghosts enjoy?
Hide-and-shriek!

What do you give a lumberjack as a
housewarming present?
Chopsticks!

What did the train driver get for
Christmas?
A play-station!

What did the theatre director get for
Christmas?
A dream-cast!

What did the burglar give his mother for her
birthday?
Something appropriated!

What do you give a gymnast for a house-
warming present?
A tumble drier!

What does a really busy person get for their
birthday?
Stuffed dates!

What did the shipwrecked sailor do for his
mother's birthday dinner?
He washed up afterwards!

What do you give a cat for its birthday?
A surprise purrcel!

What do you give a fairy as a housewarming
present?
A wishing-machine!

What do you give a pig for its birthday?
A gold pen!

What do you give a tailor for his
birthday?
Anything suitable!

What do you give a DJ as a house-warming
present?
A mixer!

What do you give a golfer for his birthday?
Driving lessons!

What do you give a duck for its birthday?
A pond of chocolates!

What do you give an antique collector for her
birthday?
Any old thing will do!

What did Superman get for his birthday?
A birthday cape with candles!

What did the truant get for his birthday
present?
Skipping lessons again!

What did the boy say when his mum gave him
a duvet for his birthday?
"Huh! Another hand-me-down!"

What did the philosopher want for his
birthday?
Anything—it's the thought that counts,
after all!

Why did the historian love birthdays?
Because they were something to look
forward to for a change!

Why did the judge take his birthday gifts to
work with him?
Because without his presents (presence), the
case couldn't continue!

What did the fortune-teller get for her
birthday?
Prescience (presents)!

Bill — "I don't mind what I get for my
birthday as long as it's wrapped up in
paper, and given with real warmth!"
Will — "Here you are then—fish and
chips!"

How do you get revenge on a pilot?
Land him one!

How do you take revenge on a burglar?
Get your own back!

How do you get revenge on a waiter?
Keep him waiting!

How do you get revenge on a mechanic?
Put a spanner in his works!

How do you get revenge on a teacher?
Teach her a lesson!

How do you get revenge on a doctor?
Give him a taste of his own medicine!

How do you get revenge on a carpet fitter?
Floor him!

How do you get revenge on a sailor?
Deck him!

How do you get revenge on a miser?
Play a mean trick on him!

How do you get revenge on a gardener?
Turf him out!

How do you get revenge on a surgeon?
Cut him out of your will!

How do you get revenge on a plumber?
Get him into hot water!

How do you get revenge on a sewage
worker?
Do the dirty on him!

How do you get revenge on a tennis player?
Beat him at his own game!

How do you get revenge on a magician?
Play a trick on him!

How do you get revenge on a postman?
Sort him out!

How do you get revenge on an Arsenal
supporter?
Send him to Coventry!

How do you get revenge on a parrot?
Demand an a-polly-gy!

How do you get revenge on a golfer?
Take a swing at him!

How do you get revenge on an underwear
salesman?
Give him a sock!

How do you get revenge on a lumberjack?
Cut him down to size!

How do you get revenge on a tailor?
Stitch him up!

How do you get revenge on a travel agent?
Trip him up!

How do you get revenge on a pedestrian
crossing?
Double-cross it!

"They call me Dictionary Dave!
—I'm never at a loss for words!"

"They call me Abacus Al!
—You can count on me!

"They call me Bill the Balloon!
—I'm full of hot air!"

"They call me Double Glazing Dave!
—You can see right through me!"

"They call me Hairpin Hattie!
—They think I'm round the bend!"

"They call me Galloping Gus!
—I'm always horsing around!"

"They call me Dogtail Dan!
—I'm a bit of a wag!"

"They call me Table-lamp Ted!
—I'm a shady character!"

"They call me Encyclopedia Ernie!
—I have an answer for everything!"

"They call me call me Limerick Larry!
—I'm full of nonsense!"

"My name is Armstrong
—I'm a weightlifter!"

"My name is Ford
—I live across the river!"

"My name is Matt
—People walk all over me!"

**"My name is Luke
—but I never stop and listen!"**

*"My name is Mona
—I never stop complaining!"*

"My name is Mima
—I'm the silent type!"

**"My dog's name is Spot
—I picked it myself!"**

*"My name is Neil
—I can't stand it!"*

"My name is Hugh
—I'm a colourful character!"

**"My name is Belle
—why don't you give me a ring?"**

*What do you call a man with a stamp on his head?
Frank!*

What do you call a girl with a fish on her head?
Annette!

**What do you call a man with a spade on his head?
Doug!**

*What do you call a woman with a frog on her head?
Lily!*

What do you call a woman with a target on her head?
Miss!

**What do you call a man with a sou'wester on his head?
Mac!**

*What do you call a man with a bill on his head?
Owen!*

What do you call a man with a kilt on his head?
Scott!

**What do you call a man with a baby's bed on his head?
'Scot!**

*What do you call a man with a boat on his head?
Bob!*

What do you call a woman with a snail on her head?
Shelley!

**What do you call a man with a loudspeaker on his head?
Mike!**

*What do you call a man with piles of rock on his head?
Cairns!*

What do you call a man with a potato on his head?
Spud!

**What do you call a man with the contents of the vacuum cleaner on his head?
Dusty!**

*What do you call a man with nothing on his head?
Just Ed!*

What do you call a man with a haystack on his head?
Rick!

**What do you call a man with a petrol pump on his head?
Phil!**

*What do you call a woman with a small car on her head?
Minnie!*

What do you call a woman with a horse on her head?
Winnie!

**What do you call a man with a legal document on his head?
Will!**

*What do you call a man with a crane on his head?
Derek!*

What do you call a woman with a chimney on her head?
Ruth!

What do you call a woman with a radiator on her head?
Anita!

What do you call a man with a car number plate on his head?
Reg!

What do you call a man with a wig on his head?
Aaron!

What do you call a man with a map on his head?
Miles!

What do you call a woman with a spring on her head?
April!

What do you call a man with a purple and blue bump on his head?
Bruce!

What do you call a man without a spade on his head?
Douglas!

What do you call a woman with a Christmas tree on her head?
Carol!

What do you call a woman with red berries on her head?
Holly!

What do you call a man with a seagull on his head?
Cliff!

What do you call a man with a paper bag on his head?
Russel!

What do you call a woman with two lavatories on her head?
Lulu!

What do you call a man with a plank on his head?
Edward!

What do you call a man with a car on his head?
Jack!

What do you call a man painted scarlet all down one side?
Alfred!

What do you call a woman with a tap on her head?
Flo!

How many names did the little star in the nursery rhyme have?
Three— Howie, Wanda and Watt!

What was the name of the German hairdresser?
Herr Cutt!

What was the name of the Russian millionaire?
Ivan Ovolotov Roubles!

What did Mr and Mrs Potts the gardeners call their daughter?
Fleur!

What did the Reverend Spray and his wife name their daughter?
Lettice!

"My name is Raoul—Raoul Ett. I'm game for a night out!"

"My name is Juan Jack. Fate has dealt me a poor hand!"

Mr Browning the chef lives with his old, grey-haired mother, called Violet.
She is known to her friends as Grey V.!

"My dog's name is Daisy
—she was the best of the bunch!"

"I called my dog Banana
—I found him a-peeling!"

"My name is Archy—I'm a bridge-builder!"

"Remember darling, don't be late home—
we're having Rose Lamb for dinner!"

Old MacDonald couldn't pay his bills
—so he just sent some e-i-e-i-o-u's!

Mr and Mrs Master named their young son Ed.
He didn't make many friends at school!

Major T Deer was very popular in the officers' canteen!

Mr and Mrs Day had twins—a boy and a girl.
They named them Sonny and Renee!

Mr and Mrs Green had a baby daughter.
They named her Theresa!

Mr and Mrs Lee had a baby son.
They named him Ernest!

Mr and Mrs Hill had a baby son.
They named him Ant!

Mr and Mrs Fields of Home Farm had a baby daughter.
They named her Tilda!

Mr and Mrs Eigg had a baby son.
They named him Hammond!

Mr and Mrs King enjoy walking.
When they had a baby son, they named him Ike!

Mr and Mrs Binn had a baby daughter
They named her Lydia!

Mr and Mrs O'Reilly had a baby!
Oh, really?
No—O'Reilly!

Mr and Mrs Bott had a baby daughter.
They named her Rhonda!

Mr and Mrs Lastek had a baby daughter.
They called her Lucy!

"I'm a pump attendant at the local filling station. The people around here call me Beans."
"Why is that?"
"Because I give them gas!"

"My name's Jack—anyone need a lift?"

"I call my dog Milkbottle
—I found him on the doorstep!"

"My old car's called O' Flaherty!
— O' Flaherty will get you nowhere!"

What is the most popular hobby for gardeners?
Studying the family tree!

What do dentists do when they're not working?
They fill in time!

What do orthopedic surgeons do in their spare time?
They hang around some broken-up joint!

What do boxers do in their spare time?
They hit the town!

What do nurses do in their spare time?
Needlepoint!

What do nuclear scientist do in their spare time?
Fission!

What do taxidermists do when they get hungry?
They stuff their faces!

What do geologists do in their spare time?
They go to rock concerts!

Take up abseiling —
You'll soon get the hang of it!

Have you heard about the new fishing craze?
It's catching!

Take up caving —
It's a hole lot of fun!

What—me? Take up lacemaking?
Get knotted!

Take up yacht racing —
Become a passed-mast-er!

Tired of playing the straight guy?
Take up contortionism!

Blowing eggs is easy —
Believe me, I'm an egg-spurt!

Go camping —
The excitement is in-tents!

Take up baton-twirling —
Have a fling!

When do philosophers go to the supermarket?
Schopenhauer!

What do watchmakers do in their spare time?
They just unwind!

What do teachers have hanging on the back of their bedroom doors?
Dressing-downs!

What do ice skaters wear when they're relaxing at home?
Slippers!

What do refrigeration engineers do in their spare time?
They chill out!

What do burglars do in their spare time?
They take it easy!

What do musicians do after they die?
They decompose!

What do dishonest people do when they're not working?
They lie about the house!

Stamp-collecting is for losers —
Philately will get you nowhere!

What do bakers wear ion their days off?
Loafers!

What do photographers do when they're tired?
They snap at the children!

What do train drivers wear when they're relaxing?
Tracksuits!

"I'm studying the family tree—did you know that my Great-great-great grandfather was called Richard, just like me, and so was his son, and so was his son. . and so on? I've counted it all up, and I'm the seventh Richard!"
"Fascinating!"
"Fascinating? It's Add-Dick-tive!"

What happens when philosophers take a break?
They become thoughtless!

What do golfers wear when they go to bed?
Night-tees!

What do lawyers do in their spare time?
They go courting!

What happens when plumbers get tired?
They feel drained and sink into bed!

How do racing drivers relax?
They just slow down a bit!

Why did the taxi driver take his taxi out to sea?
He was cruising for business!

What do farmers do when they're tired?
They hit the hay!

What do mathematicians do when they're tired?
They put on their pi-jamas!

What do atoms do in their spare time?
Very little!

Advice from a gardener to his son —
"Don't let the grass grow under your feet, my lad!"

Advice from a photographer to his fed-up son — "Come on son, don't be so negative—just snap out of it!"

Advice from a cook to her daughter —
"Remember dear, save your dough and don't stir up trouble for yourself!"

Advice from a barber to his son —
"Remember, son—look trim and take shortcuts!"

Advice from a sailor to his son — "Don't take too much on board!"

Advice from a doctor to her daughter —
"Remember dear—listen to your heart!"

Why did the dairy farmer's son not do as his father advised?
Because he hadn't herd!

Advice from a comedian to his son — "Don't take life too seriously!"

Advice from a fish to her children — "Cleanliness is next to codliness!"

Advice from a flea to her children — "Always keep up to scratch!"

Advice from a bus-driver to his children — "Remember kids, life isn't always fare!"

Advice from a dancer to her children — "Take things one step at a time!"

Advice from a lawyer to his children — "Remember, kids, where there's a will, there's a way!"

Advice from an accountant to her daughter — "Remember my dear, things don't always add up!"

Advice from an actor to his children — "If things go wrong, kids—make a scene!"

Advice from a refuse collector to his children — "Don't throw away your opportunities!

Advice from a supermarket manager to his children — "Remember kids, you've got a lot to offer!

Advice from a nurse to her children — "Whatever happens, keep your patients!"

Advice from a mountaineer to his children — "Aim for the top!"

Advice from a dry-cleaner to his children — "Grime doesn't pay!"

Advice from a balloon seller to his daughter — "Don't blow things up out of all proportion, dear!"

How did the mathematician announce the birth of his first child?
"We have a new addition to the family!"

**Why do racing drivers not like babies?
Because they only go at a crawl!**

*What did the lawyer name her children?
Will and Sue!*

What did the policeman do when his dog had puppies?
He arrested her for littering!

**Why was the bald man delighted when his wife gave birth?
Because at last he had a(n) heir!**

Larry the lifeguard and his wife had a baby. It was a buoy!

Henry the hairdresser and his wife had a baby.
It was a little curl!

**Did you hear about the racing driver's son?
He was a real tear-away!**

*Why was the ghost upset?
Because her children were whoo-ligans!*

Why was the librarian mother-to-be upset?
Because her baby was overdue!

**Why was the glow-worm disappointed in her son?
He was rather dim!**

*Why was the gardener disappointed?
Because his children were late bloomers!*

Scientist — "What's the matter, son?"
Son — "I don't know, Dad—I haven't finished analysing it yet!

**What does the chef do when he sees his children crying?
He asks them what the batter is!**

*What does the electrician do when he sees his children crying?
He asks then Watt is wrong!*

Why was the train driver upset?
His son was going off the rails!

**Why was the baker fed-up with his children?
They wouldn't rise in the mornings!**

*Why did the musician stop his children from fighting?
He didn't want any disharmony in t he house!*

Did you hear about the private investigator's children?
They were such curious little things!

**Did you hear about the actress's children?
They were very play-ful!**

*Did you hear about the demolition worker's children?
They were terribly spoiled!*

Why did the butcher rush into the burning shop?
Because his children's lives were at steak!

**Why did the garbage man spoil his children?
He couldn't refuse them anything!**

*What did the butcher call his children?
Ham and Patty!*

Why was the monster proud of his children?
Because they were little horrors!

**Why was the stuntman proud of his children?
Because they were such little dare-lings!**

*Did the tennis player give his children pocket money?
Not exactly—he passed them a backhander from time to time!*

**Why was the confectioner so proud of his children?
They were little sweeties!**

*Why was the golfer proud of his children?
Because they were real queue-tees!*

How did the florist die?
She kicked the bouquet!

**What happens to gardeners when they die?
They push up the daisies!**

*Why did the lady with a sore throat call the undertakers?
To take away her coughin'!*

Did you hear about the dairy farmer's funeral?
It was a cream-ation!

**Here lies the body of chef David Bold
Just like his cooking, he's mouldy and cold!**

*How do old footballers die?
They just pass away!*

Here lies the body of Jeremy Devon—
He made a stink bomb and smelled to high heaven!

**Here lies the body of William Firth—
Once under the weather, now under the earth!**

*Here lies the body of Sarah-Jane Bell—
She TOLD her mother she didn't feel well!*

Here lies the body of Wilberforce Brown—
He discovered a mine-shaft and then he fell down!

**Here lies the body of Ron the Rover—
He smelled his own feet—and then he keeled over!**

*Here lies the body of Annabelle Stout
—Her boat took in water and washed her out!*

What happens to very old watchmakers?
They wind up dead!

**If a man was born in France to an Italian mother and a German father, lived all his life in England and died in the USA, what would that make him?
Dead!**

*Two children are looking at a mummy on display in the museum.
1st child — "3550 BC—what does that mean?"
2nd child — "It's the licence-plate number of the car that killed him!"*

What happens to robots when they die?
They rust in peace!

**What happens to broken robots when they die?
They rust in pieces!**

*Little boy on beach — "Mum! Mum! I'm seeing tiny spots in front of my eyes!"
Mum — "Wash the sand off your sunglasses, son!"*

A man was rushed into hospital. He didn't look too bad, but he kept mumbling the lines of 'Tam o' Shanter' and 'To a Haggis' over and over again.
Sadly, he died the next day.
Diagnosis?— fatal Burns!

Boy on beach — "Dad! Dad! There's a man in the water trying to signal to us!"
Dad — "He's using semaphore! Hang on, I'll see what he's saying. . . 'G-E-T Y-O-U-R D-I-R-T-Y F-E-E-T O-F-F M-Y T-O-W-E-L'!"

What do you call an octopus with nine legs?
An octoplus!

What do you do when a fish comes to dinner?
Set an extra plaice!

Two sharks shoot out of the torpedo tubes of a sunken submarine.
"What I can't understand," says one to the other, "is why they got rid of a fantastic water-ride like that!"

What flies around the seashore with wooden planks attached to its feet?
A ski-gull!

What's flat, yellow and juicy and lives in the sea?
A lemon sole!

What do you call an inky sea creature with a gun?
A firing squid!

Mo (on beach) — "What's wrong with that seagull, Molly? It looks sick!"
Molly — "I think it's just eaten one of your sandwiches, Mo!"

How do squid move around under the sea?
In an octobus!

When is the tide like a mean dog?
When it turns on you!

What did the mummy fish say to the naughty baby fish?
"This time, you're in deep trouble!"

Did you hear about the underwater nightclub?
It's a bit of a dive!

What do fish wear when they're swimming around the coral?
Reef-er jackets!

Why did the fish get all dressed up?
He was going out with his gill-friend!

Why did the octopus get all dressed-up?
She was going out with her buoy-friend!

Where did the whales go for a night out?
To a clamburger restaurant!

Why could the ray not take his girlfriend out at the weekend?
He was flat broke!

Where did the cod go when he needed his tonsils removed?
He made an appointment with the sturgeon!

Where do fish sit when they go to the movies?
In the cod's roe!

What lives in waters of the Caribbean and plays reggae music?
Bob Marlin!

Captain — "Sailor, have you swabbed the decks and polished the brasses?"
Sailor — "Yes sir, and I swept the horizon with my telescope!"

What lives in the sea and fills teeth?
A dental sturgeon!

1st diver — "I caught a bigger shark than you did!"
2nd diver — "All right—just don't go harpoon on about it!"

What did one wreck say to the other?
"I never thought I would sink this low—did you?"

How much fuel does a treasure diver need?
Ten miles to the galleon!

What did the old sailor call his children?
Eb and Flo!

What did one rock pool say to the other?
"Show me your mussels!"

"Whenever I see a baby, I remember my summer holidays—wet and windy!"

Bobby (picnicking on beach) — "Did you pack a jelly for pudding, mum?"
Mum — "No, dear!"
Bobby — "Then I've just eaten a jellyfish!"

Mum — "Look at your clothes, Annie! They're soaking!"
Annie — "I know—I wanted to keep warm when I went in for a swim!"

Mum — "What's that great big stone in your bag for, son?"
Dad — "That's for Grandpa—he asked me to bring him back some seaside rock!"

Why did the electrician take a voltmeter out to sea?
He wanted to sea how strong the current was!

What's the waves' favourite game?
Tide and sea-k!

Annie — "Will you come to the seaside with me, Bob?"
Bob — "For a romantic stroll along the sand?"
Annie — "No—to blow up my li-lo!"

Maisie — "I don't fancy being a seagull at all!"
Fred — "Why is that?"
Maisie — "Sand in your sandwiches all day, every day!"

Why do octopuses laugh when they go camping?
Because their tent-tickles!

What flower do hypnotists like best?
Daze-ies!

What flower should never be placed near balloons?
The poppy!

What do mountaineers grow in their gardens?
Climbers, mostly!

When is a flower like a child from outer space?
When it's an ork-kid!

Little boy — "What are you doing?"
Beachcomber — "I'm looking for flotsam and jetsam!"
Little boy — "What kind of dogs are they?"

Bill (in hotel room) — "Ah, the silver sands of Blackpool!"
Will — "But this is Menorca!"
Bill — "I know—I was talking about my plimsolls—I haven't cleaned them out since our last holiday!"

What does the notice say outside the shellfish's house?
Whelkhome!

What do monsters grow in their gardens?
Bein' sprouts!

When is a flower like a coward?
When it has a yellow streak!

What do you do when the caterpillars have eaten all your cabbages?
Open a tin of peas!

How do you know when the Lone Ranger is in the garden?
You hear him calling, "I hoe, Silver!"

What's the canteen lady's favourite flower?
Ladle-weiss!

Why was the plumber surprised in the garden?
Because he planted cabbage seed, but up sprang a leek!

What do comedians grow in their gardens?
No flowers—just corn!

What do gymnasts have in their gardens?
Tumbleweed!

What do cartoonists grow in their gardens?
Daffy-dills!

What are the most polite garden flowers?
The prim-roses!

Why was the hoe ashamed?
Because her father was an old rake!

How do you illuminate your garden?
Plant some light bulbs!

What do cheeky children grow in their gardens?
Raspberries!

What do shopkeepers grow in their gardens?
Sell-ery!

Teacher — "What do we call trees that lose their leaves in autumn?"
Pupil — "Careless!"

Why did the cowslip?
Because it saw the bullrush!

Why did the snow drop?
Because it heard the crow-cuss!

What kind of trees do cows like best?
Heiffergreens!

What flower do sprinters like best?
The speedwell!

What does the comedian say to his gardener?
"Hoe-hoe-hoe!"

What does the driving instructor wear when he's working in the garden?
He wears a seed-belt!

When is a herb like a dance?
When it's a chive!

What does the cook do when he's working in the garden?
He feeds the lawn!

What herb do sailors grow in their gardens?
Bay!

How do you confuse a carpenter?
Pick up a screwdriver and tell him "That's all (awl)!"

How do you confuse a waiter?
Order a rare steak and when he brings it, shout "Well done!"

How do you confuse a bus driver?
Get on an overnight bus and ask for a day return!

How do you confuse a bell-ringer?
Ask him to peel the potatoes!

How do you confuse the man in the parcel office?
Ask him to send the shipment by air!

How do you confuse a navigator?
Tell him to get lost!

How do you confuse a gardener?
Plant the seeds of doubt in his mind!

How do you confuse a taxi driver?
Ask him to take the next turning, and when he asks, "This one on the left?" shout "Right!"

How did the mother confuse her son when he asked her for some money?
She said, "Take it from me—you're not getting anything!"

What did the plumber do to help prepare the dinner?
He drained the vegetables!

What can hypnotists cook best?
Stare-fry!

What do vampire hunters cook best?
Stake pie!

What do demolition experts cook best?
Crumble and crump-it!

What did the boxer say to his wife when it was time to do the dishes?
"You wash and I'll swipe!"

What did the lawyer for the prosecution do to help prepare the dinner?
He grilled the steaks!

What is that guy in blue tights and a red cape doing in the kitchen?
He's doing the supper, man!

What did the carpenter do to help make the dinner?
He chipped the potatoes!

What did the tell-tale do in the kitchen?
He shopped the vegetables!

What does the car mechanic do before he starts cooking?
He oils the griddle!

What kind of cooker does a famous person have?
One with a fan-assisted oven!

How does the gymnast cook his eggs?
Easy-over!

How do ballet-dancers cook their vegetables?
They sauté them!

Why were there ten hairdressers waiting in line in the garden?
They were having a barber-queue!

Why did the cook quarrel with the master of ceremonies?
They both wanted to make the toast!

Mr Dopey was reading the instructions on a packet of kidney beans. They said "Soak overnight in cold water."
With a sigh, he turned his back on his nice warm bed, and started filling the bath. . .

Bill — "What have you made for dinner, Will?"
Will — "Mushroom omelette!"
Bill — "I can't see any mushrooms in it?"
Will — "There wasn't mush-room to put any in!"

Why did the minister ask his cook to leave?
She kept giving him burnt offerings.

Will — "What are you cooking?"
Bill — "Duck!"
Will — "Roast duck?"
Bill — "No, please duck—my pancake's coming down to land!"

What did the juggler do to help prepare the dinner?
He tossed the salad!

How did the central heating engineer like his dinner served?
Piping hot!

What do business tycoons cook best?
Profit-e-rolls!

Bill — "Did the audience enjoy your concert last night?"
Will — "I don't know—she left half-way through!"

What do wrestlers like to eat for lunch?
Slami!

What is the most dangerous vegetable in the kitchen?
The asparagus spear!

What did the watchmaker make for dinner?
Clock-au-vin!

What did the confectioner make for dinner?
Mints pie!

What do lawyers cook best?
Sue-it dumpling!

What kind of curry do teachers like best?
Chicken Tick-a maths-ala!

What did the golfer do to help prepare the dinner?
He sliced the bread!

What did the prize-fighter do to help prepare the dinner?
He battered the fish!

What did the sign on the sprinter's fridge say?
"No food—I've run out!"

What do musicians have for dessert?
Flute salad!

What did the golfer do after lunch?
He went out for tee!

Notice on psychiatrist's office door — "Out to lunch"!

Bill — "Which part of your performance did the audience like best?"
Will — "When the microphone broke!"

Fred — "I gave a rousing performance last night!"
Ted — "Really?"
Fred — "Yes—the audience woke up—and left!"

Ted — "My juggling act was stunning!"
Fred — "Really?"
Ted — "Yes—I threw one of the clubs too far and knocked out a man in the front row!"

Maisie — "When I sat down to play the piano, the audience roared with laughter!"
Mo — "Why was that?"
Maisie — "Someone had taken the piano stool away!"

Bill — *"I went to see a ventriloquist last night!"*
Will — *"Was he good?"*
Bill — *"The ventriloquist was very good, but his dummy was rather wooden!"*

Molly — "Well, at least that play had a happy ending!"
Mo — "Yes—everyone was happy to see the end of it!"

When is a hospital patient like an actor? When he's in a cast!

Why did the director ask his performers to do the play one more time?
He wanted to see how they would re-act!

Maisie — "The critics said my acting was stiff!"
Mo — "How unkind! What part were you playing?"
Maisie — "The dead body!"

Molly — "I got sacked from the theatre last night!"
Maisie — "Why?"
Molly — "I was supposed to be the prompt, but I missed the bus and wasn't prompt enough!"

Mum — "So why do you think you failed your piano exam?"
Billy — "My head had learnt all the notes— but my fingers hadn't!"

Bill — "My ambition to become an actor is bearing fruit at last!"
Will — "Really?"
Bill — "Yes—last night the audience threw six tomatoes and four oranges at me!"

Did you hear about the train driver who took up acting?
He always knew his lines!

Billy — "I failed my trumpet exam!"
Mum — "Why?"
Billy — "Don't know—I just blew it!"

Jim — "And how did you get on at the talent show?"
Joe — "The audience was helpless with laughter!"
Jim — "So you did a comic routine?"
Joe — "It wasn't meant to be!"

How do you bribe a choirmaster?
Offer him a tenor!

Joe — "I failed my violin exam, Mum!"
Mum — "Why?"
Joe — "The examiner said I wasn't up to scratch!"

Annie — "The music teacher says I'm good at concussion!"
Mum — "Don't you mean percussion?"
Annie — "No, concussion—the teacher's head got in the way when I was clashing the cymbals!"

Maisie — "The choir teacher said I was to sing solo!"
Mum — "Really!"
Maisie — "Yes— so low that the audience can't hear how out of tune I am!"

Bill — "The audience were rolling in the aisles tonight!"
Will — "So your comedy act is a success, then?"
Bill — "No—they all had food poisoning and were rolling in agony!"

What's a taxi-driver's favourite song?
"Cabbie-ret"!

What's a monster's favourite song?
"Simply the Beast"!

What's a cow's favourite song?
"Moo-in' River!"

What's a horse's favourite song?
"Hay Chewed"!

What's a wasp's favourite song?
"Stingin' in the Rain"!

What's a car mechanic's favourite song?
"Oiled Lang Syne!"

What's a grocer's favourite song?
"My Weigh!"

What kind of opera do fish like best?
Anything by Gill-bert and Sole-ivan!

What's a golfer's favourite song?
"Tee for Two"!

What do patriotic insects sing?
The Gnat-ional Ant-them!

What's a dieter's favourite song?
"Don't Fry for Me, Argentina"!

What is the number one hit of all time under the sea?
"The Whales on the Bus Go Round and Round"!

What is the alligator's favourite song?
"Rock around the Crock"!

What is the postman's favourite song?
"Mailhouse Rock"!

What is the writer's favourite Michael Jackson hit?
"Thriller"!

What's the butcher's favourite song?
"Love Meat Tender"!

What's a fairy's favourite song?
"Wand-erful World"!

Albert — "My great-grandfather fought with the English, my grandfather fought with the French and my father fought with the Americans!
Annie — "Not a very friendly family, then?"

Mike — "I can tear up a telephone directory in two minutes!
Mack — "So what? I can tear up the street in thirty seconds!

Bill — "I went through hell to get here!
Will — "Did you? I went through the front door!"

Ike — "I spent a fortune on this rare work of art!"
Mike — "I spent quite a lot on the steak I had for lunch—but at least it was well done!"

Bob — "I once caught a tiger!"
Bill — "So what? I once spotted a leopard!"

Bob — "My ancestor lost his leg at Waterloo!"
Joe "Did he? I lost my suitcase at King's Cross!"

Fred;— "My ancestor fell at Waterloo!"
Ted — "Pushed off the platform, was he?"

Annie — "I learned to play the piano in no time at all!"
Flo — "So when will you learn to play in time?"

Bill — "When I play the violin, people say that the music is haunting!"
Will — "That's because you murdered the tune!"

Alf — "I own several pieces of the Caribbean—one island and three plots of land!"
Wilf — "I own several pieces of China—one teapot and four mugs!"

Fred — "I was chased all round the safari camp by a stampeding elephant, but I finally escaped by climbing a tree!"
Ted — "I was once chased round in circles by a ferocious tiger!"
Fred — "And how did you get away!"
Ted — "I got off the merry-go-round!"

Harry — "I once went water-ski-ing in the Sahara Desert!"
Henry — "Don't be ridiculous—whoever heard of water-ski-ing in a desert?"
Harry — "You just did!"

Gus — "I saw a man-eating shark in the Pacific Ocean!"
Gertie — "I saw a man eating cabbage—in the restaurant across the street!"

Wally — "I was once a criminal, till I changed my life!"
Olly — "I was once decisive, till I changed my mind!"

Ike — "I was strolling in the forest, when all of a sudden a giant grizzly bear stood right in front of me!"
Mike — "Get away!"
Ike —"That's what I said to him, but he wouldn't listen, so I turned and ran!"

Mo — "I've got a whopper of a sapphire in my engagement ring!"
Maisie — "So? I've got an ace of diamonds in this pack of cards!"

What happened when the cricketer skidded on the pitch?
He got an extra four runs in his socks!

What are the noisiest sports players?
Tennis players—they raise a racquet whenever they play!

Why did the rugby player retire?
He gave up trying!

How does a footballer eat his birthday cake?
He doesn't eat it all—he just takes a corner!

What sport do ghosts enjoy?
Ghoulf!

What game is played with an elephant, a human, and two racquets?
Squash!

What game can you play with a sieve and a ball?
Siftball!

What game do the animals of the riverbank play?
Otter polo!

Do private investigators play pool?
Yes—but they prefer snooper!

What game do photographers play?
Spool!

What game do orthodontists play?
Braceball!

What game is played by five people with racquets?
Ten-knees!

What game can you play with a stiff neck?
Crick-it!

Referee — "Why are you carrying that bit of rope onto the pitch?"
Footballer — "I'm the team skipper!"

What game do milkmen play?
Rounders!

What game do tailors play?
Darts!

What game do bakers play?
Tarts!

Did you hear about the man who shot the Spanish golfer?
He made a hole in Juan!

How do rugby players communicate?
They get in touch with one another!

You have an umpire in tennis, a referee in football—but what do you have in bowls?
Soup!

Goalie — "I can jump higher than the crossbar!"
Friend — "How do you manage that?"
Goalie — "Easy—the crossbar can't jump!"

Why did the boxer carry a suitcase?
So that he could pack a punch!

Why was the pool player always late?
Because he was always at the back of the cue!

Why did the golfer shoot his opponent?
It was a sudden death tournament!

"What was your score?"
"72—but I'll do better at the next hole!"

What do you call a compulsive golfer?
A crackputt!

Bill; — "Golf lessons don't work—how can I improve my game?"
Will — "Try cheating!"

Golfer — "I got a birdie at the fourth! Poor little sparrow, he was just flying overhead when I took my swing. . ."

Fred — "I'm saving up for a golf club!"
Ted — "Which one?"
Fred — "The Royal and Ancient!"

Golfer — "My driving's becoming better!"
Caddie — "Try chauffeuring!"

Golfer — *"I hardly recognize this course!"*
Caddie — *"It's healed up since you were last here!"*

What is the difference between a good golfer and a bad golfer?
One has to replace the turf. the other has to returf the place!

Caddie — "Remember, sir, keep an eye on the ball!"
Golfer — "Righto—I'll make sure no-one takes it!"

Golfer's wife — *"No, I don't play golf— goodness, I don't even know how to hold a caddie!"*

Golfer — *"Do you like my game?"*
Friend — *"No—I prefer golf!"*

Will — "I've just invented a game that's a bit like golf!"
Bill — "JUST invented? You've been playing that for ages!"

Golfer — *"My swing's improving—I'm getting closer to the ball each time!"*

Golfer — *"Win? No! But I got to hit the ball more than anyone else!"*

Golfer — "I got a hole in one at the tenth!"
Friend — "Yes, but you were playing the eleventh at the time!"

Woman — *"My husband's away every weekend on golfing trips!"*
Friend — *"I think I'll get my husband to take the sport up!"*

Golfer — *"How do I cut 15 strokes from my game?"*
Caddie — *"Leave out one hole!"*

Golf shop assistant — "Shall I wrap these ball for you?"
Golfer — "No need—I'll be driving them home!"

Grumpy Gus — *"I'm not playing tennis any more!"*
Friend — *"Why not?"*
Grumpy Gus — *"I'm fed up of being told to love all!"*

Bill — *"Our team didn't do too badly this season, did it? We were fourth in the league!"*
Will — *"There only were four teams in the league!"*

Manager — "And this is our latest transfer—Joe Smith. His nickname is 'Birdie'.
Reporter — "Why is that?"
Manager — "Because he was going cheap!"

Footballer — *"What'll we do? The pitch is flooded!"*
Manager — *"Bring out the subs!"*

Referee — *"Wharoop!"*
Soccer player — *"What?"*
Referee — *"Sorry! Freak hic!"*

Bill — "When I was manager of our local team, I had the crowd behind me all the way!"
Will — "All the way to the exit!"

Friend — *"New perfume?"*
Soccer player's wife — *"Yes. My husband's the (s)center!"*

What part of a football stadium is never the same?
The changing rooms!

What do rugby players like to drink?
Penal-tea!

Why do skeletons never take part in dangerous sports?
They don't have the guts for it!

Boxing manager — *"My new lad's really tough!"*
Friend — *"Really!"*
Boxing manager — *"Yes—he's so tough that he uses a hedgehog as a sponge!"*

Did you hear about the angler who took up rugby?
He kept baiting the players in the other team!

1st boxer — *"I feel too tired to fight tonight!"*
2nd boxer — *"Don't worry—two minutes in the ring with me, and you'll be fast asleep!"*

What is Robin's favourite game?
Batman-ton!

What is the hardest thing about learning to skate?
The ice!

Boxer (to opponent) — "I'll buy you a pint after the match, bruiser!—What blood group is it?"

What kind of sportsplayers are like cats?
Ten-pin bowlers—you'll always find them in alleys!

What are a boxer's favourite colours?
Anything but black and blue!

Why is a boxer always the last to know?
Because everyone watching the match knows he's lost ten seconds before he finds out!

Mr Big — "I'm teaching my son how to box—it's a skill he may have to use one day!"
Mr Little — "I'm teaching my son to run away—generally, I find it less painful!"

1st boxer — "Hey! Mauler Mack! Don't you remember me? I fought you last Saturday!"
2nd boxer — "Sorry—I didn't recognize you standing up!"

Why did the young married couple take up card-playing?
They wanted to hold hands!

Why did the swimmer take up massage?
Because he was a great backstroker!

How do you teach your puppy to swim?
Give him a doggie paddle!

"Why is that boxer called 'The Portrait'?"
"Because his head is always on the canvas!"

Did you hear about Mr Dopey's water-ski-ing holiday?
He came home because he couldn't find a lake with a slope!

Why did the boy fail his personal survival test in the pool?
Because he couldn't swim to save himself!

Phil — "I play golf with my twin brother at the same time every day!"
Lil — "And what time is that?"
Phil — "Two twin-tee!"

Boxer — "I'll say he was a featherweight—he tickled me to death!"

When is a rugby player like a bartender?
When he puts one over the bar!

What's got three legs, one wing, and plays rugby?
A fly-half!

"I'd be a great catcher if it wasn't for two things!"
"What are they?"
"My hands!"

Did you hear about the royal soccer match?
It was reigned off!

Did you hear about the chef who took up baseball?
He kept beating the batter!

Ten-bowling is a quiet sport—you can hear a pin drop!

When is a bowler like a match?
When he gets a strike!

What is the difference between a fouling rugby player and a confused bloodhound?
One's sent off, the other's off scent!

Why did the basketball team disband?
Because they were hopeless!

What do golfers do when they're posing for a photograph?
They watch the birdie!

Which golf clubs are best for taking really difficult shots?
Tiger Woods!

Why is an arrow better than a golf club?
Because with an arrow, one shot will always make a hole!

Did you hear about the archer who took up football?
He kept shooting at the centre!

Why did the golfer buy a lorry?
He wanted to be a long-distance driver!

Two grasshoppers got married on Saturday,
then divorced on Sunday. Why?
Because it was a one-day cricket match!

Golfer — "My name is George, but my
friends call me Sandy!"
Friend — "Why is that?"
Golfer — "Because I'm always in the
bunker!"

Mountaineer — "I'm at the peak of my
profession!"

Deep-sea diver — "I've sunk to an all-time
low!"

Why did the cricketer go to the doctor?
Because he had the runs!

What do you call a soccer trophy on a
merry-go-round?
The Whirled Cup!

Why did the sprinter get sunburn?
Because he'd been running in the heat!

What's the most popular sport in the Wild
West?
Dodge-ball!

What was the soccer player doing with a
felt pen at the edge of the stadium?
He was marking defence!

What do swimmers do in their spare time?
Play pool!

Why could the boxer not beat the trampolinist
in a fight?
He couldn't get him to stay down!

Why do golfers always keep their clubs in
the front seat of the car?
Because they can't stand backseat
drivers!

Why does it take a golfer so long to iron his
clothes?
Because he uses five-irons!

Why did the pitcher take all his clothes off?
He was on a winning streak!

What do you get if you cross a cricket ball
with a rug?
A throw!

Why are matches useless at baseball?
One strike and they're out!

"There's something not right about this
hockey game!"
"What is it?"
"The referee!"

A bottle of water and a river had a race.
Which one won?
The river—it ran, but the bottle kept still!

What kind of race are typists best at?
The short dash!

When is a tap like a sprinter?
When it runs in short spurts!

When do fungi compete for the cup?
On spore-ts day!

Why did the electrician miss the rugby
match?
He couldn't find his shorts!

What position did the ghost play on the
soccer team?
He played in ghouls!

Why did the musician miss the soccer
match?
He couldn't find the right pitch!

What did the soccer player say when he saw
the Gulf of Mexico?
"Look! Look! A Mexican wave!"

Why did the soccer player retire?
He'd achieved all his goals!

Why was the mathematician confused at
the football match?
Because someone told him it only took one
player to make a score!

What did the golfer say when he met his
friend?
Putt it there, buddy!

Why did the golfer lose his appetite?
Because he took a few chips at the green!

What do golfers like to write with?
An O-pen!

Diver — *"I did a double flip, pike, somersault and twist!"*
Friend — *"And then you won the trophy?"*
Diver — *"No—then I landed on the changing-room floor!"*

Why did the diver take a fish to the diving board?
To do a triple somersault with pike!

Watching a diving competition is like living through winter!
—You're always waiting for the spring!

Swimmer — *"Joe swam a length, then Jack swam a length, then Jim swam a length, and at last it was my turn!"*
Friend — *"Relay?"*
Swimmer — *"Yes—honestly!"*

Why was the caterpillar unhappy?
It wasn't chosen for the butterfly race!

Diver — "My last dive stunned the crowd!"
Friend — "It must have been spectacular!"
Diver — "Not exactly—my swimming trunks came off!"

Footballer — *"... And then the referee yelled 'Off! Off!'"*
Friend — *"Had you committed a foul?"*
Footballer — *"No— I was standing on his toe!"*

Newsflash —Rabbits have made hundreds of holes in the grass in the local football stadium. The manager has cancelled all matches but has opened the facility as a pitch-and-putt."!

Did you hear about the man who lost a pack of cards at the tennis match?
He got most of them back, but the aces were never returned!

Why did the tennis player storm out of the hotel?
Because the service was poor!

Why did the tennis player fall over?
He made a foot-fault!

Where do tennis players hang out in their spare time?
In a singles bar!

What do you get if you cross a skunk with a table tennis bat?
Ping-pong!

Why could the two gymnasts not get married?
Because the best man wouldn't let go of the rings!

Why did the gymnast build a staircase?
He wanted to make the perfect landing!

Why do gymnasts never practise in cold weather?
Have you ever hear of wintersaults?

What did the gymnast say when he turned over?
"Oh—flip!"

Where do bees hold tennis matches?
Bumbledon!

What sport do hawks enjoy watching on TV?
The Swooperbowl!

What is the name of the vampire's tennis championship?
The Grave-is Cup!

What athletic event are sailors best at?
The deck-athlon!

What athletic event are real cool dudes best at?
The hip-tathlon!

What athletic event are writers best at?
The pen-tathlon!

What is the creepiest Olympic event?
Rowing—because of all the skulls!

Did you hear about the slalom skier?
His career went downhill!

What do mountaineers keep in their fridge?
Ice poles!

Why do skiers head for the mountains?
For some piste and quiet!

1st skier — "AVALANCHE!"
2nd skier — "Yes, I packed some sandwiches in my knapsa-a-a-ah! . ."

What athletic event are rugby players best at?
The try-athlon!

How do you build a bobsleigh?
With a sledgehammer!

When is a skier like a broken-down car?
When he's on tow!

What should you do if the ski-lift breaks down?
Ask someone to send you a cable!

What do you call two Russians on their first ski-ing holiday?
Igor Toniski and E. Foloviski!

Why did the ski instructress never tell her pupils her name?
Because it was Ima Lerner!

Did you hear about the gardener who bought a ski resort?
His seedlings all died on the nursery slopes!

Where do skunks stand when they win medals at the animal Olympics?
On the poo-dium!

What did one parachutist say to the other parachutist?
"See you next fall!"

1st parachutist — "I'm really nervous!"
2nd parachutist — "Why?"
1st parachutist — "This is only my second time up, and last time I was up, my parachute didn't even open!"
2nd parachutist — "Why not?"
1st parachutist — "Because I was too scared to jump!"

Parachute instructor — "Don't jump! Don't jump!"
Pupil — "Why not?"
Instructor — "Because the plane hasn't left the ground yet!"

Where do golfers get their refreshments?
From the tee-caddie!

Water-ski instructor — "Boy, oh boy! I've never seen such a talented beginner. How did you manage to do all those jumps and twists and turns?"
Pupil — "Oh, it was nothing, really—just a wasp in my wet suit!"

"Wanted—waterproof horses for new water polo team!"

What did the footballer's mother say to him?
Don't play games with me, young man!

Why do golfers never cheat?
Because they play the fairway!

Why do dentists make bad golfers?
Because they keep filling the holes!

Why was the pothole unpopular?
Because it was a low-down creep!

Why do cavers wear torches?
So they can see a hole lot better!

What happened when the jelly played the cream at tennis?
The jelly won the first set, but the cream ended up on top!

What did the fish say when it saw the worm dangling on the end of the hook?
"This bait here be good!"

Why do anglers have buttons instead of zippers in their trousers?
Because they use their flies for fishing!

What's that man doing standing with a ruler at the side of the tennis court?
—He's the linesman!

Why do footballers eat oranges at half-time?
Because they haven't time to eat them while they're playing!

Why did the dentist not eat his pie at the football match?
He didn't like the look of the filling!

The fishermen played the sharks at football. One fisherman, wearing red socks, had one leg each eaten by sharks. The team was red-leg-ate-d!

Why do football captains shake at the start of each match?
Because they're frightened they might lose!

"How was the football match?"
"Terrible! I think the referee was a Venetian!"
"Why?"
"Because he was blind!"

"How was the football match?"
"Terrible! The pitch must have a slope on it!"
"Why?"
"Because our team had an uphill struggle all the way!"

Did you hear about the cops v. criminals football match?
The cops were robbed!

Did you hear about the match between the monkeys and the zookeepers?
The monkeys won and they're now league chimpions!

What do you say to an arctic explorer with a broken leg?
"Have an ice trip?"

What do you say to a runner at the end of a race?
"Have a good time?"

Why did the ice-hockey player's wife leave him?
She was tired of his hard-puck stories!

The bowler bowled and the batsman ducked—just in time.
"Phew! That was a hard ball!" he said.
"Don't be ridiculous!" said the bowler. "It was the same ball as I used the last time!"

Did you hear about the lumberjack who took up cricket?
He made his own stumps!

"I used to work out on the rowing machine, but I soon gave up.
—it just wasn't getting me anywhere!"

"My husband said I should do weights at the gym. I've been there three times and waited, and waited, and waited. . . but I'm still unfit!"

"I don't like the running machine at the gym. It just stands there, while I have to do all the running!"

With a terrible crash, the racing car careered into the barrier.
"Is the driver all right?" called the crowd.
"Yes—he's fine!" answered a voice, "but has anyone got any barrier cream?"

"I don't think going to the gym is helping me lose weight. I don't work up a sweat—I just work up an appetite!"

"I used to drive a power boat, pulling along water-skiers—but I got fed up of having to tow the line!"

Footballer — "Yes, there are no sore losers in this team—except one!"
Friend — "And who is that?"
Footballer — "He's the one we all kick if we don't win!"

"Why is there a cat on the photocopying machine?"
"He's the copy-cat!"

Manager — "This coffee's as black as ink— and it tastes terrible!"
Deaf Clerk — "I got it fresh from the copy machine, like you asked sir!"

Why did the manager employ a very small secretary?
He was impressed by her shorthand skills!

The telephone rang and the office receptionist answered it.
"This is Gus the ghost here," said the voice at the other end. "Can I speak to the manager, please?"
The receptionist buzzed up to the manager's office.
"I've got a dead ringer for you here sir," she said!

What do you get if you cross a sound system with a typewriter?
A stereotype!

Manager (to late employee) — "Oi! Don't you know what time we start work here?"
Employee — "No—you're always getting on with things well before I arrive!"

Manager — "You weren't ill yesterday, were you, Smithers? You were lounging about at home, doing nothing!"
Employee — "I wasn't, sir—and I've got the fish to prove it!"

Manager (to new office boy) — "Remember, son, nothing pleases me more than hard work!"
So what did the office boy do?—Nothing!

Manager — "Why do you want the day off tomorrow, Smith?"
Smith — "It's my grandmother's funeral, sir!"
Manager — "All right—but don't let it happen again!"

Mother — "You've been working in that office for two years, Mary, and you're still the office junior. When are you going to get ahead?"
Mary — "I've already got one, Mum!"

Did you hear about the dopey secretary?
She thought the fax machine was an electronic encyclopedia!

What went wrong with the manager's computer in the cake factory?
There was a loose confection!

Why did the dinosaur cross the road?
Don't be silly! Dinosaurs didn't cross roads! No-one had built any yet!

So why did the dinosaur cross the hill?
To imagine what a road might look like winding down into the valley!

The dinosaur and a pebble were standing at the top of the hill. Which went down first?
The pebble—it was a little boulder!

Why did the pebble stop at the bottom?
Because it was feeling a little rocky!

What did the dinosaur call its dog?
Tyrannosaurus Rex!

What do you call a dinosaur carrying a bottle of pills and covered in bandages?
A doctorsaurus!

What kind of music did dinosaurs enjoy?
Rap-tor music!

How do you stop a dinosaur from biting his nails?
Pull his foot out of his mouth!

What do you get if you cross a jelly with a dinosaur?
A jellodactyl!

Did you hear about the dinosaur who wrote novels?
It was a Bronté-saurus!

What do you call a dinosaur who gives you a surprise party?
A Ta-rah!-nnosaurus!

What do you call a dinosaur who makes a lot of noise when it's asleep?
A dino-snore!

What do you call a dinosaur with one horn and a wrinkly skin?
A rhino-saur!

What do you call a dinosaur who's an ace at football?
A dino-score!

What do you call a dinosaur who plays the trumpet?
A ta-ran-ta-rah-nnosaurus!

What do you get if you cross a dinosaur with a dog?
Jurassic Bark!

What do you get if you cross a dinosaur with a pig?
Jurassic Pork!

What would you be if you were a dinosaur?
Extinct!

What do you call a cute dinosaur?
A dimple-odocus!

What do you call a stupid dinosaur?
A dim-plodocus!

What do you get if you cross a dinosaur with a tree?
A stick-osaurus!

Why do elephants float on their backs?
To keep their shoes dry!

What is the difference between a pterodactyl and a canary?
If you had ever had a pterodactyl sit on your shoulder, you wouldn't have to ask!

What happens when you have a pterodactyl for Thanksgiving?
You have enough leftovers to feed an army!

What do you get if you cross a brontosaurus with a cat?
A terrible mess in the kitty litter!

What's grey, yellow, grey, yellow, grey, yellow. . .?"
An elephant rolling downhill with a daisy in its mouth!

What do you get if you cross an elephant with a whale?
A submarine with a built-in snorkel!

What kind of elephants live at the North Pole?
Cold ones!

What do you get if you cross an elephant with a kangaroo?
Enormous holes all over Australia!

Why do elephants travel in herds?
Because if they travelled in flocks they might be mistaken for sheep!

What is the difference between an Indian elephant and an African elephant?
About three thousand miles!

Why do elephants paint the soles of their feet yellow?
So that they can hide upside down in bowls of custard!

How do you get an elephant out of the water?
Wet!

How do you catch a blue elephant?
With a blue elephant net.
But what about the yellow elephants—how do you catch them?
Don't be silly! Yellow elephants don't exist!

Why are elephants wrinkly?
They're very hard to iron!

Bill — "I ran over an elephant yesterday."
Will — "How did you do that?"
Bill — I climbed up its tail, trotted along its back and slid down its trunk."

What does an elephant smell like before he takes a shower?
An elephant!

Why do elephants need trunks?
Because they don't have glove compartments!

And what does he smell like after his shower?
A wet elephant!

How do you know if there's an elephant under your bed?
Your nose is touching the ceiling!

What's brown, has four legs and a trunk?
An elephant coming back from his holidays!

What do you call a twenty-ton elephant?
Sir!

How do you get down off an elephant?
You don't. You get down off a duck!

How does an elephant get out of a phone booth?
The same way as he got in!

Why do elephants lie on their backs with their feet in the air?
To trip up low-flying birds!

What do you get when an elephant parachutes into an army camp?
A flat major!

What goes clomp, clomp, clomp, squidge?
An elephant with a wet tennis shoe!

Why do elephants have horns on their bicycles?
They can't get the bells to work!

How do you know when two elephants have been riding your bicycle?
There's a great big dent in the crossbar!

How do you make an elephant float?
Take some cola, several scoops of ice cream, and an elephant. . .

What is beautiful, grey, and has only one glass slipper?
Cinderelephant!

How do elephants talk to each other?
By 'elephone!

Where do elephants with spots go?
To the pachydermatologist!

Why do elephants dry the dishes with a pink dishtowel?
Because they're wet!

What's enormous, grey and really hard to spot?
A stain-resistant elephant!

Which have better memories—elephants or turtles?
Turtles—they have turtle recall!

How do you know if an elephant has been sleeping in your bed?
There are peanut shells under the pillow!

What do you get if you cross an elephant with a mouse?
Enormous holes in the skirting board!

What's large and grey, and goes round and round?
An elephant stuck in a revolving door!

Why did the elephant burn his diary?
He wanted to forget!

Why do elephants paint their toenails pink?
To match their tutus!

Why do elephants wear tutus?
Because their leotards are in the wash!

How do you stop an elephant from charging?
You take away his credit card!

What did the currant bun say to the elephant?
Nothing—currant buns can't talk!

Fred — "Did your pet elephant cost a lot, Ted?"
Ted — "Not really—and its trumpet came free!"

Which is more powerful—a fireman's hose or an elephant's trunk?
An elephant's trunk, because a jumbo jet can keep 500 people thousands of feet up in the air for hours.

What did the grape say when an elephant stood on it?
Nothing—it just gave a little wine!

What would you get if you crossed an elephant with a sparrow?
A broken bird table!

How do you know when an elephant has been in your fridge?
Footprints in the butter!

How do you know when there is an elephant in your fridge?
You can't get the door shut!

What do you call an elephant teacher?
A tuskmaster!

What do you call a superstitious elephant?
Mumbo-Jumbo!

What do you call an elephant that speaks with its mouth full?
Mumble-Jumbo!

What do you call a clumsy elephant?
Fumble-Jumbo!

What do you call an elephant that studies Latin American dancing?
Mambo-Jumbo!

What do you call baked elephant pudding?
Crumble-Jumbo!

Why did the elephant buy running shoes?
To jog his memory!

How do you eat an elephant?
One bite at a time!

What's white on the outside and grey on the inside?
An elephant sandwich!

Did you hear about the elephant who sucked up ten tons of peanuts?
He sneezed, and shot down a herd of zebra!

Did you hear about the elephant who sucked up a gallon of glue?
He couldn't get his trunk open for two weeks!

How do you stop an elephant going through the eye of a needle?
Tie a knot in its tail!

Why is it best to cremate a dead elephant?
Because burying it would be an enormous undertaking!

Did you hear about the elephant with hay-fever?
It didn't last long—with the first sneeze he blew away all the flowers in a ten-mile radius!

What's big, grey, and goes up and down?
An elephant doing press-ups!

How many elephants can you see from the top of the hill?
It depends how many are at the bottom!

How many elephants can you see from the bottom of a hill?
None—they all look like rocks from where you're standing!

Did you hear about the elephant who swallowed ten tons of TNT?
It's now a space station!

How do you play a tune on an elephant?
Tickle its ivories!

Where will you find an elephant in an orchestra?
In the trumpet section!

What did the elephant say when it walked into the bank?
"Ow!"

How do you know when an elephant is passing your window?
It goes really dark inside!

Why did the elephant stay in bed all day?
He was doing undercover work!

What did the architect say to the builders?
"I've got great plans for you!"

10,000 slates were stolen from the building site today. Police say the criminals were roofless.

Who is that man with the briefcase, standing at the edge of the building site?
He's the lawyer for de-fence!

A terrible crime was carried out on the building site today.
Two hundred doors were hung!

Why did the demolition expert buy a pile of bricks?
He got them at a knock-down price!

What's a demolition worker's favourite film?
"Start Wreck—The Movie"

Why did the wall hit the roof?
It was put up to it!

What did the carpenter use to play computer games?
A joist stick!

When is the roof like the sun?
When the roof beams!

The architect fell into the drains on the building site today.
He says his plans are in the pipeline!

Why did the builder go to the optician?
He was having problems with his site!

1st bricklayer — "Seen Bill?"
2nd bricklayer — "Bill? He's twelve blocks down from me!"

What do you call a wheelbarrow with no wheel?
Useless!

Builder (answering call on mobile phone) — "Can't talk now, dear, I'm up to my ears in plaster!"
Builder's wife — "Are the walls nearly finished, then?"
Builder — "No—I fell off the scaffolding!"

Did you hear about the burglar who fell into the concrete mixer?
He's now a hardened criminal!

Client — "These walls aren't straight!"
Builder — "Stand over there, close one eye, screw up the other one, tilt your head to the side a bit and they'll look all right!"

Why do builders wear big boots?
To keep their big feet warm!

What did the pile of bricks say to the crane?
"Can you give us a lift?"

Newspaper advertisement "Ladders for hire. Cranes for even higher!"

Did you hear about the cake that fell in the cement mixer?
It became a real tough cookie!

Did you hear about the builder who could shovel sand faster than any other person on the building site?
They called him the Ace of Spades!

Gravel-voiced, sandy-haired, stony-featured, muscles of iron, nerves of steel — the perfect construction worker!

Why did the journalist go into the ice-cream parlour?
For a big scoop!

Why did the journalist interview the chicken?
For an eggs-clusive story!

The editor of the Daily Blurb passed away last night. The story hit the deadlines.

Why was the type on the newspaper very faint?
Because it was printed weekly (weakly)!

Why did the journalist go to the seashore?
To report on current events!

Did you hear about the horoscope writer who stopped writing for the newspaper? She said there was no future in journalism!

What did the editor say when he fired the journalist?
"You're yesterday's news!"

What newspapers did the doctor buy?
Three Times daily!

There was a problem with printing the Daily Drivel yesterday. Everything was printed squint. Readers say the editor should try and get his facts straight!

What newspaper did the hospital patient buy?
The Chronic-ill!

Which newspaper does the mailman buy?
The Post!

Which newspaper do private investigators buy?
The Observer!

Which newspaper sells best in the mountains?
The Echo!

Which part of the newspaper do dieticians like best?
The supplements!

Which part of the newspaper do grouches like best?
The crossword!

Which part of the newspaper do monsters like best?
The horrorscopes!

Which part of the newspaper do mathematicians like best?
The ads!

Which part of the newspaper do doctors read?
The agony column!

Which part of the newspaper do dentists read?
Extracts from the back!

Which part of the newspaper was written in Trafalgar Square, London?
Nelson's Column!

Which part of the newspaper do electricians like to read?
Watts On!

Which part of the newspaper do athletes like to read?
The small (s)print!

Why did the editor close the curtains?
Because he was putting the paper to bed!

What did the reporter say when he tore the newspaper?
"Holed the front page!"

Where do gardeners retire?
Idaho(e)!

Where did the hippie's wife live?
Missis-hippie!

Where was 'Singin' in the Rain' filmed?
Sing-a-pour!

Where can you find honourable sheep?
The Ewe-knighted Kingdom!

Where do American doctors learn to stitch wounds?
Connect-i-cut!

Where do electricians go to learn their trade?
Switcherland!

Which American state was named after the end of the Gold Rush?
Ore-gon(e)!

Where should you go if you want to lose weight?
Hungary!

Where is Felixstowe?
On the end of his foot!

How do you get to Bury St Edmonds?
First, you need a big spade. . .

Where can you never win a tennis match?
Thailand!

Who was the most dangerous president of the United States?
Ronald Raygun!

Who was the most honest president of the United States?
Truman!

Who was the most houseproud president of the United States?
Hoover!

Why did Nicholas II take acting lessons?
Because he wanted to be a tsar!

Which famous person in history invented cross-country car-racing?
Raleigh!

Who was the first man in history to have hay-fever?
Julius Sneezer!

What lives in the Himalayas and is never on time?
The not-yeti!

Why did Shakespeare write plays?
Because with a name like that, he couldn't throw the javelin, could he?

What was the name of America's most famous private eye?
Martin Sleuther King!

Ivan was angry. His horse wouldn't move. It spent all day, Lenin against the stable door. "No more Stalin!" shouted Ivan, "On your Marx, get set, Gogol!" and he gave it a little Pushkin. At last, it started to Trotsky, and within seconds, it was really Russian!

Mo — "My brother's really stupid. He saw a moose's head on the wall of the castle we visited yesterday. . . so he went into the adjoining room to see what the rest of it looked like!"

Betsy — "My brother opened a shop."
Mo — "Really? What's he doing?"
Betsy — "Six months. . . he opened the shop with a brick!"

Annie — "My brother broke his arm in two places."
Molly — "What did you say to him?"
Annie — "I told him he'd better not go back to those places again!"

Fred — "I'd like a puppy for my little brother, please!"
Pet shop owner — "Certainly—would you like to choose your puppy?"
Fred — "I'd like this one please—and here's my little brother, just as we arranged!"

Little sister — "My hair needs cut badly!"
Big sister —"It was cut badly last time—why don't you get a decent style for once?"

Katie — "My brother's always flying off the handle!"
Kit — "Why is that?"
Katie — "Because he has a screw loose!"

Fred — "My sister's really ugly!"
Ted — "That's not a very nice thing to say!"
Fred — "But it's true— she's so ugly that every time I pull her hair she says 'Oink!' "

Billy's sister — "I've made a cake for your friend Joe!"
Billy — "Why? What harm has he ever done to you?"

Fred — "My sister's boyfriend loves the simple things in life —That's why he chose her!"

Bill — "There's nothing my sister likes better than listening to Puccini as she relaxes in a bathful of bubbles."
Will — "Oh—she's a soap opera fan, is she?"

Fred — "Whenever my sister's down in the dumps, she buys herself some clothes!"
Ted — "So that's where she gets them!"

My sister's so stupid that she lost her job as an elevator operator because she couldn't remember the route!"

Ted — "My sister has only two faults. . .Everything she says and everything she does!"

Bill — "D'you think my sister smells funny?"
Will — "Why do you ask?"
Bill — "She told me she got some toilet water from her boyfriend for Christmas!"

Joe — "My sister put on a mud-pack today!"
Jim— "And did it make her look any better?"
Joe — "Only for a few minutes—then she washed it off!"

Fred — "Every time my sister passes a boy, he sighs. . . with relief!"

Fred — "My sister's always singing. I told her she should be on the radio. . . then I could switch her off!"

Ted — "Ignorance is bliss—so my sister's a happy little thing!"

Ted — "My girl-friend said I was half daft!!"
Ted's brother — "She's half-right, then, isn't she!"

Ted — "My brother's so stupid that he thinks a dessert spoon is for eating sand!"
Fred — "That's nothing! My brother's so stupid, he thinks a brainwave is a kind of hairstyle!"

Annie — "My brother's really stupid!"
Mo — How stupid is he?"
Annie — "He once spend three days in a revolving door, looking for the handle!"

What's that planet up there?
Mars!
And the one beside it?
Pa's!

Bill — "My little brother's a dab hand!"
Will — "At what?"
Bill — "A dab hand at finger-painting!"

Mike — "My brother was sent out of the school concert for bad behaviour last week."
Mo — "Was he upset?"
Mike — "Well, he was certainly disconcerted!"

Annie — "My brother's built the wrong way round!"
Mo — "Why do you say that?"
Annie — "Because his feet smell and his nose runs!"

Annie — "My brother's so lazy that when he has a runny nose, he sticks it out the window so that the wind will blow it for him!"

Annie — "My brother's giving up playing the violin!"
Mo — "Why is that?"
Annie — "He's been blowing and blowing for three months and he still can't get a sound out of it!"

Bill — "I ran away from home at six!"
Will — "And did your parents miss you?"
Bill — "No—I was home by quarter past!"

Molly — "My parents had a blazing row last night!"
Mo — "What was it about?"
Molly — "Who was going to put out the fire in the living-room!"

A little boy was out riding his bike while his mother watched from the window. The first time he passed, he called out, "Look, Ma, no hands!" Then there was a loud crash. After a moment or two, the little boy rode past the window again. This time he called out to his mother, "Look Ma, no teeth!"

And of course, there is the story of the little German boy who went mountain-climbing with his brother and his mother. His mother fell of the edge of the mountain, and the little boy turned to his brother and said "Look Hans, no Ma!"

Son — "I'm going to be a rap star when I grow up!"
Mum — "Is that so? Well, you can make a start now with these Christmas parcels. Get wrapping!"

**Son — "I'm going into the pop business when I grow up!"
Dad — "Well, in that case you can pop out and buy me a paper!"**

*Mum — "I've got good news and bad news!"
Dad — "Tell me the good news first."
Mum — "That dreadful dog's run away!"
Dad — "So what's the bad news?"
Mum — "He's taken your dinner with him!"*

Mum — "Where is the pie I left on the table, son?"
Son — "I'm just warming it up, Mum!"
Mum — "Warming it up?"
Son — "Yes, inside my stomach!"

**What do you call a clone of the worst behaved boy in the family?
Double trouble!**

*Mum — "Why is the dog scratching like that?"
Son — "I took him to the flea circus and he stole the show!"*

Billy — "What's the matter, Dopey—have you lost your key again?"
Dopey — "Oh, I can find my key all right. Trouble is, I've forgotten where I left my house!"

**Billy — "How's your new baby sister, Bobby?"
Bobby — "She's just like a bad joke —a real howler!"**

*Son — "I think I'm going to be an athlete!"
Mum — "What makes you say that?"
Son — "Teacher said I was in for the high jump!"*

Dad — "Bath night tonight, Joe!"
Joe — "Uh-oh! Looks like I'm going to be in hot water again!"

**Billy — "I wouldn't have that yogurt if I were you, Bobby—it's past its sell-by date!"
Bobby — "Oh, that's all right—I'm not going to sell it. I'm going to eat it!**

*Auntie, visiting — "My, my George! I hardly recognised you!"
George (glumly) — "I know— Mum made me have a bath before you arrived!"*

Billy — "Dopey! You're covered in bruises! What happened?"
Dopey — "I was ironing Mum's curtains and I fell out of the window!"

**It's Christmas time.
Mum — "Why are you boiling Grandma's hat?"
Son — "I'm making some Granberet jelly!"**

*Dad — "Christmas day, Joe, and you're being as naughty as ever!"
Joe — "It's the season of goodwill, Dad, not the season of good Joe!"*

Little girl — "Mummy said I came from a gooseberry bush!"
Brother — "No wonder you're such a goose!"

**Joe — "Dopey! You're wearing one of your mother's high-heeled shoes!"
Dopey — "Thank goodness for that! I thought I had a terrible limp!"**

Neighbour — *"What's the matter, George?"*
George — *"I lost my ball!"*
Neighbour — *"Shall I help you look for it?"*
George — *"I don't think that would be a good idea!"*
Neighbour — *"Why?"*
George — *"It went through your sitting-room window!"*

Billy — "Isn't that amazing! Cedric won the 100m sprint!
Bobby — "He, heh—yes, with that nasty dog from across the street a close second—hard on his heels!"

Auntie Ethel — "I'm going home tomorrow, Betty—are you disappointed?"
Betty — "Just a bit—I thought you were going home today!"

Billy — *"Mum, how do you spell 'sigh'?"*
Mum — *"S-I-G-H. What are you writing about?"*
Billy — *"My favourite hobby—cycling!"*

Mum — "Go on, Joe, let your little brother play with your marbles!"
Joe — "He doesn't want to play with them—he wants to keep them!"
Mum — "What makes you say that?"
Joe — "He's swallowed ten already!"

Mum — "Where did you get those sweets from?"
Son — "I got them from the boy next door for doing him a favour!"
Mum — "What did you do for him?"
Son — "I stopped hitting him!"

Mother — *"My little boy ran away from home with the dog today!"*
Friend — *"That's terrible!"*
Mother — *"I know—I'm really going to miss that dog!"*

Little Betty got a bottle of perfume and a penny whistle for her birthday. Her posh Granny and Grandpa came for the birthday tea, and Betty sat down next to them. She was looking forward to showing off her presents after they had finished eating, and had been keeping it all a big secret. But just before the birthday cake came out, she whispered to her Grandparents — "After tea, if you hear a little noise and smell a little smell, it'll be me!"

Mother — "Get off that wall, Jimmy, it's far too high!"
Jimmy — "Don't worry, Mum, I'll be fine!"
Mother — "All right, but if you fall off and break both your legs, don't come running to me to complain!"

Cannibal boy — *"Mum! Mum! It's boiling in here!"*
Mother — *"Good—five more minutes and you'll be done to a turn!"*

Little boy — "Mum, you like toast, don't you?"
Mother — "Yes, dear—why?"
Little boy — "I've just set fire to the bread bin!"

Little boy — "Mum, I don't want a games console for my Christmas any more!"
Mum — "Why not?"
Little boy — "Because I found one under your bed!"

Mother — *"Our children really brighten the home!"*
Friend — *"So do ours—they never turn the lights off!"*

Little boy — "Mum, can I go out to play?"
Mum — "But it's pouring wet out there!"
Little boy — "But I'm not going to play out there—I'm going to play at the park!"

Why did the little horror drop his baby sister?
His mother said she was a bouncing baby!

Never trust teenagers—they lie in bed till all hours!

Father — "That was a short call. You were only on the phone for half an hour!"
Teenager — "I know—it was a wrong number!"

Father — *"My daughter runs up terrible telephone bills!"*
Friend — *"So does ours—in fact, we call her Bait!"*
Father — *"Why?"*
Friend — *"Because she's always on the end of a line!"*

Little girl, leaning over the side of a cruise ship — "I'm sorry sir, but I can't help you—my Dad says he'll kill me if I play with the lifebelts!"

Mike — "My wife's an angel!"
Ike — "My wife's still alive!"

Proud father — "My son's got a fine head on his shoulders!"
Other father — "My son's got a good head too—in fact, it's hardly been used!"

Friend — "Are you close to your children?"
Father — "Yes, but never quite close enough to catch them!"

Billy — "Were you in the war, Grandpa?"
Grandpa — "Yes—I fought with all my heart and soul—but they still made me go!"

Bobby — "My big brother taught me to swim!"
Jimmy — "How did he do it?"
Bobby — "He took me out into the middle of the lake in a boat, and threw me over the side, so that I had to swim back to shore!"
Jimmy — "That sure was a tough way to learn to swim!"
Bobby — "Oh, the swimming was quite easy—the hard part was finding my way out of the sack first!"

Bobby — "Does your mother cook on gas?"
Billy — "I don't know—I've never tried to cook her!"

Old Lady — "And is your new sister all soft and pink?"
Little boy — "No—she's nasty sort of yeller!"

Bobby — "My father's missing! He went to catch us a trout for our dinner yesterday, and he fell in the lake!"
Joe — "What did your mother do?"
Bobby — "She cooked hamburgers instead!"

Dopey teenager — "You won't catch me bungee-jumping—if the rope snapped, I would just die of embarrassment!"

Scrawled on bicycle-shed wall — "Get angry—it's all the rage!"

Bill — "Someone told me you buried your dog last week—what happened?"
Fred — "He died!"

Fred — "My wife's nearly forty-five, but she doesn't look it, does she?"
Ted — "No—I'd have guessed she was about sixty!"

Little boy — "I help my two brothers clear up every day after dinner!"
Old Lady — "What do you do?"
Little boy — "They clear the dishes off the table, and I pick up the pieces!"

What did the Mummy bin say to the baby bin?
"No more junk food!"

Little boy — "My Grandad's glad he's one hundred!"
Friend — "Why is that?"
Little boy — "Because if he wasn't one hundred, he'd be dead!"

The world might be different today, if Eve had said —
"No thanks, I don't like apples much!"

The world might be very different today, if Christopher Columbus had said —
"America? Not on your life!—don't you know I get horribly seasick?"!

The world might be very different today, if Isaac Newton had said —
"I'm not sitting under that apple tree—the grass is wet!"

The world might be very different today, if Sir Walter Raleigh had said, "I've brought you back some potatoes, your majesty. . . No, no, you can't EAT them, you're supposed to throw them at the enemy!"

Dear Auntie Emma. Thanks for the turtle-neck sweater. I'm choked. . .

Dear Uncle Charlie. Thank you for the giant balloon you sent for my birthday. I've blown it up and it sure is swell.

Dear Aunt Agnes, Thank you for the sweater you knitted for my Christmas. My ankles have never been so warm. . ."

Stupid question —"How much is a dollar return?"

Stupid question — "When does the two o'clock train go?"

Stupid remark — "You wouldn't catch me dead in the cemetery!"

Stupid question — "How long have you had that birthmark?"

Stating the obvious — "Whispering is not allowed!"

Stupid remark — "When my mother woke me this morning, I was fast asleep!"

Strange but true — The heavy end of a match is the light end!

Think about it — A piece of string has two ends. But where's the beginning?

Marvellous invention — a saddle for a clothes horse.

Marvellous invention — sheets for the sea bed.

Marvellous invention — An underwater hairdrier.

Marvellous invention — An inflatable dartboard.

"Dear son, I'm writing this very slowly, because I know you can't read fast. . ."

Marvellous invention — An open-top tent.

"Dear son, your grandmother has had all her teeth taken out and central heating put in. . ."

For sale —Tallboy with assorted ladies' clothing.

For sale — Bureau for lady with elegantly carved legs.

Job Advert — Opening for a doorman. Apply within.

Advert —Room to Let for two ladies, 14ft by 15ft with cheerful outlook.

For sale — Bicycle for five-year old boy in good condition.

Marvellous invention — A soundless violin.

"Dear son, I hope this letter reaches you, because the rescue party didn't. . ."

Dear Aunt Effie, Thank you for the socks that you knitted for me. It's a pity that one of them is full of holes, but never mind —I will make sure I put my best foot forward. . ."

Motto for a boxer — "He who hesitates is sloshed!"

Motto for a criminal — "If at first you don't succeed, lie, lie and lie again!"

Motto for a grubby child — "Cleanliness is next to impossible!"

Motto for a burglar — "The best things in life are free!"

Motto for a doctor — "Leave well alone!"

Motto for a carpenter — "Least sawed, soonest mended!

Motto for a ghost — "Spook before you sleep!"

Motto for a historian — "You can't have archaic and eat it!"

Get married in summer—Bride comes before the fall.

Keep the bathroom floor dry—Look before you leak.

Never let the gardener look after the royal furniture—People who live in glass houses shouldn't store thrones.

Leave a light on to deter burglars—A switch in time saves crime.

Good-natured Hansel manufactures garden implements— Merry Hans makes light forks.

Hot food—self-service only!—Ask me no questions and I'll sell you no pies.

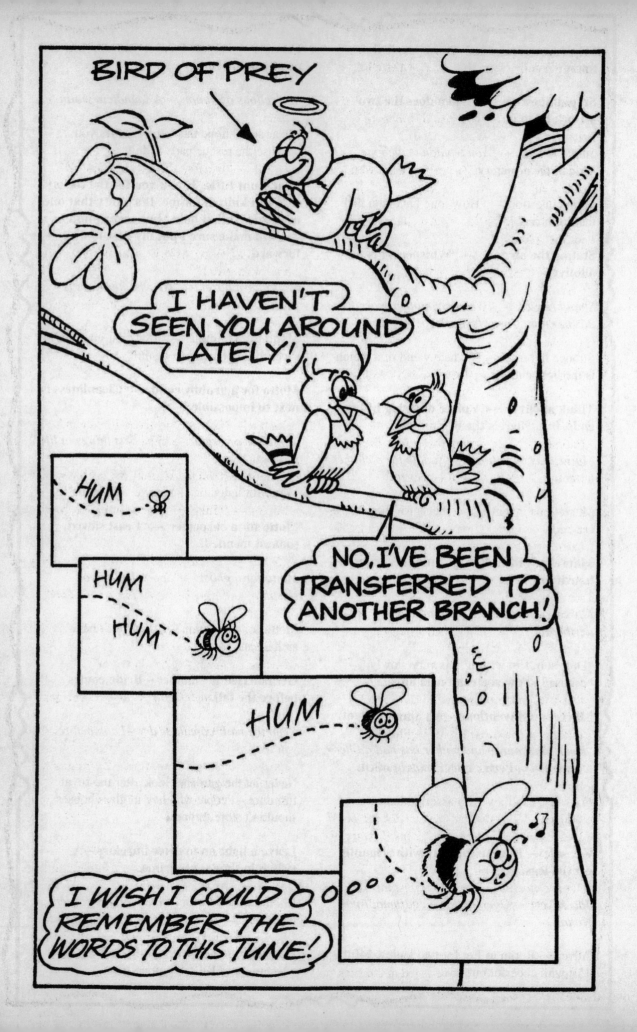

Hairdressers are only human!—There's many a slip 'twixt the cut and the clip.

Lumberjacks have terrible trouble with their feet—Hell hath no fury like a woodman's corns!

Motto for an oil prospector — "Oil's well that ends well!"

Motto for a jeweller — "All that glitters can be sold!"

Doctor — "Same old complaints, Mrs Green?"
Mrs Green — "No— something different!"
Doctor — "Then that's easy to diagnose—it's new-moan-ia!"

Romeo — "Doctor, doctor! I don't feel well at all, and nor does Juliet!"
Doctor — "That'll be romantic fever!"

Patient — "Doctor, doctor! I feel like an apple!"
Doctor — "You'll soon be cored!"

Patient — "Doctor, doctor! My wife says I'm a pig!"
Doctor — "I'll soon cure you!"

Patient — "I'm not going to the local hospital for my operation!"
Doctor — "Why not?"
Patient — "I've seen the sign outside— 'Guard Dogs Operating!' "

Doctor — "I'm afraid your husband doesn't have long to live!"
Wife — "But he's hungry! I'm in the middle of making him an egg for his breakfast!"
Doctor — "Better make it soft-boiled, then!"

Surgeon — "I'm sorry, Mr Macdonald, but it seems a rubber glove was left inside you after your last operation. We're going to have to open you up again!"
Mr Macdonald — "No need for that, Doc! Here, have a fiver! Buy yourself another pair!"

Doctor — "Stick your tongue out farther!"
Patient — "I can't! It's fastened at the back!"

Doctor — "Stick your tongue out farther!"
Patient — "Okay, son!"

Patient — "Doctor, doctor, I fell in the cement mixer!"
Doctor — "You'll be hard to cure!"

Patient — "Doctor, doctor, where am I?"
Doctor — "You're on the road to recovery!"

Patient — "I've had four broken legs, you know!"
Doctor — "Well, at least the ones you have now seem fine!"

Doctor — "Your husband's off the danger list, now!"
Wife — "Is he!"
Doctor — "Yes—he's dead!"

Patient — "Doctor, doctor, will I ever be better?"
Doctor — "Get a job as a repair man and you'll soon be on the mend!"

Patient — "Doctor, doctor, my whole world is grey!"
Doctor — "Take off your sunglasses, Miss Smith!"

Patient — "Doctor, doctor, I hear music in my head!"
Doctor — "Must be the band on your hat!"

Patient — "Doctor, doctor, I feel light-headed!"
Doctor — "Your wig has fallen off!"

Patient — "Doctor, doctor, will I ever get better?"
Doctor — "At what?"

Patient — "Doctor, doctor, the baby cries whenever I take him out in his pram!"
Doctor — "Guess he doesn't like being pushed around!"

Doctor's wife — "Coffee, darling?"
Doctor — "Yes, but I'm taking something for it!"

Patient — "Doctor, doctor, sometimes I feel like a marquee, sometimes I feel like a tepee!"
Doctor — "You're two tents!"

Patient — "Doctor, doctor! I feel like an enormous boiled sweet!"
Doctor — "That's a bit hard to swallow!"

Patient — "Doctor, doctor, I feel like an old jersey!"
Doctor — "Well, darn it!"

Patient — "What can I do about my flat feet?"
Doctor — "Try a foot pump!"

Why did the undertaker go to the doctor?
To ask about his terrible coffin!

Patient — "Doctor—I've got seconds to live. . ."
Doctor — "Wait a minute, please!"

Doctor — "Drink a cup of warm milk after a warm bath, and that should help you sleep!"
Patient — "Sleep? After drinking all that bathwater??"

Patient — "Mackintosh, MacGregor, Campbell, Robertson. . ."
Doctor — "Mr MacDougall, you have a Clan-dular disorder!"

Did you hear about the man who took four baths a day?
His doctor had told him to take his pills in water!

Patient — "Doctor, doctor, every time I go to put on my hat, a white rabbit pops out of it! And every time I wash behind my ears, I find an egg"
Doctor — "Hmm! Tricky problem!"

Patient — "I've been getting pains in different places!"
Doctor — "Whatever you do, don't go back to any of these places!"

Patient — "Doctor, I tend to put on weight in certain places!"
Doctor — "Where?"
Patient — Restaurants!"

Patient — "Doctor, doctor! I've got skin trouble!"
Doctor — "Have you?"
Patient — "Yes—I can't peel this banana!"

Wife — "Get the doctor! The baby just swallowed my engagement ring!"
Husband — "Don't worry—the diamond wasn't real anyway!"

Doctor — "What happened to you?"
Patient — "I was driving in my car when my boss 'phoned me and told me I had been promoted. I got such a shock that I swerved the car. Then he called me again and said I had been promoted higher up. I swerved the car again. Then he called me a third time and told me I had been appointed vice-chairman of the company! Well, I was so shocked that I swerved the car again, and this time I drove onto the verge and hit a tree!"
Doctor — "Oh, dear!"
Patient — "Yes—I careered off the road!"

A man goes to the doctor with a bad leg.
"Say Aaah," says the doctor.
"Why?" says the man.
"Because my budgie died yesterday," says the doctor.

Patient — "Doctor, doctor, it's my hat!"
Doctor — "What's wrong with it?"
Patient — "It's white and peaky!"

A man went into the dentist's surgery and sat down. Most dentists' chairs go up and down, but the man was surprised to discover that this one went back and forwards.
Then the dentist told him to get out of the filing cabinet drawer!

A man comes into the doctor's surgery with a pair of pants over his head, flowers sticking out of his ears, blue spots on his cheeks and his hair dyed green and purple. The doctor tries hard to keep a straight face, and asks the man, "What seems to be the trouble?"
"Well," says the man, "It's like this. . .I'm terribly worried about my brother!"

Doctor — "Does it hurt when you do this?"
Patient — "Yes, it does!"
Doctor — "Me too! Isn't it strange? I wonder what the matter is with us!"

Doctor — "Mrs Jones, you have acute lumbago!"
Mrs Jones — "Oh, Doctor, you flatter me!"

Doctor — "And does it hurt when you do this?"
Patient — "Yes, it really hurts!"
Doctor — "You'd better not do it again, then!"

Patient — "Doctor, Doctor! I've got water on the knee!"
Doctor — "Here—have a prescription for drainpipe trousers!"

Patient — "Doctor, doctor, I've still got water on the knee!
Doctor (picks up hammer) — "I'll give you a little tap on the leg!"

Patient — "Doctor, doctor, I think I'm a kettle!"
Doctor — "Does that bother you?"
Patient — "Bother me? It makes my blood boil!"

Patient — "Doctor, Doctor, I still think I'm a kettle!"
Doctor — "Then perhaps you are a kettle!"
Patient — "Aw, Doc, you're putting me on!"

A man walked into the doctor's waiting room with a pile of fruit on his head, chicken legs dangling from his ears, butter all over his face, slices of ham and cheese sticking out of his pockets and slices of bread stuck to the chest.
"What's wrong with me, Doctor?"
he said.
"It's quite clear," said the Doctor, "You're two sandwiches short of a picnic!"

A woman takes her canary took the vet's.
"He's lost his voice—can you help him?"
"I'm sorry," says the vet, "he's untweetable!"

A man walks into the vet's with his dog.
"What can you do about distemper?" he asks.
"You'll have to learn to control dat temper!" says the vet. "And now, what can I do for de dog?"!

What do you give a moose with indigestion?
Elk-aseltzer!

What do you give a cockatoo with a headache?
Parrot-cetamol!

What do you give a snake with a sore throat?
Asp-irin!

What do you get if you cross a kangaroo with a fur coat?
A furry jumper with pockets!

What do you get if you cross a sheep and a porcupine?
An animal that knits its own sweaters!

Why did the farmer give the cow a hot-water bottle?
It was Friesian!

Why is a fox like a carpenter?
Because it can make a chicken run!

Why did the farmer put the cow in the wardrobe?
It was a Jersey!

What has feathers and grumbles?
Moody Woodpecker!

Why did the kitten not want to go to school?
She didn't like the mew-niform!

Why did the little bee not like school?
They gave him too much hum-work!

What do you say when a sheep sneezes?
Bless ewe!

Did you hear about the baby kangaroo who ran away from home?
He had to come home because the experience left him out of pocket!

The posh people down the street have got two new dogs.
They call them Reauveux and Fideaux!

A man is walking home with his pet elephant one day, when suddenly the elephant collapses and dies, right in the middle of a busy road The man shrugs his shoulders, wipes away a tear, turns, and walks away, leaving the dead animal blocking the traffic.
"Oi!" calls a bus driver. "You can't leave that lyin' there!"
"What else am I to do?" says the man, "—and besides, it's not a lion, it's an elephant!"

What do you call an otter with a washing machine on its head?
An otter-matic!

What do sheep say to each other at Christmas?
"Season's bleatings!"

How many skunks does it take to clear a building?
A phew!

How many sheep does it take to knit a jumper?
Don't be stupid! Sheep can't knit!

1st cow — "How do you like the new bull?"
2nd cow — "At a safe distance!"

Did you hear about the stupid worm?
He fell in love with his other end!

Did you hear the joke about the cattle?
It's laugh-a-bull, really!

Customer — "You told me this dog was house-trained!"
Pet-shop owner — "So he is. He won't go anywhere else!"

How do you say goodbye to a mouse?
"See you next squeak"!

How did the duck pay for lunch?
He put it on his bill!

How do hedgehogs play leapfrog?
Very carefully!

Billy (at zoo) — "Look! Look! Dangeroos!"
Mum — "Don't you mean 'kangaroos', son?"
Billy — "I know what I meant! I read it on a sign; 'These animals are dangeroos'!"

Motto for all rabbits — "Don't worry, be hoppy!"

What do bees chew?
Bumble gum!

Two large black and white bears started a fight at the zoo today, all over a piece of bamboo. . .
—zookeepers say it was panda-monium!

Did you hear about the dog who swallowed a bunch of keys?
He got lockjaw!

Two kangaroos crossed the English Channel from Dover to Calais.
They went by hoppercraft!

Two cleaners raced them to the other side. . .
—they were in a hoovercraft!

They never saw the football player who beat them all to Calais. Why?
Because he was a sub!

A man went to sleep and dreamt he was eating candy floss.
When he woke up, his wife was bald!

Why did the fraud go to the blacksmith's?
To forge some documents!

Singer (sings) — "And for bonnie Annie Laurie, I would lay me down and die!"
Voice over the tannoy — "Is there a Miss Laurie here? We need her help!"

What's a donkey's favourite TV programme?
Bray Watch!

1st robber — "How can we get all this stuff back to the den?"
2nd robber — "I know! We'll steal a car!"
1st robber — "Don't be stupid! Neither of us has a driving licence!"

Will — "You'd never think this car was second-hand!"
Bill — "No—I thought you'd made it yourself!"

"I've got a lot on my hands just now!"
"So I see! You'd better go and wash it off!"

Dreary Dierdre — "I must be the unluckiest person in the world! I got sick, so my friend sent me a birthday card. . .
—and I got a paper cut opening it!"

"Why is that goat wearing a stetson?"
"He thinks he's Billy the Kid!"

What lives in a Scottish loch and grumbles all day long?
The Loch Ness Moanster!

Son — "Do elephants always walk in single file?"
Father — "I've only seen one elephant—but he certainly did!"

Fred — "both my dog and I enjoy a good novel!"
Ted — "Really?"
Fred — "yes—I read it, then he eats it!"

Why did the man take his dog to the Chinese supermarket?
They were just going for a wok!

When is a good dog like an old shoe?
When it's down-at-heel!

What did Mr Toad say to Mrs Toad?
"I love you, warts and all!"

Thought for the day — Where does a snake begin when it wants to wag its tail?

A leopard escaped from the zoo the other day. However, it was quickly found.
Vets tranquilized it on the spot!

What do you call a curious pig?
A nosey porker!

What are the most dangerous mountains for cats?
The Catskills!

Did you hear about the snake who worked at the carwash?
He was the windscreen viper!

What is the badgers' favourite movie star of all time?
Brock Hudson!

What did one dove say to the other?
"How are you doo-oo-ing?"!

What do you get if you cross a wildcat with a pig?
Sausage lynx!

What's mad, bad, black and sits in trees?
A raven lunatic!

Who has a parrot that shouts 'pieces of four!'?
Short John Silver!

What do you get if you cross a blood-sucking creature with a pig?
A Hampire!

Did you hear about the smart dog who could read? He came to a lamppost with a notice on it saying "Wet Paint"...
—so he did!

What is a skunk's favourite fairy story?
"Cindersmeller"!

"Darling! I can hear the patter of tiny feet!"
"Are you expecting a baby, my love?"
"No—there are mice in the cellar!"

Ben was worried about Sven. He seemed depressed. Ben decided he would go to the shops to get something nice to cheer Sven up, so he set off, leaving Sven to mope. Not long after Ben left, Sven brightened up.
"I know what I would really like!" he said to himself, "some German sausage! I'll try and catch Ben before he gets to the shops and perhaps we can buy some together."
So, smiling at the thought of biting into a delicious German sausage, Sven put on his coat, and set off up the road after Ben.
For company, he took his pet bird, a tern he had found on the seashore one day.
They went as fast as they could, and pretty soon they caught up with Ben.
"I thought you were too depressed to go out!" said Ben.
"I was," said Sven, "but now I'm taking a tern for the wurst!"

What did one sardine say to the other?
"Hey—we're locked in—and the key's outside!"

Polly joined the army...
she wanted to become a parrot-trooper!

Polly bought a new dress...
she was sick of putting the same old kettle on!

What do you call a brightly coloured bird on a slide?
A parrot-chute!

Fred — "Why is your dog wriggling?"
Ted — "I gave him worm tablets!"

Hickory dickory dock,
Three mice ran up the clock. . .
The clock struck one
—so he was gone. . .
But the other two got away with minor cuts and bruises.

Ted — "So your dog thinks he's funny, does he?"
Fred — "Yes—he's a bit of a wag!"

What do you call an anaesthetized rabbit?
The ether bunny!

What goes "oo! oo! OO!"?
A cow with sore lips!

Someone told Mr Dopey he should try parascending. . .
So he wrapped up Polly, and took her to the post office!

What does a 500lb canary say?
TWEET!

What did one frog say to the other?
"Time's fun when you're having flies!"

What has more lives than a cat?
A frog—it croaks hundreds of times a day!

Why did the chicken go to the railtrack?
To lay it on the line!

Bill — "Why is your cat in disgrace?"
Will — "He took first prize at the bird show!"

How do you make a rabbit glamorous?
Use a little hare spray!

What was the pony's favourite TV programme?
"Little Horse on the Prairie"!

What was the mosquito's favourite TV programme?
"Big Bother!"

Three big ducks stepped on a little duck.
The little duck felt downtrodden!

Maisie — "Why do you call your dog Marge?"
Mo — "I don't have any but her!"

Did you hear about the wolf who ran straight through the mesh fence round the chicken shed?
He strained himself!

Betty — "Your puppy's a dear little thing!"
Bertha — "I'll say—he cost me £500!"

Did you hear about the fly on the cow?
It went in one ear and out the udder!

What do you call a pig with laryngitis?
Disgruntled!

Are there any wild animals in Illinois?
Of course—haven't you heard of the Chicago Bears!

Why do bees have sticky hair?
They use honeycombs!

Why did no-one buy Bambi?
He was a little deer!

What's short and sharp and found in ponds?
A terra-pin!

What do elephants tuck their vests into?
Their elly-pants!

A dog walks into an employment agency.
"I'm looking for a job!" he tells the man.
A talking dog! The man in the employment agency is amazed!
"I'll have no trouble at all finding a smart dog like you a job," he says. "They'll be delighted to take you on at the circus!"
"The circus?" says the dog. "Don't circuses move round from place to place?"
"Yes," says the man, "What's the problem with that?"
"Well, says the dog, "Why would they want a landscape gardener?"

What did the bee give his girlfriend for her birthday?
Bumblebath!

Farmer — "My cow's in love!"
Friend — "How adore-a-bull!"

Farmer — "The bull's stuck in the cow-shed door!"
Farm hand — "So the shed's in-access-a-bull!"

How do you know if a snail has gone off?
Check its shell-by date!

When do skunks stop stinking?
When they're past their smell-by date!

There was no shortage of beer in the bear's cave. . .
—he was always Bruin!

Farmer — "You know, I've had this bull for so long, that I've come to know him very well. I just have to look at him to tell what he's thinking!"
Farm hand — "Understand-a-bull in these circumstances!"

What extreme sport do budgies do?
Budgie-jumping!

What extreme sport do cockatiels take part in?
Parrot-gliding!

What do you get if you cross a car horn with a cat?
A peeping tom!

How did he monkey hear all the jungle gossip?
On the apevine!

What did the termite say when it walked into the pub?
"Is the bar tender here?"!

"Have you ever seen whales canoeing?"
"No—but I've seen cod roe!"

Where do baby frogs come from?
The spawn shop!

Why did the librarian keep looking at her hand?
She was consulting her index finger!

How did Bill get the job at the puppet theatre?
Somebody pulled a few strings on his behalf!

What's the difference between a farmer and a dressmaker?
The farmer gathers what he sows and the dressmaker sews what she gathers!

How did the plumber split up with his girlfriend?
He said "It's over Flo!"

What do you get if you cross a comedian with an electrician?
Shock-a-lot-sauce!

Musician — "Are you familiar with Chopin's works?"
Mr Dim — "No—what do they make there?"

Where does a boxer keep a record of his fights?
In a scrap book!

1st gardener — "Did the storm damage your greenhouse?"
2nd gardener — "Dunno! Haven't found it yet!"

Did you hear about Mr and Mrs Hand and their children?
They were all electricians. Outside their shop was a notice which read like this —
"Many Hands make light work!"

Man in water — "Help! Help! Throw me a lifebelt!"
Tailor — "What size round the waist, sir!"

Will — "How was work today, Fred!"
Fred — "Terrible! The computer system broke down so we all had to do sums and think!"

Lady in butcher's shop — "Do you keep dripping?"
Butcher — "Yes! I'm sorry, but it's terribly hot and sweaty in here!"

Mike — "I was told to do two new things at work today!"
Ike — "What were they?"
Mike — "Get out and stay out!"

How do you say goodbye to a dentist?
"Goodbye for Now-ow-OW!"

Why are boxers like stamps?
If they're well licked, they stay down!

Why did the musician have to get rid of his double bass when he moved?
His new house didn't have a bass-ment!

Mr B. wakes up in the middle of the night, to the sound of crashing and thumping downstairs. He goes down to investigate and finds a man with a scarf tied round his eyes, holding the television in his arms, staggering round the room and bumping into furniture.

"What on earth are you doing?" Mr B. asks.

"Isn't it obvious?" said the man. "I'm robbing you blind!"

1st robber — "It's pitch black in there! Did you remember your torch?"
2nd robber — "No need—I'm light-fingered!"

Why did the golfer have to walk home?
He lost his driver somewhere on the course!

Favourite song of Scottish plumbers — "100 pipers!"

Barber — "I was shaving a customer when my wife rang to tell me she was expecting a baby! . .
—if it's a boy, we're going to call him Little Nick!"

Chauffeur — "I had to give up my last job because my boss and his wife fell out!"
Friend — "What had that got to do with you?"
Chauffeur — "I was driving the car they fell out of!"

**What kind of underwear do runners wear?
Short pants!**

What kind of underwear do railway porters wear?
Trunks!

What kind of underwear do lawyers wear?
Briefs!

**What kind of underwear do philosophers wear?
Why-fronts!**

"I entered a doughnut competition today. I got to the final, but the other man won.
—I guess he just got the batter of me!"

What is a doctor's least favourite musical?
"Saturday Night Fever"!

Builder — "This house is going to be a bit draughty!"
Workman — "Why?"
Builder — "We're building it with breeze blocks!"

Why is the pen mightier than the sword?
Because no-one has invented a ballpoint sword!

Where did the sandwich maker go on holiday?
New Delhi!

**What has twenty two feet and wings?
A football team!**

Why is a teacher like a racing driver?
Because they both like to keep a strong position at the front!

Why was the army quartermaster sacked?
He couldn't make a rational decision!

**Why did the mad woman marry a horse breeder?
He was a stable-izing influence!**

What did the light technician do when his girlfriend smiled at him?
He beamed right back at her!

The gardener kept all his tools in a shed, carefully cleaned and sharpened ready for use. He loved his tools, Hoe, Spade, Rake and Trowel, and he talked to them just as he talked to his flowers. In the shed. beside the tools, the gardener kept an assortment of garden twines — green for the green climbing shoots, brown for the twigs, blue for blue flowers. . .—and for special occasions, he had even once bought a ball of silver garden string.
One day, remembering that his wife's birthday was drawing near, he decided to make her a special bouquet, and tie it with silver twine. But he couldn't remember whether there was any left. "I know," he said, "I'll go and ask the tools if there is any in the shed." So he trotted to the foot of the garden, opened the shed door, and sang out —
"Hi, Hoe! Silver Twine in?"

**How do you fool a weaver?
Spin him a yarn!**

Why did the minister walk into church on his hands?
It was Palm Sunday!

Rock-a-bye baby, on the treetop. . .
Dad promises your bedroom will be finished by Friday!

Business tycoon — "Young man, do you know the way to succeed?"
Little boy — "Nope! You'll have to ask a policeman!"

Bob — "My sister Claire went to a fancy dress party covered in chocolate sauce!"
Bert — "Why?"
Bob — "She was a chocolatey Claire!"

Bobby — "Mum! The other kids keep calling me bighead!"
Mum — "Don't worry, son, I'm sure there's nothing in it!"

The new gardener's assistant was pretty slow, but at last they found the perfect job for him. . .
—chasing snails off the flower beds!

"Ding-dong"
"Darling, I've just been to answer the door. There's a terrible smell out there, but I can't see anyone!"
"Must be the gas man, dear!"

Will — "My uncle's a lumberjack!"
Bill — "Do you like him?"
Will — "Oh, yes—he's a fine feller!"

"Why were you disqualified from the walking race last year?"
"I won it two years running!"

"But why did they disqualify you this year?"
"I won it for the third time on the trot!"

How do you become a university professor?
You do it by degrees!

Why did Annie not want to throw a ball at the fair?
She was coconut shy!

Why do gardeners fence off their vegetable plots?
In case the cabbage leaves!

What do actors have for breakfast?
Coco-Props!

Why did the weatherman take his moneybox outside?
He was expecting some change in the weather!

What does a campanologist do when he's worried?
He wrings his hands!

Did you hear about the campanologist who murdered his wife?
He wrung her neck!

Did you hear about the kindly judge?
He refused to hang the wallpaper without a fair trial!

Office manager — "Why were you off work last week, Smith?"
Smith — "I had my appendix taken out, sir!"
Manager — "Well, see it doesn't happen again!"

Become a wig-maker!
It's a million-hair lifestyle!

What was the hairdresser's favourite bedtime story?
"Ali Barber"!

What was the photographer's favourite bedtime story?
"The Little Prints"!

Do chemists take their dogs for walks?
No—they just exercise them in a compound!

What do body builders like to eat?
Mussels!

What does the minister water his vegetable patch with?
Lettuce spray!

What does the invisible man drink?
Evaporated milk!

Burglar (to his wife) — "I've brought you some hot chocolate, dear!"
Wife — "Don't tell me— you broke into the sweet shop again!"

What do gardeners do on Sunday afternoons?
They relax with the Sunday peppers!

Why is a banker like a cowboy?
Because a banker is a Loan-Arranger!

Why did the butcher put his knives in the
fridge?
His customer wanted cold cuts!

How do you become a ballet dancer?
One step at a time!

Jim — "And do you work full-time as an
undertaker?"
Joe — "No—I only work mournings!"

Betty — "And does being a teacher make you
feel special?"
Netty — "Oh yes—I'm in a class of my
own!"

Why do singers hate camping?
They can never find the perfect pitch!

Why is a betting shop owner like a
librarian?
They're both book-keepers!

How can you recognise a mathematician's
garden?
It's full of square roots!

Why did the novelist go mad?
He lost the plot!

Mo — "I used to be a sandwich maker, you
know!"
Maisie — "Why did you have to give it
up?"
Mo — "I didn't cut the mustard!"

Maisie — "I've been working in the sandwich
business for five years, and I haven't had a
pay rise yet!"
Mo — "You'll have to butter up the boss!"

A— "My father works in the church;—he's a
canon!"
B — "Why, you old son-of-a-gun!"

Will — "I hope this rain keeps up!"
Bill — "Why?"
Will — "Because I don't want it to fall
down!"

Prisoner — "I sneezed and the man in the
house woke up!"
Lawyer — "So you were caught red-
handed?"
Prisoner — "No—red-nosed!"

Annie — "Have you seen my blue shoes?"
Betty — "Are you sure you had them on
when you took them off?"

Maisie — "That self-lighting stove works
beautifully!"
Mo — "Does it?"
Maisie — "Yes—I set light to myself the
first time I used it!"

"My daughter was born while I was painting
a wall. . .
so we called her Muriel!

Convict — "Warder! There's nothing on my
bread!"
Warder — "Then stick it in the door and
jam it!"

What's the difference between a gorilla and
a biscuit?
You can't dip a gorilla in your tea!

What did the artist say to his wife?
"Darling, you look a picture!"

"When my son was born our house was
burgled. . .
—so we called him Robin!"

Bill — "I got a Christmas parcel full of
salt, pepper and spices yesterday!"
Will — "What did the card inside say?"
Bill — "Seasonings Greetings!"

Bill — "And inside the pepper pot was
another note!
Will — "What did it say?"
Bill — "Sneezin's greetings!"

Bill —"And the next day I got another parcel,
full of tiny bits of cheese!"
Will — "And what did the note say this
time?"
Bill — "Season's Gratings!"

Bill — "What's roulette?"
Will — "It's a thing you roll under your
arms every day to make you smell nice!"

Little Jack Horner sat in a corner. . .
The rest of the family had taken all the chairs.

Mum — *"Do you want some meat, Minnie?"*
Minnie — *"Oh, yes!"*
Mum — *"Potatoes?"*
Minnie — *"Yes!"*
Mum — *"Peas?"*
Minnie — *"Yes!"*
Mum — *"What's that other little word, dear?"*
Minnie — *"Gravy!"*

Professor Potty's daughter — "I've just come to say goodnight, Daddy!"
Professor Potty — "It'll have to wait till the morning, dear. I'm very busy just now!"

Sailor — "My bed was made in the last war, and it's eight feet long!"
Friend — "What a lot of old bunk!"

There was an old woman tossed up in a basket
Seventy times as high as the moon. . .
"Oh help!" she said. "I think I've left the iron on!"

English football supporter (to small boy) — "So you're a Scotland fan, are you? Why is that?"
Little boy — "Because my mum and Dad are Scotland fans!"
England fan (nastily) — "If your Mum and dad were both idiots, what would that make you then?"
Little boy — "That would make me an England fan!"

Photographer — "Do you want a large photo or a small one?"
Client — "Just a small one!"
Photographer — "Then keep your mouth shut!"

Man (to little boy in the street) — "Can you tell me the way to the bank?"
Little boy — "I'll tell you for £5!"
Man — "What a cheek! Who do you think you are?"
Little boy — "A bank director!"

Little Miss Muffet sat on a tuffet. . .
—Her sofa was being re-upholstered.

"Goosey, Goosey Gander, whither do you wander?"
"Not very far," she said. "There's a great big fence round the farmyard!"

What did one bookworm say to the other bookworm?
"Can I have a little word with you?"

Why did the footballer shoot himself?
Because there was no-one to pass the ball to!

Little girl at swimming pool — "I'm going to swim a whole length today. . .
—even if it takes me a week to do it!"

Convict — "I hope it's not porridge and milk for breakfast again!"
Warder — "You're in luck! It isn't!"
Convict — "What is it then?"
Warder — "Just porridge!"

Actor — "When I was performing in 'King Lear', crowds stormed the box-office every day!"
Friend — "To get their money back?"

"Who's that man in a microlite buzzing round Sir Lancelot's head?"
"Just some fly-by-knight character!"

"I fell off a twenty-foot wall yesterday!"
"Didn't it hurt, falling all that distance?"
"The falling didn't hurt at all—but the landing was terribly painful!"

Billy (to friend in swimming in sea) "Is the water very cold today, Bobby?"
Bobby — "Freezing! I wouldn't have come in swimming, but my Dad told me not to!"

Optician — "You have very small pupils, Miss Brown!"
Miss Brown — "Yes—I'm a kindergarten teacher!"

Optician — "But your irises are a beautiful colour of blue!"
Miss Brown — "Thank you! They won a prize at the flower show last week!"

"Why did your parents call you Nicholas? Were you born at Christmas?"
Nicholas — "No—I was born without any underwear!"

Little boy (to man who has just hauled him out of the river) — "Thanks, mister! My mum would have killed me if I had drowned!"

Billy — *"Dad, I've got something to tell you!"*
Dad — *"Spit it out, then!"*
Billy — *"I wish I could! I've just swallowed a £1 coin!"*

Office manager — "That new cleaner is very quiet!"
Director — "I know—he doesn't even disturb the dust!"

Did you hear about the inflatable man? His inflatable girlfriend let him down!

How did the high-jumper feel when his girlfriend dumped him?
He was over her in no time!

When is a question like a fishing net?
When there's a catch in it!

"Pussy cat, Pussy cat, where have you been?"
"Good grief," thought the cat, "I'm seventeen years old and they still don't trust me!""

Boss (on telephone to employee) — "I'd like to see you in my office now!"
Employee — "I'm afraid that's impossible, sir—I'm downstairs in my own office at the moment!"

Boss (on telephone to employee) — "Come and see me in my office, Jones!"
Jones — "Why, sir?"
Boss — "Because I look very grand in these surroundings!"

1st cowboy — "Is Texas Pete around here?"
2nd cowboy — "Nope!"
1st cowboy — "But I heard tell he lived within shooting distance of you!"
2nd cowboy — "Yep! That's why he ain't here no more!"

"There was a terrible rainstorm the night our son was born. . .
—so we called him Mac!"

Will and Bill are out in a rowing boat in the middle of the lake.
Will — "Look, Bill! The boat's full of water! What will we do?"
Bill — "Let's drill a hole in the bottom to let it out!"

What did one tent say to the other tent? "Let's spend the weekend with the guys!"

Mary had a little lamb. . .
—then a big yellow dog came and ate it all up.

Annie — "Where are my glasses?"
Betty — "On your head!"
Annie — "Thank goodness for that! If you hadn't told me where they were, I might have gone off without them!"

Batty Betty — "I lost two stones last week. . .
—they must have fallen out of my handbag!"

What's a textbook?
A book that tells you how to send messages on your mobile phone!

Why did the ballerina go to the pub?
To do her exercises at the bar!

Have you heard the old song about mobile phones?. . .
"Ring-tone, ring-tone, ring-tone, ring-tone, ring-tone tiddle-I-po!"

Why is an electrician like a gymnast?
He can manage high volts!

Hey, diddle diddle, the cat and the fiddle. . . were left behind when the family moved to America.

Will — "My old mother has offered her body to medical research, but they don't want it!"
Bill — "Why not?"
Will — "After all the operations she's had, there won't enough left to look at!"

Charlie the comedian doesn't need to take his pills in water.
He tells them a joke and they dissolve into laughter!

Man at boating pond — "Come in number 99—your time is up!"
Assistant — "There is no number 99!"
Man — "Oh? Right then. . .Are you in trouble out there, number 66?"

Man at baseball game — "Strike One! Strike Two! Str. . .
—Oops! Run out of matches!"

"This egg is unusual!"
"Yes—it's an egg-centric!"

Will — "See this cut? The stitches have to stay in for five days!"
Bill — "That's nothing! Hear this joke and you'll be in stitches for a fortnight!"

"My uncle's a basketball player. . .
—he's a dodgy character!"

Son (doing homework) — "Dad! Where are the Appalachians?"
Dad — "I don't know, son—try the drawer in the sideboard!"

"What's thirty two thousand dollars plus two thousand dollars plus ten thousand dollars, plus twenty thousand dollars?"
"Ah! The sixty-four thousand dollar question!"

Football manager — "We'll have to buy some new players this season!"
Coach — "How about a sweeper?"
Manager — "Maybe—but we'll need a new dustbin to match!"

Why did the psychiatrist keep his wife under the bed?
She was a little potty!

Lady in butcher's shop — "Do you have chicken legs?"
Butcher — "Yes—but I have a lovely personality!"

Little boy — "Our family car journeys are very quiet. . .
—Mum makes us belt up in the back!"

Why did the farmer open a betting shop in his field?
So the lambs could gambol to their hearts' content!

"That's a curious pen!"
"Yes! It's a Nosey Parker!"

A man walks into the cafe across the road from the hospital. He's obviously a patient—he's wearing pyjamas and a dressing gown, and he's wheeling a drip on a stand beside him. He orders coke, pizza, salad, beans, chips, and for afters, ice cream and chocolate sauce. The waitress brings him his order and he says, "You know, I shouldn't be eating all this with what I've got!"
"What have you got?" asks the waitress.
"15 pence!" says the man.

"That weevil is very small compared to the one beside it!"
"Yes—it's the lesser of two weevils!"

"Where do weevils come from?"
"The root of all weevils!"

"I've heard of him! He was a French painter, wasn't he?"
"That's right. . .
Monet is the root of all weevils!"

What do you call a very selfish girl?
Mimi!

A man is standing at a bus stop beside a teenage boy. Suddenly the man notices a half-eaten sandwich discarded on the pavement at the boy's feet.
"Is that yours?" he asks the boy sternly.
"No—you saw it first," says the boy politely, "you have it!"

Builder — "I can't work out how much cement we'll need for this job!"
Friend — "Why not?"
Builder — "It's just too hard!"

Mr Dopey managed to make a cake yesterday. It didn't look too bad. . .
—until he put it in the freezer to ice it!

Did you hear about the lighthouse keeper who joined the orchestra?
He played the foghorn!

Customer — "This painting's a fake!"
Art dealer — "Not exactly, sir—it's an authentic replica!"

Mo — "Why is there one shoe in the fridge?"
Maisie — "I couldn't find the other one!"

What goes up and never comes down?
Your age!

Will — *"Why are you wearing a wig?"*
Bill — *"I'm travelling under an assumed mane!"*

Mo — "I went camping on a steeply sloping mountainside last week!"
Maisie — "Did you like it?"
Mo — "Not really—I was inclined to regret it!"

"I'll be back very late tonight, Darling!"
"Righto, sweetheart! But remember to wake me as soon as you get in—you know I can't sleep a wink if you're not there!"

Alice — *"One of my children wants to be a nun!"*
Anne — *"What did you have to say about that?"*
Alice — *"I told him I didn't think he was the right sort of person!"*

How do you recognize a dogwood tree?
by its bark!

Why could the bicycle not stand up by itself?
It was two-tyred!

Mother — *"I've run a lovely warm bath for you!"*
Grubby little boy — *"It's okay—you can have it!"*

Dopey and Dim shared a house. One day, they went out and bought two kittens to have as pets. In order to tell which one was Dopey's and which one was Dim's, they tied a blue ribbon round the neck of Dim's kitten. But they got up the next day and the ribbon had come off.
"What will we do?" said Dopey. "How will we tell which one is yours and which one is mine?"
"I tell you what," said Dim. "You have the black one, and I'll have the white one!"

What moisturiser did the matador use?
Oil of Olé!

If you get H2O inside a fire hydrant, what do you get outside?
K9P!

Stallholder at market — "Interested in cheap pirate videos?"
Woman — "No thanks! I didn't think much of 'Treasure Island'! "

What's the difference between a hunter and a fisherman?
A hunter lies in wait and a fisherman waits and lies!

Bald man — *"I don't know what to do with my money after I die. . .*
—I've got no surviving hairs!"

Fred — "Which hand do you use to eat your soup?"
Ted — "Neither—I use a spoon!"

How do you confuse a mathematician?
Ask him, "Is the square around here?"!

A (to B and C) — *"You two look very alike—are you twins?"*
B — *"I don't know about him, but I'm not!"*

Miser(on ferry) — "How can I stop myself being seasick?"
Friend — "Easy! Hang your head over the side and hold a £1 coin between your teeth!"

A — "I collect stamps!"
B — "I collect coins!"
C — "I collect my old-age pension!"

What do you call a pheasant with blonde feathers?
Fair game!

What happened to Mary Poppins?
She retired from her job as a nanny and went to California, where she became famous for her skills as a fortune teller. She did not use a crystal ball, nor did she read palms or tarot cards. Instead, she could tell a person's future simply by smelling their breath. The sign outside her house read like this —
"Super California Mystic Expert Halitosis"!

Will — "I'd like to be buried at sea!"
Bill — "Well, don't expect me to dig the grave!"

How do you stop a runaway tank?
Give it a tank-uillizer!

Prisoner — "Thirty years in prison? I'll never live to serve it!"
Judge — "Never mind; just do as much as you can!"

The monastery had an open day. Visitors were given a tour of the premises and then treated to a slap-up meal of fish and chips. The fish was so delightful that one visitor wanted to compliment the cook personally, so she went into the kitchens. "Excuse me," she said to the first man she met, "are you the fish friar?" "No," the man replied, "I'm the chip monk!"

Will — "I've just been to Greece!"
Bill — "How did you find it there?"
Will — "Same way as we do here—there's a little picture of a man on the door!"

Man looking at painting — "You say this is a painting to represent the saying 'Life is a bowl of cherries'?
Artist — "That's right!"
Man — "So what's that black thing in the middle?
Artist — "That's my raisin for living!"

Ringmaster — "We used to have a human cannonball at this circus."
Visitor — "Really?"
Ringmaster — "Yes—but he was no good, so we got shot of him pretty quickly."

Ringmaster — "I remember the human cannonball we had in the circus when I was a child. He was unbeatable!"
Visitor — "Can't you find another one who is just as good?"
Ringmaster — "No—we'll never find one of the same calibre!"

Maisie — "I never give away a secret. . . I just exchange it for another one!"

Did you hear about the identical twins, Juan and Amahl?
Once you've seen Juan, you've seen Amahl!

Will — "My shoes need to be soled!"
Bill — "Nobody would want to buy them!"

What do you get if you cross a minister and an athlete?
A holy sweater!

1st scientist — "Oh, look! I've split the atom!"
2nd scientist — "Glue's on the top shelf!"

Will — "I know the real meaning of dismay!"
Bill — "What's that then?"
Will — "I went to the doctor's to get a tetanus shot, and he said to me, 'Dis may hurt a bit!' "

"Back in a minute!"
"Don't be long!"
"Can't be—I'm only 5ft!"

Little boy to baby — "it's a waste of time learning to speak. As soon as you can do it, they'll start telling you to shut up!"

What's the name of the world's fattest puppet?
Mr Paunch!

Bill — "Busy day, Ted?"
Ted — "Oh, yes! I washed the kitchen floor, scrubbed the front step, washed the dishes and wiped them dry!"
Bill — "Anything else?"
Ted — "Oh, yes! I polished off the biscuits in the cupboard!"

Singer — "I performed in the town hall last night!"
Friend — "Did the audience clap?"
Singer — "He clapped his hands over my mouth!"

Comedian — I performed at the policeman's ball last night!"
Friend — "Did the audience clap?"
Comedian — "Yes—they clapped me in handcuffs!"

Fred — "That's a nasty cut! Did you have to get stitches?"
Ted — "Stitches? Why, the doctor had to send out for a sewing machine!"

Friend — "So how did you know the guide was lying when he told you the mountain wasn't steep?"
Climber — "I tumbled to the truth!"

Something to think about —
Can a short-sighted woman have a faraway
look in her eyes?

Why did Dr Who go to Wales?
To see the Dai-leks!

Bill — "Why did you give me that nasty
look?"
Will — "I didn't give it to you—you were
born with it!"

How would you describe an old, bald bear?
Over the hill and fur away!

Office manager — "You need to be pushy to
get into this office!"
Friend — "Why?"
Office manager — "Because the door's really
heavy!"

A man rushes onto a plane and screams
"Hijack!"
"Hi, Bill!" says the steward. "Take a seat!"

Why did the cowboy go skydiving?
For a chute out!

Fred — "Keep your eyes peeled!"
Ted — "What do you think I am—a potato?"

A man is lying on the road, dazed. He's just
been knocked down by a bus. He hears a
voice above him
"Don't worry sir, I'll look after you—I'm a
professional!"
"Doctor?" asks the man.
"No," the voice replies, "undertaker!"

A man walks into a bar and orders a drink.
While he's waiting he nibbles on some
peanuts that are sitting in a dish on the bar.
But every time he puts a peanut to his mouth,
he hears voices. . .
— "You're looking very nice sir!"
— "Love the jacket!"
— "Blue suits you very well!"
"Is it my imagination," he asks the barman,
"or are these peanuts talking to me?"
"They are indeed, sir," says the barman.
"The peanuts are complimentary here!"

Where can you find a three-footed police
officer?
Scotland Yard!

How do you get Mr Dopey in a twist?
Ask him to stand on his head!

Old man — "It's tough being old and bent!"
Young man — "Not as tough as being young
and broke!"

1st neighbour — "My cat just fell down your
wishing well!"
2nd neighbour — "It works! It works!"

How can you land a jumbo jet on water?
Easy—it's plane sailing!

Mike — "My dad invented a way of telling
people's futures!"
Ike — "Did it work?"
Mike — "Yes—he made a fortune!"

Banker — "And do you have any other liquid
assets, Mr Jones?"
Mr Jones — "I've got a couple of cans of
beer in the cupboard at home!"

Fred — "That's a nice new scarf!"
Ted — "You have it—it's too tight
for me!"

Customer — "These tights you sold me have
ladders in them!"
Assistant — "What do you expect at that
price? A marble staircase?"

Driving pupil — "Good grief! There's a man
lying in the middle of the road in front of us!"
Instructor — "I know! You just reversed over
him!"

Maisie — "I tried becoming a nudist, but it
wasn't for me."
Mo — "Why not?"
Maisie — "It just left me cold!"

Why did the actor travel to the Wild West?
To hire a stagecoach!

Billy — "Dad got a new book on woodwork
and it helped him fix our wobbly table!"
Bobby — "Was it easy to understand?"
Billy — "Oh, he didn't read it—he put it
under one of the table legs!"

Ike — "I tried bareback riding once too!
Mike — "What happened?"
Ike — "I fell off the bear!"

Mike — *"I once tried bareback riding!"*
Ike — *"Did you like it?"*
Mike — *"Well, the clothes didn't half suit me!"*

Billy — "Mum! There's a man outside from the optician's. He's brought your new glasses!"
Mum — "Tell him I can't see him yet!"

**One morning, a man gets on the bus and puts some bacon, eggs, toast and butter on one of the seats. Then he sits down on it.
"What are you doing that for?" asks the driver.
"My mother told me to go to work on a good breakfast!" answers the man.**

Barty the Bore — "I walked all the way across America and I kept myself going on tins of soup!
Friend — "It might have been easier if you had worn shoes!"

A man walks into a fortune teller's and sits down on a pack of tarot cards that have been left on the chair.
"Before we start," says the woman, "I can tell you are sitting on a fortune!"

**Barty the Bore — "I once swam the English Channel!"
Friend — "I tried that once too, but I got tired 100 metres from the other side and had to swim back!"**

Mo — "I'd love a three-piece suite!"
Maisie — "Here—break up this humbug!"

What did one mind-reader say to the other mind-reader?
"Hello! How am I?"

**"Wow! Where did you learn to swim like that?"
"In the water!"**

A woman walks up to an ice cream stand in the park.
"Ice cream?" says the man at the counter.
"Yes please," says the woman.
"Hundreds and thousands?" asks the man at the counter.
"No, thanks," says the woman, "just the one!"

Did you hear about the boy who broke into a fireworks factory?
The police let him off!

**And what about the boy who stole a car battery?
The police charged him!**

And what about the boy who stole an amber traffic light?
He got off with a caution!

A little boy had been warned before church that he wasn't to say anything about the vicar's rather large and very red nose.
The family went to church and sure enough, there was the vicar, his nose beaming a bright welcome to all who came in at the door. Just as the family passed through the door, the little boy announced to his mother
"It's all right, Mum, I'm not going to say anything. . . I'm just going to have a good look!"

**"My sister speaks through her nose!"
"Why?"
"Because she's worn her mouth out!"**

"My sister is always out of breath!"
"Why?"
"Her tongue keeps running ahead of her!"

What did Mr Spock say when he fancied a fight?
"Beat me up, Scottie!"

**"Darling, what did you do before you met me?"
"Anything I wanted!"**

How do jelly babies keep their feet dry?
Gum boots!

A man is in a wine shop, studying a bottle of white wine on the shelf. The assistant tries to make polite conversation.
"Looks like rain, sir!"
"So it does," says the man. "I think I'll have a bottle of red wine instead!"

**Manager of shop — "Any orders while I was out?"
Assistant — "Yes! I was ordered to put my hands up and tell them the safe combination!"**

Bob — "Why do you call your dog Buttons?"
Betty — "Because you often see him attached to trousers!"

A dog walks into a telegraph office in New York and asks if he can send a telegraph to a friend in Texas.
"What do you want to say?" asks the woman at the desk.
"Bow-wow, bow-wow, bow-wow-wow!" says the dog.
"You can add another 'bow-wow' and it won't cost any more," says the lady behind the desk.
"Maybe," says the dog, "but it sounds kind of stupid!"

What do you call a man who lets you off a parking offence?
A terrific warden!

Mo and Fred went out in a boat. They started having a heated discussion. Then they began arguing.
—Then they fell out!

Mum — "I've just had a letter from your aunt!"
Son — "But she only lives next door—why did she write you a letter?"
Mum —"We're not on speaking terms!"

Lady (in electrical goods store) — "But this fridge is tiny! Whatever could I keep in a fridge this size?"
Assistant — "Condensed milk and nibbles!"

Man in bank — "This is a muck-up!"
Cashier — "A stick-up?"
Man — "No—a muck-up! I forgot my gun!"

Friend — "Why did you become a professional golfer?"
Golfer — "To earn my bread and putter!"

Maisie — "I share a comb with my sister!"
Mo — "Do you?"
Maisie — "Yes—it's partly mine!"

A man runs into a bank holding a twig aloft.
"This is a stick-up!" he cries.
"So what?" says the cashier, dumping an enormous log on the desk in front of her.
"This is a major branch!"

Fred — "I go to work almost every day!"
Ted — "How many days did you work last week?"
Fred — "None—but I almost went five days!"

Why did the chicken jump into the cement mixer?
It wanted to become a bricklayer!

Did you hear about the man whose job was stringing tennis rackets?
He needed a lot of guts for his work!

Will — "Our local team has a new coach!"
Bill — "How many seats?"

What's the difference between an useless soccer team and a tea-bag?
The tea-bag stays longer in the cup!

What toy hates to be touched?
Lego!

Maisie calls round to Mo's house one night and finds her all dressed up.
"Going out?" she asks.
"Yes!" said Mo. "Almost ready now!"
And she goes into the kitchen and takes a steaming little brown thing out of the microwave.
"What's that?" asks Maisie.
"Oh—" says Mo. "That's my hot date!"

Farmer — "We once had a cockerel called Robinson!"
Friend — "Why did you call him that?
Farmer — "Because he crew so!"

Billy (in French restaurant) — "Mum! Can I have frogs' legs?"
Mum — "No, dear. You're stuck with the ones you were born with!"

Dave had a date with a new girl, Rosie. She was bringing along her friend Evelyn and he was taking along his friend Sam. He really hoped the evening would be a success, and that he would be able to impress Rosie.
When he got home later that night, his mother asked him how he got on.
"Not too good," he said. "I don't think Rosie likes me much. Still, the evening wasn't a disaster for all of us—
Sam enchanted Evelyn!"

Bill — "I got a surprise package from my mother today!"
Will — "What was in it?"
Bill — "Nothing—that was the surprise!"

Fred — "You been eating cake again?"
Ted — "No—why?"
Fred — "You look crummy!"

Why is the truth like an old bell?
Because it's rarely tolled!

What did one snooker ball say to the other?
Get to the end of the cue!

When is a ship not a ship?
When it's a dot on the horizon!

Why did Moses never win any races?
Because God told him to come forth!

Passenger (to bus conductor) — "I'm sorry, but my dog has just eaten my bus ticket!"
Conductor — "Then you'll just have to buy him a second helping!"

A painter was once asked to paint the windows on the local church, and to save money he thinned the paint with water to make it go further. The job looked all right at first, but the night after it was finished, the rain came, and washed off most of the paint. When the painter got up the next morning, there was a note from the vicar pinned to his door.
"Repaint and thin no more!"

How do you make a paper tissue dance?
Blow a boogie into it!

How do you hold a party in outer space?
You planet!

How did the duck meet a new partner?
Through an intro-duck-tion agency!

Billy — "Bobby! There's two feet of ice at the far end of the village pond!"
Bobby — "So what? I have two feet of ice at the end of my legs!"

Boxer — "How do I look, dear?"
Wife — "Stunning!"

Did you hear about the explosives expert who got a job at the football stadium?
He blew up all the balls!

Lady visiting zoo — "Now, Mr Keeper, what can you tell me about the parrots?"
Keeper — "The parrots? They speak for themselves, madam!"

Why were the soldiers tired on April 1st?
They were at the end of a thirty-one day March!

Why did the apple fall off the tree?
Because it was careless!

Plumber (on doorstep) — "Here we are, bang on time, with all our tools, at the ready. . ."
Householder — "—and at the wrong house!"

How do you distract a golfer?
Putt him off his game!

Old Granny Dopey's getting hard of hearing. She went out to play bingo for the first time last night. After a few minutes, she thought she was getting the hang of it, when someone suddenly shouted "HOUSE!"
Granny screamed and stood on a chair!

Actor — "After my performance of 'Macbeth', the audience took half an hour to leave the theatre!"
Friend — "Why? Was he lame?"

When can you hear a pin drop twenty yards away?
When it's a rolling pin!

Al — "My mother hasn't seen sight of my face for ten years!"
Hal — "Perhaps you should shave off your beard then!"

Mrs A — "How can I stop my husband from singing in the bath?"
Mrs B — "Have the bath taken out!"

Mum — "Butter cheese AND jam in your sandwich, Jimmy? Isn't that a bit greedy?"
Jimmy — "Not really—I'm saving bread!"

Why is the ticket collector on the train cruel?
Because he punches the tickets!

Old woman — "I've been cooking Christmas dinner for the family for twenty years now!"
Friend — "Good grief, the turkey won't half be tough!"

Prisoner — "Before you sentence me, judge, I think you should know that before I committed this crime, I had been out of trouble for twenty-five years!"
Judge — "Twenty five years, eh? Where did you spend these twenty-five years?"
Prisoner — "In prison, your honour!"

A — "It's funny, but I get dizzy whenever I take myself for a walk!"
B — "You've got to get out of this lighthouse, you know!"

Shopkeeper — "This £10 note doesn't look right!"
Customer — "That's exactly what I said to the man who made it for me!"

Will — "Do you know Lanky Larry?"
Bill — "No. Do you know Fat Burns?"
Will — "No."
Bill — "Well, it does!"

When is a singer like a burglar?
When he breaks into song!

How do you get revenge on a boring speaker?
Make him swallow his words!

Fred — "I always take a handkerchief with me to the golf course."
Ted — "Why?"
Fred — "In case I get a bogey!"

Mary had a little lamb;
The doctor was surprised. . .
When Old Macdonald had a farm
The doctor nearly died!

Did you hear about the jockey who took up golf?
He won the Ryder cup!

Why is Popeye so healthy?
He does all his cooking with Olive Oyl!

What do you call a cowboy who treats his girlfriends badly?
Billy the Cad!

There were once four boys who grew up as friends, but also as competitors. Whatever they did—schoolwork, sport or hobbies, each one tried to be better than all the rest. The boys grew up and became men, and the rivalry continued. Even when they were old and grey, they competed fiercely at cards, dominoes, and hobbling along the road as fast as they could to the shops. Then one of them died. The other three put on their smartest clothes for the funeral, and stood at the graveside watching their friend's coffin being lowered into the ground. Then they noticed the gravestone, standing nearby, waiting to be put on the grave. Peering through tired old eyes, they could just make out the inscription that was on it. . .
— "BEAT YOU!"

Wife — "I know the doctor said you weren't allowed to drink alcohol, but I've put something in your orange juice to make it a little bit special tonight?"
Husband (rubbing his hands together in delight) — "Oh, goodie! What is it?"
Wife — "An ice cube!"

Did you hear about the mathematician who had a brick dropped on his head?
He was out for the count!

A man walked into a library and cut off the foot of one of his trouser legs and handed it to the librarian.
"Here's a turn-up for the books," he said!

Wife — "You should try working on the railway!"
Husband — "Why?"
Wife — "Because you're such a sound sleeper!"

A woman is walking down the street when she comes across a man standing on a corner wearing an anorak. Whenever someone passes him, the hood of his anorak starts jiggling up and down, and the passer-by throws a coin in it.
"Whatever have you got there?" asks the lady.
"Oh," says the man, "it's my livelihood!"

What is the most talkative creature in the world?
The yak!

Why was the archeologist miserable?
His career lay in ruins before him!

Trainer (to boxer, after fight) — "Looks bad!
I'd better get you something for it!"
Boxer — "What can you get me?"
Trainer — "A new passport photograph for
starters!"

**Fred — "There's a price on your head, you
know!"**
Ted — "Why? What have I done?"
**Fred — "Forgotten to take the label off
your new hat!"**

Who invented curtains?
Sir Francis Drape!

Why did the wig go crazy?
Because it was off its head!

**Did you hear about the Lord Mayor's busy
day?**
**He opened a new bank, a new hospital, a
garden fete and an extension to the town
hall.**
**Then he went home and opened a tin of
beans for his supper!**

*What do you get if you cross a cowboy and a
banana skin?*
Billy the Skid!

Who whipped Russia into shape?
Beater the Great!

**A man comes back to his car to find a note
saying 'Parking Fine' stuck to his
windscreen. Before he drives away, he
writes a little note and sticks it to a nearby
lamppost
"Thanks for the compliment!"**

*Electrician — "Hold these two wires for me,
will you?"*
Assistant — "These two?"
*Electrician — "That's right! Now, do you feel
anything?"*
Assistant — "No!"
*Electrician — "Good. Now whatever you do,
don't touch the other two or you'll get a nasty
shock!"*

Fred — "People think I'm quite a comedian!"
Ted — "You're joking!"

**Boring Barnaby — "I have a fine family
tree, you know!"**
Nasty Nick — "Yes—and you're the sap!"

*What's black and slow-moving and appears
on stage at Christmas time?*
A pantomime hearse!

How do golfers stave off hunger on the golf
course?
They take a sand wedge with them!

**Boring Barnaby — "I throw myself
wholeheartedly into everything I do!"**
**Nasty Nick — "How about digging an
enormous hole?"!**

*A woman parks her car on a double yellow
line and goes into a nearby shop. When she
comes out, a traffic warden is standing by her
car.*
"Parking fine here for you!" he says.
*"I'm glad it is," replies the old lady, "but
where are other people allowed to park?"*

1st watch — "You're a bit slow!
2nd watch — "Look who's tocking!"

**You can't win if you play cards with a
cornet player. . .**
You play any card and he'll trumpet!

How did Ghengis Khan get fit?
He ran up and down the Steppes!

Mo — "I've lost a packet of sponge fingers!"
Maisie — "Don't worry about trifling things
like that!"

**Actor — "I appeared at the Globe last
week!"**
Friend — "What in?"
Actor — "Row G seat 32!"

Actor — "I was on the telly last night!"
Friend — "Really?"
*Actor — "Yes—I stood on it to change a
lightbulb in the lounge!"*

Did you hear about the very neat
mathematician?
He made a tidy sum!

Why did the man give up Sumo wrestling?
He didn't have the stomach for it!

A farmer walked into library and handed a large vegetable to the librarian.
"Here's a turnip for the books," he said!

Singer — "I slipped a disc at EMI last week!"
Friend — "Don't you mean 'cut a disc?' "
Singer — "No—I tripped coming out of the lift!"

The Lone Ranger rode into town with Tonto. They had been out in the desert all day and the horses were sweating.
"Tell you what," said the Lone Ranger, "You run round the horses flapping your blanket to cool them down, and I'll go into the saloon for a quick drink. Then we'll swap over."
So Tonto got out his blanket and started trotting round the horses, flapping the blanket to cool them down. The Lone Ranger went into the saloon and ordered a beer. He drank it down in no time.
"Another?" said the bar tender.
"No thanks," said the Lone Ranger. "I'm in a hurry. I've left my injun runnin'!"

Bill — "Basher Bloggs is such a colourful fighter!"
Will — "Yes—he's black and blue all over!"

How can a good boxer help a bad boxer?
He can show him the ropes!

What did one boxer say to the other before he punched him?
"Sleep well!"

What do teddy bears have for breakfast?
Teddy Brek!

Bill — "The first time I met your puppy, he bit my toes. . .then he got a bit bigger, and he bit my ankles. . . He's still getting bigger, and today he bit my leg! What have you got to say about it?"
Will — "You'd better wear thick underwear the next time you come!"

Captain — "Hard-a-port!"
Elderly passenger — "Did you? What did it sound like?"

How did Gulliver get to know the people of Lilliput?
Little by little!

Motorist — "Why have you stopped me, officer?"
Police officer — "You were driving at 95 miles an hour!"
Motorist — "Impossible! I only left home five minutes ago!"

How does a dentist learn to drill teeth?
Bit by bit!

What do dentists do when they go on holiday?
They get someone to fill in for them while they're away!

What do opticians eat for breakfast?
Ready-Spec!

Why is Great Britain so wet?
Because it has a reigning monarch!

Did you hear about the kindly mathematician?
He gave a generous sum to charity!

Mum(in cafe) — "Billy! Where are your manners?"
Billy — "I think I must have left them at home!"

What did the mathematician do when his children were naughty?
He took away a number of their toys!

Dad — "Don't make that noise when you're eating—haven't you got any manners?"
Son — "Yes—but I don't want to wear them out too soon!"

A man walks up to a woman in the street. The woman is reading a map. "I don't suppose," says the man, "you could find your way to lending me a fiver?"

Annie — "What happened to you, Katie?"
Katie — "Our school was putting on a performance of 'Grease'—and I slipped in it!"

What did Joan of Arc have for her last meal?
A hot stake!

Why did the stable hand take a watering can to work?
To water the horses!

Three hunters were out hunting one day, when they came across some tracks. "It's a deer!" said the first hunter. "It's a rabbit!" said the second hunter. The third hunter was trying to decide which one was right when a train came and ran them all over!

What did Mary Queen of Scots have for her last meal?
A cold chop!

Why are old-fashioned sailing ships more environmentally friendly?
Because you get thousands of miles to the galleon!

Did you hear about the film they made at the local jail recently?
It's due for release in two years' time!

Fisherman — "I haven't had a bite all day—I feel terrible!"
Postman — "I haven't had a bite all day, and I feel great!"

How do you tune an underwater piano?
With a tuna fork!

Did you hear about the man who solved a great mystery by accident?
They called him Sheerluck Holmes!

What do you call a Scottish skeleton in a kilt?
Boney Prince Charlie!

Did you hear about the famous Scottish queen who invented a cure for acne?
She was known as Mary Cream of Spots!

Why are there no dominoes in hospital?
Because the doctors clear up the spots!

Why did the farmer build a straight path from the field to the milking shed?
He didn't want the milk to turn!

What kind of ship was invented by a hairdresser?
A clipper!

Will — "Our dog's just swallowed the title deeds to the house!"
Bill — "Oops! He's eaten you out of house and home!"

What kind of ship was invented by an apprentice hairdresser?
A tug!

Did you hear about the ladies who worked at the bread counter in the supermarket?
They started a pop group—The Slice Girls!

The Lone Ranger's friend had highlights put in his hair. . .
—now they call him Tinto!

Did you hear the joke about the aeroplane?
It's probably way over your head!

Why did the mushroom love her boyfriend?
Because he was a fun guy (fungi)!

Bill — "The doctor told me I had a dicky ticker!"
Will — "You have something wrong with your heart?"
Bill — "No—something wrong with my watch—I was late for my appointment again!"

Where does the Lone Ranger go on holiday?
He goes camping with his trusty tento!

A — "My wife is an angel!"
B — "My wife is a devil!"
C — "My wife is still alive!"

Son — "Dad! Dad! I've hit the big time!"
Dad — "What did you do, son?"
Son — "I crashed into the town hall clock!"

Great idea! Hang bells on your bathroom scales at Christmas. . .
—and jingle all the weigh!"

What did the cornfield say to the farmer?
"Stop pulling my ears!"

It's been a long day at medical school. The students learned arteriosclerosis, pneumothorax, and myocardial infarction. . .
And now that they can spell them, the tutor can explain what the words mean!

What's a bus driver's favourite musical?
"My Fare Lady!"

Mr Dopey — "I can't understand why I crashed into that tree. . .
—I hooted my horn in plenty of time!"

Why did Cinderella go to the milking shed?
To visit her dairy godmother!

What did the butcher say when his cat sat on the scales?
"Get out of the weigh!"

Man on aeroplane — "Alp! Alp!"
Steward — "Did you call for help, sir?"
Man — "No—we're heading straight for a mountain!"

Billy — "My dad hammers nails in like lightning!"
Bobby — "Really fast?"
Billy — "No—he never strikes twice in the same place!"

What was the burglar's favourite fairy story?
"Sleeping Booty"!

What happened at the sea scout summer camp?
All the tents sank!

Why was the stupid comedian booed off stage?
Because he was witless!

Explorer — "Luckily, I found water in three different places in the desert!"
Bored listener — "Well, well, well!"

A new maternity hospital opened in town yesterday. . .
they're offering free delivery to all their clients!

When is a batsman like a clock?
When he strikes one!

Fred — "That's a nice scarf, Ted!"
Ted — "You can have it—it's too tight for me!"

Bob — "My wife said she was sick of all her clothes. She wanted to be seen in something long and flowing!"
Bert — "And what did you say?"
Bob — "I told her to jump in the river!"

Bus driver — "Move farther down the bus, please!"
Passenger — "Which one is your father?"!

Mum — "Katie, soon your baby brother will be learning to feed himself!"
Katie — "You'd better get him some L-plates, then!"

Bob — "Our next-door neighbour is a robber!"
Bill — "What a dangerous way to live?"
Bob — "Not really—he's a safe robber!"

Why did the campanologist travel to the Amazon?
To play jungle bells!

Billy — "I've got some stuff in a jar that goes 'bang' when you mix it with water!"
Bob — "So what? My sister puts stuff on her face that cracks when she smiles!"

Burglar's next-door neighbour — "Someone's stolen your car!"
Burglar — "It's all right—it wasn't mine anyway!"

Who was the father of the Black Prince?
Old King Coal!

Tourist — "What a lovely colour that cow is!"
Farmer — "It's a Jersey!"
Tourist — "Really! And I thought it was its own skin!"

Pharmacist — "Did the medicine help? Is your cough looser?"
Customer — "No—but my teeth are—that stuff shrank my gums!"

Did you hear about the paper boy?
He blew away in a gale!

Bill — "How far can you drive a golf ball?"
Will — "It all depends how much petrol is in the car!"

Did you hear about the cowhand who had bandy legs?
He couldn't keep his calves together!

What's a gymnast's favourite dance?
The vaultz!

Bill — *"I never gamble!"*
Will — *"Why not?"*
Bill — *"It's a dicey business!"*

Two cowboys are sitting in the cinema. A person behind them starts opening a large bag of sweets.
"Call the sheriff!" yells one cowboy. "There's rustlers in here!"

"What's that?"
"It's a plane, stupid!"
"A plane stupid what?"

1st astronaut — "Let's fly to the sun!"
2nd astronaut — "Can't—it's too hot!"
1st astronaut — "We'll go at night!"

A man walks up to a restaurant where a notice on the door announces proudly, "Our food speaks for itself!"
Then he hears a little voice coming from inside — "Help! Help! I'm burning!"

Assistant — "Coach! Coach! I've got all the boots mixed up! I can't tell which ones belong to the 'A' team and which belong to the 'B' team!"
Coach — "No problem, son. The 'B' team's boots are the ones that hum!"

Why was the climber upset?
He had mountin' problems!

Who is the fastest Russian on water?
Ivor Jetski!

Bill — "My boss is just like a balloon!"
Will — "A real high-flyer?"
Bill — "No—full of hot air!"

Mo — "How much is that goose?"
Butcher — "£30!"
Mo — "Forget it—I can't afford the bill!"

Mike — "I have my father's nose, you know!"
Molly — "Doesn't he look pretty stupid without it?"

Molly — "I want a small bird for Sunday lunch, please!"
Butcher — "Do you want a pullet?"
Molly — "No—I want to put it in my shopping bag!"

A man hands his ticket to the ticket collector. The ticket collector takes it, then 'Wham!' he hits the man, right on the nose.
"Why did you do that?" asks the man.
"Orders, sir," said the ticket collector.
"They said 'Take their tickets and punch them'! "

What do you get if you pour soda in your ears?
Hearing-ade!

What are the most common birds that are kept in captivity?
Jailbirds!

Why do nuns always wear black?
It's a habit they get into!

Bill is doing press-ups in the front room.
Will — "Are you working out?"
Bill — "No fear! It's pouring down with rain—I'm staying in!"

Fred — "My brother plays rugby like Cinderella!"
Ted — "Graceful on his feet?"
Fred — "No—he runs away from the ball!"

Businessman (on phone) "Honey! I'm flying home tonight!"
Wife — "I'll leave the landing light on for you!"

Will — "First my boss tells me to keep my nose to the grindstone. . ."
Bill — "Yes?"
Will — "Then he tells me to put my shoulder to the wheel. . ."
Bill — "And then?"
Will — "Then says I've to sharpen my wits!"
Bill — "So?"
Will — "So the doctor says I'm scarred for life!"

Fred (drawing up in his car) — "Hi, Maisie! Need a lift?"
Maisie — "No thanks! I live in a bungalow!"

Will — "My friend's apartment collapsed while he was inside!"
Bill — "How is he now?"
Will — "Flat on his back!"

Husband — "This suit's a bit tight—do you think I should wear it tonight?"
Wife — "Yes, but keep your stomach in!"
Husband — "If my stomach stays in, then the rest of me does too!"

The football pitch was covered with spent matches.
—then the referee sent the striker off!

Did you hear about the kindly old lady who went into hospital to have an operation?
Just before they anaesthetized her, she said to the surgeon, "Go on! Help yourself!"

Maisie — "How did you win that set of saucepans?"
Mo — "It was pot luck!"

A man from a sales company calls up a house and a tiny whispering voice answers "Hello?"
"Hello," says the man. "Is your mummy in?"
"Yes" whispers the voice, "but you can't speak to her. She's too busy!"
"Is your daddy in. then?" asked the man.
"Yes," whispers the voice.
"Can I speak to him?"
"No," whispers the voice, "he's busy too!"
"Is there anyone else there?" asks the caller.
"Well. . ." whispers the voice, "the police are here, but they're pretty busy right now as well!"
"Anyone else there?"
"The ambulance people," whispers the little voice, "and the fire brigade!"
"Anyone else?"
"There are some other people here too," whispers the little voice, "but you can't speak to any of them—they're all terribly busy!"
The caller is puzzled. "You seem to have an awful lot of people in your house," he says, "and they're all very busy! What exactly are they doing?"
And the little voice whispers back, quieter than ever. . .
"They're looking for me!"

Motorist — "I'm so sorry—I've just run over your dog—but I'll gladly replace him!"
Dog owner — "All right—but remember—you're not allowed on the sofa!"

Butcher — "I've got to take the feathers of 150 turkeys before Christmas!"
Customer — "Gosh! That'll take some pluck!"

What did the magician's visitors say when they left his house?
"Thanks for halving us!"

Bar tender (interviewing someone for a job) — "Have you any experience working behind bars?
Applicant — "Yes! I did two years for burglary!"

A — "Have you got a light, mate?"
B — "No—he weighs over 20 stone!"

Tennis player's boyfriend — "Don't you love me?"
Tennis player — "Love? Love means nothing to me!"

Molly — "I have a model husband!"
Minnie — "Why so glum, then?"
Molly — "He's not a working model!"

Will — "I met an angel today!"
Bill — "Really? What did you say to her?"
Bill — "Halo there!"

What do chatterboxes have for breakfast?
Waffles!

What do elephants sing at Christmas?
Noel-ephants, Noel-ephants!

How did the hairdresser get over the wall?
He made a style for it!

Maisie — "Mum, can I have new shoes for gym?"
Mum — "No! Tell Jim to get his own shoes!"

Why did the football team wear black and yellow strips?
Because it was the 'B' team!

What do you call a cowboy covered in carrots and gravy?
Hopalong Casserole!

What did the musician call his dog?
Bitehoven!

What do you call a western sheriff with a face like a clock?
Wild Bill Ticktock!

Two cowboys called Billy live under the sea. Who are they?
Billy the Squid and Billy the Cod!

Agnes and Bill had been going out together for forty-five years. One day, sitting over lunch at a restaurant, Bill said to Agnes, "Don't you think it's about time we got married?"
"Yes," said Agnes, "but who would have us at our age?"

What is the greasiest rugby team in the world?
The Oil Blacks!

Why did the farmer go to the hairdresser?
To get a good crop!

Why was the boxer barefoot?
He'd used up all his socks!

What do grouches have for breakfast?
Grumbled eggs!

The favourite Christmas carol of hairdressers?
"While shepherds washed their locks. . ."!

Why did the jelly baby go to the bowling alley?
To see his friends the Skittles!

Billy — "I really got my sister confused yesterday!"
Bobby — "How?"
Billy — "I drew a circle in the middle of the floor and told her to sit in the corner!"

How do you repair a broken freezer?
With a frost aid kit!

Bill — " 'The Mousetrap' is a great play!"
Will — "Really?"
Bill — "Yes—I was completely caught up in it!"

Who invented the first fountain pen?
The Incas!

What's green and red and very hot?
A dragon holding its breath!

What did the fraud have for breakfast?
Con Flakes!

Granny — "You must come and pick something from the garden, Annie. There are so many things to see; foxgloves, lady's mantle, lady's smock, monkshood. . ."
Annie — "I don't think any of them would suit me, Granny!"

How can you spot a mariner's house at Christmas?
It's the one with the ferry at the top of the tree!

A — "My son was born on St George's day, so we call him George!"
B — "My son was born on St David's day, so we call him David!"
C — "My son was born at Christmas, so we call him Noel!"
D — "Isn't that a coincidence! MY son was born on a special day too!
Others — "So what's his name?"
D — "Pancake!"

How do you say goodbye to the woman in the ice cream shop?
Waifer off!

Maisie — "I'm going to get fit, so I've got myself a trainer!"
Mo — "But what about your other foot?"

What do cyclists have for breakfast?
Tricicles!

The school nurse is giving a talk to one of the classes.
"And now," she says, "Personal hygiene!"
"And a personal 'Hi!' to you too!" calls a voice from the back!

How do you say goodbye to a surveyor?
Tell him "So long!"

Fred — "I sent my watch away to have it gold-plated!"
Ted — "So it's been on a gilt trip!"

Maisie — "Sometimes our dog doesn't come in when we call him!"
Mo — "And when is that?"
Maisie — "When the door's shut!"

How do you say goodbye to a stamp?
Tell it to gum back soon!

How do you find the way to the dentist's?
Go toothy end of the road!

Why was the hunter sad?
He missed his wife!

1st nun — "What a lovely day!"
2nd nun — "Let's ask if we can go out to pray!"

What is the difference between the son of the monarch and a bearded father?
One is the heir apparent and the other is a hairy parent!

How do you get a writer started?
Give him a propelling pencil!

What nationality are knots?
Tie-one-ese!

What nationality are apples?
Core-ean!

What nationality are eyes?
Eyes-landic!

Where does Bo Peep live?
Bo-livia!

Where do happy cats come from?
Purr-u!

Where do algae come from?
Algae-ria!

What nationality are bacteria?
Germ-an!

What nationality are fish?
Fin-ish!

What are the world's most fruitful mountains?
The Apple-achians!

What are the world's most useful mountains?
The 'Andes!

What is the name of the most discontented mountain range in Scotland?
The Grumpians!

What is the most common kind of car in Norway?
The Fjord!

What are the most musical mountains in the world?
The Humalayas!

Will — "I hurt my foot climbing a volcano!"
Bill — "Mount Etna?"
Will — "No! Kraka-toe-a!

How do you say goodbye to a queen?
Tell her "Tiara-for-now!"

How do you say goodbye to a piccolo player?
Say "Tootle-oo!"

Sailing instructor (to elderly lady pupil) —
"Righto, you can cast off now!"
Lady — "I thought we were sailing, not knitting!"

Will — "I can't come round to your house tonight. I'm going to see 'The Swiss Family Robinson'. "
Bill — "I tell you what. . .why don't you bring them along too?"

What do you call a boomerang that doesn't come back?
A plank!

Air steward — "During the flight, we will be serving a light snack of cabbage and beans. . .
—later on in the flight, you may experience a little turbulence!"

Which Star Wars character wears the biggest boots?
Darth Wader!

Who is the tallest character in Star Wars?
Luke Skyscraper!

What do the Star Wars characters do on their days off?
They take an R2D Tour!

1st sailor — "I'm bored. Let's play cards!"
2nd sailor — "Can't do that!"
1st sailor — "Why not?"
1st sailor — "Captain's on the deck!"

A little boy comes into the hospital with his father. His Dad hasn't told him yet, but there's a wonderful surprise waiting for him. Mum's had twins!
His father takes him into a room, where Mum is lying in bed with a baby in each arm.
"Well, what do you think of these?" she asks.
The little boy has a good look at the babies.
"Let's have the one on the left," he says!

It was a very bumpy flight. Bill and Will weren't feeling too good. After a while, the stewards served the passengers a meal, and when Will got his, he started taking the dishes off his tray and packing them into his sick bag.
"What are you doing that for?" asked Bill.
"I'm just seeing how much of this will fit in when it comes back later!" said Bill.

Did you hear about the baby who liked Heavy Metal music?
He rocked himself to sleep!

Fred — "My dog swallowed a bell!"
Ted — "What happened to it?"
Fred — "Now it's a dingo!"

Trainer — "Why did you lose the match?"
Boxer — "It was all on account of. . ."
Trainer — "On account of what?"
Boxer — "On a count of ten!"

What's Captain Kirk's favourite musical?
"The Klingon I"!

Why was the undertaker's assistant sacked?
Because he made a grave mistake!

They've got new bells in the village church. . .
—dings have changed around here!

Did you hear about the monster who had a feeding frenzy in the parking lot?
He passed three cars on the way home!

Molly — "My brother fell off our garden wall into the next-door neighbour's empty swimming pool!"
Minnie — "Did he break anything?"
Molly — "No—it's made from solid concrete!"

An English tourist walks into a car-hire office in a small town in Spain.
"So you're here on a holiday from England!" says the man behind the desk.
"Yes," says the tourist.
"Have you come for the fiesta?" enquires the man behind the desk.
"Well," says the tourist, "As long as it's reliable, I'm not particularly bothered what kind of car I get!"

Later on that day, the same tourist returns to his hotel and asks the receptionist for the keys to his room. He looks tired.
"Siesta?" enquires the receptionist.
"No—I haven't seen her since I left England!" replies the tourist!

Why did the skylark refuse to play in goals?
Because it was used to being on the wing!

Fred — "I've taken up ski-jumping!"
Ted — "How are you getting on?"
Fred — "Great! I can jump over four skis now!"

Will — "Whenever I have dinner in a Chinese restaurant, I feel as if I'm being watched."
Bill — "That'll be the Peking duck!"

The x-ray technician at the local hospital had a new boyfriend.
No-one could understand what she saw in him!

Mo — "You remind me of the hero in a book I once read!"
Fred — "Who?"
Mo — "Big Ears!"

Ancient Roman news reporter — "So, Brutus, why did you kill Caesar?"
Brutus — "Because he had been eating my smarties!"
Reporter — "And have you proof of that?"
Brutus — "Yes! He confessed as he was dying!"
Reporter — "What did he say?"
Brutus — "Et two, Brute!"

When you drop a piece of bread and butter, why does it always land butter side down?
Because you always butter the wrong side!

Maisie — "My boyfriend says my face is like fine porcelain!"
Mo — "That's because of your glazed expression!"

Ted — "I lost two stones when I was in hospital!"
Fred — "But you don't look any thinner!"
Ted — "They were kidney stones!"

1st hippy — "I ate twelve tins of beans yesterday, man!"
2nd hippy — "Wow, man! How did you feel?"
1st hippy — "I tell you, man, I was blown away!"

Parachutist's friend — "And do you see much of your family?"
Parachutist — "I drop in one them every once in a while!"

What did the judge say when he looked in the mirror?
"Who is the fairest of them all?"

Who's the grumpiest person in the Louvre?
The Moany Lisa!

Bob — "My wife sat on a trifle yesterday!"
Bert — "How did you tell her?"
Bob — "I said she had a sweet behind!"

What did Stoneage man do on Saturday nights?
He went out clubbing!

Why did Mrs Bell call her son Alexander Graham?
The name had a ring to it!

Why did the miser never see his family?
He was too mean to pay them a visit!

Why did the sprinter have no breakfast?
He needed a fast start!

Annie — "There was such a cross bee on the dining room door today!"
Betty — "How do you know it was cross?"
Annie — "It flew off the handle!"

At cookery school last week, the students had to fry two strips of bacon and make an omelette.
It was an eggs-ham-ination!

A man walks into a travel agents and says he wants to book a holiday in China.
"Peking?" enquires the travel agent.
"No," says the man, "I want to take a good long look at everything there is to see!"

Tourist — "Who is that man weeping by the market cross?"
Local — "That's the town crier!"

Fred — "As soon as I saw my horse come in last in the race, I knew what time it was!"
Ted — "And what time was it?"
Fred — "Five past one!"

Bill — "Don't talk to me about matadors—it makes me so mad!"
Will — "How?"
Bill — "It's just like showing a red rag to a bull!"

Did you hear about the very rich Italian tenor?
His name was Hava-lotti!

Why did the greedy man visit the witch twice?
He wanted extra potions!

Why did the stockbroker dip his clients' documents in bleach?
To give them fair shares!

Will — "At least I know I can count on my friends!"
Bill — "But not very high—you only have three!"

Why did the grandfather clock take the little clock to the speech therapist?
Because it wouldn't tock properly!

Why did the piece of knitting feel unwanted?
Because it was cast off!

Why are chemists good at crosswords?
They know all the solutions!

What's soft and fluffy and guarded by beefeaters?
The Towel of London!

When did the first bus appear in America?
1492—it was Colum-bus!

What is the name of the famous grunting bell in London?
Pig Pen!

Why are vampire cricket games confusing?
There are so many bats!

Many people enjoy taking their bicycles out for a long ride in the country. Ernie the electrician is different.
He just does short circuits!

What is a greedy person's favourite spot in Italy?
The Leaning Tower of Pizza!

Who was the first man in Scotland?
MacAdam!

What did Adam say when he first caught sight of his future wife?
Eve-ho!

What has two feet and flies?
A helicopter pilot!

What has two legs and flies?
A pair of trousers!

What race always starts with a tie?
A three-legged race!

Where do sugar lumps come from?
Cuba!

Which Roman emperor made up puzzles?
Julius Teaser!

Don't eat very hot curry. . .
—You'll spend too much time Vin-da-loo!

Nasty Nora — "My sister was one of only two entrants in a beauty contest. She came in second. . .
—and her dog took first prize!"

What has no legs, is scared of birds, and flies?
A worm in an aeroplane!

Who is the footballing hero of all bananas?
Peel-e!

Why is a sculptor destined to die horribly?
Because he makes faces and busts!

Why is a novelist like a monster?
Because he has a tale coming out of his head!

What is brought to the table, cut, but never eaten?
A pack of cards!

What happens when one card player leaves the table?
All the rest follow suit!

What does a dead liar do?
Lie still!

What kind of stories do butterflies like best?
Myths!

Why is O the noisiest vowel?
Because the other four are inaudible!

What bridge will you never cross?
The bridge of your nose!

Who is the oldest woman alive?
Anne Tiquity!

What lock can a burglar never pick?
A lock of hair!

Why did the gardener's wife get cross with him?
Because he was always raking up the past!

Will — "I'm hungry!"
Bill — "Lie down and have a roll, then!"

Why did the chicken go to the library?
To get a buk-buk-buk!

Why did the postman dump his girlfriend?
She wasn't his sort!

Why is aeroplane coffee never very hot?
So that the passengers don't get scalded when the steward pours it into their laps!

Holidays Italian style — "I like to Rome. Turin is my hobby! I travel all over Italy in Mi-lan-drover. All the same, I'm quite glad Venice time to go home again!

"And what are you making for dinner tonight, dear?"
"Reservations at a restaurant, sweetheart!"

Tourist — "I've cut my hand—can you stitch it?"
Nurse in local surgery — "Certainly! Just hold still, while I get my needle and thread!"
Tourist — "What? No anaesthetic?"
Nurse — "Sorry—you're not from around these parts, and I'm only allowed to give local anaesthetics!"

Why is the sea so destructive?
Because it's full of breakers!

What do you call a basement full of grouches?
A whine cellar!

Murphy's Law — If anything can go wrong, it will.
Cole's Law — Shredded cabbage, carrot and mayonnaise!

What did the frog say when he returned his book to the library?
"Reddit! Reddit!"

Did you hear about Gypsy Rose Lee's new crystal ball?
It cost her a fortune!

What did one piece of clay say to the other piece of clay?
"I'm going to be a model!"

What do you call an absent-minded acorn?
A forget-me-nut!

Lethargic Len — "I helped my mum with the housework today!"
Dozy Dave — "Yeh?"
Lethargic Len — "Yeh! I lifted my feet while she vacuumed under them!"

What do you get if you put vinegar in your ears?
Pickled hearing!

What happens if you put gravel in your ears?
You go stone deaf!

Old Effie — "My husband was electrocuted twenty years ago, and I can still remember his last words!"
Old Isa — "And what were they?"
Old Effie — "I'll fix it!"

What is the definition of a university professor?
A person who talks in other people's sleep!

1st lawyer — "You can't win this case—I know the law better than you do!"
2nd lawyer — "Perhaps. . . But I know the judge better than you do!"

Fred — "My mother brings me my meals in a nosebag whenever I go to see her!"
Ted — "Why?"
Fred — "Because she thinks I eat like a horse!"

Mum — "Did you make your bed, Son?"
Son — "No! Some bloke in a factory did!"

Did you hear about the baker's accident?
He fell off his pie-cycle!

What do you call a dentist who grows fruit trees?
An orchard-dontist!

What do you call a Russian snooker player?
Inoff the Red!

What has ten legs and makes a fearful sucking noise?
A basketball team eating oranges!

Who owns the video store in the jungle?
Tarzan of the Tapes!

Two experienced soldiers and a dim-witted recruit are being chased through farmland by enemy soldiers. They come across a pile of old sacks and decide to hide in them. The enemy soldiers appear after a few minutes, and decide to investigate the sacks. As they start to open the first sack, the soldier inside makes a mewing sound. "It's just a sack of kittens," say the enemy soldiers. They turn to the second sack, and as they start to open it, the soldier inside makes a yelping sound. "It's just a bag of puppies," say the enemy soldiers. So they turn to the third sack, in which the dim-witted recruit is hiding. And just as they are about to open it, a voice from inside calls out. . .
"Potatoes!"

Why did the comb visit the dentist?
To have its teeth cleaned!

Will — "I'm broke! I'd do anything for a buck or two!"
Bill — "Try rodeo riding!"

What happens if you put cement in your ear?
You become hard of hearing!

What did one end of the giraffe's neck say to the other?
"So-o-o long!"

Why was the maths teacher angry with his son?
Because his son totalled the car!

What turns up at the polling station going "putt-putt"?
An outboard voter!

What did Miss Muffet say to the spider?
"Get out of my whey!"

And what did the spider say to Miss Muffet?
"Fancy a game of curds?"

Where can you get ice cream in a forest?
In a pine tree—it's full of cones!

When is a chicken like a fencing master?
When it's foiled!

How far can you walk into a tunnel?
Half-way—after that, you're on the way out!

How do gardeners mend their trousers?
With vegetable patches!

Did you hear about the gardener's novel?
It had a fertile plot!

Why did Cinderella quit the football team?
Her coach turned into a pumpkin!

Why do skeletons never eat curry?
They haven't the guts to digest it!

How do you get Pikachu on a bus?
Pokemon!

How did the canary become famous?
It made a chart-topping seed-D.!

Soccer player — "I'm so annoyed that I missed that chance at goal—I could kick myself!"
Friend — "You'd probably miss!"

Why did the ballroom dancer leave her partner?
It was time he stood on his own two feet!

What does the sign of three golden balls mean under the sea?
Prawnbroker's shop!

Fred — "My next-door neighbour's got a gold tooth!"
Ted — "How do you know?"
Fred — "It came out in conversation!"

Salesman — "Want to buy some special mouthwash?"
Lady — "No, thank you!"
Salesman — "Never mind—would you like one of my sweets?"
Lady — "Oh, that's very kind of you—UGH! They taste like poison! I need something to take the taste away!"
Salesman — "How about some special mouthwash?"

Joe — "I pay all my bills with good grace!"
Jim — "I have to use money!"

How did the penniless watchmaker get his weekly groceries?
On tick!

Customer — "I'd like to buy that television on the bottom shelf over there!"
Assistant — "Certainly, sir—have you thought about hire purchase?"
Customer — "No—I want the one on the bottom shelf!"

Tourist (in New York) — "Excuse me, how do I get to the Carnegie Hall?"
Musician — "Practise!"

Man watching grand funeral procession —
"What a crowd! Who's died?"
Little boy — "The person in the coffin!"

Maisie — "I have a rare gift!"
Mo — "What's that?"
Maisie — "A present from my brother—he's never given me anything before!"

Mum — "What was that noise?"
Son — "Don't worry Mum, it was just Dad's ladder falling over!"
Mum — "Oh, no! Did Dad fall too?"
Son — "No—he's fine—he's hanging from the roof guttering!"

Visitor to maternity hospital — "Have any great people been born here?"
Midwife — "No—just hundreds of babies!"

Judge — "And why did you steal your friend's car?"
Prisoner — "I didn't steal it—I just took it for a joke!"
Judge — "Where did you take it?"
Prisoner — "I took it to London!"
Judge — "Well, that's taking a joke too far!"

Customer — "I'd like to return these mothballs—they're no use!"
Shopkeeper — "Why?"
Customer — "I've been throwing them at the moths all day and haven't killed one!"

Farmer —"Officer! My pigs have all gone missing!"
Police officer — "Probably a hamburglar, sir!"

A traveller arrives late at night at a country hotel where he has booked a room. The hotel is locked up, but he rings the doorbell and waits for an answer.
The hotel manager appears at a window overhead. "What do you want at this time of night?" he demands.
"It's all right," says the traveller, "I'm staying here for the night!"
"Fine then," says the hotel manager, "Stay there!" and he goes back to bed!

Guest — "I want another room!"
Receptionist — "Why?"
Guest — "Because mine's on fire!"

Who is the most popular general ever known?
General Holiday!

Two vultures are checking in their bags before a long flight. "What about these bags there?" asks the man at the check-in desk.
"We're taking them with us," say the vultures. "They're carrion bags!"

Traveller(leaning into a gale) — "Is this place always so windy?"
Local — "Oh, the wind stops blowing about once a year!"
Traveller — "And then?"
Local — "Then we all fall down!"

Two travellers are lost in the desert. They are running out of food. Then one of them finds two slices of bread in the pocket of his rucksack.
"Perfect!" he says. "We can make a sandwich!"

Traveller — "Give me a day return for Florence please!"
Ticket clerk — "But Florence is in Italy!"
Traveller — "No she isn't, she's standing right beside me!"

Traveller — "Does this village have a mobile library?"
Local — "No, but there's a revolving bookstand in the newsagent's!"

Traveller — "I went on holiday for the change and the rest!"
Friend — "And?"
Traveller — "The hotel porter got my change and the hotel manager got the rest!"

Traveller — "I want a return ticket please!"
Ticket clerk — "Where to, madam?"
Traveller — "Back here, of course!"

1st traveller — "I wish I'd brought my bookcase with me!"
2nd traveller — "Why?"
1st traveller — "Because I left the plane tickets on top of it!"

Why did the boy take his bicycle on board a double-decker bus?
He wanted to ride on the top deck!

"Has your wife ever been on safari before?"
"Not safaris I know!"

"What are you doing with all these boxes?"
"I'm taking them on a package tour!"

Traveller — "Give me a room and a bath!"
Receptionist — "I can give you the room, but you'll have to bath yourself!"

What do you call a twelve-inch sausage?
A frank-footer!

1st traveller — "When I went swimming in Spain last year, a jellyfish stung me one the foot!"
2nd traveller — "Which one?"
1st traveller — "Dunno—there were so many of them, and they all looked the same!"

Traveller — "Why is the station so far from town?"
Local — "To make it close to the railway line!"

Why is the hot dog the noblest creature of all?
Because it feeds the hand that bites it!

What did the hot dog say when it finished the race?
"I'm the weiner!"

What's Chicken Tarka?
The same as Chicken Tikka—but 'otter!

What is the most popular dance at barbecues?
The char-char!

Why was the potato arrested on the motorway?
It broke the spud limit!

What's a vampire's favourite fruit?
A neck-tarine!

What is the name of the opera about cooking outdoors?
The Barbecue of Seville!

What's the difference between bogeys and broccoli?
Kids don't eat broccoli!

Where did the hazelnut meet the toffee?
At the candy bar!

What do you call a cow spying on another cow?
A steakout!

What has hundreds of legs, eats, drinks and flies?
A boy scouts' picnic!

What do electricians like to eat for dessert?
Shock-a-lot mousse!

Why did the lettuce go limp?
Because it saw the meat loaf!

Where do biscuits sleep at night?
Under the baking sheets!

What does woodworm have for breakfast?
Oakmeal!

Why did the hungry robot go to the hardware store?
To get some assorted nuts!

What did one date say to the other?
"Well, stone me!"

What do pastry chefs drink?
Baking soda!

What do boy bands have for breakfast?
Pop-star-ts!

What did one pretzel say to the other?
"Let's twist again!"

What's a gherkin's favourite musical?
"Hello Dilly"!

Why did the pastry go to the dentist?
To get a filling!

What do you eat at breakfast but drink at dinner?
Toast!

Buy a cookbook today!
It's a stirring read!

"My hen just laid a 5lb egg! Can you beat that?"
"Yes—with a very big whisk!"

"But really—a five pound egg! What do you think?"
"I think it's an eggs-aggeration!"

"Seen the lettuce bat?"
"No, but I've seen the salad bowl!"

Did you hear about the greedy boy who drank eight cokes?
He brought 7-Up!

Where do you go to preserve strawberries?
Jamaica!

Why do snakes not need cutlery?
Because their tongues are forked!

Why did the potato get beaten by the onion?
Because the onion was too strong for it!

What do you call a troublesome potato?
An agi-tater!

How do you blow up a squash?
With a pump-kin!

Why was the roast beef expensive?
Because it was rare!

Maisie — "I found an egg on the street yesterday—where do you think it came from?"
Mo — "A hen!"

Why did the salad go to the psychiatrist?
Because it was all mixed up!

Who is the superhero of the vegetable patch?
Beetman!

Will — "I want to make the perfect burger. First comes the bun, then the meat, then the cheese. . .what comes after the cheese?"
Bill — "The mouse!"

What's purple and can be seen from outer space?
The Grape Wall of China!

Where did the ice cream learn to read?
At Sundae school!

What did Guy Fawkes have for his last meal?
Bangers, crackers and pop!

What's brown an knobbly, wears a space suit and makes great chips?
Spud Lightyear!

Why did the coffee call the police?
It was mugged!

What kind of monkeys grow on vines?
Grey apes!

Why did Bill sit in front of the TV with a bowl of milk?
He was waiting for his favourite cereal!"

Did you hear about the thirsty man from Vancouver?
He drank Canada Dry!

How did the egg feel about its new spectacles?
Egg-sighted!

Did you hear the joke about the loaf of bread?
It's a bit stale!

What did the pie say to the rhubarb?
"Stop stalking me!"

What did one melon say to the other?
"Honeydew want to marry me?"

When is a nut like hay fever?
When it's a-cashew!

What's the swamp monster's favourite pudding?
Bloopberry pie and mudcake!

Why did the carrot not like the cabbage?
Because the cabbage had a big head!

What did the rotisserie say to the chicken?
"Do you come around this way often?"!

Where does spaghetti dance?
At the meatball!

Where do you find lettuces in the theatre?
In the dressing room!

You can have a blind date. . .
—But you can't get a deaf prune!

Why did the surgeon spend all day in the garden?
He was transplanting his kidney beans!

What's orange and goes SLAM! SLAM! SLAM! SLAM!
A four-door pumpkin!

Mum — "I've changed my mind about spinach. It can't be all that healthy!"
Friend — "What makes you say that?"
Mum — "My children like it!"

What do dogs eat at the movies?
Pupcorn!

What was the maggot doing in the middle of the olive?
It was making a pit-stop!

What was the policeman doing in the vegetable patch?
Patrolling the beet!

What's green and sings 'Jailhouse Rock'?
Elvis Parsley!

I like bananas
—I find them a-peeling!

What do penguins like in their salad?
Iceberg lettuce!

What kind of dinosaur likes herbs?
The Dill-plodocus!

What do martial arts experts like to drink?
Kara-tea!

Why did the cracker crack a joke?
To cheer up the blue cheese!

Great idea! Eat 6,000 oranges. . .
—Then swim in the Vitamin C!

What do you call a musical gherkin?
A pickle-o!

What do you get if you cross a cabbage with a novel?
A vegetable that needs its head read!

What do you call an egg with a straw in its mouth?
A yolkel!

What kind of nut gives you sore feet?
An ache-corn!

What's a dentist's favourite flavour of ice cream?
Toothy Frutti!

Why did Eve eat the apple?
Because she couldn't get a date!

Why did the baby corn cry?
It had sore ears!

What do you call a baby hot dog?
A teeny weenie!

What did the celery say to the carrot stick?
"Shall we go for a dip?"

How do you make a pear drop?
Let go of it!

Did you hear the joke about the ice?
I can't tell you it— it's slipped my mind!

What is the most musical kind of ice cream?
Tooty-frutti!

"You're a peach!"
"Because I'm soft and delicious?"
"No—because you have a heart of stone!"

"Why have you brought a goat on the picnic?"
"You told me to bring the butter!"

Where do gherkins go on holiday?
Dill-adelphia!

Is it alright to play football on a full stomach?
No—it's better to play on a football pitch!

Why did the teacher get cross with the orange juice?
Because it wouldn't concentrate!

Where do monsters dine out?
At a beastro!

Why did the witch turn into a peapod?
She wanted a peas-full life!

Why does the cheese stick to the pizza?
Because of the tomato paste!

When is a potato like old paint?
When it's peeled and chipped!

Diner — "Do you serve shrimps?"
Waiter — "Oh, sir, you're not all that small!"

Diner — "This strawberry cake has no strawberries in it!"
Diner — "That's because it's a strawberry shortcake!"

Diner — "Waiter! I asked for some bread with my meal!"
Waiter — "Yes, sir—it's in the sausages!"

Diner — *"What are your mussels like?"*
Waiter — *"Not bad—I work out in the gym regularly!"*

A diner has been sitting in a restaurant for a very long time, waiting for his Christmas dinner.
"Waiter!"
Waiter — "Yes, sir?"
Diner — "Forget the Turkey! Just bring me an Easter egg!"

Diner — "Is this a popular restaurant?"
Waiter — "I wouldn't describe it that way, sir!"
Diner — "Well, what's the food like?"
Waiter — "Like a tennis ball!"
Diner — "Like a tennis ball?"
Waiter — "Yes, sir—served, but never eaten!"

Girl — "What's the soup like?"
Waiter — *"Quite nice—but really thick!"*
Girl — *"Sounds just like my boyfriend!"*

Diner — "It says here that the chef can make anything on request!"
Waiter — "That's right, sir!"
Diner — "I bet he can't make me a yeti sandwich!"
Waiter — "Oh, dear, you've caught us out there, sir—we just used up the last of the bread!"

Diner — "What's this?"
Waiter — "It's bean casserole!"
Diner — "I know it's been casserole, but what is it now?"!

Diner — *"No change on the menu today?"*
Waiter — *"No, sir. We keep the change for tips!"*

Diner — "How much for dinner?"
Waiter — "£50 a head, sir!"
Diner — "I'll just have a couple of ears, then!"

Waiter — "Genoa cake, sir?"
Diner — "Yes, I know a cake when I see one!"

Why was the waiter sacked?
He wouldn't take orders from anyone!

Resident in hotel — "Waiter! There are six cornflakes on the tablecloth!"
Waiter — "That'll be the new six-part cereal, sir!"

Diner — "There's a dead woodlouse in the bottom of my teacup! What is the meaning of this?"
Waiter — "Search me, sir—I'm no fortune teller!"

Diner — *"This tea could do with some carrots and onions!"*
Waiter — *"Why?"*
Diner — *"Because it's stewed!"*

When do plankton have family get-togethers?
Every once in a whale!

Naval captain — "All hands on deck!"
New cadet — "Not likely! Someone will step on my fingers!"

Will — *"I went sea fishing today. I caught a cod and a panfer!"*
Bill — *"What's a panfer?"*
Will — *"Cooking the cod in!"*

Who is the fishiest nursery rhyme character?
Old King Cole—he was a merry old sole!

What's a fisherman's favourite TV game show?
"Name That Tuna"!

What's a flat fish's favourite musical?
"Kiss me Skate!"

What's large and black and flies around the ocean in a 747?
The pilot whale!

What are the busiest fish in the sea?
The ant-chovies!

Bill — *"How do you know you're having fish for dinner?"*
Will;— *"My wife laid a plaice on the table for me!"*

Maisie — "I've just thought of a great invention!"
Mo — "What?"
Maisie — "An underwater lighthouse for submarines!"

Why did the man drive his car into the sea?
Because a policeman told him to dip his headlights!

There was once a gardener went to see a concert. It was the craziest concert ever. . .

There was a computer expert there. . .
Selling programmes!

There was a dog on stage. . .
He was the lead singer!

There was a man dressed up like a valuable note. . .
He was the tenner!

There was a coal merchant on stage. . .
He was playing sacks!

There was an ice cream van on stage. . .
It was for the cornet players!

There were hieroglyphics scrawled on the back wall. . .
They were the symbols!

There were twelve people eating baked beans on stage. . .
They were the wind section!

Twenty lengths of twine hung from the ceiling. . .
They were the strings!

A fisherman stood beside the strings. . .
Playing carp!

Beside him, a banker tuned his instrument. . .
He was on the fiddle!

Two convicts stood at his side. . .
In front of their cell-os!

Clouds of smoke came from the side of the stage. . .
The pipers were blowing hard!

There was a man with a tape deck in the corner. . .
He was playing recorder!

Two chickens joined the band. . .
They were playing cluckenspiel!

A tailor crouched in the corner. . .
He was waiting for his sew-low!

Several people were waving scraps of material in the air. . .
They were playing ragtime!

Twelve people with wooden spoons stood at the back. . .
They were beating time!

A distracted woman wandered across the stage, muttering. . .
She had lost the key!

A man with a ticket machine stood in front of everybody. . .
He was the conductor, of course!

And there was a terrible mess on the piano stool! — What was it?
Beethoven's last movement!

But the gardener wasn't impressed. He got up and left. Why?
Because he preferred Mow-zart!

How do you get revenge on a bus driver?
Show him where to get off!

How do you get revenge on the school janitor?
Wipe the floor with him!

Will — "I've made peace with my vacuum cleaner!"
Bill — "How?"
Will — "I stopped pushing it around!"

Earth for sale — Dirt cheap!

Bricks for sale — Knock-down prices!

Psychiatric advice free — Head straight here today!

Hay-fever tablets for sale — End of sneezin' special!

Great bargain —yacht for sail!

Cow sheds for sale — Great byre gains to be had!

Engines for sale — Everything must go!

Notice in Baker's window — "Cakes 99p. Upside-down cakes, 66p!"

Pick-axes for sale — Earth-shattering prices!

Coconut shy for sale — Going at a fair price!

Dartboards for sale — Not to be missed!

Duvets and pillows on special offer — Everything is down!

Trainers on special offer — Quick, before they run out!

FOR SALE —Baker's business; smart premises with oven. Present owner has been in it for twenty years.

Visitor — "I tell you, Inspector, the men in this station are like fancy lawnmowers!"
Inspector — "Sharp? Efficient? A cut above the rest?"
Visitor — "No—they need a good shove to get them going, and even then they don't work half the time!"

Visitor to police station — "Excuse me, officer, but can you tell me where the lost property office is?"
Police officer — "If I could tell you that, madam, it wouldn't be lost, would it?"

Police officer (to suspicious-looking man, carrying a sack over his shoulder) — "Oi! You! What have you got in that sack?"
Man — "Can't exactly say, officer—it was dark when I filled it!"

Driver — "Are my back tyres completely flat, officer?"
Policeman — "No, sir—only a little bit at the bottom!"

What do you call a crow who joins the police force?
A rookie!

A police officer is out walking his beat when he spots a man shinning up a drainpipe on a block of flats.
Police officer — "What do you think you're up to?"
Man — "The second storey, officer!"

The police officer tells the man to come down, so he slides down the drainpipe and stands beside the police officer.
Police officer — "Now, I'll ask you again— what are you up to?"
Man — "Your shoulder, officer!"

The police officer arrests the man and they head back towards the police station. They pass a friend of the arrested man. "Hi, mate!" calls the friend. "What are you up to?"
"Nothing," answers the man, "it looks like I'm going down this time!"

A lady has parked on a double yellow line outside the theatre while she nips in to book seats for the next performance. When she comes out, a policeman is standing by her car.
"Officer! Don't tell me you're going to give me a ticket!" she says.
"At that price? Not likely!" says the officer, "Not even for the back stalls!"

Constable — "Sergeant! I've been stung by a wasp!"
Sergeant — "Put some cream on it, then!"
Constable — "I can't! It'll be miles away by now!"

PC Plod — "Anyone reported a large black cat with a white collar missing?"
Sergeant — "No!"
PC Plod — "Oops! I've just run over the vicar in my squad car!"

Sergeant — "What is the suspect's name, Constable?"
Constable — "His name's unpronounceable, Sarge!"
Sergeant — "And how do you spell that? . . ."

Man coming into police station — "Can I speak to the officer in charge? I'm a criminal lawyer!"
Police officer — "Aha! Come to give yourself up, have you?"

What did the policeman say when he saw two whales coming along the road? "Whale, whale, what have we here, then?"!

PC Plod — ". . . and I gave the young vandals a piece of my mind, sir!"
Sergeant — "Are you sure you could spare it?"

Tourist — "Officer, do you know the way to Clapham?"
Police officer — "Yes—just keep your palms straight and smack them together like this!"

Witness — ". . . And then I looked more closely, and saw that it was the body of a man. There was a large axe embedded in a deep wound in the chest, and the head had been completely severed and was lying approximately three feet to the right of the body."
Police officer — "And what led you to the conclusion that the man was actually dead?"

Sergeant — "Has the suspect been arrested for burglary before, constable? "
Constable — "No, Sarge—he's always been arrested afterwards!"

Tourist — "Officer, can you tell me the way to Fulham?"
PC Plod — "I'm afraid not, sir—these villains are smarter than me!"

PC Plod — "Oh, Sergeant, I have fallen in love with such a clever woman!"
P.C. Plod's mother — "So it's true then! Opposites attract!"

Sergeant — "So you arrested him for dangerous driving, did you—what speed was he doing?"
Constable — "55 miles an hour, Sergeant!"
Sergeant — "55 miles an hour? And what gear was he in?"
Constable — "Blue jeans and a white tee-shirt!"

Sergeant — "I need a responsible officer for this job!"
Constable Clod — "That's me Sarge! At my last station, whenever there was a disaster, I was responsible!"

Newsflash — Twenty gondolas go missing in Venice. Italian police say there are some dodgy punters going around!

A police constable had just returned to the police station after a visit to the football stadium, where there had been a break-in.
"Well," said the sergeant, "did the burglars take any of the cups?"
"No," said the constable, "they didn't get into the cafeteria!"

What's the difference between a triangle and the local police football team?
A triangle has three points!

1st detective — "If we follow these footprints this way, we can find out where the murderer is headed!"
2nd detective — "No. . .let's follow them in the other direction and find out where he's been!"

PC Plod — "Sergeant! I bumped into your Dad earlier this evening!"
Sergeant — "And how was the old so-and-so?"
PC Plod — "He seemed a little dazed, so I scraped him off the road and called an ambulance!"

What did the policeman sing to his tie?
"I've got you under my chin!"

Police officer (to suspect's wife) — "Mrs Brown, your husband is like an advertisement. . .
I can't believe a word he says!"

Why are there no ice cubes in the freezer at the police station?
Someone stole the recipe!

The C.I.D. were working on a big case. They had an idea who the mastermind behind was behind the recent crime wave, but they weren't quite sure. Then it all fell through. The uniformed officers arrested the detectives for suspicious behaviour!

Old lady — "I swear officer, policemen are getting younger and younger these days!"
Police officer — "I'd love to stand and chat madam, but I've got to get home or my mum'll kill me!"

Police officer — *"I'm afraid I'm going to have to ask you to accompany me to the station, ma'am!"*
Woman — *"Why, officer?"*
Police officer — *"Because it's dark and scary and I'm afraid to go all by myself!"*

Sergeant — "Has the prisoner spent a quiet night in his cell?"
Constable MacTavish — "No, sergeant, I've been here too!"

How do you say goodbye to a policeman?
Give him a crime wave!

Reporter — "Who's in charge of the murder inquiry?"
Constable — "Inspector Bradshaw, over there, sir!"
Reporter — "And who's that over there, sleeping on the sofa?"
Constable — "That's the a-resting officer!"

Who is the superhero who bumps into buildings?
Splatman!

Why did Batman have so much trouble with the Penguin?
He couldn't get the wrapper off!

Who is the hero of all photographers?
Flash Gordon!

What is the name of the superhero with a sore back?
Stooperman!

Who is the nosiest superhero ever known?
Snooperman!

What's the name of the teeny-tiniest superhero?
Gnatman!

He slips into action and chutes off to save the world. Who is he?
Sliderman!

What does Robin say when Batman asks him a tricky question?
"Dunno, dunno, dunno, dunno, Batman!"

What is the name of Batman's inflatable boat?
Bobbin'!

Who is the grouch with his pants over his tights?
Supermoan!

Who torments Batman and leaves damp patches all over Gotham City?
The Widdler!

Knock-knock!
Who's there?
Scot!
Scot who?
Scot nothing to do with you!

Knock-knock!
Who's there?
C!
C who?
C for yourself!

Knock-knock!
Who's there?
Rose!
Rose who?
Rose chicken and chips!

Knock-knock!
Who's there?
Beth!
Beth who?
Beth you donth know who thith ith!

Knock-knock!
Who's there?
Mayonnaise!
Mayonnaise who?
Mayonnaise have seen the glory. .

Knock-knock!
Who's there?
Don!
Don who?
Don ask me so many questions.

Knock-knock!
Who's there?
Fi!
Fi who?
'Fi ruled the world. . .!

Knock-knock!
Who's there?
Everest!
Everest who?
Everest of this ice cream—I've had enough!

Knock-knock!
Who's there?
Hugh!
Hugh who?
Hugh who! I can see you through the letter-box!

Knock-knock!
Who's there?
Lil!
Lil who?
Lil' ol' me!

Knock-knock!
Who's there?
Terry!
Terry who?
Terry-fied of the dark!

Knock-knock!
Who's there?
Lentil!
Lentil who?
Lentil my change to my friend—got none left for the bus home!

Knock-knock!
Who's there?
Tooth!
Tooth who?
Tooth company, threeth a crowd!

Knock-knock!
Who's there?
Lotta!
Lotta who?
Lotta-ry tickets for sale!

Knock-knock!
Who's there?
Yetta!
Yetta who?
Yetta nother door-to-door salesman!

Knock-knock!
Who's there?
Alf!
Alf who?
'Alf yer knocker's come away in me 'and!

Knock-knock!
Who's there?
House!
House who?
House about letting me in?

Knock-knock!
Who's there?
Waiter!
Waiter who?
Waiter minute! I think I've just knocked on the wrong door!

Knock-knock!
Who's there?
Hall!
Hall who?
Hall me friends have left me halone out 'ere!

Knock-knock!
Who's there?
Wilma!
Wilma who?
Wilma dad come and fix your doorbell for you?

Knock-knock!
Who's there?
Castle!
Castle who?
Castle look out of the window and you'll see who it is!

Knock-knock
Who's there?
Manor!
Manot who?
Manor woman—whoever you are, open the door!

What do you call a ghost who hasn't learned to walk?
A creepy crawlie!

Why did the monster buy trainers?
To join the human race!

What do dinosaurs have for breakfast?
Tricera-pops!

What's a ghost's favourite TV sitcom?
"The Ghoul Cosby Show"!

Where do monsters go to get their teeth fixed?
The awfuldontist!

1st cannibal —"What a great day for eating al fresco!"
2nd cannibal —"And how does Al feel about that?"

Why are dinosaurs good pupils at school?
Because they pass with extinction!

What has four legs, three arms and two heads, and hums?
A cannibal's freezer!

1st cannibal — "I really don't know what to make of this man!"
2nd cannibal — "How about a nice stir-fry?"

Why do ghosts never take a shower?
It dampens their spirits!

What do monsters cook for breakfast?
Soft-boiled ughs!

What do wizards do when they lose their busfares?
They witch-hike home!

What happens when zombies go sky-diving?
They land dead on target!

What is monstrous and frightening and makes your wishes come true?
A scary godmother!

What did the Cyclops' wife say to him?
"You're the one eye love!"

How can you make a witch behave rashly?
Take away her 'W'!

What do you call a fruit bat with no teeth?
A fruit gum!

Why did the zombie go to bed early?
Because it was dead on its feet!

What's a monster's favourite TV sitcom?
"Fiends"!

In which part of town do the zombies live?
The dead centre!

Did you hear about the cannibal who went on a cruise ship?
When he went for dinner, he didn't ask to see the menu. . .
—he asked to see the passenger list!

What do you call a dinosaur burger?
A Ptero-snack-dyl!

1st vampire — "So what kind of job are you looking for?"
2nd vampire — "Something I can really get my teeth into!"

What's a monster's favourite colour?
Terror-cotta!

1st monster — "You should take up professional tennis!"
2nd monster — "Why is that?"
1st monster — "Great four hands!"

How do you become a zombie?
Take a stiff test!

"The Greatest Collection of Singalong Songs Ever" by Carrie Oakey.

"My Life as a Chimney Sweep" by Sue T Lumsden.

"Bingo for Beginners" by Colin Numbers.

"Gambling for Cheats" by Mark D. Cards.

"How to Deal with Garden Pests" by Stan Don M. Quick.

"Confessions of a Tea Addict" by Mustapha Cuppa.

What are the most observant letters of the alphabet?
ICU!

What are the smartest letters of the alphabet?
IIQ!

What are the hottest letters of the alphabet?
BBQ!

What are the coldest letters of the alphabet?
IC!

What is the wettest letter of the alphabet?
C!

What is the scariest place in the alphabet?
L!

What are the most spiteful letters of the alphabet?
IHU!

What is the most hesitant letter of the alphabet?
M!

What is the most nutritious letter of the alphabet?
P!

What is the most inquisitive letter of the alphabet?
Y!

What letter of the alphabet makes people impatient?
Q!

What is the most thirst-quenching letter of the alphabet?
T!

What is the most surprised letter of the alphabet?
O!

Teacher — "What is an optimist?"
Pupil — "Someone who tests your eyes!"

Teacher — "Where is the Acropolis?"
Pupil — "That's where Superman lives!"

Teacher — "What is an autobiography?"
Pupil — "It's the life story of a car!"

Teacher — "What's one fifth of a foot?"
Pupil — "A toe!"

Teacher — "I'm not happy with your report!"
Billy — "I'm in no hurry! Take your time, try again, and make a better job of it!"

Teacher — "Children! Behave! 'Romeo and Juliet' is a serious play—it is NOT a pantomime!"
Voice from back of room — "Oh yes it is!"

Teacher — "Remember what I said, children. Whatever some people at the back of the class think, this is NOT a pantomime. Let's get on with it! Now, where did I put my copy of the play?"
Voice from back of room — "It's behind you!"

Teacher — "What is the opposite of woe?"
Pupil — "Gee-up!"

Billy — "I'm not playing a duet with my sister ever again!"
Music teacher — "Why not?"
Billy — "Because she always finishes first!"

Teacher — "What is a magnet?"
Pupil — "It's a wiggly thing that you find in apples!"

Pupil — "I want to follow my father's profession when I grow up!"
Teacher — "What do you want to become?"
Pupil — "A detective!"
Teacher — "So your father is a detective, is he?"
Pupil — "No— he's a burglar!"

How did the sports therapist let her friends know they were invited to dinner?
She sent them a massage!

Teacher — "What is the name of Jacob's brother?"
Pupil — "See-saw!"

Teacher — "What is a molecule?"
Pupil — "A one-eyed spectacule!"

Teacher (to former pupil) — "I remember you—you were such a little fool!"
Pupil — "But I've changed! Now I'm a big idiot!"

Teacher — "So you're going to follow in your father's footsteps are you, young man?"
Pupil — "Yes—he's giving me his old shoes!"

What happened when the maths teacher died?
He left his family a small sum in his will!

Teacher — "If I say the sentence 'I am beautiful', what tense am I using?
Pupil — "Pre-tense, miss!"

Billy — "Our teacher talks to herself!"
Bobby — "So does ours—but she thinks we're listening!"

Annie was late for school yesterday.
"Don't you dare walk into my classroom late again!" said the teacher.
So Annie didn't walk in late today.
She came in on rollerblades!

Pupil (at violin lesson) — "What would you like me to play?"
Music teacher — "Truant!"

Teacher — "Half an hour ago, I caught you eating chocolate, and now you're chewing gum! What explanation have you got to offer for it?"
Pupil — "I finished all the chocolate!"

Teacher — "Tomorrow, we're going to the art gallery to see some Old Masters."
Pupil — "Why? We've got plenty of them here!"

Pupil — "I've just discovered the hardest piece of furniture in the world!"
Teacher — "And what is that?"
Pupil — "The multiplication table!"

History teacher — "And if we look at the evidence, we can see how the death rate in Great Britain has changed over the last twenty years. . ."
Pupil — "But it hasn't changed at all! It's still one death per person!"

Did you hear about the teacher who took up golf?
He won the Masters trophy!

Teacher — "What have you got in your mouth, Billy?"
Billy — "Toothache!"

A man appeared in court recently on a charge of stealing a number of stringed instruments from a music shop. He was found guilty and sentenced to prison.
The newspaper headline read as follows — "Man sentenced to six months in violin case"!

Lost — Large dog lost by local family with black spots and a vicious temperament.

Lost — Silver bracelet belonging to lady with several charms.

Police statement — "I arrived at the scene of the hit-and-run and was told by witnesses that the culprit was a man in a station wagon with a black moustache and a blue suit."

Statement to police after car accident — "The other driver was all over the road. I was forced to swerve several times before I hit his car."

Police statement — "The dead man had brown hair, blue eyes and a foreign accent."

When is a pain like a PE teacher?
When it makes you jump!

Motto for judges — "Try, try and try again"!

Motto for lawyers — "Where there's a will there's a pay"!

Motto for useless boxers — "'Tis better to have gloved and lost, than never to have gloved at all"!

Motto for drop-outs — "Don't worry, be hippy"!

Motto for bakers
— "Make loaves not war"!

Insurance claim — "I thought the glass door was open but I discovered it was shut when I ran through it."

Letter to hospital staff —
"I am writing to thank you all for your kind assistance in the recent death of my mother-in-law. . ."!

Bumper sticker — "Don't read this! Watch the road!"

Inscribed on the tomb of a farmer —
"A great man—outstanding in his field!"

Inscribed on the tomb of a judge — "At last, his earthly trials are over!"

Inscribed on the tomb of Moaning Minnie — "Her final complaint was fatal!"

Inscribed on the tomb of a man who was killed by a bear — "The victim of a grizzly crime!"

Teacher – A camel can go a whole week without touching water!
Wilfrid – So could I if my mother would let me!

Inscribed on the tomb of a fisherman —
"He has earned his plaice in heaven. May his sole rest in peace!"

**Inscribed on the tomb of a historian —
"The past caught up with him."**

Inscribed on the tomb of a doctor — "A fine doctor once. . . now never better!"

Inscribed on the tomb of a gardener —
"Planted; spring, 1999!"

**What's this? "Snip, snip, snip!"
—A cutting comment!**

*What's this? "Brush, brush, brush!"
—A sweeping statement!*

What's this? "Anyone seen the general?"
—A general enquiry!

**What's this? "Clean, ironed, polished, combed!"
—A smart remark!**

*What's this? "Needle!"
—A sharp retort!*

What's this? "4 a.m.!"
An early response!

**What's this? "120 miles an hour! 200 kilometres per second!"
Fast talking!**

*What's this? "Stand clear! All clear! Clear up!"
—Clear instructions!*

What were all of the above?
Stupid questions!

**Fortune-teller – You will suffer much from poverty for twenty-five years.
Davie – And then?
Fortune-teller – And then you will get used to it!**

*Inscribed on the tomb of a philosopher —
"Here I lie. . .but is it I?"*

Teacher – If that tooth were mine, I'd have it out.
Pupil – So would I, if it were yours.

Rob (to his brother) – You greedy thing! You grabbed the biggest apple just as I was going to take it myself.

**Man – What's happened, little boy?
Davie – My coat fell in the pond.
Man – But you're soaking.
Davie – Well I was inside the coat.**

*Barber – What do you think of our new shaving foam, sir?
Customer (spluttering) – Worst I've ever tasted.*

Auntie – Well, Dennis, I'm going home tomorrow! Are you sorry?
Dennis – Yes, Auntie!
Auntie – That's nice of you, Dennis! Why are you sorry?
Dennis – I thought you were going home today!

**A — "I want to marry a geologist—
he's my rock!"**

*B — "I want to marry a chili grower—
he's hot stuff!"*

C — "I want to marry a plumber—but he keeps running hot and cold!"

**Little Alan (to big brother) – I wouldn't like to be in your shoes tomorrow.
Big brother – Why?
Little Alan – They'd be too big for me!**

*Guest (wakening hotel manager at two o'clock in the morning) – I want another room.
Manager – Surely you can wait till morning? What's wrong with your room?
Guest – Well, for one thing, it's on fire.*

Mum – Hurry up, Jimmy, or you'll be late for school.
Jimmy – It's all right, Mum. It stays open all day.

**Uncle – You're not looking very happy, Tom. What's the matter?
Tom – Well, Auntie said I could eat as many cakes as I wanted, and I can't.**

*Dad – You see that man over there, Johnny? He's six feet in his socks.
Johnny – Go on, Dad. You'll be telling me next he's two heads in his hat.*

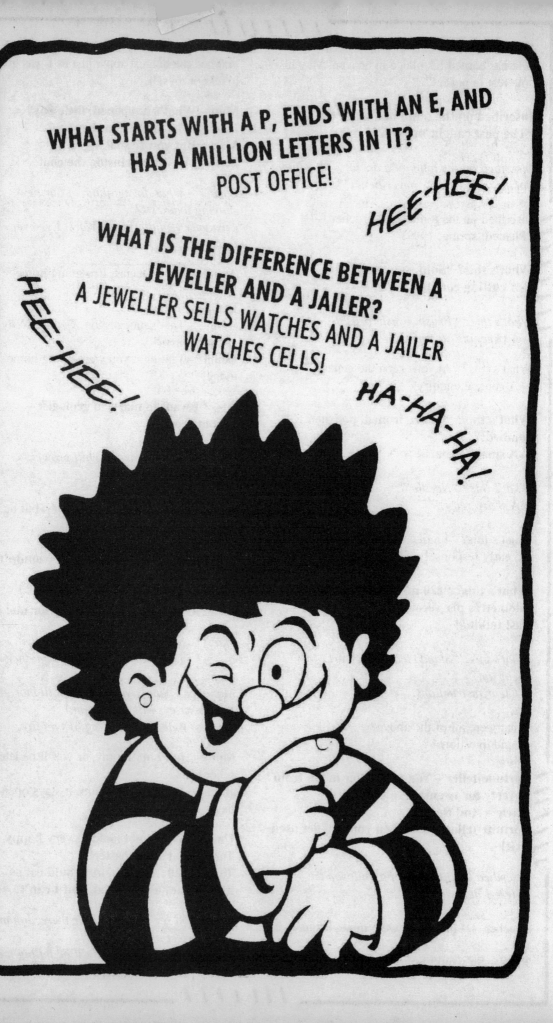

Knock! Knock!
Who's there?
Murry.
Murry who?
Murry Christmas, Happy New Year.

Knock! Knock!
Who's there?
Franz.
Franz who?
Franz is just across the channel.

Knock! Knock!
Who's there?
I used.
I used who?
I used to be able to reach the doorbell but now I can't.

Knock! Knock!
Who's there?
Russell.
Russell who?
Russell up some breakfast.

Knock! Knock!
Who's there?
Daryl.
Daryl who?
Daryl never be another you.

Knock! Knock!
Who's there?
Scott.
Scott who?
'S got you up out of your chair.

Knock! Knock!
Who's there?
Ewan.
Ewan who?
Ewan me are in a knock knock joke.

Knock! Knock!
Who's there?
Howard.
Howard who?
Howard is it raining out here?

Knock! Knock!
Who's there?
Tick.
Tick who?
Tick 'em up. I'm the tongue tied cowboy.

Knock! Knock!
Who's there?
Dona.
Dona who?
Dona sit under the apple tree with anyone but me.

Knock! Knock!
Who's there?
Waiter.
Waiter who?
Waiter a minute while I tie my shoe.

Knock! Knock!
Who's there?
Hi.
Hi who?
Hi who? (sings) It's hi ho! Hi ho! Hi ho! It's off to work we go.

Knock! Knock!
Who's there?
House.
House you?
House it going?

Knock! Knock!
Who's there?
Cows go.
Cows go who?
No, silly. Cows go Moooooo!

Knock! Knock!
Who's there?
Canoe.
Canoe who?
Canoe come out to play?

Knock! Knock!
Who's there?
Accordian.
Accordian who?
Accordion to the TV, it's going to rain tomorrow.

Knock! Knock!
Who's there?
Butter.
Butter who?
I butter not tell you.

Knock! Knock!
Who's there?
Toodle.
Toodle who?
Toodle-oo to you, too.

Knock! Knock!
Who's there?
Shamp.
Shamp who?
Why, do I have lice?

Knock! Knock!
Who's there?
Dime.
Dime who?
Dime to tell another Knock! Knock! joke.

Knock! Knock!
Who's there?
Radio.
Radio who?
Radio not, here I come!

Knock! Knock!
Who's there?
Winner.
Winner who?
Winner you gonna get this door fixed?

Knock! Knock!
Who's there?
Alaska.
Alaska who?
Alaska one more time … let me in!

Knock! Knock!
Who's there?
Cyril.
Cyril who?
Sir ill? Hope he get better soon.

Knock! Knock!
Who's there?
Mister.
Mister who?
Mister window and knocked on 'er door.

Knock! Knock!
Who's there?
Ice cream soda.
Ice cream soda who?
Ice cream soda neighbours wake up.
(I scream so the neighbours wake up.)

Knock! Knock!
Who's there?
Sheena.
Sheena who?
Sheena shcarlet shportsh car?

Knock! Knock!
Who's there?
Disk.
Disk who?
Disk is a recorded message. Please leave your message after the beep.

Knock! Knock!
Who's there?
Aladdin.
Aladdin who?
Aladdin the rain. Let me in.

Knock! Knock!
Who's there?
Saul.
Saul who?
Saul I'm going to tell you.

Knock! Knock!
Who's there?
Jonah.
Jonah who?
Jonah doorbell?

Knock! Knock!
Who's there?
Elsie.
Elsie who?
Elsie you when you open the door.

Knock! Knock!
Who's there?
Carmen.
Carmen who?
Carmen to the garden. Maude.

Knock! Knock!
Who's there?
Thor.
Thor who?
Thort you'd ask me that.

Knock! Knock!
Who's there?
Claire.
Claire who?
Claire to see you don't know.

Knock! Knock!
Who's there?
Petula.
Petula who?
Petulaugh at this gag.

Knock! Knock!
Who's there?
Hugo.
Hugo who?
Hugo away from this door now.

Knock! Knock!
Who's there?
Ammonia.
Ammonia who?
Ammonia (I'm only a) little girl who can't
reach the door bell.

Knock! Knock!
Who's there?
Judy.
Judy who?
Judeliver milk in the mornings?

Knock! Knock!
Who's there?
Icon.
Icon who?
Icon tell you another joke. Do you want me
to?

Knock! Knock!
Who's there?
Joan.
Joan who?
Joan this old place?

Knock! Knock!
Who's there?
Peg.
Peg who?
Peg your pardon, wrong door.

Knock! Knock!
Who's there?
Dougal.
Dougal who?
Do gulls live near the sea?

Knock! Knock!
Who's there?
Jeff.
Jeff who?
J-effer hear this joke before?

Knock! Knock!
Who's there?
Francis.
Francis who?
France is next door to Spain.

Knock! Knock!
Who's there?
Janet.
Janet who?
Janetor from the school.

Knock! Knock!
Who's there?
Ivy?
Ivy who?
Ivish you vell.

Knock Knock!
Who's there?
Empty.
Empty who?
Empty V
(MTV)

Knock! Knock!
Who's there?
Liz.
Liz who?
Liz is getting ridiculous.

Knock! Knock!
Who's there?
Ken.
Ken who.
Ken't you recognise my voice?

Knock! Knock!
Who's there?
Andy.
Andy who?
Andy knock knock jokes just keep on coming
and coming.

Knock! Knock!
Who's there?
Rufus.
Rufus who?
Rufus get a hole in it, carpet's getting wet.

Knock! Knock!
Who's there?
Wanda.
Wanda who?
Wanda saints go marchin' in.

Knock! Knock!
Who's there?
Ralph.
Ralph who.
Ralphabet goes from A-Z.

Knock! Knock!
Who's there?
Little old lady.
Little old lady who?
I didn't know you cold yodel.

Knock! Knock!
Who's there?
Joy.
Joy who?
Joil your roller skates yesterday?

Knock! Knock!
Who's there?
Michael.
Michael who?
My collection of knock knock jokes is brilliant.

Knock! Knock!
Who's there?
Dino.
Dino who?
Dino the answer.

Knock! Knock!
Who's there?
Wood.
Wood who?
Wood you marry me?

Knock! Knock!
Who's there?
Mona.
Mona who?
Mona lawn for you.

Knock! Knock!
Who's there?
Doctor.
Doctor who?
You just said it.

Knock! Knock!
Who's there?
Donald.
Donald who?
Donald come baby, cradle and all.

Knock! Knock!
Who's there?
Darren.
Darren who?
Darren young man in the flying machine.

Knock! Knock!
Who's there?
Dina.
Dina who?
Dinah shoot until you see the whites of their eyes.

Knock! Knock!
Who's there?
Diploma.
Diploma who?
Diploma to fix the leak.

Knock! Knock!
Who's there?
Dimitri.
Dimitri who?
Dimitri is where the burgers grow.

Knock! Knock!
Who's there?
Don Juan.
Don Juan who?
Don Juan to go to school today.

Knock! Knock!
Who's there?
Dennis.
Dennis who?
Dennis says I need to have a tooth out.

Knock! Knock!
Who's there?
Dozen.
Dozen who?
Dozen anyone ever answer the door?

Knock! Knock!
Who's there?
Deanna.
Deanna who?
Deanna-mals are restless, open the cage.

Knock! Knock!
Who's there?
Dawn.
Dawn who?
Dawn leave me out here in the cold.

Knock! Knock!
Who's there?
Daisy.
Daisy who?
Daisy plays, nights he sleeps.

Knock! Knock!
Who's there?
Dragon.
Dragon who?
Dragon your feet again!

Knock! Knock!
Who's there?
Willube.
Wllube who?
Will you be my valentine?

Knock! Knock!
Who's there?
Water.
Water who?
What are friends for!

Knock! Knock!
Who's there?
Dummy.
Dummy who?
Dummy a favour and go away.

Knock! Knock!
Who's there?
Disguise.
Disguise who?
Disguise the limit.

Knock! Knock!
Who's there?
Dana.
Dana who?
Dana talk with your mouth full.

Knock! Knock!
Who's there?
Arncha.
Arncha who?
Arncha going to let me in? It's freezing out here!

Knock! Knock!
Who's there?
Dotty.
Dotty who?
Dotty way the cookie crumbles!

Knock! Knock!
Who's there?
Doris.
Doris who?
Doris slammed on my finger. OUCH!

Knock! Knock!
Who's there?
Duane.
Duane who?
Duane the bath, I dwowning.

Knock! Knock!
Who's there?
Nobel.
Nobel who?
No bell so I'll knock.

Knock! Knock!
Who's there?
You.
You who?
Are you calling me?

Knock! Knock!
Who's there?
Ketchup.
Ketchup who?
Ketchup or you'll be left behind.

Knock! Knock!
Who's there?
Cargo.
Cargo who?
Car go beep! beep! beep! beep!

Knock! Knock!
Who's there?
Police.
Police who?
Police open the door.

Knock! Knock!
Who's there?
Banana.
Banana who?
Knock! Knock!
Who's there?
Banana.
Banana who?
Knock! Knock!
Who's there?
Orange.
Orange who?
Orange you glad I didn't say banana???

Knock! Knock!
Who's there?
Boo.
Boo who?
Don't cry.

Knock! Knock!
Who's there?
Water.
Water who?
Water you, a gorilla?

Knock! Knock!
Who's there?
Wednesday.
Wednesday who?
Wednesday saints go marching in!

Knock! Knock!
Who's there?
The Sultan.
The Sultan who?
The Sultan pepper.

Knock! Knock!
Who's there?
Donna Mae.
Donna Mae who?
Donna Mae-k you an offer you can't refuse!

Knock! Knock!
Who's there?
Army.
Army who?
Army and you still friends?

Knock! Knock!
Who's there?
Doughnuts.
Doughnuts who?
Doughnut open until Christmas.

Knock! Knock!
Who's there?
Ya.
Ya who?
YAHOO? Is there a party going on in there?

Knock! Knock!
Who's there?
Mice.
Mice who?
Mice to meet you.

Knock! Knock!
Who's there?
Smore.
Smore who?
Can I have some smore marshmallows please?

Knock! Knock!
Who's there?
Lettuce.
Lettuce who.
Lettuce out, it's cold in here!

Knock! Knock!
Who's there?
Pam.
Pam who?
Pamission to enter please.

Lady Posh – Good gracious, Jessie, why are you feeding the cat with bird seed? I told you to feed the canary!
Maid – That's where the canary is, madam.

Lady – You shouldn't knock a little boy down like that.
Tough boy – How should I knock him down then?

Boss – You know, my boy, you must always start at the bottom.
Office boy – How about when you're digging a well?

Policeman – You can't stay here.
Motorist – I can't, eh?
Policeman – No.
Motorist – You don't know this car like I do.

PC 49 – We're looking for a man with a monocle.
Old lady – Wouldn't it be better to look for him with a telescope.

Swimming teacher – Now don't forget that a hollow body can't sink. Next lesson I will show you how easy it is to keep your head above water.

Editor – I don't like the end of the story.
Author – What's wrong with it?
Editor – It's too far from the beginning.

Tall youth (to friend) – Have you ever tried listening to films with your eyes shut?
Gent (behind) – Have you ever tried listening to them with your mouth shut?

Jackie – Dad, when a thing is bought, it goes to the buyer doesn't it?
Dad – Why yes.
Jackie – Well, why is it when you buy coal it goes to the cellar?

Will:- "Can I tap you for a fiver?"
Bill:- "Can I punch you for a tenner?"

Bill:- "Can I press you for a fiver?"
Will:- "No thanks-I like being crumpled!"

Pete:- "Can I press you for a tenner?"
Mike:- "No-it would leave me flat broke!"

Fred:- "Can you give me fifteen pounds?"
Ted:- "No-but I can give you a bunch of fives!"

Ted:- "Can I ask you for a loan?"
Fred:- "Of course you can ask-but don't expect to get it!"

Sue:- "Can I trouble you for a pound?"
Lou:- "You trouble me all the time, but you've never given me any money for it before!"

Ike:- "Can you lend me ten pounds for a week, old man?"
Mike:- "Get the weak old man to ask for it himself!"

Will:- "I sent the builder three letters last week!"
Bill:- "What did they say?"
Will:- "I. O. U."!

Fred:- "You remind me of Eddie Brown!"
Ted:- "Why is that?"
Fred:- "He owes me money just like you!"

A crooked chef was arrested last week. Police say he's in the cooler!

What do electricians do at the gym?
Circuit training!

"My husband's a cross-country car racer!"
"Really?"
"No-rally!"

Did you hear about the two bridges across the same river?
They were arch rivals!

Why did the chess player have trouble with his children?
He coldn't keep them in check!

What kind of word games do zombies like best?
Crypt-ic crosswords!

Mr Jones:- "Mr Brown! How are you? I heard you had a nasty fall!"
Mr Brown:- "Yes-in fact the weather's been bad all year in these parts!"

Tailor:- "That suit fits you like a second skin, sir!"
Customer:- "I think I like my first skin better-at least I can sit down in it!"

Thought for the day:- Do gardeners write in flowery prose?

Why did the musician go to the north pole?
He wanted to make cool music!

Will:- "How did you break your arm?"
Bill:- "Raking leaves!"
Will:- "Did you trip over the rake?"
Bill:- "No-I fell out of the tree!"

Maisie:- "I've given up climbing. I guess I'm just too old for it now."
Mo:- "Over the hill, eh?"

Thought for the day:-Once you make up your mind to step into a revolving door, there's no going back!

Thought for the day:- Can a walking stick get blisters?

An artist dropped his keys on the way home. How did he find them?
He re-traced his footsteps!

It's a stormy day when Ernie sets out from home. The wind is blowing and the rain is pouring down. The further he goes, the stronger the wind blows until he finds he is caught in the teeth of a mighty gale. He has never been out in weather like this before.
"Well, blow me down!" he says.
Immediately, a huge gust of wind lifts him right off his feet and drops him flat on his back on the ground.
He picks himself, dusts himself off and struggles on. Suddenly, a deafening roll of thunder fills the air and the sky is lit up by a great flash of lightning.
"Well, strike me down!" says Ernie.
Seconds later, another bolt of lightning shoots out of the sky and hits him-wham!-just like that. When Ernie wakes up, he can hear beautiful music. He is lying on something white and fluffy and a man with golden wings is standing over him.
"Who in heaven are you? . . ." gasps Ernie in amazement.
"I'm an angel," says the man, "I've come to welcome you!"
"Well, I'll be damned!" says Ernie.
"You shouldn't have said that!" says the angel, and Ernie feels himself falling, falling, falling. . .

Why did Mr Dopey throw away his new guitar?
It had a hole in the middle!

Notice on Dr Who's tardis door:- "Back in time for lunch."

How can you tell a Mexican carpet?
Underlay! Underlay!

Think about this:- You can find me in your memory, but you won't see me in a thousand years! (Look at the words!)

Will:- "You know I'd go to the ends of the earth for you!"
Maisie:- "Off you go then, and when you get there, jump off!"

A boxer's fiancée and her friend are watching him in a boxing match. He's doing quite well until the third round when his opponent whacks him hard on the side of the head. He is knocked out cold and as he lies on the canvas, the referee begins to count, "One. . two. ."
His fiancée doesn't seem worried at all, however. "Four. . . five. . ." the referee is still counting. "He's out cold!" says her friend. "He might lose the match! Doesn't it bother you?"
"No," says the boxer's fiancée. "It'll be fine. He promised faithfully he'd come round and see me at nine!"

Bill:- "How's your new job at the aquarium?"
Bob:- "Not bad-but I don't think the manager likes me!"
Bill:- "Why not?"
Bob:- "He told me to stroke the pirhana fish yesterday!"

How many seconds are there in a year?
Twelve-January the second, February the second. . .!

Did you hear about the goalkeeper who saw a little boy jumping from a burning building?
He caught him safely in his arms. . .
then bounced him three times and kicked him over a nearby wall!

Where do snooker players spend their leisure time at home?
In the potting shed!

The leader of the city orchestra was dismissed for unprofessional behaviour. . .
He didn't know how to conduct himself!

How do you get rid of an angler?
Tell him to sling his hook!

"I'm saving for my retirement fund!"
"You're not that old!"
"No-my car has four punctures!"

Motto for an undertaker:- Never put the cart before the hearse.

Railway guard (to breathless man):- "Missed your train, sir?"
Traveller:- "No-I couldn't stand the sight of it, so I chased it out of the station!"

Why did the Frenchman boil his hat in suger?
To make blackberet jelly!

"Have you got a remote handset for your television?"
"No-I've just got one on the table beside me!"

Why was the lightswitch depressed? It couldn't go on any more!

Friend:- "Why did you give up your job as a joiner?"
Joiner:- "I couldn't stop biting my nails!"

Mike:- "How are you getting on with your piano lessons?"
Ike:- "Great! I've mastered the first steps!"
Mike:- "I didn't know you could play the piano with your feet!"

Thought for the day:- Are cartoonists colourful characters?

What has two arms, four legs and wings?
A man holding a duck!

What has two arms, two legs and flies?
A man holding a garbage bag!

Why did the robber have a nervous breakdown? He just couldn't take any more!

Why did the office boss quit his job?
He couldn't manage it any longer!

What's the difference between a person who arranges funerals and a person who steals motor-bikes?
One's an undertaker, the other's a Honda-taker!

Mother:- "That was little Billy on the phone. He says he's run away to London!"
Father:- "That's it! He's gone too far this time!"

How do you make a Mexican chilli?
Take his clothes off!

Cross an amphibian with a dove and what do you get?
Don't know what it'll look like, but it's sure to be pigeon-toad!

What did one dollar bill say to the other? "I wouldn't change you for the world!"

Why did the goalkeeper go to the bank?
To ask about his savings!

Why did the monster leave home?
His mother told him it was time he stood on his own two feet!

A magician got a job on an ocean liner, performing card tricks while the passengers dined. Unfortunately, his act was spoiled every night by the captain's parrot, who kept giving the tricks away. "It's up his sleeve! It's up his sleeve!" the parrot would cry, or "Look under his hat! Look under his hat! Behind his ear! Behind his ear!"
Well, the magician got mightily sick of all this, and was looking forward to the day when the cruise was over. However, two days from shore, the ship sank. The magician, luckily, found a lifebelt and jumped overboard before the ship disappeared under the waves. As he floated in the water, wondering what to do next, the parrot flew up to him and landed on his head.
"All right!" said the talkative bird, "I give up-where did you put the ship?"

What's gooey and plays the piano?
Meltin' John!

A woman is out driving one day when a lorry coming in the opposite direction suddenly skids, veers across the road, and crashes right into her. She is taken into hospital, but she is very badly injured. When her husband comes in to see her, the doctor takes him aside.
"The news is not good, I'm afraid," says the doctor.
"I know," says the husband. "The police say the car's a complete write-off!"

Bank robber:- "Life is all about give and take. . .
-give them a fright and take their money!

What's green and dances in the herb garden?
Chive Bunny!

Have you heard about the toy rabbit that goes after bloodsuckers?
Fluffy the vampire slayer!

Lady Muck:- "Did you plant the herb garden today?"
Gardener:- "No Ma'am-I didn't have the thyme!"

Why did the angel go to hospital?
She had harp failure!

My name is Mr Sharp-but I'm sometimes quite blunt!

My name is Mr Stamp-but I'm not always frank!

My name is Mr Buss-and I travel by taxi!

My name is Mackintosh-and I've got you covered!

My name is Mr Gunn-and I've just been fired!

Did you hear about the lazy farmer?
He covered his cattle in flour to make them self-raising!

Doctor:- "What happened to you?"
Patient:- "I fell down the stairs!"
Doctor:- "Did you miss a step?"
Patient:- "No-I bounced off every single one!"

Mr Dopey went to the theatre for the first time. He bought a ticket at the box office and set off towards the auditorium. Two minutes later, he was back at the box office, buying another ticket. Once again he set off towards the auditorium, but yet again, he came back to the box office. The box office attendant was curious.
"Why have you come back for a third ticket?" she asked. "Have you met a friend?"
"No," said Mr Dopey, "it's just that every time I try to go inside to see the show, this big bully at the door grabs my ticket and tears it in half!"

Thought for the day:- Selling newpapers improves the circulation!

Billy:- "I came real close to getting the right answers in my maths test today!"
Mum:- "How close?"
Billy:- "Two seats!"

Mum:- "What's your new teacher's name?"
Bobby:- "Wanda Howe!"
Mum:- "Are you sure?"
Bobby:- "Yes! She came in and she said, "I, Wanda Howe, I can possibly teach you lot!"

Harry got a new book about outer space. It was such an interesting book that Harry, who didn't usually like reading, spent all afternoon reading it in his bedroom. He kept on reading until well after his suppertime. Downstairs his parents were getting more and more concerned.
Eventually, Harry finished another chapter, put the book aside, and went downstairs.
"Where did you get to?" asked his Mum.
"Oh," said Harry, "just to the end of the universe!"

"My husband had an accident last weekend."
"What was he doing? DIY?"
"No-PE! He had to go to hospital!"
"ICU?"

"No-A&E! The doctor says he'll be OK after some R&R, so we're going on holiday."
"USA?"
"Yes-LA!"
"How will you get there-TWA?"
"No-BA!"
"Have a good time -and don't forget to send me a PC!"

Irate customer:- "You told me that car would go like a bomb!"
Car salesman:- "Did I, sir?"
Irate customer:- "And I suppose you were right-it blew up this morning!"

Sheriff:- "What's your name, cowboy?"
Cowboy:- "Tex!"
Sheriff:- "So you're from Texas, are you?"
Cowboy:- "Nope-Carolina!"
Sheriff:- "So why do you call yourself Tex?"
Cowboy:- "It's better than Caroline!"

Will:- "How many Valentines cards did you get last year?"
Bill:- "Twelve-but I forgot to post them!"

What did one Egyptian say to the other Egyptian?
"Have I seen your fez somewhere before?"

What do you call a disused satellite?
A waste of space!

1st poacher:- "I can catch more rabbits than you!"
2nd poacher:- "Shut your trap!"

Did you hear about the builders who tried to climb Mount Everest?
They got within thirty feet of the top and ran out of scaffolding!

Billy:- "My mum can lift five hundred pounds with one hand!"
Bob:- "How does she manage that?"
Billy:- "She works at the bank!"

Why is an electrician like a news reporter?
They're both concerned with current events!

Why did the wizard go round to see his friend?
He had some good newts for him!

Why did the artist have to go and see his bank manager?
Because his account was overdrawn!

Did you hear about the man who took up breeding spaniels?
His life went to the dogs!

Burglar's wife:- "Where have you been?"
Burglar:- "Can't tell you, dear-the sign outside said 'Strictly No Admittance'!"

Molly:- **"That's a lovely diamond ring, Mo!"**
Mo:- **"Yes-I told my husband that the doctor said I needed to put on a stone!"**

Diner:- "Are these fresh vegetables?"
Waiter:- "Yes-they've been giving me cheek all night!"

Doris at the dairy was sick. . .
-so her friends sent her a get-well curd!

A man marched into the bank and slammed four posters on the counter.
"Stick 'em up!" he said.

Five minutes a squirrel came, in and tipped a pile of nuts in front of the teller.
"This is a hoard-up!" he said.

No sooner had the squirrel left than a string quartet marched into the bank and waved their instruments at all the staff.
"What's the meaning of this?" asked the manager.
"Can't you tell?" replied one of the musicians.
"It's robbery with violins!"

Tourist:- **"Can you put me up for Christmas?"**
Hotel receptionist:- **"Sorry sir, but the manager insists we always have a real tree!"**

Why was the peanut butter happy?
He'd just fallen in love with a little honey!

What did the robber say when he held up the watchmaker's shop?
"Tick 'em up!"

What did the cabbage say to the cook?
"You've broken my heart!"

How can you recognise a table-tennis player's house?
Listen for the doorbell. . .
-Ping-pong!

A motorist had to stop his car on a country lane to mend a puncture, but he found he had terrible trouble getting the wheel off. He was beginning to give up hope when a farmer's lad came strolling along towards him.
"Can you help me?" said the motorist. "I've just got a flat-it's nothing much!"
"You're lucky!" said the farmer's lad. "A flat! I've only got one dingy little room and I have to share it with my brother!"

Little Annie's mother had invited some ladies round for tea and Little Annie was kept busy handing cakes round the guests. When everyone had been served, she went back and stood beside Mrs Green, a rather large woman, and stared at her intently.
"What's the matter, dear?" asked Mrs Green.
"Nothing," replied Annie. "I'm just waiting for you to do your trick!"
"My trick?" said Mrs Green.
"Yes," said Annie, "My mum says you can eat like a horse!"

Will:- "I want to die with my boots on!"
Bill:- "Why?"
Will:- "So I don't stub my toe when I kick the bucket!"

Texas Pete:- **"Hi, y'all, it sure is great to be in Scotland!"**
MacTavish:- **"Hauv ye come ower tae learn the language, then?"**

Aggie:- "My husband thinks I look a picture in this outfit!"
Maggie:- "Really?"
Aggie:- "Yes-he said 'If you wear that dress you deserve to be hung!'!"

Little boy:- "Look, Mum, there's Keepie-uppie, Kev, the famous soccer player!"
Mum:- "how do you know it's him?"
Little boy:- "He's heading towards us!"

Angler:- **"I fought for an hour to get that salmon!"**
Friend:- **"I don't suppose the man who caught it wanted you to have it!"**

Cyclist:- "Is there a cycle path running through the park, officer?"
Policeman:- "If there was, sir, we'd be after him straight away!"

Mike:- "Will you be my wife?"
Mo:- "Perhaps one day. . .
-but not a moment longer!"

Teacher:- **"What's this big black smudge on your maths, Billy?"**
Billy:- **"You told us to finish our work, and step on it!"**

Tourist:- "I shot fifteen lions on holiday!"
Friend:- "How do you know they were on holiday?"

Tourist:- "No- what I mean is I shot fifteen lions when I was on holiday in Africa!"
Friend:- "What did you use?"
Tourist:- "Just a polaroid!"

Receptionist:- "The only room we have left is one with a sea view, and that's £10 extra, sir!"
Hotel guest:- "I tell you what, I'll keep the curtains closed and pay £10 less!"

Did you hear about the vicious card player?
He beat his opponent with a club!

Little boy:- "Dad! Dad! Barry's up to his ankles in mud?"
Dad:- "What's so bad about that?"
Little boy:- "He's in head first!"

Patient:- "Doctor, doctor, I've got a huge boil on my neck!"
Doctor:- "Which side?"
Patient:- "The outside!"

Someone sent Mr Dopey an electric toothbrush.
But he sent it back. . .
-he didn't have electric teeth!

Man at speaker's corner:- "Repent! Repent! The end of the world is nigh!"
Little boy:- "Don't be stupid! The world is round!"

How many days of the week start with T?
Four: Tuesday, Thursday, today and tomorrow!

What did one bell say to the other?
"How's dings with you?"

Careful when you open your electricity bill. . .
-you might get a shock!

Why do lightbulbs stay out of the sun?
They prefer to sit in the shade!

"Mum, can I go out to play?"
"No!"
"Can I ask a friend round to play?"
"No!"
"Can I have a biscuit, then?"
"No!"
"Huh! No-it-all!"

What can go up and down at the same time?
A yo-yo in an elevator!

Will:- "You're just a big girl's blouse!"
Bill:- "Don't you get shirty with me!"

Son:- "Everyone says I'm hopeless at cricket!"
Father:- "Practise hard, son. . .
-you'll soon be a little batter!"

Why did Mr Dopey take his music stool back to the shop?
He couldn't work out how to play it!

What do you do when a football player's down?
Cheer him up!

Flo:- "My husband used to be a pirate, but he's a refuse collector now. You might have seen him in the street with his refuse lorry!"
Mo:- "How would I know which was his lorry?"
Flo:- "It's the one with the skull and cross-bins painted on the side!"

Why can't you steal a canal?
It has too many locks!

Father:- "You're lying!"
Son:- "how do you know?"
Father:- "Your lips moved!"

Robber's wife:- "Can you nip down to the bank and get some money out for me, dear?"
Robber:- "Sorry, sweetheart, it's still open-you'll have to wait!"

Did you hear about the prisoner with chickenpox?
He broke out in a rash!

Who's the most unwanted man in the world?
Bill!

Who's the least known man in the world?
Hugh?!

Who's the smelliest man in the world?
Pugh!

Who's the brightest man in the world?
Ray!

Who's the most cowardly man in the world?
Fred!

How can you recognise a librarian?
Look for the volume-inous clothes!

Why did the lumberjack have to do overtime?
He had a backlog of work to catch up on!

Fred:- "I've just bought a second-hand computer-do you think it'll be reliable?"
Ted:- "I wouldn't count on it, if I were you!"

Teacher:- "Can anyone give me a sentence using the word 'writhe'?"
Pupil:- "I have Writhe Krithpieth for breakfatht every morning!"

"Why did you givce up your job filling shelves at the supermarket?"
"Thing just kept stacking up on me!"

What did one spade say to the other?
"Shovelong a bit, will you?"

Landlord:- "I've come to collect the rent!"
Gardener:- "But the rent's spade!"

Landlord:- "I've just increased the rent-you owe me £10!"
Gardener:- "But I can't fork out any more money!"

How can you recognise a gardener's home?
His and Hers trowels hanging in the bathroom!

"Busy at the fishing net factory?"
"Nope-there's knot much doing!"

Where do you find three-footed police officers?
Scotland Yard!

How did the gas man feel when he met his wife?
Very pleased to meter!

Did you hear about the two granny Smiths who fell in love?
They lived appley ever after!

Sheriff:- "The prisoner's escaped! Call out the posse!"
Deputy:- "Here, posse, posse, posse!"

Teacher:- "What is a spokesperson?"
Pupil:- "Someone who repairs bicycles!"

Pharmacist:- "Take three tablets twice a day."
Patient:- "That's a very large dose!"
Pharmacist:- "So? Your ears are enormous!"

Bill:- "These photos don't do me justice!"
Will:- "You don't want justice-you want mercy!"

Fred:- "That new football captain is useless!"
Ted:- "Why?"
Fred:- "He doesn't pay any attention to what's going on behind his back!"

Mr Dopey was dismissed from his job as a railway guard. . .
-he threw the driver off the train because he didn't have a ticket!

Did you hear about the comedian who died in a restaurant?
He choked on a quip!

What's green and goes backwards?
A gooseberry in reverse!

What else?
Sniff and you'll see!

Why did the gymnast buy a packet of crisps?
Because the shop had run out of Hula-Hoops!

What did the torch say to the battery?
Glad you popped in-I was just about to go out!

Will:- "My brother used to be a bodybuilder."
Bill:- "Really?"
Will:- "Yes-you should have seen the thighs of him!"

Why did the stage manager go to the doctor's?
He kept seeing stars!

Why did the flower fairy go to the doctor's?
She kept having daisy spells!

Why did Mr Dopey take a bucket out surfing?
He wanted to catch a wave!

What's the difference between sea and surf?
When the sea's wild, you see the surf-bored!

"Can you tell me the way to Bury St Edmonds?
"Start by digging a big hole!"

Headmaster:- "What are you doing out in the corridor, boy? Shouldn't you be in a music lesson?"
Pupil:- "Yes, sir-bu I was told to wait outside for a minuet!"

Thought for the day:- Scrambled eggs are not always what they're cracked up to be!

Thought for the day:-Gravity gets you down!

Little boy:- "My mum bought a new watch today. . .
-she said she needed some time to herself!

French teacher:- "Can anyone tell me the meaning of 'aperitif'?"
Pupil:- "A set of dentures!"

Where did B go?
To C D!

Why did Big Chief Sitting Bull drive up the middle of the motorway?
He was looking for the central reservation!

A quick argument:-
"I H U!"
"I H U 2!"
"I Z it first!"

A swift invitation:-
"i 1 2 c u!"

Notice from the ladlady:-
"Q 4 T at 5!"

A little poem:-
1-1 was a race horse,
2-2 was1-2;
1-1-1-1 race 1 day,
2-2-1-1-2!

1st lady:- "My son's very quick at picking things up, you know!"
2nd lady:- "Just like my husband-until he was arrested!"

Bob:- "My dog wouldn't hurt a hair on your head!"
Rob:- "No-he goes straight for the ankles!"

Will:- "I need a new job-something I will find absorbing!
Bill:- "Absorbing? Try working in a kitchen roll factory!"

Fred:- "How did you meet your new girlfriend, Ted?"
Ted:- "I was out fishing one day and I caught her eye!"

Ike:- "Look at the size of your stomach! You should diet!
Mike:- "I know-what colour do you think would look best?"

Mo:- "My brother broke the world record for lying under a sunbed. . .
-now he's the toast of the town!"

Will:- "I ran a mile in two minutes!"
Bill:- "How did you manage that?"
Will:- "I took a short cut!"

Driving instructor:- "You should look in your rear view mirror, Mrs Jones!"
Mrs Jones:- "Why? Does my bottom look too big in these trousers?"

A motorist had a puncture while out driving one day, so he stopped his car, jacked it up and lifted the wheel off. Just as he lifted it off, however, he dropped it-thump!-right on his foot. just at that moment, a breakdown truck drove up and the man in the breakdown truck leaned out of the window to speak to the car driver.
"Need a toe?" he asked!

What did the gardener say to his children before they took part in the school sports?
"I'll be rootin' for you, kids!"

Why do policemen enjoy their holidays?
Because a change is as good as arrest!

Molly:- "Why did you leave your job in the laundry of the convent?"
Mo:- "I was worried about picking up dirty habits!"

How do you greet a radio operator?
Give him a short wave!

Teacher:- "Who is the first person mentioned in this novel?"
Pupil:- "Chap One, miss!"

How can you ask for a drink using only three letters of the alphabet?
N E T ? !

How can you make a firelighter?
Take out half of the sticks!

Did you hear about the barber detective?
He called himself Hairlock Holmes!

"What kind of rock is this, Sherlock?"
"Sedimentary, my dear Watson!"

For Sale:- Grand piano-nothing to play for nine months!

Notice on fishmonger's window:- "Sorry-shoaled out!"

For Sale:- Christmas carols-going for a song!

For Sale:- Scissors-a snip at the price!

For Sale:- Second hand car with free saddle-for the ass that buys it!

Where does a prison officer keep his clothes?
In a warder-robe!

Did you hear about the waiter who poured hot soup over the judge?
He was asked to serve a sentence!

Man in park:- "Does this plant belong to the creeper family?"
Gardener:- "No-it's the property of the Town Council!"

Where does a bodybuilder keep his clothes?
In a big chest!

Where does an artist keep his clothes?
In drawers, of course!

What did the sailor say to the crane driver?
"A-hoist there!"

Harry the highland dancer needed a holiday. . .
-so he packed a few flings and left!

A man goes into a baker's shop and has a look round to see what he wants to buy. As he's looking, he hears a voice coming from a cake box in the corner. "Buy me," says the voice, "I'm sweet and rich and chocolatey!" What? Cakes don't talk! The man decides his ears must be deceiving him and carries on looking round, but seconds later, the voice speaks again. "Have a look at me," says the voice this time. "I'm the best cake you've ever seen. I have strawberries on top, and cream in the middle, and plump, ripe cherries round the side. I have your name written in pink icing right in the centre. Look at me!"
The man looks over in the corner, but still, all he can see is a cake box. So he decides to ask the baker about the voice. Does he really hear what he thinks he is hearing? A talking gateau? A confection that speaks?
"Oh yes," says the baker. "You heard it all right. But don't listen to a word of it. It's all rubbish. That one in there's a real fruitcake!"

What did the undertaker give his daughter for her birthday?
Hearse-riding lessons!

One of Bart Simpson's family was in the newspaper yesterday! It was Marge. . .
-she made a double page spread!

Who made a map of Peter Rabbit's garden?
Beatrix Plotter!

What cartoon do skunks like best?
Phew-turama!

When does Homer Simpson sound like a dog?
"Bart! Bart!"

What kind of deer is like Homer Simpson?
Doe!

When do the Teletubbies sound like Pikachu?
When they shout "Po! Come on!"

Why did the undertaker's stay open all night?
They were expecting a late delivery!

"Can I speak to X!"
"Y?"
"I Z X!"
"And I Z Y!"
"O...U...I want to speak to X I Z!"
"O...I C!...X! Sorry, you" have to wait in a Q!"
"O-G!"

Two small boys are playing war games.
"Bang-Bang!" says one boy. "I've shot you!"
"Who cares?" says the second boy. "Rumble-Rumble! I'm a tank!"

Traveller:- "I'd like to book a ticket to   . London!"
Ticket salesperson:- "Return?"
Traveller:- "Um-let me come back to you on that one!"

Why did S go home?
It was time for T!

Will:- "Why do you think your dog is a secret agent?"
Bill:- "He leaves little messages under the bench in the park every morning!"

Will:- "I tried to join the lacemaking society!"
Bill:- "Really?"
Will:- "Yes, but they told me to get knotted!"

Will:- "Then I tried a woolencraft society!"
Bill:- "That sounds interesting!"
Will:- "It was-until they told me to get knitted!"

Will:- "Then I tried needlecraft!"
Bill:- "Oh?"
Will:- "But it was sew hard, I gave up!"

Will:- "The last class I attended was furniture assembly. And nothing could drag me away from that!"
Bill:- "Why?"
Will:- "I superglued myself to the wardrobe I was making!"

Why are saints never ill?
They always feel good!

Why are army officers untidy?
They spend a lot of time in a mess!

How did the telephone engineer keep his children busy?
He gave them one hundred lines!

"Why did you give up your job in the stationery shop?"
"I kept feeling feint!"

The scotch broth in the police canteen tasted revolting. . .
-so they called in the souperintendent!

Two old ladies called at Snow White's front door selling apples. She didn't know what to do. . .
-she couldn't tell which was witch!

Two cartons of cream had a fight.
"Right!" said one after fifteen minutes of squabbling. "That's it! I'm off!"

Why did the bartender hire a crane?
To lift his spirits!

Why was Snow White confused?
Because Doc said he was Grumpy and Happy said he was Sleepy!

Why did Mr Spock agree with his ears?
He could see they had a point!

Merlin:- "Wow!"
Assistant:- "What?"
Merlin:- "I've just had a wizard idea!"

How do you get in touch with the manager of a safari park?
Drop him a lion!

Farmer A:- "Are you sure you can afford to lend me all this hay?"
Farmer B:- "Oh, yes-I've got stacks of the stuff!"

Farmer A:- "And what about the manure?"
Farmer B:- "Oh, yes-I've got heaps to spare!"

Farmer A:- "But are you sure you can lend me this chickenfeed?"
Farmer B:- "Of course! I've got bags of the stuff!"

Farmer A:- "Goodness me-what a big heavy cow you have in that field over there!"
Farmer B:- "Cow?-that's a load of old bull!"

The REAL meeting of the three witches in Shakespeare's 'Macbeth'....
1st witch:- "When will we three meet again?"
2nd witch:- "Ooh, now, let me see...how about Tuesday, around twelve-ish?"

Why did the three witches call in the plumber?
Hubble, bubble, toilet trouble!

What did Louis Armstrong sing when he got off the helter-skelter?
"What a wonderful whirl!'"

What's a prizefighter's favourite Disney Film?
"The Punchback of Notre Dame"!

Will:- "My cat swallowed a car horn!"
Bill:- "Really?"
Will:- "Yes-now he's a peeping tom!"

How did the spider make a big entrance at the party?
He stood in the doorway and at the top of his voice shouted "Ta-ran-tu-la!"

"Can I speak to the doctor, please? I've hurt my ankles and can't walk!"
"The doctor's busy-you'll have to crawl back later, please?"

What do you get if you cross a chicken with a snake?
A feather boa!

Will:- "Your cat just threw up all over the piano!"
Bill:- "He just loves to make mew-sick!"

Why did the egg need a box?
To keep its albumen!

Did you hear about the pig who wanted to be on stage?
He joined a hamateur theatre group!

Thought for the day:- Are chicken jokes hentertaining?

Why did the rooster go to the gym?
to work on his pecks!

What is a third of three needles and three parrots?
One point one repeater!

What is a chicken's favourite musical?
"The Bantam of the Opera"!

What is a chicken's second favourite musical?
"My Fair Lay-day"!

Why did the pig buy paper and envelopes?
To write to his pen-friend!

What do you get if you cross a sheep with a porcupine?
An animal that knits its own clothes!

Why are ducks more clever than chickens?
You don't get Kentucky Fried Duck, do you?

What do you call a brave pigeon?
A daring doo!

How do dolphins punish their children?
They keep them in after school!

What do you call a kangaroo with sore legs?
Hopless!

Why did the chicken farmer hire an assistant?
He couldn't coop on his own!

What kind of dog is hardest to please?
A moan-grel!

Teacher:- "We talk about a gaggle of geese and a school of dolphins. but how do we describe a group of donkeys?"
Pupil:- "An assassination!"

"Can I speak to Mr Brown?"
"Can I have your name, please?"
"No-it's mine!"

What did one carousel horse say to the other?
"I'll be coming rond to your place in a sec.!"

"Can I speak to Rod?"
"Hold the line one moment!"

"Can I speak to Mr Hook?"
"Hang on a minute, please!"

"Can I speak to Mr Chance?"
"You bet!"

"Can I speak to Mr Plane?"
"Sorry-he just took off somewhere!"

"Can I spesak to the navigator?"
Off course you can!"

"Can I speak to the barber, please?"
"Sorry-he can't comb to the phone just now!"

"Hello?"
"Is that Al?"
"Why-what else do you want me to say?"

"Can I speak to Mr Brown?"
"Sorry, Mr Brown's not here at the moment!"
What?"
"No-Mr Watt's out as well!"

"Well, eh. . ."
"Oh-Willie! He's here! Hold on and I'll get him for you!"

"Can I speak to the dentist?"
"Sorry, he's out of the orifice just now!"

"Can I speak to the butcher?"
"Sorry-he's in a meating!"

"Can I speak to Mr Barr?"
"I'll see if he's inn!"

"Is Mr Smith there, please?"
"Can I say who's calling?"
"Not until I tell you!"

Police Sergeant:- "And what is the suspect's name?"
Constable:- "Zoblinski, sir!"
Sergeant:- "And how do you spell that?"
Constable:- "T-H-A-T!"

"Will Bet be available to come to the phone later?"
"Well, you can always try your luck!"

"Is Mr Jones there, please?"
"Yes, sir-can I say who's calling?"
"I don't know. . . it's Mr Zchendrokypopozchopakitski. . . can you say that?"

"Can I speak to the bride?"
"Sorry-she's una-veil-able!"

"Can I speak to my fiancé?"
"Sorry-he's otherwise engaged!"

"Can I speak to Doug?"
"Sorry-he's in a bit of a hole!"

"Can I speak to Beau?"
"Sorry-he's all tied up just now!"

"Can I speak to Bet?"
"Chance would be a fine thing!"

"Can I speak to Dawn?"
"She'll be up in a moment!"

"Do you know Mike Roe phoned?"
"Of course I know what what a microphone is!"

"I'm calling to see how Bob is!"
"Oh-he's up and down!"

"Can I speak to Mr Flame?"
"Sorry-he's just gone out!"

"Can I speak to Mr Targett?"
"Sorry-you just missed him!"

"Can I speak to Pete?"
"I'll see if I can turf him out for you!"

"Can I speak to the manager about this sweater I bought-it looks terribly motheaten!"
"One moment, madam, I'll put you on holed!"

"Can I speak to Mr Sharp?"
"Sorry-he is out on an appointment!"

"Can I speak to Sandy, please?"
"Sorry-he's all at sea just now!"

"Is Sandy available yet?"
"Sorry-he's tide up until four!"

"Is Sandy available to speak to me yet?"
"He shore is!"

"Can I speak to Mr Cork?"
"Sorry-he just popped out a moment ago!"

"Can I speak to the undertaker?"
"I'm sorry-you'll have to call back tomb-orrow!"

Message on CIA agent's answering machine:-
"I'm sorry, but I can't tape your call at the moment. . ."

Knock-knock!
Who's there?
Theo!
Theo who?
Theo-wner of the house! Get out before I call the police!

Knock-knock!
Who's there?
Ron!
Ron who?
Ron away! The house is on fire!

Knock-knock!
Who's there?
Marmite!
Marmite who?
Marmite let me ask you for tea if I'm good!

Knock-knock!
Who's there?
Arfur!
Arfur who?
Arfur got!

Knock-knock!
Who's there?
Fiona!
Fiona who?
Fiona dog you have to exercise it!

Knock-knock!
Armageddon!
Armageddon who?
Armageddon sick of waiting for you to answer!

Knock-knock!
Who's there?
Toot!
Toot who?
I don't care what you're wearing! Just open the door!

Knock-knock!
Who's there?
Ma!
Ma who?
Ma kilt's caught in the letter box!

Knock-knock!
Who's there?
Watney!
Watney who?
Watney name of goodness took you so long to answer?

Knock-knock!
Who's there?
Canter!
Canter who?
Canterford a doorbell, eh?

Knock-knock!
Who's there?
Alma!
Alma who?
Alma little teapot, short and stout. . .

Knock-knock!
Who's there?
Rowan!
Rowan who?
Rowan the back! No-one answered the front door!

Knock-knock!
Who's there?
Bracken!
Bracken who?
Bracken the door down with my fist!

Knock-knock!
Who's there?
Ivy!
Ivy who?
Ivy very sore hand from all this knocking!

Knock-knock!
Who's there?
Beech!
Beech who?
Beech you at golf yesterday!

Knock-knock!
Who's there?
Privet!
Privet who?
Privet Potter reportin' for duty, sah!

Knock-knock!
Who's there?
Willow!
Willow who?
Willow-will you let me in?

Knock-knock!
Who's there?
Pine!
Pine who?
Pine in the neck!

Knock-knock!
Who's there?
Fir!
Fir who?
Fir goodness' sake, let me in!

Knock-knock!
Who's there?
Saul!
Saul who?
Saul the shopping done-what's next?

Knock-knock!
Who's there?
Wide!
Wide who?
Wide-on't you open the door?

Knock-knock!
Who's there?
Few!
Few who?
Few were the only girl in the world. . . !

"My parents worked on the oil rigs. . .
-so they called me Derrick!"

"My parents were sprinters. . .
-so they called me Spike!"

"My parents were ice hockey fanatics. . .
-so they called me Chuck!"

"My parents enjoy playing cards. . .
-so they called me Patience!"

"My parents love fried potatoes. . .
-so they called me Chip!"

"My mother gave birth to me in a field of hay. . .
-so she called me Rick!"

"My parents own a florist's business. . .
-so they called me Posy!"

"My parents are D.I.Y. fanatics. . .
-so they called me Andy!"

Did you hear about the business tycoon's twin
sons?
They were called Hiram and Phairam!

Did you hear about the dart player's twin
daughters?
They were called Amy and Missy!

What do you call a man with a tin hat on his
head?
Helmutt!

What do you call a man with a radio on his
head?
Roger!

What do you call a girl with a griddle on her
head?
Barbie!

What do you call a man with a shower on his
head?
Wayne!

What do you call a man with a gutter on his
head?
Dwayne!

What do you call a girl with a piece of glass on
her head?
Claire!

"Interior Design Magic" by Evan-Lee
Holmes.

"Smoking-A Filthy Habit" by Dawn T.U. Dewitt.

"Learning Through Repetition" by Yetta Gain.

"Planting a new garden" by Douglas Tier.

"Plastering Techniques" by Dot Anne Dab.

"A Sideways Glance" by Ima Crabbe.

"Missed opportunities" by I. Bluitt.

"Success in Second-Hand Car Sales" by Dod G.
Deal.

"Conquering Travel Sickness" by Eve Inder-
Carr.

"The Uses of Ink" by Philippa Penn.

"Traditional English Entertainment" by Maurice
Dancer.

"Winning at Whist" by Shona Trump.

"Perfume Manufacture" by Watt A. Pugh.

"Striving to Win" by Buster Gutt.

"Marine Life" by C. Anne Enemy.

What's the ice dancer's favourite song from
"Aladdin"?
"A Whole New Whirl"!

What did the hairdresser sing to her babies to
get them to sleep?
"Barber black sheep. . .!"

What is an angler's favourite song?
"Salmon-chanted evening"!

Newsflash:- The takings of the local bank
were stolen today by a man dressed only in
his underwear:-Police say they have a brief
description of the robber.

What did the gardener sing as he cut the grass?
"Getting to Mow You"!

What song do they sing at the local Chinese
carry-out?
"Wok on By"!

What did the artist's wife sing to him?
"Lavender's BLUE, Silly Billy"!

"Here lies Ebenezer Fogg:-Sadly mist."

"Here lies George the Glazier:-Free from pane
now."

"Here lies Hypochondriac Harry:-He always
said there was something wrong with him."

"Here lies Pete the petrol pump attendant:- he
lived a fuel life."

"Here lies Shoemaker Sam, along with his
tools:-Peace at last."

"Here lies Alice from Australia:-Gone back
down under."

"Here lies Ice Skater Imogen:-Slipped away
peacefully."

"Here lie Bert the Baker and his dearly beloafed
wife."

"Here lies Bob, the famous bald bear:-Gone
but not fur-gotten."

"Here lies Vera, the Voice of the Speaking
Clock:-She said her time had come."

"Here lies Wally the window cleaner:-he kicked
the bucket."

"Here lies Mr Bone the Butcher:-a happy
families man."

What's an archeologist's favourite film?
"The Remains of the Day"!

What's a hunter's favourite film?
"The Three Moose-get-eers"!

What's a Canadian Police Officer's Favourite
Film?
"The Full Mounty"!

What's an artctic explorer's favourite film?
"Chilly Elliot"!

Geography teacher:- "Today, class, we're going
to do some work on the French Alps!"
Pupil:- "Will be back in time for P.E.?"

Why did the mailman go to the cinema?
To see "Postin' Powers"!

Have you heard of Wacky Films Ltd? They've
just made a new film about a cement mixer. . .
-it's called "Dryhard"!

Their last film was ever so exciting! It was the
story of a sledgehammer. . .
a real blockbuster!

What's a philosopher's favourite film?
"The Bridge Over the River-Why?"!

What's a Yeti's favourite film?
"The Snowman"!

What's a fox's favourite film?
"Chicken Run"!

What's a cleaner's favourite film?
"Bleaches"!

Teacher:- "Why did the Americans design
rockets to take men to the moon?"
Pupil:- "Because they couldn't fly themselves!"

Teacher:- "Does anyone know the meaning of
'propaganda'?"
Pupil:- "A very polite male goose!"

Teacher:- "Name three people who set sail in
the Ark. . .
-and I'm not taking Noah for an answer!"

Teacher:- "Billy! Did I see you looking at your
neighbour's answers?"
Billy:- "Hopefully no, sir!"

Gym teacher:- "Come on, Jimmy! Ten more
press-ups! Work your forearms!"
Jimmy:- "But I've only got two arms!"

Teacher:- "Are you chewing gum?
Pupil:- "No-I'm Willie Smith!"

Teacher:- "Are you trying to be smart?"
Pupil:- "That's what I came to school for!"

Teacher:- "So you think you're witty!"
Pupil:- "No-Willie!"

Teacher:- "Pay attention, Billy!"
Billy:- "But I've only got 50p!"

History teacher:- "And what happened when the
Germans attacked the Poles?"
Pupil:- "All the telephone wires fell down!"

Teacher:- "Can anyone spell 'jealousy'?"
Pupil:- "N.V.!"

"Why did the Cold War come to an

...ecause the snow melted?"

...her:- "Can anyone briefly describe what ...vacuum is?"
Pupil:- "M.T.!"

Why did the battery go to the doctor's?
It was feeling run down!

Doctor:- "That's a nasty wound-we'll have to put several stitches in it!
Patient:- "Well, I'll be darned!"

**Peter called the doctor in the middle of the night. He was in terrible pain. The doctor got dressed and ready to leave.
"Why are you going out again?" asked his wife. The doctor told her.
"Oh, for Pete's ache!" she said.**

Why did the bottle of gin go to the doctor's?
To get a little tonic!

Newsflash:- Mysterious explosion destroys house:- Police suspect home-icide.

Newsflash:- Two thousand felt-tipped pens stolen from factory:- Police say the robber is a marked man.

Newsflash:- Man falls from bike and breaks his leg:- Police say he is the victim of a notorious cyclepath."

Newsflash:- Thirty-three bathroom suites stolen from factory:- Police say there's a ruthless gang of criminals on the loos.

Newsflash:- A man was caught today, setting fire to Farmer Brown's pea crop:-Police have charged him with grievous pod-ily harm.

Sergeant:- "Very funny constable! How do you write 'Zoblinski'?"
Constable:- "Holding the pen in my right hand!"

Traffic cop:- "Watch your speed, sir! The road through these parts is very dangerous. One person is knocked down by a motor vehicle every week!"
Driver:- "Goodness! That person must be getting mightily sick of it!"

**A motorist is stopped by a traffic cop on the motorway.
"Where are your rear light?" says the traffic cop.
"Rear lights?" says the motorist. "Never mind about them-where's my caravan?"!**

Why did the Baby strawberry cry?
Beacause his parents were in a jam

Why did the golfer take a spare pair of socks?
In case he got a hole in one!

**What's a bird's favourite programme?
The feather forecast.**

What do you call a kitten which looks at other people's exam answers?
A copy cat.

Why did the traffic light turn red?
You would too if you had to change in the middle of the street!

Which monkey was defeated at Waterloo?
Napoleon Baboonaparte.

**Why was Cinderella thrown off the football team?
Because she ran away from the ball!**

If you were surrounded by Dracula, Frankenstein's monster, a werewolf and a ghost, where would you be?
At a fancy dress party.

What's round and dangerous?
A vicious circle!

Which dessert looks at you while you eat it?
Eyes-cream.

**How was the stupid kidnapper caught?
He sent a stamped addressed ransom note.**

How many psychiatrists does it take to change a lightbulb?
Just the one, but the lightbulb has to really want to change.

What do you call a man who crosses a river twice and doesn't take a bath?
A dirty double crosser!

**Why does Santa have three gardens?
So he can ho ho ho!**

What do you get when you corss Frosty the Snowman with a vampire?
Frostbite.

Why were the basketball players so hot and sweaty?
Because all their fans went away!

**Which weighs more, a ton of bricks or a ton of feathers?
Neither they both weigh a ton!**

WHAT IS THE BEST WAY TO CALL FRANKENSTEIN'S MONSTER?

LONG DISTANCE!